The Case
for
Auschwitz

The Case for Auschwitz

Evidence from the Irving Trial

Robert Jan van Pelt

Indiana University Press
Bloomington and Indianapolis

This book is a publication of

Indiana University Press
601 North Morton Street
Bloomington, IN 47404-3797 USA

http://iupress.indiana.edu

Telephone orders   800-842-6796
Fax orders   812-855-7931
Orders by e-mail   iuporder@indiana.edu

The paper used in this publication meets
the minimum requirements of American
National Standard for Information
Sciences—Permanence of Paper for
Printed Library Materials, ANSI
Z39.48-1984.

Manufactured in the United States of
America

**Library of Congress Cataloging-in-
Publication Data**

Pelt, R. J. van (Robert Jan), date
   The case for Auschwitz: evidence from
the Irving trial/Robert Jan van Pelt.
      p. cm.
Includes bibliographical references and
index.
   ISBN 0-253-34016-0 (alk. paper)
   1. Irving, David John Cawdell, 1938-—
Trials, litigation, etc. 2. Lipstadt,
Deborah E.—Trials, litigation, etc.
3. Penguin (Firm)—Trials, litigation, etc.
4. Trials (Libel)—England—London.
5. Auschwitz (Concentration camp)
6. Holocaust denial literature—Great
Britain. I. Title
   KD379.5.I78 P45 2002
   345.41'0256—dc21
                    2001002615

1 2 3 4 5 07 06 05 04 03 02

Preparation and publication of *The Case for Auschwitz* was generously assisted by the Conference on Jewish Material Claims Against Germany.

The publisher gratefully acknowledges the generous support of the following sponsors:

Douglas and Sandra Barton

Shirley Efroymson-Kahn

Ellen and Tom Ehrlich
in honor of Alvin Rosenfeld, Director, Jewish Studies Program,
Indiana University

Irving M. Glazer

Leonard and Ruth Goldstein

Mr. and Mrs. Hart N. Hasten

J. William Julian

Barton L. Kaufman

Herbert M. Levetown

Sandy and Art Percy

Frances M. and M. Mendel Piser

Alvrone and Ron Sater

Phyllis and Gary Schahet

Mrs. Ruby Schahet

Melvin Simon

CONTENTS

Preface
and
Acknowledgments

This book grows out of my involvement as an expert witness in the libel trial brought by David Irving before the British High Court in January 2000, in which Irving sued American historian Deborah Lipstadt, author of *Denying the Holocaust,* and her British publisher, Penguin Books, for labeling him a Holocaust denier. For the trial I prepared, and subsequently defended in cross-examination, a 700-page report addressing a core issue of the proceedings: the historical evidence for the gas chambers at Auschwitz. The bedrock of Irving's claim that the Nazis had no systematic program to murder all the Jews of Europe, and that the Jews who had died had succumbed to the ordinary violence of war, was his insistence that the Germans had not built extermination camps to kill Jews. Irving justified this assertion by reference to the claim made by one Fred A. Leuchter that there had been no homicidal gas chambers at Auschwitz. In 1988 Irving had seized upon Leuchter's report as "shattering in the significance of its discovery" and had become its publisher and advocate. Irving reasoned that if Auschwitz had no gas chambers, neither did the other extermination camps, and if all the death camps were figments of a perverse imagination, the German murder of six million Jews was a hoax. Irving claimed that the available evidence, or the lack thereof, justified such a conclusion. Lipstadt had argued that Irving had betrayed his vocation as a historian and falsified history when he had accepted Leuchter's conclusions without considering the massive amount of evidence that pointed to the existence and operation of the gas chambers at Auschwitz. It was my task, therefore, to help the defense barristers Richard Rampton, Heather Rogers, and Anthony Julius convince the judge that no serious historian who had considered the evidence would have serious cause to doubt that there were gas chambers at Auschwitz. We were successful. On April 11 Justice Charles Gray stated in his verdict that, on the basis of "the convergent evidence relied on by the Defendants," he had concluded that "no objective, fair-minded historian would have serious cause to doubt that there were gas chambers at Auschwitz and that they were operated on a substantial scale to kill hundreds of thousands of Jews."[1]

The Case for Auschwitz tells the story of how and why Auschwitz became central in the Irving-Lipstadt trial, and why the so-called question of the gas chambers has become a pivot of Holocaust denial, or negationism, as I will call it. More importantly, this book presents the bulk of the evidence I submitted to the court in my expert report—evidence of the use of Auschwitz as an extermination camp in which more than a million people died. Most of these were Jews, and most of them died in gas chambers. Finally, this book explains how Rampton, Rogers, and Julius used this evidence to defeat Irving, and in what way Irving tried to challenge that evidence in court. The material here may, or may not, be sufficient to convince every skeptic that Auschwitz was indeed an extermination camp. It proved sufficient to convince Justice Gray, and it may prove useful to others who may find it necessary to present the case for Auschwitz.

This book not only aims to provide those engaged in the struggle against Holocaust denial with the material introduced and defended in the Irving-Lipstadt trial. It also seeks to respond to the unexpectedly great interest the case generated among the public at large. The day after the verdict *The Daily Telegraph* commented in its lead article that "the Irving case has done for the new century what the Nuremberg tribunals or the Eichmann trial did for earlier generations."[2] And while only future generations will be able to judge if such an assessment was justified, the fact remains that like the earlier war crime trials that first exposed the full measure of Nazi brutality and the special character of the Nazi war against the Jews, the trial was closely followed by the media and generated a lot of discussion.

Press coverage, which had kept up during the more than two months of proceedings, reached its high point on April 12, the day after Justice Gray ruled for the defendants and pronounced Irving a falsifier of history, a right-wing pro-Nazi polemicist, an anti-Semite, and a racist. Cartoonists had their day. *The Guardian* showed Hitler in the fires of hell, with a guardian demon telling him: "Tough luck. He lost. You stay." *The Daily Telegraph* showed a display table in a bookstore marked "David Irving's New Book." The title of the book advertised is *That Libel Trial Never Happened*. *The Times* showed a man sitting in his chair reading Irving's autobiography. He tells his wife, "I'm at the bit when he's recounting his stunning court victory." On a more serious note, the Israeli daily *The Jerusalem Post* reported that Prime Minister Barak sent Lipstadt a message declaring the outcome of the trial a "victory of the free world against the dark forces seeking to obliterate the memory of the lowest point humanity ever reached."[3] *The New York Times* quoted Rabbi Marvin Hier and Rabbi Abraham Cooper of the Simon Wiesenthal Center in Los Angeles as having said that "Irving tried to manipulate the British legal system in order to put the victims murdered in the gas chambers on trial; instead, the net result is that he will be relegated to the garbage heap of history's haters." In short, the ruling was a "victory of history over hate."[4] In London, Stephen Moss of *The Guardian* added that the verdict was also a victory "for the historians who had left their seminar rooms and lined up with the defendant, Deborah Lipstadt, in court to attempt to destroy David Irving's reputation as a historian."[5]

Historians and the practice of writing history were credited with much that day. In a leading article *The Independent* noted that "the cogency of the testimony presented by the defence" had vindicated "the great liberal principle, enunciated by John Stuart Mill, of the marketplace of ideas in which false coin is tested and replaced by true."[6] In a tough editorial, *The Irish Times* applauded the destruction of Irving's reputation; it noted that his defeat was not the result of some "argy-bargy on university campuses" and it had not occurred under a "hail of rotten eggs and the shouting down of his message by strident adolescent voices." The hero, in this case, was "the clinical, forensic examination of his credo, a calculated and methodical destruction of his untruthful version of history."[7] Indeed: the trial once again reminded the world that "truth is no shining city on a hill," *The Guardian* pronounced.

> It has to be worked at; the credibility of those who claim to express it is critical. Even a casual reader of the case reports could quickly see how painstaking genuine historical scholarship is; it builds detail upon detail, avoiding casual inference and thin deduction. Eventually, a plausible narrative is pieced together but even then it has to withstand the slings and arrows of competitive scholars. And the Holocaust is now hot history. Due, in part, to the persistence of the deniers, academic effort has been redoubled. Among the many Irving assertions to be comprehensively demolished was the suggestion that thought police prevent open challenge to received historical wisdom. It is precisely because of the historians' efforts from the early 50s on that there is now no room for doubt, despite the false trails and the lacunae left by a Nazi bureaucracy as assiduous about destroying the signs of its crimes as realising the final solution. Other jurisdictions make denying the Holocaust a crime. After this case, we can rely on empiricism and the sheer weight of evidence.[8]

All the articles published that day conveyed that a case that should never have gone to court had come to a fitting and, more importantly, a final end. Even negationists found some solace. Michael A. Hoffman II compared Irving to St. George before the dragon, Christ before the mob and David before "Golipstadt." He placed his hope on the future. "Great libel trials are dramas that stick in the memory for generations and posterity often takes a very different view than contemporary received opinion," Hoffmann wrote. "The trial of Oscar Wilde is but one example of a protagonist whose cri de coeur, *De Profundis* (from out of the depths) resonates down the corridors of time in his vindication." Yet, he admitted his deep disappointment that instead of a "world-shaking miracle" the final result of the trial was merely "another revisionist weed pushing itself up through hairline cracks in the Jewish concrete that covers our planet."[9]

As I read these comments and editorials on April 12, and as I listened to Mr. Justice Gray's verdict the day before, I enjoyed an increasingly rare satisfaction in this post-historical age: namely, an awareness that the practice of history not only offers a pleasant occupation, but that the way we historians go about our business also matters. For most of my life, my pursuit of the past had seemed largely irrelevant to the questions of the day. I remember well that I wrote my first high school essay on the iconography of the bedroom of Slangenburg Castle in eastern Holland during the 1968 student uprising against the perceived feudal structures of Dutch society. When a little more than a decade later I began my dissertation research on the Holy of Holies of the Temple of Solomon in the pleasant confines of the Warburg Library in London, Polish students supporting workers in their demands for such fundamental rights as the freedom of association were arrested and imprisoned. When, another decade later, I traveled to a Poland liberated from the tyrannical oppression of "the emergency" because of the tenacity of those same workers and students, I questioned whether my research on the construction of the gas chambers at Auschwitz really mattered, given that the government of Israel was then handing out gas masks to all its citizens in anticipation of a missile strike from Baghdad. Indeed, every time I became enthusiastic about some chosen aspect of the past, the papers told me that the real action was somewhere else. Teaching compulsory courses in cultural history at a Canadian architecture school did not give me much reason to change my perspective: while in general my students were kind enough to write in the teaching evaluations that they liked what they had been forced to read and what they had suffered to hear, it was also clear that they would have preferred to use the time spent with Aquinas, Descartes, and Schopenhauer to draw their projects and build their models.

That April day a year ago I was proud to be a historian, and I remembered fondly those who taught me to love the past and the practice of history: my *Opa* Hans Bunge and my primary school teacher *Meester* Jan Neuteboom, my high school history teachers *Meneer* Sietse Haagsma and *Meneer* Jan Modderman, and my university professors Jan Terwen and Moses Gans, my Warburg tutors Perkin Walker and Dame Frances Yates, and my *Promotor* Jan van Dorsten. From them I learned that the study of history is truly the way to unite oneself with a larger purpose, a greater whole. I remembered, also, Ben Weinreb, a very special tutor in the art of living. The preparations for the trial had allowed for regular visits to Ben in Yarley Hill, in Somerset. In early 1999 I traveled there with a copy of my 770-page expert report in my bag. My old mentor was only marginally impressed and certainly not pleased. "Studying the architecture of a death camp is not good for the soul," he admonished me. That was the last time I saw him. He died a few weeks later.

I thought of those more senior colleagues who had helped me to mature as a historian and who, at crucial moments, had given me their vote of confidence: Bill Westfall and George Hersey, Raul Hilberg and Michael Berenbaum. The first person I phoned after the verdict had come down was the historian who, more than any other teacher or colleague, had prepared me for the ordeal in court: my friend and writing partner, Debórah Dwork. Without her, I would not have chosen to become a Holocaust historian, and without her, I would not have persevered in this vocation. She also accepted, if reluctantly, that I would have to interrupt a joint project to write a short history of the Holocaust to participate in the defense of Lipstadt.

The day of the judgment, outside the courtroom I was able to thank my mother, Judy Jolly, Sir Martin Gilbert, and Mike and Anne Rossiter, who had given crucial support when, prohibited from communicating with the other members of the defense team, I faced cross-examination alone, and to express my appreciation to Eva Menasse for her exceptional daily reports in the *Frankfurter Allgemeine*. At a party that the solicitors held in the Bank bar and restaurant that day, I tried amidst the general noise to convey my gratitude to the individuals who had come to mean so much to me during our two years of common effort. But it is not clear that Anthony Julius, James Libson, Kevin Bays, or Helen Peacock could have heard my heartfelt "Thank you!" I was able on that occasion to thank Laura Tyler and Mark Bateman, who had offered me crucial support in acquiring all the documents from Irving's discovery. Some of the lawyers who had offered great help in an earlier phase of the case had been assigned to another case by the time we went to court, so I could not thank Harriet Benson and Veronica Byrne on that occasion. Deborah Lipstadt and Richard Evans were not present, so I could not tell them how much I envied their colleagues in Atlanta and Cambridge for having the continuing opportunity to work with them.

Professional relations had grown into deep friendships, and that evening researcher Tobias Jersak and expert witness Hajo Funke joined Richard and Carolyn Rampton, Heather Rogers, and me for dinner at the Livebait fish restaurant on the South Bank. The involvement of Tobias and

Hajo, both German, had been crucial, as it demonstrated that the issue at stake in the trial concerned all people of goodwill—whether Jew or gentile, Englishman or German. The dinner turned out to be an unexpectedly melancholy affair, and I did not give the toast I had prepared to tell Richard and Heather how much I had come to love them, and how profoundly they had changed my outlook on life and scholarship. More than anyone else, they made me realize that what I had to contribute to the case truly mattered.

The next day, on my return to Canada, I was moved to hear from the many friends who gave me practical, intellectual, and spiritual support during the time I worked on my expert report and testified in London: Djamel Zeniti from Vienna, Errol and Julia Morris from Cambridge, Topher Elliot from Minneapolis, and Daphna Arbel from Vancouver; from Toronto my friends from Tuesday Lunchgroup, my neighbors Gordon Joscelyn, David Ayrth and Elizabeth Burridge, my colleagues Donald McKay, Rick Haldenby, Robert Wiljer, Ryszard Sliwka, and Andrew Levitt, and my friends Sheila Davis, Joanne Younge, Anne Sliwka, and Isabel Silva. They had conveyed their support in unique ways: one gave me his lucky penny and another his lucky tie; a third gave me an old Hebrew amulet to protect me from evil; a fourth gave me a book on how to adopt a *Yiddishe Kop* in the face of pressure; a fifth, the advice never to crack a joke on the witness stand; a sixth, the practical support of organizing my regular commute between Pearson and Heathrow airports; all of them offered a stiff drink when the calculations on Zyklon B use in Auschwitz became too much. I, in turn, had the pleasure of expressing my appreciation to Jed Braithwaite and Wayne Austin, who helped me produce the visual reconstructions of the crematoria which proved so crucial to the presentation of our case, and to Omer Arbel for his practical support during our trip to Oswiecim and for his unstinting friendship and loyalty during the trial. I had no opportunity after the trial to toast my friends at the Auschwitz-Birkenau State Museum in Oswiecim, who have been steady supporters of my work and graceful hosts whenever I was in Poland, so I will state here the high esteem in which I hold Barbara Jarosz, Teresa Swiebocka, and Wojtek Smolen; it is thanks to their commitment and professionalism that the infernal legacy of Auschwitz will be preserved for the education of future generations.

Soon after Justice Gray had handed down his verdict, I attended the Passover meal hosted by Debórah and Shirley Dwork and Ken, Miriam, and Hannah Marek. Gathered around the table was my adopted North American family who had been a rock of support in all of my endeavors and a source of continuous counsel. Sadly absent, however, was Bernard Dwork, who had died two years earlier, just at the time that I had begun work on my report. He, more than anyone, had shown me early on that the life of a scholar can be well balanced if approached with a broad sense of humor and without too much pretense. I miss him dearly.

In the year that followed, when I faced the need to respond to Rudolf's affidavit, I received invaluable help from Richard Green, who spared me the need to earn a Ph.D. in chemistry to answer Rudolf's pseudo-scientific arguments. I am profoundly grateful to Stig Björklund, who forgave me for my frequent lapses of communication and who kept me informed of the research being done on the location of the holes. I express my deep gratitude to Harry Mazal, Daniel Keren, and Jamie McCarthy for undertaking this work and for allowing me to submit their results to the Appeal Court. I thank Morden Yolles and Paul Zucchi for reviewing the work of Mazal c.s., and for giving me a crash course on concrete slab technology. Writing my rebuttal to Rudolf's affidavit, I was fortunate to have Green,

Mazal, Keren, and McCarthy as partners in a daily conversation that quickly also included John Zimmerman, Ken Stern, Peter Maguire, and Stephen Prothero. Their criticisms and suggestions helped to shape the final product. Finally, at Mishcon de Reya in London, Juliet Darell-Brown provided the necessary infrastructure that kept everything together.

Now that I am finally able to close the manuscript and the story of what happened and the evidence presented is about to become a book, I wish to thank my agent, Anne Borchardt, for having found a perfect home for the book at Indiana University Press, and my editor, Janet Rabinowitch, for all her work, her judgment, and, most important of all, for her friendship. I am in debt to those anonymous and ultimately also not so anonymous reviewers who recommended publication of the manuscript to Indiana University Press, including Richard Rampton, John Efron, and Michael Berenbaum. I am very grateful for all the support of Roman Kent. Finally, I would like to express my thanks to Kate Babbitt for the tough love with which she copyedited the manuscript, Marvin Keenan for the precision with which he read and corrected the proofs, and Sharon Sklar for the grace and good sense of the design.

Pnina Rosenberg of the Ghetto Fighters Museum helped me to obtain good photos of the work of David Olère. Before the trial Menashe Arbel helped me understand the art and purpose of cross-examination and successfully traced Yehuda Bacon, who subsequently told me about the circumstances under which he made three drawings of the gas chambers in 1945. Yehuda graciously granted me permission to include these unique drawings in this book. Susan Nashman Fraiman of the Yad Vashem Art Museum provided copies for reproduction. Serge Klarsfeld generously permitted me to quote significant parts of Henryk Tauber's testimony first published in Jean-Claude Pressac's 1989 *Auschwitz: Technique and Operation of the Gas Chambers,* a landmark in the history of Auschwitz scholarship.

I am profoundly grateful to Priscilla Coleman for allowing me to include in the book her drawing of the last day of the trial. Jesse Dormody and Andrew Haydon eagerly responded to an urgent call for assistance and produced a lucid diagram. At short notice Marc Downing drew the axonometric and interior views of Crematorium 4, an axonometric view of Crematorium 2, and the gas chamber of that building. Scott Barker remembered just in time that he had promised me a reconstruction of the gas columns of Crematorium 2, and as a result chose to forgo a weekend of adventure in London to deliver a beautiful drawing. Thank you, my friends.

Finally, I would like to acknowledge the loyal financial support for my research on Auschwitz that I have received over many years from the Social Sciences and Humanities Research Council of Canada. In a situation where the provincial government of the richest province in Canada has allowed its *per capita* support to its universities to slip close to (and according to some even below) the poorest jurisdiction in the United States, it is good to know that a federally funded agency is charged with the support of research. The Conference on Jewish Material Claims Against Germany generously provided a substantial subvention which allowed us not only to include a variety of unique illustrations that were difficult to obtain, but also to make possible publication of this work at a price that makes it more widely accessible. Finally, I also render thanks to the Center for Holocaust Studies at Clark University both for practical support given and for its crucial role in establishing Holocaust history as an academic discipline in its own right.

At the end of a writer's acknowledgments one often reads the statement that any errors or mistakes are the writer's own. This applies to *The Case for Auschwitz*. Unlike most writers, in this instance I must specifically acknowledge one deliberate misrepresentation that appears in the subtitle of this book. Calling it *Evidence from the Irving Trial* distorts the fact that it was actually the Penguin/Lipstadt trial, as Penguin Books and Deborah Lipstadt were the defendants and Irving the plaintiff. With due apologies to Penguin and Lipstadt, I believe that in this case the formal designation does not reflect historical reality, because the successful (and in libel cases common) defense strategy turned the *de jure* plaintiff Irving into the *de facto* defendant. This strategy proved so convincing that many observers mistakenly came to believe that the trial had been initiated against Irving, and that his right to free speech, and not Lipstadt's, was at the core of the case.

It is good to recall, in this context, that Lipstadt wrote at the beginning of *Denying the Holocaust* that she did not advocate "the muzzling of deniers."

> They have the right to free speech, however abhorrent. However, they are using that right not as a shield, as was intended by the Constitution, but as a sword. There is a qualitative difference between barring someone's right to speech and providing him or her with a platform from which to deliver a message.[10]

Lipstadt recognized the paradox that, in analyzing the phenomenon of Holocaust denial, she in fact provided its proponents with a platform for their ideas and a certain stature for their cause. Her decision to defend herself against Irving's assault only reinforced that paradox: the trial provided Irving a lot of publicity, and given the fact that in a court of law both sides receive an equal opportunity to make their case, it often appeared as if there were two sides to what seemed to all too many to be the core of the case: the question of whether or not the Holocaust happened. As a result, many believed that, indeed, the Holocaust was on trial—a gross misrepresentation of the fact that formally Lipstadt stood accused of libel, and effectively Irving stood accused of routinely and perversely distorting and falsifying history with the aim of serving a racist and anti-Semitic agenda.

As I close this manuscript I share the anxiety Lipstadt expressed at the beginning of her book. Undoubtedly, the very existence of this book will be hailed by some deniers as proof that their enterprise is alive and well. So be it. In the end I trust that the public and dramatic collision of evidence with deliberate falsehood that occurred in the British High Court and that is described in the following pages will have produced, as John Stuart Mill intended, a clearer perception and livelier impression of the truth. But this does not diminish the great ambivalence I felt, and continue to feel, about the whole enterprise, which has carried from the beginning a paradoxical if not surreal signature.

I therefore will end with the simple observation that the use of the preposition "for" in the title of this book reflects some of the bitter ironies raised in the trial.

The Case
for
Auschwitz

One

The Negationists' Challenge to Auschwitz

> When the surrounding world, which remembers the Armenian atrocities (against which it could have intervened), takes offense at tortures, which required more imagination to think them up than to invent them, it gets as an answer: "Believe us, the lack of understanding that our measures often meet with saddens us all." They don't mean it like this, but always otherwise. They feel it a violation when they are thought capable of the very acts they commit. Such acts they then describe as "alleged"—a brief but efficient formula based on the resolve not to engage such things and derived from the indisputability of a political morality based on allegations of what has not happened. In order to win the incompetent a position, the pickpocket accuses the civil servant of greed, and as one prefers to send this person to a concentration camp instead [of] to the courts, the suspicion hardens that he who was so capable in his position was capable of anything. In that way the alleged becomes real, and the real alleged, and exactly marks the breakthrough to a new civilizatory type, which writers describe: that the murderer, who also lies, has not murdered, and that the very cowardice of the murder gives him a hero's stature. It is the principal camouflage which the little word "alleged" generates— the little word that crops up again and again in the comments on current events.
>
> —Karl Kraus, *Die Dritte Walpurgisnacht* (1933)

"I don't see any reason to be tasteful about Auschwitz. It's baloney. It's a legend." These provocative words, first spoken by David Irving in 1991, were echoed nine years later in the Royal Courts of Justice in London by barrister Richard Rampton QC. The occasion was Rampton's opening statement for the defense in the libel case of *David John Cawdell Irving versus Penguin Books Limited and Deborah Lipstadt*. Continuing to read from Irving's speech, which was given in Calgary, Alberta, Rampton noted that Irving's Canadian audience had been sympathetic. There had been laughter when Irving remarked that when he was called a "moderate fascist," he strongly objected to the adjective "moderate." Irving's pronouncements about Auschwitz made clear why. Rampton quoted from Irving's lecture:

> Once we admit the fact that it was a brutal slave labour camp and large numbers of people did die, as large numbers of innocent people died elsewhere in the war, why believe the rest of the

baloney? I say quite tastelessly in fact that more people died on the back seat of Edward Kennedy's car in Chappaquiddick than ever died in a gas chamber in Auschwitz.

Turning to Mr. Justice Charles Gray, who heard the case alone without a jury, Rampton emphasized the important issue of the libel case:

My Lord, this is obviously an important case, but that is not however because it is primarily concerned whether or not the Holocaust took place or the degree of Hitler's responsibility for it. On the contrary, the essence of the case is Mr Irving's honesty and integrity as a chronicler—I shy away from the word "historian"—of these matters, for if it be right that Mr Irving, driven by his extremist views and sympathies, has devoted his energies to the deliberate falsification of this tragic episode in history, then by exposing that dangerous fraud in this court the Defendants may properly be applauded for having performed a significant public service not just in this country, but in all those places in the world where antisemitism is waiting to be fed.[1]

With this statement the first day of the trial came to an end.

Rampton's decision to quote one of Irving's many tasteless remarks about Auschwitz and Auschwitz survivors at the end of his short opening statement reflected the central importance of Auschwitz in the case. Irving's libel action against the American academic Deborah Lipstadt, the author of *Denying the Holocaust,* and her publisher, Penguin Books Limited, touched on a number of issues: Irving accused Lipstadt of libeling him by labeling him a Holocaust denier, accusing him of falsifying history in order to put Hitler in a more favorable light, and charging that he had stolen documents from a Moscow archive. Irving agreed with none of these accusations. In his own opening statement he submitted that Lipstadt's charge that he was a Holocaust denier was intolerable. "For the chosen victim, it is like being called a wife beater or a paedophile," Irving said. "It is enough for the label to be attached for the attachee to find himself designated as a pariah, an outcast from normal society. It is a verbal yellow star."[2] Both sides agreed that Holocaust denial—revisionism, as Irving calls it, or negationism, as I prefer to call it—stood at the center of the case, and both parties accepted that at the center of Holocaust denial was Auschwitz, the largest of the extermination camps.

Irving dramatized the centrality of Auschwitz to the trial during his cross-examination of myself, the expert witness for the defense for matters concerning Auschwitz. He had constructed an argument that assumed that the evidence for the function of Auschwitz as an extermination camp ought to be the presence of an underground gas chamber in Crematorium 2, and that the evidence for that gas chamber ought to be the presence of some holes in the remains of the concrete roof of that space. According to eyewitnesses, the SS had introduced the gas into the gas chambers through those holes, which connected to hollow wire-mesh columns in the gas chambers that allowed for the gas to disperse. In my own expert report to the court, I had stated that "today, these four small holes that connected the wire-mesh columns and the chimneys cannot be observed in the ruined remains of the concrete slab." However, my report continued:

Yet does this mean they were never there? We know that after the cessation of the gassings in the fall of 1944 all the gassing equip-

Richard Rampton

ment was removed, which implies both the wire-mesh columns and the chimneys. What would have remained would have been the four narrow holes in the slab. While there is not certainty in this particular matter, it would have been logical to attach at the location where the columns had been some formwork at the bottom of the gas chamber ceiling, and pour some concrete in the holes, and thus restore the slab.[3]

Developing a line of argumentation easily summarized by negationist Robert Faurisson's pet expression "No holes, no Holocaust," on the eleventh day of the trial, Irving offered to abandon his libel suit against Penguin and Lipstadt if I could show archeological evidence of those holes. I responded that this was impossible, as the concrete roof of the gas chamber was too badly damaged. Yet Irving did not give up, trying to get me at least to accept the principle that a causal chain existed in which the holes would prove the gas chamber, the gas chamber would prove the use of Auschwitz as an extermination camp, and the use of Auschwitz as an extermination camp would prove the Holocaust.

> [Irving]: "And do you accept, do you not, that if you were to go to Auschwitz the day after tomorrow with a trowel and clean away the gravel and find a reinforced concrete hole where we anticipate it from your drawings, this would make an open and shut case and I would happily abandon my action immediately?"

> [Van Pelt]: "I think I cannot comment on this. I am an expert on Auschwitz and not on the way you want to run your case."

> [Irving]: "There is my offer. I would say that that would drive such a hole through my case that I would have no possible chance of defending it any further."[4]

Irving's obsession with Auschwitz was a reflection of the general negationist creed that Auschwitz was indeed the linchpin of the so-called Holocaust Hoax. The reasons for the negationist preoccupation with attacking Auschwitz are many. Here it suffices to mention the most important and at the same time most paradoxical one: the presence of overwhelming eyewitness evidence and substantial documentary evidence for the history of Auschwitz as an extermination camp.

First of all, one of the very few full confessions given by any German official involved in a key role in the Holocaust is the comprehensive explanation made by Auschwitz Kommandant Rudolf Höss. Other key figures in the Holocaust either died before the end of the war (Reinhard Heydrich), committed suicide immediately after the German defeat (Heinrich Himmler), or made less than full confessions (Adolf Eichmann). Höss acknowledged the central role of Auschwitz in the Holocaust, and he described the organization, development, procedures, and problems of the extermination program in great detail on various occasions. For example, in his interrogation at Nuremberg, Höss gave a detailed account of the numbers of Jews who had arrived in Auschwitz: 250,000 from Poland, 65,000 from Greece, 100,000 from Germany, 90,000 from Holland, 110,000 from France, 90,000 from Slovakia, 20,000 from Belgium, and 400,000 from Hungary. When asked how he could accommodate all these people in a camp designed to hold 130,000, Höss answered: "They were not supposed to be employed in work there, but they were supposed to be exterminated."[5]

Rudolf Höss (facing the camera, middle), attending to a conversation between Reichsführer-SS Heinrich Himmler (left, with glasses) and IG Farben engineer Max Faust (right, in civilian attire). Auschwitz, July 17, 1942. Courtesy Archive Auschwitz-Birkenau State Museum, Oswiecim.

In an affidavit which he corrected and ultimately signed, Höss admitted that he had overseen the extermination, "by gassing and burning," of at least two and a half million human beings—mostly Jews:

6. The "final solution" of the Jewish question meant the complete extermination of all Jews in Europe. I was ordered to establish extermination facilities at Auschwitz in June 1941. At that time there were already in the general government three other extermination camps; BELZEK, TREBLINKA and WOLZEK.[6] These camps were under the Einsatzkommando of the Security Police and SD. I visited Treblinka to find out how they carried out their exterminations. The Camp Commandant at Treblinka told me that he had liquidated 80,000 in the course of one-half year. He was principally concerned with liquidating all the Jews from the Warsaw Ghetto. He used monoxide gas and I did not think his method was very efficient. So when I set up the extermination building at Auschwitz I, I used Cyclon B, which was crystallized Prussic Acid we dropped into the death chamber from a small opening. It took from 3 to 15 minutes to kill the people in the death chamber depending upon climatic conditions. We knew when the people were dead because their screaming stopped. We usually waited about one-half hour before we opened the doors and removed the bodies. After the bodies were removed our special commandos took off the rings and extracted the gold from the teeth of the corpses.

7. Another improvement we made over Treblinka was that we built our gas chambers to accommodate 2,000 people at one time, whereas at Treblinka their 10 gas chambers only accommodated 200 people each. The way we selected our victims was as follows: we had two SS doctors on duty at Auschwitz to examine the incoming transport of prisoners. The prisoners would be marched by one of the doctors who would make spot decisions as they walked by. Those who were fit for work were sent into the Camp. Others were sent immediately to the extermination plants. Children of tender years were invariably exterminated since by reason of their youth they were unable to work. Still another improvement we made over Treblinka was that at Treblinka the victims almost always knew that they were to be exterminated and at Auschwitz we endeavoured to fool the victims into thinking that they were to go through a delousing process. Of course, frequently they realized our true intentions and we sometimes had riots and difficulties due to that fact. Very frequently women would hide their children under the clothes but of course when we found them we would send the children in to be exterminated. We were required to carry out these exterminations in secrecy but of course the foul and nauseating stench from the continuous burning of bodies permeated the entire area and all of the people living in the surrounding communities knew that exterminations were going on at Auschwitz.[7]

On Monday, April 15, 1946, the affidavit was read out in court. Under cross-examination by American prosecutor Colonel John Harlan Amen, Höss confirmed that he had signed it voluntarily.[8] After he was extradited to Poland, Höss provided extensive explanations of the operation of Auschwitz during his trial, wrote a long essay on the Final Solution as it affected Auschwitz, composed his memoirs, and produced a great number of smaller essays on individual SS men with whom he had worked.

Höss was an important witness, and therefore any attempt to refute the Holocaust must engage and refute Höss. Furthermore, our knowledge of Auschwitz is based not only on Höss's testimony but also on a powerful convergence between eyewitness accounts, physical remains of the camp, the extensive building archive of the Auschwitz Central Construction Office (which survived the war), and various other archival sources. The evidence for the role of Treblinka, Belzec, and Sobibor—sufficient as it may be to come to a moral certainty about the wartime history of those places—is much less abundant. There are very few eyewitnesses, no confession that can compare to that given by Höss, no significant remains, and few archival sources.

Given this situation, negationists decided that it made strategic sense to concentrate their energies on debunking the Höss account and showing that Auschwitz could not have accommodated an extermination program. In 1982, the well-known American negationist Arthur R. Butz explained that impartial scientific, forensic, and scholarly analysis of the evidence would reveal that Auschwitz had not been a center of extermination. "It follows," Butz argued, "that the basic tactic of the defenders of the [extermination] legend, in controversies to come, will be to attempt to make claims that cannot be tested by the normal method of placing them as hypotheses in appropriate historical context and seeing if they cohere." According to Butz, those who maintained that the Holocaust existed despite evidence to the contrary would prefer to discuss extermination camps such as Belzec, Sobibor, and Treblinka—places of which little remained in terms of physical or archival relics and knowledge of which is largely based on witness testimony of survivors such as Jankiel Wiernik and postwar confessions of Treblinka commandant Stangl and others. "The consequence," Butz concluded, "is that it is much easier to disprove the legend as it applies to Auschwitz than as it applies to the others." The remains of the Auschwitz crematoria and the surviving archival sources pointed to a non-genocidal intent and use, Butz claimed. Therefore Butz declared that, confronted with Auschwitz, "the defenders of the [extermination] legend are in an impossible position." He predicted that it would be "very easy to bring down the legend as it applies to Auschwitz and Auschwitz in turn, on account of the nature of the evidence involved, brings down the rest of the legend with it."[9]

Butz called for an attack on Auschwitz because the evidence provided enough technical data to refute the accepted historical record (he said). Irving aimed at Auschwitz because he recognized the great symbolic value of the camp for our knowledge and understanding of the Holocaust. In a speech given at the Tenth International Revisionist Conference, organized in 1990 by the negationist Institute for Historical Review, Irving raised the question of why he and everyone else had been fooled for so long into thinking that the Holocaust had happened. His answer was simple: "We have been subjected to the biggest propaganda offensive that the human race has ever known." The main weapon in this campaign was "the great battleship Auschwitz!" Therefore Irving adopted as his battle cry: "Sink the Auschwitz!"[10] This call to arms invoked Churchill's 1941 order "Sink the Bismarck!," immortalized in the 1960 movie *Sink the Bismarck*, which described the Royal Navy's hunt for Hitler's proudest and deadliest battleship which, as some believed at the time, could have turned the course of history with her eight 15-inch guns. Irving's substitution gives an inkling of the topsy-turvy geography of the negationist world, in which Jews displace Germans as perpetrators of the Holocaust and Germans displace Jews as victims.

Irving's designation of Auschwitz as the most powerful "battleship" of the opposing side reflected his appreciation for the central symbolic significance of Auschwitz. At least since 1951, when Theodor Adorno stated that "to write a poem after Auschwitz is barbaric," the word Auschwitz has become a synecdoche for the Holocaust in general.[11] As Hans Jonas explained, the single name of Auschwitz serves "as a blindingly concentrating lens" to gather the widely dispersed reality of the Holocaust. "Auschwitz," he said, "marks a divide between a 'before' and an 'after,' where the latter will be forever different from the former."[12] Originally formulated by Adorno, "after Auschwitz" has become a linguistic marker within philosophical and theological discourse to denote the great historical rupture wrought by the Holocaust.[13] As Jürgen Habermas explained, "Auschwitz" changed the world because there the fundamental solidarity of all human beings was destroyed. Therefore "Auschwitz altered the conditions for the continuation of historical life contexts—and not only in Germany."[14] Trying to comprehend his own experience, Elie Wiesel came to the conclusion that "Auschwitz signifies not only the failure of two thousand years of Christian civilization, but also the defeat of the intellect that winds to find a Meaning—with a capital M—in history. What Auschwitz embodied has none."[15]

Philosophers have identified Auschwitz as a historical watershed. Historians have more empirical reasons to identify Auschwitz as the symbolic center of the Holocaust. First of all, it was the site where the single largest group of Jews were murdered. According to Raul Hilberg's rather conservative figures, which I hold to be the most reliable estimate of total Jewish deaths, the Holocaust claimed 5.1 million Jewish lives. Of this number, over 800,000 Jews died as the result of ghettoization and general privation, over 1.3 million were murdered in open-air shootings, and up to 3 million died in the camps. Of these, Auschwitz had the highest mortality with 1 million Jews, followed by Treblinka and Belzec with 750,000 and 550,000 Jews respectively.[16]

Second, Auschwitz may be considered a symbolic center of the Holocaust because the camp became the destination of a greater variety of Jews than any other. Jews were deported from at least twelve European countries to Auschwitz; the history of Auschwitz testifies to the pan-European character of the Holocaust.[17] But beyond that, Auschwitz was the place where the Germans killed many non-Jews: Romani, Poles, and Russians. These people died with Jews and died with the dead of the Jews; because of this, they give Auschwitz a particularly universal character which makes it different from Belzec, Sobibor, and Treblinka.

Auschwitz may be seen, then, as a particularly pointed attempt to destroy not only Jews but also the soul of Judaism. As the great Jewish philosopher Franz Rosenzweig reminded the generation that was to succumb in Auschwitz, the Jews were the first to understand that the son is born so that he may bear witness to his father's father: "The grandson renews the name of the forebear. The patriarchs of old call upon their last descendant by his name—which is theirs."[18] Thus, God planted eternal life in the midst of the Jewish people. Rosenzweig observed how the Jewish concept of a linked sequence of everlasting life goes from grandparent to grandchild; the Jewish people know that its eternity is present in the child of its child. Because of this, Jews could forgo claiming its eternity by

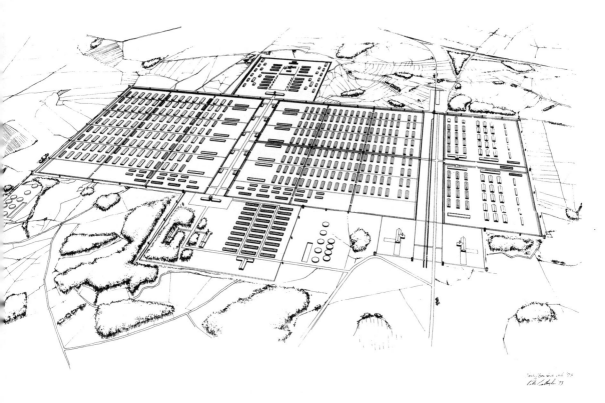

Bird's-eye view of Auschwitz-Birkenau, as planned in February 1943. The view is from the west to the east. Closest to the viewer are, left to right, a sewage treatment plant, Crematorium 5 (surrounded by trees), Crematorium 4, the so-called Central Sauna with the thirty storage barracks known as Canada, another sewage treatment plant, Crematorium 3, and Crematorium 2. The railway spur connecting to the main railway corridor runs east to west to end between Crematorium 2 and Crematorium 3. On the eastern side of the camp, one can see the SS compound. The northern part of the camp, on the left of the picture, was only partly completed. Drawing by Robert Jan van Pelt, Peter Gallagher, and Paul Backewich.

means of the possession of land. In the grandchild, the Jewish nation knew itself to "begin again." As Elie Wiesel wrote in a commentary on the new beginning Adam and Eve made after they had been thrown out of Paradise, "It is not given to man to begin." This, so he argues, is God's privilege. "But it is given to man to begin again—and he does so every time he chooses to defy death and side with the living."[19] This, in a nutshell, is the eternal foundation of a people which defines itself in the relationship between the old and the young. In Auschwitz, the Germans annulled this link and tried to destroy the very basis of Jewish existence: on arrival the old and the young, the grandparents and the grandchildren, were immediately sent to the gas chambers. The linked sequence of the everlasting life which, for the Jews, goes from grandparent to grandchild, was to be destroyed from the very beginning. The generation in between was allowed to live for somewhat longer in the barracks adjacent to the ramps where the selection took place, under the smoke of the crematoria. The whole camp system was designed to make fathers strangers to their sons and mothers strangers to their daughters, to set brother against brother and sister against sister. Primo Levi commented in his *The Drowned and the Saved* that in Auschwitz "almost everybody feels guilty of having omitted to offer help."[20] Those whose ancestors had given the world knowledge of a God who had created a good world from nothing were confronted with the truth of Auschwitz—the revelation that "man, the human species—we, in short— had the potential to construct an infinite enormity of pain, and that pain is the only force created from nothing, without cost and without effort. *It is enough not to see, not to listen, not to act.*"[21] Auschwitz has remained an enormous challenge to the survival of Judaism, a religion that centers on a covenant of life between God and Abraham, a covenant that stipulates that the stronger will bear witness to the suffering of the weaker in a world that God acknowledged to be "good."

Furthermore, and perhaps more important for those concerned with the general cultural-historical impact of Auschwitz, the camp may be considered the symbolic center of the Holocaust because it was thoroughly "modern" in its technology and organization. For Henry Feingold, Auschwitz marked the juncture where the European industrial system went awry. "Instead of enhancing life, which was the original hope of the Enlightenment, it began to consume itself." Therefore Auschwitz was "a mundane extension of the modern factory system" in which people were the raw material "and the end product was death, so many units per day marked carefully on the manager's production charts."[22]

As the nexus of technological prowess, bureaucratic discipline, and ideological determination, Auschwitz was not only thoroughly modern but also "civilized." As Franklin H. Littell observed, the death camps were not planned, built, and operated by illiterate, unschooled savages. "The killing centres were, like their inventors, products of what had been for generations one of the best university systems in the world."[23] The architect who designed Birkenau was a Bauhaus graduate. Dr. Josef Mengele had a degree in philosophy from the University of Munich and a degree in medicine from the University of Frankfurt am Main; he believed himself to be a herald of a new era. Inspired by Mengele, German dramatist Rolf Hochhuth had the camp doctor state in his controversial play *The Deputy* that Auschwitz marked the end of the old and the beginning of a new age, an age marked by the gospel that "life as an idea is dead."[24]

In Hochhuth's analysis, the modernity of Auschwitz was partly embodied in the crematoria, which offered in their logical arrangement of undressing rooms, gas chambers, and crematoria ovens a carefully thought out production facility of death. Yet the modernity of this technology of mass destruction is embodied not merely in the statistics that state that the gas chambers could kill so many people in so many minutes and the ovens could reduce so many corpses to ashes in so many hours. It is also embodied in the anonymity of the killing procedure itself. Ancient German law, going back to the pre-Christian era, stipulated that sentences of death should be pronounced in the midst of the community in the open air and that the judges who had condemned a person to death should be present at the execution, which likewise had to take place in full view of the community and the gods. All of this embodied a profound sense that when humans decide to take the life of another human being on behalf of society, they inflict a wound in the created world and should accept public responsibility for this. In the modern world, issues of personal responsibility and accountability tend to become diffused. At no point has this become so clear as in the case of Auschwitz, where Jews were executed without having been subjected to a clearly established judicial procedure and where the killing itself took place hidden from the world, in (mostly) underground gas chambers.

For French historian Pierre Vidal-Naquet, the gas chambers represented more than the industrialization of death with its attendant anonymity. They also offered an epistemological shift by introducing the negation of the crime within the crime itself. Vidal-Naquet quoted the sophistry of one of the attorneys for the accused in the Frankfurt Auschwitz Trial (1963–1965), who argued that those involved in the selection of the arriving Jews were not separating those fit for work from those unfit for work; they were separating those who would be sent to replace the disappeared work force from those who would be killed right away. As the decision to kill all Jews had been made before, those involved in the selection ought to be considered not killers but saviors of Jews, and those throwing the Zyklon B into some innocent-looking vents were only following orders. To Vidal-Naquet, this lawyer expressed the reality of the near-disappearance of responsibility expressed in the question: "Who, then, was the killer at Auschwitz?"[25] The very modernity of Auschwitz—that is, the anonymity of the killing—is embodied in the uniquely modern phenomenon that has arisen from it: the fact of Holocaust denial. As Vidal Naquet noted, "The crime can be denied today because it was anonymous."[26]

American theologian Richard L. Rubenstein explored some other dimensions of the "modern humanitarianism" of Auschwitz. Rubenstein defined Auschwitz as the supreme example of absolute domination that, thanks to technology and bureaucracy, has become possible in the modern age. As a place which combined extermination with slave labor, Auschwitz constituted a new kind of society which allowed, so Rubenstein believes, a prophetic vision of a future increasingly confronted with the assumed problem of "surplus populations."[27] Rubenstein believed that, as things are going, Western urban civilization is doomed to culminate in Necropolis, the new city of the dead. As the Holocaust was to him "an expression of some of the most significant political, religious and demographic tendencies of Western civilisation in the twentieth century," so Auschwitz was the terminal expression of the icon of modernization: the city. "The camps were thus far more of a permanent threat to the human future than they

Crematorium 3, Spring 1943. Courtesy Archive Auschwitz-Birkenau State Museum, Oswiecim.

Lageplan des Kriegsgefangenenlagers
Auschwitz O.S.

Maßstab 1:2000.

Bauabschnitt 1.

Bauabschnitt 2.

Brunnengalerie

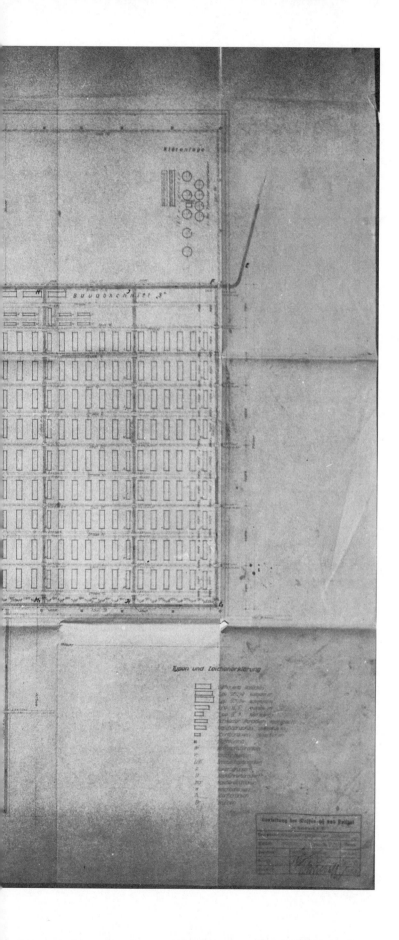

Plan of Auschwitz-Birkenau, 1943. On the west side (top of drawing) are, from left to right, Crematorium 2, Crematorium 3, a sewage treatment plant (Kläranlage), the so-called Central Sauna with the thirty storage barracks known as Canada (Effektenlager), Crematorium 4, Crematorium 5, and a second sewage treatment plant (Kläranlage). Courtesy Archive Auschwitz-Birkenau State Museum, Oswiecim.

could have been had they functioned solely as an exercise in mass killing.
An extermination center can only manufacture corpses, a society of total
domination creates a world of the living dead."[28]

Because not all deportees were killed on arrival, many more survived
Auschwitz than any of the other death camps. Of the 1.1 million Jews who
were deported to Auschwitz, some 100,000 Jews left the camp alive. Many
of those survivors were to succumb during the death march to the West or
during their stay during the spring of 1945 in concentration camps such as
Buchenwald and Bergen-Belsen. But tens of thousands saw liberation and
testified about their ordeal after the war. Some even did so during the war.
The most important wartime report on the German genocide of the Jews,
sponsored by the War Refugee Board, was written by two escapees from
Auschwitz who described the extermination installation in some detail. Of
the 100,000 gentile survivors of Auschwitz, of whom the Poles, with
75,000, were the largest group, all who could do so bore witness to the use
of the camp as an extermination center for Jews.

The technology of mass destruction as it existed in Auschwitz also
points to another important issue: the significance of the so-called Final
Solution of the Jewish Problem as a state-initiated, state-sponsored, and
state-controlled program of genocide. Like any major historical problem,
there has been, is, and probably will remain legitimate disagreement among
historians about various aspects of the history of the Holocaust. Yet there
has been, is, and probably will remain a general consensus that the German
destruction of at least five and possibly as many as six and a half million
European Jews was *not* the result of countless individual initiatives taken,
as Irving phrased it in 1984, by "Nazi criminals, acting probably without
direct orders from above."[29] The evidence of the operations of the Einsatzgruppen in the German-occupied parts of the Soviet Union, of the ghetto
clearings in Poland and the subsequent mass killings in the death camps,
and of the deportations of Jews from many countries over long distances to
the killing centers in Poland reveals a high level of organization involving
many state officials. Furthermore, Auschwitz was constructed in the middle
of the war, at a time when there was a general building stop in Germany,
with public funds. Many levels of the German bureaucracy were involved
in the process, providing special construction permits and rationed building materials. The German state railways cooperated when it gave, after
careful consideration, permission for the construction of a railway spur
connecting the existing railway tracks at Auschwitz to the crematoria in
Birkenau. The staged transformation of Auschwitz from a prison camp for
Poles to a death camp for Jews occurred on the initiative of, and under
control of, the state—primarily as it was embodied in Reichsführer-SS
Heinrich Himmler in his capacity as chief of the German police.

Finally, Auschwitz is considered the center of the Holocaust because
enough of the two most important parts, the Stammlager (main camp) at
Auschwitz (also known as Auschwitz I) and its huge satellite camp Auschwitz-Birkenau (also known as Auschwitz II), still remain to give the visitor
a sense of the nature and scale of the operation. Treblinka, Belzec, and
Sobibor, which together hosted the murder of 1.5 million Jews, were small
camps that were demolished by the Germans at the end of 1943. Very little
to nothing of the original arrangement can be seen. Only recently in Belzec,
with the uncovering of the enormous mass graves, has it become possible
to acquire, at the location of the massacre, some visual sense of the
atrocities that passed there.

In Auschwitz I and, more important, in Auschwitz II, the case is
different. When the SS evacuated the camps, they were able to dismantle

the gas chambers and blow up the crematoria. But the Soviets found the rest of the Stammlager and Birkenau largely intact. In 1947, the Polish parliament adopted a law "Commemorating the Martyrdom of the Polish Nation and other Nations in Oswiecim," and the minister of culture included both Auschwitz I and II in the new Auschwitz-Birkenau State Museum.

Given the many remains of the death camps—the guard towers, the barbed-wire fences, the gatehouse, the tracks, the barracks, the ruins of the crematoria, and so on—it is not surprising that in a largely visual culture dominated by photography, film, and television, the landscape of Auschwitz has become an icon of the Holocaust. Alain Resnais and Jean Cayrol's magnificent 1955 movie *Night and Fog* was largely shot in and around Birkenau. The opening scenes showed the banal, seemingly innocent fields around the camp. Their filming of the remains at Birkenau allowed the horror to slowly emerge from the midst of banality. As the camera pans the empty barracks in Birkenau, the narrator immediately warns us not to take the image of the present for the reality of the past. "No description, no picture can restore their true dimension: endless, uninterrupted fear. . . . We can only show you the shell, the shadow."[30]

Resnais tried to evoke an impression of the deportations by filming what remained of the deportees in the showcases of the museum at Auschwitz I. As he films their contents, the narration, which until then has so quietly recalled and probed, becomes halting, as the unimaginable and unspeakable is brought home. Finally it stops—as if there is nothing more to say about the world of the camp. Resnais constantly returns with his camera to the fields of Birkenau, and with every scene he confirms the factuality of the events that happened there and the centrality of Auschwitz for the modern understanding of the world. Revolutionary in its visual language and brilliant in its counterpoint of image and sound, past atrocity and present landscape, *Night and Fog* simultaneously established and confirmed the central role of the landscape of Auschwitz in the modern imagination of atrocity.

All of this combined in what Irving labeled "the battleship Auschwitz" that had to be sunk if the negationists were to convince the world that the Holocaust was, in the words of Butz, "The Hoax of the Twentieth Century." Irving was right. Because of its symbolic significance, Auschwitz was, is, and will remain the crucial battleground.

Irving's obsession with Auschwitz also carried a personal if not an existential dimension. In 1988, a quick perusal of an engineering study of the Auschwitz crematoria was the occasion for Irving's turn to negationism, which in turn had made him into a protagonist in Lipstadt's *Denying the Holocaust*. In his opening statement for the defense at Irving's libel case, Rampton summarized the circumstances of that fateful conversion.

> So, my Lord, I pass on to Mr Irving and Holocaust denial. Between the publication of the first edition of *Hitler's War* in 1977 and its second edition in 1991, Mr Irving's views about the Holocaust underwent a sea change. In the 1977 edition he accepted it as an historical truth in all its essentials, systematic mass murder of Jews in purpose-built extermination factories, but in the 1991 edition all trace of the Holocaust in this sense had disappeared. Auschwitz, for example, has been transformed from a monstrous killing machine into a mere slave labour camp.
>
> What are the reasons for this astounding volte-face? The

principal reason can be expressed in one word: Leuchter. In 1988 a man of German origin, Ernst Zündel, was put on trial in Canada for publishing material which, amongst other things, denied the existence of homicidal gas chambers at Auschwitz. In defence of this charge, Mr Zündel's lawyers recruited a man called Fred Leuchter, who seems to have made his living as some kind of consultant in the design of execution facilities in the USA. Mr Leuchter was duly dispatched to Auschwitz to seek evidence of the use, or otherwise, of homicidal gas chambers. He took some samples from various parts of the remains of Auschwitz which he later had analysed in America and then wrote a report describing his findings and summarizing his conclusions. These were that there were never any homicidal gas chambers in Auschwitz.

Unfortunately for Mr Zündel, Mr Leuchter's report was declared inadmissible by the Canadian judge on the grounds that Mr Leuchter had no relevant expertise.

Now it happened that Mr Irving also gave evidence for Mr Zündel at that trial. In the course of that visit he had read the Leuchter Report. Shortly thereafter he declared himself convinced that Leuchter was right and that there were never any homicidal gas chambers at Auschwitz. So enthused was he by the Leuchter Report that he published it himself in this country, with an appreciative foreword written by him and introduced it to the public at a press conference in London, at which he declared that the validity of Leuchter's laboratory reports was unchallengeable.

So it was that the Leuchter Report became the main weapon in Mr Irving's campaign to "Sink the Battleship Auschwitz," as he calls it. The essence of this campaign is that the Holocaust symbolized by Auschwitz is a myth, legend or lie, deployed by Jews to blackmail the German people into paying vast sums in reparations to supposed victims of the Holocaust.

According to Mr Irving, the Leuchter report is "the biggest calibre shell that has yet hit the battleship Auschwitz" and has "totally exploded the legend." Unfortunately for Mr Irving, the Leuchter Report is bunk, and he knows it.[31]

The Zündel trial and its aftermath turned out to be a watershed in Irving's life. With his endorsement of Leuchter's conclusions he lost his standing in the community of historians. Before 1988, Irving was known mainly as the author of mostly well-written but controversial historical studies of the Third Reich. His books appeared under the imprint of respected houses such as Viking, Macmillan, Cassell & Company, Simon & Schuster, and Hodder & Stoughton and received accolades from other historians. After 1988, Irving came to be seen as the rabble-rousing speaker at gatherings of the extreme right who ended up accused and convicted in German and French courts, a man who rapidly turned into a pariah of the historical community. It is clear from a study of the evidence that Irving is largely to blame for his own fate. He did not embrace negationism in the rush of the moment but accepted it deliberately, after a long period of gestation. To understand Irving's journey to the Royal Courts of Justice, it is necessary to sketch the outline of his intellectual biography.

David John Cawdell Irving was born in Britain in March 1938, the month that Hitler annexed Austria. His father served as a naval officer on the Murmansk convoys. He survived the sinking of the ship in which he

The ruined chimneys of
Auschwitz-Birkenau.
Photo by Rod Shone.

served, but he never returned home. His mother, a commercial artist, raised David and his three siblings in strained circumstances. Already at grammar school, Irving showed his desire to achieve notoriety when, awarded a book as a school prize, he asked for Hitler's *Mein Kampf*. After a short stint at the University of London, he left for Germany to work in a Thyssen steel mill. There he rose to the position of third smelter and perfected his German and for the first time encountered in the stories of his fellow workers a German perspective on the Second World War—one that defined the Germans not as perpetrators but as victims. One of them came from Dresden and told Irving about the Allied fire-bombing of that city in February 1945. His story proved a catalyst, and Irving decided to write a history of what he had come to see as a major Allied war crime. Published in 1963, Irving's well-written *The Destruction of Dresden* not only became a best-seller but its allegation that the bombing of the city was "the biggest single massacre in European history"[32] gained him access to Germans who, after 1945, had chosen to remain out of the public eye. These Germans were happy to share with Irving their memories and some old documents which they had kept under lock and key since 1945. As a result, Irving gained among professional historians the enviable reputation for finding hitherto unavailable historical material. Irving, in turn, developed a profound disdain for the work of other historians, whom he accused of intellectual incest because they copied each other's conclusions without bothering to dig up new evidence. In quick succession Irving published, among other books, the memoirs of Field Marshal Wilhelm Keitel (1965), a history of the Nazi atomic research program (1967), a biography of Air Force Field Marshal Erhard Milch (1973), and a biography of Field Marshal Erwin Rommel (1977). Irving's friendship with Hitler's SS adjutant Otto Günsche proved fateful. Günsche introduced him to many members of Hitler's staff: his adjutants such as Karl-Jesco von Puttkamer, Gerhard Engel, and Nicolaus von Below; secretaries such as Traudl Junge and Christa Schroeder; servants; and many others. These people who had lived very close to Hitler trusted Irving as a sympathetic Englishman who had no anti-Nazi axe to grind, and they entrusted him with their diaries and private papers.

After more than a decade of research, Irving published his massive *Hitler's War* (1977). Written in a gripping narrative style, *Hitler's War* was very different from the dry studies that preceded it. The first sentence effectively set the tone. "Late on the evening of September 3, 1939, Hitler exchanged the elegant marbled halls of the Chancellery for the special train, Amerika, parked in a dusty Pomeranian railroad station surrounded by parched and scented pine trees and wooden barrack huts baked dry by the central European sun."[33] Showing a keen eye for the texture of life, Irving wrote the book in the style of a historical novel. It read as if he had somehow crawled into the skins of the main protagonists—a quality that does not surprise because Irving relied heavily on the interviews, diaries, and memoirs he had obtained from the members of Hitler's inner circle. The general public loved it. Professional historians were not enthusiastic. True, many praised Irving's energy in turning up new sources, and some welcomed it because *Hitler's War* offered an absolutely original perspective on Hitler's career as a military leader. But most historians were deeply troubled by the fact that Irving had uncritically accepted as truth the views of those who had a vested interest in putting Hitler in the best possible light. The result resembled the account of his life during the war that Hitler never came to write.

Irving's sympathy for Hitler led to what most reviewers considered the offensive core of *Hitler's War*: Irving's theory that the Holocaust had been initiated behind Hitler's back by men such as Reichsführer-SS Heinrich Himmler, SS-Obergruppenführer Security Police Chief Reinhard Heydrich, and Gauleiter Artur Greiser. In the introduction to the book, Irving raised this theory in the context of his attempt to "expose the 'unseaworthiness' of many current legends about Hitler." The "most durable" legend concerned Hitler's involvement in the extermination of the Jews. Irving proposed that the killing had been ad hoc, "the way out of an awkward dilemma, chosen by the middle-level authorities in the eastern territories overrun by the Nazis—and partly a cynical extrapolation by the central SS authorities of Hitler's anti-Semitic decrees." Hitler had aimed only to deport the Jews to the East, but the Germans there were unable to deal with the arrival of many Jews in the already overcrowded ghettos. "Partly in collusion with each other, partly independently, the Nazi agencies then simply liquidated the deportees as their trains arrived, on a scale increasingly more methodical and more regimented as the months passed."[34]

According to Irving, these massacres happened not only without Hitler's permission but even in violation of Hitler's express wish that the Jews be spared. To support this assertion, he provided rather flimsy arguments such as the notion that as a pragmatic politician, Hitler would not have approved of moving "millions of Jews" to the East with the single purpose of killing them there, "nor would he willingly destroy manpower, for which his industry was crying out."[35] Significantly, *Hitler's War* contained only two photos. One showed what Irving described in the introduction as the "incontrovertible evidence"[36] for Hitler's alleged protection of the Jews. It is a facsimile page from Himmler's phone log of November 30, 1941. That day Himmler was at Hitler's headquarters. In Himmler's Gothic handwriting the log recorded that at 1:30 P.M. Himmler had called Heydrich in Prague. The topic of discussion: "Jew transport from Berlin. No liquidation."[37] Irving did not transcribe Himmler's log entry but wrote as a caption "at 1:30 P.M. the SS chief telephones Heydrich in Prague from Hitler's bunker in the Wolf's Lair, ordering that there was to be 'no

David Irving, author of Hitler's War. *Photo by Ted Bath. Courtesy* The Times.

liquidation' of Jews."[38] It is important to note that the phone log referred to a "Jew transport" (singular), not to "Jew transports" (plural). In the main narrative Irving wrote that "on November 30, 1941, [Himmler] was summoned to the Wolf's Lair for a secret conference with Hitler, at which the fate of Berlin's Jews was clearly raised. At 1:20 pm Himmler was obliged to telephone from Hitler's bunker to Heydrich the explicit order that Jews were *not to be liquidated.*"[39] By changing the wording of Himmler's phone log of November 30, Irving conveyed the impression that Hitler had intervened on behalf of the Jews and had "obliged" Himmler to call the operation off.

While Irving tried to lift the burden of guilt from Hitler's shoulders, misquoting evidence to make his point, he did not deny that the Holocaust had occurred. To the contrary: he made a number of references to the role of Auschwitz as an extermination camp. Writing about the spring of 1942, Irving stated that the Germans began to round up Jews in France, Holland, Belgium, and Slovakia to send them to Poland. "Upon arrival in Auschwitz and Treblinka, four in every ten were pronounced fit for work; the rest were exterminated with a maximum of concealment."[40] The major reason for that concealment, as Irving argued in the next few lines, was to dupe Hitler. "The concealment was almost perfect, and Himmler's own papers reveal how he pulled the wool over Hitler's eyes."[41] Writing about the Hungarian Action in 1944, when more than 400,000 Jews were deported to Auschwitz, Irving noted that "in Auschwitz, the defunct paraphernalia of death—idle since late 1943—began to clank again as the first trainloads from Hungary arrived."[42] Yet this time the policy of concealment was to fail. "Himmler's ghastly secret was coming out, for two Slovak Jews had escaped from Auschwitz extermination camp, and their horrifying revelations were published in two reputable Swiss newspapers in early July."[43] At this time Irving accepted that Auschwitz had been an extermination camp. He was to reverse himself eleven years later.

If Irving had hoped that *Hitler's War* would earn him the respect of the historical establishment, he must have been disappointed. Hugh Trevor-Roper, Regius Professor of Modern History at Oxford, praised Irving's "indefatigable scholarly industry" and then launched into an attack on Irving's method, concluding that Irving's judgment could not be trusted. Trevor-Roper observed that Irving's discussion of Hitler's attitude toward the Jews was highly implausible. The Himmler phone log of November 30 did not refer to the liquidation of Jews in general but to the liquidation of one transport. Trevor-Roper rightly observed that "one does not veto an action unless one thinks that it is otherwise likely to occur." Irving's argument showed his greatest fault as a historian: "He seizes on a small but dubious particle of 'evidence'; builds upon it, by private interpretation, a large general conclusion; and then overlooks or re-interprets the more substantial evidence and probability against it. Since this defective method is invariably used to excuse Hitler or the Nazis and to damage their opponents, we may reasonably speak of a consistent bias, unconsciously distorting the evidence."[44]

In Germany, Martin Broszat, director of the Institute for Contemporary History in Munich, published a devastating 36-page critique in his institute's quarterly; and in the United States, Charles W. Sydnor, Jr., undertook considerable original research before demolishing *Hitler's War* in a 30-page review that not only claimed that "an inflexible bias is the shaky foundation of Mr. Irving's revisionist edifice" but also judged Irving's claim to have surpassed all earlier scholarship on Hitler as "pretentious twaddle." Concerning Irving's reliance on his conversations with Hitler's staff, Sydnor concluded that "Mr. Irving's mining efforts have yielded more lead than gold." The collective testimony of those who had served Hitler on a day-to-day basis in no way provided the foundation for a "credible revisionist argument about what he did or did not know, order, do."[45]

If *Hitler's War* generated the indignation of professional historians, it attracted the sympathetic attention of negationists. Until the publication of *Hitler's War,* no historian of reputation had come even close to their views. They recognized in Irving a kindred spirit who could lend their case legitimacy, and they actively began to cultivate him as a fellow traveler. In 1980, Irving received his first invitation to speak at a negationist conference.[46] Irving was apprehensive. A condition of his participation would be not having to share the same platform with notorious negationists such as Arthur Butz. "This is pure Realpolitik on my part," he admitted in a letter to the conference organizers. "I am already dangerously exposed, and I cannot take the chance of being caught in Flak meant for others!"[47] Irving was not (yet) prepared to be associated too publicly with well-known negationists, particularly because he aimed to establish his own right-wing political party. He was, however, quite willing to establish an ongoing commercial relationship with negationists by granting the Institute for Historical Review the right to distribute his books. While projecting toward the outside world an image of success, with a flat in Mayfair and a Rolls-Royce, Irving was having financial difficulties and was in need of help.

In 1983, Irving finally agreed to attend the annual conference of the Institute for Historical Review. His political ambitions had been thwarted, so he had greater freedom to associate with whomever he wished. But, perhaps most important of all, Irving's confidence was buoyed by the reaction to his highly visible role in the debunking of the Hitler diaries as forgeries. Endorsed as authentic by eminent British historian Lord Dacre (Hugh Trevor-Roper), prominent American historian Gerhard Weinberg, and German scholar Eberhard Jäckel, the diaries were scheduled to be published by the German magazine *Der Stern,* the British *Sunday Times,* the American *Newsweek,* the French *Paris Match,* and several smaller journals. Resisting the tide, Irving maintained that the diaries were fake. His conviction derived from the fact that he knew the collection from which the diaries had come as one riddled with forgeries. In fact, he was in possession of copies of many of these fakes. Editors of magazines who had missed the scoop of the Hitler diaries and who had a vested interest in protecting their own circulations by showing that they were not genuine courted Irving as never before. It made him a lot of money. More important, in a remarkable *coup de théatre,* the Hitler diaries affair had allowed him to appear as a prophet of truth. On Monday April 25, one of *Der Stern*'s competitors, the *Bild Zeitung,* smuggled Irving into the *Der Stern* press conference to announce the discovery. In his *Selling Hitler,* Robert Harris described what happened when David Irving leapt to the microphone in the center of the hall to announce that the diaries had come from a source that mostly yielded forgeries.

> "Reporters stormed towards me," recalled Irving, "lights blazing, and microphones were thrust at me." A Japanese film crew was trampled in the rush and a fist fight broke out. Chairs and lights were scattered as chaos rippled across the crowded floor. From the platform, Koch shouted that Irving should ask questions, not make speeches. Irving's microphone was switched off. But it was too late. Irving challenged *Stern* to say whether the

diaries' ink had been tested for its age. There was no answer. "Ink! Ink!" shouted some of the reporters. "Torpedo running," whispered Irving to one of the journalists sitting next to him as he sat down. The local NBC correspondent approached and asked if he would leave immediately to take part in a live link-up with the *Today* show, now on the air in America. Irving agreed. "All most exhilarating," he noted, "and I left a trail of chaos behind me."[48]

Irving carried the day and earned tens of thousands of dollars from the media, which was clamoring for his story. His vindictive and very public triumph over Trevor-Roper, who had so fiercely criticized *Hitler's War* six years earlier, reinforced his neurotic sense of pride and his grandiose sense of self-importance. Recalling the event five years later, the man who took pride in being an outsider without a title admitted that it gave him an incredible pleasure to see important people—the doctors, professors, and lords of this world—with "egg on their face."[49]

The *Der Stern* press conference marked a turning point in Irving's career, but he undercut some of the credit he had won when, several days later, he changed his mind and declared the diaries to be authentic. This disclosure brought him to the front page of *The Times,* but a few weeks later the forensic investigations of the ink and paper, which Irving had advocated, definitively proved that Irving had originally been right and that the diaries were a postwar forgery. As a result, he was to be remembered as the first person to declare the diaries to be fake and the last person to declare them authentic.[50] But while the outcome for his professional reputation was mixed, the Hitler diaries affair seems to have emboldened him, and the earlier caution he had shown in mixing with negationists began to disappear. Speaking later that year at the annual conference of the Institute for Historical Review, Irving was willing to share a platform with well-known negationists such as French academic Robert Faurisson and German judge Wilhlem Stäglich.

David Irving at Stern *press conference, 1983. Courtesy* Stern.

If his hosts expected a repetition of the excitement Irving had generated on April 25, they must have been disappointed. Yet his rambling speech was revealing. At the beginning, Irving freely admitted that he conducted his activity as a historian with a keen eye to the publicity he could receive. "I have at home . . . a filing cabinet full of documents which I don't issue all at once," Irving told his audience. "I keep them; I issue them a bit at a time. When I think my name hasn't been in the newspapers for several weeks, well, then I ring them up and I phone them and I say: 'What about this one, then?'"[51] He mentioned that his collection contained not only genuine documents but also forgeries, which allowed him to launch a curious description of his role in the Hitler diaries affair. After a preview of some of the controversial elements in his forthcoming Churchill biography, Irving turned to his *Hitler's War* and the violent response it had generated in Jewish circles. He repeated his opinion that Hitler had ordered the resettlement of the Jews in the East and that he suspected that the atrocities that befell the Jews there were the result of initiatives taken by "local criminals on the spot." He admitted that he could not prove his thesis. "I haven't gone into that, I haven't investigated that particular aspect of history but from the documents I have seen, I've got the kind of gut feeling which suggests to me that that is probably accurate."[52] Such remarks must have been none too welcome to most of those present, but the comparison he subsequently developed must have been more acceptable. The fate of the Jews in the East was no different from that of the Palestinians in Sabra and Chatilla. "Isn't it right for Tel Aviv to claim now that David Irving is talking nonsense and *of course* Adolf Hitler must have known about what was going on in Auschwitz and Treblinka, and then in the same breath to claim that, *of course,* our beloved Mr. Begin didn't know what was going on in Sabra and Chatilla. You can't have one without the other; rather like a horse and carriage."[53] Irving's conclusion was that Hitler had been "so busy being a soldier that he didn't really pay too much attention to what crimes may or may not have been going in various far-flung parts of the Reich." To which he added: "I'm not going to go into the controversy here about the actual goings-on inside Auschwitz, or the other extermination camps or concentration camps." Immediately after declaring that he did not want to engage Auschwitz, he stated that he had been "deeply impressed by Mr. Friedrich Berg's lecture earlier this afternoon."[54] The thesis of Berg's lecture had been that accounts of the alleged diesel gas chambers at Belzec, Sobibor, and Treblinka were false, because it was hard to imagine "a more hideously clumsy, and inefficient, method of committing mass-murder." Hence "the Diesel gas chamber claim is rubbish."[55] Irving was cautious, he admitted, because he was being watched and risked a total boycott by the American publishing industry. "I am right out in the front line. The artillery fire is beginning and the shot and shell are falling all 'round me."[56]

Irving did not explicitly embrace negationism at the 1983 conference, but the occasion was to have far-reaching consequences: it marked his first encounter with hard-core negationist Dr. Robert Faurisson. That meeting began a process that would lead to Irving's 1988 endorsement of the Leuchter Report and, twelve years later, culminate in the libel trial in the Royal Courts of Justice.

Faurisson was a one-time lecturer in French literature at the University of Lyons-2. He had emerged from a school of literary interpretation known as New Criticism. This school went back to the early 1940s, when two prominent American critics, Monroe C. Beardsley and William Kurtz

Wimsatt, proposed that the contemporary approach of interpreting poems in their autobiographical, historical, political, or cultural contexts was bankrupt. Instead, a critic should read a poem as a verbal icon—an autonomous verbal structure—and foreclose any appeal to history, biography, or cultural context. Even the poet's intention did not matter when judging a poem.[57] French student of literature Robert Faurisson adopted Beardsley and Wimsatt's ontologically grounded aesthetic isolationism but abandoned its pragmatic aim to encase it in a particularly dogmatic set of rules. His "Ajax method" (because "it scours as it cleans as it shines"), centered on the proposition that while words may have more than one meaning if taken in isolation, they acquire one specific meaning only within a text. And while texts may generate different responses, this does not mean that they have different meanings. In short: "Texts have only one meaning, or no meaning at all."[58] Refusing to consider any external evidence, the only access to truth was now to be through Faurisson's own technique of textual exegesis.

Robert Faurisson, 1988. Courtesy Canadian Jewish News.

Faurisson's work would have remained a footnote in the history of postmodern literary theory if not for his desire to apply the "Ajax method" to the study of history. It was, at first sight, a natural extension of his activities. "The historian works with documents" declared a nineteenth-century French handbook on historical methodology in its opening sentence. And it concluded its opening paragraph with the succinct formula: "No documents, no history"[59]—an adage which, incidentally, would inspire Faurisson to coin his own maxim: "No holes, no Holocaust." Langlois and Seignobos's classic *Introduction to the Study of History* (1897) stressed the importance of a critical approach to documents because "criticism is antagonistic to the normal bent of the mind."[60] Writing in a time which clearly remembered how historians cultivated an "empty and pompous species of literature which was then known as 'history,'"[61] Langlois and Seignobos pressed their case that historians should not make easy assumptions about documents written a long time ago by people who may have used language differently.[62] But they also wrote that contemporary documents could be taken at face value. Ignoring Langlois and Seignobos's observation that it was not necessary to apply the most rigorous internal criticism to contemporary documents because the author and the historian shared language and outlook, Faurisson condemned historians who habitually failed to "attack" the documents they were using and instead tried to fit those texts into their various contexts.[63] In other words, historians sinned against the ground rule of Faurisson's theory of criticism, seemingly justified by Langlois and Seignobos, that nothing should distract from the exegesis of the sacrosanct "word on the page."

Faurisson's attempt to apply his rule of textual exegesis to history was ill founded. First of all, it was a clear example of the kind of hypercriticism against which Langlois and Seignobos had warned. "There are persons who scent enigmas everywhere, even where there are none. They take perfectly clear texts and subtilise on them till they make them doubtful, under the pretext of freeing them from imaginary corruptions. They discover traces of forgery in authentic documents."[64] Applied without restraint, hypercriticism destroyed the possibility of history.

Furthermore, Faurisson's approach very clearly departed from Beardsley and Wimsatt's own method of exegesis, which applied only to poetry because in poems "all or most of what is said or implied is relevant." For the interpretation of "practical messages," the critic had to "correctly infer the intention."[65] However, Faurisson had no qualms about launching his theory of literary criticism into a colonizing drive beyond the boundary of the poetic to treat historical texts as merely rhetorical, purely discursive operations that have no link to external evidence.

Faurisson was not the only one to dissolve the boundary between literature and history. In fact, a whole school arose which, under the banner of New Historicism, began to apply the lessons of adherents of New Criticism to the discourse of history. The new historicism claimed that the materials of historical investigation—chronicles, correspondence, bills, minutes, memoirs, court proceedings, eyewitness testimonies, and so on— were at an ontological level not different from, for example, poetry. Fair enough. Yet they also charged that the accounts historians wrought from those elements—their "histories"—were no different from poems or novels or epics. In effect, they erased the fundamental distinction between fact and fiction—a distinction that had in a rough-and-ready fashion defined the boundary between history and literature since the ancient Greeks.

Faurisson could be seen as just another exponent of post-structuralist historiography if not for the fact that he attempted to apply this theory to a unique ideological agenda. To be sure, many in the New Historicist camp had a mission of their own: to challenge the dominant understanding of history as just another hegemonic discourse. The New Historicists aimed to create a place in history for the hitherto repressed—that is, everyone who was not white, straight, or male. In other words, by dissolving "History" into "histories," they tried to reveal new riches hitherto suppressed under the totalitarian discourse that centered on a Whig interpretation of history as progress. Faurisson, however, had a different axe to grind: he did not desire to make our reading of the past more inclusive. To the contrary: he aimed to narrow history by scouring the Holocaust from the record. If the champions of New Historicism intended to increase the truth content of history by allowing different and contradictory "truths" to float simultaneously, Faurisson desired to use the same technique to debunk a central truth of contemporary history as a lie.

In this mission, Faurisson was inspired by another French ideologue, Paul Rassinier.[66] Born in 1906, Rassinier had been a communist in his youth, but he was expelled from the party in 1932. A pacifist in the 1930s, Rassinier applauded the Munich agreement. He served in the French army in 1940, joined the French Resistance in 1942, and edited the clandestine magazine *La Quatrième République*. Arrested on November 29, 1943, by the Gestapo, he was deported to the concentration camp of Buchenwald in January 1944. After a period of quarantine there, he was brought to the concentration camp at Dora-Mittelbau, where he was imprisoned for fourteen months.

When Rassinier entered the camps he saw no basic difference between the democratic West, National Socialist Germany, and communist Russia, between the First World War and the Second. He was simply not prepared to acknowledge that the National Socialist regime was different or that its concentration camps were unique. "The problem of the concentration camps was a universal one, not just one that could be disposed of by placing it on the doorstep of the National Socialists."[67] Rassinier believed that the horror of camp life was the result not of German policies but of the common practice, found in every country, of letting trusted inmates, who were referred to in the French penitentiary system as *Chaouchs*, run the prison on behalf of the jailers. "From morning to night, our *Chaouchs*, throwing out their chests, plumed themselves on the power that they said that they had to send us to the *Krématorium* for the least indiscretion and with a single word."[68] According to Rassinier, the SS kept a distance and were even ignorant of what happened inside the camp. If they had involved themselves with the day-to-day lives of the inmates, the situation would have been better.[69] After having formulated the thesis that the SS was really not in control and that all the horror of inmate life was due to the petty cruelty of the Kapos, Rassinier came to a logical conclusion: the atrocity stories about the use of the camps as factories of death could not be true, because these stories implied an organized system of terror that transcended the cruelty of the Kapos. To account for the fact that such stories circulated nevertheless, Rassinier postulated "the complex of Ulysses' lie, which is everyone's, and so it is with all of the internees." Camp inmates had an inborn need to exaggerate their suffering "without realizing that the reality is quite enough in itself."[70]

After he was liberated in April 1945, Rassinier returned to France. He had no patience for or empathy with his fellow deportees who "came back with hatred and resentment on their tongues and in their pens." They were caught in "a treadmill of lies. . . . So it was with Ulysses who, during the course of his voyage, each day added a new adventure to his Odyssey, as much to please the public taste of the times as to justify his long absence in the eyes of his family."[71] To Rassinier, the proof of the fact that the ex-inmates were lying was their constant return to the (to him) obviously absurd proposition that camps had been equipped with homicidal gas chambers. As time progressed, he became more and more obsessed with the issue of the gas chambers, which had ceased to be the result of mere "lies of Ulysses" and had become a massive fabrication created with a political aim in mind.

This shift in explanation from psychology to conspiracy was due to the notorious Kravchenko trial, which dominated the French media in the first half of 1949. In 1944, Victor Kravchenko, a top official of the Soviet delegation in Washington, D.C., defected to the West. In his best-selling book *I Chose Freedom* (1946), Kravchenko described the Soviet Union as a totalitarian nightmare in which the successes that had been trumpeted all around the world, especially the ruthless collectivization of agriculture, had been achieved through the application of terror backed by an extensive system of concentration camps. The Soviets and their communist allies in the West answered through a campaign of defamation against Kravchenko, which resulted, among other things, in an article published in the French magazine *Les Lettres Francaises*. It claimed that Kravchenko was too stupid to have written the book, and that his so-called revelations had been manufactured by American intelligence. In response, Kravchenko filed a libel suit against the magazine, and in early 1949 the trial began in Paris. It lasted for two months. In the end Kravchenko won, but many never surrendered the idea that the whole gulag had been an invention of the American intelligence service, designed to discredit the Soviet Union.[72] Rassinier drew the conclusion that if the Russian concentration camps had been concocted in Washington, D.C., the stories about German extermination camps with large crematoria equipped with homicidal gas chambers must also have been the product of some propaganda apparatus.

Rassinier spent the rest of his life trying to debunk the myth of the camps. As a known Nazi sympathizer and anti-Semite, Faurisson was attracted to Rassinier's thesis that the Holocaust was a hoax and the gas chambers the stuff of legend.[73] Exposed to an alleged deception of such dimensions, Faurisson lost his interest in sonnets, odes, and novels and began to subject accounts about Auschwitz to his "Ajax method." As he surveyed the literature, the great debunker found many contradictions in, among other things, statements about the total number of victims who had died in Auschwitz. Shortly after the liberation the Russians had given the number of 4 million victims. Commandant Rudolf Höss had mentioned at one time 3 million victims, of whom two and a half million had been gassed—the rest having died from "natural causes," and at another time he had mentioned a number of some 1,130,000 victims. And historians such as Gerald Reitlinger had estimated that "only" 700,000 Jews had died in Auschwitz. Faurisson discovered other contradictions in the literature: for example, the plan of the crematoria published in the wartime War Refugee Board report, based on the testimony of two escaped prisoners and released in November 1944, showed little relation to the plans of the crematoria published after the war. And of course, many eyewitness testimonies contradicted each other, while some plagiarized other texts. Faurisson concluded that all these contradictions pointed at only one possible conclusion: the story that Auschwitz had been an extermination camp was a hoax.

Until 1978, Faurisson did not have access to the public at large. The prestigious daily *Le Monde* refused to publish his letters, and elsewhere the mainline press ignored him. Only the extreme-right *Défense de l'Occident* (Defense of the West) was interested, and in June 1978 it published an article entitled "Le 'problème des chambres à gaz'" ("The 'Problem of the Gas Chambers'").[74] Because of its limited circulation, Faurisson sent an off-print to a number of important people, adding a convenient summary of his arguments.

> Conclusions (after thirty years of research) of revisionist authors: (1) Hitler's "gas chambers" never existed. (2) The "genocide" (or: the "attempted genocide") of the Jews never took place; clearly, Hitler never ordered (nor permitted) that someone be killed for racial or religious reason. (3) The alleged "gas chambers" and the alleged "genocide" are one and the same lie. (4) This lie, which is essentially of Zionist origin, has allowed a gigantic politico-financial swindle of which the principal beneficiary is the State of Israel. (5) The principal victims of this lie and this swindle are the German and the Palestinian peoples. (6) The tremendous power of the official information channels has, until now, assured the success of the lie and censored the freedom of expression of those who denounce the lie. (7) The supporters of the lie know now that their lie is in its last years; they misrepresent the purpose and meaning of revisionist investigations; they label what is just a return to a concern for historical truth as "resurgence of Nazism" or "the falsification of history."[75]

Not many of the recipients gave the material a second thought. Yet the Nazi-hunters Beate and Serge Klarsfeld—the former a German by birth, the latter a Holocaust survivor—saw a gathering storm, and they invited Joseph Billig, who had assisted in the Nuremberg prosecution of the Nazi ideologist Alfred Rosenberg, and Georges Wellers, editor of *Le Monde,* to contribute to a volume entitled *The Holocaust and the Neo-Nazi Mythomania* (1978). Wellers, a survivor of Auschwitz, wrote two essays united under the heading "Reply to the Neo-Nazi Falsification of Historical Facts concerning the Holocaust." One of the two essays dealt with Paul Rassinier's demographic "proof" that the Holocaust was a hoax, and the other essay is entitled "The Existence of the Gas Chambers." In his introductory remarks, Wellers summarized the allegations of the negationists and noted the paradox that a Frenchman and former resister, Rassinier, had laid down the foundations of negationism. "The paths marked out by Rassinier are faithfully followed by his imitators, who constantly refer to the master, citing him as a 'classic' who has 'definitively' demonstrated this or that," Wellers observed. Yet the pupils had started to go beyond the master, denying even the few concessions Rassinier had made to historical truth. Wellers mentioned them briefly, ending with the remark that "finally, for a certain R. Faurisson, everything is crystal clear: 'The time is ripe,' it is the 'imposture of genocide.'"[76]

If Klarsfeld's aim was that the publication of *The Holocaust and the Neo-Nazi Mythomania* would finish the issue, he must have been disappointed. In the fall of 1978, shortly after the book appeared, the existence, technology, and operation of the gas chambers became an object of public contention in France. The catalyst was a notorious *L'Express* interview with Louis Darquier de Pellepoix. Living in comfortable exile in Spain since the end of the war, the former commissioner general for Jewish affairs of the Vichy government alleged that the Holocaust had not occurred, that there had been no gas chambers in Auschwitz. He claimed: "Only lice were gassed in Auschwitz."[77]

The Darquier interview provided Faurisson with the opportunity he needed. Within days, he published an article in the socialist newspaper *Le Matin*. Faurisson commented that the Darquier affair ought to convince the French that the Holocaust was fiction and the gas chambers fabrications and proclaimed "that the massacres in so-called 'gas chambers' are a historical lie."[78] A few weeks later *Le Monde* was forced, under the threat of legal action, to publish a letter by Faurisson entitled "'Le problème des chambres à gaz' ou 'le rumeur d'Auschwitz'" ("'The Problem of the Gas Chambers' or 'The Rumor of Auschwitz'"). The letter began with the declaration that "no-one contested the use of crematoria ovens in certain German camps." The high mortality due to epidemics had made those incineration facilities necessary, he claimed. "It is the existence of 'gas chambers,' true slaughterhouses for humans, which is contested."[79] Faurisson argued that any visitor to Auschwitz or Majdanek could observe that the gas chambers could not have worked because it would have resulted in a "catastrophe" for the perpetrators, who would be killed themselves. Furthermore, it would have been impossible to cram 2,000 people in a room of 210 square meters, and it would have been ridiculous to then sprinkle them with pellets of an insecticide. Faurisson argued that the plans that did exist showed that the alleged gas chambers were typical morgues and that the gas would have taken too long to be extracted from the room. Finally, he noted that in all the trials no one had been able to produce German documentation for Bunkers I and II. Faurisson concluded with the statement that "Nazism is dead, quite dead, and also its Führer. Today only the truth remains. Let us dare to proclaim it: The non-existence of the 'gas chambers' is good news for poor humanity. Good news like this should no longer be suppressed."[80]

Publication of such language in the influential and prestigious *Le Monde* brought the negationist denial of the gas chambers into public prominence for the first time anywhere. Until then, such ideas had circulated only within the fringe. Now denial was to stay in the public arena. Worried by the effect of Faurisson's letter, the editors of *Le Monde* asked for a response from Wellers, who was well prepared to answer Faurisson. Wellers's letter, "Abondance de preuves" ("An Abundance of Evidence") appeared next to Faurisson's. While Wellers competently refuted the latter's arguments, the publication of his letter proved a mistake: the publication of the two letters on the same page created the appearance that Faurisson's and Wellers's arguments were in principle commensurate in intellectual respectability—that, in short, there were (as the negationists have tried to establish all along) a "revisionist" and an "exterminationist" thesis concerning the Holocaust, the advocates of which ought to be given equal opportunity to plead their cases.

According to a nineteenth-century French law, Wellers's direct attack on Faurisson gave the latter a right of response. Faurisson did not hesitate to make use of it, and *Le Monde* printed his reply to Wellers on January 16. He claimed that he believed in the gas chambers until he read the work of Rassinier and that he had reflected on the issue for fourteen years and researched it assiduously for another four. "I have analyzed thousands of documents. . . . I have searched in vain for a single deportee capable of proving to me that he has seen, with his own eyes, a 'gas chamber.' I certainly did not want an illusory abundance of proofs; I would have been satisfied with only one proof, only one proof. That proof I never found."[81]

Many regarded the publication of Faurisson's letters with confusion and mortification, and responsible historians who feared an unending cycle of negationist assertions and professional rebuttals joined together to end the farce. Well-known Holocaust historian Léon Poliakov and Pierre Vidal-Naquet, historian of ancient Greece, wrote a declaration that was endorsed by thirty-five other prominent French historians and published in *Le Monde* on February 21. Entitled "La politique hitlérienne d'extermination. Une déclaration d'historiens" (The Hitlerian Policy of Extermination: A Declaration by Historians"), the manifesto pronounced that "the question of how technically such a mass murder was possible should not be raised. It was technically possible because it occurred. This is the necessary starting point for all historical investigation of the subject. It has fallen to us to recall that point with due simplicity: there is not nor can there be a debate over the existence of the gas chambers."[82]

Faurisson wrote a rebuttal of the statement, but it was refused for publication. In this letter, entitled "A proof . . . one single proof," which Faurisson published a year later in his book *Mémoire en défense,* he offered (what seemed to be) a constructive proposal. "Instead of repeating ad nauseam that there is a superabundance of proofs that attest to the existence of 'gas chambers' . . . I propose that, to begin at the beginning, one supplies me with a proof, one single precise proof of the actual existence of one 'gas chamber,' one single 'gas chamber.' Let us examine this proof together, in public."[83] If we compare the spirit of "A Declaration by Historians" and Faurisson's "A proof . . . one single proof," one can, on a first view, feel some sympathy for Faurisson's attitude. After all, we are heirs to a rational, liberal, and individualistic culture that accepts as one of its formative myths the conflict between the Church and Galileo. It is all too easy to see in the statement of the historians a dogmatic pronouncement by a new intellectual inquisition aiming to repress evidence and logic for the sake of doctrine and to see in Faurisson a champion of free inquiry. And, indeed, negationists have tried to exploit this seemingly obvious parallelism between the heroes of the scientific revolution and themselves for all it is worth.

Faurisson had become well known in France. Fame came, however, at a high personal price. Students at the University of Lyons-2 staged demonstrations against him, and in response the university administrators suspended his lectures. The staff of the Center of Contemporary Jewish Documentation in Paris, which had been Faurisson's main source of information, refused to serve him. Faurisson also became known abroad. In August 1979, the Italian magazine *Storia illustrata* printed a long interview in which Faurisson's statements were left unchallenged. Hitler, so the French scholar declared, had not engaged in genocide any more than

Roosevelt had. Both had interned enemy aliens in internment camps: the latter the Japanese and the former the Jews. Yet because he had not been able to intern all Jews, Hitler had forced those who were left in the cities and villages to wear a sign. Faurisson compared them with paroled prisoners and argued that Hitler had ordered the Jews to be marked so that he could ensure the safety of the German soldier: "The German soldier would otherwise have been unable to distinguish the Jews from the non-Jews."[84] Thus, the segregation of Jews from the non-Jews occurred not for ideological but for military reasons. To Faurisson, the fact that the Jews built 700 bunkers in the Warsaw ghetto proved their threat. Even the children challenged the military situation. "There exist today enough accounts and memoirs in which Jews tell us about the way they engaged, even as children, in all kinds of illicit activities or resistance against the Germans."[85] Faurisson's logic was allowed to go unchallenged.

Shortly after giving his interview to the *Storia illustrata,* Faurisson crossed the ocean to begin his missionary activity in the United States. In fact, his name had already become known in progressive circles: a French academic had been hindered in his pursuit of knowledge, and in response to that violation of academic freedom, several hundred scholars signed in the fall of 1979 a text that protested the "vicious campaign of harassment, intimidation, slander and physical violence" designed to silence Faurisson and strongly supported "Professor Faurisson's just right of academic freedom."[86] The most prominent signatory was Noam Chomsky. To the famous linguist and public intellectual, who showed open disgust for the general subservience of the mainstream intelligentsia to the propaganda systems of their own governments, Faurisson must have appeared a fellow traveler worthy of support. The same year that he signed the petition in support of Faurisson, Chomsky derided the proven willingness of many intellectuals to "disseminate propaganda concerning the evil practices, real or fabricated, of current enemies of the state. It is remarkable to see how susceptible intellectuals have been, over the years, to the machinations of the atrocity fabrication industry."[87] Faurisson did not belong to the herd, and therefore he deserved support.

Faurisson's first stop was California, where he attended the first congress sponsored by the Institute for Historical Review. There he was to present a paper entitled "The Mechanics of Gassing," but because he felt that his English was rather bad, Faurisson asked a Canadian participant, Ernst Zündel, to read his paper on his behalf. Zündel was an appropriate choice: he was the publisher of, among other negationist books, Thies Christophersen's *The Auschwitz Lie.* Zündel's presentation of Faurisson's paper marked the beginning of an interesting relationship.

Faurisson's paper began with a discussion of the difficulty of gassing people because it imposed severe risks for the executioner. Therefore Höss's recollection that the crews began clearing the gas chambers *sofort* ("immediately") after the gassings did not make any sense, because too much hydrogen cyanide would have remained in the bodies and in the air pockets between them. "What kind of superpowerful fan is able to instantly disperse so much gas drifting through the air and hidden in air pockets?" the paper asked, and it continued with the observation that "it is abundantly clear from Höss's description that the fan in question must have been endowed with magical powers in order to be able to disperse all the gas with such flawless performance . . . that there was no cause for concern or need for verification of the absence of the gas!"[88] Then the paper reviewed the instructions for handling Zyklon B from its manufacturer, Degesch, which stipulated that rooms fumigated with the agent should be aired at least for twenty-one hours and discussed the danger of explosion at some length. The paper once more considered the issue that, according to Höss, the Sonderkommandos had entered the gas chambers "immediately" after the deaths of the victims. "I contend that this point alone constitutes the cornerstone of the false evidence, because this is a physical impossibility," Faurisson wrote (and Zündel said). "If you encounter a person who believes in the existence of the 'gas chambers,' ask him how, in his opinion, the thousands of cadavers were removed to make room for the next batch?"[89] As far as we know, no one at the meeting rose to point out that, after gassing 2,000 people in the basement of Crematorium 2 in one operation, even the Germans had to allow some time before "the next batch." After all, it would take the crematoria ovens of that same crematorium more than a day and a half to incinerate the bodies.

Turning to the remains in Auschwitz, the paper mentioned that the gas chamber of Crematorium 2 had been merely a morgue and that it would have been too small to accommodate the between 2,000 and 3,000 victims mentioned by Höss. Then it mentioned the idea that the Germans attempted to blow up the crematoria to erase the traces of their alleged crimes. "If one wishes to obliterate all trace of an installation which would be intrinsically quite sophisticated, it must be scrupulously dismantled from top to bottom so that there remains not one shred of incriminating evidence."[90] The paper did not mention that eyewitnesses mentioned that, indeed, the gas chambers had been "scrupulously dismantled" and that only after the perforated columns and ventilators had been removed were the rooms dynamited.

Then the paper turned to what was to become a focus of Faurisson's studies in the next years: the design, technique, and operation procedures of American gas chambers. "The real gas chambers, such as those created in 1924 and developed by the Americans around 1936–1938 offer some idea of the inherent complexity of such a method of execution," the paper proclaimed. There followed a lengthy description of the gassing procedure in American prisons and the extensive safety precautions taken to prevent any accidents.

After discussing American gas chambers, the paper returned to the German gas chambers. "If the Germans had decided to gas millions of people, a complete overhaul of some very formidable machinery would have been absolutely essential." The construction of gas chambers would have involved many experts, commanded huge financial resources, and consequently generated a lot of paperwork. "Had this occurred in a state such as the Third Reich, a wealth of evidence would surely have survived."[91]

Faurisson's paper generated a discussion; Zündel especially liked its approach. Comparison of the structures in Auschwitz and American gas chambers was to be the key to the future of negationism and was to provide the basis for Leuchter's involvement in the second Zündel trial in 1988—an involvement that directly led to Irving's adoption of the negationist position.[92] On his return trip to France, Faurisson made a stop in Washington, D.C., to give a lecture at the headquarters of the National Alliance, the American neo-Nazi party. Faurisson made use of his stopover to visit and photograph the gas chamber in the state prison in Baltimore, Maryland. He sent those photos to Zündel who, as Faurisson testified in the second Zündel trial, became obsessed with the American gas chambers and urged Faurisson to continue his investigations in that direction. But, as Faurisson testified in Zündel's 1988 trial, "I had some trouble after that that I could not really work on this question."[93]

Indeed, on his return home to France Faurisson became, once again, the center of public debate. In April 1980 the so-called Faurisson Affair was given new life with the publication of Serge Thion's 350-page-long book *Vérité historique ou vérité politique? La dossier de l'affaire Faurisson. La question des chambres à gaz* (*Historical Truth or Political Truth? The File of the Faurisson Affair—The Question of the Gas Chambers*). With the strong declaration of the thirty-five French historians published in *Le Monde* on February 21, 1979, Faurisson had become the underdog opposed by the defenders of the status quo. For the champions of the radical left, Faurisson became a hero of the search for a new cause that would unmask the hypocrisy of the bourgeoisie, and they began to fashion, in imitation of the Dreyfus Affair, a so-called Faurisson Affair. Those who rallied to Faurisson's side were the same radicals who believed that the reporting on the Cambodian genocide had actually served the interests of the establishment. "The West's best propaganda resource is Pol Pot's regime," Régis Debray observed in discussion with Noam Chomsky. "We needed that scarecrow."[94] And Chomsky provided, together with Edward Herman, a lengthy analysis of the way the liberal press averted its eyes from the "terrorizing elites" at home and used the news of atrocities abroad to help maintain the political, social, and economic status quo.[95] Thus, the atrocities ascribed to Pol Pot (or Stalin) allowed the elites in the United States to discredit every form of socialism as a highway to the Gulag and to resist the creation of national health insurance, the improvement of welfare programs, and the growth of the labor movement.

Contemporary atrocities were not the only ones to be exploited by the reactionary establishment. Hitler also proved a convenient "scarecrow." For the French ultra-Left of the 1970s, National Socialism had been the ultimate political emanation of capitalist society, created to stop the historically necessary advance of the working classes. As such, it was a tool of the bourgeoisie, the same bourgeoisie that shaped and dominated postwar liberal-democratic society. Yet the bourgeoisie denied the fundamental identity between liberal democracy and Hitler's regime, and their main argument was, as some ultra-Left ideologists had discovered, the Holocaust. The strategists of the proletariat formulated the thesis that the fundamental identity between the two political systems would become clear only if the Holocaust, the principal foil of capitalism, were to be removed from the historical record.[96]

Finally intellectual fashion played into Faurisson's hands. The generation that began to dominate the intellectual world in the late 1970s had been the same that, ten years earlier, had seen its hopes of progress through radical change defeated. As the promise of change had not materialized, the students of 1968 felt that "history" had betrayed them and became skeptical of any "grand narrative" of historical development that led to some social, political, and economic resolution at the end. This, in turn, led to the conception of a different kind of understanding of the past, or, for that matter, of the present. Instead of one privileged narrative that told of the progress of God's people from fall to redemption or of the progress of (Western) civilization from cave to lunar colony or of the progress from slavery to freedom, the generation of 1968 formulated the idea that one should allow, paraphrasing Chairman Mao, a thousand parallel "histories" to bloom. And they carried on their banners Nietzsche's observation that objective reality is not accessible, that what we call truth is a "mobile army of metaphors, metonyms, and anthropomorphisms" in the service of political, social, and economic power.[97] Armed with Nietzsche's slogan that one's obligation to truth was just one's pledge to lie herd-like according to a fixed convention, these revolutionaries stormed the bastille of the "grand narrative" which, so they believed, disenfranchised all but the (generally) white male carriers of "the idea." These radicals preached that one should stop searching for "the truth" and become engaged in recovering many alternative "truths," such as the histories of the underprivileged class (the common folk, slaves), gender (women), race ("colonials"), and so on. In short, in an effort to defeat the cultural imperialism of the West and the cultural arrogance of its intellectual tradition, historians began to practice a principled relativism that demanded an absolute suspension of judgment when faced with "otherness" or concepts expressed in such neologisms as "alterity," "illeity," and "différance." In seeking the stranger and the for-eigner, they hoped to find themselves.[98] As a result, many of the generation of 1968, who reveled in the rhetoric of "difference," "textuality," "in-commensurable phrase-regimes," and the like, were fascinated by Fauris-son—the ultimate stranger, the champion of an alternative history that was incommensurable with the hegemonic narrative of the Holocaust.

For example, philosopher Jean-François Lyotard became interested in the Faurisson Affair because it illustrated a number of difficult issues that arise when one accepts, as Lyotard does, that questions of historical truth and falsehood are wholly defined within the context of language games and the incommensurability of discourses. Lyotard argued that any attempt to dismiss Faurisson by pointing to the massive amount of evidence concern-ing Auschwitz or to Faurisson's mistakes in logic would deny the narrative "differend" between his and our version of events. Therefore one ought to encounter Faurisson by suspending judgment and see in him a champion of the war on totality. In arguing his case, Lyotard provided what remains the classic summary of Faurisson's logic. "His argument is: in order for a place to be identified as a gas chamber, the only eyewitnesses I will accept would be a victim of this gas chamber; now, according to my opponent, there is no victim that is not dead; otherwise, this gas chamber would not be what he or she claims it to be. There is, therefore, no gas chamber."[99]

To Lyotard, Faurisson's submission that we can have no knowledge, no *evidence* of what actually occurred in the gas chambers at Auschwitz since there exist no survivors who can vouch for the facts as a matter of firsthand empirical witness had a philosophical significance. He did not, however, become one of Faurisson's champions. Others found sufficient reason to take a more active role. The prominent left-wing radical Serge Thion rallied to Faurisson's case, presenting his support as the logical consequence of his commitment to the principles of freedom of thought and his political activism on behalf of the unassimilable "Other." Faurisson was "by all standards, a man alone."[100] Remarkably enough, Thion moved beyond accepting Faurisson as the stranger that must be embraced and actually assimilated Faurisson's point of view, categorically dismissing the great abundance of evidence that attests to the historical reality of the Holocaust. The confessions of Höss and other SS men were without value. "Once one is prepared to imagine the situation of those defeated men, gambling with their own lives between the hands of their jailers, a paltry game in which truths and lies are the basic tokens in a tactic of survival, one will not be prepared to accept all their declarations as valid currency."[101] A true defender of the underdog, be it the Algerians in their battle with the French Republic, the Vietnamese in their battle with the United States, or Faurisson in his battle with the establishment, Thion had no difficulty feeling sympathy for even men such as Höss or Frank when they were in the dock. To Thion, the Nuremberg War Crimes Tribunals had been not much different from the Stalinist show trials, and therefore they had no evidentiary value.

Within months after bringing Thion's book on the market, Faurisson published his *Mémoire en Defense—contre ceux qui m'accusent de falsifier l'histoire. La question des chambres à gaz* (*Testimony in Defense—Against Those Who Accuse Me of Falsifying History: The Question of the Gas Chambers*). The true significance of the book was to be found in Noam Chomsky's ill-advised preface. As we have seen, in 1979 Chomsky had signed a petition in support of Faurisson's academic freedom to challenge the inherited account of the Holocaust, and one thing had led to another. Entitled "Some Elementary Commentaries on the Right to the Freedom of Speech," Chomsky reviewed the reasons why he had signed the 1979 petition and dismissed the outcry that had resulted from it. He stated that he had often signed petitions on behalf of people whose ideas he found detestable—Russian dissidents who supported American policies in Indochina, for example—and observed that in those cases no one had raised an objection. "If someone had, I would have regarded him with the same contempt that those who denounce the petition in favor of Faurisson's right deserve, and for the same reasons."[102] Then Chomsky went on to contrast the freedom-loving practice in the United States with the stifling intellectual climate in France. Back home, he proudly stated, Arthur Butz ("whom one may consider the American equivalent of Faurisson") was not subjected to harassment, negationists had not been hindered in running an international conference, and the American Civil Liberties Union had defended the right of neo-Nazis to march through the largely Jewish town of Skokie, Illinois. The French, in other words, had much to learn. In his final paragraph, he addressed the tricky question of Faurisson's anti-Semitism. This did not remove the obligation to defend Faurisson. On the contrary: Chomsky declared that it made the defense of Faurisson more necessary. "It is exactly the right to express the most dreadful ideas freely that must be defended most rigorously."[103]

The Chomsky preface initiated a second wave of publicity for Faurisson, which led, among other things, to a radio interview on December 17, 1980. Faurisson said that the alleged Holocaust was a historical lie that served a huge political and financial swindle that benefited the State of Israel at the expense of the German and Palestinian peoples. This statement led to Faurisson's indictment under France's Race Relations Law. At the same time Faurisson was also indicted under Article 382 of the civil code for willfully distorting history. Finally, Faurisson faced a libel suit initiated by French historian Léon Poliakov, whom Faurisson had accused of fabricating his sources with reference to an important historical document on the Belzec extermination camp. The first two trials certainly put Faurisson in the position of the Dreyfusian underdog persecuted by the system and brought him much publicity, even sympathy, especially when he was convicted in each case.

By the time Irving met Faurisson, the latter had set his sights on the English historian, sensing that Irving could be a potential convert to his cause. Scheduled to speak after Irving, Faurisson began his talk with a challenge: if Irving believed that a Holocaust had happened, but behind Hitler's back, he had better prove it.[104] Faurisson followed up in an article entitled "A Challenge to David Irving," published in the negationist *Journal for Historical Review* in 1984. Faurisson first summarized his general thesis that the extermination camps had not existed. So much was known about the concentration camps, he claimed, "but about the gigantic homicidal gas chambers, we have nothing. That is magic."[105] Then he turned to Irving. Faurisson observed that Irving "sometimes gives in to the temptation to maintain opinions that, from his own point of view, he ought not to maintain since he has not studied the question."[106] Faurisson proceeded to attack the various statements Irving had made about the Holocaust in which he had admitted to various liquidations done at various locations by various criminal elements of various ethnic backgrounds without direct orders from above. As to Irving's account of the extermination procedures, Faurisson observed that it contained "too much metaphysics, not enough materialism."[107] Faurisson counseled that it was time for Irving to begin at the beginning. "Let me tell you that the moment has come for a historian of your importance to get into the subject and to study it for yourself in your own fashion."[108]

But Faurisson was soon to forget about Irving. More pressing issues had come up. A few months after the end of the conference, Faurisson was approached by Ernst Zündel, the man who had read his presentation at the 1979 conference. Zündel was a kindred spirit, if only for having published Richard Verrall's (alias Richard Harwood) *Did Six Million Really Die?* This book began with the claim that it offered "irrefutable evidence that the allegation that 6 million Jews died during the Second World War, as a direct result of official German policy of extermination, is utterly unfounded." The Holocaust, in short, was a "most colossal piece of fiction and the most successful of deceptions."[109] Harwood's conclusions were not shared by many, and in 1983 Holocaust survivor Sabina Citron issued a private complaint against Zündel. The Crown assumed the carriage of the charge and in 1984 indicted Zündel under Section 177 of the Criminal Code of Canada for willfully publishing statements that he knew to be false and for causing injury to a public interest. Zündel decided that he would defend himself by arguing that Harwood's book did not contain false statements because no gassings had taken place in Auschwitz. Zündel asked Faurisson to direct the defense team and act as an expert witness. Faurisson accepted. Zündel also asked Irving to testify as an expert witness. Irving responded that he had been a successful expert witness in two German trials and that he could be persuaded to go. He cautioned Zündel, however, that "in *some* respects my evidence may be disadvantageous, but on balance it would help."[110] It is likely that Irving's warning gave Faurisson second thoughts, and in the end Irving's services were not required.

In early 1985, the case was heard by District Court Judge Hugh Locke in the District Court of Ontario. Attorney Peter Griffiths represented the Crown, and attorney Douglas Christie acted on behalf of Zündel. Because it was a public trial, Canadians got for the first time a taste of the tenor of negationism. In his cross-examination of one of Zündel's expert witnesses, Swedish negationist Ditlieb Felderer, Griffiths exposed the vituperative language of negationism. Griffiths presented Felderer with some of the negationist flyers he had published.

[Griffiths]: "Could you read us that pamphlet?"

[Felderer]: "This one here?"

Q.: "Yes please."

A.: "Yes. It says, '*Please accept this hair of a gassed victim.*'"

Q.: "Why would it say that if there was no hair in it?"

A.: "Why would it say this?"

Ernst Zündel, 1988. Courtesy Canadian Jewish News.

Q.: "Yes."

A.: "Well, because sometimes the people don't mail, I suppose, any hair. I don't know. You have to ask those people who mail it."

Q.: "Are they supposed to put hair on it?"

A.: "Yes. If they wish. There are other things that are mentioned in the back."

Q.: "Read it from the start, Mr. Felderer."

A.: "'*Hair of a gassed victim. Next time you cut your hair do not discard it! No, mail it instead to Mr. Smolen* . . . (Now, Mr. Smolen is the director of Auschwitz, I will just bring that in.) . . . *at the Auschwitz Museum or to any of the addresses found on the next page—to be exhibited in the display of hair of gassed victims. Your hair has a much better claim to be exhibited there than the phony samples of commercial wigs and hair hitherto exhibited. Also collect together the hair of all your friends, dogs, and other animals. Send it all in a plastic bag to Mr. Smolen. He will remember you for it. It can be mailed as "Printed Matter" by placing the term "Sample" on the special delivery.*' Typical Voltaire satire, I would say. And then it continues on. It says: '*To Mr. K. Smolen and Staff, Auschwitz Museum, Oswiecim,*—Auschwitz —*Poland. Dear Mr. Smolen: In appreciation of your deep concern for gas victims, I am hereby forwarding my personal trophy for your permanent Museum exhibits. I understand that you are intensely involved with the subject of gassing. Personally I feel rather miserable. Not even Zyklon-B would cure me! This is much on account of the fact that I am getting gassed to death by a slow poison procedure. Our air is full of filth, poison, gasses, harmful chemicals and other disgusting elements. Matters are no better in your city. Your city is virtually saturated with deadly gasses emanating from your Monowitz chemical factory. In fact the place is not fit even for crows. I urge you to pay it a visit. Surely the Nazis never had a factory in such deplorable condition. But it is not necessary for you to go there as the factory's poison gasses reaches your very own office at Auschwitz which is situated close to the former Nazi brothel.*' And I must say here that this is in fact Block 24."

Q.: "I am not asking you to say. Please read that."

A.: "Which the inmates used."

Q.: "Just read that, Mr. Felderer."

A.: "'*In case of urgency I suggest you to put on a gas mask immediately. You may collect one at the private Museum displays in Block 24. Please be sure it has the special "J" filter. The poison at Auschwitz is deadly. You need to take the utmost precautions. My package of hair to you is a very* personal *proof of the fact that I am being gassed to death. Should you doubt it, I beg your experts to analyze it. I am therefore donating this private gift to you with the hope of that countless of your Museum's avid onlookers may gaze at it in wonder and give a solemn prayer in memory of a victim doomed to extinction due to environmental poison gassing.*'"

Q.: "All right. . . ."[111]

As an expert witness, Faurisson was not as offensive as Felderer, but if Zündel had hoped that Faurisson's Gallic wit would shine in the court, he must have been disappointed. The strategy of the defense was to prove that the Auschwitz gas chambers had been a hoax, and in order to do so, they had to destroy the credibility of a wartime report on Auschwitz written by Rudi Vrba and Alfred Wetzlar after their escape from Auschwitz in April 1944. A summary of the Vrba-Wetzlar report had been cabled from Switzerland to the United States in early July 1944 that described the procedure and machinery of destruction in some detail.

At the end of February 1943 four newly constructed crematoria and gassing units were put into operation in B two larger and two smaller the larger type consisted of vast central hall flanked on one side by furnace room and on other by long narrow gas chamber. About 2000 persons at once were crowded into central hall which was camouflaged to resemble a bathing establishment made to undress given a piece of soap and towel and then herded down a short stairway into ad[j]oining lower gas chamber this is hermetically closed and SS men wearing gasmasks mount [the roof] and shake down into room from three openings in ceiling a powdered cyanide preparation labelled cyklon manufactured in Hamburg. Within a few minutes everyone in gas chamber is dead, latter is aired and Sonderkommando proceeds with gruesome work of transporting bodies on small flat cars running along track passing under central hall to furnace room here there are nine ovens each with four openings with high smokestack rising in middle each opening can incinerate three normal bodies within one-half hours. Daily capacity of larger crematoria is 2000 of two smaller about 1000 each, total of all four units is some 6000 daily.[112]

The full report was published only in November 1944 by the War Refugee Board, and it was consequently known as the "War Refugee Board Report."

Faurisson believed that the War Refugee Board Report was one of "the three pillars of the story of the gas chamber,"[113] and therefore he had to demolish its credibility. During his examination-in-chief, Faurisson tried to convince the court that the discrepancy between a sketch plan of a crematorium drawn by Vrba after his escape and the remains of that crematorium in Auschwitz proved the report to be without any value at all.

[Christie]: "Any other reason why you say we should not believe the W.R.B. Report of Dr. Vrba and others?"

[Faurisson]: "The plan of Auschwitz, the plan of the crematorium."

Q.: "What about them?"

A.: "They do not—they are nothing."

Q.: "What do you mean, they're nothing?"

A.: "When you see the reality of the place . . ."

Q.: "Yes."

A.: ". . . It does not stand, that's all. When you see on the same level a gas chamber, then a track to put the people, the bodies in the furnaces, and when you see that in fact this place which was a mortuary was underground, that you had a little lift, and on the—at the other level you had the furnaces . . ."

Q.: "Yes."

A.: ". . . And the furnaces are not at all like they have been drawn by Dr. Vrba, and he said . . ."

Q.: "What do you conclude from that, doctor?"

A.: "I conclude that it is not exact."

Q.: "What do you conclude about the author of that, if he says it is exact?"

A.: "I say, 'You say something which is not exact.'"

Q.: "All right. . . ."[114]

It was not a great performance, given the fact that, two days earlier, Vrba had explained why the plan of the crematorium was "not exact." It had been a conflation of the plans of two different types of crematoria, drawn up in haste with the objective of warning the Hungarian Jews of their fate in Auschwitz.[115]

The testimony of defense witness Dr. William Lindsey proved a particular disappointment. A chemist who had worked for DuPont, Lindsey had traveled to Auschwitz, where he had made a cursory examination of the gas chamber of Crematorium 1. Furthermore, he had studied the German documentation of Zyklon B. He had earned respect in negationist circles after his publication of an article in *The Journal of Historical Review* entitled "Zyklon B, Auschwitz, and the Trial of Dr. Bruno Tesch." In this article, Lindsey argued that the allies had originally "invented" the Holocaust during the war as part and parcel of the usual atrocity propaganda and that after the war, they had decided to continue to push that story, against all evidence to the contrary, to cover up their own misdeeds and create a foundation for postwar Allied solidarity.

> With no "Holocaust" to take their place in the columns of the world's newspapers, the many surreptitious, undercover activities, plans and responsibilities of Franklin D. Roosevelt and his proto-United Nations conspirators prior to, during and after the war—today still too-little publicized—would have come under immediate, murderous, and lasting scrutiny. This would have resulted in the United Nations wartime charges and the (still-vulnerable) "integrity" of this organization being ripped asunder in a manner which would have made the revelations about the Allied lies found in the World War I Bryce Committee Report on propaganda charges look by comparison like reports on a love feast. If the many plans already formulated diplomatically and formally or informally in war conferences were to be fully, irreversibly implemented as the planners wished, the "New" United Nations organization would have to meet the full support of those who might otherwise strongly oppose it. The wartime "atrocity propaganda" charges made by the victors to inflame their soldiers and citizenry, and to justify and condone their own use of progressively more violent, ruthless measures against Germany and Japan, *simply had to be sustained after the war.*[116]

On paper, Lindsey showed the kind of eloquence and argumentation which attracted Zündel and Faurisson, and he also seemed to know a fair amount about hydrogen cyanide in general and Zyklon B in particular. But as an expert witness, Lindsey's performance was not very satisfactory. When Christie asked if he believed that either 2.5 million or even 1 million people had been gassed in the crematoria, Lindsey answered that "I find it, from my point of view, I find it is absolutely impossible to believe that. The method as described, the rate at which they can burn these bodies and carry out the gassing procedure, I find it's impossible."[117] In the witness stand, Lindsey showed very little eloquence, and, contrary to the impression he had given in the many notes that accompanied his article, Lindsey proved unable to back up his opinions with demonstrable scientific facts. His testimony failed to provide the negationist breakthrough Faurisson had hoped for.

The case ended with Zündel's conviction for publishing *Did Six Million Die?,* and Thomas sentenced him to a prison term of fifteen months. Not deterred by the facts, negationists celebrated "The Great Holocaust Trial" as a watershed: it had given them the first public platform in North America. Thus, negationists celebrated Zündel's legal defeat as a resounding victory for the negationist cause. "For the first time in modern history, the consensus reality most accurately described as Exterminationism, was tested and challenged in a court of law," one of Zündel's supporters claimed. Zionists, Holocaust historians, and the public at large had been shown to have no answer to "the revisionist revelations within the Great Holocaust Trial." Instead of addressing the "radical questions [the trial] has raised and the bedrock of previously censored facts it has unearthed," those who pushed the Holocaust Hoax had only turned up "the volume on their hysterics."[118]

The Zündel trial encouraged many negationists to believe that their cause was on the rise. Sensing a change, Irving began to move closer to the position occupied by hard-core negationists, and he began to engage the issue that was at the core of the negationist challenge to the historical

William Lindsey on his way to the Ontario District Court, accompanied by Zündel's bodyguards, 1985. Courtesy Canadian Jewish News.

record: the camps. In 1986, he told an audience in Australia that the photos of the concentration camps taken by the English and American soldiers in the spring of 1945 did not provide evidence of German atrocities. "The starvation, the epidemics, the typhoid had only broken out in the last two or three weeks of the war." The Allies, not the Germans, probably carried the blame because of the deliberate bombing of the German transportation and industrial infrastructure.

> We had deliberately created the conditions of chaos inside Germany. We had deliberately created the epidemics, and the outbreaks of typhus and other diseases, which led to those appalling scenes that were found at their most dramatic in the enclosed areas, the concentration camps, where of course epidemics can ravage and run wild. And so it is symbolic of the hypocrisy that existed at the end of the Second World War that we picked on those awful photographs, which were of course good television one would say nowadays, they were good newsprint, they were good photos, they were very photogenic those scenes, those piles of corpses. We picked on them as being evidence that the war was a just war and that our journey had not been in vain.[119]

Irving was not (yet) prepared to explicitly deny the Holocaust as such or the fact that many Jews had died. But he did become silent about Himmler's role: obviously Himmler was too close to Hitler, and it was not very probable that Himmler could have exterminated a good part of European Jewry without Hitler's knowledge. Instead, Irving began to shift the responsibility to the actions of "nameless criminals" of various nationalities. In a radio interview given during the same Australian trip, he stated that between hundreds of thousands and millions of Jews had been liquidated "by the Germans, or the Latvians, or the Ukrainians, or all the rest who carried out liquidations."

> They were the victims of a large number of nameless criminals into whose hands they fell on the eastern front. Mostly around Eastern Europe the liquidations occurred. And these men acted on their own impulse, their own initiative, within the general atmosphere of brutality created by the Second World War, in which of course the Allied bombings played a part.[120]

When his interviewer Terry Lane asked him if his remark about the "hundreds of thousands or millions" of Jews implied that he rejected the figure of 6 million Jewish victims, Irving evasively replied that "when you are a statistician as I am, and you've studied statistics, you know that figures don't compact [sic], they don't come rounded up to six figures like that, with zeroes at the end. There is one school of thought that says 4 million. Another school of thought may say 6,500,000. Another school of thought, right out at the fringe, says it was only 100,000."[121] Irving was not willing to come down on one side or the other.

Irving was not the only historian who seemed open to negationist propositions. In Germany, Ernst Nolte, professor of history at the Free University in Berlin, had come to the conclusion that Hitler's persecution of the Jews was not unique and that the German concentration camp system had been in everything except the construction of gas chambers just a copy of the Soviet Gulag. The Nazi attempt to kill all Jews, "a universal nation," was a reply to Stalin's destruction of the bourgeoisie, "a universal class." Nolte believed that the Nazi policy against the Jews was created in defensive response to the real, or at least honestly perceived, threat of Judeo-

Bolshevism and was therefore not much different in kind from the American internment of Japanese citizens after Pearl Harbor. But he acknowledged that, as an act of self-defense, Auschwitz was "excessive."[122] This judgment appeared in his monumental *Der europäische Bürgerkrieg 1917–1945* (*The European Civil War, 1917–1945*), completed in 1986 and published in 1987. In this book, Nolte did more than try to explain why the Germans had been forced to kill Jews or share his judgment of why Auschwitz had been a somewhat excessive response to the threat of the Jews. Even worse, he also threw doubt on the historical record of the Holocaust. The historiography of the Holocaust, Nolte argued, had been a largely Jewish affair, and as a result it had crystallized in simplistic schemes that defined the Holocaust in terms of German murderers and Jewish victims. Nolte noted that, as far as he was concerned, the verdict was out about what had happened in the extermination camps. He noted that various authors who had no neo-Fascist leanings and who were not German, and who therefore had no axe to grind, sincerely doubted the existence of the gas chambers and he mentioned that "not rarely is [it] stated that mass gassings of that scale were technically impossible with the means available."[123] In a footnote, Nolte made it clear that he was quite sympathetic to the negationist argument that the Wannsee Conference, held to discuss the Final Solution of the Jewish Problem, had never happened. And he called on established historians to engage these arguments constructively instead of condemning out of hand.[124] In declaring the negationists as partners in a historical debate, Nolte had de facto legitimized them. It seemed that as far as the Holocaust was concerned, the climate of opinion was about to change.

In 1986, David Irving visited Toronto on a world-encompassing lecture tour. He had arranged for a driver to pick him up at the airport, but instead Zündel showed up to greet him. According to Zündel, Irving was visibly shocked. "He wanted nothing to do with me, even then, because of the bad reputation that I had in conservative circles in England and Europe. He thought I was some 'Revisionist-Neo-Nazi-Rambo-Kook!'"[125] In order not to give the wrong impression to his audience, Irving asked Zündel not to show up at his lecture. Zündel complied, and so did his supporters. As a result, attendance at Irving's lecture was very poor. Worst of all, journalists stayed away. After Irving left, Zündel sent him a long letter in which he reviewed the disappointing results of the trip and told him bluntly: "Please make sure that you have someone competent handle your next appearance. You deserve the best!" In the remainder of the letter, Zündel persuasively laid out various schemes that would enrich Irving. Both "handsome" and "witty," Irving was a promoter's dream. "You speak beautifully, with a well-modulated voice. You can be combative and abrasive when necessary and also humble and charming."[126] All of these talents were, of course, wasted if no one marketed them properly. Zündel, who identified himself as "an advertising man," made it clear that he saw all the possibilities.

Flattered, enticed by the potential for profit, and encouraged by the ever-more-public willingness of Nolte and others to consider the necessity of a historical revision of the Holocaust, Irving allowed himself to be drawn into Zündel's orbit and closer to Zündel's continuing legal battle. On appeal, the 1985 ruling against Zündel had been overturned on procedural grounds, and a new trial had been ordered. This time District Court Judge Ron Thomas was to preside, and John Pearson and Catherine White were to conduct the prosecution. Christie was to represent Zündel again, and, as it soon became clear, Faurisson was once more to head the research team. It had become obvious to Zündel that witnesses of the caliber of

Felderer had done him no good and that he needed the endorsement of a public personality like Irving. In late 1987, Zündel asked Irving to act as an expert witness in what Zündel modestly defined as "The Second Great Holocaust Trial." Irving would have to testify on Churchill's responsibility for the outbreak of the Second World War. "Undoubtedly, the prosecution will ask you about 'mass-gassings' and 'Hitler's orders for the extermination of Jews,'" Zündel warned Irving. "I assume that you will give him the same statements you have made in this regard during your various lectures and talks. I think the Defence can live with that!"[127] Zündel proved a master of persuasion: he suggested that Irving could use his stay in Canada to give lectures and promote his books from coast to coast. Zündel noted that Irving would profit from the publicity derived from his courtroom appearance and that he would provide "frontmen" to organize the book-promotion campaign.

Zündel repeated his presentation of the trial as a catalyst for a successful book tour in another letter sent in early January 1988. After expressing his dismay over the fact that Irving had had to personally deliver his books to London booksellers and once more offering to organize help with such pedestrian chores so that Irving could concentrate on the important task of revising history, Zündel came to the point: his "thoughtcrime trial" was to begin on January 18, 1988. He notified Irving that he expected him to testify in late March or early April. Zündel predicted that in his testimony Irving could create a proverbial "bang" to begin a promotional tour. "Your timely appearance at the 'Hitler Diary' debate was excellent in this regard, and the forthcoming trial here in Toronto promises to be a well-covered media event."[128]

Irving remained cautious. In his reply to Zündel, he established clear conditions to make the whole thing worth it to him: the whole operation was to be essentially risk free as far as his ability to travel in the future to Canada and the United States. He also warned Zündel that he could not endorse all of his claims. "I accept that a great tragedy did happen but do not accept the present versions as to how." Irving added that he expected "adequate compensation for my time and travel."[129]

While Zündel and Irving were courting each other, Faurisson worked out the details of what was to serve as the defense's trump card: a scientific report on the Auschwitz gas chambers. In his 1980 paper "The Mechanics of Gassing," he had called for an analysis of the Auschwitz gas chambers in terms of the gas chambers used by some American states, and now the opportunity had arisen to realize that ambition. Faurisson identified Bill Armontraut, warden of the Missouri State Penitentiary in Jefferson City, Missouri, as a potential expert witness. Armontraut's prison included a gas chamber operated by cyanide gas. Constructed in 1939, it had been used thirty-nine times. Zündel's legal aide Barbara Kulaszka wrote to Armontraut, who responded in a January 13, 1988, letter, suggesting that she contact a certain Fred Leuchter. "Mr. Leuchter is an engineer specializing in gas chambers and executions. He is well versed in all areas and is the only consultant in the United States that I know of."[130]

Faurisson had found the man he had been looking for. He called Leuchter and gave him, as Leuchter recalled a year later, "a very shocking history lesson" which left the engineer questioning "that fifty-year-old Holocaust lie and the application of that lie to generations of children."[131] After a few initial telephone conversations, two trips to Boston by Faurisson, and one trip to Toronto by Leuchter, Leuchter agreed to investigate the ruins of the crematoria. He left for Poland on February 25, accompanied by his wife, a draftsman, a videocameraman, an interpreter, and, "in spirit,"

Zündel and Faurisson, "who for obvious reasons could not accompany us in person, but who nevertheless were with us every step of the way."[132] The party returned on March 3, having spent three days at Auschwitz and half a day at Maidanek. In those camps, Leuchter studied the layout of the crematoria—or, better, of what remained of them—and illegally took various samples of the brickwork and plaster, which he brought back to the United States to be analyzed by Alpha Analytical Laboratories in Ashland, Massachusetts, for residual cyanide content.

A week after Leuchter's return from Poland, Zündel suddenly became nervous about Irving's appearance when two of the expert witness he had called—Dr. Russell Barton and Dr. Kuang Fann—agreed during cross-examination with the Crown's argument that the Nazis had murdered 6 million Jews and that *Did Six Million Really Die?* was a repugnant book. He contacted Irving again, writing that he could not afford anymore to have one of his witnesses "in the final analysis agreeing with the Crown prosecutor that 'It really did happen.'" If cross-examined on the Holocaust, Irving ought either say that he could give no expert opinion on that matter because he had done no research in that area or that he had done research and that it showed "major problems" with current knowledge about the Holocaust. "To affirm that mass gassings took place, or that there was an official policy of 'Judenausrottung' coming from your lips would be a disaster for me. Please let me know exactly how you feel."[133]

Then Zündel received Leuchter's report, and it appeared that Faurisson's strategy had been successful: unlike Lindsey in 1985, Leuchter had delivered the goods. "The author finds no evidence that any of the facilities normally alleged to be execution gas chambers were ever used as such, and finds, further, that because of the design and fabrication of these facilities, they could not have been utilized for execution gas chambers." Furthermore, Leuchter stated that "an evaluation of the crematory facilities produced conclusive evidence that contradicts the alleged volume of corpses cremated in the generally alleged time frame."[134] Leuchter's conclusion gave Zündel the opportunity to force the issue with Irving. The question became now very easy: Would Irving be prepared to endorse, in court, Leuchter's findings? In an interview given in 1998, Zündel told American filmmaker Errol Morris that he had phoned Irving in Florida, telling him about Leuchter's investigation in Auschwitz and the analysis of the samples he had taken there. According to Zündel, Irving responded: "Why did I not think of that myself?" Irving agreed to travel to Toronto, meet Leuchter, and then decide if he would testify.

Fred Leuchter holding an electrocution helmet for an electric chair. Courtesy Fourth Floor Productions.

> And so David Irving was in Toronto. He saw the Leuchter Report. He met Fred Leuchter, he looked at all the stuff that he had brought, the video footage, and the drawings that Fred had brought with him. And he said, "This is a shattering document. The Leuchter Report is a shattering document. It is a stroke of genius by the defense. As a historian," he said, "anybody that will write history, the history of the Second World War that does not take into consideration what Fred Leuchter has found and unearthed, will henceforth do so at their peril because they will write propaganda. Not history."[135]

For Zündel, the chase had ended. Irving was to testify on his behalf, unequivocally endorsing Leuchter's findings.

Irving testified on Friday, April 22, and Monday and Tuesday, April 25 and 26, 1988. As an expert witness for the defense, Irving endorsed the main object of legal contention in general terms, Harwood's *Did Six*

Million Really Die?—a book that claimed that the Holocaust was a piece of Allied atrocity propaganda not that different from the stories that had circulated in the First World War that had credited the Germans with transfixing Belgian babies on bayonets and operating "corpse factories" in which they extracted fat and other useful commodities from the corpses of their own dead. Irving judged "over ninety percent of the brochure *Did Six Million Really Die?* to be factually accurate."[136] Through his general endorsement of *Did Six Million Really Die?*, Irving implicitly endorsed the theory that the stories about gassings were Allied atrocity propaganda. Later in his examination-in-chief, Irving became more explicit when he noted a contradiction between the alleged Nazi policy "for the deliberate, ruthless, systematic extermination of the Jews in Auschwitz and in other places of murder" and the existence of many survivors. "So either the Nazis had no such program or they were an exceedingly sloppy race, which isn't the image that we have of them today."[137]

During his examination-in-chief, Irving even called Hitler as his witness to support his contention that nothing in Auschwitz had been out of the ordinary.

> [Christie]: "And have you in your examination of the records of Adolf Hitler's headquarters' activities, discovered what was said on the occasion when Auschwitz was captured? Do you know what was going on?"
>
> [Irving]: "On January the 26th or January the 27th, 1945, the Russian troops overran Auschwitz and on this day, the stenographers, who took down in Hitler's headquarters every word he spoke, recorded a passage which has survived. We have the fragment of what he said. General Guderian reported to the Führer, 'Yesterday the Russians overran Auschwitz,' and Hitler just replied 'Oh, yes.'"[138]

"Oh yes," and not, as Irving added, "Well, let's hope they manage to get rid of it or they're not going to find anything."[139]

Irving did not retract his remarks when, during cross-examination, Crown Attorney Pearson confronted him with a passage from his *Hitler's War* in which he had written about the Holocaust as a historical fact. Pearson confronted Irving with a sentence in which he declared that "the secret extermination camps did not begin operating until December 1941."

> [Pearson]: "Sir, aren't you suggesting there, stating to the reader that the secret extermination camps did not begin operating until December 1941?"
>
> [Irving]: "I think I have to say here that this sentence falls into the category of sentences that I would not repeat in 1988. At the time I wrote that in the 1960's, 1974 thereabouts when I wrote—wrote that introduction, I believed. I believed everything I had heard about the extermination camps. I wasn't investigating the extermination camps. I was investigating Hitler."
>
> Q.: "But you told us that you did ten years of extensive research on the National Socialist regime?"
>
> A.: "Yes."
>
> Q.: "And you had no problem making that statement, did you?"
>
> A.: "Because I believed."

David Irving in Toronto, April 1988. Courtesy Canadian Jewish News.

Q.: "Right."

A.: "I believed what I had read up at that point. I hadn't gone to the sites of Auschwitz and Treblinka and Maidanek and brought back samples and carried out analysis. I hadn't done any research into what is called the Holocaust. I researched Hitler and his staff."

Q.: "You haven't done that, have you, since?"

A.: "I haven't."

Q.: "You haven't done those things?"

A.: "I have carried out no investigation in-depth in equivalent depth of the Holocaust."

Q.: "But your mind changed?"

A.: "My mind has now changed."

Q.: "You no longer believe it?"

A.: "I have now begun to challenge that. I understand it is now a subject open to debate."

Q.: "But your belief changed even though you didn't do any research; is that what you're saying?"

A.: "My belief has now changed because I understand that the whole of the Holocaust mythology is, after all, open to doubt and certainly in the course of what I have read in the last few days, in fact, in this trial, I am now becoming more and more hardened in this view."

Q.: "As a result of what you've read here in the last few days?"

A.: "Indeed."[140]

As he explained, the reading matter that had changed his mind was Leuchter's conclusion that "none of the facilities examined were ever utilized for the execution of human beings and that the crematories could never have supported the alleged work load attributed to them."[141] In court, Irving publicly embraced Leuchter's conclusions: "I'm very impressed, in fact, by the presentation, by the scientific manner of presentation, by the expertise that's been shown by it and by the very novel conclusion that he's arrived at." Irving admitted that "as a historian I'm rather ashamed it never occurred to me to make this kind of investigation on the particular controversy." In conclusion, Irving endorsed the report wholeheartedly. "I think it is shattering in the significance of its discovery."[142]

After the trial, Irving could have chosen to pack up, return to London, forget about it, and continue his studies of the Nazi pantheon. Probably his reputation would not have suffered much, and he would still have enjoyed the pleasures of a scholar's life without many controversies and court actions. Yet he chose a different route: he decided that Leuchter's Auschwitz was to be his Rubicon and a turning point in the history of history. As he was to state two years later in his notorious "Battleship Auschwitz Speech," his stance in the Toronto courtroom had been foreshadowed by his dramatic and effective intervention in the *Der Stern* press conference five years earlier. He introduced his account of his Toronto testimony by saying "Just picture me seven years ago, in 1983."

> I'm at the press conference of the West German Magazine *Der Stern,* in Hamburg. . . . I was the first one to have a chance to ask the people at *Der Stern* certain questions. I said right out: "The Diaries are fake—the Adolf Hitler diaries are fake!" They'd spent nine million deutschmarks on them! And all the German historians had said they were genuine. Eberhard Jäckel had said they were genuine, so they must be genuine—but they weren't.
>
> I got the same kind of feeling about the Holocaust. . . .
>
> This is how it was when I was in Toronto a couple of years ago.[143]

Having tied his 1988 Toronto appearance to his 1983 Hamburg intervention, Irving denied himself the opportunity to reflect on what he had done and, with that, the possibility of retreat. His destiny as a historian came to be tied up with the historical record concerning Auschwitz.

From the moment he left the courtroom, Irving began to aggressively trumpet his own conversion as a world-historical event. Undoubtedly flattery played a role: one negationist magazine, *Instauration,* celebrated his testimony as "traumatic for world Jewry."[144] Willis A. Carto of the Institute for Historical Review wrote Irving that with his support, negationism was to triumph. "It's not everyone who has a chance to be instrumental in a historic turnaround. The practical consequences of destroying the holocaust myth are almost indescribably potent."[145]

Such attention triggered a whole range of behavior patterns that had little to do with the professional conduct of historians in search for the truth and much to do with the narcissism of a man caught in a no-man's-land between an inflated sense of his own superiority as a historian and a sense of inferiority vis-à-vis the historical establishment. In a lecture given in 1988 in Canada, Irving admitted that since he had been a small boy he had enjoyed seeing important people, or people with reputation and prestige, with "egg on their face." With Holocaust denial, he had found a way to act out his boyhood dream: "Just imagine the omelet on their faces if we manage to expose that other six million lie [as opposed the six million marks *Stern* paid for the Hitler diaries]. This is the prospect that is now opening up in front of me."[146] The reference to the Hitler diaries was revealing, because his intervention in the Hitler diaries affair had been an occasion when he had indeed played a useful public role. Again and again he was to compare his role in the Hitler diaries affair with his endorsement of Leuchter's results. Irving predicted that soon he would bring the whole exterminationist edifice down with a new book on Auschwitz. "This is why I hope that people will recognize that I managed to pull off a coup even more spectacular than exposing the Hitler diaries as a fake. From one six million lie to another. That I will see then that some of the world's most famous historians and politicians have the biggest omelet of all times all over their face."[147]

In a hurry to see the omelet on their faces, Irving bought from Zündel the right to publish the British edition of the Leuchter Report through his own publishing venture, Focal Point Publications. In the spring of 1989, when everything was ready for the book launch, an event occurred that removed whatever restraint Irving may have had. A storm broke loose in the United States about a book published half a year earlier by respected Princeton historian Arno Mayer. Entitled *Why Did the Heavens Not Darken? The Final Solution in History,* it proposed that the Holocaust, which he termed "Judeocide," was not the result of anti-Semitism but of anti-Bolshevism. It was the result not of the National Socialist fantasy concerning the so-called "Jewish Question" but of German frustration after the Wehrmacht failed to defeat the Soviet Union in the summer and fall of 1941.[148]

While this thesis could perhaps be accepted for the operations of the Einsatzgruppen, Mayer went farther: Hitler's invasion of the Soviet Union also provided the cause and context for the death camps, including Auschwitz. Mayer's book included a whole chapter on Auschwitz which provided enough clauses, sentences, and paragraphs to raise the enthusiasm of negationists everywhere. While Mayer did not deny the presence and importance of the gas chambers, he attached particular importance to typhus as a cause of death in Birkenau, which he described as the place where the ailing and dying from the other camps in the Auschwitz complex were sent. "The result was an unspeakable death rate."[149] Mayer offered a well-meant but ill-considered reflection on the causes of death in Auschwitz that concluded with the sentence that "from 1942 to 1945, certainly at Auschwitz, but probably overall, more Jews were killed by so-called 'natural' causes than by 'unnatural' ones."[150] Mayer did not provide a scholarly apparatus to support his statements.

Mayer's thesis that typhus had been one of the main causes of death in Birkenau could only bring happiness to negationists such as Robert Faurisson, who had advised Zündel about his defense and who had set Leuchter's research agenda. Faurisson had always maintained that all the Zyklon B shipped to Auschwitz could be easily explained because of the (in his opinion) endemic prevalence of typhus-bearing lice in the camp. Yet none of those connected with the Institute of Historical Review noticed Mayer's book. That changed in April 1989, when *The New Republic* published an angry and devastating 6-page review entitled "False Witness," written by Daniel Goldhagen. He summarized Mayer's book as "an artful construction of half-truths" that was "riddled with extraordinary factual errors, which amount to a pattern of falsification and distortion."[151] Goldhagen observed that Mayer's "outrageous" account of Auschwitz showed "the spirit of revisionist apologia."[152] He had no difficulty in demolishing Mayer's account of Auschwitz. His review, however, had unintended consequences: it alerted the negationists to the fact that a major historian had produced a work that, with admittedly considerable distortion, could be presented as an endorsement of their own position. Consequently, the May issue of the newsletter published by the Institute of Historical Review carried a review entitled "The Holocaust: A Sinking Ship?" It described Mayer as "one of the leading lights of his profession" and his book as a justification of "the approach and methodology of Revisionist scholars of the Holocaust like Paul Rassinier, Arthur Butz, Robert Faurisson, Wilhelm Stäglich, Walter Sanning, David Irving, Mark Weber, Fritz Berg, Carlo Mattogno, Henri Roques and a growing cohort of other researchers."[153] It defined Mayer's text as a "minefield of hoax-boasting concessions"—a place "where Exterminationist angels fear to tread" but an "intrepid Harvard graduate student" had rushed in. And it ended with the question "What to make of it all?"

> Is the crew of the good ship *Holocaust* preparing a rush for the lifeboats (and women and children be damned!), or are damage control teams working feverishly below decks in an effort to keep the stricken hull afloat? Will the (largely Gentile) suckers for what passed not so long ago, even among academics, as "the best

documented event in history" stick to their berths in steerage, as the hoax capsizes and begins its last lonely hurdle to the watery graveyard of historical frauds?[154]

In his review of *Why Did the Heavens Not Darken?*, published later that year in *The Journal of Historical Review*, Robert Faurisson did not hide his pleasure either. One sentence had given him particular joy: "Sources for the study of the gas chambers are at once rare and unreliable."[155] Faurisson observed how far revisionism had come. He reminded his readers that in 1979, leading French scholars had publicly stated that there could be no debate about the gas chambers.

> We had to wait until 1988 for an established historian like Arno Mayer to say, in his chapter on Auschwitz, that sources for the study of the gas chambers, far from being *abundant* and *reliable,* as people asserted, are only *rare* and *unreliable.* This is just a single example of the significant progress that Historical Revisionism has made in the scholarly community.[156]

With the apparently partial "conversion" of a prominent member of the historical establishment to a negationist position vis-à-vis the Auschwitz gas chambers, the prospects of the Leuchter Report to attract establishment support looked good indeed. In a letter to negationist Robert Countess, Irving judged Mayer's book to be "remarkable, though not quite as 'revisionist' as the reviews of it (Newsweek etc) suggest. Still, it is a breakthrough."[157] With the "breakthrough" of *Why Did the Heavens Not Darken?*, Irving gained the confidence to put his whole reputation on the line: the provocative press statement issued by Focal Point—that is, Irving—was not only grandiose in its claims for the historic significance of the Leuchter Report, but also unequivocal in the (self-)aggrandizement of Irving as a debunker of falsehood. There was no doubt where Irving stood: the pamphlet announced that on June 23, 1989, Irving was to make the "epochal announcement" that the gas chambers of Auschwitz had not existed. Claiming that "scientists, using the same ultra-modern equipment and methods that detected the centuries-old fraud of the Turin Shroud," had established the Auschwitz gas chambers to be a fraud, the pamphlet stated that Irving "has placed himself at the head of a growing band of historians, worldwide, who are now sceptical of the claim that at Auschwitz and the other camps there were 'factories of death' in which millions of innocent people were systematically gassed to death." Reminding the reader that Irving had been the first to unmask the Adolf Hitler diaries as fraudulent, it stated that "now he is saying the same thing about the infamous 'gas chambers' of Auschwitz, Treblinka and Majdanek. They did not exist—ever—except, perhaps, as the brainchild of Britain's brilliant wartime Psychological Warfare Executive (PWE)." It added that "the survivors of Auschwitz are themselves testimony to the absence of an extermination programme."[158]

The press release more or less followed Irving's introduction to the Leuchter Report. In it, Irving clearly established his contempt for the historical establishment and his aim to use the report as a weapon in his battle with mainline historians.

> Unlike the writing of history, chemistry is an exact science. Old fashioned historians have always conducted endless learned debates about meanings and interpretations, and the more indolent among them have developed a subsidiary Black Art of "reading

THE LEUCHTER REPORT

The First Forensic Examination of Auschwitz

With a Foreword by DAVID IRVING

Focal Point Publications
London

The Leuchter Report, Focal Point (190 pp.). Courtesy Fourth Floor Productions.

between the lines," as a substitute for wading into the archives of World War II documents which are now available in embarrassing abundance.[159]

Saying that "more daring" historians had begun to use modern technologies to dispel "some of the more tenaciously held myths of the twentieth century," Irving presented his own record as a debunker of the faked Hitler diaries through laboratory analysis of the ink used. The results of "laboratory analysis" of Auschwitz, he claimed, were unequivocal: "While significant quantities of cyanide compounds were found in the small delousing facilities of the camp where the proprietary (and lethal) Zyklon B compound was used, as all are agreed, to disinfect the plague-ridden clothing of all persons entering these brutal slave-labour camps, no significant trace whatsoever was found in the buildings which international opinion—for it is not more than that—has always labelled as the camp's infamous gas chambers." He added that he did not expect "incorrigible historians, statesmen and publicists" to change their view that the Nazis used gas chambers at Auschwitz to kill human beings. "But it is now up to them to explain to me as an intelligent and critical student of modern history why there is no significant trace of any cyanide compound in the building which they have always identified as the former gas chambers," Irving wrote. "The ball is in their court."[160]

Confident of his contribution to world history, and seeking maximum publicity, Irving sent copies of the preface to members of Parliament. It was met with an immediate response. On June 20—three days before the official launch of the Leuchter Report—Hugh Dykes, M.P. introduced an "early-day motion" with the title "David Irving and Holocaust Denial."

> DESCRIPTION: That this House, on the occasion of the reunion of 1,000 refugees from the Holocaust, most of whose families were killed in gas chambers or otherwise by Nazi murderers is appalled by the allegation by the Nazi apologist David Irving that the infamous gas chambers of Auschwitz, Treblinka and Majdanek did not exist ever, except perhaps, as the brainchild of Britain's brilliant wartime Psychological Warfare Executive: draws attention to a new fascist publication, the Leuchter Report, in which this evil calumny appears: and condemns without qualification such pernicious work of Hitler's heirs.[161]

Eighty-eight of the members present signed the motion.

The only effect of this public opposition to Irving's claims was to strengthen his sense that he was the instrument of destiny. In a letter to Hugh Dykes, copies of which were sent to the media, Irving asked if his motion was "the best that the gallant but dwindling band of gullible believers in the 'gas chambers' can do?" And he warned him that "if you persist in believing in 'gas chambers' at Auschwitz you are on a loser."[162] A year later, Irving sent another batch of Leuchter Reports to Parliament, this time to members of the House of Lords. The occasion was the War Crimes Bill designed to give British courts greater jurisdiction over certain war crimes committed in Germany and German-held territory during the Second World War. In an accompanying letter, Irving predicted that "five years from now even the dourest academic will accept that the 'gas chambers' displayed at Auschwitz are as false as the one removed at Bonn's insistence from the site at Dachau—a propaganda legend just like the 'soap made from victims of the Nazis,' which Israeli historians last month finally admitted was also a grotesque wartime untruth."[163]

Casting himself as the central protagonist in a great historical drama and making prophetic statements, Irving tied his reputation ever more doggedly to Auschwitz. At the press conference he declared that he was "quite happy to nail my colours to the mast" and inferred from Leuchter's conclusions concerning the Auschwitz gas chambers that there had been no gas chambers anywhere. When a journalist asked him if this implied that he also denied the gas chambers of Sobibor and Treblinka, Irving answered "I think *prima facie* if they turned out to have been faked at Auschwitz then it's equally likely that they'd turn out to be fake at the other places behind the Iron Curtain too."[164]

His position was remarkable, given the fact that within weeks after launching the Leuchter Report he received a first indication that Leuchter had produced a dud. A fellow traveler from South Africa, David A. Crabtree, had obtained a copy of the Leuchter Report through his daughter, who had attended a lecture Irving had given in Johannesburg. He wrote Irving that he found it interesting reading and that its major conclusion was "well founded." Yet he was troubled by the "elementary errors of fact and reasoning in the text."[165] Crabtree enclosed a 5-page critique in which he defined some of Leuchter's observations as "total rubbish, good evidence to brand the author as a scientific ignoramus."[166] On page after page he corrected Leuchter's figures and challenged his reasoning. Crabtree's observations troubled Irving, and he shared his concerns with Zündel. In his response, Zündel accepted that the report could be vastly improved but said that a court order forbade him to do so. If he violated the order, he would lose his right to appeal, he would forfeit the bond that kept him out of prison pending his appeal, he would immediately be arrested and, after completing his sentence, he would automatically be deported. As an alternative to tinkering with the Leuchter Report, Zündel suggested that a new expedition could be mounted to Auschwitz, this time accompanied by a professional television crew. Irving should join as a narrator. "This would give you 'instant expert' status and let you talk more forcefully and convincingly with 'eyewitness status,'" Zündel told Irving. In addition, Irving's presence "would make the whole thing a serious archaeological history endeavour."[167] Zündel also suggested that if the Poles made it impossible to take samples, they would amalgamate the new discoveries with the Leuchter samples. And even if the whole thing were to end in scientific failure, Zündel saw the commercial benefits: Irving would end up with "a very marketable product in the Irving image of media Razzle Dazzle."[168]

Crabtree's critique, written from a perspective sympathetic to Leuchter's effort, was not the only indication that there were profound problems with the Leuchter Report. In early August Irving received from Mark Weber an anonymous 23-page German critique, entitled "A critical Comment on the So-called Leuchter Document" ("Kritische Stellungnahme zum sogen. Leuchter-Dokument"). Written by octogenarian German retired civil servant and amateur historian Werner Wegner, it was to be published in 1990 as a chapter in the monumental *Die Schatten der Vergangenheit: Impulse zur Historisierung des Nationalsozialismus* (*The Shadows of the Past: Impulses towards a Historicization of National Socialism*), published by Propyläen Verlag.[169] Weber told Irving that he was worried about the impact of the essay.[170] He had reason to do so: Wegner amply demonstrated that Leuchter's science did not pass critical muster.[171] Irving had to admit that Wegner's chapter was "*very* cogent."[172]

A final blow to the credibility of the Leuchter Report materialized a few months later, when Irving received through the good offices of Colin M. Beer another utterly devastating critique of the Leuchter Report, written, allegedly, by an unnamed "friend" of Beer.[173] In the first six conclusions, the report dismantled Leuchter's science. The seventh conclusion proved harsh to Irving, while the eighth and last conclusion turned the Leuchter Report into a boomerang returning into the face of the negationists:

> 7) The Leuchter Report on its own does not conclusively prove that the buildings in question were used as gas chambers. Equally its conclusions that they could not have been do not stand up to rigorous analysis. Contrary to Irving's assertions forensic science is not exact except in detective fiction. At best it is a matter of

balancing probabilities. In all such cases it must be considered in the light of all available evidence. In this context the omission of all other evidence from the Leuchter Report is damning.

Leuchter is not, in spite of his undoubted (if gruesome) expertise, a forensic scientist. He is also not a historian. Had he been either his first reaction should have been that his investigation contradicted the mass of available evidence. Where this occurs there are the following probabilities.

a) The mass of evidence is wrong
b) His conclusions are wrong
c) The contradiction is due to a significant factor being wrong or omitted.

Leuchter, having correctly analysed the problem in the light of his own experience then simply assumed that this conclusion invalidated all the other evidence available and reported accordingly. A forensic scientist or skilled historian then would have asked what factor would have eliminated the contradiction. The reports of a 30–45 minute death time would have pointed him at 100 ppm gas concentration and lead to a fundamental reassessment of his report. Once the 100 ppm assumption is made, all the Holocaust evidence falls into place and the accurate and detailed evidence of the Leuchter Report confirms them. Which leads to our final conclusion.

8) The evidence of the Leuchter Report, when taken in the context of the times and in full consideration of all other evidence[,] is consistent with that other evidence and together strongly supports both the fact and the scale of the massacres in the gas chambers of Birkenau provided that assumption is made that the gas chambers operated at relatively low toxic concentrations.[174]

The report was devastating. Irving had to admit as much when he responded to it in a letter to Mr. Beer. As to the general thrust of its argument, he wrote that "I agree, in fact, with many of your friend's criticisms."[175]

In conclusion: within six months after the publication of the Focal Point edition of the Leuchter Report, it had become clear to Irving that he had tied his fortune to a dud. But Irving refused to retreat. Instead, he revised his magnum opus, *Hitler's War*, to remove all references to the use of Auschwitz as an extermination camp. For example, in the original edition, Irving described how in the spring of 1942 the Germans rounded up Jews in France, Holland, Belgium, and Slovakia to send them to Auschwitz where, upon arrival, "four in every ten were pronounced fit for work; the rest were exterminated with a maximum of concealment." In the new edition, Irving dropped the reference to the selection and the killing and replaced it with a sanitized account of Himmler's visit to Auschwitz in July 1942. After having toured "the immense synthetic rubber plant being erected by forced labor," Himmler inspected the camp accompanied by, among others, Gauleiter Fritz Bracht. Introducing a false analogy, Irving wrote that "whatever later historians would claim, Hitler never visited any concentration camp, let alone Auschwitz. Historians would also claim that Himmler witnessed the 'liquidation' of a trainload of Jews on this occasion. This is apocryphal—devoid of any documentary substance." Indeed, there is no wartime German document that provides a detailed schedule of Himmler's visit of the camp—his service calendar tersely mentions "Inspection of the camp of the inmates and the women's camp"[176]—but in 1946

Höss provided an extensive report of Himmler's visit, and it contained a description of Himmler attending the arrival and selection of a transport from the Netherlands. "Himmler very carefully observed the entire process of annihilation. He began with the unloading at the ramps and completed the inspection as Bunker 2 was being cleared of the bodies. At that time there were no open-pit burnings. He did not complain about anything."[177] Irving did not refer to this evidence but instead quoted a postwar statement by Bracht's deputy, Albert Hoffmann, who had accompanied Himmler around Auschwitz.

> Conditions were, he volunteered, considerably worse than those he had seen at Dachau in 1938. "Maltreatment did occur, and [he] has actually seen the [crematory] ovens where bodies were being burned." But Hoffmann's interrogation report significantly added, "He totally disbelieves the accounts of atrocities as published in the press." (By late 1945 the world's newspapers were full of unsubstantiated, lurid rumors about "factories of death" complete with lethal "gas chambers.")[178]

And thus Irving transformed fact into parenthetical rumor.

In the 1977 edition of *Hitler's War,* Irving described the deportation of more than 400,000 Hungarian Jews to Auschwitz and wrote that "in Auschwitz, the defunct paraphernalia of death—idle since late 1943—began to clank again as the first trainloads from Hungary arrived."[179] The new edition recorded that "four hundred thousand Jews were being rounded up in Hungary; the first trainloads arrived in Auschwitz as slave labor for the now completed I.G. Farben plant."[180] And whereas in the 1977 edition Irving described Auschwitz as "Himmler's ghastly secret," which was revealed in the "horrifying revelations" of Vrba and Wetzlar published in "reputable Swiss newspapers in early July,"[181] the 1991 edition contained none of this evidence.[182]

Irving invited Leuchter and Faurisson to help him launch the publication of the new edition of *Hitler's War* with personal appearances. Preparations began in the early summer, when Irving began to inform the press. Some proved less than excited about the prospect of a Leuchter speech in Britain. On July 12, the *Jewish Chronicle* ran the headline "Keep Holocaust 'Apologists' Out of Britain, Home Secretary Is Told." The article quoted David Winnick, M.P., who said that "revisionists and apologists for Nazism are highly offensive to the memory of all those who were murdered. It contaminates British soil to have them here." Irving was said to be unmoved by the protests: "I won't be intimidated, I won't knuckle down."[183] In the end, anti-Irving activists were able to convince the government that Leuchter's presence would not serve public interest, and, while still in the United States, Leuchter had been informed by the Immigration and Nationality Department that the Home Secretary had given directions "that you should not be given entry to the United Kingdom on the grounds that your presence here would not be conducive to the public good."[184] Both Irving and Leuchter decided to ignore this letter, the former because he needed Leuchter to attract the attention of the media, the latter because he had been convinced by Zündel that a lecture tour to Europe could be profitable: the latter had lined up some "catacomb meetings" in Germany where Leuchter would speak before his appearance with Faurisson in London. The date for Leuchter's appearance was set for November 15. To mark the importance of the occasion, Faurisson was to give an introductory lecture while Irving was to function as the host.

On November 11, 1991, Faurisson and Leuchter arrived in Britain, despite the exclusion order. Notwithstanding, Irving had distributed a flyer to advertise the launch of the expurgated edition of *Hitler's War* that announced in large type "Leuchter Is Coming!"[185] This publicity triggered a dramatic chain of events which undoubtedly served Irving's desire for publicity but brought Leuchter and his wife some very uncomfortable hours in a London police station and the indignity of immediate deportation. The setting was the Chelsea town hall, which was rented for the occasion. In his welcoming word, Irving described the "revisionist" project he, Faurisson, and Leuchter had undertaken as "the greatest intellectual adventure of the twentieth century."[186] Irving praised Faurisson as a scholar experienced in "microscopic textual analysis, the analysis of words in enormous detail," and concluded his introduction with the statement that "Faurisson is one of the bravest historians I know."[187]

The French academic talked for some time about the impossibility of the gas chambers and then vacated the platform for the main speaker of the evening: Leuchter. According to an article in the *Sunday Telegraph* entitled "Death's Salesman Cut Off before His Time," Irving introduced Leuchter with "Boy, have we got a treat for you," and proceeded to tell the audience how he had smuggled Leuchter into the country. According to the article, Leuchter started in form. "It was like listening to a lesson in how to gas people"—a lesson meant to show that the Germans had not done so. The police were present in case of trouble, but because Irving had publicly told the audience that Leuchter ought not be there, they had checked to see if indeed there was an exclusion order. Confirmation came within five minutes. A police officer standing in the wings interrupted Leuchter and asked him to come with him. A chief inspector explained to the disappointed crowd: "Fred Leuchter has been made subject of an exclusion order to this country and in order to resolve the matter, a gentleman who goes by that name has agreed to come to the police station in order to resolve the matter."[188] The article also recorded Irving's answer when asked if he was mad: "When you're working on the edge of intellectual hyper-strain, sometimes you must say: 'Have I flipped?' Unfortunately, there's no intellectual thermometer you can slip in your mouth to find out."[189]

The same day that the *Sunday Telegraph* ran the story, Leuchter issued his own press release, stating that the United Kingdom had "joined the ranks of terrorist nations of the world." The Home Secretary had violated international law when he incarcered Leuchter in a frigid cell "with known felons (a dangerous and potentially lethal place for a maker of execution equipment)." It was defiantly signed by "Fred A. Leuchter Jr., Citizen of the United States of America."[190]

Later that month *The Independent* ran a long article about the event and its context in an article entitled "David Irving Resells Hitler's War." It carried a photo of Irving and Leuchter just before the intervention by the police. Interestingly enough, it also provided a telling quotation the *Sunday Telegraph* had not chosen to print: "Mr. Irving told his Chelsea audience that in the new edition of *Hitler's War* they would 'not find one line on the "Holocaust." Why dignify something with even a footnote that has not happened?'"[191]

Irving's defiant language signified his decision to advance ever more aggressively. With that, an increasingly aggressive rhetoric took the place of his earlier calls to science. If the statements he made about Auschwitz were not so appalling, Irving's predicament following the exposure of Leuchter's ineptitude could be described as tragic. But his statements were appalling. For example, in a lecture given in Toronto in 1990 he not only proclaimed what was to become his favorite summary of case on the Holocaust—"more people died on the back seat of Senator Edward Kennedy's motor car in Chappaquiddick than died in the gas chamber in Auschwitz"—but also provided another example of his infinite ability to mock the victims. Obviously comfortable with maritime terms and undoubtedly inspired by the review of Mayer's book that had appeared in the newsletter of the Institute for Historical Review, Irving embroidered the metaphor of the cruise ship Holocaust. It was a huge vessel "with luxury wall-to-wall fitted carpets and a crew of thousands" and "marine terminals established in now virtually every capital in the world, disguised as Holocaust memorial museums." But Irving predicted that the ship was in for rough seas, because the Russians had made available "the index cards of all the people who passed through the gates of Auschwitz." (This, by the way, was a lie; the Russians had provided access to the death books that recorded the deaths of registered inmates of Auschwitz.) As a result, "a lot of people are not claiming to be Auschwitz survivors anymore." Irving predicted that the hoax would collapse as people began to challenge the survivors, beginning with the tattoos on their arms. "Because the experts can look at a tattoo and say, 'Oh yes, 181,219 that means you entered Auschwitz in March 1943.'" Irving advised the survivors that "if you want to go and have a tattoo put on your arm, as a lot of them do, I am afraid to say, and claim subsequently that you were in Auschwitz, you have got to make sure a) that it fits in with the month you said you went to Auschwitz, and b) that it is not a number which anyone has used before."[192]

In lectures given in Europe, North America, and Australia, Irving dragged Auschwitz down and was in turn dragged down with it. In early 1990, Irving declared in a lecture given in the German town of Moers that perhaps 30,000 people had been killed in Auschwitz. "Bad enough. No-one of us would like to approve of that. Thirty thousand people in Auschwitz from beginning to end—that is as many as we English killed in Hamburg in one night." The camp had not been an extermination camp, he argued, and it did not have homicidal gas chambers. Therefore the gas chambers in Auschwitz shown to the tourists were phony. "I say the following thing: there were no gas chambers in Auschwitz. There have been only mock-ups built by the Poles in the years after the war."[193] On April 21, 1990, Irving made the same argument to 800 people assembled in the Löwenbraukeller in Munich.[194] A Bavarian public prosecutor decided to take action. After 1979, the German penal code defined Holocaust denial as a punishable offence that carried a maximum sentence of two years in prison. On July 11, 1991, a magistrate's court convicted Irving for his remarks and fined him DM 7,000. Irving appealed. On May 5, 1992, the District Court of Munich convicted Irving for defamation in conjunction with the offense of denigrating the memory of deceased persons and fined him DM 10,000. Irving appealed again, claiming that there was no evidence for the operation of the Auschwitz gas chambers. He lost this second appeal in 1993. The 25th Criminal Chamber of the Regional Court of Munich increased his fine to DM 30,000. The language of the judgment was harsh for a man who claimed to be the preeminent historian of the Third Reich. "Had the Accused applied his endeavours in an unprejudiced manner, not marked by any ideology of the Right, he would always have been in a position to assess accurately the numerous historical sources and witnesses."[195] His conviction not only gave him a criminal record but also led to a decision by the German Ministry of the Interior to ban Irving from using German federal archives. This was followed by his exclusion from the very country to which he had devoted his life. In Germany, Irving had become persona non grata.

Irving had chosen Auschwitz as his battlefield—one that he (incidentally) had never visited. In January 1992, the *Jewish Chronicle* characterized him as "describing himself as a 'field marshal' who would tour the 'battlefield' only once the final victory had been achieved."[196] But victory had not come his way. Auschwitz had proved to be Irving's Waterloo. It had made him into a felon, and it had subjected him in Canada to the indignity of arrest and deportation. If he was to clear his name, it could only be by proving that he had been right all along—an attitude that came naturally to the man who described himself in his press statement announcing the publication of the Leuchter Report as "controversial—but always right." For Irving, therefore, there was no escape from Auschwitz. In private, he was willing to admit that his endorsement of Leuchter's conclusion had been a disaster. In early 1993, he wrote Zündel that his life had been perfect until they crossed paths. "In April 1988 I unhesitatingly agreed to aid your defence as a witness in Toronto. *I would not make the same mistake again.* As a penalty for having defended you then, and for having continued to aid you since, my life has come under a gradually mounting attack: I find myself the worldwide victim of mass demonstrations, violence, vituperation, and persecution."[197] Irving's reasoning was, of course, fallacious. His problems did not derive from his willingness to support Zündel but from his eagerness to exploit the Zündel trial for his own purposes.

But whatever disaster his involvement with Auschwitz had brought him, Irving remained unable to publicly retreat from the issue, and he continued to make it the focus of provocative and ill-considered pronouncements. In 1993, he claimed that probably 100,000 Jews had died in Auschwitz—"but not from gas chambers. They died from epidemics." Of these probably 25,000 had been murdered. "If we take that generous figure, then I would say that 25,000 people murdered in Auschwitz in three years is still half the number of people that we murdered in Hamburg, burning them alive in one night in 1943." As to the "real" fate of the Jews, Irving reached back to one of his earlier ideas: most Jews had been killed by Allied bombs after having been evacuated from the camps in the winter of 1944/1945. "The concentration camp inmates arrived in Berlin or in Leipzig or in Dresden just in time for the RAF bombers to set fire to those cities," Irving claimed. "Nobody knows how many Jews died in those air raids."[198]

Irving not only added new themes to his lecture offerings, he also looked for new publishing initiatives, and in this he remained fatally attracted to Auschwitz. In 1992, a book entitled *Air Photo Evidence* appeared in Canada which formed, together with the Leuchter Report, the bookends of revisionist obsession with the gas chambers. If Leuchter had tried to prove through the chemical analysis of some wall samples that no gassings had taken place, John C. Ball from Delta, British Columbia, thought he could do the same through the study of air photos of Auschwitz and Birkenau taken by Allied planes on April 4, May 31, June 26, August 25, and September 13, 1944. Ball's reasoning was simple: "Nothing is hidden from air photos. Looking at the air photos will be just as if we went back in time to World War II to take a series of airplane flights over the different areas." His alleged aim was equally simple. "My objective was to *analyze* World War II German controlled detention camps in Poland for evidence to confirm the claims that mass murders, burials, and cremations had been conducted there"[199]—a statement that, given the contents of the book, reminds one of Leuchter's often-repeated assertion that he went to Auschwitz to prove that the gas chambers had been efficient killing mass installations. Of course, like Leuchter, Ball came to the opposite conclusion: "There is *no* evidence mass murders and cremations occurred at or near the Birkenau crematoriums, which were visible from both inside and outside the camp, or the Auschwitz I or Majdanek detention camps."[200] In fact, as a 16-page insert that accompanied the Ball book declared, the situation was quite the opposite of what all witnesses had described: "Auschwitz inmates enjoyed a wide range of healthy activities."[201]

Unlike the Leuchter Report, Ball's book, published by the author, did not have much of an impact. Yet both Zündel and Irving believed that it had potential. It was exceedingly well illustrated with many seemingly informative air photos from the National Archives in Washington. The problem was the text, which was in fact nothing more than a series of captions to the photos. In 1993, Zündel bought the German rights for the book, but at the same time Irving found a right-wing German publisher who would distribute the book under Irving's Focal Point imprint. The deal was that Irving would write a foreword as he had done for the Leuchter Report that would, as he explained to Zündel, make the book understandable.[202] In the end, the whole project collapsed. Ball was not to be another Leuchter, and *Air Photo Evidence* was not to be another Leuchter Report. As a publisher of path-breaking negationist pamphlets, Irving had begun to lose his touch.

Irving increasingly began to reap the bitter harvest of the carelessly phrased seeds sown in the years before. He always had taken pride in his prophetic gifts, and in 1991 he had announced that the Holocaust "hoax" would have only another two years of life. "Gradually the word is getting around Germany," he had told a Canadian audience. "Two years from now too the German historians will accept that we are right. They will accept that for fifty years they have believed a lie."[203] But in 1994 he had to admit that his prophecy had not been realized and that the "rotting corpse" of the "profitable legend" of the Holocaust still had some life in it.[204] In an interview he gave to the New York–based author Ron Rosenbaum, Irving expressed defiant pride in having made negationism highly visible. "So what started out as a historical footnote in my *Hitler's War* in 1977 has now become so important that prime ministers and presidents have to [denounce] it," Irving claimed proudly. But pride was mixed with regret, and as he talked to Rosenbaum he admitted even a sense of embarrassment in conjunction with the people he had come to associate with. "I'm not blind," Irving told Rosenbaum. "I know these people have done me a lot of damage, a lot of harm, because I get associated then with those stupid actions."[205]

But Irving did not give up hope that some deus ex machina would redeem his 1988 conversion by revealing the "real history" of Auschwitz. In January 1995, Irving believed that his moment had come, with the apparent bouleversement of a prominent French magazine on the issue of Auschwitz. In order to mark the fiftieth anniversary of the liberation of Auschwitz—an occasion that testified to the universally shared significance of Auschwitz as the central symbol of the Holocaust—the French magazine *L'Express* carried a section with articles about the camp. One of these, written by journalist and historian Eric Conan, concerned the problems of historic preservation, restoration, and presentation.[206] Conan's article provided a solid account of problems conservator Witold Smerk faced in controlling the decay of the remaining barracks, which had been erected as temporary structures more than fifty years earlier, and the degradation of the hair, shoes, and other exhibits in barracks not equipped with any climate control.[207] And then there was the great problem the museum authorities faced in removing from the presentation the overly communist interpretation of the murders that had taken place at the site—one that had inflated the number of victims while simultaneously suppressing the Jewish identity of the vast majority of those killed. Conan quoted a senior advisor to the museum and to the Ministry of Culture, who said that there was now a unanimous resolve "to make an end to the nationalist-communist discourse at the place, and find for the genocide of the Jews a central place in the memory of Auschwitz." In the five years since the fall of communism much had been achieved. "The biggest blunders have been rectified but the main discussions are never-ending and far from being settled. I may even say that the essential debates, distressing and sometimes unexpected, are only beginning."[208]

Conan described the ongoing discussions of the museum with people from all over the world about how to improve the presentation, including a short description of a conference that I attended in 1993. And then he turned to two "delicate" subjects: the issue of the hair, which many Jews would like to see removed from the exhibition and buried, and the problem of ill-considered restorations done shortly after the war. The most important was the reconstruction of the gas chamber in Crematorium 1. "Everything there is wrong: the dimensions of the gas chamber, the locations of the doors, the openings for pouring in Zyklon B, the ovens that were rebuilt according to the recollections of some survivors, the height of the chimney."[209]

Conan's discussion about the problems of the restoration, conservation, and presentation of Crematorium 1 were perfectly justified. Yet his article would prove excellent raw material for negationists. Indeed, they immediately hailed Conan's article as a breakthrough.

Irving celebrated Conan's article in the May 1995 issue of his newsletter named *Action Report*.

> **L'Express: "Tout y est faux"—Everything About It Is Fake**
> *French Make a Clean Breast: Admit Forty-Seven-Year Auschwitz "Gas-Chamber" Fraud*
> Paris—Braving the risk of prosecution under France's draconic new Fabius-Gayssot Law, the mass circulation national weekly magazine L'Express has admitted that the gas chamber shown to tourists at Auschwitz is a fake—built by the Polish Communists three years after the War.
> This was the claim which British writer David Irving made in Munich in April 1990: a remark for which the German government fined him DM 30,000 ($22,000) and banned him from Germany in 1993.[210]

Although he remained silent about Conan's discussion of the wartime history of Crematorium 1, Irving defined the "admission by L'Express that 'everything is fake' about the Auschwitz gas chamber" as "the fourth great triumph for the world-wide revisionist movement"—the other three were the admissions that "there were never homicidal gas chambers in Dachau," that "the soap story was a propaganda lie," and that not four million, but only between one and 1.5 million people had been murdered in Auschwitz. "Now the Auschwitz gas chamber legend is finally crumbling too. Just as the leading revisionists promised that it would."[211]

As Irving had indicated, the issue had great personal importance for him because he had been convicted in Germany for stating that the gas chambers shown in Auschwitz were fakes. Ignoring the fact that he had made a statement about all the gas chambers, and that Conan's article only concerned the gas chamber in Crematorium 1—those of Crematoria 2, 3, 4, and 5 were never reconstructed—Irving felt that the time had come to call for a revision of the case, and he called all his supporters "to tell German diplomatic officials and journalists about the article and its findings."[212] Irving's reaction to Conan's article once again clearly revealed that he felt that his own reputation was tied up with Auschwitz.

Irving refused to recant his position on the Auschwitz gas chambers even when, in 1995, he showed a surprising willingness to abandon the extremely offensive position he had adopted in 1988. When interviewed in July 1995 on Ron Casey's morning radio show in Australia, Irving remarked that if Churchill had accepted Hitler's 1940 peace offer, "the world would have been spared a lot of suffering and would also, incidentally, have been spared what is now called the Holocaust." When Casey pointed out to Irving that he had admitted that the Holocaust had happened, Irving tried first some evasive action. "I don't like talking about the Holocaust as though there was only one Holocaust, it's just that I get a bit unhappy about the fact that the Jewish community have tried to make a monopoly of their own suffering." Casey did not give up and elicited from Irving a statement that up to 4 million Jews had died in the concentration camps "of barbarity and typhus and epidemics."[213] Thus, by the middle of 1995, Irving seemed to abandon the extreme negationist position he had taken in his Battleship Auschwitz speech given at the Tenth International Revisionist Conference and in fact conceded that up to 4 million Jews had been killed in concentration camps, a number that actually exceeded Raul Hilberg's estimate, based on a careful study of the evidence, that of the total number of 5.1 million Jewish victims up to 3 million Jews had been killed in the camps.[214] Yet even in retreat Irving did not change his views concerning the Auschwitz gas chambers. He attributed the deaths to "barbarity and typhus and epidemics," carefully avoiding mentioning the gas chambers.

Irving's remarks generated much anxiety in negationist circles, especially after they had been picked up by the anti-Fascist monthly *Searchlight* and published in their September issue. In response, Faurisson wrote Irving on September 29, 1995, to ask him if he had indeed had admitted to the killing of 4 million Jews.[215] Irving did not respond, claiming later that he had not received the letter. He only engaged Faurisson's complaint when the latter published his letter in the newsletter of the negationist Adelaide Institute. In response, Irving wrote a letter to Faurisson which suggested the possibility that the interview had been edited "to fake what I actually said," and repeated that while the number of victims could have been as high as 4 million, the causes of death would have been "air raids, forced marches, starvation, disease, epidemics, old age."[216] Faurisson was not impressed. He waited for three days and then responded curtly, asking him for his evidence that perhaps 4 million Jews had died. "Why not 5,100,000 as Hilberg says? Or any other figure?" Faurisson asked.[217]

Rigid as ever, Faurisson was very disappointed, and on July 7, 1996, he sent a letter to the Adelaide Institute, which published it as their lead article in August. In it Faurisson reviewed Irving's career as a negationist. In the early 1980s he had been like a "half-pregnant woman," reluctant to jump in 1988 onto the revisionist bandwagon in Toronto, yet "benefiting from the enormous work I had done for years and under the worst circumstances for my family and myself, and benefiting also from the fact I had won F. Leuchter to both E. Zündel's and my revisionist views." Yet in 1991, Faurisson began to have doubts about Irving's willingness to suffer both jail time and financial ruin for his beliefs. "In recent years I have watched Irving become more and more upset, and trying to distance himself from the revisionists. . . . We are, in this way, getting back to the 'half pregnant woman'!" He counseled Irving that "if he stops changing and shifting, if he decides to repeat clearly what he first said about the 'shattering' *Leuchter Report* and the 'sinking battleship, Auschwitz,' without desperately trying to regain the favour of the 'Establishment,' he will be respected and feared by everybody, including his worst enemies: It is the best tactic."[218]

Faurisson's public criticism challenged Irving's idealized image. By the time Faurisson's letter appeared in print, Irving's retreat had ceased, and he announced publicly that he would make a stand. His battle was to take the form of a libel action against Penguin Books Limited and Professor Deborah Lipstadt of Emory University in Atlanta, respectively publisher and author of a study of negationism entitled *Denying the Holocaust*.

To have a fight one needs two, and Irving chose wisely when he decided to initiate his suit against Lipstadt. Of all the people who had said nasty things about him, Lipstadt was the least likely to give in without a fight. Born in New York City in 1947, she received an intensive Jewish education. At the City College of New York, she read political science and history. She spent two academic years in Israel (1966–1968) and was there during the Six-Day War. This experience triggered a turn to Judaism, and after her return to the United States she enrolled in the graduate program of Judaic studies at Brandeis University. On receiving her doctorate, she was appointed first at the University of Washington, then the University of California Los Angeles, and following that at Occidental College in Los Angeles. In Los Angeles she became interested in the indifference of the American press to the fate of the Jews in Nazi Europe. The result was a passionate book, *Beyond Belief: The American Press and the Coming of the Holocaust 1933–1945* (1986).

As she researched the largely unconscious patterns of denial that had marked contemporary American reporting of the Holocaust, Lipstadt became interested in the highly conscious patterns of negationism that had gained increasing visibility in the early 1980s. In 1984, Lipstadt proposed to Professor Yehuda Bauer, head of the Vidal Sassoon Centre for the study of Anti-Semitism at the Hebrew University of Jerusalem, that she write a book on the historical and historiographic methodology of American negationists. In the original proposal, Lipstadt mentioned that negationists "find it expedient to associate themselves with those such as David Irving who do not deny that the Holocaust took place but seek to shift the blame to others." One of the particular questions the book was to answer was the measure in which World War I revisionism had influenced "people such as App and Butz and those such as David Irving who, though they may not deny the existence of the Holocaust, do shift the blame from Hitler."[219] In 1988, Bauer and Lipstadt arrived at a formal agreement. After four years of research the first draft was completed; it treated Irving as a minor figure in the story of negationists. In a critique of the manuscript, Bauer urged Lipstadt to adopt a more worldwide perspective, as it limited itself to American and French negationists. "Americans are so provincial anyway," Bauer noted. "I would not like to strengthen that." Reviewing Lipstadt's treatment of negationism in various other countries, Bauer observed that

"Irving is mentioned, but not [as] the mainstay of Holocaust denial today in Western Europe."[220]

Bauer's call was justified, and Lipstadt recognized this. She immediately set out to find more material on Irving. When asked for help, Antony Lerman of the Institute of Jewish Affairs in London obliged and sent her some clippings. When the book finally appeared, Irving had become an important protagonist in the story. Lipstadt, who had by then moved to Emory University in Atlanta, now defined Irving as "one of the most dangerous spokesmen for Holocaust denial." She charged that "familiar with historical evidence, he bends it until it conforms with his ideological leanings and political agenda."[221]

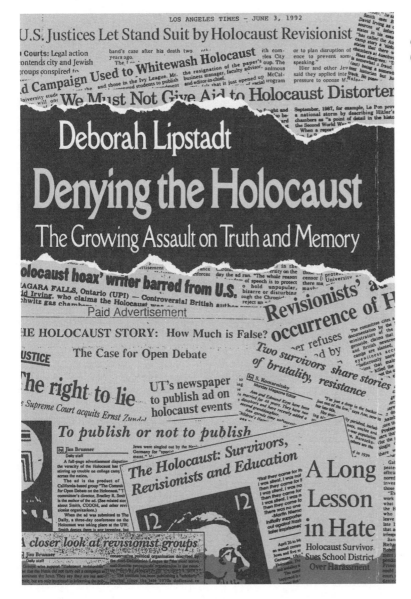

Cover, Denying the Holocaust *(1993). Collection of author.*

Lipstadt's book first appeared in 1993 in the United States under the imprint of The Free Press, a subsidiary of Macmillan. In 1993, Irving did not act. First of all, the American libel laws made success very unlikely: not only would the burden of proof be on him, but following the Supreme Court judgment in the case of *New York Times vs. Sullivan,* as a public figure Irving would have to prove that Lipstadt had made her criticisms of him with knowledge of falsehood or with reckless disregard for the truth. The book appeared in Britain in 1994 under the imprint of Viking, a subsidiary of Penguin. If he were interested in a suit, he had a chance: singularly and strikingly, British libel law favors the plaintiff and not the defendant. The plaintiff only needs to make the charge that certain remarks are defamatory. Unless the defendant claims that the plaintiff misunderstood the ordinary meaning of the words at issue, or their innuendo, the law requires that the defense justify the words by proving the alleged libel to be "substantially" true.

Yet for two years nothing happened. Irving was not interested in pursuing Lipstadt in the courts. In fact, Irving enjoyed confronting her directly in the hustle and bustle of the free market of ideas. On November 11, 1994, he joined the audience for a lecture about negationism Lipstadt was to make at DeKalb College, located in Atlanta, Georgia. During the question-and-answer period Irving rose to hijack the meeting in a manner not much different from his tactic at the 1983 *Der Stern* press conference. He charged that Lipstadt's claim that there were abundant proofs for the gas chambers in Auschwitz was false and that there was no blueprint for the gas chamber showing the holes through which the Zyklon was inserted. He offered a thousand-dollar reward if she could produce that document. As the meeting dissolved into chaos, he unrolled a large wartime aerial photograph of Auschwitz, challenging Lipstadt to show him the mountains of coke necessary to incinerate the alleged number of victims. Then he offered those present free copies of his Göring biography. In the diary account that he wrote the next day and which he immediately faxed to his supporters, he described his offer as an attempt to get the better of Lipstadt in her own backyard. Many students accepted the free copies. Irving noted in his diary that not since his intervention in the *Der Stern* press conference "had success smelt so sweet, and been (in my view) so richly deserved."[222]

The paths of Irving and Lipstadt parted again. Both had other things on their minds. Lipstadt had been appointed to the United States Holocaust Memorial Council, the body that oversees the United States Holocaust Memorial Museum in Washington, D.C. Miles Lerman, the chairman of the Council, asked Lipstadt to run the Education Committee, which supervised the Education Department of the museum, and appointed her to the museum's Executive Committee. She was too busy to be concerned about Irving. This changed, however, in the spring of 1996. The New York publishing house St. Martin's Press was about to publish Irving's biography of Goebbels. Many protested, but Deborah Lipstadt was particularly vocal in her opposition to the publication of the Goebbels biography, accusing Irving and St. Martin's Press of killing the victims of the Holocaust a second time. At the last moment, St. Martin's Press stopped publication. The collapse of the deal meant a great financial loss to Irving—he was to claim later that he had lost $500,000. Irving blamed a Jewish conspiracy, and much of his anger was focused on Lipstadt. According to the *Washington Post,* Lipstadt compared the publication of Irving's Goebbels biography with the publication of a treatise on pedophilia by Jeffrey Dahmer, the murderer and cannibal of a dozen young men. Irving resented being compared to a pedophile, as he was to state four years later in his opening statement in the Royal Courts of Justice in London. "It is enough for the label to be attached, for the attachee to find himself designated as a pariah, an outcast from normal society." He intended to teach Lipstadt a lesson. In July, Irving announced his response in his *Action Report*: "Prof. Lipstadt is about to receive a writ from me for her tract Denying the Holocaust which she has foolishly started peddling within the jurisdiction of the British Courts."[223]

On September 5, 1996, Irving issued a writ of summons, which triggered an action in which Penguin and Lipstadt, if they chose not to settle, would have to prove that the statements that Irving considered libelous were justified. His complaint involved, apart from the quote given above, six other passages and one footnote. Two of the passages were crucial, and both related to Irving's involvement with the Leuchter Report. In the first passage, Lipstadt wrongly claimed that Irving had been involved in the preparation of the Leuchter expedition to Auschwitz. "Both Irving and Faurisson advocated inviting an American prison warden who had performed gas executions to testify in Zündel's defense, arguing that this would be the best tactic for proving that the gas chambers were a fraud and too primitive to operate safely."[224] Irving did indeed have a point. Lipstadt was in error. As we have seen, Irving was not involved in this stage of the Zündel defense.

The second passage was more damaging to Irving.

> David Irving, who during the Zündel trial declared himself converted by Leuchter's work to Holocaust denial and to the idea that the gas chambers were a myth, described himself as conducting a "one-man intifada" against the official history of the Holocaust.
>
> In his foreword to his publication of the Leuchter Report, Irving wrote that there was no doubt as to Leuchter's "integrity" and "scrupulous methods." He made no mention of Leuchter's lack of technical expertise or of the many holes that had been poked in his findings. Most important, Irving wrote, "Nobody likes to be swindled, still less where considerable sums of money are involved." Irving identified Israel as the swindler, claiming that West Germany had given it more than ninety billion deutsche marks in voluntary reparations, "essentially in atonement for the 'gas chambers of Auschwitz.'" According to Irving the problem was that the latter was a myth that would "not die easily." He subsequently set off to promulgate Holocaust denial notions in various countries.[225]

The language of the passages was plain enough, and in the "Statement of Claim" attached to his writ of summons, Irving charged Lipstadt with having "falsely and recklessly" written these defamatory words, and he charged that Penguin "falsely and recklessly" published them. Referring to the "natural and ordinary meaning of the words complained of," Irving made eleven complaints, one of which concerned his integrity as a historian:

> (iii) that the Plaintiff routinely, perversely and by the way of his profession but essentially in order to serve his own reprehensible purposes, ideological leanings and/or political agenda
> • distorts accurate historical evidence and information
> • misstates
> • misconstrues
> • misquotes

- falsifies statistics
- falsely attributes conclusions to reliable sources
- manipulates documents
- wrongfully quotes from books that directly contradict his arguments in such a manner as completely to distort their authors' objectives and while counting on the ignorance or indolence of the majority of readers not to realise this.[226]

Three of his complaints directly concerned Auschwitz:

(vi) that before Zundel's trial began in 1988 in Toronto the Plaintiff, compromising his integrity as an historian and in an attempt to pervert the course of justice, and one Faurisson wrongfully and/or fraudulently conspired together to invite an American prison warden and thereafter one Fred A. Leuchter an engineer who is depicted by the Defendants as a charlatan to testify as a tactic for proving that the gas chambers were a myth.

(vii) that the Plaintiff after attending Zundel's trial in 1988 in Toronto having previously hovered on the brink now denies the murder by the Nazis of the Jews;

(viii) that the Plaintiff described the memorial to the dead in Auschwitz as a "tourist attraction."[227]

In addition, Irving complained of the innuendo of having been identified as a "Holocaust denier."

10. The Plaintiff will show at the hearing of this action that the true or legal innuendo of the words "Holocaust denier" is that any person described as such wilfully perversely and with disregard to all the existing historical evidence denied and continues to deny all and any occurrence of one of the worst crimes known to history namely the mass murder by whatever means by Hitler's agents and their associates of the Jewish people and hence genocide and a crime against humanity.[228]

Irving claimed an entitlement to aggravated damages because Lipstadt would have pursued a "sustained malicious vigorous well-funded and reckless world-wide campaign of personal defamation" against Irving which had brought him, among other things, "hatred, ridicule, contempt, risk of personal injury, and/or assassination."[229]

It was difficult to argue that Irving had misunderstood either the ordinary meaning of Lipstadt's text or its innuendo. And so Penguin and Lipstadt had a simple choice: either to give in or to engage Irving in court. With some hesitation at first, the publishers and lawyers at Penguin convinced first themselves and then its new parent company Pearson, who was to have the ultimate financial liability, that in defending *Denying the Holocaust* it would continue a line that had begun years earlier when it had refused to withdraw from publication D. H. Lawrence's *Lady Chatterley's Lover* and, more recently, Salman Rushdie's *The Satanic Verses*. For Lipstadt, there was no need to convince herself. She was resolved to engage Irving from the outset. But it was also a difficult course of action, because it would be necessary to prove in court that Lipstadt had been *substantially* right in her claim that Irving had distorted historical evidence and manipulated documents to serve his own ideological purposes. While the defendants did not have to prove the truth of every detail Lipstadt had written, they had to justify the truth of the sting of the defamatory charges. This meant that, among other things, the defense would have to demonstrate that Irving had misrepresented the historical record concerning Auschwitz. In order to determine the instances that he had engaged in special pleading, suppression of evidence, or even the invention of evidence as it related to that camp, the legal team that was to be assembled would need an expert on the history of Auschwitz.

Two

Marshaling the Evidence for Auschwitz

My journey to Courtroom 73 of the Royal Courts of Justice in London began in 1985 in the dean's conference room at the architecture school of the University of Virginia. I had recently been appointed as visiting assistant professor of architectural history and attended a faculty meeting to discuss the 750 buildings which students of architectural history were to know for their comprehensive exam. My colleagues offered me an opportunity to review the existing list and suggest alterations. Having earned a doctorate with a dissertation on the cosmic speculations on the Temple of Solomon a year before, I proposed its inclusion in the University of Virginia canon. There were no objections. The Tabernacle of Moses and the Tower of Babel also proved acceptable. Then I nominated Crematorium 2 of Auschwitz. A stunned silence followed, broken by one professor's acid observation that obviously I was not serious. When I said I was, another academic suggested that perhaps I ought to consider an alternative career.

By the time I arrived in Virginia, I had become increasingly vexed by the way my colleagues circumvented the questions raised by the camps. It seemed that most historians were embarrassed by the camps, preferring to consider these places as aberrations that belonged to a footnote. And architectural historians had ignored the camps altogether. Auschwitz did not appear in any architectural history—not even in specialized studies of Nazi architecture. This troubled me because I had come to the conclusion that interpretations of history that ignore evil were doomed to remain shallow and ultimately meaningless. I did not underestimate the historiographical pull away from systematic investigations of the presence of evil in history: as I wrote my dissertation, I had become acutely aware of the extent to which historians possess an artistic bent for building. They assemble isolated pieces of historical evidence into a coherent story that fits the constructive ideology of causal thought. The practice of historiography makes it inevitable that historians are at ease when they describe the constructive efforts of past generations—be it in economics, politics, speculative thought, science, art, or architecture—and that they feel lost when confronted with evil, because in its negative and purely destructive character evil denies meaning and, as such, refuses to fit modes of historical narration that imply in form and causal structure the presence of meaning. Having studied narrations of the destruction of the Temple of Jerusalem, I realized that manifestations of evil in some remoter past can be molded into an aesthetic form. But when the memory of victims has not yet died, this is more difficult.

My proposal to include Crematorium 2 among the key buildings of architectural history was based on the assumption that its construction was an event of crucial significance in the history of architecture. The gas chambers changed the whole meaning of architecture. When I reconstruct the path that led to this thesis, I can point to two or three landmarks. One was an early speculation about the typological relationship between the Holy of Holies of Solomon's Temple, a forbidden place where a man could attain knowledge at the price of his life, and the gas chamber of Auschwitz, a place forever inaccessible to our knowledge and, perhaps more important, imagination. Even before I finished my dissertation, I felt that temple and crematorium were united in a diptych, and that having studied one panel, I should not avert my gaze from the other. And then there was, of course, the German philosopher Karl Jaspers. As a teenager, I had found in my grandfather's library his masterful *The Origin and Goal of History*, written immediately after the war. If it were not for that book, I probably would not have become a historian. Jaspers believed that the practice of history had become particularly urgent because humanity had reached a hinge point of destiny and faced the real possibility of slipping into "a sombre malignancy destitute of humanity."

> What man may come to has today, almost in a flash, become manifest through a monstrous reality that stands before our eyes like a symbol of everything unspeakably horrible: The national socialist concentration camps with their tortures, at the end of which stood the gas-chambers and incinerators for millions of people—realities that correspond to reports of similar processes in other totalitarian régimes, although none but the national socialists have perpetrated outright mass murder by the gas chamber. A chasm has opened up. We have seen what man can do—not according to a plan drawn up *in toto* at the outset, but in a circle along which he moves at ever increasing speed once he has set foot upon it. It is a circle into which the participants are dragged without the majority of them knowing or desiring what they will suffer or do as they advance unceasingly around it.[1]

In the camps, "men ceased to be human." Therefore, the world of the camps "provides an intimation of future possibilities, before which everything threatens to vanish. After dealing with reports of the concentration camps, one hardly dare continue to speak."[2]

I accepted Jaspers's judgment that the camps were a hinge in history. Auschwitz was the place where 5,000 years of architecture and thinking about architecture, which had begun with the erection of a small acropolis in northern Iraq, not far from today's Mosul, terminated in Crematorium 2. The depression that remained after the dismantling and dynamiting of Morgue 1, the basement room that had served as the core of that factory of death for some eighteen months, was the black hole that refuted the premise that architecture adds to our world. Those 2,500 square feet, in which the Germans produced perhaps as many as 500,000 corpses, was to the modern age what the Parthenon had been to the Greek polis, what the Chartres Cathedral had been to Christendom. As the station of total collapse, it could be the site from which architecture could rise again, a place of renewal ex nihilo. Therefore my attempt to include Crematorium 2 in the University of Virginia canon was not a merely theoretical exercise to mark a rite of passage for architectural historians; it was the foundation of a curriculum for aspiring architects.

My thesis was based on the premise that Crematorium 2 was a work of architecture and that it properly belonged to the history of architecture. My colleagues at the University of Virginia challenged this proposition with the argument that the aesthetics of the building were not worthwhile and that the architects involved were not of sufficient reputation to warrant the inclusion of Crematorium 2 in a history of architecture. Their definition of what makes a building a work of architecture, and therefore worthy of attention, was misguided. My own point of departure was that the question of meaning ought to define what deserves our attention. A building that makes us shudder is likely to be more meaningful than a work that gives us joy.

Having faced initial rejection, I embarked on a more systematic undertaking to find a place for Crematorium 2 in architectural history. Taking the question of meaning as my point of departure, I initially turned for inspiration to Martin Heidegger's fundamental ontology. But I did not find what I was seeking: it seemed that the magus of Todtnauberg postulated that the basic understanding of meaning had remained constant over time. I had come to the conclusion, however, that meaning was specific to time and culture—that meaning was embodied in the ideals of institutions. While what gave these institutions legitimacy was undoubtedly the assumption of a stable and eternal moral order, their embodiment of that presupposed order was historical. Works of architecture were, in that context, embodiments of the ideals on which the life of institutions depended. These ideals all centered on the problem of death and the hope for what Robert Jay Lifton labeled symbolic immortality. I began to discern a close and essential link between culture, death imagery, ideologies of immortality, and history. This link, which determined the history of cities and their institutions and the embodiment of those institutions in monumental architecture, was the struggle to cope with the anxiety generated by the knowledge of death in a constructive fashion.

From this perspective, Auschwitz posed a radical challenge not only to culture but also to our institutions, and therefore to architecture. The camp suggested the emptiness of all immortality ideologies. This raised more than the question of whether culture was still possible; it also raised the question of whether architecture, understood as the record of efforts to embody a collective sense of immortality in the human-made environment, was still conceivable. And I began to speculate about whether the history of architecture had come to an end in Auschwitz—if indeed Crematorium 2 had been "the last building." I began to see Auschwitz as the final nadir of an urban civilization which, having lost the stability of the traditional institutions, feared death so completely that it had no recourse but to build cities of corpses in order to refute death. Crematorium 2 was the temple of a people—the Nazis—who had lost all knowledge of placating their anxiety of death except through an unspeakable convulsion of continuous murder.

My thoughts on this matter acquired shape in a book entitled *Architectural Principles in the Age of Historicism* (1991). The volume was conceived as a dialogue, with the odd-numbered chapters by me and the even-numbered chapters by Carroll William Westfall, the only colleague present at that meeting in the dean's conference room who had been willing to continue the conversation. Karl Jaspers's *The Origin and Goal of History* provided the firm foundation for my own contribution to the project. To write my contribution, I read widely in the fields of architectural history, Holocaust history, historiography, philosophy, and theology, but I did not do original archival research on the history of Auschwitz. My interest in Crematorium 2 was a general theoretical one. As I read, I encountered the most important negationist literature available at the time: works by Paul Rassinier, Arthur Butz, Robert Faurisson, and Fred Leuchter.

I ventured into the world of negationism for three reasons. First of all, I did not think that I should reject a priori any potential source of information. If negationists could help me understand the history of Crematorium 2, I would be happy to learn from them. More important, I believed in Karl Popper's criterion of falsifiability as an essential tool in the testing of hypotheses. When I became interested in Auschwitz, I was convinced that at least Birkenau had been conceived and designed as a factory of death, and that, in accordance with its designer's intentions, it had operated as an extermination camp. The way to prove this thesis was to look at the evidence and see if the evidence could be used to argue that Birkenau had *not* been conceived and designed as a factory of death and that it had *not* operated as an extermination camp. As I will discuss in greater detail below, my attempt to apply the falsifiability criterion led to the results set out in a book I wrote with Debórah Dwork, which was published in 1996. In it we came to the conclusion, after having reconstructed in detail Himmler's attempt to create a model city in Auschwitz, that while Birkenau had not been conceived and designed as a factory of death, it did change its purpose in mid-1942 to evolve into an extermination camp.

There was, however, a third reason why I had become interested in the negationists. One of the main aims of *Architectural Principles* was to deal with relativism, and in my readings in that field I had come across Lyotard's *The Differend*. I came to see from this book that the specific issue of negationism was intimately connected to the larger issue of a relativism in which questions of historical truth and falsehood are wholly defined within the context of language-games and the presumed incommensurability of discourses. However, in the writing of *Architectural Principles*, the issues raised by Lyotard drifted into the background, and with that the arguments of the negationists. In the end only a trace remained, a residue that I believed at the time to be my farewell to the negationist landscape in which 6 million murdered Jews are merely a chimera. In an endnote, I commented that the hours spent reading those negationist writings "were among the worst I have had in my professional work." Characterizing this literature as an insult to the intellect, I observed that "their 'evidence' is doctored, and in their attempts to reveal a great 'conspiracy' to blot the reputation of Germany, these 'scholars' . . . ignore half of the evidence, and that part of the evidence they attempt to discredit they butcher and mutilate beyond recognition."[3] My verdict was an angry, visceral outburst that betrayed more than intellectual irritation. The negationist tracts had gotten under my skin in a way the historical material did not: I felt that I had come face to face with a dangerous personal abyss. An article in the *Partisan Review,* published a decade earlier, revealed that my crisis was not unique. Reporting on Robert Faurisson's trial in Paris, Erika Apfelbaum got to the heart of why the negationist assault on history turns into an assault on the self:

> Current Jewish history is deeply rooted in Auschwitz as the general symbol of the destruction of the Jewish people during the Holocaust. For someone whose past is rooted in Auschwitz, the experience of reading through the revisionists' tortured logic and documentation is similar to the psychologically disorienting experience of sensory deprivation experiments or solitary confinement in prison, where one loses touch with reality. The insidious effect of reading this literature is ultimately to lose one's identity as a survivor and, more generally, as a Jew. Therefore, the revisionist allegations serve to dispossess the Jews from their history, and in doing so, in seeking to destroy a people's history, a symbolic genocide replaces a physical one.[4]

And so I turned away from the negationist literature. I thought that, as a historian, the negation of history was not my business and that I could settle my quarrel with relativists without having to engage Faurisson and company. I sincerely believed that the curse of negationism could be exorcised through a couple of lines safely hidden in one endnote.

Having considered some of the historiographical questions that arose from the absence of Crematorium 2 in our narratives of architectural history, I decided to research and write the kind of history of Auschwitz that I would have liked to have read. At that time, I thought that this would be the kind of philosophical history suggested in *Architectural Principles*—a history that culminated in the ruined camp grounds I knew so well—a symbolic landscape of perdition marked by hundreds of broken chimneys. But there were anomalies I could not explain. One day, when I walked through the town of Oswiecim, I noted the substantial German wartime civic construction. Why would the Germans have invested heavily in the development of a place meant to be in the shadow of crematoria? Clearly, the town was not the back of beyond, the "Asshole of the World," as the Germans had called it. The solidity of the German architecture so close to the camp forced the question: *Where* was Auschwitz, the Auschwitz of the Holocaust?

I realized that having grown up in a culture that had defined itself as one "after Auschwitz," I had ignored descriptions of historical contingency in my analysis of Auschwitz in *Architectural Principles*, preferring to make assertions about some unchanging nature of the site. In an early essay entitled "A Site in Search of a Mission," I summarized the problem as one of mythification.

> Banished from the world of description, analysis, and conclusion, Auschwitz has become a myth in which the assumed universality of its impact obscures the contingencies of its beginning. I use the word myth in the sense that Barthes gave to it in his essay "Myth Today." Mythification, he argued, occurs when language empties a narrative of its historical contingency to fill it with an unchanging nature. "In passing from history to nature, myth acts economically: it abolishes the complexity of human acts, it gives

them simplicity of essences." The result is an account of "blissful clarity" in which there are no contradictions because statements of fact are interpreted as explanations; "things appear to mean something by themselves." Few events can rival the mythic power of "Auschwitz."[5]

I realized that the mythification of Auschwitz, in which I had participated unwittingly, had blinded me to a more complex reality. I decided that I had to stop philosophizing about Auschwitz and begin with an investigation of the archives in Poland. For this project my friend Debórah Dwork joined me as a writing partner. She had recently completed her book on Jewish children in the Holocaust, *Children with a Star,* and had begun to consider the history of Auschwitz from the perspective of the victims.

It proved a happy collaboration on an unhappy subject. We recovered Auschwitz as a *place*—a prewar ordinary town with a 700-year history followed by a 5-year wartime history which sundered it from its past and put it into the realm of myth and metaphor. We stripped away the myth of a necropolis of night and fog closed in upon itself, its victims, and its executioners and laid bare the place as it operated within the ordinary financial, economic, and other constraints imposed by its location in a particular municipality (Auschwitz), a particular province (Upper Silesia), and a particular region (the so-called German East). We discovered that between October 1939 and January 1945, Auschwitz was officially incorporated into the German Reich and that it belonged to a region that had been given the highest priority for political, social, economic, and—yes—architectural redevelopment. Auschwitz was the focus of much discussion immediately after the 1939 annexation, and none of it concerned the Holocaust. Instead it was seen as a place that had once been German and that was to be redeemed from centuries of non-German rule. Auschwitz was part of what the Nazis celebrated as "the German East," a land that signified a return to the pristine, lost past of medieval German achievement and betokened opportunity and promise to new generations. It was, in short, a paradise to be regained. Reichsführer-SS Heinrich Himmler acquired responsibility for the redevelopment of the area as Reich commissioner for the consolidation of the German nation, and he created an organization to support and advise him. In most areas under his control, he practiced a policy of ethnic cleansing by deporting Poles and Jews and bringing in Germans. But that formula did not work in Auschwitz. Some of the local Polish population could not be deported because they were employed in industry and there were no skilled ethnic German workers to replace them. Himmler's response to this purely local condition was to build a concentration camp in the suburbs of the town to terrorize the local population. It would keep them in check. In the rural areas immediately south of Auschwitz, ethnic cleansing did take place, and Himmler organized the immigration of ethnic Germans into the area. In order to provide practical support to help the new arrivals establish economically viable farms, Himmler made the camp the center of a huge agricultural experiment estate, a scientific farm. The camp claimed increasingly larger territories for this new function, and Himmler began to see that its future might be different from what he had originally envisioned: as a concentration camp it was assumed to be a temporary facility; as an agricultural estate it claimed permanence.

We began to understand that once the small compound surrounded by a double barbed-wire fence had grown into a 15-square-mile SS "zone of interests," a huge influx of money and building materials was needed to develop this zone. This forced us to look more closely at the significance of the camp as a pawn in Himmler's attempt to generate income by attracting the huge chemical giant IG Farben to Auschwitz. The terms of the bargain were that the camp was to supply labor to construct Farben's synthetic rubber or Buna plant, and a new camp, Birkenau, to be populated by Soviet prisoners of war, was to provide labor to improve the town of Auschwitz into a place worthy of an IG Farben enterprise. In return, IG Farben was to finance and supply Himmler's Germanization project in the area with building materials. As we discovered, Farben's money stimulated the growth of the camp and its integration into Europe's industrial and transport infrastructure.

The architects expected many deaths from endemic and epidemic disease in a camp which was meant to house 125,000 Soviet prisoners of war in Birkenau and 30,000 Polish prisoners in the main camp in Auschwitz. The old crematorium was obviously too small. A very large state-of-the-art crematorium to cope with the anticipated "normal" mortality in a slave labor camp with 130,000 inmates was designed in the fall of 1941. As conceived in the autumn of 1941, this was to be a crematorium to accommodate the mortality of the concentration camp at Auschwitz and the prisoner-of-war camp in Birkenau. It was not meant to provide execution facilities: nothing in the original conceptual sketches of the crematorium or in the blueprints which date from January 1942 suggest homicidal gas chambers or their use in the Final Solution.

When large-scale mass murder of Jews began in the summer and fall of 1941 in the wake of Operation Barbarossa, the SS in Auschwitz was still fully committed to Himmler's project to develop the town and the region. It was when Göring directed Soviet POWs from Auschwitz to German armament factories in January 1942 that Himmler began to consider the systematic use of the Final Solution of the Jewish Problem within the context of what he called "The Auschwitz Project." Yet this did not mean that Himmler wanted to use the camp as a site of continuous mass murder of Jews. In early 1942, he was still very much committed to making Auschwitz the centerpiece of his racial utopia. But he had modified his plan: now the utopia was not to be created on the backs of Soviet prisoners of war; Jewish slave laborers were to take their place. The Wannsee Conference gave Himmler (through Heydrich) the power he needed to negotiate with German and foreign civilian authorities for the transfer of Jews to his SS empire. The first transports of Jews fit for labor started to leave Slovakia for Auschwitz-Birkenau soon thereafter.

When the Slovak government suggested that Himmler also take Jews unfit for labor in exchange for a cash payment, Himmler dispatched SS Construction Chief Hans Kammler to Auschwitz. Kammler toured the site and ordered that a peasant cottage there be converted into a gas chamber. Two months later, on July 4, 1942, the first Jews from Slovakia were sorted out. Those who could work were admitted to the camp. Those who could not were killed in the peasant cottage, now known as Bunker I. Killing at Auschwitz of selected categories of Jews had now changed from an "incidental" practice, as had happened with some transports of Jews from Upper Silesia in late 1941, into what one could call "continuing" practice, but it had not yet become policy. Bunker I was still a particular solution to a situation created by the combination of Slovak unwillingness to provide for old and very young Jews and German greed. The main purpose of Auschwitz, *at this time,* remained construction (of a plant, a city, and a region), not destruction (of Jews).

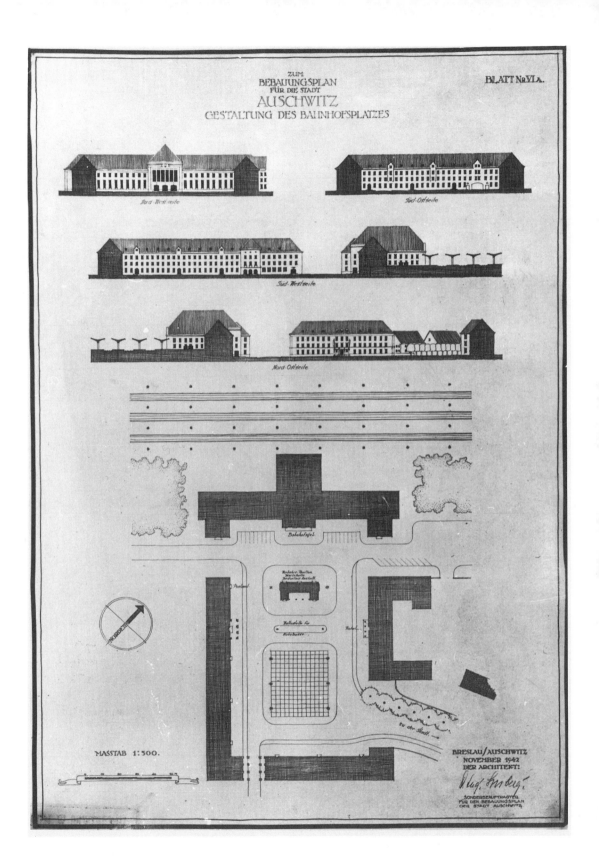

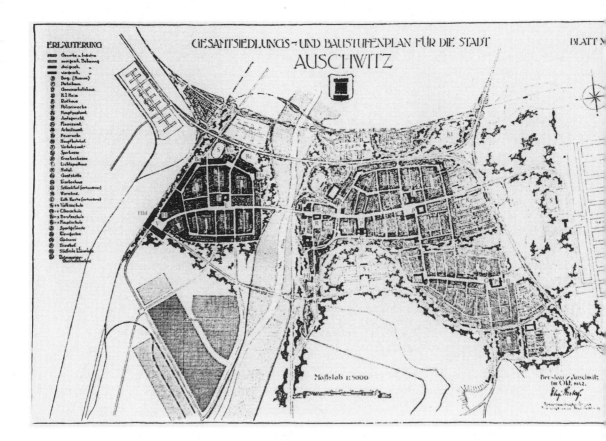

Design for the new town of Auschwitz, 1942. Architect Hans Stosberg. The railway corridor with the station is on the west side of the town (left), the IG Farben works on the east side of the town (right). The two gray areas south of the railway station, labeled as Wehrmachst-anlagen *(army installations), are in fact the concentration camp and the SS barracks. This area did not belong to the municipality of Auschwitz, and therefore Stosberg did not specify an urban design. The camp at Birkenau, which was to provide the labor for the construction of the new town, was located west of the railway corridor, or at the utmost left side of this urban plan. Courtesy Niels Gutschow.*

Design for the expansion of the Stammlager at Auschwitz and an adjacent SS village. Architect Lothar Hartjenstein, 1942. This design was made in the SS headquarters in Berlin for the area under SS control. Courtesy Archive Auschwitz-Birkenau State Museum, Oswiecim.

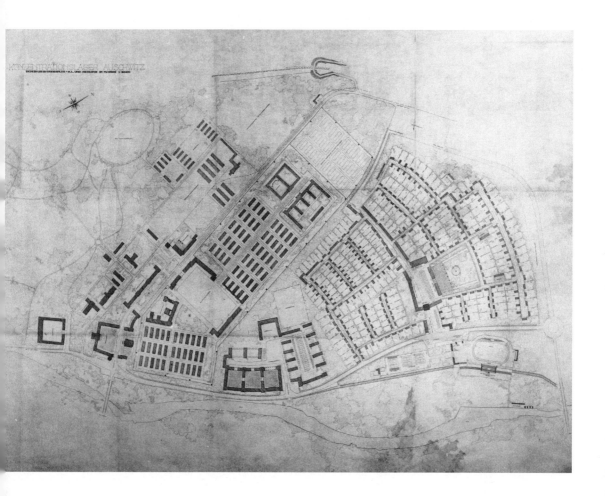

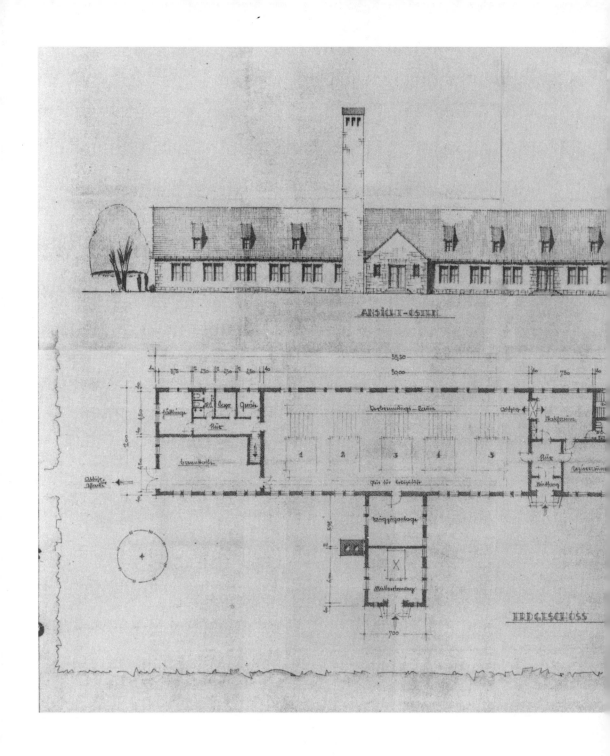

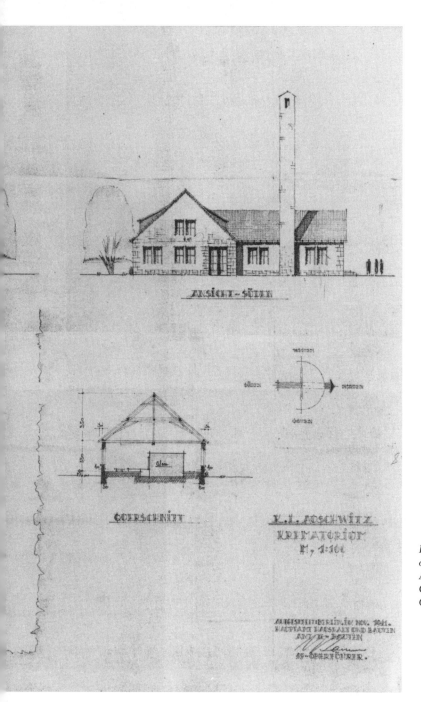

ANSICHT-SÜDEN

QUERSCHNITT

K.L. AUSCHWITZ
KREMATORIUM
M, 1:100

*Front elevation and main floor
of a new crematorium at
Auschwitz, fall 1941. Architect
Georg Werkmann. Courtesy
Osobyi Archive, Moscow.*

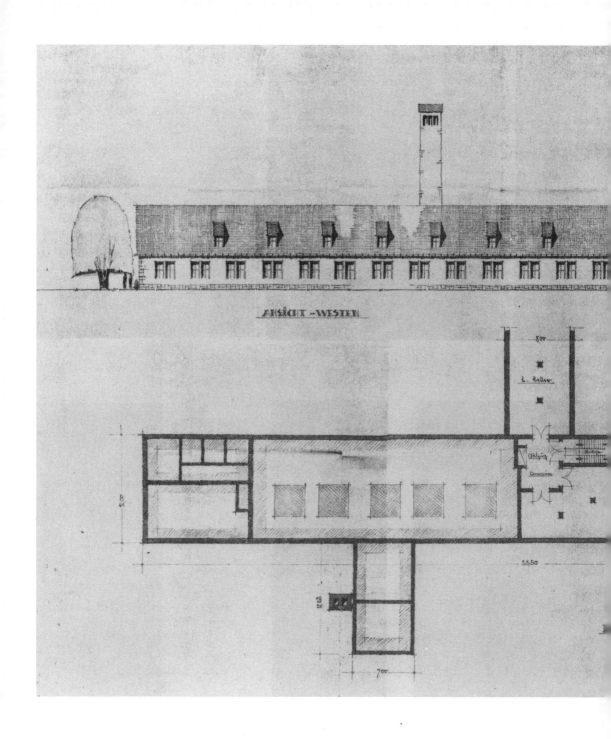

ANSICHT –WESTEN

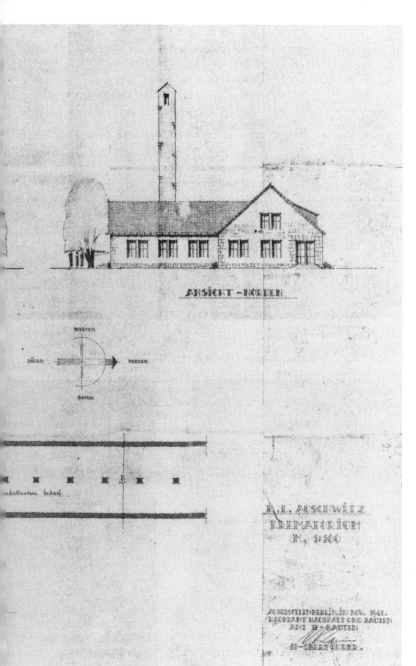

Back elevation and basement of a new crematorium at Auschwitz, fall 1941. Architect Georg Werkmann. Courtesy Osobyi Archive, Moscow.

Around mid-July 1942, Himmler acquired the responsibility for German settlement in Russia—an authority that he had coveted for more than a year. His view of Auschwitz and his plans for Auschwitz changed rapidly and dramatically. The "Auschwitz Project" was no longer of interest to him. The camp could be used to serve the systematic killing of Jews. Practice became policy. The camp architects got the order to design crematoria equipped from the outset with homicidal gas chambers on August 20, 1942. As Birkenau had become a site for mass murder, all pretence of civility and civilian rules were shed: the Heimat style of Auschwitz I, which characterized Crematoria 2 and 3, was replaced by the functional vernacular of Birkenau. Crematoria 4 and 5 were to look like simple sheds, and they were equipped from the outset with gas chambers. And Crematoria 2 and 3, which were under construction, were retroactively fitted with homicidal gas chambers. The architects of Auschwitz had no difficulty with adaptive reuse. SS architect Walther Dejaco transformed the basement design, changing one of the two underground morgues into an undressing room and the other into a gas chamber.

In the late winter and early spring of 1943, when the killing was at its height, the first of the new crematoria in Birkenau came into operation. By the time all four crematoria had been handed over to the SS, the Holocaust itself had peaked. The genocide had begun in 1941, and the Germans killed some 1.1 million Jews that year. In 1942, they murdered another 2.7 million Jews, of whom approximately 200,000 died in Auschwitz. The year the crematoria of Auschwitz came into operation, the number of victims dropped to 500,000, half of whom were killed in Auschwitz. All the Jews whom the Germans had been able to catch easily had been trapped. By the end of 1943, the Germans closed down the death camps built specifically to exterminate Jews: Kulmhof (150,000 Jews), Sobibor (200,000 Jews), Belzec (550,000 Jews), and Treblinka (750,000 Jews). In these camps there was no selection process; nearly everyone who was shipped in was killed within hours of arrival. In terms of mortality, at the end of 1943 Auschwitz ranked behind Treblinka and Belzec. But it was the only camp that remained to mop up the remnants of the Jewish communities of Poland, Italy, France, the Netherlands, and the rest of occupied Europe. In 1944, another 600,000 Jews would be killed in Auschwitz. With more than 1.1. million victims, it was the most lethal death camp of all.

And because it was the last to be in operation, it was also the camp remembered best. "Auschwitz" became a synonym for "Holocaust."

Dwork and I wrote *Auschwitz: 1270 to the Present* in response to the challenge of present-day mythification. We wrote in order to ensure that, by remembering the Holocaust, we would deny the Nazis another victory. Every historian struggles to rescue some part of the past from oblivion. But for the historian of the Holocaust, this task is even more important; those who conceived and executed it wanted it to be, in the words of Reichsführer-SS Heinrich Himmler, "an unwritten and never-to-be-written page of glory."[6] As can be understood from the admonishment which, according to Primo Levi, a guard gave to concentration camp inmates, the rank and file of the SS shared their leader's aim.

> However this war may end, we have won the war against you; none of you will be left to bear witness, but even if someone were to survive, the world will not believe him. There will be perhaps suspicions, discussions, research by historians, but there will be no certainties, because we will destroy the evidence together with

Selection of a transport of Hungarian Jews, spring 1944. The selection is about to begin. Women and children are lined up to the left, men to the right. Courtesy Yad Vashem.

you. And even if some proof should remain and some of you survive, people will say the events you describe are too monstrous to be believed: they will say that they are exaggerations of Allied propaganda and will believe us, who will deny everything, and not you. We will be the ones to dictate the history of the Lagers [camps].[7]

Not only did the murderers seek to deny the genocide, but the bystanders proved willing to see without seeing and hear without hearing. Alexander Donat, who ascribed his survival to his sense of having been entrusted with the sacred mission of salvaging the record of the Warsaw ghetto uprising, wrote in his book *The Holocaust Kingdom* how a friend anticipated the difficulties the survivors would have in preserving their story. Even if some were to survive to "write the history of this period of blood and tears—and I firmly believe we will—who will believe us? Nobody will *want* to believe us, because our disaster is the disaster of the entire civilized world. . . . We'll have the thankless job of proving to a reluctant world that we are Abel, the murdered brother."[8] As we wrote our history of Auschwitz, we consciously adopted Donat's mission to confront a reluctant world with an unmasterable past. What had begun as a crusade to do justice to Auschwitz within architectural history had slowly turned into a commitment to those who were killed in Auschwitz. Dwork and I felt that we had become witnesses for those who had been silenced. Recently I was happy to find a clear articulation of this sense of duty in a book by Edith Wyschogrod, in which she argued that the primary responsibility of the historian is not to the living—be they right or wrong, good or evil—but to the dead. "Responsibility thus interpreted is Janus-faced: its moral authority is expressed in its disinterestedness, but its psychological force is experienced as a sense of inescapable urgency." Thus, the historian is torn between "an impassioned necrophilia which would bring to life the dead others" and the need to produce "a dispassionate relation to events."[9]

In our book, Dwork and I did not directly engage current negationism, and in this our perspective clearly differed from that of Jean-Claude Pressac's magnum opus, *Auschwitz: Technique and Operation of the Gas Chambers* (1989), which was explicitly conceived, written, and published to respond to Faurisson's negationist challenge to provide him with "a proof, one single precise proof of the actual existence of one 'gas chamber,' one single 'gas chamber.'"[10] Pressac assembled massive documentation of the gas chambers, which culminated in one chapter entitled "'One Proof . . . One Single Proof': Thirty-Nine Criminal Traces."[11] We had no need or desire to repeat Pressac's work.

But while we were not interested in Faurisson and his followers, some people alarmed by negationism were interested in our work. Even before our book was published, Michael Shermer and Alex Grobman sought contact. As founder and editor of the quarterly *Skeptic,* Shermer was interested in negationism as a particularly potent example of a large group of fringe sociocognitive phenomena that also include belief in cryonic suspension, creationism, repressed memory syndrome, and millenarianism. Grobman directed the Martyrs Memorial and Holocaust Museum in Los Angeles and was interested in negationism from an anti-defamation perspective. They were interested in the way Dwork and I had studied many different kinds of evidence—blueprints, photographs, ruins, requisition forms, transportation vouchers, planning permissions, bills of sale, bills of receipt, eyewitness accounts, confessions, diaries, and letters—to create a narrative history that, in Shermer and Grobman's words, "tells a story and tests a hypothesis."

> The hypothesis [Dwork and van Pelt] test is that Auschwitz was originally planned to be an extermination camp. They reject this hypothesis and in its stead present a contingently functional hypothesis—that Auschwitz *evolved* into an extermination camp from its original plans.[12]

We had shown the history of Auschwitz to be quirky and unpredictable, and we had shown that an understanding of that history was only possible on the basis of a convergence of many different strands of often contradictory evidence that, in the end, all pointed to a history that could be understood as a story.

Shermer himself had reflected on the convergence of evidence and the problem it posed to negationists. By way of introduction, he sent me an issue of *Skeptic* that included a long article on negationism. Shermer's almost satirical reflection on the epistemological difficulties negationists faced proved particularly good reading.[13] But Shermer's and Grobman's interest made me feel uneasy. I realized that, having become experts on the history of Auschwitz, negationism was closing in on Dwork and myself. And I did not like it.

My worst fears were realized when one day Shermer, Grobman, and a friend of theirs, Israel Shaked, arrived at my office at the University of

Waterloo to see my research collection on Auschwitz. When they had finished examining my files, Shermer facetiously suggested that we visit Ernst Zündel, who happened to live in nearby Toronto. A couple of hours later Shermer, Grobman, Shaked, and I found ourselves in Zündel's basement headquarters. We were there not to debate or argue, just to listen. And we were not disappointed. Zündel talked and talked. A large roguish fellow who could have been quite a pleasant companion during a night on the town—assuming that one did not understand a word he said—Zündel cheerfully and candidly counseled us to use our influence to turn the Jews from the disastrous path they had chosen: if they continued to peddle the lie of the Holocaust and hoodwink the gentiles into paying absurd amounts of money, they would trigger a terrible response which would unleash a real Holocaust, one for which they themselves would be to blame. After enduring the two-hour monologue, I left Zündel's headquarters shaken, but not without having received a warm recommendation for a Kosher restaurant acceptable to Grobman and Shaked. On the way out I noticed some big posters announcing a lecture by David Irving. In the picture Irving looked like a gentleman, and I wondered how he had gotten involved with Zündel, who seemed to relish his role as a lout and a buffoon. Little did I surmise that, four years later, I would enjoy the mixed blessing of reconstructing the history of their impetuous partnership.

A year later I met Shermer and Grobman again in Los Angeles. On the day of my visit they had made an appointment to meet Nevin Bryant, supervisor of Cartographic Applications and Image Processing Applications at NASA's Jet Propulsion Laboratory in Pasadena, and they suggested I join them. On the freeway to Pasadena, I got a quick briefing: a few years earlier Canadian negationist John Ball had published under his own imprint a glossy book, *Air Photo Evidence: Auschwitz, Treblinka, Majdanek, Sobibor, Bergen Belsen, Belzec, Babi Yar, Katyn Forest.* The cover included an aerial photo of Birkenau, one statement, and two questions: "World War II photos of alleged *mass murder* camps!" "Does evidence *confirm* or dismiss eye witness stories?" "Were *gas chamber* marks put on by *C.I.A. workers?*" Ball's book was an answer to a CIA report, published in 1979, that was written by Dino A. Brugioni and Robert G. Poirier. *The Holocaust Revisited: A Retrospective Analysis of the Auschwitz-Birkenau Extermination Complex* had claimed that aerial photos of Birkenau taken by American bombers attacking the IG Farben Buna works just east of Auschwitz proved that the camp had been used for mass exterminations. Quite specifically, Brugioni and Poirier had identified in blowup photos of Crematorium 2 small marks on the roofs of the underground gas chambers. "On the roof of the sub-surface gas chambers, we can see the vents used to insert the Zyklon-B gas crystals."[14] Ball's book challenged the CIA report and not only claimed that the aerial photos made clear that there had been no extermination but that the marks on the roof of the gas chambers had been drawn on the negative by hand, presumably by CIA officials. Using the most up-to-date technology to enhance the pictures digitally, Bryant was to settle the question once and for all.

We visited him at his office, and he offered his first guess about why certain dots seemed more irregular than one would have expected, given the presumed architectural order of the Zyklon B insertion points. It was probably due to a moire effect that occurred on a molecular level within the film. I felt uncomfortable with the way the conversation was going. Having reviewed the main evidence, Ball had made assumptions to justify his conclusions. It was clear that most of his assertions about Birkenau were unfounded, and it seemed therefore that Shermer was embarking on what easily could become a wild goose chase to counter a totally unfounded suggestion. Weren't we giving too much attention to Ball's ideas? Did the negationists deserve our energy?

Our book appeared in the spring of 1996 as *Auschwitz: 1270 to the Present.* Publication had two unexpected consequences. In late 1997, documentary filmmaker Errol Morris called me. I knew Morris as the director of *Gates of Heaven* (1978), *The Thin Blue Line* (1988), and (my personal favorite) *Fast, Cheap & Out of Control* (1997), an amazing cinematographic fugue in which the obsessions of a lion tamer, a builder of robots, a topiary gardener, and an expert on naked mole rats provided the raw material for a contrapuntal, playful, and at times puzzling reflection on the human condition. Morris was in deep trouble. He had just finished a rough cut of a movie about negationist Fred Leuchter, whom he sarcastically described to me in our first conversation as "the Maytag Man from Hell." He described the first part of the movie, which was later to be given the more neutral title *Mr. Death: The Rise and Fall of Fred A. Leuchter, Jr.,* as a kind of follow-up to *Fast, Cheap & Out of Control.* Only this time electric chairs, gallows, lethal injection machines, and gas chambers had taken the place of lions, robots, bushes, and rats as the objects of loving engagement. So far so good. The problem came in the second part of the movie, which included video footage of Leuchter's trip to Auschwitz. Following his own rigid rule only to show his subjects and never to include voiceovers, narration, or any form of outside expertise, Morris had tried to tell Leuchter's trip entirely through his eyes, using only his celebrated editing skills to introduce a measure of ironical distance that would allow the audience to perceive Leuchter's self-delusion. In this case, Morris's magic did not work. At a trial screening at Harvard, one half of the audience thought that Morris agreed with Leuchter's conclusions about Auschwitz and the other half came to agree with Leuchter's conclusions about Auschwitz. Not surprisingly, both views horrified Morris. He turned for advice to Deborah Lipstadt, who had described Leuchter's engagement with Auschwitz in some detail in her *Denying the Holocaust.* Lipstadt saw the rough cut, agreed that Morris was in trouble, and told him of a new book on Auschwitz that she had identified a year earlier as "a work of tremendous importance."[15] Morris contacted Debórah and me, and after some long discussions with my writing partner, I came to be involved with *Mr. Death,* first as a consultant and then as "talent."

As I prepared for my first meeting with Morris, I took the by now yellowing photocopy of the Leuchter Report that I had made ten years earlier when researching *Architectural Principles.* I noticed that after a decade-long engagement with Auschwitz, my first reaction was not disgust but amusement. The whole account seemed a parody of a forensic report. Two sentences stood out. "None of these [gas] chambers were constructed in accordance with the known and proven designs of facilities operational in the United States at that time. It seems unusual that the presumed designers of these alleged gas chambers never consulted or considered the United States technology, the only country then executing prisoners with gas."[16] My opinion did not improve when, at my first meeting with Morris, I saw parts of the videotape recording Leuchter's trip to Auschwitz. Leuchter hacked away at the remaining structures of what he always called the "alleged" gas chambers; his probe was a parody of a forensic investigation.

My involvement with *Mr. Death* brought Leuchter into my life just at the time that Lipstadt's lawyers at the British legal firm of Mishcon de Reya realized that they needed a historian of Auschwitz on the team. Dwork or

Poster Mr. Death. *Courtesy Fourth Floor Productions.*

van Pelt were obvious names to consider. In January 1998, I was contacted to see if either of us was interested and, if so, available to join the team of experts to be assembled for the defense. Debórah and I discussed the matter, and as I had become by then somewhat conversant with Leuchter, we decided it was to be me. I had read Lipstadt's book, browsed a cheap paperback edition of Irving's *Hitler's War*, had actually perused a rather unknown work he had written in favor of Germany's recovery of Silesia, Pomerania, and East Prussia, and knew (thanks to Robert Harris's *Selling Hitler*) about Irving's Janus-faced role in the unmasking of the Hitler diaries. I knew too that Irving had published the British edition of *The*

Leuchter Report and, thanks to Morris, I had actually studied the report in some detail. But I knew nothing about the case.

On my way to Auschwitz, where I was to film with Morris, I passed through London to have a general meeting with Lipstadt's solicitor, Anthony Julius, who had acquired fame as Princess Diana's divorce lawyer; lawyer Harriet Benson, who seemed to be in charge of the day-to-day management of the case; and well-known historian Richard Evans, who had written extensively on modern German history and who was to assemble and coordinate a team of experts. In conversation with Evans, Benson, and Julius, I made it clear that I was an expert on Auschwitz and, despite my recent reacquaintance with Leuchter, not an expert on negationism. I suggested that if they were looking for an expert on negationism, they ought to consider Michael Shermer. They replied that they needed someone who had worked in the Auschwitz archives and who had authority as an Auschwitz scholar. We turned to various points of contention. Benson gave me copies of Irving's 2-page "Writ of Summons," his 8-page "Statement of Claim" that gave the exact passages from Lipstadt's book which Irving considered libelous, the 60-page "Defence of Second Defendant" drafted by a lawyer who had since left the case, and Irving's 44-page "Reply to Defence of Second Defendant." I only had time to glance at the bundle. They asked me to consider only one statement from the "Defence of Second Defendant"

> 6. Further, or in the alternative, the said words are true in substance and in fact. The meanings the Second Defendant will justify are:
> (i) that the Plaintiff has on numerous occasions (in the manner hereinafter particularised) denied the Holocaust, the deliberate planned extermination of Europe's Jewish population by the Nazis, and denied that gas chambers were used by the Nazis as a means of carrying out that extermination;
> (ii) that the Plaintiff holds extremist views, and has allied himself with others who do so, including individuals such as Dr Robert Faurisson, and Ernst Zündel.[17]

It seemed a transparent case, and I did not quite see why they needed an Auschwitz scholar for that: a sampling from Irving's speeches which any intern could compile should do. Julius told me that it might still be necessary to demonstrate that what Irving had said was untrue and that this meant that the defense would have to submit some kind of report on the gas chambers and exterminations at Auschwitz.[18] This seemed straightforward enough, and I agreed to join the team.

Later that day I began reading the file, giving special attention to the issues concerning Auschwitz. The "Defence of Second Defendant" quoted various statements Irving had made about Auschwitz. These included assertions that there were no gas chambers at Auschwitz, that Auschwitz was not an extermination camp, that the gas chambers were a figment of British wartime propaganda, that the "gas chamber legend" was based on "baloney," and that the gas chambers presently visible in Auschwitz were erected in Poland for the tourists. The same document also contained some of the replies to Irving's allegations.

> After an experiment on Soviet prisoners of war in the main camp of Auschwitz on 3 September 1941 in which 600 of them were murdered using Zyklon B gas, extermination camps in Poland such as Chelmno, Belzec, Sobibor, Treblinka, Auschwitz-Birkenau and

Majdanek were used and/or established with (save for the latter two, which were also labour camps) the sole purpose of murdering every person brought to them, irrespective of age or sex.[19]

This rebuttal was imprecise, if not wrong. It suggested a causal connection between the experiment in Auschwitz and the establishment of the death camps at Belzec, Sobibor, and Treblinka. In fact, the precedent for the latter camps was to be found in Operation T4, the program to kill the mentally handicapped in carbon-monoxide gas chambers built in various asylums in Germany.

Turning to Irving's "Reply to Defence of Second Defendant," I found that while he had not picked up on the historical inaccuracy, he had nevertheless produced a clever response:

> The Plaintiff is not aware of any authentic wartime archival evidence for the allegations raised in this paragraph by the Defendants. In the case of Auschwitz-Birkenau the Plaintiff is troubled by the refusal of the authorities to call for site examinations, forensic tests and other investigations, the more so since documents in the National Archives indicate that equal tonnages of Zyklon-B pesticide granules were delivered to Auschwitz and Oranienburg camps, at which latter camp nobody has ever suggested that gas chambers existed, and to camps in Norway, and since documents have now been found in the Auschwitz files held in the former German archives indicating that Auschwitz prisoners were actually released to the outside world again upon completion of their sentence, which seems incompatible with the character of a top-secret mass extermination centre.[20]

If wartime archival evidence meant a wartime German document, Irving was right: knowledge of the experimental gassing of the Soviet prisoners of war was based on eyewitness testimony. In this particular case, I knew that this testimony had already become available in 1942: the London-based *Polish Fortnightly Review* carried a report of this gassing on July 1, 1942.[21] The issue, of course, was whether the lack of archival evidence implied a lack of evidence. Irving was obviously playing a variation on Faurisson's game: give me one proof, one single archival proof! Obviously he was going to argue that only wartime archival evidence could be used to establish the facts.

Anticipating that scenario, I remembered one of the first lessons I had received as a graduate student of history: the variety of historical evidence is infinite. Not only testimony, but everything that people produce can be used as evidence if it can be made to correspond to similar evidence. The great French historian Marc Bloch, who was executed by the Germans in 1944, was one of my mentors, thanks to his posthumously published *The Historian's Craft* (1953). Bloch taught that one should not expect that a particular historical question (for example, whether a homicidal gas chamber was installed in Auschwitz in the late summer of 1941) can be proved only by turning up one particular piece of evidence (for example, a blueprint dated August 1941 showing a building or room designated as "gas chamber"). He had made clear that it would be foolish to require for each historical question the presence of a unique type of document with a specific sort of use. "On the contrary," he wrote, "the deeper the research, the more the light of the evidence must converge from sources of many different kinds."[22] This meant that one should be flexible and judge with a practical wisdom and on a case-by-case basis what could be admitted as evidence and what could not. John Wilkins, Bishop of Chester and one of the founders of the Royal Society, said as much in 1675, when he proposed that "things of several kinds may admit and require several sorts of proofs, all which may be good in their kind."

> The Philosopher has long ago told us [Aristotle, *Eth. Lib. 1, cap. 3; Metaph. lib.1, cap ult.*], that according to the divers nature of things, so must the Evidences for them be; and that 'tis an argument of an undisciplined wit not to acknowledge this. He that is rational and judicious will expect no other kind of Arguments in any case than the subject-matter will bear. . . . All things are not capable of the same kind of Evidence. . . . From whence I infer this, That it is not, ought not to be, any prejudice to the Truth or Certainty of any thing, that it is not to be made out of such kind of proof, of which the nature of that thing is not capable, provided it be capable of satisfactory proofs of another kind.[23]

It was obvious that Irving would maintain that each particular historical question concerning Auschwitz calls for one particular piece of evidence, and that in addition each of these pieces ought independently to prove the use of the camp as a death factory. The defense, in turn, would have to heed Bloch's counsel and argue that knowledge of Auschwitz was based on a convergence of many different types of evidence.

Irving's argument concerning the equal deliveries of Zyklon B could be easily investigated and possibly rejected, because it was based on some invoices from 1944 which had found their way into the Nuremberg trial and not from the more substantial information about deliveries of Zyklon B to Auschwitz and Oranienburg that had emerged in the Bruno Tesch trial in 1945. I did not recall the exact amounts that had been delivered but did remember that it seemed out of proportion to the deliveries to other concentration camps.

I found it difficult not to smile when I read "upon completion of their sentence," as if the Auschwitz prisoners had been actually sentenced by some kind of court. But, more important, this document gave me a sense of the quality of Irving's challenge to the historical record. As Dwork and I had demonstrated in *Auschwitz: 1270 to the Present,* the camp had had many different functions, and as a result it had been a very complex place with a tangled, complex, and confusing history—or, better, histories, because it would be possible to write many different histories of Auschwitz: Auschwitz as a concentration camp for Poles, Auschwitz as an agricultural estate, and so on. Each of these histories had their own political, institutional, and financial context; each had its own unique spatial impact on the site and its own temporal regularities, variabilities, and times of crisis and change. As we had shown, at times these histories ran at cross-purposes, at times they ran parallel without interfering with one another, and at times they communicated, converged, and united. Therefore any conclusion about any aspect of the history of Auschwitz had to take into account an often labyrinthine context, made even more difficult to negotiate because of intentional camouflage of certain aspects of the camp's history during the war and the willful destruction of archival and other material evidence at the end of the war. As I read Irving's argument, I remembered the Russian proverb that one ought not drive straight on a twisted lane. Irving's conclusion was groundless. And it was relatively easy to see why. Irving's conclusion was based on the combination of two syllogisms:

Released prisoners are free to divulge information.
Prisoners were released from Auschwitz.
Therefore Auschwitz was not a top-secret place.

Mass extermination is a top-secret operation.
Auschwitz was not a top-secret place.
Therefore Auschwitz was not a top-secret mass extermination center.

These syllogisms were fallacious when applied to Auschwitz because the term "Auschwitz" covered a very manifold and complex reality. If Auschwitz had only been a (top-secret) mass extermination center, located in one place, Irving's argument could have been conclusive. Yet Auschwitz encompassed many different sites, and as an institution it was engaged in many different functions. Furthermore, it functioned as a (top-secret) mass extermination center for only part of its history. If the released prisoners had included the so-called Sonderkommandos who operated the crematoria, Irving would have a point. They did not. In fact, no Jews were ever included in the category of *Erziehungschäftlinge*, or "re-education inmates," the only prisoner category from which releases (some 1,500 out of a total of 10,000) did occur.[24] Most of the Sonderkommandos were put to death after a few months on the job to protect secrecy. The few who survived did so because they either escaped from the death march that concluded the camp's history or because, amid the chaos of Germany's collapse, they were able to merge (after the death march) with the general camp population in the receiving concentration camps in the West.[25]

At that moment it became clear to me that I would face a great task in educating the jury and the judge—I did not know yet that in the end the trial would be conducted without a jury. Because of the dichotomy between the very complex nature and history of Auschwitz and the habit of many of considering the camp only as a "top-secret mass extermination center," I had to make clear that many people, including bona fide historians, survivors, and less than bona fide negationists, often commit the fallacy of composition: they reason from the properties of the part of Auschwitz that was engaged with mass extermination to the properties of Auschwitz as a whole. For example, negationists argue that the presence of a swimming pool in Auschwitz I, with three diving boards, shows that the camp was really a rather benign place and therefore could not have been a center of extermination. It is a fallacious argument, because the swimming pool was built as a water reservoir for the purpose of fire-fighting (there were no hydrants in the camp), the diving boards were added later, and the pool was only accessible to SS men and certain privileged Aryan prisoners employed as inmate functionaries in the camp. In short, the presence of the swimming pool does not say anything about the conditions for Jewish inmates in Auschwitz and does not challenge the existence of an extermination program with its proper facilities in Auschwitz II.

There were other points of contention. The "Defence of Second Defendant" contained a second paragraph dealing directly with Auschwitz.

Auschwitz-Birkenau began operating as an extermination camp in March 1942. At its height, it had 4 gas chambers in use, using Zyklon B. Over 1 million Jews were murdered there, as were tens of thousands of Gypsies and Soviet prisoners of war, until it was closed in November 1944.[26]

As I read this statement, I shook my head: at its height, in 1944, Auschwitz had five extermination installations in use (Crematoria 2, 3, 4, and 5 and Bunker 5), which counted a total of 13 gas chambers (Crematorium 2 had 2, Crematorium 3 had 1, Crematorium 4 had 3, Crematorium 5 had 3, and Bunker 5 had 4). But in his "Reply to Defence of Second Defendant" Irving had not picked up on the mistake in the gas chamber count. Instead he made a broader argument that suggested that there had been no gas chambers at all.

> Auschwitz-Birkenau. The Plaintiff is not aware of any authentic wartime archival evidence for the allegations raised in this paragraph by the Defendants. Notwithstanding that the Defendants assert that it had four operating gas chambers in use, Adolf Eichmann writing privately in 1955–6 about his inspection visits to Auschwitz, was never shown them (although he was shown an open-air pit with cadavers burning in it).
>
> Auschwitz commandant Rudolf Höss reported daily to his superiors in Berlin in top secret SS cipher on prisoner statistics. From the spring of 1942 to the spring of 1943 these daily signals were read by British codebreakers. They reported the number of inmates, the number of arrivals, and the "departures by any means"—primarily deaths, according to British Intelligence; the signals also distinguished between Jews, Poles, other Europeans and Russians. "The returns from Auschwitz . . . mentioned illness as the main cause of death, but included references to shootings and hangings. There were no references in the decrypts to gassing" (Professor Sir Frank H Hinsley et al., British Intelligence in the Second World War: Its Influence on Strategy and Operations, Cambridge, 1979–84, 3 vols., vol. 11, appendix, page 673).
>
> The Defendants have not explained what became of the one million cadavres [sic] which they claim were produced by killing operations at Auschwitz.[27]

These three paragraphs revealed, first of all, that Irving employed a double standard. He demanded "authentic wartime archival evidence" for the gas chambers and then invoked such evidence with a postwar statement by Eichmann, who would have had every reason to have forgotten about the gas chambers. I had to admit that I did not know Hinsley's book, but from the quotation given, it seemed that the statistics referred to the deaths of registered inmates and not to the murder of those who were selected for the gas chambers immediately after their arrival. Subsequent research was to confirm my initial hunch. Irving's final claim that the defendants had not accounted for the 1 million corpses seemed just a waste of paper, as it was clear that most of the gas chambers were conveniently located in crematoria.

It was going to be very tedious. Or perhaps not: both the "Defence of Second Defendant" and the "Reply to Defence of Second Defendant" included much material concerning the Leuchter Report and Irving's 1988 "conversion" to negationism that was new to me. Some of Irving's statements seemed hallucinatory. For example, in February 1989, Irving told the participants of the Ninth International Revisionist Conference organized by the negationist Institute of Holocaust Review that Holocaust historians realized "that they are way out of line with the Auschwitz story, and they are frantically engaged in damage control at present."

They're pulling their entire army of liars back from the main battlefront, into the second line, because all the artillery that's coming down on the front line now is making it too dangerous for them.[28]

As a person who had just joined the alleged "army of liars," I had noticed nothing of either the bombardment or the subsequent retreat. There was an obvious gap between events as I had witnessed them and history as told by Irving.

One part of the "Defence of Second Defendant" left me in shock. It quoted at length parts of the speech that Irving had given in October 1990 at the Tenth International Revisionist Conference. Introducing Irving, conference organizer Mark Weber referred to a speech Irving had given in Dresden earlier that year in commemoration of the city's destruction forty-five years earlier, in which he said "Ladies and gentleman, survivors and descendants of the holocaust of Dresden, the holocaust of Germans in Dresden really happened. That of the Jews in the gas chambers of Auschwitz is an invention. I am ashamed to be an Englishman."[29]

Irving's 1990 speech revealed to me that if I were to join the case and engage Irving in court, I would face a showman with a great sense of drama who would, without doubt, occupy center stage. It was an unattractive prospect. His account of his initial reaction to the Leuchter Report revealed the way he handled historical evidence, though.

> I was called as an expert witness as a historian to give evidence at the Ernst Zündel case, where Zündel's researchers showed me the *Leuchter Report,* the laboratory tests on the crematoria and the gas chambers. As a person who, at the University of London, studied chemistry and physics and the exact sciences, I knew that this was an exact result. There was no way around it. And suddenly all that I'd read in the archives clicked into place. You have to accept that, if there is no evidence anywhere in the archives that there were any gassings going on; that if there's not a single German document that refers to the gassings of human beings— not one wartime German document; and if there is no reference anywhere in the German archives to anybody giving orders for the gassings of people, and if, on the other hand, the forensic tests of the laboratories, of the crematoria, and the gas chambers and Auschwitz and so on, show that there is no trace, no significant residue whatsoever of a cyanide compound, then this can all only mean one thing.[30]

Later in his speech, he raised the specter of the Battleship Auschwitz. Having declared the Holocaust a hoax, Irving scoffed at Auschwitz as the main weapon in "the biggest propaganda offensive that the human race has ever known." I was both annoyed, perturbed, and tickled. Whatever else one could say, Irving's call to "Sink the Auschwitz!" brought some relief amid the legal tedium. I could not but admire the consistency with which he had exploited this metaphor when he announced that the crew of the battleship was already fighting on the bridge, "boxing and engaging in fisticuffs." Undoubtedly inspired by recent newspaper reports that, based on detailed studies, the Auschwitz Museum was about to revise the official death toll of the camp to a little over a million, Irving had enthusiastically claimed that "the Auschwitz has been steering amongst the icebergs, and finally it has begun to scuttle itself."

They've begun to haul down the flag of the battleship Auschwitz. They've taken down the placard, they've taken down the memorial to the four million, and they've replaced it with a rather smaller memorial to one million.

Of course that's not the end of the story. I'm convinced that it's just the "interim memorial." I think it is on cardboard, if you have a close look, because why waste money on an expensive memorial when you're going only to have to change it again in a few months time! . . . To me, Auschwitz is unimportant—I'm happy that the ship is scuttling itself. It's vanishing. It's going to be left like the battleship Arizona at Pearl Harbor—if you ever go to Hawaii and have a look at it—with just its mast sticking out of the water to mark where once a great legend stood. And when people go there a hundred years from now and say: "Down there is the most incredible legend that people believed for fifty years: it's the great battleship Auschwitz, it was scuttled by its crew!"

Why don't we have to believe it? Well, you know about the *Leuchter Report*.[31]

I continued to read with increasing disbelief. The "Defence of Second Defendant" provided a short account of how Zündel commissioned Leuchter's investigation. It included some interesting tidbits about Zündel I did not know, such as the fact that he had written a book entitled *UFOs: Nazi Secret Weapons?* which claimed that UFOs had been developed as one of Hitler's secret weapons and that they were still in use at underground bases in the Antarctic. The text also described Irving's reaction when confronted with Leuchter's results. It quoted, once again, Irving's central statement from the 1990 speech, adding (perhaps unwisely) some words between brackets:

You have to accept that, if there is no evidence anywhere in the archives that there were any gassings going on; that if there's not a single German document that refers to the gassings of human beings—not one wartime German document; and if there is no reference anywhere in the German archives to anybody giving orders for the gassings of people, and if, on the other hand, the forensic tests of the laboratories, of the crematoria, and the gas chambers and Auschwitz and so on, show that there is no trace, no significant residue whatsoever of a cyanide compound, then this can all only mean one thing . . . [no gassings of human beings (at Auschwitz-Birkenau) in gas chambers].

Not surprisingly, in his "Reply to Defence of Second Defendant," Irving challenged "the admissibility of the concluding sentence in square brackets."[32] I was rather surprised that the lawyer who had drafted the "Defence of Second Defendant" had been so unsure about the intelligence of the reader. In my view, the innuendo of the original statement ought to have been left alone.

A final part in the "Defence of Second Defendant" that touched my area of expertise was a long attack on the Leuchter Report. One long paragraph demolished Leuchter's standing as an expert.

Fred Leuchter had no expertise in the manners upon which he purported to give an expert view in the Report, and his evidence as a self-styled expert was (rightly) rejected (save to a very limited extent) by the Canadian Court, for that reason. Moreover, the scientific validity and methodology of the Report were fundamentally flawed. Though Leuchter claimed an expertise in engineering, he had none. Indeed in June 1991, 2 weeks before Leuchter was due to go on trial in Massachusetts for practising or offering to practice engineering without a license, Leuchter signed a consent agreement admitting that he was not and never had been a professional engineer.[33]

This contention did not convince me: the issue of his formal credentials seemed moot. In a world in which bicycle mechanics had introduced the age of aviation, one ought to consider a person's actual abilities and expertise. In this instance, it seemed that Irving's response—if true—was to the point: Leuchter was a "professional consultant who had routinely and for a fee advised these penitentiaries on electric-chair and gas-chamber execution procedures and safety precautions."[34]

Although I owned a photocopy of the American edition of the Leuchter Report, I had never read Irving's introduction to the British edition. I was surprised to discover Irving's contempt for the historical establishment and his alleged aim to use the Leuchter Report as a weapon in his battle with mainline historians, whom he accused of utter laziness and of ignoring "documents which are now available in embarrassing abundance."[35]

Having met Zündel in his lair, I was not surprised to read that Irving credited the British Psychological Warfare Executive with having invented the gas chambers as a propaganda story which had been put to adaptive reuse after the war to swindle 90 billion Deutschmarks from the Germans. Nor was I surprised that Irving invoked his own credentials as a debunker of the Hitler diaries. I was somewhat amused by his humble admission at having failed to subject "Auschwitz" to laboratory analysis.

> And yet I have to admit that it would never have occurred to me to subject the actual fabric of the Auschwitz concentration camp and its "gas chambers"—the holiest shrines of this new Twentieth Century religion—to chemical tests to see if there was any trace of cyanide compounds in the walls.
>
> The truly astounding results are set out in this report: while significant quantities of cyanide compounds were found in the small de-lousing facilities of the camp where the proprietary (and lethal) Zyklon B compound was used, as all are agreed, to disinfect the plague-ridden clothing of all persons entering these brutal slave-labor camps, no significant trace whatsoever was found in the buildings which international opinion—for it is not more than that—has always labeled as the camp's infamous gas chambers. Nor, as the report's gruesomely expert author makes plain, could the design and construction of those buildings have made their use as mass gas-chambers feasible under any circumstances.
>
> For myself, shown this evidence for the first time when called as an expert witness at the Zündel trial in Toronto in April 1988, the laboratory reports were shattering. There could be no doubt as to their integrity. I myself would, admittedly, have preferred to see more rigorous methods used in identifying and certifying the samples taken for analysis, but I accept without reservation the difficulties that the examining team faced on location in what is now Poland; chiseling out the samples from the hallowed site under the very noses of the new camp guards. The video tapes made simultaneously by the team—which I have studied—pro-

vide compelling visual evidence of the scrupulous methods that they have used.

Until the end of this tragic century there will always be incorrigible historians, statesmen and publicists who are content to believe, or have no economically viable alternative but to believe, that the Nazis used "gas chambers" at Auschwitz to kill human beings. But it is now up to them to explain to me as an intelligent and critical student of modern history why there is no significant trace of any cyanide compound in the building which they have always identified as the former gas chambers.

Forensic chemistry is, I repeat, an exact science.

The ball is in their court.[36]

I did not really know whether or not forensic chemistry was an exact science. But even if it was, and even if Leuchter had been an excellent forensic scientist, it seemed that all the forensic data would not change the inherent problems with the evidence from Auschwitz if one wanted to arrive at a historical proof. When I read Irving's statement, I recalled how I received regular admonitions as a graduate student not to apply the paradigm of scientific inquiry to history. We were told that, unlike scientists, historians could not conduct repeated experiments to find evidence and construct a proof. After all, unlike scientists who operate in a universe ruled by natural laws, we studied a world shaped by incessant and unrelenting contingency. Therefore a historical proof was a difficult thing. Unlike scientists, who could design laboratory experiments that offered the ideal situation to study a particular phenomenon, we often worked with scraps of evidence that had accidentally survived the times or with the testimony of witnesses who were absolutely not qualified to bear witness, and so on. The application of some scientific techniques, such as carbon dating, did not challenge the inherent unscientific character of any historical judgment. It seemed that Irving tried to circumvent the issue of judgment by invoking some scientific result that stated that the walls of the homicidal gas chambers had a low residue of cyanide compounds and the walls of the Zyklon B delousing chambers a high residue. But all the troubles of historical proof remained. If the "alleged" homicidal gas chambers had not functioned to kill people, why would they have any traces of cyanide compounds at all? Because Irving challenged a well-established historical record, it was up to him to provide an explanation.

The text of Irving's introduction to the Leuchter Report was interesting and revealing about the man, but I could not see exactly how quoting it at length served Lipstadt's defense. Irving responded in his reply to Lipstadt's lawyers by stating that he did voice in his introduction to the Leuchter Report "his own measured concerns about what he saw as methodological flaws," and, more important, claimed that Polish investigations made to disprove Leuchter "broadly confirmed Mr Leuchter's affidavit."[37] I seemed to remember the results of the Polish tests differently: didn't the Polish researchers come to exactly the opposite conclusion of Leuchter when they proved that the presence of cyanide compounds in the walls of the gas chambers confirmed the gassings?

A final issue that was directly relevant to me was raised by a passage in "Defence of Second Defendant" that accused Irving of uncritically accepting evidence that exculpated Hitler while ignoring evidence that did not. This passage unwisely included the name of Auschwitz commandant Rudolf Höss, who would not have been in a position to know if Hitler knew, or did not know, about the Holocaust. Irving's response to "Defence of the Second Defendant" did not address the historical fallacy of introducing Höss as a potential witness to Hitler's knowledge of the Holocaust. Instead, it contained a broader attack on the general credibility of Höss's testimony. He argued that Höss would have made his statements under circumstances of duress that would have made his testimony unacceptable to a British court.

> SS *Obersturmbannführer* Rudolf Höss, commandant of Auschwitz, was manhandled upon capture. After making self-incriminating (and often self-contradictory) confessions at Nuremberg he tried to smuggle a letter out to his wife apologising that he had made them only because he had been tortured (the letter is now in private hands in the USA). Höss's subsequent memoirs, written in Polish captivity, before his execution, bristle with inconsistencies, inaccurate statistics, anachronisms and data so egregiously false that historians quoting the memoirs have been obliged to omit these passages for fear of bringing discredit on the whole. Adolf Eichmann, told of Höss's confessions, described these while still in hiding in Argentina in 1956 as downright lies; shown a printed text of Höss's memoirs, Eichmann scribbled scornful remarks in the margin (the Plaintiff has a copy of these pages with Eichmann's handwritten marginalia). Told that Höss confessed to killing 2.8 million Jews in Auschwitz, Eichmann asked sarcastically where Höss was claiming to have obtained the seven million or so Jews from (of which the "2.8 million" would have been the "unfit residue")—"Certainly not from me." In the absence of satisfactory collateral evidence of a forensic or documentary nature, the self-serving oral testimonies of Nazi criminals like Höttl and Höss alone are not enough for a scrupulous historian.[38]

I must admit that the information about Höss's letter to his wife was new to me. The "inconsistencies, inaccurate statistics, anachronisms" of Höss's memoirs were well known, and Dwork and I had addressed them in our book. While they did present problems, there was in fact sufficient "collateral evidence of a forensic or documentary nature" to resolve them. Irving's attempt to use Eichmann's memoirs to discredit Höss gave me some pause. The memoirs were published in 1980 in Germany, and I thought I knew the passages well where Eichmann discussed his dealings with Auschwitz and Höss. I did remember that Eichmann had challenged Höss's victim count of 2.5 million (not 2.8 million) Jews but did not recall that Höss had received "seven million or so." On my return to Canada, I immediately checked my copy of Eichmann's memoirs. It revealed that, at least in the published memoirs, Eichmann did not mention "seven million or so":

> Like the testimony of Hauptsturmführer Wisliceny, also Höss's Nuremberg testimony, that he killed 2.5 million Jews in Auschwitz, seems to have been made under pressure. I knew Höss as a decent comrade, a good family man, decorated in the First World War with the Iron Cross, a man who, because of his national socialist belief, served many years in prison before the Machstübernahme.
>
> Höss told me once that the Reichsführer had inspected the whole process of destruction and that he had said that "the coming generations will not need to fight these battles"—a statement that inspired him to fulfil his difficult duty.
>
> The number of 2.5 million Jews liquidated in Auschwitz I

Rudolf Höss after his arrest.
Courtesy Auschwitz-Birkenau
State Museum, Oswiecim.

always considered to be beyond belief, because the camp did not
have such a capacity. Besides which I have never brought so many
Jews to Auschwitz. It is true that I was not the only one who
deported [Jews to Auschwitz], but also other authorities like the
Sipo (Security Police), but even when we add all up, 2.5 million
could not have gone to Auschwitz and certainly could not have
been destroyed. After 1945 the so-called "Auschwitzer" emerged
like mushrooms after the rain, and still today hundreds of thousands enjoy a good health, just because they were put to work.[39]

More to the point, however, seemed the fact that in using Eichmann as a
witness against Höss on the basis of the latter's claim to have killed 2.5 (or
2.8) million Jews, Irving did not provide a fair and honest account of Höss's
own assessment of how many Jews he had killed. During his initial interrogations, Höss seems to have confirmed an initial assessment by his interrogators that 3 million people had been killed in Auschwitz.[40] In Nuremberg, he gave different numbers on different occasions. During his
interrogations, he gave a detailed list of numbers for each nationality that

came to over 1.1 million deportees.[41] In his affidavit, however, he stated that "at least 2,500,000 victims were executed and exterminated [in Auschwitz] by gassing and burning, and at least another half million succumbed to starvation and disease, making a total dead of about 3,000,000."[42] He confirmed this number in a conversation with prison psychologist Dr. Gilbert. "He readily confirmed that approximately 2½ million Jews had been exterminated under his direction."[43] However, when given again the opportunity to make his own calculations, he returned to the lower number of 1.1. million. In a short memorandum which he wrote for Gilbert later in April, Höss credited Eichmann with having given him the information that 2.5 million Jews had been shipped to Auschwitz—a figure he considered much too high, as he could account for only 1,125,000 victims.[44]

Höss substantially repeated this argument in his memoirs written in Polish captivity:

> During my earlier interrogations I gave the number of 2.5 million Jews who arrived at Auschwitz to be exterminated. This figure was given to me by Eichmann, who had given this figure to my superior, SS General Glücks, when Eichmann was ordered to make a report to Himmler shortly before Berlin was surrounded. Eichmann and his deputy, Günther, were the only ones who had the necessary information to calculate the total number of Jews annihilated. . . . I myself never knew the total number, and I have nothing to help me arrive at an estimate. I can only remember the figures involved in the larger actions, which were repeated to me by Eichmann or his deputies.
>
> | From Upper Silesia and the General Government | 250,000 |
> |---|---|
> | Germany and Theresienstadt | 100,000 |
> | Holland | 95,000 |
> | Belgium | 20,000 |
> | France | 110,000 |
> | Greece | 65,000 |
> | Hungary | 400,000 |
> | Slovakia | 90,000 |
>
> I can no longer remember the figures for the smaller actions, but they were insignificant by comparison with the numbers given above. I regard the number of 2.5 million as far too high. Even Auschwitz had limits to its destructive capabilities.[45]

Thus, a quick review of the evidence had made quite clear that Irving was less than scrupulous in his interpretation: the figure of "seven million or so" seemed a figment of his imagination, the figure of 2.8 million seemed a product of sloppiness, and the figure of 1.1 million was suppressed.

As I considered Irving's attempt to discredit Höss's testimony, I became convinced that the defense argument concerning Auschwitz as it had been put down in "Defence of Second Defendant" aimed at the wrong target. It seemed that the central question was not "What happened in Auschwitz and how did Irving deny it?" but "What is the evidence of what happened in Auschwitz and did Irving make statements about Auschwitz with a reckless disregard for that evidence?" In other words, the center of the dispute would not be "the facts" but "the evidence" of those facts. Irving's invocation of Eichmann's memoirs against Höss seemed to offer a prime example of his tendency to distort, misstate, misconstrue, and misquote historical evidence. Julius and Evans, who themselves seemed less than enthusiastic about the "Defence of Second Defendant" as time passed, assented. After various telephone conversations, we agreed that I was to provide a report of the true numbers of Jews killed by gassing at Auschwitz and elsewhere and establish that these numbers were falsified by Irving when he claimed that 100,000 people had died in that camp from all causes but gassing. I was also to research the nature and the content of the statements Irving had made about Auschwitz and determine if Irving's denial of mass gassings and of the existence of gassing facilities at Auschwitz and elsewhere did or did not agree with the evidence and could, therefore, be understood as a fair presentation or as a falsification of history. Finally, I was to establish if the supposed "scientific" evidence presented by Irving had been false or misleading.[46]

On my return to Canada, I took some time to reflect on my new task, which filled me with a sense of bleak irony. I had come to Auschwitz because I had been interested in the large historiographical questions surrounding the place of Crematorium 2 in our understanding of architectural history. This had triggered the much more empirical engagement with the historical facts that resulted in *Auschwitz: 1270 to the Present*. Now the descent seemed complete, and for the duration of the case I was to engage the most tedious task of all: proving the obvious. Having become comfortable with the world view of common law, I had come to accept that the court was an important forum where society, through battle, finds out and defines what it stands for. While my work as an expert was going to be dreary, it was also going to be honorable and possibly historically significant.

I had been instructed that, as an expert, I would be an amicus curiae who would write a report without prejudice for the defendants and against the plaintiff. We all had our role to play, and as I was to engage Irving, I hoped that he would prove a worthy opponent. But there was something else too: compared to the subject matter which was to be the object of our battle—the way we know of and remember the murder of more than 1 million people in Auschwitz—the fortunes of either Lipstadt or Irving or even myself were of no great consequence. I clearly saw that I faced the twofold loyalty Wyschogrod had described: one to dispassionate scholarship, and the other to the victims of Auschwitz.

As I tried to imagine the pitfalls ahead, I ran again into the conundrum of historical proof. I was to write a report on the evidence for our knowledge about Auschwitz fifty-five years after the world had first learned of the atrocities in that camp, amid a society that had reached a consensus about what had happened at Auschwitz. I began to jot down notes, some of which, in an edited form, I was to include in my expert opinion. My first problem was rather straightforward: the evidence for Auschwitz was undoubtedly problematic. Since the day the first revelations of the concentration camps appeared, their existence has fit with great difficulty in our understanding of the world. Those who survived the camps most often testified to their inability to tell the world what it had been. Some compared themselves to those who, according to the Greek legend, turned into stone upon seeing the hideous head of the Gorgon Medusa. They were muted. Israeli writer and survivor Aharon Appelfeld explained on Canadian radio that Auschwitz could not be an object of observation. "It is like the sun," he said. "You cannot look at the sun." As a result, one could not speak or even utter what the Holocaust had been. "You can only surround it. . . . We know it before and after, and we can guess."[47] And even those who wanted to communicate had to admit that ordinary language did not work. Reflecting on his memoir of Auschwitz, Elie Wiesel wrote that its language was not human but an almost animal-like shouting, screaming, howling, moaning. "This is the concentration camp language / It negated all other language, and took its place."[48] Ordinary language was not capable of bearing testimony, which was forever to fluctuate between the obligation to share the silence of the murdered and the pressure to scream.

Another survivor, Primo Levi, reflected that there was no common vocabulary between those who experienced the extremities of living and who witnessed the extremities of dying within the camps and those who had not. But the situation was worse than that. If a silence separated the survivors from the rest of humanity, a double silence existed between those who had not survived and us.

> I must repeat: we, the survivors, are not the true witnesses. This is an uncomfortable notion of which I have become conscious little by little, reading the memoirs of others and reading mine at a distance of years. We survivors are not only an exiguous but also an anomalous minority: we are those who by their prevarications or abilities or good luck did not touch the bottom. Those who did so, those who saw the Gorgon, have not returned to tell about it, or have returned mute, but they are the "Muslims," the submerged, the complete witnesses, the ones whose deposition would have general significance. They are the rule, we are the exception.[49]

Levi was not the first to recognize that the survivors were not the ultimate witnesses of the reality of the camps as death camps. In 1945, American scholar David P. Boder traveled from displaced persons camp to displaced persons camp to interview survivors. A small selection of his very important collection of transcripts was published under the title *I Did Not Interview the Dead.*[50]

The impossibility for survivors to verbalize their experiences reaches to the heart of the problem of what one may call "the evidence for Auschwitz." If indeed Auschwitz is the center of an event of such silencing power, how can language faithfully record its history? Lyotard considered the implications of this situation in his essay written in response to the Faurisson Affair. While I believe that Lyotard was mistaken in arguing for a suspension of judgment vis-à-vis Faurisson so as not to impose a totalitarian view on the discourse of Auschwitz, his reflections on the problem of evidence made more sense. His point of departure was a diary entry made by one of the camp doctors: "It's not for nothing that Auschwitz is called the 'extermination camp.'" Annihilation, Lyotard argued, not only affected human beings but also the evidence for that annihilation. "Many of the means to prove the crime or its quantity were also exterminated." The documents, the gas chambers: all of that was destroyed. "With Auschwitz, something new has happened in history (which can only be a sign and not a fact), which is that the facts, the testimonies which bore the traces of *here's* and *now's,* the documents which indicated the sense or the senses of the facts, and the names, finally the possibility of various kinds of phrases whose conjunction makes reality, all this has been destroyed as much as possible." This created a unique epistemological challenge.

> But the silence imposed on knowledge does not impose the silence of forgetting, it imposes a feeling. Suppose that an earthquake destroys not only lives, buildings and objects but also the instruments used to measure earthquakes directly and indirectly. The

impossibility of quantitatively measuring it does not prohibit, but rather inspires in the minds of the survivors the idea of a very great seismic force. The scholar claims to know nothing about it, but the common person has a complex feeling, the one aroused by the negative presentation of the indeterminate. *Mutatis mutandis,* the silence that the crime of Auschwitz imposes upon the historian is a sign for the common person.[51]

Those who would study Auschwitz ought not to apply the most restrictive cognitive rules for the establishment of historical reality; that would not do justice to the history of the camp. Therefore the historian of Auschwitz was to look not only at positive evidence but also to venture forth "by lending his or her ear to what is not presentable under the rules of knowledge." This, of course, applies to every fact of history, in which one moves from the evidential to what it implies. But in the case of the Holocaust, this was even more valid. Lyotard concluded that "Auschwitz is the most real of realities in this respect."[52]

The problem of the eyewitnesses would not be so profound if the Germans had not made such a systematic effort not to put things on paper as they proceeded and to destroy whatever had been put on paper the moment it was practically possible. Finally, when in late 1944 the Germans closed and dismantled the Auschwitz gas chambers and, shortly thereafter, dynamited the crematoria and burned the camp archives, they did so in order to destroy whatever remained of the immediate material evidence of what the camp had been between 1942 and 1944. And at the same time, Allied bombers completed the destruction of primary evidence by successfully bombing SS offices in Berlin. As a result, when Dwork and I set out to reconstruct the development and operation of Auschwitz as an extermination camp, we had to rely in a greater measure than we felt comfortable on what Marc Bloch identified as "intentional evidence"—narrative sources such as testimonies, confessions, memoirs, and so on. Following Bloch's definition, all these accounts are "consciously intended to inform their readers."[53] While very important as a historical source, the problem with intentional evidence is that the historian should always assume the possibility that it might have been created to mislead us. In a sense, as historians of Auschwitz, we were thrown back into an epistemological situation that existed before the modern development of historiography, which saw a great shift from a reliance on narrative sources to one on the evidence of witnesses in spite of themselves. This may include written "documents" such as inscriptions, charters, deeds, letters, government papers, bills, ledgers, inventories, wills, and death books or archeological traces such as bones, flints, shards, tombs, ruins, or any other trace accidentally left by earlier generations. As graduate students, we were taught that we should not rely heavily on what those in the past explicitly wanted posterity to know, such as an individual's memoirs or an institution's official hagiographies, but to free ourselves from the perspective that the past tried to impose on us to interrogate the past by overhearing what was never intended to be preserved.

By destroying most of the "non-intentional evidence," the Germans placed us in an embarrassing position. First of all, we had to rely more on eyewitness evidence than we felt comfortable with, given the paradigms of modern historiography, and with that all the problems of inaccuracies of perception, errors of memory, and unconscious self-deception took on a central significance. "There is no reliable witness in the absolute sense," Bloch observed. "There is only more or less reliable testimony."[54] Reliable testimony presupposes first of all an accuracy of perception, and many witnesses of Auschwitz made their observations under the most difficult circumstances: suffering from hunger and fatigue amid utter squalor, shorn of their former identity, at best demoralized and more usually at the edge of absolute despair, these people lived without any ability to control even the smallest part of their existence in a completely unintelligible world marked by random violence. Even the most basic conditions for a careful examination of the facts were absent. As a result, even within valuable testimonies one often finds a great range of credibility, ranging from the obviously factual through the plausible to the implausible. But I realized that in the same way that Auschwitz survivors often make poor witnesses in trials because of the problems of language and silence discussed above, much of the evidence I would present would be vulnerable to attack in cross-examination. Since Rassinier, negationists had been more than willing to exploit any error of detail, whether made in good or bad faith, in order to throw doubt on the reliability of the evidence as a whole. I did not expect Irving to be different.

There was a second problem: the impossibility of coming to any "objective" assessment of the "facts." As I considered the genealogy of our knowledge about Auschwitz, I realized that it included more than evidence such as confessions by SS men, sworn depositions by Jewish and Polish eyewitnesses, original German documents, substantial residues of cyanide in the ventilation covers of the gas chambers of Crematorium 2, and Polish forensic investigations done in 1945. Since 1945, other genres of knowledge had emerged: memoirs of survivors, interpretations of writers, evocations by filmmakers, symbolic monuments designed by architects and sculptors, public rituals of commemoration, theological speculation, and so on. In other words, I was fully aware that my own knowledge of "Auschwitz," like that of anyone else, was a mixture of learning and secondhand memory, of public political discourse and private anxiety. As such, it had detached itself from the knowledge of present matters of fact —confessions, sworn depositions, documents, traces of residual cyanide, forensic opinions—and acquired a life of its own. With that its epistemological status had changed, definitively and irrevocably. Mediated by social factors, my knowledge of Auschwitz (or for that matter of any historical event) did not reflect David Hume's thesis, presented in Section IV of Part III of Book I of *A Treatise Concerning Human Nature* (1739–1740), that all historical knowledge is based on valid inferential arguments based on direct and certain pieces of evidence available in the present—that is, that historical knowledge ultimately stems from a direct apprehension of "the facts."[55] Instead, my knowledge about Auschwitz followed Alexis de Tocqueville's observation, in *Democracy in America,* that social factors mediate perceptions and understandings and that only a small part of any individual's knowledge is based on original, unmediated perception of evidence, while most of that person's knowledge is transmitted as one's patrimony through social networks.[56] In other words, as Auschwitz was part of my intellectual patrimony, I was engaging Auschwitz as a historical fact after I had come across it as an already accepted item of knowledge. I recognized the paradox that resulted from this, namely, that I and Irving, and everyone else for that matter, shared a cultural consensus about Auschwitz—that, in short, the upcoming battle about what was to be considered evidence and how to interpret that evidence was only possible because we shared a consensus about its history. If Irving did not share that consensus, he would not have bothered to put his career on the line for it, to bring all his energies to bear to "Sink the Battleship Auschwitz." Part of a shared cultural and historical inheritance, our knowledge of Auschwitz had become more or less independent of the potential or actual availability of evidence, and as a result my effort to establish the evidence for our knowledge about Auschwitz would be a somewhat ritual exercise, because neither judge nor jury would be able to separate themselves from our own culture and judge the inherited account of Auschwitz on the basis of documentary evidence. Instead they, like everyone else, would interpret the evidence within the context of the belief for which it would seem to provide evidence. This, I began to realize, was the great pitfall in asking anyone to judge the evidence of any event that had become part of one's cultural patrimony. The evidence for the crime of an unknown individual citizen could be the basis of a legitimate verdict, but the evidence for a crime that had become a universally accepted symbol of criminality could not.

Having come to this disturbing point, I found Leon Pompa's reflection on the dependency of historical knowledge upon a set of accepted historical beliefs particularly enlightening. Pompa confirmed the validity of my anxiety.[57] But Pompa made an interesting observation which did prove helpful. Using the case of Caesar's assassination, first employed by Hume in his discussion of the foundations of historical knowledge, Pompa stated that "it may seem a conceptual possibility that Caesar never existed, but it cannot be a historical possibility."[58] He argued, in my view convincingly, that because facts are interrelated to each other and progressively entrenched in the account as it is transmitted from one generation to the next, the very assumption that Caesar had not been assassinated would force us to abandon our belief in much of Roman history.[59] Applying Pompa's observation to Auschwitz, I found it useful to consider Irving's thesis about the Auschwitz gas chambers to be a conceptual possibility but not a historical possibility, because the historical existence of those gas chambers has come to be the a priori of most of our knowledge of the Second World War. Our knowledge of the gas chambers is not independent of, for example, our knowledge of the ideological radicalization of the Nazis after the beginning of Operation Barbarossa. In our understanding of the history of the Second World War, the operations of the Einsatzgruppen in the East, the deportations of German Jews from the West, the German treatment of Soviet prisoners of war, the expansion of the concentration camps, the first experimentations with Zyklon B as a killing agent, and the adaptation of the morgues of Crematoria 2 and 3 in Auschwitz into gas chambers are interrelated to each other. It became clear that Irving's denial of the gas chambers challenged not only the history of the Holocaust but much of the history of the war itself.

These reflections gave me some pause. When I had accepted the invitation to join the defense team, I had assumed that in the courtroom Irving and I would engage the contentious issue of Auschwitz on a level playing field. I now realized that it would not be so, and that in choosing to challenge a social consensus which he paradoxically shared himself he would find it almost impossible to convince not only the judge and jury, but even himself, that the evidence could be interpreted substantially differently from the way it had been done. In other words, he would engage the evidence epistemologically divided against himself. The trial was to show that this was indeed the case. Every time that Justice Gray tried to establish Irving's conclusion about the evidence under discussion, he received confused answers that in the end affirmed that the evidence stated that the alleged gas chambers were designed and used as gas chambers. Only by claiming that these had been rooms to gas corpses could Irving reach a compromise between his two sides, the one that had declared war on the consensus and the other that, despite everything, had remained part of it. As I watched him struggle with the paradoxes he had summoned up, I sometimes felt sorry for him. But then, again, I remembered what he had said about Auschwitz—"I don't see any reason to be tasteful about Auschwitz. It's baloney. It's a legend."

Both Irving and I were going to be handicapped. My evidence was marked with the sign of silence, and his propositions would make little sense given the cultural consensus shared by all in the courtroom—including Irving himself. Thus, paradoxically, Irving would face the same burden in communicating with the judge as the survivors had faced when they attempted to speak about Auschwitz.

Most of my report was to be based on original archival research I had done in the past, such as the history of the construction of the crematoria, or on new research which I was to do for the purposes of the trial. This new work included a critique of what negationists had written about Auschwitz. In only one issue was I to rely on the scholarship of others. This was the question of the number of victims.

The victim count of Auschwitz was important because Irving had been particularly irresponsible in his public statements about that issue. In a lecture given in Germany in March 1990, Irving speculated that 30,000 people had been killed in Auschwitz: "That is as many as we English killed in Hamburg in one night."[60] Later that year, after he learned that the Russians had released the Auschwitz death books, he gloated that the release of the death books was "an ugly blow for the battleship Auschwitz and its crew. Because the Russians, by releasing the forty-six death books of Auschwitz, which cover the years 1942 completely, 1943 almost completely, and 1944 incompletely—the Russians have revealed that the set of Auschwitz death books, which they have released, now shows, a total of 74,000 deaths, 74,000 deaths by all causes."[61] In fact, Irving was wrong on two points: first of all, 1942 was not complete, and there is not one book for 1944. Second, these books record a total of 68,864 and not 74,000 deaths.[62] Most important, these forty-six volumes only recorded the deaths of registered inmates. Most of the people who died in Auschwitz were murdered on arrival without having been admitted to the camp. Irving could not claim ignorance on this point, because he wrote in the original edition of his *Hitler's War* that 60 percent of the arrivals at Auschwitz were immediately killed "with a maximum of concealment."[63] Yet thirteen years later, in 1990, he chose to suppress the fate of the (in his original estimate) 60 percent of arriving Jews not deemed fit for work. He did not even allude to a potential problem. Of the alleged 74,000 deaths by all causes, Irving believed half of them to have been by natural causes. "Which means less than half of 74,000 people were killed in Auschwitz. Let's be generous and say 40,000 may have been killed in Auschwitz over three years—that's a bad figure! That's a grave crime, it's almost as many people as we British killed in one night."[64] Three years later, Irving proposed that 100,000 Jews had died in Auschwitz, "but not from gas chambers. They died from epidemics." And he speculated that of those 100,000 victims "a quarter were murdered. 25,000 people murdered in Auschwitz in the three years, if we take that generous figure, then I would say that 25,000 people murdered in Auschwitz in three years is still half the number of people that we murdered in Hamburg, burning them alive in one night in 1943." And he added that "we are looking at crime and crime. They are both crimes.

One crime gets all the publicity. One crime is the only one that is referred to in the media today and the other crime you put up a statue to commemorate the man who carried it out. There is something wrong about that."[65]

It was clear that when he made such guesses Irving had not done any original research himself and had disregarded solid scholarship. To show that he was a falsifier of history, it was necessary to establish that there was substantial research on the number of victims. Contrary to what negationists asserted, serious historians had not turned off their critical faculties when they considered the number of victims. After a thorough examination of the evidence, in the early 1990s they had accepted and endorsed a major downward revision of the death count of Auschwitz from 4 million to 1.1 million. To document this scholarship, I wrote a short history of research on the victim count, concentrating on the major revision undertaken in the 1980s by Dr. Franciszek Piper, chief historian of the Auschwitz-Birkenau State Museum. I include here a somewhat abridged version of this essay, which was included in Chapter 2 of my report.

A Short History of Scholarship concerning the Number of Victims of Auschwitz

Before we begin, it is important to note that the Germans did not keep any records of the number of people killed in the gas chambers. There are many German testimonies to that effect. One of them is from SS-Unterscharführer Pery Broad, who worked in the Political Department at Auschwitz—the office that served, among other things, as a liaison between Berlin and the camp for the purpose of the Final Solution. Immediately after the war, Broad gave some valuable information regarding record-keeping. He stated that transport lists were destroyed immediately after its arrival.[66] Broad's statement was confirmed by Commandant Rudolf Höss, who wrote after the war in a document that was submitted and accepted as evidence in the Eichmann trial that he had not been allowed to keep records. Eichmann was "the only SS officer who was allowed to keep records concerning these liquidation operations, according to the orders of the Reichsführer-SS. All other units which took part in any way had to destroy all records immediately."[67] And Oswald Pohl, who ran the central administration of the SS, testified during his trial that while he received regular information about the mortality of registered prisoners, he was not informed about the number of deportees killed in the gas chambers upon their arrival in Auschwitz.[68]

Franciszek Piper. Courtesy Auschwitz-Birkenau State Museum, Oswiecim.

The first postwar attempt to establish within the context of a forensic investigation the total number of dead was undertaken by the Soviet "Extraordinary State Committee For the Ascertaining and Investigation of Crimes Committed by the German-fascist Invaders and Their Associates On Crimes Committed by the German-fascist Invaders in the Oswiecim Death Camp." The committee came to the conclusion that 4 million people had been killed in Auschwitz. Their conclusion was based on an assessment of the capacity of the crematoria. Crematorium 1, the committee estimated, had a monthly incineration capacity of 9,000 corpses. It was in operation for 24 months, and the committee assumed that it had a burning capacity of 216,000 bodies. Crematoria 2 and 3 were estimated to each have had a monthly capacity of 90,000 corpses. As they had been in operation for 19 and 18 months, they would have been able to incinerate together a total of 3,330,000 corpses. The committee estimated that Crematoria 4 and 5 processed 45,000 bodies per month, and as they had been in function for 17 and 18 months, they had together over that time a cremation capacity of 1,575,000 bodies. The five crematoria would have been able to burn, at least in theory, 5,121,000 bodies.[69] Added to that was the extra capacity provided by the pyres.

> Making allowances for possible undercapacity operation of the crematoriums and stoppages, however, the Commission of technical experts established that during the existence of the Oswiecim camp the German executioners killed in it no less than four million citizens of the USSR, Poland, France, Jugoslavia, Czechoslovakia, Rumania, Hungary, Holland, Belgium, and other countries.[70]

In addition to the engineering approach to the question of how many people had died in Auschwitz, a second method emerged to establish the number of victims. It was based on an analysis of the number of deportations to the camp. As early as 1946, Nachman Blumental, using this method, came to an informed guess that the number of victims ought to have been somewhere between 1.3 and 1.5 million.[71] In the early 1950s, Gerald Reitlinger also tried to make a rough guess of the number of victims on the basis of the number of deportees.

> As to the total number of Jews brought to the selection place at Auschwitz, it is possible to estimate fairly closely for the Western and Central European countries and the Balkans but not for Poland. There is no real guide to the percentage gassed. It was low before August, 1942, and generally low again after August, 1944, but in the meantime gassings might vary between fifty and nearly a hundred per cent. The following list makes allowances for a number of French and Greek transports sent to Majdanek and 34,000 Dutch Jews who went to Sobibor:
>
> | | |
> |---|---:|
> | Belgium | 22,600 |
> | Croatia | 4,500 |
> | France | 57,000 |
> | Greater Reich [. . . direct transports only]* | 25,000 |
> | Greater Reich [via Theresienstadt] | 32,000 |
> | Greece | 50,000 |
> | Holland | 62,000 |
> | Hungary (wartime frontiers) | 380,000 |
> | Italy | 5,000 |
> | Luxembourg | 2,000 |
> | Norway | 700 |
> | Poland and Baltic States* | 180,000 |
> | Slovakia (1939 borders) | 20,000 |
> | | 840,800 |
>
> (* uncertain)
>
> Of this total, 550,000 to 600,000 may have been gassed on arrival and to this must be added the unknown portion of the 300,000 or more, missing from the camp, who were selected.[72]

It is important to note that when he was confronted with different estimates about the number of victims, Reitlinger systematically chose the lowest one. The first reason was that exaggeration would serve those who wished to deny the Holocaust. Reitlinger explained this reason for his extremely cautious approach in the preamble to his calculation of the total number of Jewish victims of the Holocaust, which he set at between 4,194,200 and 4,581,200 people:

> Since the reading of the Nuremberg indictment in November, 1945, naming the figure of 5,700,000 Jewish victims of Germany, the round number of six millions has become a generally accepted assumption in most circles that are interested in the matter. But in the course of writing this book I have been forced to the conclusion that, while it cannot be determined even within a half-million degree of accuracy, the true figure may be considerably smaller. In submitting my following estimates I realise that I may be accused of belittling the sufferings of the persecuted communities, but I believe that the nature of the book is a guarantee of my good faith in that respect. The figure used in Nuremberg was supplied by the World Jewish Congress at a moment when little reputable data were available. Constant repetition of that figure has already given anti-semitic circles on the Continent and in Germany in particular the opportunity to discredit the whole ghastly story and its lessons. I believe that it does not make the guilt of the living German any less, if the figure of six million turns out to be an over-estimate and that the accurate assessment, *if it can be ever obtained,* will not weaken the Jewish case for sanctions against recurrences of these symptoms. Whether six million died, or five millions, or less, it will still be the most systematic extermination of a race in world history. Moreover, once the principle of the murders is proved, there is no particular magic in additional millions. As a German, Walter Dirks, has written: "It is shameful that there should be Germans who see a mitigating circumstance in reducing the sum from six millions to two millions!"[73]

A second reason must be located in his unusually cheerful disposition vis-à-vis the whole story, which was rooted in his very bleak assessment of human nature: as he wrote the book, he always reminded himself that it could have been worse. In the end, almost half of Europe's Jews survived.

> I have spent close to four years among these documents and I found their company neither gloomy nor depressing. For on many pages darts and gleams that thing which prevents all government becoming a living hell—human fallibility. Eichmann fails to fill his death trains, the satellite-government Ministers refuse to answer letters, someone gets the figures wrong, and someone else gives the show away too soon. And so the immense disaster was partly whittled down. How much worse it would have been if the French had not been inconsistent, if the Italians had not been easygoing, the Hungarians jealous, the Rumanians corrupt, and the Germans wedded to protocol.[74]

In my ten years of studying Auschwitz, I found little occasion to share Reitlinger's optimism.

Let us return to the victim total at Auschwitz. The different assessments made by Commandant Rudolf Höss were also an important source. As I have discussed earlier in this chapter, he made two important guesses, one allegedly based on Eichmann's number of 2.5 million victims and one based on his own calculations of 1.1 million victims.[75]

Thus, by the beginning of the 1950s, there were basically three estimates of the number of victims, each based on different sources: a high one of 4 million based on the assumed capacity of the crematoria, a low one of around 1 million based on the number of transports and Höss's final assessment, and a middle one of around 2.5 million, based on Eichmann's number as related by Höss, which he initially substantiated in his Nuremberg affidavit.

Until the early 1980s, no original scholarship was undertaken to come to a resolution of the unacceptably great range between the lowest and highest estimate. The Cold War was largely to blame: the figure of 4 million had been established by the Soviets, and the figure of 1 million had been first proposed in the West. As relations between the East and West deteriorated after the war, with the largest part of Germany becoming part of NATO and with that country refusing to recognize the legitimacy of the postwar Polish annexation of the former German territories of East Prussia, Pomerania, and Silesia, the number of victims became a political issue. The communist rulers of Poland were unwilling to give an inch on their claims against Germany as long as the Bonn government did not recognize the territorial integrity of the People's Republic of Poland, and therefore they continued to maintain, as a matter of policy, that 4 million people had been killed in Auschwitz. In the West, most historians of the Holocaust were unable to do original research in the matter. They tended to accept, with reservations, the middle figure of 2.5 million. Initially only Raul Hilberg, who did important statistical analysis on the number of victims of the Holocaust, supported the lower figure of 1 million. He reasoned—with justification—that given the total number of victims of the Holocaust (5.1 million in his conservative estimate), and given more or less reliable assessments about the number of Jews who died of general privation in the ghettos, who were executed in open-air shootings, and who died in other extermination and concentration camps, the total number of Auschwitz victims could not have been more than 1 million.[76]

The advent of Solidarity and the election of the Pole Karol Wojtyla as Pope John Paul II (1978) changed the intellectual climate in Poland. While the government was still committed to the official figure of 4 million victims, Dr. Piper of the Auschwitz Museum, who had been banned until then from researching the issue, began to focus his attention on the question of how many people had died in the camp. A catalyst for his research were new figures produced in France by Georges Wellers, who had come to the conclusion that 1,613,455 persons had been deported to Auschwitz (of whom 1,433,405 were Jews) and that 1,471,595 of them had died (of whom 1,352,980 were Jews).

Piper brought his work to a first completion in 1986. Given the fact that he largely endorsed the figures that had been proposed in the West by Reitlinger and Hilberg, he decided to proceed carefully—a smart move considering that Poland was under military rule in the mid-1980s. He first subjected his conclusions to a process of internal review within the museum and then to a thorough external review by the leading Polish research institute on the Nazi era, the Main Commission for the Investigation of Nazi Crimes in Poland. In 1990, after endorsement of his findings (and with the first post-communist government in power), Piper made his new estimate of 1.1 million victims known to the international community. This figure has been endorsed by all serious, professional historians who have studied the complex history of Auschwitz in some detail, by the Holocaust research institute at Yad Vashem in Jerusalem, and by the United States Holocaust Memorial Museum in Washington, D.C.[77]

When he began his work, Piper realized that the remaining papers of the camp administration, which the SS had largely destroyed before they abandoned the camp, would provide little help in establishing the total number of people deported to and killed in the camp. All the deportees who had been selected for the gas chambers on arrival had never been registered as inmates, so no administrative record about them within the camp had ever existed except for reports made by the head of the labor allocation of the inmates to his superiors in Berlin, stating that of such-and-such transport that contained so many deportees a certain number had been selected as "fit for work," while the rest, judged to be "unfit for work," had been subjected to "Special Treatment" ("*wurden sonderbehandelt*") or had been "specially lodged" ("*gesondert untergebracht*")—an obvious euphemism for killing as, first, there was no accommodation in the camp to provide "special lodging" for those declared "unfit for work," and second, with one exception, these people subsequently disappeared without a trace. Three such reports survive. One is a telegram of February 20, 1943, that concerns three transports from Theresienstadt which arrived on January 21, 24, and 27, 1943. These transports counted a total of 5,022 Jewish men, women, and children. Of these, 930 (614 men and 316 women) were selected for labor allocation; the rest (4,092 people) were determined to be "unfit for work" and were "lodged separately" ("*gesondert untergebracht*"). The second is a telegram of March 8, 1943, that concerns three transports from Berlin and Breslau which had arrived on March 5 and 7. They counted a total of 3,223 Jews. Of these, 1,324 (973 men and 351 women) were selected for work, the rest (306 men and 1,593 women and children) were "treated specially" ("*wurden sonderbehandelt*"). A final telegram of March 15, 1943, concerns a transport from Berlin of 964 Jews. Of these, 365 were selected for work, and the remaining 126 men and 473 children were "specially lodged" ("*gesondert untergebracht*"). There is no record in the Auschwitz archives about any special accommodation for those who were to be "specially lodged" after having been determined to be "unfit for work" at a selection.[78] According to Pery Broad of the Political Department of Auschwitz, similar reports were sent by his department to Eichmann at the nerve center of the whole operation to kill the Jews: the Reich Security Main Office. None of these survive. As we have seen above, Broad declared that the Political Department was under instruction to destroy all records immediately after the numbers had been dispatched to Berlin.[79]

The one exception to the general rule that those arriving Jews judged "unfit for work" were killed without being admitted to the camp was the admission without selection of 10,000 Theresienstadt Jews in the so-called family camp. Created in subsection BIIb of Birkenau, the family camp was created in September 1943; its inmates included old people and children. The purpose of the family camp was to produce a paper trail to refute reports that those taken to Auschwitz were killed. During Red Cross visits to Theresienstadt, the postmarked messages of people who had been sent six months earlier to Auschwitz were given to the delegates to counter rumors that Auschwitz was an extermination camp. These inmates were also kept alive because some Red Cross delegates to Theresienstadt had mentioned their wish to visit these people in Auschwitz. When the SS proved able to convince the delegates of a Red Cross visit to Theresienstadt on June 23, 1944, that no transports had left the ghetto and that "Hitler's gift to the Jews" was indeed a permanent abode and not a transit point to Auschwitz, the delegation deemed that there was no need to visit Auschwitz. Subsequently, the SS liquidated the family camp in Birkenau, killing the inmates. The circumstances that led to the creation and destruction of the family camp—the only place in Auschwitz where inmates who could have been considered unfit for work (if they had been selected) were lodged—were unique, and they cannot be used to explain the references to "special lodging" for those declared "unfit for work" after the selection at arrival in Auschwitz.[81]

Piper also decided not to use the estimates from eyewitnesses of the number of people murdered. With one exception—Kommandant Rudolf Höss—none of the German personnel who confessed after the war and none of the survivors of the camp who had belonged to the resistance organization within the camp, worked in administrative offices, or slaved as Sonderkommandos in the crematoria had been in a position to gather sufficient aggregate data over the whole period of the camp's history to establish a credible figure.

Piper also discarded the early attempts by Soviet and Polish forensic investigators in 1945 to establish the total number of victims on the basis of the incineration capacity of the crematoria. As we have seen, the experts had decided that over the period of their existence, the crematoria could have incinerated up to 5,121,000 corpses. To be on the safe side, they had assumed that the crematoria had operated at four-fifths capacity, and therefore they finally assumed a number of 4 million. But Piper knew that the investigators had probably overestimated the incineration capacity of the crematoria, because he had in his possession a German wartime document that made clear that the official incineration capacity of Crematorium 1 had been 340 corpses per day (or 10,200 corpses per month), while Crematoria 2 and 3 had an official daily cremation capacity of 1,440 each (or 43,200 per month each) and Crematoria 4 and 5 had an official daily cremation capacity of 768 each (or 23,040 per month each).[81] After multiplying the monthly incineration rates of the crematoria with the number of months each had been in operation, Piper knew that the maximum number of corpses that could have been incinerated would have been 2.6 million, or half the Soviet estimate. However, given the fact that the crematoria had been idle for sometimes considerable time, Piper concluded that it would be difficult to reach conclusions on that basis alone.

The best approach, so he argued, was to follow Nachman Blumental's method and proceed on the basis of research on the numbers of people who had been deported from the various countries to Auschwitz. Analysis of the transports had been the basis for Reitlinger's guesstimate that some 900,000 people had died in the camp and Wellers's conclusion that 1,471,595 people had died in Auschwitz. Yet Piper was skeptical of Wellers's figures. Wellers, so he argued, had used some arbitrary premises, had not considered data of great importance, and had combined approximate figures with precise numbers. Failing to take into account transfers of inmates to other camps, inmates who had been released, and inmates who had escaped, he had underestimated the number of survivors by 80,000. Added to that, Wellers had overestimated the number of deportees to Auschwitz by around 320,000 people, chiefly by overcalculating the number of Polish Jews brought to the camp (622,935 instead of 300,000).[82]

On the basis of archival research done by scholars in various countries, especially the three-decade-long project known in the Auschwitz archive as the "Kalendarium," which was undertaken by the Polish scholar Danuta Czech, Piper was able to come to an estimate of the number of Jews deported to Auschwitz. The Kalendarium—a day-by-day, fully annotated chronicle of the history of the camp—is a massive reference work which has been the core of the long-term research policy of the Auschwitz-Birkenau State Museum since 1956. Early installments of the Kalendarium were published in the late 1950s and early 1960s. Work continued throughout the 1960s, 1970s, and 1980s, with constant refinements as more source material became available. Finally, in 1989, the German publishing house Rowohlt published the massive German edition of the Kalendarium, followed a year later by the English-language edition entitled *Auschwitz Chronicle: 1939–1945*.[83] This work includes, after 12 pages of introductory remarks, 805 pages chronicling almost every day of the camp's operation until its liberation on January 27, 1945. Added to that are 19 pages with short biographies of the major perpetrators, a 4-page glossary, and an 8-page bibliography.

A typical entry, randomly chosen, reads as follows:

November 14 [1942]

Prisoner No. 69656 is shot at 5:40 A.M. by the SS sentry on duty at Watchtower B of the main camp "while escaping."

The standby squad is ordered to the unloading ramp at 1:45 A.M. to take charge of a transport.

2,500 Jewish men, women and children arrive with an RSHA transport from the ghetto of the Zichenau District. After the selection, 633 men and 135 women are admitted to the camp and receive Nos. 74745–75377 and 24524–24658. The remaining 1,732 are killed in the gas chambers.

1,500 Jewish men, women and children arrive with an RSHA transport from the ghetto in the Bialystok District. After the selection, 282 men and 379 women are admitted to the camp and receive Nos. 75378–75659 and 24659–25037. The remaining 839 deportees are killed in the gas chambers.

71 male and two female prisoners sent to the camp by the Sipo and SD for the Krakow District receive Nos. 75660–75730, 25038, and 25039.

The SS Camp Doctor makes a selection in the prisoners' infirmary. He selects 110 prisoners, who are taken to Birkenau and killed in the gas chambers.[84]

The Kalendarium must be regarded as the basis of any research into the history of deportations to Auschwitz, but it must be pointed out that it is not perfect. Especially with regard to the final liquidation of the Lodz ghetto and the subsequent deportation of its remaining population to Auschwitz, the absence of a clear indication of the size of eleven of the twelve listed transports is troublesome. The transport of September 18, 1944, had a size of 2,500 deportees. If this was a typical transport, this would mean that the ten listed transports account for a total of 25,000 deportees. However, the Statistical Office of Lodz shows that in August and September, 73,563 Jews were deported from Lodz; most of them were sent to Auschwitz. This means that all records of a maximum of twenty transports (some 50,000 people) are lost, at least in the account of the Kalendarium. This "disappearance" of up to twenty transports seems, in my opinion, to be the single greatest anomaly in the Kalendarium.

Using both the Kalendarium and the research done by historians in various countries on the precise number of Jews of each national group deported—in the case of France, the total number of victims was established by Jacob Letschinsky in early 1947;[85] in the case of the Netherlands, all deportation lists were found intact and included in the Parliamentary Report on the German occupation, and so on—Piper was able to come to precise estimates of deportations to Auschwitz of Jews from the following national groups (rounded up or down to the next thousand for all numbers larger than 10,000):

(i) France: 71 transports between March 27, 1944 and August 22, 1944; transport lists total to a number of some 69,000 deportees;

(ii) The Netherlands: 68 transports between July 15, 1942 and September 3, 1944; transport lists total to a number of 60,000 deportees;

(iii) Greece: 22 transports between March 20, 1943 and August 16, 1944; railway tickets show the deportation of some 49,000 Jews from Saloniki to Auschwitz, and transport lists show the deportation of another 6,000 Jews from Athens and Corfu to Auschwitz;

(iv) Bohemia and Moravia: 24 transports between October 26, 1942 and October 28, 1944; transport lists total a number of some 46,000 deportees;

(v) Slovakia: 19 transports between March 26, 1942 and October 20, 1942; various other transports in the fall of 1944; transport lists total a number of some 27,000 deportees;

(vi) Belgium: 27 transports between August 4, 1942 and July 31, 1944; transport lists total a number of some 25,000 deportees;

(vii) Italy: 13 transports between October 18, 1943 and October 24, 1944; transport lists total a number of some 7,500 deportees;

(viii) Norway: 2 transports between December 1, 1942 and February 2, 1943; transport lists total a number of 700 deportees.

This brings a subtotal of some 290,000 deportees based on relatively straightforward archival information. All the deportees were either killed on arrival, and therefore not registered, or admitted to the camp and registered.

The figures concerning the Jews from various other countries demanded more involved analysis. In one case, Hungary, there are precise figures for the number of deportees, but a significant number of those not killed on arrival were *not* admitted or registered in the camp. These so-called *Durchgangsjuden* (transit Jews) were housed temporarily before being dispatched to concentration camps in the Reich.

(ix) Hungary: according to a telegram dated July 11, 1944, sent by the German ambassador in Budapest to the Foreign Ministry in Berlin, a total of 437,402 (438,000) Jews were deported to Auschwitz. The total number of transports was 148. Of the 438,000 Jews, as much as 25,000 could have been qualified as *Durchgangsjuden.*

This brings a revised subtotal of 728,000 deportees—all Jews—from nine countries. In all the foregoing cases, Piper's numbers came close to those of Wellers.

Finally there are the countries for which the data, for various reasons, proved less straightforward, or for which, at one point or another, there has been substantial disagreement between scholars.

(x) Poland: there is relatively reliable information, based on records kept by the camp resistance movement, about the number of regular transports with Polish Jews (except those from Lodz) that arrived in Auschwitz between May 5, 1942 and August 18, 1944. These 142 regular transports averaged some 1,500 people each; three had as many as 5,000 people (June 1942 from Bielsko-Biala, August 1942 from Bendzin, September 1943 from Tarnow), three had more than 4,000 people (June 1942 and January 1943 from Lomza, November 1943 from Szebnie), and thirteen transports had between 3,000 and 4,000 people. The usual size of Polish transports was either 1,000 or 2,000 people. Thirty-six transports counted less than 1,000 people. The total number of deportees from these transports were some 221,000 people. Added to this number should be the transports that liquidated the Lodz ghetto in August and September 1944. Of these, ten transports are listed. In July 1944, the ghetto counted a little below 74,000 people. By the end of September there were none. Most of the transports went to Auschwitz. Hence, the total number of Polish Jews deported to Auschwitz was between 280,000 and 290,000. Piper rounded this up to 300,000 people to accommodate possible discrepancies.

This round figure of 300,000 Polish Jewish deportees to Auschwitz also seems confirmed by a consideration of the fate of all the Jews of prewar Poland. Before the war, some 3.1 million Jews lived in Poland. After the Polish Campaign of 1939, the Germans gained control of some 1.8 million Polish Jews. With Operation Barbarossa, another million Polish Jews came under German control, which brings a total of 2.8 million Jews. Of these, 100,000 survived. Polish historian Czeslaw Madajczyk determined that some 200,000 Polish Jews were executed through shooting by Einsatzgruppen or police units and 500,000 died in the ghettos. Some 2 million Polish Jews were killed in the German camps. Madajczyk estimated that between 1.6 million and 1.95 million Jews were killed in Treblinka, Belzec, Sobibor, and Chelmno; Hilberg estimated the number at 1.7 million. Of these 1.7 million, 100,000 victims came from Germany, the Netherlands, and Czechoslovakia, and the rest (1.6 million) from Poland. Which leaves (2 million–1.6 million) = 400,000 Polish Jews unaccounted for at this point in our calculation. Between 50,000 and 95,000 Polish Jews were killed in Maidanek, from which one may conclude that at least 300,000 and possibly as much as 350,000 Polish Jews died in Auschwitz.

This figure is roughly half the figure of 622,935 Polish Jews assumed by Wellers.

(xi) Germany and Austria: according to research done by the German Federal Archive in Koblenz, 38,574 German Jews were killed in Auschwitz. Of these, a number had found refuge in France, Belgium and Holland before the war and were included in transports from those countries to Auschwitz. Others were first deported to Poland or Bohemia and Moravia (Theresienstadt) and were included in transports from those places. In order not to count these people twice, their number (some 15,000) must be deducted from the 38,574. The resulting figure is some 23,000 German Jews who were deported directly from Germany to Auschwitz.

(xii) Yugoslavia: the data for Yugoslav Jews are confusing. Between 60,000 and 65,000 Yugoslav Jews were killed during the war. Most of them were killed in Yugoslavia, through public executions, in pogroms, or in camps organized by Croats or Serb fascists. From some of these camps, Germans deported groups of Jews to Auschwitz—some 5,000 in total. After the Italian capitulation in 1943, the 4,000 remaining Jews in Croatia were deported to Auschwitz in May 1943. Adding in some smaller transports in 1944, Piper estimates the total number at around 10,000.

This brings a revised subtotal of 1,061,000 Jews deported to Auschwitz.

Finally, a number of Jews, some 34,000 in total, arrived in Auschwitz from other concentration camps (not including Theresienstadt or the transit camps in the various countries mentioned above). This brings a final total of 1,095,000 (1.1 million) Jews deported to Auschwitz—a figure that came close to Höss's informed assessment of 1.1 million deportees.

How many of these deportees were killed on arrival? There are precise data for the number of registered inmates. The registration numbers ran consecutively, and once a number had been issued, it was never reissued again. In total, 400,207 numbers were issued for six categories of prisoners:

a. General number system, given to gentiles and Jews (May 1940 and later): 202,499 men and 89,325 women. Total: 291,824 inmates.

b. Jews, A series (May 1944 and later): 20,000 men and 29,354 women. Total: 49,354 inmates.

c. Jews, B series (May 1944 and later): 14,897 men.

d. Reeducation prisoners: 9,193 men and 1,993 women. Total 11,186 inmates.

e. Soviet prisoners of war: 11,964. Total 11,964 inmates.

f. Romani: 10,094 men and 10,888 women. Total 20,982 inmates.

Total: 400,000 registered inmates.

Groups b and c total 64,251 Jewish inmates. On the basis of calculations that took into account the facts that virtually no Jews were registered in the camp before March 1942 and that after that date all the transports sent by the Reich Security Main Office contained exclusively Jews, Piper came to the conclusion that slightly less than half of the 291,824 inmates registered under the general number system were Jews. This brings a total of some 205,000 (64,000 + 141,000) registered Jews.

Given the facts that 1,095,000 Jews were deported to Auschwitz and 205,000 were registered as inmates in the camp, it follows that 890,000 Jews who arrived were not registered. Of these some 25,000 would have been *Durchgangsjuden,* which leads to the conclusion that 865,000 Jews were killed on arrival.

The mortality of the registered Jews is more difficult to determine. It is clear that, of the registered inmates, 190,000 were transferred to other concentration camps—most of them after the death marches of January 1945. A total of 8,000 inmates were liberated by the Red Army on January 27, 1945, some 1,500 inmates were released, and some 500 escaped. This means that some 199,500 inmates, or roughly half of all the registered inmates, are accounted for. The rest, or 200,000, must have died in the camp. According to Piper, the mortality rate for the general camp population (mainly Poles and Jews), was around 50 percent over the life of the camp—for the Soviet prisoners of war and the Romani it was much higher. As a result, Piper came to a rough estimate of 100,000 registered Jews that died in the camp. The result is that the total mortality of Jews in Auschwitz was 960,000.

Added to this number are a number of other victim groups, such as unregistered Poles sent for execution to Auschwitz by the Gestapo Summary Court, registered Polish inmates, unregistered Romani, registered Romani, unregistered Soviet prisoners of war sent for execution, registered Soviet prisoners of war, and others (Czechs, Russians, Belorussians, Ukrainians, Yugoslavs, Frenchmen, Germans, Austrians, and so on):

1. Jews: 860,000 unregistered and 100,000 registered inmates. Total 960,000 victims.

2. Poles: 10,00 unregistered and 64,000 registered inmates. Total 74,000 victims.

3. Romani: 2,000 unregistered and 19,000 registered inmates. Total 21,000 victims.

4. Soviet prisoners of war: 3,000 unregistered and 12,000 registered. Total 15,000 victims.

5. Others: 12,000 registered inmates. Total 12,000 victims.

Total: 1,082,000 victims.

Since its publication, Piper's assessment that some 1.1 million people died in Auschwitz has found only one substantial challenge. In 1993, French researcher Jean-Claude Pressac came to the substantially lower figure of around 800,000 in a 5-page appendix to his *Les Crématoires d'Auschwitz.* The major reason for Pressac's disagreement with Piper is in Pressac's belief that both the number of Hungarian and Polish Jews killed in the camp were substantially lower than Piper assumed. Pressac agreed with Piper that 438,000 Hungarian Jews were deported to Auschwitz, yet he assumed that 118,000 of them were *Durchgangsjuden* who were transferred to other camps immediately after selection.[86] Piper assumed that only 25,000 of these Hungarian Jews had been *Durchgangsjuden,* which meant that Pressac felt justified, on the basis of this assumption alone, in reducing the mortality of Auschwitz to (118,000–25,000) = 93,000 people. Pressac also assumed, on the basis of a very quick and rough calculation, that instead of 300,000, only 150,000 Polish Jews were deported to Auschwitz.[87] As a result, Pressac came to a total number of 945,200 Jews deported to Auschwitz, of whom 118,000 were *Durchgangsjuden* (Piper's number is 1.1 million, of whom 25,000 were *Durchgangsjuden*). Subtracting from that number 200,000 registered Jews, Pressac assumed that 630,000 Jews were gassed on arrival (Piper's number is 860,000). Because Pressac also assumed a lower mortality for registered inmates (130,000 instead of 200,000) while assuming the same numbers for the Soviet prisoners of war (and "forgetting" the Romani!), he arrives at a total mortality of (630,000 + 130,000 + 15,000) = 775,000 dead (or roughly 75 percent of Piper's numbers).[88]

In the German translation of *Les Crématoires d'Auschwitz,* which appeared in 1994 under the title *Die Krematorien von Auschwitz: Die Technik des Massenmordes,* Pressac changed his mind. In an 11-page appendix, he presented a substantially lower figure of *at least* between 631,000 and 711,000 dead. This new range of figures was the result of a new assumption that the number of Hungarian Jews deported to Auschwitz was substantially lower than both Piper and Pressac himself had assumed. Instead of 438,000 Hungarian Jews, Pressac now used a number of between 160,000 and 240,000.[89] As a result, Pressac came to a total number of between 667,200 and 747,200 Jews deported to Auschwitz (Piper's number is 1.1 million), and, subtracting from that number 200,000 registered Jews, Pressac assumed that between 470,000 and 550,000 Jews were gassed on arrival (Piper's number is 860,000). Because Pressac also assumed a lower mortality for registered inmates (126,000 instead of 200,000) while assuming the same numbers for the Soviet prisoners of war and the Romani, he arrives at a total mortality of between 630,000 and 710,000— or roughly between 57 and 65 percent of Piper's number.

Are Pressac's challenges to Piper's numbers to be taken seriously? Let us first consider the general credibility of his research. There is no doubt

Selection of a transport of Hungarian Jews, spring 1944. The selection is under way. The mother with the baby has been directed to the right—the direction of Crematoria 2 and 3. Courtesy Yad Vashem.

that Pressac has rendered important service to the historiography of Auschwitz through his research on the development of the gas chambers and the crematoria. Yet it is also true that, having achieved a deserved recognition through the study of one aspect of the history of Auschwitz, Pressac did not hesitate to pronounce himself, at least in my own presence, not only the ultimate expert in all matters relating to the history of Auschwitz, but the expert in all matters relating to the Holocaust. Pressac did not hesitate to make far-reaching claims on issues he had not studied, and which were beyond his judgment. His desire to "escape" the narrow perspective of his study of the gas chambers by offering his contribution to the question of the number of victims is a case in point. His lack of demographic expertise becomes clear when one considers how he radically changed his assessment of the number of people murdered in Auschwitz from one edition to the next.

As I review his arguments, it seems to me that Pressac could have a point, which he however fails to prove, when he claims that Piper was too low in his assessment of the number of Hungarian Jews who were qualified as *Durchgangsjuden* on arrival in Auschwitz. Because of the German policy during the Hungarian Action of using Auschwitz as a selection station, I have always had some problems with Piper's number—but I did not have data to prove him wrong. If Pressac were to be right, or somewhat right, on this issue, then it could be that the total number of Jewish people murdered in Auschwitz would be lower than 960,000 and that the total number of victims would be closer to 1 million than the 1.1 million people which Piper calculated.

Pressac's argument that between 150,000 and not 300,000 Polish Jews were deported to Auschwitz was, however, based on some very arbitrary observations regarding the liquidation of the ghettos of Bendin and Sosnowitz in early 1943. It is clear that in the first week of August, more than 30,000 Jews from these ghettos arrived in convoys of either 2,000 or 3,000 people in the camp and that more than 22,000 of them were killed in the gas chambers. Pressac reasoned that the average killing and incineration rate was close to 4,000 per day during this period. Theoretically, this was possible, given the fact that the official daily incineration capacity of the crematoria was 4,756 corpses.[90] Pressac believed, however, that in the first week of August the total incineration capacity of the camp was less than halved because of problems with Crematoria 2 and 5 and that as a result the camp incinerators could not have "accommodated" the (close to) 22,000 victims within the given period. Hence, Pressac assumed that because the incineration capacity of the crematoria was halved during this period, the number of victims was also half, and that therefore the number of Bendin and Sosnowitz Jews deported to Auschwitz was half—ignoring the fact that there was independent confirmation from the chief of police of Sosnowitz of the number of 30,000 deported Jews. Undeterred by this, Pressac argued that because the number of deportees was half, the size of each of the transports was half (that is 1,000 or 1,500 people per transport and not 2,000 or 3,000 people per transport) and, committing the fallacy of composition, he now assumed that all transports of Polish Jews were half of what they were supposed to have been and that therefore the total number of Polish Jews was half of the 300,000 people Piper assumed.[91] Thus, a potentially legitimate observation that during the first week of August 1943 half of the ovens were out of order led Pressac to conclude that over the whole history of the camp, only 150,000 and not 300,000 Polish Jews had been deported to the camp. And he "saved" these 150,000 Polish Jews in an argument that takes a little over a page.

I concluded my review of the scholarship on the victim count of Auschwitz with the observation that Pressac's methodology, and hence his revision of the number of Polish Jews deported to Auschwitz, could not be taken seriously, and that Piper's numbers remained the only ones supported by substantial investigation into the matter. I reviewed Piper's methodology and his conclusions in conversation with him, through study of his writings, and by considering the evidence he presented, and I felt that he had put the matter to rest.

I must admit that I had some second thoughts when I included this essay in my expert opinion. While its strategic aim was to provide an account of the scholarship that had been done, which showed Irving's statements on the victim count to have been unworthy of a serious historian, I also realized that the inclusion of this essay would expose me to the possibility of cross-examination on the matter. I did not look forward to that because I feared that Irving would easily twist the case and would argue that the inclusion of this essay demonstrated that I claimed special expertise in the matter of the victim count and that he would now expose me as something less than an expert on the number of victims. In fact, he tried this approach when he challenged my credentials at the beginning of my cross-examination, arguing that I had claimed to be an architect—which I had not—and that he had exposed me as a "pseudo architect." Yet I also realized that Irving would raise the issue of the victim count at his own peril. While he could easily get me to admit that I had not done original research in that matter, it would also open him up to the potentially fatal riposte that, as a responsible historian, I did take the scholarship of others seriously. If cross-examined on this essay, Irving would risk losing much for the prospect of little gain, and I assumed that he would try not to attract attention to it. The trial proved me right.

When I accepted the task of writing an expert opinion on Auschwitz, I was largely an Internet illiterate. I despised electronic mail, did not know what a Web site was, and was hardly in a position to learn because I was working with a 10-year-old computer that did not take kindly to the demands of Web search engines and the like. As I had agreed to enter Irving's world, I had to catch up with the electronic media. On June 17, Richard Evans informed me in an electronic message that I should have a look at Irving's Web site, because it included "correspondence" with me.[92] I was utterly surprised. I responded immediately, telling Evans that I would ask a colleague of mine to visit Irving's Web site, explaining that "my own computer is so antique that it barely does e-mail." And I added, "By the way: I never received any letter or e-mail or telephone call from Irving. So I wonder what claims he makes about our correspondence."[93] An hour later I sent Evans a follow-up report. "I have accessed Irving's site, and printed the letter which I had never seen before. Maybe he should spend money on a stamp and envelope, if he wants me to read it!"[94] During the trial it became clear that Irving had sent me a copy but addressed it incorrectly. Whatever may have happened, when I began to read the letter I was at first pleasantly surprised.

> I expect you will be familiar with my name. I have been reading your book on Auschwitz with close attention over the past few days—in fact I have made time to read it right through, from left to right. My attention was drawn to it by Dr. David Cesarani's review of it in *The Jewish Chronicle* which made it seem—I am

sure this was not Cesarani's intention!—to be a work of almost revisionist thrust!

Ninety percent of what you write is new to me—by which I refer to the mediaeval history, the architecture, and the town planning aspects of Auschwitz. What a fascinating study, and why did nobody before you think of building up to the grim centerpiece on such a broad canvas? A lot of it is familiar: the recurrent theme in your book is the prevalence over the centuries of lethal epidemics both in that marshy region and in the camps built there by the Nazis.[95]

With the last sentence, flattery turned into a remarkable exercise in misreading, misconstruction, and special pleading. For example, our book did not claim that Auschwitz was plagued over the centuries by lethal epidemics. It did mention the effect of the Black Death in 1349, which affected the whole of Europe, but that is the only attention we gave epidemics. Irving's attempt to hijack our book to support his often-repeated claim that the fear of typhus justified the building of four large crematoria in Birkenau may have been based on wishful thinking, but it was not based on the words on the page.

I was not surprised that Irving had paid particular attention to our discussion of Crematorium 1 in our epilogue:

You quote Broad on pages 301–2 describing, in a 1991 book of memoirs, the "effective gas chamber which could hold 900 people" in the main camp (i.e. Auschwitz I), but on pages 363–4 you confirm that there was never a gas chamber at Auschwitz I, and that the one shown to tourists since the war was a fake built by Polish communists.

The quote is as follows:

The morgue of the crematorium in the main camp had been transformed in September 1941 into an effective gas chamber which could hold 900 people, so there was plenty of room to kill the elderly Jews with ease. Shortly before their arrival, the SS closed off the roads and emptied the offices that had a view of the crematorium. "A sad procession walked along the streets of the camp," Pery Broad remembered after the war. "All of them had large, yellow Jewish stars on their miserable clothes. Their worn faces showed that they had suffered many a hardship."

It was not an ideal situation from the camp management perspective, Broad noted. Using the crematorium as a killing station for a transport of old people interrupted the life of the camp. Broad's superior Maximilian Grabner, who had overseen the whole operation, had even had to run a truck engine to drone out the death cries of the victims. While the Germans had felt no need to camouflage the execution of Polish hostages or resistors "duly" sentenced by a court of justice, the murder of elderly Jews was another matter. It was not a useful deterrent against resistance activities.

On pages 363–364 we wrote the following:

There have been additions to the camp the Russians found in 1945 as well as deletions, and the suppression of the prisoner reception site is matched by the reconstruction of crematorium 1 just outside the north-east perimeter of the present museum camp. With its chimney and its gas chamber, the crematorium functions as the solemn conclusion for tours through the camp. Visitors are not told that crematorium they see is largely a post-war reconstruction.

When Auschwitz was transformed into a museum after the war, the decision was taken to concentrate the history of the whole complex in one of its component parts. The infamous crematoria where the mass murders had taken place were ruins in Birkenau, two miles away. The committee felt that a crematorium was required at the end of the memorial journey, and crematorium 1 was reconstructed to speak of the history of the incinerators at Birkenau. This program of usurpation was rather detailed. A chimney, the ultimate symbol of Birkenau, was re-created; four hatched openings in the roof, as if for pouring Zyklon-B into the gas chamber below, were installed, and two of the three furnaces were rebuilt using original parts. There are no signs to explain these restitutions, they were not marked at the time, and the guides remain silent about it when they take visitors through this building that is presumed by the tourist to be the place where *it happened*.

When one compares our text to Irving's interpretation of it, it was clear that he was once again involved in a case of misconstruction. We did not "confirm that there was never a gas chamber at Auschwitz I, and that the one shown to tourists since the war was a fake built by the Polish communists." Instead, we clearly stated that the crematorium was a "reconstruction," which is a representation of a situation that had existed earlier that had disappeared. As such, a reconstruction was clearly different from a fake, which would have been a representation of a situation that had never existed. Because the chimney was "re-created" and because "two of the three furnaces were rebuilt using original parts," neither the chimney nor the furnaces were fakes either. Given the context of the sentence, and the definition in the next sentence of all postwar construction at the crematorium as "restitutions," it ought to have been clear to Irving that the clause "four hatched openings in the roof, as if for pouring Zyklon-B into the gas chamber below, were installed" also referred to an attempt to reconstruct an earlier situation.

Irving went on at length, sometimes raising a legitimate question but most often just trying to neutralize any wartime German evidence. I was irritated, but as I knew that at some future date I was to face Irving in court, I was grateful for having received valuable intelligence and decided to accepted Irving's letter as a blueprint of his strategy of cross-examination. With this in mind, I began to annotate the various points he raised. For example, Irving challenged the fact that the Germans would have been able to cremate the alleged number of victims.

Now my next point: You have signally failed to address the question of the disposal of the masses of bodies. I calculate that about ten bodies go to a cubic meter; disposing of 355,000—one such gassing spree alleged to have taken three weeks (May 14, 1944 onward)—therefore requires a pit of about 35,000 m³, which would surely have been visible on aerial photos. If they were cremated, it is an iron rule that each cadaver consumes 30–40 kilos of coke. So cremating 355,000 bodies would require some ten to fifteen thousand tons of coke. The fuel cellars in the crematoria would not hold more than about twenty tons. The real coke consumption is given from documents which show that from November 1942 to October 1943—when the crematoria were not exactly standing idle, according to your book and your source, Danuta Czech—a total of 760 tons of coke were delivered to the crematoria, enough to dispose of up to 25,000 cadavers, which is well within the figures assessed by revisionists.

Considering this, I wrote the following "Note To Self."

How Many Bodies Could Be Incinerated with 760 Tons of Coke in the Auschwitz Crematoria?

On 12 March 1943, the (civilian) engineer Rudolf Jährling wrote and signed the document in which he calculated the coke use of Crematoria 2 to 5, which were still under construction.

In 12 hours, Crematoria 2 and 3 were to use 4,200 kg coke each under normal circumstances, but when they were in constant use, this was to drop to 2,800 kg coke each. In 12 hours, Crematoria 4 and 5 were to use 932 kg each. Remarkably enough, the sum total of 2,800 + 2,800 + 932 + 932 was, according to Jährling, 8,264 kg coke (instead of 7,464 kg coke).

SS architect Karl Bischoff, who countersigned the estimate, did not notice the mistake in Jährling's calculation. But someone did, and five days after the original calculation, on March 17, 1943, Jährling wrote and signed a second document in which he recalculated the coke use of Crematoria 2 to 5. The numbers for Crematoria 2 and 3 remained unchanged: In 12 hours, Crematoria 2 and 3 were to use 4,200 kg coke each under normal circumstances, but when in constant use, this was to drop to 2,800 kg coke each. But the numbers for Crematoria 4 and 5 were different this time: in 12 hours, Crematoria 4 and 5 were to use 1,120 kg each (instead of 932 kg each). As a result, Crematoria 2 to 5 would use 7,840 kg coke in 12 hours, or 654.3 kg per hour when in constant use. The capacity of the crematoria was calculated on a 24-hour basis as being 1,440 for Crematoria 2 and 3 and 756 for Crematoria 4 and 5, or ([1,440 + 1,440 + 756 + 756]/24) = 183 corpses per hour. This implies that, according to Jährling, on average one needs (654.3/183) = 3.5 kg coke to incinerate one corpse.

As coke delivery in 1943 was around 844 tons, this would have allowed for the incineration of 241,000 bodies. According to Piper's calculations based on transport lists, around 250,000 people died in Auschwitz in 1943.

As I predicted, Irving turned to the issue of coke consumption during cross-examination. My note proved good preparation.

In court he also followed up on a suggestion made in his letter that the four great crematoria planned in 1942 and completed in 1943 could be explained as a response to the fear of typhus. This suggestion made me create the following note.

Does the Fear of Typhus Justify the Construction of Crematoria 2–5?

The number of dead from typhus was great in 1942, but it pales in comparison with the incineration capacity of the crematoria. Of the 68,864 death entries in the Auschwitz death books, only 1,637 are listed as caused

Bftgb.: 34757 /43/Jä/Lm   Auschwitz, am 12.3.1943

Aktenvermerk

Betr.: Schätzung des Koksverbrauches für Krematorium II KGL
nach Angaben der Fa. Topf u. Söhne (Erbauer der Öfen)
vom 11.3.43.

10 Feuerungen = 350 kg/stdl.
in 12 Std. = 12 . 350 = 4 200 kg, 2 Krematorien demnach 8 400 kg.

Bei Dauerbetrieb vermindert sich diese Menge wesentlich, sodass
mit 2/3 der Menge gerechnet werden kann. Für Krematorium II u.
III demnach Verbrauch in 12 Stunden $\frac{350 \cdot 12}{3 \cdot 2}$ = 2800 . 2 = 5600 kg.

– – – – – – – – – – –

Krematorium IV + V:

mit je 4 Feuerungen = 8 Feuerungen zusammen =
$\frac{350 \cdot 4}{3 \cdot 2}$ = 932 . 2 = 1864 kg in 12 Stunden.

– – – – – – – – – – –

Krematorium II   = 2 800 kg
"   III = 2 800 "
"   IV = 932 "
"   V = 932 "

zus.   8 264 kg in 12 Stunden

– – – – – – – – – – –

Dies sind Spitzenleistungen! Ein Jahresbedarf lässt sich nicht
angeben, da vorher nicht bekannt ist, wieviel Stunden bezw. Tage
geheizt werden muss.

Jährling

Verteiler
2 Verwaltung KL
2 Sachbearbeiter
1 Registr. BW 30 KGL

Jährling's first calculation of coke use in the Birkenau crematoria, March 12, 1943. Collection Zentralbauleitung, File BW 30/34, page 68. Courtesy Auschwitz-Birkenau State Museum, Oswiecim.

Bftgb.: 24 757/43/Jä/Lm   Auschwitz, am 17.3.1943

A k t e n v e r m e r k

Betr.: Schätzung des Koksverbrauches für Krematorium II KGL
nach Angaben der Fa. Topf u. Söhne (Erbauer der Öfen)
vom 11.3.43.

10 Feuerungen = 350 kg/stdl.

in 12 Std. = 12 . 350 = 4 200 kg. 2 Krematorien demnach 8 400 kg.

Bei Dauerbetrieb vermindert sich diese Menge wesentlich, sodass
mit 2/3 der Menge gerechnet werden kann. Für Krematorium II u.
III demnach Verbrauch in 12 Stunden = $\frac{350 \cdot 12}{3}$. 2 = 2800 . 2 = $\frac{5600}{kg.}$

- - - - - - - - - - - - - - - - - -

Krematorium IV + V:

mit je 4 Feuerungen = 8 Feuerungen zusammen =

$\frac{35 \cdot 4 \cdot 12}{3}$. 2 = 1120 . 2 = 2240 kg in 12 Stunden (1 Tagesbet.)

- - - - - - - - - - - - - - - - -

Krematorium II = 2 800 kg
"   III = 2 800 "
"   IV = 1 120 "
"   V   = 1 120 "

zus. = 7 840 kg in 12 Stdt.(1 Tagesbetr.)

- - - - - - - - - - - - - - - -

Dies sind Spitzenleistungen! Ein Jahresbedarf lässt sich nicht
angeben, da vorher nicht bekannt ist, wieviel Stunden bezw. Tage
geheizt werden muss.

Verteiler:
2 Verwaltung KL
2 Sachbearbeiter
1 Registr. BW 30 KGL

Jährling's second calculation of coke use in the Birkenau crematoria, March 17, 1943. Collection Zentralbauleitung, File BW 30/34, page 54. Courtesy Auschwitz-Birkenau State Museum, Oswiecim.

by typhus. Of course, most of the causes of death listed are fictitious, but still one wonders why so few deaths were ascribed to typhus if typhus was to be the official justification for building the four new crematoria, which had together a daily capacity of 4,392 corpses.

The Auschwitz death books record that the total mortality of the registered prisoners during the worst months of the 1942 typhus epidemic was as follows:

July 1942:	4,345 inmates
Aug 1942:	8,507 inmates
Sept 1942:	7,199 inmates
Oct 1942:	4,492 inmates

With a daily capacity of 4,392, Crematoria 2–5 would take two days to incinerate the inmates who died in the month of August 1942, the peak of the typhus epidemic. At that time, Auschwitz had a size of 24,000 inmates. In other words, mortality of registered inmates in August 1942 was 18.3 percent. For a short time in August 1942, Auschwitz was planned to have a size of 200,000 inmates. If we assume, for the sake of argument, that the crematoria had been designed to deal with a monthly mortality of 18 percent of 200,000 inmates (which assumes that the designers of the camp did not think themselves capable of improving on the catastrophic hygienic conditions in the camp), they should have had a capacity of 36,000 corpses per month. Crematoria 2–5, however, had a monthly capacity of 131,760 corpses, or more than 3.5 times the capacity needed to address the August 1942 mortality figure in a setting of 200,000 inmates. By September 1942, the projected size of the camp had been reduced, but all the crematoria continued to be built. [N.B.: In fact, I made a mistake in this note: while Birkenau was projected to have a size of 200,000 inmates, I had forgotten to add Auschwitz I, with another 30,000. This changed the figures some-what: a monthly mortality of 18 percent of 230,000 would have produced 41,400 corpses per month, which meant that the crematoria had 3.2 times the capacity needed. Note added July 4, 2000.]

Responding to Irving's challenge gave me a taste of what was to come, but it also distracted from the immediate task at hand, to write an account of what evidence existed to support the thesis that Auschwitz had been an extermination camp and in what ways negationists from Rassinier on had chosen to either ignore, misconstrue, or falsify that evidence. I had to turn away from Irving and his challenges. I was very aware that his cross-examination of me would have only one purpose: to destroy the authority of my report. And so I began to create a text which, following the principles of battleship design, could if necessary absorb heavy punishment in its presentation of the case for Auschwitz and in the end deliver a decisive blow in its case against the negationists.

As I researched the main issues to be included in my report—the evidence for Auschwitz and the evidence for the corrupt methods of the negationists when they challenged the history of Auschwitz—I wrote a number of other smaller essays on it, some of which were included in the final report. One of these essays was my attempt to think through the thesis that Irving was right when he suggested, for example at the press conference to celebrate the launch of the so-called Leuchter Report, that the gas chambers of Auschwitz, Treblinka, and Majdanek were a piece of atrocity propaganda. As we saw in the last chapter, the flyer that announced the press conference claimed that the gas chambers were "the brainchild of Britain's brilliant wartime Psychological Warfare Executive."[96] In his foreword to the Leuchter Report, Irving added to his claim that the gas chamber story had been manufactured by the Psychological Warfare Executive the observation that "as late as August 1943 the head of the PWE minuted the Cabinet secretly that despite the stories they were putting out, there was not the slightest evidence that such contraptions existed, and he continued with a warning that stories from Jewish sources in this connection were particularly suspect."[97] Asked about this at the press conference, Irving discussed this issue in some detail, changing his accusation against the Psychological Warfare Executive insofar as he dropped the explicit charge that the accounts of mass gassings of Jews were instances of atrocity propaganda manufactured by a British government agency to bolster morale to replace it with the thesis that propagandists presented unproven rumors about the gas chambers as proven facts.

> I think that, as I have said often before, that in wartime governments produce propaganda. The propaganda flywheel starts to spin, [and] nobody at the end of the war has a motive to stop the propaganda flywheel spinning. It should be the job of the historians, but the historians have become themselves part of the propaganda process. Now we find in the British archives a lot of evidence that we willingly propagated the gas chamber story because it was a useful propaganda line for us to take. However it was based on such tenuous evidence, as you can see from the document in the press pack, that the people who themselves spread the lie then urged that Her Majesty's Government should not even attach their name because for fear that eventually it should be shown up.[98]

A year later, speaking in Germany, Irving changed his tune once again when he claimed that the head of the Psychological Warfare Executive, Victor Cavendish-Bentinck, had admitted in a minute written in August 1943 that "the whole assertion of German extermination measures against Jews with gas chambers and so on have no foundation in fact and are merely a lie that we have spread against the Germans."[99]

Curious about the evidence for Irving's charge, I obtained from the Public Record Office a copy of Foreign Office file 371/34551, which contained Cavendish-Bentinck's note. It became clear that his note was written in response to two telegrams the Foreign Office had sent to the British Embassy in Moscow concerning a forthcoming Allied public declaration about German atrocities in occupied Poland. The first telegram, sent at 4:25 P.M., explained the context:

> Polish Government recently expressed to us their concern over extension of German campaign of mass murder and deportation against population of Poland and asked that His Majesty's Government should issue a declaration warning the Germans of the consequences of such action.[100]

The German action referred to was a systematic program of ethnic cleansing taking place in the Zamosc area.

A second telegram, sent an hour later, gave more specific information.

> Trustworthy information has reached His Majesty's Government in the United Kingdom regarding crimes committed by the German invaders against the population of Poland. Since the autumn of 1942 a belt of territory extending from the province of Bialystok southwards along the line of the River Bug has been sys-

tematically emptied of its inhabitants. In July 1943 these measures were extended to practically the whole of the province of Lublin, where hundreds of thousands of persons have been deported from their homes or exterminated.

These measures are being carried out with the utmost brutality. Many of the victims are killed on the spot. The rest are segregated. Men from fourteen to fifty are taken away to work for Germany. Some children are killed on the spot, others are separated from their parents and either sent to Germany to be brought up as Germans or sold to German settlers or despatched with the women and old men to concentration camps, where they are now being systematically put to death in gas chambers.[101]

The next day Cavendish-Bentinck wrote a comment on the second telegram. This text was what Irving identified as the crucial piece of evidence from which one could extrapolate that the killing of Jews in the gas chambers had been conceived as a piece of British atrocity propaganda.

In my opinion it is incorrect to describe Polish information regarding German atrocities as "trustworthy." The Poles, and to a far greater extent the Jews, tend to exaggerate German atrocities in order to stoke us up. They seem to have succeeded.

Mr. Allen and myself have both followed German atrocities quite closely. I do not believe that there is any evidence which would be accepted in a Law Court that *Polish* children have been killed on the spot by Germans when their parents were being deported to work in Germany, nor that *Polish* children have been sold to German settlers. As regarding putting Poles to death in gas chambers, I do not believe that there is any evidence that this has been done. There have been many stories to this effect, and we have played them up in P.W.E. rumours without believing that they had any foundation. At any rate there is far less evidence than exists for the mass murder of Polish officers by the Russians at Katyn. On the other hand we do know that the Germans are out to destroy Jews of any age unless they are fit for manual labour.

I think that we weaken our case against the Germans by publicly giving credence to atrocity stories for which we have no evidence. These mass executions in gas chambers remind me of the stories of employment of human corpses during the last war for the manufacture of fat, which was a grotesque lie and led to the true stories of German enormities being brushed aside as being mere propaganda.[102]

After I read Cavendish-Bentinck's note, it was clear that Irving could have only come to the conclusion he did by the most dogmatic application of Faurisson's "Ajax method" to selected parts of the text. It meant, first of all, that he had to ignore the direct occasion of the minute—two telegrams dealing with the alleged atrocities of Germans against the gentile Polish population. That the Poles referred to were gentiles is clear from the information contained in the second telegram, which clearly refers to the Zamosc Action, which took place in the Lublin province from November 1942 to August 1943. The Zamosc region had been identified as a settlement area for ethnic Germans, and the violent deportation of the local population occurred under terrible conditions. In fact, many Zamosc Poles ended up in Auschwitz, a fact to which the second telegram alluded.

Cavendish-Bentinck understood well that the telegram referred to the deportation and killing of gentile Poles and not to the killing of Polish Jews—in fact, the mass murder of Polish Jewry had largely come to its successful end by August 1943. That month the Germans closed Treblinka. Sobibor had already been transformed from an extermination camp into an ordinary concentration camp, and Belzec had been closed since the Spring of 1943. These camps that had been built to liquidate Poland's Jews had done their work by August 1943. Cavendish-Bentinck took care to underline twice in his note the adjective Polish, and he made a clear distinction between his skepticism about the alleged gassing of these (gentile) Poles and his certainty about the fate of the Jews. Therefore, when he stated that he did not believe that there was evidence for the killing of Poles in gas chambers, he did not address the issue of whether there was evidence for the killing of Jews in gas chambers. And when he expressed regret that the Psychological Warfare Executive sometimes played up these rumors on the basis of "many stories" which were not necessarily believed, he only admitted that British propagandists were happy to use anything available to discredit the Germans, but he did not say that they had actually invented those stories. And while he did mention that "mass executions in gas chambers remind me of the stories of employment of human corpses during the last war for the manufacture of fat," he did not state that this association discredited those stories a priori. He only warned the government to remain careful in assessing the evidentiary value of stories about mass killings of people in gas chambers. In short, whatever the minute tells us about the skepticism of a senior British government official, it does not provide even the smallest piece of historical evidence that the whole assertion of the German extermination of Jews in gas chambers has no foundation in fact and was propaganda lie.

So much for Irving's claim that the gas chamber story belonged to a genre of official disinformation and that it originated in the Psychological Warfare Executive. Yet having demonstrated to myself that his allegation was based on a distortion and misrepresentation of one particular piece of evidence and the suppression of other pieces of relevant evidence, I felt that the issue deserved a second look. Since my days as a graduate student, I have always been fascinated by the "what if" question, or counterfactual question, as it is more appropriately known in academia, as a serious tool for historical research and not merely as a frivolous parlor game. Just at the time that I began work on my dissertation, Hugh Trevor-Roper (who would later mistakenly identify the Hitler diaries as genuine) said in his valedictory lecture as Regius Professor of History at Oxford that every historian is obliged to "restore to the past its lost uncertainties, to reopen, if only for an instant, the doors which the *fact accompli* has closed." This, so he admitted, "requires an effort of the imagination. But it is surely a necessary effort if we are to see history as a reality, and not as a convenient scheme."[103] My mentor, Dame Frances Yates, who had devoted her career as a historian to researching the so-called lost moments of history, was at the lecture. On her return, she told me about it. "Remember his call for an open history," she told me at the time.

As I explained before, when we began work on Auschwitz, Dwork and I had consciously applied to the evidence the question "What if Auschwitz had not been intended to become the 'asshole' of the world?" That question had produced a remarkable revision of our understanding of the history of the camp. I felt that Irving's charge that the Psychological Warfare Executive had invented gas chamber stories for propaganda purposes raised the question of whether such a scenario would have been even remotely plausible. Assuming that Cavendish-Bentinck and his colleagues acted according to the dictates of reason, one would have to assume that they would have gained something by spreading those stories. Would the soldiers have been braver in the field? Would the sailors have been more resilient on the Murmansk run? Would the laborers have accepted longer hours in the factories? Cavendish-Bentinck's note already suggests that atrocity propaganda was a potential boomerang: in the First World War the "grotesque lie" that the Germans used human corpses for the manufacture of fat had "led to the true stories of German enormities being brushed aside as being mere propaganda." With this statement he referred to his own reluctance, shared by his contemporaries, to believe accounts of atrocities because they knew well how they had been fooled by wild stories and outright lies a quarter-century earlier.

The source of their skepticism was Arthur Ponsonby's best-selling 1928 study *Falsehood in War-Time*. Chapter 28, entitled "The Manufacture of News," consists of only one page and offers an account of five short newspaper clippings recording the fall of Antwerp.

The Fall of Antwerp.
November 1914.

> When the fall of Antwerp got known, the church bells were rung (meaning in Germany).
>
> *Kölnische Zeitung.*

> According to the *Kölnische Zeitung,* the clergy of Antwerp were compelled to ring the church bells when the fortress was taken.
>
> *Le Matin.*

> According to what *Le Matin* has heard from Cologne, the Belgian priests who refused to ring the church bells when Antwerp was taken have been driven away from their places.
>
> *The Times.*

> According to what *The Times* has heard from Cologne via Paris, the unfortunate Belgian priests who refused to ring the church bells when Antwerp was taken have been sentenced to hard labour.
>
> *Corriére della Sera.*

> According to information to the *Corriére della Sera* from Cologne via London, it is confirmed that the barbaric conquerors of Antwerp punished the unfortunate Belgian priests for their heroic refusal to ring the church bells by hanging them as living clappers to the bells with their heads down.
>
> *Le Matin.*[104]

Remarkably enough, Ponsonby's account was based on his inability to catch the irony of an article entitled "What Can Be Made Out of a News Item" that had appeared in 1915 in the *Norddeutsche Allgemeine Zeitung*. The article was a spoof on Allied propaganda. Ponsonby read it shortly after publication and, not realizing that it was a hoax, reprinted it in Britain as a demonstration of the way rumors develop in war. To make the cycle of absurdity complete, almost a year later the same German paper carried the identical story, citing Ponsonby as authority. The German editors had forgotten that it had originally been German irony. Like many propagandists, they had succeeded in talking themselves into believing a legend of their own creation.[105]

By the end of the 1930s, Ponsonby's account of the living clappers had become the staple of textbooks, and his more general conclusions, such as that "in war-time, failure to lie is negligence, the doubting of a lie a misdemeanor, the declaration of the truth a crime,"[106] had become part and parcel of common parlance. The overall effect of the relentless exposure of the atrocity stories was, however, a general resentment of the public against those who had roused its passion, inflamed its indignation, exploited its patriotism, and desecrated its highest ideals by government-initiated concealment, subterfuge, fraud, falsehood, and trickery. Significantly, in the context of the history of Auschwitz, the most notorious symbol of the atrocity story was the gruesome account of the *Kadaververwerkungsanstalt* (corpse exploitation establishment) operated behind the front lines by the *DAVG—Deutsche Abfall-Verwertungs Geselschafft* (German Offal Utilization Company, Inc.). The author of this particular piece of atrocity propaganda, which claimed that the Germans used the corpses of their own fallen soldiers for the manufacture of soap, was Brigadier General J. V. Charteris, Chief of Intelligence of the British Army. His aim was to turn the Chinese, who revere the dead, against the Germans.[107] But the story returned to Europe, and a detailed account of the *Kadaververwerkungsanstalt* appeared in *The Times* on April 17, 1917. Its source, so the editorial introduction claimed, was a Belgian newspaper published in England, which in turn had received it from another Belgian newspaper published in neutral Holland. The article described a large factory where trains arrived full of corpses. Men wearing oilskin overalls attached the bodies to hooks connected to an endless chain.

> The bodies are transported on this endless chain into a long, narrow compartment, where they pass through a bath which disinfects them. They then go through a drying chamber, and finally are automatically carried into a digester or great cauldron, in which they are dropped by an apparatus which detaches them from the chain. In the digester they remain from six to eight hours, and are treated by steam, which breaks them up while they are slowly stirred by the machinery.
>
> From this treatment result several products. The fats are broken up into stearin, a form of tallow, and oils, which require to be redistilled before they can be used. The process of distillation is carried out by boiling the oil with carbonate of soda, and some of the by-products resulting from this are used by German soap makers. The oil distillery and refinery lie in the south-eastern corner of the works. The refined oil is sent out in small casks like those used for petroleum, and is of yellowish brown colour.[108]

It was a lie, but it was plausible, and it was not possible to completely refute it during the war. In the weeks that followed, *The Times* published many letters that seemed to corroborate the account. On April 25, the satirical magazine *Punch* included a cartoon entitled "Cannon-Fodder—and After," showing the Kaiser and a German recruit. Pointing out of a window to a factory with smoking chimneys and the signs "*Kadaververwerkungs[anstalt],*" the Kaiser tells the young man: "And don't forget that your Kaiser will find a use for you—alive or dead."[109] On April 30, the issue

CANNON-FODDER—AND AFTER.

Kaiser (*to 1917 Recruit*). "AND DON'T FORGET THAT YOUR KAISER WILL FIND A USE FOR YOU—ALIVE OR DEAD."

[At the enemy's "Establishment for the Utilisation of Corpses" the dead bodies of German soldiers are treated chemically, the chief commercial products being lubricant oils and pigs' food.]

"Cannon Fodder—and After."
Cartoon published in Punch,
April 25, 1917.

was raised in the House of Commons, but the government refused to endorse the news. In the months that followed, the account of the *Kadaververwerkungsanstalt* gained international circulation but, remarkably enough, never expanded beyond the few lines printed in *The Times*. No eyewitnesses ever appeared, nor did any report amplify the original report. By the end of the war, the story of the *Kadaververwerkungsanstalt* died, only to be revived by General Charteris in an after-dinner speech at the National Arts Club in New York. Finally, in 1928, the legend of the corpse factories was put to rest in Ponsonby's *Falsehood in War-Time*.

The long-term effect of stories that told of human clappers in Belgian bell towers or human bodies used as raw material for the production of soap was that few were prepared to be fooled once again by such a fabrication. Indeed, during the late 1930s and 1940s, most people tended to disbelieve anything that did not fit their customary, liberal view of the world. English historian Tony Kushner described this resistance in his excellent *The Holocaust and the Liberal Imagination* (1994). Before the war, German Jewish refugees were often not believed when they told what had happened to them. Dr. Ludwig Gutmann, one-time director of the Jewish hospital in Breslau, recorded that when he told his acquaintance, philosopher F. A. Lindemann, of the events of Kristallnacht, Lindemann "somewhat sneeringly interrupted me, saying 'You must not tell me atrocity legends.'"[110] And Lindemann was a staunch anti-Nazi.

During the war, reports of German atrocities were commonly interpreted as exaggerations at best. *Time* mockingly referred to news from Poland as "the 'atrocity' story of the week,"[111] and when the Polish government-in-exile published a long report of the Nazi policy of terror in German-occupied Poland in March 1940, one American editorial felt the need to warn its readers that, twenty years earlier, "a great many of the atrocity stories which were so well attested and so strenuously told, so indignantly believed and so commonly repeated, were found to be absolute fakes."[112] When the British Foreign Office received a fully corroborated account of Jewish life in German-occupied Poland in April 1940, Assistant Under-Secretary Reginald Leeper dismissed the report. "As a general rule Jews are inclined to magnify their persecutions," Leeper commented. "I remember the exaggerated stories of Jewish pogroms in Poland after the last war which, when fully examined, were found to have little substance."[113] Three years later, when the British government had become well aware of the mass extermination of Jews, senior Foreign Office officials such as Victor Cavendish-Bentinck still refused to believe what they knew.

Arthur Koestler, a Hungarian-Jewish refugee in Britain, expressed often in public his great frustration with the English unwillingness to believe the news that trickled in from Poland. "The trouble with being a contemporary in times like this," Koestler said in a broadcast talk, "is that reality beats the imagination every step. . . . For an educated Englishman it is almost easier to imagine conditions of life under King Canute on this island than conditions of life in, say, contemporary Poland."[114] In an article published in early 1944 in the *New York Times Magazine,* Koestler lamented that so very few were prepared to believe the reports of the exterminations. Nothing seemed to make a difference. "So far three million have died. It is the greatest mass-killing in recorded history; and it goes on daily, hourly, as regularly as the ticking of your watch," he told his readers. But he was unable to convince the many people he had lectured to. "You can convince them for an hour, then they shake themselves, their mental self-defence begins to work and in a week the shrug of incredulity has returned like a reflex temporarily weakened by the shock."[115]

Bill Lawrence, the *New York Times* correspondent in the Soviet Union, was one of those who remained skeptical. When, for example, Lawrence reported in the fall of 1943 on the mass killing of Jews in Babi Yar near Kiev, he employed a language not much different from that used today by more sophisticated negationists. After mentioning that "Kiev authorities asserted today that the Germans had machinegunned from 50,000 to 80,000 of Kiev's Jewish men, women and children in late September 1941," Lawrence made it absolutely clear that he regarded the claim with great skepticism. "There is little evidence in the ravine to prove or disprove the story," he wrote.[116] After the war, Lawrence showed considerable embarrassment about his skepticism, and he explained that "I grew up in the generation between the two world wars—a generation which had a natural scepticism and inherent disbelief of all wartime atrocity stories. In our most formative years, we had found out that the propagandists for the Western Allies, including our own government, had fabricated some of the most lurid tales of German behavior to arouse their people to wartime fervor."[117]

Even when the war came to an end and the Allied armies liberated the camps, there remained a great resistance to face the facts. One of the 500 diarists who kept a daily record for the English social survey organization Mass Observation wrote after the liberation of Bergen-Belsen that the revelations were beyond belief. "I have not forgotten the recent controversy over the last war atrocity stories, and to me they have always smacked of propaganda—the Germans are our enemies, therefore we must hate the Germans, so additional evidence must be given us to whip up this hatred."[118]

General Dwight D. Eisenhower made it his business to change such attitudes. Immediately after the liberation of the concentration camp at Ohrdruf he visited it, as he wrote to his superior General Marshall on April 15, "in order to be in a position to give *first-hand* evidence of these things if ever, in future, there develops a tendency to charge these allegations merely to 'propaganda.'"[119] On April 19, he cabled to Marshall the proposal that prominent members of Congress and journalists visit "one of these places where the evidence of brutality and cruelty is so overpowering as to leave no doubts in their minds about the normal practices of the Germans in these camps."[120] President Truman accepted Eisenhower's proposal, and on April 22 a plane left Washington for Weimar via Paris with six senators and six representatives. The next day a plane with a similar destination left New York. On board were eighteen prominent American journalists. Many were skeptical. Malcolm W. Bingay, editor-in-chief of the *Detroit Free Press,* admitted a month later in a meeting at the Economic Club of Detroit that he was "frankly sceptical about the atrocity charges. Having lived through the first world war, I realized too many of them had been exploded as myths and I went over in the attitude of 'being from Missouri.'"[121] Joseph Pulitzer, the publisher of the *St. Louis Post-Dispatch,* also changed his mind.

> I came here in a suspicious frame of mind, feeling that I would find that many of the terrible reports that have been printed in the United States before I left were exaggerations, and largely propaganda, comparable to reports of crucifixions and amputations of hands which followed the last war, and which subsequently proved to be untrue. It is my grim duty to report that the descriptions of the horrors of the camp, one of many which have been and which will be uncovered by the Allied armies have given less than the whole truth. They have been understatements.[122]

In the end, even the most stalwart supporters of the thesis that all the stories about the systematic extermination of the Jews had been merely atrocity propaganda had to face the facts for what they were. The American magazine the *Christian Century,* which in 1944 had still chided American newspapers for giving much attention to the discoveries made by the Soviets in Maidanek—claiming at the time that the "parallel between this story and the 'corpse factory' atrocity tale was too striking to be overlooked"[123]—had to (hesitantly) admit in 1945 that it had been wrong, and that the parallel with "the cadaver factory story of the last war" did not hold. "The evidence is too conclusive. . . . The thing is well-nigh incredible. But it happened."[124] When even the *Christian Century* admitted that it had been wrong, it seemed that the world was finally ready for the truth.

There is no historical justification for judging and dismissing the accounts of German atrocities during the Second World War within the context of the atrocity propaganda of the First World War: the attitude of the public of 1939–1945 was radically different from that of twenty-five years earlier, and it is clear that any attempt to generate the kind of propaganda symbolized by the notorious *Kadaververwerkungsanstalt* would have merely generated mockery. To understand the difference in the way people experienced these two wars, it is important to remember that the sudden, all-devouring fire of the First World War caught people, who had experienced more than a century of peace and progress, by surprise. No one could really explain why the war had come and why it ought to be fought. There was so little relationship between the trifle of Sarajevo and the cataclysm of Verdun. Tens of millions of men, coerced into the mass armies, faced incredible suffering amid a general unintelligibility of events caused by a senseless, overwhelming force. Facing death without knowing why, the demoralized and dejected men who fought in the trenches lost their self-respect. In such circumstances, values collapsed: as the individual act had become irrelevant and individual judgment impossible, the distinction between truth and lie, fiction and reality had become obsolete. Manufacturing useful lies such as the stories of the *Kadaververwerkungsanstalt* was no better or worse than the generals' practice of masking the defeat of their strategies by sacrificing extra armies in order to steal a very small local success that could be trumpeted as a major victory.

The Second World War was different. Instead of confusion, there was resolve. From the very beginning, the Allies knew that the war would be grim. "No one can predict, no one can even imagine, how this terrible war against German and Nazi aggression will run its course or how far it will spread or how long it will last," Churchill told the House of Commons on October 8, 1940—in the midst of the blitz against London. "Long, dark months of trials and tribulations lie before us. Not only great dangers, but also many misfortunes, many shortcomings, many mistakes, many disappointments will surely be our lot."[125] Fighting Hitler under the inspired leadership of men such as Churchill and Roosevelt, the Allies had no need for atrocity propaganda. In the case of England, Churchill expressed his superb and passionate historical imagination with the consciousness that his words, and those spoken by all Englishmen, would remain the object of scrutiny and judgment for many generations—"Let us therefore brace ourselves to our duties, and so bear ourselves that, if the British Empire and its Commonwealth last for a thousand years, men will still say, 'This was their finest hour.'"[126] Evoking a dramatic image of what England was and what Englishmen stood for, and giving surprisingly little attention to what Germany and the Germans had become, Churchill was able to mobilize a nation without the need to engage in the very kind of all-too-easily dismissable atrocity propaganda that the weak leaders in the First World War found necessary to employ to bolster morale. Indeed, if the caricature of the *Kadaververwerkungsanstalt* was the legacy of Allied propaganda of the First World War—a legacy that continues to embarrass—the bold and dramatic language of Churchill became the legacy of the Second World War—a language that, almost sixty years later, still never fails to inspire.

Public opinion in the Second World War was not receptive to atrocity propaganda, and this makes clear that it is highly implausible that the

Psychological Warfare Executive would have circulated invented atrocity stories that could not be backed up. It was not effective propaganda because the death camps could not be imagined. In early 1945, Theodor Adorno brought this problem into philosophical focus. He claimed that with the creation of the camps something had come to pass that had changed the whole perception of what is a lie and what is truth.

> When the National Socialists began to torture, they not only terrorized the peoples inside and outside Germany, but were the more secure from exposure the more wildly the horror increased. The implausibility of their actions made it easy to disbelieve what nobody, for the sake of precious peace, wanted to believe, while at the same time capitulating to it. Trembling voices persuade themselves that, after all, there is much exaggeration: even after the outbreak of the war, details about the concentration camps were unwanted in the English press. Every horror becomes, in the enlightened world, a horrific fairy-tale.[127]

Adorno noticed that, with the war's end, the situation that had existed before the Nazis had begun to confound truth and lies had not been restored. As lying had come to sound like truth, and truth had come to sound like lying, it had become "a labour of Sisyphus to hold on to the simplest piece of knowledge." And Adorno concluded, with melancholy: "So Hitler, of whom no-one can say whether he died or escaped, survives."[128]

In 1948, American Judge Michael A. Musmanno, who had served on the Nuremberg Military Tribunal II to hear the case against Oswald Pohl and other members of the SS Wirtschafts- und Verwaltungshauptamt (SS Economic and Administrative Main Department), concluded that, after having sat through 194 sessions of the tribunal, reviewed 1,348 different pieces of written evidence and 511 affidavits, and listened to 48 witnesses and testimonies by the defendants, the world of the death camps was still beyond comprehension. In his concurring opinion, Musmanno observed that, when writing of the extermination of the Jews, "the ink runs heavy, the words falter, and a sadness akin to a hopeless resignation enters the soul."

> How can one write about a planned and calculated killing of a human race? It is a concept so completely fantastic and so devoid of sense that one simply does not want to hear about it and is inclined to turn a deaf ear to such arrant nonsense. Barbarous tribes in the wilds of South Pacific jungles have fallen upon other tribes and destroyed their every member; in America, Indian massacres have wiped out caravans and destroyed whole settlements and communities; but that an enlightened people in the 20th century should set out to exterminate, one by one, another enlightened people, not in battle, not by frenzied mobbing, but by calculated gassing, burning, shooting, poisoning is simply blood-curdling fiction, fit companion for H. G. Wells' chimera on the invasion from Mars.
>
> Adolf Eichmann, chief of the Jewish section of the Gestapo, estimated that the Hitler-Himmler extermination policy of the Jews resulted in the liquidation of 6,000,000 Jews, of which 4,000,000 were killed in extermination institutions. The murder of 6,000,000 human beings is entirely beyond the capacity of man's imagination and one instinctively refuses to believe. But the

curtain of incredulity has lifted and the armor of incomprehensi-bility no longer protects. The evidence is in and what was utter fantasy and a mere macabre playing with numbers, is proved fact.[129]

Musmanno was right: by 1948 the evidence about the Holocaust in general, and about Auschwitz in particular, was in. In the next two chapters, we will see how, against the backdrop of a skeptical world, that evidence emerged in the three years before and the three years after the liberation of Auschwitz on January 27, 1945.

Three
Intentional Evidence

On Wednesday, January 19, 2000, during the sixth day of the Irving libel trial, Richard Rampton accused Irving of having betrayed his vocation as a historian in his quick endorsement of the Leuchter Report. "A man in your position does not enter the arena waving flags and blowing trumpets unless he has taken the trouble to verify in advance what it is that he is proposing to say, particularly when what he is proposing to say is something of great sensitivity and importance to millions of people throughout the world." Irving responded that historians cannot regard the sensitivities of people when they write history. He denied having entered arenas blowing trumpets and waving flags. "I am not a Holocaust historian," he said. "I am a Hitler historian." This prompted Rampton to ask "Why do you not keep your mouth shut about the Holocaust?"[1]

Later that day, Rampton repeated his charge when Justice Gray asked him to summarize his case on Auschwitz, which was to be the subject of Irving's cross-examination the next day. Rampton replied that he did not intend to prove that Auschwitz had homicidal gas chambers. His main aim was to demonstrate that Irving, "on the back of a piece of so-called research which is not worth the paper it is written on jumped up and said he was perfectly certain that there were never any gas chambers at Auschwitz." Rampton added that Irving had repeated that statement in meetings attended by people who were likely to be anti-Semites, which had given his pronouncements on Auschwitz a political dimension. "As an insight into Mr Irving's credentials as a so-called historian, it is extremely illuminating," Rampton stated, adding "and that is the whole of my argument."[2] It was not original, to be sure. Twenty-three years earlier Hugh Trevor-Roper had similarly charged that, motivated with a desire to exonerate Hitler, Irving was prone to build large conclusions based on minimal evidence, ignoring more substantial evidence against it.[3] More to the point, perhaps, Rampton's summary of the defendants' case on Auschwitz paraphrased Lipstadt's accusation that Irving was prepared to bend historical evidence "until it conforms with his ideological leanings and political agenda." The case for Auschwitz was, therefore, central to the defendant's plea of justification.

Two years before Rampton spoke those words in court, I had adopted Trevor-Roper's analysis of the twofold character of Irving's distortion as the foundation of my own report. I have shown how on the basis of a misrepresentation of the Auschwitz death books Irving was quite prepared to make wild and unsubstantiated guesses about the number of victims of Auschwitz without considering Piper's careful scholarship. In the case of Irving's involvement with the Auschwitz gas chambers, the "small but dubious particle of evidence" on which he seized as the basis for his pronouncements was the Leuchter Report. The more substantial evidence he had overlooked was the historical record established on the basis of both eyewitness and documentary evidence.

As I began preparing my presentation of the Auschwitz evidence, I was guided by an item I found on Irving's Web site. It contained what appeared to be a scholarly piece of some 71 pages with 449 endnotes written by a person who identified him/herself as "Samuel Crowell." Subsequent investigation suggests that the author is male, a graduate-school dropout who is employed as a teacher at a middle school in the United States. Entitled "The Gas Chamber of Sherlock Holmes: An Attempt at a Literary Analysis of the Holocaust Gassing Claim," the article promised "to deliberately review the gassing claim, with the object, not to prove that gassings did or did not take place, but rather investigate whether a plausible basis for revisionist doubt exists."[4] Nothing could be more reasonable, at least to the uninformed visitor of this site. And indeed, at first I was pleasantly surprised to find what appeared to be literary analysis. Crowell's model was Elaine Showalter's study *Hystories: Hysterical Epidemics and Modern Media* (1997), which explains claims of alien abduction, chronic fatigue syndrome, recovered memory, the Gulf War syndrome, and multiple personality disorder as psychogenic epidemics in which the narrative similarity between independent accounts of, for example, instances of alien abduction, does not mean that these events actually took place.

> Literary critics . . . realize that similarities between two stories do not mean that they mirror a common reality, or even that the writers have read each other's texts. Like all narratives, hystories have their own conventions, stereotypes, and structures. Writers inherit common themes, structures, characters, and images; critics call these common elements *intertextuality*. We need not assume that patients are either describing an organic disorder or else lying when they present similar narratives of symptoms. Instead, patients learn about diseases from the media, unconsciously develop the symptoms, and then attract media attention in an endless cycle. The human imagination is not infinite, and we

are all bombarded by these plot lines every day. Inevitably, we all live out the social stories of our time.[5]

Taking Showalter as his model, Crowell had embarked on a study of the emergence of the gassings claims from early 1942 through the end of the Nuremberg and Auschwitz Trials in 1947.[6] Identifying the story elements of "the gassing claim story," and revealing their "textual links" to other texts, Crowell argued that the gassing claim, "featuring a shower-gas-burning sequence," could have arisen spontaneously in response to ignorance of East European Jews with delousing procedures, the creation of gas-proof air-raid shelters, and anxiety about cremation as a means of disposal of the dead. Rejecting earlier negationist claims that the stories about gas chambers were the result of a conspiracy, Crowell blamed the emergence of the gassing claim on the prevailing "social and cultural climate" of the 1930s and 1940s, a little "solicitous fraud," and a general "willingness to believe the worst about one's enemies."[7] In other words, the gassing claim was a classic example of the power of intertextuality to create a massive "hystory."

> The gassing claim of the Holocaust derives from a complex of delusion and censorship. We are now in a position to encapsulate how both tendencies reinforced each the other. The gassing legend seemed to have been endemic in Europe for several years before the outbreak of World War Two. At that time, and in conjunction with the National Socialist euthanasia program, conducted in secret, the rumor of gassing developed more widely. Once the Germans began large-scale deportations in the Spring of 1942, the typical disinfection rumors arose, as they had in previous decades, but this time they tended to focus on the gassing claim. These rumors passed through the BBC, which gave the rumors authority, and in turn created the feedback loop for their further development. In this respect the growth of the gassing rumors should be distinguished from such phenomena as the *War of the Worlds* panic, because in the latter case official denunciation of the claim was immediate. But in this case there were no official pronouncements about the extermination rumors at all, but simply the repetition of these claims.
>
> The combination of frightful epidemic scenes in the Western camps combined with a series of Soviet Special Commissions, including the Auschwitz report, set the seal on the story, providing the canonical Holocaust, which, in its function was scarcely distinguishable from one of the manuals of interrogation from the days of the great witch hunts or the Inquisition. The evolution of the Canon continued at the postwar trials, where the presentation on the alleged mass gassings and exterminations was in the hands of a state which had already demonstrated its schizophrenic tendencies in its approach to handling various internal crises while following a path of rapid and forced industrialization and modernization in the previous two decades. The residue of such rapid change is furthermore well understood to be anomie, disorientation, and other social pathologies, and these also profoundly affected the Jews of eastern Europe, who were themselves not only subject to almost continuous persecution during this time but also to the disorientation and social disintegration characteristic of grand socioeconomic transformations.

This is the context in which the claim of mass gassing and extermination arose and found its fulfilment.[8]

Crowell's attempt to explain the origin and development of "the gassing claim" brought negationist discourse to a new level. It had begun to redress the single largest liability of the negationists: their inability to produce, in forty years of effort, a plausible counter-narrative to the inherited history of the Holocaust or, more particularly, the history of Auschwitz. Claiming to be revisionist historians, they had yet to produce a history that offered a credible, "revised" explanation of the events in question. Until Crowell's piece appeared, Rassinier and his disciples had an exclusively nihilist agenda—to attack the inherited account on the unproven assumption of some general conspiracy. But they were unable, or unwilling, to produce one product of serious revisionist historiography that reconstructed the origin and development of this conspiracy and why and how it seized on, of all places, Auschwitz as the fulcrum of its effort to hoodwink both gentiles and Jews, to leverage the international community in general, and to defraud the Germans and the Arabs in particular. Crowell's essay offered at least the appearance of a plausible narrative that engaged with issues of relevancy and causation.

Given the fact that Irving had deemed Crowell's essay of sufficient importance to make it accessible to anyone visiting his Web site, I considered it likely that either directly or indirectly Crowell's (mis)reading of the evidence would inform Irving's strategy during the trial and direct whatever torpedoes he would fire at the "battleship Auschwitz." Hence it seemed to make sense to organize my presentation of the evidence in a course roughly parallel to Crowell's argument, beginning with the emergence of the first information about the use of Auschwitz as an extermination camp equipped with homicidal gas chambers and following the trail of the way information about Auschwitz became available until the death of Höss. If Irving would introduce the thesis that the Auschwitz gas chambers were not history but hystory, the application of Ockham's razor to both my and Crowell's explanation of the evidence would clearly demonstrate mine to be more, and Crowell's to be less, probable. While the assumption that the gas chambers had indeed existed would easily explain the various forms of evidence that had emerged since 1942, a presentation of the material in court based on Crowell's explanation of "a complex of delusion and censorship" would not be able to account for all the evidence. At the same time, a systematic consideration of this historical record would make amply clear that in 1988 Irving had ignored substantial evidence against Leuchter's conclusions that there had been no gas chambers in Auschwitz and would serve in that sense an offensive purpose in the trial.

There was, however, also another reason to organize the material in this manner. Crowell's proposition that the Holocaust was a product of intertextuality is an updated version of a theory first proposed in the 1970s by German negationist Wilhelm Stäglich. In 1944, Stäglich had served with an anti-aircraft battery unit near Auschwitz. In order to obtain food, Stäglich had gone a few times to the camp, which had its own slaughterhouse and bakery. In 1973, the monthly *Nation Europe* published Stäglich's recollections of Auschwitz.

> If memory serves, I was inside the camp three or four times altogether. On none of these visits did I see gassing installations, crematoria, instruments of torture, or similar horrors. The camp gave one the impression of being well-kept and very well-orga-

nized. On none of these visits did I find that inmates—at least the ones present in the camp, for example, inmates employed in the various workshops or on clean-up details—were badly, much less inhumanly, treated. . . . None of the inmates behaved as though they were in fear of mistreatment, let alone death.[9]

Publication of his eyewitness evidence of Auschwitz brought him a lot of praise from the extreme right, and, flattered by the attention he had received, Stäglich went to work on his magnum opus: his massive *Der Auschwitz Mythos* (*The Auschwitz Myth*), which was published in 1979. Stäglich's aim, as set out in the introduction, was "to survey, examine, and assess as objectively as possible the evidence that has thus far been presented for the claim that Auschwitz was a 'death factory.'" Stäglich acknowledged that other camps were connected to the Holocaust. But he did not feel obliged to consider them. As Irving was to pronounce a decade later, Stäglich was convinced "that the extermination thesis stands or falls with the allegation that Auschwitz was a 'death factory.'"[10]

Because he claimed to be an eyewitness himself, and because his observations were so different from those of the survivors, he postulated the thesis that mass suggestion was the cause for the atrocity stories.

> The investigation of this phenomenon, in regard to the alleged extermination of Jews in the "gas chambers" of so-called extermination camps, would certainly be a worthwhile task for psychologists and sociologists. For even if the extermination of Jews had taken place, it would be unrealistic to assume that the laws of mass suggestion could not have had any influence on the description of the extent and nature of killings of Jews that actually took place. Probably this influence was far greater than one would imagine.[11]

According to Stäglich, the camps, closed off from the world, were therefore ruled by rumor and provided the perfect context for the emergence of mass suggestion. Invoking the work of the French psychologist Gustave Le Bon (1841–1931) on self-delusions of "psychological crowds," Stäglich claimed that "the many accounts of the alleged mass gassings in Birkenau have their origin in mass hallucinations or mass suggestion inspired by propaganda." In short, inmates would have heard Allied radio broadcasts claiming gassings in the camps, and as a result had started to fantasize about such gassings in their own situation. "It is easy to find examples substantiating the view that many accounts of the alleged mass gassings in Birkenau have their origin in mass hallucinations or mass suggestion inspired by propaganda, for the observations upon which such reports are based can usually be explained in a completely natural way," Stäglich argued. That those deemed "unfit for work" left the place of selection in the direction of the crematoria could be explained because in that vicinity was also a hospital for inmates, and a bath house, he claimed.

> An equally natural explanation can be given for the observation, variously reported, that corpses were removed from the cellar of one of the crematoria, or a room next to the crematorium, to the incineration area of the crematorium. It is well-known that the death-rate in the Auschwitz camps was high at times—especially during the frequent typhus epidemics. It is understandable that all these dead people could not be cremated at once. They must have been stored in a special area until they could be cremated. This

was the "corpse cellar" of the crematorium, mentioned in various documents, or an annex serving the same purpose. The removal of corpses from such an area was a completely normal procedure. But many an inmate who observed such a procedure may, under the mass suggestive influence of rumors that were in circulation, have come in all good faith to the conclusion that he was witness to a "gassing."[12]

But then, what about the testimonies about living people descending into those "corpse cellars"?

Stäglich was not concerned about the fact that so many people unanimously attested that gassings occurred. "In the nature of things," he observed, "the unanimity of many groups of witnesses is itself the result of mass suggestion."[13] Stäglich then formulated his rules for accepting eyewitness evidence:

> As evidence for the alleged gassing of the Jews, reports that do not contain specific details about it, but are limited to quite vague allegations of this type—as is usually the case—must be rejected at once. Such general statements are just as worthless as hearsay testimony, since they cannot be proved. Further, only statements free of contradictions, which do not stand in contradiction to other circumstances and facts, may lay claim to credibility. Finally, to have probative value, a statement must contain nothing improbable, something that may seem obvious to most people, but—as we shall see—is not always the case with reports about the Birkenau crematoria.[14]

There were several problems with Stäglich's approach. First of all, he abused Le Bon's theory about the psychology of the crowd when he applied the latter's theories to the world of the camps. Le Bon's book was a straightforward critique of modern society as a whole. Civilization with its shared ideals and its unity of sentiment had given way to a confused agglomeration of individuals who had lost "the genius of the race" to become a crowd "at the mercy of every chance."[15] Consequently, all people today were victims of mass suggestion, Le Bon posited. It was inappropriate to single out the world of the camps. If Stäglich had used Le Bon's thesis correctly, he should have argued that, given the fact that all of society has disintegrated into a crowd, it had become impossible to make any determination about the truth or falsehood of any testimony, and that if one could claim on the basis of this that Auschwitz was a myth, so was the whole World War, including his own experiences of that war. In other words, Stäglich would have had to draw the epistemological consequences from his invocation of Le Bon and admit not only that no piece of evidence about any fact has any probative value, or that the Auschwitz Myth was just a part of the Reality Myth, but that even Le Bon's *Psychologie des foules* had no authority because it was conceived, published, and read by people in the crowd.

More important, however, was that Stäglich's critique of the eyewitness evidence was based on the supposition that very little was known about Auschwitz after the war. Located in Soviet-controlled territory, the camp generated rumors that could not be checked, he wrote: "Details were generally avoided when reference was made to the concentration camps in the Auschwitz region."[16] And so Stäglich assumed that there was little information about the gassings. "One of the first comes from the Austrian

Jewish socialist leader Benedikt Kautsky," Stäglich wrote. Kautsky had been an inmate of Auschwitz-Monowitz who wrote in his memoir *Teufel und Verdammte* (1946) that he thus escaped the gas chambers at Birkenau but that "nevertheless the gas chambers were close enough to obtain reliable information about them."[17] Kautsky provided some particulars that were partly right and partly wrong. For Stäglich, Kautsky's mistakes and the fact that he did not provide the names of the inmates who had given him the information about the gas chambers provided sufficient reason to condemn his whole report as "a product of pure fantasy." He commented cynically, "He also failed to give a convincing explanation of why he, a *Volljude*, was not 'gassed.'"[18] Apparently, the fact that a Jew survived Auschwitz was proof that it was not an extermination camp for Jews. Nine years after Stäglich published his book, Irving was to make the same argument in a Toronto court. The survival of Jews contradicted the thesis that the Nazis had planned to systematically exterminate Jews in Auschwitz because if they had such a policy, there would have been no survivors.[19]

Stäglich also tried to destroy the credibility of another "very early 'testimony' of the gas chambers of Birkenau," Eugen Kogon's *Der SS-Staat* (1946). A former inmate of Buchenwald, Kogon reported the testimony of a "young Jew named Janda Weiss," who described that the gas entered the gas chambers through "ventilation pillars." Stäglich had no difficulty dismissing all of it:

> How one is to visualize the aforesaid "ventilation pillars" is Kogon's secret. Kogon's informant, Janda Weiss, has never stepped forward. Kogon was never in Auschwitz, but—like Rassinier—was a Buchenwald inmate. His book is completely worthless as a historical source, even though anti-German propaganda constantly attempts to classify it as such.[20]

Kautsky and Kogon proved convenient straw men. However, they were not considered to be eyewitnesses of the gassings. Stäglich's negationism simply denied the abundance of evidence about the Auschwitz gas chambers that was available in the first years after the war. According to Stäglich, because so little was known, rumors easily filled the void. In the same manner that Irving repeated Stäglich's insinuation that Kautsky's survival testified against a policy to kill Jews, Irving suggested on various occasions that there were only very few early postwar testimonies about the gas chambers. In 1988, for example, he told a Canadian audience that after his endorsement of the Leuchter Report he had been searching the archives, "looking for the evidence myself because, if Auschwitz, just to take that one cardinal tent pole of the case, itself was not an extermination factory, then what is the evidence that it was?" And he told them that "if you then start going all your way back down the pipeline to find out where this evidence comes from, you come up with one or two or three documents and eyewitness accounts and that is all."[21]

The assertion that our knowledge about Auschwitz is a fabrication balancing precariously on a very narrow evidentiary basis is patently false. A great deal of information about Auschwitz was available in 1945. Let us review the question of how the gas chambers, or to be more precise, the gas chambers at Auschwitz, became known to the world. According to Crowell, in 1942 reports emerged whose main motif was the so-called shower-gas-burning sequence: "Victims would be led into a bathing facility of some kind, and then be executed (the claimed method focussing on gas more and more as time went by), and then burned so that no trace would remain."[22] In fact, the earliest report about gassing in Auschwitz did not contain the "shower-gas-burning sequence." On July 1, 1942, an article entitled "Documents from Poland: German Attempts to Murder a Nation" appeared in the *Polish Fortnightly Review,* an English-language newspaper published by the Polish government-in-exile. It mentioned Auschwitz as a particularly violent concentration camp and also mentioned a second camp nearby. "The prisoners call this supplementary camp 'Paradisal' (presumably because from it there is only one road, leading to Paradise). The crematorium here is five times as large as the one in the main camp."[23] The report listed various forms of torture and stated that German doctors used inmates as guinea pigs for medical experiments in the camp. It also included a short discussion of an experiment to gas inmates.

> Among the other experiments being tried on the prisoners is the use of poison gas. It is generally known that during the night of September 5th to 6th last year about a thousand people were driven down to the underground shelter in Oswiecim, among them seven hundred Bolshevik prisoners of war and three hundred Poles. As the shelter was too small to hold this large number, the living bodies were simply forced in, regardless of broken bones. When the shelter was full gas was injected into it, and all the prisoners died during the night. All night the rest of the camp was kept awake by the groans and howls coming from the shelter. Next day other prisoners had to carry out the bodies, a task which took all day. One hand-cart on which the bodies were being removed broke down under the weight.[24]

It is important to note that after the war various witnesses confirmed that in early September the Germans had used Block 11 in Auschwitz as an experimental gas chamber.[25] The report did not include any reference to showers. In fact, there are no showers in Block 11.

Two weeks later the *Polish Fortnightly Review* once again drew attention to Auschwitz. It noted the excessive mortality attributed to the rigors of the camp and carried a report on a press conference given by Polish Minister of Home Affairs Stanislaw Mikolajczyk that referred to the ever-increasing size of the inmate population.[26] It also reported on statements given during the same press conference by two members of the Polish National Council on the extermination of Polish Jewry and a final remark by the Polish minister of information that at least 700,000 Polish Jews had died since the beginning of the war. Yet at this time knowledge of the concentration camp system and the emerging awareness of the Holocaust were not yet brought into connection.

Only later that year did the *Polish Fortnightly Review* begin to mention camps as execution sites of Jews. Many reports had reached the Polish government-in-exile about deportations from the Warsaw ghetto. In the fall of 1942, an eyewitness to the fate of the deportees had made his way to England. The Polish underground fighter Jan Kozielewski (better known by his underground name Jan Karski) had visited an extermination camp at Belzec disguised as a Latvian policeman and had witnessed the destruction of a transport of Jews. Karski informed the Polish government-in-exile, and on December 1, 1942, the *Polish Fortnightly Review* published as its main item an article entitled "Extermination of Polish Jewry," in which it reported that the Warsaw ghetto had been subject to daily deportations of 7,000 people per day since July 24. Those who were too ill to travel were killed on the spot or at the Jewish cemetery. The others were loaded in trains and taken to Treblinka, Belzec, and Sobibor. "Here the trains were unloaded, the condemned were stripped naked and then killed, probably by poison gas or electrocution. For the purpose of burying the bodies a great bulldozer has been taken to Treblinka, and this machine works without stopping." The report concluded that it had not been possible to ascertain whether any deportees had been left alive. "We have information only of extermination."[27]

Remarkably, the *Polish Fortnightly Review* did not publish all of Karski's observations at Belzec but chose to print as an annex to the report an earlier description of the "Jew-extermination Camp at Belzec." Dated July 10, 1942, it was obviously based on hearsay. After describing the arrival procedure, it mentioned that "the men go to a barracks on the right, the women to a barracks situated on the left, where they strip, ostensibly in readiness for a bath. After they have undressed both groups go to a third barracks where there is an electrified plate, where the executions are carried out."[28] In the summer of 1942, when the report was written, no one who was not part of the execution team had left Belzec alive, and thus the description of the method of killing was largely based on rumor.

After drawing attention to the fate of the Jews in the *Polish Fortnightly Review,* on December 10, 1942, the Polish government-in-exile issued a note to the other Allies concerning the mass extermination of Jews in Poland, repeating in substance the information from the article.[29] In all this publicity, the names of Belzec, Sobibor, and Treblinka appeared again and again, but there was no mention of Auschwitz. This can be explained by the fact that before the late fall of 1942, Auschwitz did not play a significant role in the liquidation of Polish Jewry.

It is more difficult to understand why the Polish government-in-exile did not act on a report broadcast in March 1943 by a secret radio station operated by the Polish resistance that was received in London.

> The statistics for Oswiecim from the establishment of the camp until December 15 [1942] show that more than 640,000 people perished there, with 30,000 still alive. 65,000 Poles have been executed, hanged, tortured, gassed, or have died from starvation and disease with 17,000 still alive. More than 26,000 Soviet POW's have been liquidated; 100 still alive. More than 520,000 Jews have been gassed, including 20,000 from Poland, and the rest from France, Belgium, Holland, Yugoslavia, etc. 6,800 women are alive, mainly Poles, 19,000 have died. Only a portion are registered in the camp records. Thousands are dying without being identified—e.g. almost all Jews.[30]

In 1943, when the four crematoria came into operation in Birkenau, the name "Birkenau" occasionally surfaced in relation to the Holocaust, but no one connected it with Auschwitz.[31] There remained a kind of interpretative "gap" between the few accounts of the camp at Auschwitz as a particularly violent concentration camp meant mainly for Polish resistors, Birkenau as a destination for Jews of unknown geographical location, the Holocaust in general, and the town of Auschwitz as a site of massive industrial activity. Probably the industrial activity in the Auschwitz region, with its use of slave labor, camouflaged the main purpose of Birkenau.[32] In June 1944, when the truth about the use of Birkenau as a site of systematic extermination finally became known as the result of the escape of Rudi Vrba and Alfred Wetzlar from Birkenau in April 1944, the senior representative of the Jewish Agency in Geneva, Richard Lichtheim, wrote to the

Jewish Agency executive in Jerusalem that up until then he had always assumed that any reference to deportations of Jews to Auschwitz concerned the German purpose "to exploit more Jewish labour in the industrial centres of Upper Silesia."[33]

The many atrocities the Germans performed elsewhere also proved an effective screen. In April 1943, for example, an otherwise unidentified member of the Polish resistance went to the town of Oswiecim to try to find out what was happening in the camp. He learned that Auschwitz had become a major extermination camp for Jews and that gas chambers were used as means of killing.[34] He reached London in early 1943 and drafted a report in April of that year which he added to a long description of the Warsaw ghetto—just at the time of the Warsaw ghetto uprising. The revolt made the record of the Warsaw ghetto in the report obsolete, and as a result the Polish government-in-exile shelved the whole account, including the description of Auschwitz, which had lost none of its validity.

If the Germans aimed to keep the killings in Birkenau secret, the Polish Labor Group in New York City and the American Office of War Information in Washington, D.C., inadvertently aided them in their mission. In 1942, before the mass killings of Jews had started, the Polish underground had published a book on Auschwitz entitled *Oboz Smierci* (*Camp of Death*), which chronicled the first two years of the camp's existence—the period in which it played only a marginal role in the Final Solution. Nevertheless, the account was grim. Smuggled out of Poland, the text was translated into English and published in March 1944 by the Polish Labor Group in New York City as *Oswiecim, Camp of Death: Underground Report*. The book included a long description of gassings in Block 11. It did not mention showers and concluded that "no one emerges alive from the darkness of the underground cells to tell a word, and yet, in the first bit of dawn, the secret of 800 dead men filters through. A trip to Oswiecim, a flight of steps into the 'underground,' and death by gas."[35] As we know today, the account was correct: both Pery Broad and Rudolf Höss would later corroborate it.

While the outside world knew little about what was happening in Auschwitz, knowledge about the gassings became slowly known in the concentration camps as the result of the occasional arrival of skilled craftsmen from Auschwitz in the other camps. In 1943, for example, a group of thirty-eight printers and fifty-three watchmakers were transferred from Auschwitz to Sachsenhausen. The printers were given the task of counterfeiting Allied currency, and the watchmakers were to clean and, if necessary, repair the hundreds of thousands of watches that were recovered from incoming deportees before they were given to "deserving" Germans. In Sachsenhausen, both the printers and the watchmakers were isolated in their own block, and they did not merge with the general camp population. But while the printers were kept in strict isolation, the watchmakers were free to roam the camp, and they could be visited.

One of the inmates who sought contact with these men was Odd Nansen, the son of the famous Norwegian polar explorer and statesman Fridjof Nansen. From the time of his arrest in January 1942, Nansen kept a secret diary, which survived the war. On November 11, 1943, Nansen wrote down that the previous day he had talked to a Jewish watchmaker named Keil, who had lived as a German refugee in Norway from 1936 onward.

> He came here from Auschwitz in Poland. An extermination camp of the worst type. What he told me about that camp was so

horrible, so incomprehensible in ghastliness, that it defies all description. He told me that of the Norwegian Jews who were sent there, and I should think all of them were sent, only a very few are still alive; about twenty-five out of twelve hundred was his estimate. I think twelve hundred is too high (Or is it rather hope?) Most of them were gassed. Whole transports went straight into the gas chamber and thence into the crematory. Men, women, and children of all ages, from every corner of Europe and every social class. There were five crematories in the camp, and they were going day and night—and had been for several years.[36]

Nansen went to see the Jews on November 16, and again on November 29, when he got "a little more peace to listen to the ghastly stories of Lublin, Warsaw, and other towns and camps." Nansen began to realize that something unique was happening in the east.

Beside the drama of horror thus unfolded, all the other stories, atrocities, and massacres we know in the whole history of mankind go, as it were, for nothing. It's impossible—completely impossible to form any picture of the evil revealed here; human comprehension and imagination fall short. One can "follow" up to a point, imagine thousands of Jews, young and old, being sent out in the death transports, see them marching in endless columns, day and night, week after week, month after month, yes year after year, into annihilation. And yet what one can imagine is still assuredly nothing but a pale reflection of the reality.[37]

Those who were killed on arrival were relatively lucky. To Nansen, the fate of those who were forced to work the machinery of death was the worst:

Hundreds of thousands of the strongest and best—healthiest and finest young people in their full bloom had first to be "exploited"—their strength had first to be made use of in the death gangs—moving corpses, burning, hanging! And it was their own people they were moving, burning, and hanging—their own! No! I won't make any attempt to repeat what I heard; I can't yet. I must get back from it a little, and also I must hear still more.[38]

Yet Nansen was not to have any more contact with his informants.

In the middle of 1944, substantial information about the use of Auschwitz as a site of systematic genocide became available as the result of the successful escape from Auschwitz of two young Slovak Jews, Rudolf Vrba and Alfred Wetzlar. After having been imprisoned for two years in Auschwitz, they fled the camp on April 10, 1944, and returned to Slovakia in the hope of warning Hungarian Jews. There they were debriefed by the Jewish underground. The result was the first substantial report on the use of Auschwitz as a factory of death.

The first mention of gassing in the Vrba-Wetzlar report concerns the killing of prisoners in the summer of 1942. At this time Vrba had been the administrator of the sick barrack, hence he knew of the selections. "Twice weekly, Mondays and Thursdays, the camp doctor indicated the number of prisoners who were to be gassed and then burned. These 'selectees' were loaded into trucks and brought to the Birch Forest. Those still alive upon arrival were gassed in a big barrack erected near a trench used for burning the bodies."[39] This description of the killing in Bunker 2 was to be largely confirmed after the war both by Sonderkommando Shlomo Dragon, who

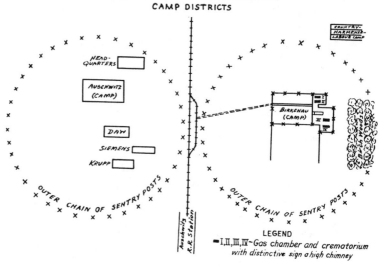

Situation sketch of the location of
the Stammlager, the railway
corridor, Auschwitz-Birkenau,
and the birch forest west of
Birkenau. War Refugee Board,
The Extermination Camps of
Auschwitz (Oswiecim) and
Birkenau in Upper Silesia (1944),
p. 40.

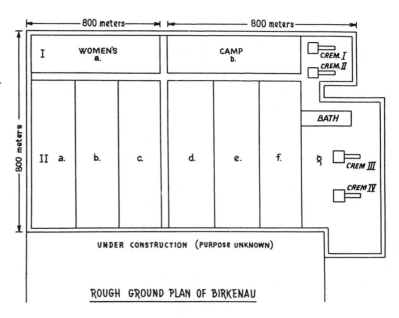

Plan of Auschwitz-Birkenau,
showing the location of the four
crematoria. All the crematoria are
depicted as identical structures.
War Refugee Board, The
Extermination Camps of
Auschwitz (Oswiecim) and
Birkenau in Upper Silesia (1944),
p. 22.

worked at that site, and by the archeological remains. The only mistake was that the "big barrack" served as an undressing barrack, and from there the victims were led to the adjacent gas chamber, located near the cremation trench.

In their report, Vrba and Wetzlar also correctly described the changing procedure of killing in early 1943. "At the end of February, 1943 a new crematorium and gassing plant was inaugurated at BIRKENAU. The gassing and burning of the bodies in the Birch Forest was discontinued, the whole job being taken over by the four specially built crematoria."[40] There followed a long description of Crematoria 2 and 3 (numbered I and II in the report).

> Those of type I and II consist of 3 parts, i.e.: (A) the furnace room; (B) the large hall; and (C) the gas chamber. A huge chimney rises from the furnace room around which are grouped nine furnaces, each having four opening[s]. Each opening can take three normal corpses at once and after an hour and a half the bodies are completely burned. This corresponds to a daily capacity of about 2,000 bodies. Next to this is a large "reception hall" which is arranged so as to give the impression of the antechamber of a bathing establishment. It holds 2,000 people and apparently there is a similar waiting room on the floor below. From there a door and a few steps lead down into the very long and narrow gas chamber. The walls of this chamber are also camouflaged with simulated entries to shower rooms in order to mislead the victims. The roof is fitted with three traps which can be hermetically closed from the outside. A track leads from the gas chamber towards the furnace room.[41]

A sketch illustrated this description. It is clear that the account of the layout of the interior is based on second-hand information, derived from members of the Sonderkommando. Indeed, in a sworn deposition Vrba made in 1961 and in his later book *I Cannot Forgive* (1963), Vrba stated that he and Wetzlar received all the specific information on the crematoria from Sonderkommando Filip Müller and his colleagues.[42] In his autobiographical *Eyewitness Auschwitz,* Müller confirmed Vrba's story. "I had described to them in full detail the process of extermination so that they would be able to report to the outside world exactly how the victims had their last pitiful belongings taken away from them; how they were tricked into entering the gas chambers; how after the gassings their teeth were wrenched out and the women's hair cut off; how the dead were searched for hidden valuables; how their spectacles, artificial limbs and dentures were collected; and everything else that took place."[43]

At first sight, the Vrba-Wetzlar account appears to include a number of mistakes. In 1985, during the Zündel trial, Vrba, under cross-examination by Zündel's counsel, Doug Christie, gave the following explanation. (N.B.: Vrba uses a different nomenclature than the Germans: Krematorium I [Vrba] is Krematorium 2 [German], Krematorium II [Vrba] is Krematorium 3 [German], and so forth.)

> [Mr. Christie]: "How do you explain the fact that you've drawn on the diagram that I showed you every crematorium the same shape in 1944, when you drew the diagram upon your escape?"

> A.: "Because I had only two days to write the whole report, and to try to depict the crematoria. There was a great urgency with

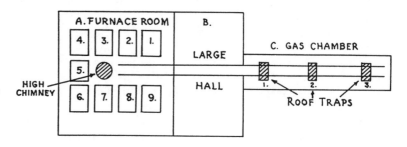

Plan of a crematorium. War Refugee Board, The Extermination Camps of Auschwitz (Oswiecim) and Birkenau in Upper Silesia *(1944), p. 15.*

ROUGH GROUND PLAN OF
CREMATORIA: TYPES I & II IN BIRKENAU

that plan, because the objective of the plan was to get it to Hungary and to use this whole report towards the Hungarian Jews of imminent deportation. Under that condition I didn't lose much time with details like what is the difference between Krematorium I and II and Krematorium II and III, but I limited myself to depict the position of the gas chambers and crematoria [on] one side, and the geographic position of the whole murderous complex on the other side."

Q.: "Sure. I now produce and show to you a diagram which came from, I suggest, your War Refugee Report of 1944 in which you depicted a crematorium. Correct?"

A.: "That's right."

Q.: "Is it accurate?"

A.: "This I cannot say. It was said that as we were not in the large crematoria, we reconstructed it from messages which we got from members of the Sonderkommando working in the crematorium, and therefore, that approximately how it transpired in our mind, and in our ability to depict what we have heard."[44]

When one compares the plans and ruins of Crematoria 2 and 3 (or I and II, according to Vrba), and those of Crematoria 4 and 5 (III and IV), to Vrba's plan, it is quite easy to reconstruct the genealogy of his "errors." Crematoria 2 and 3 were visible from some distance, and it was not difficult to notice that the one chimney did not arise from the main body of the crematorium but from a projecting wing. Not knowing that the incinerators were placed in a large hall in the main building and were connected with underground flues to the chimney, Vrba must have logically assumed that the projecting wing was the furnace room with the ovens placed around the central chimney. This then left the purpose of the main wing of the crematorium unaccounted for. As Vrba had been told that there was a large undressing room and an underground gas chamber, it was logical for him to assume that the undressing room would occupy the main body of the crematorium. Thus he had come to two adjacent rooms, one large aboveground "reception room" and an incineration room—an arrangement similar to that of Crematoria 4 and 5. But if the latter buildings had three small aboveground gas chambers at the other end, then Crematoria 2 and 3 had one large underground gas chamber, which Vrba depicted in roughly the right position. Its description is quite precise, except that it was equipped with four instead of three traps.

The description of the crematoria in the War Refugee Board report contains errors, but given the conditions under which information was obtained, the lack of architectural training of Vrba and Wetzlar, and the situation in which the report was compiled, one would become suspicious if it did not contain errors. Vrba and Wetzlar did not claim to provide an exact description of the crematoria. Their reconstruction of the killing installations was a good-faith attempt, based on whatever information they had been able to obtain, to convince the world that an unimaginable event was taking place in the heart of Europe—an event that still staggers and numbs the mind. Given the circumstances, the composite "crematorium" reconstructed by two escapees without any architectural training is as good as one could expect.

The Vrba-Wetzlar report also described the gassing procedure.

> The gassing takes place as follows. The unfortunate victims are brought into the hall (B) where they are told to undress. To complete the fiction that they are going to bathe, each person receives a towel and a small piece of soap issued by two men clad in white coats. Then they are crowded into the gas chamber (C) in such numbers that there is, of course, only standing room. To compress this crowd into the narrow space, shots are often fired to induce those already at the far end to huddle still closer together. When everybody is inside, the heavy doors are closed. Then there is a short pause, presumably to allow the room temperature to rise to a certain level, after which SS men with gas masks climb on the roof, open the traps, and shake down a preparation in powder form out of a tin labelled "CYKLON" "For use against vermin," which is manufactured by a Hamburg concern. It is presumed that this is a "CYANIDE" mixture of some sort which turns into gas at a certain temperature. After three minutes everyone in the gas chamber is dead. No one is known to have survived this ordeal, although it was not uncommon to discover signs of life after the primitive measures employed in the Birch Wood. The chamber is then opened, aired, and the "special squads" cart the bodies on flat trucks to the furnace rooms where the burning takes place. Crematoria III and IV work on nearly the same principle, but their capacity is only half as large. Thus the total capacity of the four cremating and gassing plants at BIRKENAU amounts to about 6,000 daily.[45]

Finally, the report mentioned how, in March 1943, Crematorium 2 was inaugurated with the gassing and burning of 8,000 Cracow Jews. "Prominent guests from Berlin" were present at that occasion. They were all satisfied with the results, "and the special peephole fitted into the door of the gas chamber was in constant use."[46] In fact, Vrba was partly mistaken here: while there were guests from Berlin, the transport of Cracow Jews had only counted 1,492 people—only 52 more than the official daily incineration capacity of that crematorium. It was, indeed, almost a laboratory experiment.

In June 1944, the Vrba-Wetzlar report reached Switzerland, and by the middle of the month, various copies were circulating. On June 19, Richard Lichtheim, the senior Jewish Agency representative in Geneva, wrote to the Jewish Agency executive in Jerusalem that it had now become possible to ascertain "what has happened and where it has happened." The systematic killing of Jews not only occurred in the by then well-known camps such as Treblinka, but also in "similar establishments situated near or in the labour camp of Birkenau in Upper Silesia." Knowing well the confusion that existed about the what and where of Birkenau, Lichtheim felt compelled to stress that "there *is* a labour camp in Birkenau just as in many other places in Upper Silesia, and there *are* still many thousands of Jews working there and in neighbouring places (Jawischowiz etc.)." Yet the use of Birkenau as a labor camp did not preclude an even more grim purpose: it also housed "specially constructed buildings with gas-chambers and crematoriums."[47] Lichtheim also explained that Birkenau was formally subordinated "to the camp of Auschwitz (Oswiecim) which is 4 km from Birkenau." This camp, he observed, was generally known because of its violent regime as a "Death Camp." Yet for all its horror, Lichtheim wrote, it was now revealed to be a pale foreshadowing of Birkenau. The gentiles imprisoned in Auschwitz "have not been slaughtered wholesale on arrival like 90 per cent of the Jews arriving in Birkenau."[48]

Lichtheim's confidence in the truth of the Vrba-Wetzlar report was strengthened when a second report arrived, this time from Poland. It had been written by Polish gentile Jerzy Tabeau shortly after his escape from Auschwitz on November 19, 1943.[49] Tabeau's report, which had an independent origin, corroborated the Vrba-Wetzlar account of the use of Birkenau as a site of mass extermination. It mentioned that the first large transports of Jews began to arrive in the spring of 1942. "Certain large scale preparations had to be made to receive these mass transports and a special concentration camp was opened at BIRKENAU (The Polish name of the village is RAJSKO)."[50] It described the selections in detail and the killing in the summer and fall of 1942 of the Jews in the gas chamber in the birch forest. Tabeau addressed the problems with getting rid of the corpses before the construction of the crematoria.

> Mass graves were dug at that time into which the corpses were simply thrown. This continued into the autumn of 1942. By this time extermination by gas was being intensified and there was no more time as such for summary burial. Row upon row of bodies of murdered Jews, covered only by a thin layer of earth, were widely dispersed in the surrounding fields, causing the soil to become almost marshy through the putrefaction of the bodies. The smell emanating from these fields became intolerable. In the autumn of 1942 all that remained of the bodies had to be exhumed and the bones collected and burned in the crematoria (by that time four had been completed). An alternative was to gather the remains of the unfortunate victims into heaps, pour gasoline over them, and leave it to the flames to finish the tragedy.[51]

With exception of the clause "and the bones collected and burned in the crematoria (by that time four had been completed)," everything that Tabeau described was corroborated after the war.

These revelations about the purpose and function of Birkenau occurred at a time when the Germans were in the process of dispatching daily trains full of Hungarian Jews to that location. The Jewish Agency in Jerusalem was likely to do little, but the British Government in London would perhaps do more, so Lichtheim contacted the British legation in Geneva with the request (if they would be willing) to cable a text Lichtheim had written to the Foreign Office in London. The British diplomats agreed, and on June 27 the Lichtheim telegram was sent to London under the signature of the British minister in Berne. It noted that he had received "fresh reports from Hungary stating that nearly one half total of 800,000 Jews in Hungary have already been deported at a rate of 10,000 to 12,000 per diem." Most of these Jews had been sent to Birkenau, where they were killed. "We have detailed reports about the numbers and methods employed."[52] A week later, the Foreign Office received an 8-page summary of the Vrba-Wetzlar report from the acting Czechoslovak Minister of Foreign Affairs, Hubert Ripka, who had obtained it from the Czechoslovak representative in Geneva.[53]

By the time the facts about Auschwitz reached London, they were also known in Washington, D.C. On June 24, Dr. Gerhart Riegner, who represented the World Jewish Congress in Geneva, had given the representative of the War Refuge Board in Berne, Roswell D. McClelland, a summary of the report, and that same day the latter had cabled the most important elements to Washington, D.C.[54] In fact, it was to take McClelland two weeks before he was able to telegraph an 8-page summary to Washington on July 6, promising that "when mailing facilities permit, microfilm copies of the two reports 'in extenso' will be sent."[55] McClelland's desire to corroborate the report explains the time lag. A member of the Bratislava Papal Nunciature, who had personally interviewed Vrba and Wetzlar, told McClelland that their story had been thoroughly convincing and also explained that they had been closely cross-examined by senior members of the Bratislava Jewish community. The latter had taken care that the material finally incorporated into the report included only that about which there was no uncertainty or equivocation.[56]

Having received the assurances he had sought, the American diplomat decided to put his career on the line, and he cabled a summary of the report to Washington, D.C. It described the location, the huge size, and the atrocious living conditions of Auschwitz, identified as camp "A," and Birkenau, identified as camp "B." After a short account of various medical experiments and the methods of executions through shooting or phenol injections, the summary addressed the core issue: the role of Auschwitz in the Holocaust. "Jews who were brought to A toward end of 1941 were for most part Polish political prisoners and killed by various methods as such," it observed. "Not until spring of 1942 were transports of Jews en masse sent to B (constructed principally for them) to be exterminated on purely racial grounds."[57] These transports to Birkenau had been subjected to selection, and the able-bodied men and women were admitted to the camp. "Balance including elderly people, women with small children, those ill or otherwise unsuited for work and abandoned children were taken directly to Birkenwald in trucks and gassed."[58] The summary then provided a detailed description of the crematoria and the gassing procedure.[59] After providing details of various transports that had been subjected to selection and extermination, the telegram concluded with a frightful statistic. "Authors set number of Jews gassed and burned in B between April 1942 and April 1944 at from 1.5 to 1.75 million."[60]

By the time McClelland's summary arrived in Washington, D.C., the *New York Times* had already run three stories on Auschwitz. The first, published on June 20, was only twenty-two lines long. Entitled "Czechs Report Massacre," it reported the death of 7,000 Czech Jews. "The report said that the victims were dragged to gas chambers in the notorious German concentration camps at Birkenau and Oswiecim."[61] Two weeks later, the coverage had increased fourfold in an article entitled "Inquiry Confirms Nazi Death Camps," subtitled "1,715,000 Jews Said to Have Been Put to Death by the Germans Up to April 15." The author, the *New York Times* correspondent in Geneva, Daniel Brigham, still hedged his language, but three days later, in an even longer article entitled "Two Death Camps Places of Horror," he had lost all doubt: the report had received "incontrovertible confirmation of the facts."[62]

By the middle of July 1944, many had become convinced that the Germans were engaged in the systematic annihilation of Jews in extermination camps and that Birkenau was one of the most important of these camps. But few people could really imagine what such places were like. The world of the camps remained intangible. This changed on July 23, 1944. Five days earlier, the Soviet army had broken through German lines at Kowel, and on July 23 the Eight Guards Army took the town of Lublin. In Lublin's suburb of Maidanek, General Chuikov's soldiers found a large concentration camp, which the Germans had largely evacuated in the preceding months, but which for unknown reasons they had failed to destroy. The crematorium and some of the gas chambers were captured largely intact. For the first time, it became possible to fully imagine what the word "Birkenau" meant. On August 29, the Soviet Embassy in Washington published the first installment of a long, two-piece article by Konstantin Simonov entitled "Lublin Annihilation Camp." The article began with a statement that was to be repeated almost literally by dozens of journalists as they reported, in the nine months that followed, of the things they witnessed in the German concentration camps upon their liberation: "What I am now about to relate is too enormous and too gruesome to be fully conceived." Simonov admitted that it would take a painstaking inquiry to establish all the facts about the camp. Yet, having seen the place and talked to around 100 witnesses, he could not wait. "A man who has seen what I have cannot hold his peace and cannot wait to speak."[63] He described the gas chamber as a room of some 400 square feet. "A single steel door hermetically closes the entrance to the chamber." Unlike the delousing chambers, it was equipped with "a little spy hole, a small square window barred on the inside by a stout steel grid fitted into the concrete. A thick panel of glass covers the outer side of the aperture so that it cannot be reached through the grid." When the victims were packed into this room, "specially trained operators wearing gas masks poured the 'cyclone' out of the cylindrical tins into the chamber." The executioner could easily follow what happened. "The spy hole was set into the wall at roughly the height of a human face. He had no need to look down, for the people were packed so close they did not fall as they died, but continued in an upright position." Simonov added to his report that, "incidentally, 'cyclone' really is a disinfecting substance. It was actually used for the disinfection of clothes in neighbouring sheds. Everything seemed fair and above-board. It all depended on the dose which was poured into the chambers."[64]

The victims' shoes piled in front of a warehouse, Maidanek, 1944. Main Commission for the Prosecution of Crimes against the Polish Nation, courtesy USHMM Photo Archives. (opposite page)

In a second part of his report, published a few days later, Simonov reported on the crematoria with their five ovens. "Each furnace was built to accommodate six bodies. If the six bodies would not fit into the crematorium the operators hacked off the protruding parts of the body, an arm, a leg or a head, and then hermetically closed the door." Initially, incineration time of one load was 45 minutes, "but gradually by raising the tem-

peratures in the furnaces the Germans doubled the handling capacity of the crematorium and incinerating process; instead of 45 minutes they took 25 and even less."[65] The sight that shocked Simonov most was a large shed filled with shoes. "There may be a million, there may be more. They spill over out of the hut through the windows and the doors. In one spot the weight of them pushed out part of the wall, which fell outwards together with piles of shoes." The shoes were the silent witnesses of those who had been killed and incinerated, and hence "it is hard to imagine anything more gruesome than this sight.[66]

One day after the Soviet Embassy in Washington published the first installment of Simonov's account of Maidanek, the American public found confirmation in the *New York Times*. On August 30, it carried on the front page an article entitled "Nazi Mass Killing Laid Bare in Camp," written by the same Bill Lawrence who, nine months earlier, had shown such skepticism about the alleged mass killing of Jews in Babi Yar. This time Lawrence did not hedge his statements. "I have just seen the most terrible place on the face of the earth—the German concentration camp at Maidanek, which was a veritable River Rouge[67] for the production of death." He reported that he had spoken with captured Germans "who admitted quite frankly that it was a highly systemized place for annihilation, although they, of course, denied any personal participation in the murders," and concluded that he had never been confronted with such complete evidence of a crime. "After inspection of Maidanek, I am now prepared to believe any story of German atrocities, no matter how savage, cruel and depraved."[68]

While seeing Maidanek may have convinced Lawrence that his earlier skepticism had been inappropriate, the editors of the *Christian Century* felt no need to let go of the skepticism they had shown all along about the atrocity stories coming from Europe. On September 13, 1944, they provided, under the heading "Biggest Atrocity Story Breaks in Poland," a short summary of Lawrence's account and noted that "chief evidence for the charge that 1,500,000 persons had been killed in this manner was a warehouse 'about 150 feet long' containing clothing of people of all ages who were said to have been done to death in the camp." It did not convince the editors back home in America. "Many newspapers gave the Lublin charges the big headline of the day, but the parallel between this story and the 'corpse factory' atrocity tale of the First World War is too striking to be overlooked."[69] And thus the editors of one of the leading Christian magazines in the United States concluded their coverage of the discovery of Maidanek.

The editors of *Time* showed less hesitance to accept facts for what they were. On August 21, they had provided a first account of the "gigantic murder plant," largely taken from notes by Russian war correspondent Roman Karmen.[70] Three weeks later, they printed an almost full-page article entitled "Murder, Inc." written by their Moscow correspondent Richard Lauterbach, who had visited the camp some time earlier. He was puzzled by the banality of the camp. "I took notes calmly, feeling little emotion. It was all so cold and bare." After having inspected the gas chambers, his guide, the secretary of the Soviet Atrocities Commission, Dmitri Kudriavtsev, showed him some cabbage patches covered with some gray-brown powder. "'This,' said Kudriavtsev, 'is fertilizer. A layer of human bones, a layer of human ashes, a layer of manure. This is German food production. Kill people; fertilize cabbages.'"[71] Lauterbach noted the Soviet expert's explanation of the ultimate result of capitalist logic without comment. Nor did he dispute the expert's interpretation of German efficiency when he was shown the crematorium. "'There was great economy,' said Kudriavtsev. 'These furnaces also heated the water for the camp.'"[72] Lauterbach ended with an extensive description of the warehouses with shoes. The shoes obviously bothered him, and a week later he came back to them in an article he wrote for *Life*. While the gas chambers did not get to him, the full emotional shock came at a giant warehouse chock-full of people's shoes. "It was monstrous. There is something about an old shoe as personal as a snapshot or a letter. I looked at them and saw their owners: skinny kids in soft, white, worn slippers; thin ladies in black highlaced shoes; sturdy soldiers in brown military shoes."[73]

By this time a joint Soviet-Polish commission that consisted of three Russian and eight Polish members (which included a priest, the president of the Lublin Red Cross, two academics, and two lawyers), which was assisted by a six-member Board of Medico-Legal Experts and a four-member board of Technico-Legal and Chemical Experts, had begun a systematic forensic investigation, following procedures that had been well established in nineteen earlier inquiries into German atrocities.[74] They were lucky in that they had been able to obtain not only testimonies from former inmates but also testimony from a number of SS men who had not been able to escape in time. Furthermore, some parts of the camp administration had been captured and, as we have seen, the gas chambers and crematoria remained intact and were available for forensic investigation. In October, the commission issued its report, the English-language version of which was made available by the Soviet embassy in Washington, D.C., on October 17.[75]

Tins of Zyklon B discovered in Maidanek. Main Commission for the Prosecution of Crimes against the Polish Nation, courtesy USHMM Photo Archives.

After a short introduction, the report came immediately to the point. "The Hitlerite hangmen set up a huge death factory at Maidanek in Lublin. They named it 'Vernichtungslager' (Extermination Camp)."[76] The bulk of the report was devoted to an extensive description of life in the camp, the constant starvation and exhaustion, the diseases, the humiliations, the beatings, the tortures, and the hangings. One chapter chronicled the mass shootings, which had culminated on November 3, 1943, in the execution of 18,400 people on one day. Another chapter described extermination by gas in six gassing "cells." "There were six such cells. Some had been used for killing people with 'C.O.' gas, others for killing with the poisonous chemical substance called 'cyclone.' On the camp territory there were discovered 535 drums of 'Cyclone-B2' preparation and several steel cylinders containing carbon monoxide."[77]

The next chapter dealt with the technology of incineration. The crematorium had been completed in 1943 and had five furnaces designed to burn continuously. "The furnaces were intended for burning bodies and designed to function uninterruptedly. Four bodies with hacked off extremities could be placed in one furnace at a time. It took 15 minutes to burn four bodies, and so with all furnaces working round the clock it was possible to burn 1,920 bodies in 24 hours.[78] There was also ample evidence that the Germans had incinerated corpses on large pyres, and the commission had found at least eighteen large mass graves within the camp area and 1,350 cubic meters of compost that consisted, among other things, of human ashes and small human bones. On the basis of the capacity of the old incinerators and the new crematorium and the assumed capacity of the pyres both inside and outside the camp, the commission estimated that some 1.5 million people had been killed in the camp. This latter figure was found suspect from the beginning and led in 1948 to a new, official estimate of 360,000 victims, based on analysis of transports, lists of the dead, and the occupancy of the barracks.[79]

By the time the report appeared, the shock of the initial discovery had passed. The forensic investigation had confirmed the initial accounts, and so it was not really news. Few newspapers paid attention. Yet the work of the commission made an impact on the German leadership. Maidanek was a public-relations disaster. Himmler determined that it would not happen again. He decided that, for all practical purposes, the Jewish Question had been solved as much as it was in his power to do, and he ordered the cessation of gassing in Auschwitz and the dismantling of the extermination installations in the crematoria.[80]

For Crowell, the Soviet liberation of Maidanek marked the end of a period during which rumors just arose spontaneously and the beginning of positive fabrication. "Many of the symbols of the Holocaust have their beginning here." After dismissing the huge piles of shoes as prima facie evidence of exterminations, he identified the gas-tight door with the peep-hole as "the most notorious element of the Majdanek report."[81] According to Crowell, the Soviet report simply copied the Vrba-Wetzlar report, which had included information that in March 1943 visiting dignitaries from Berlin had been present at the first gassing in Crematorium 2 and that "the special peephole fitted into the door of the gas chamber was in constant use."[82] The conclusion was obvious: that information had to have come from the Vrba-Wetzlar report. The problem with Crowell's assertion is, of course, the fact that at the time of publication of the Maidanek report the Vrba-Wetzlar report had not yet been published, and there is no evidence of any kind that the Soviets were in possession of the unpublished manuscript. The summary that had been circulating in Washington, D.C., which could have been available to the Soviet embassy there, did not contain the reference to the peephole. Thus Crowell's suggestion that the peephole in the Maidanek report had its origin in intertextuality is not plausible.

A month after the publication of the Maidanek report, the War Refugee Board published the Vrba-Wetzlar and Tabeau reports, to which they had added a third text drafted by Arnost Rosin and Czeslaw Mordowicz, who had escaped from Auschwitz in late May and who provided important information about the early phase of the Hungarian Action. The collated text was entitled *German Extermination Camps—Auschwitz and Birkenau.* In its press release, the Board stated that, with exceptions for the figures concerning the number of people admitted to the camps—"declared by the authors to be no more than reliable approximations"—it accepted the accounts as "a true picture of the frightful happenings in these camps."[83]

On January 27, 1945, units of the 28th and 106th Corps of the First Ukrainian Front liberated the Auschwitz camps. They found in Auschwitz-Monowitz, the slave labor camp attached to the IG Farben Buna works, 600 sick inmates. Italian Primo Levi was one of them. He observed that the soldiers "did not greet us, nor did they smile; they seemed oppressed not only by compassion but by a confused restraint." Primo Levi believed that the soldiers were burdened with shame, "the shame the Germans did not know, that the just man experiences at the other's crime; the feeling of guilt that such a crime should exist, that it should have been introduced irrevocably in the world of things that exist, and that his will for good should have proved too weak or null, and should not have availed in defence.[84]

The Red Army liberated 1,200 sick prisoners at the Auschwitz Stammlager (main camp) and 5,800 inmates at Birkenau. The rest, some 60,000 inmates, had been forced a week earlier to begin a death march to the West. In Birkenau, the Soviets also found the blown-up remains of four crematoria—the SS had learned from their public-relations debacle at Maidanek—

and a large compound with thirty-two burned storage houses. The SS had tried to avoid the embarrassment caused by the 820,000 shoes in Maidanek. And they largely succeeded this time: all that was left in the four storage barracks at Birkenau were a mere 5,525 pairs of women's shoes and 38,000 pairs of men's shoes—*and* 348,820 men's suits, 836,255 women's garments, 13,964 carpets, 69,848 dishes, huge quantities of toothbrushes, shaving brushes, glasses, crutches, false teeth, and seven tons of hair.

Immediately after the liberation, well-known Russian writer and *Pravda* correspondent Boris Polevoi wrote a first impression of the camp entitled "The Factory of Death at Auschwitz." Wired from Auschwitz, it appeared in *Pravda* on February 2. "It will take weeks of long and careful investigations by special commissions before a full picture of the truly unparalleled German outrages at Auschwitz is established," the article began. "What is noted here are only the outlines coming from a first glance acquaintanceship with the site of the monstrous outrages of the Hitlerite hangmen." And this was indeed what the article provided, "a first glance acquaintanceship." If Simonov's report on Maidanek had been characterized by utter surprise and shock, Polevoi admitted that he had been prepared for what was to be revealed. "The name of the town 'Auschwitz' has long been a synonym for bloody German atrocities in the lexicon of the peoples of the world."[85] Polevoi interpreted Auschwitz as the direct result of monopoly capitalism—a leitmotif that had been well established almost half a year earlier on the occasion of the liberation of Maidanek and that went straight back to Karl Marx's analysis of the reduction of human labor into a commodity. But, as Polevoi observed, Auschwitz was in class of its own. It was a massive factory. Freight trains, "tightly packed with people," supplied the plant with raw material. One part of the factory processed arrivals into those who could be worked to death and those who would be killed immediately, and another part of the factory sorted their possessions for shipment. Auschwitz, in other words, was a vast corporate enterprise which was unique insofar as it considered its workers to be totally expendable. Once labor had ceased to be a commodity, the body became one. "Around this industrial plant, enormous fields and enclosures were established in the Sola and Vistula river valleys. The remains of the prisoners, burned in the 'ovens,' had their ash and bones crushed in rolling mills and converted to meal, and this meal went to the fields and enclosures." The trains left the camp empty.

Then the article turned to the machinery of death, which included gas chambers. Polevoi noted that little remained because the Germans had begun to dismantle the killing installations after the liberation of Maidanek. Trying to imagine what that installation would have been, Polevoi allowed his imagination free range: the Germans would have rebuilt the gas chambers and have torn up and destroyed "the traces of the electric conveyor belt, on which hundreds of people were simultaneously electrocuted, their bodies falling onto the slow moving conveyor belt which carried them to the top of the blast furnace where they fell in, were completely burned, their bones converted to meal in the rolling mills, and then sent to the surrounding fields."[86]

In the weeks that followed, forensic investigation was to confirm the existence and use of the gas chambers and the ovens and relegate the electric conveyer belt and the blast furnace to the realm of myth. One can only speculate about the source of Polevoi's claim that the extermination installation contained an electric conveyer belt between the gas chamber and the so-called blast furnace. In Crematoria 2 and 3, an electric elevator

(Top) Russian and Polish investigators inspecting bags of human hair found in Auschwitz, 1945. Courtesy Archive Auschwitz-Birkenau State Museum, Oswiecim.

(Middle) Artificial limbs found in Auschwitz, 1945. Courtesy Archive Auschwitz-Birkenau State Museum, Oswiecim.

(Bottom) Dentures found in Auschwitz, 1945. Courtesy Archive Auschwitz-Birkenau State Museum, Oswiecim.

connected the underground gas chamber and the incineration room. In the confusion of tongues that existed in Auschwitz at liberation, Polevoi could have misunderstood references to the electric elevator. As to the blast furnace, the most likely source is patent application T 58240, which was submitted by incinerator manufacturer J. A. Topf & Söhne in Erfurt for a "Continuous Operation Corpse Incineration Furnace for Intensive Use," filed by Topf on November 5, 1942. In its design it reflects in general terms Polevoi's description. The Auschwitz Central Construction Office possessed a copy of this patent application, and it was found by the Russians when they liberated the camp. It may be possible that Polevoi was shown this document and drew his own conclusions.[87] What is important, however, is not that Polevoi described something that never existed in Auschwitz, but that the fiction of the electric conveyor belt–cum–blast furnace had no echo in later literature.

Polevoi's article was only recently translated and made available over the Internet by Crowell. He performed this service to scholarship about Auschwitz because it was important to him that "any atrocity claim should be placed in its proper historical context so that the researcher can understand either how the facts came to be known or how the fiction evolved in the popular mind." According to Crowell, Polevoi's article was important because it was different from "the version of Auschwitz that we have come to know, substituting the traditional atrocity record with another, completely imaginary one." The divergence between Polevoi's article and the current narrative suggested, according to Crowell, "not only to the inaccuracy of this initial report, but also to the artifice of all the subsequent ones."[88] Crowell's argument is a remarkable combination of the fallacies of false cause and special pleading.

The same day that Polevoi's article appeared in *Pravda*, the British weekly the *Jewish Chronicle* devoted one sentence to the event. "The Red Army has captured Auschwitz (Oswiecim), one of the most notorious of all death camps."[89] A week later, the same magazine carried a front-page article entitled "Oswiecim Revelations: Worst Death Camp Captured." The article provided a summary of Polevoi's account and ended with the grim statistic that "it is estimated that over 1,500,000 victims were done to death in Oswiecim, and hundreds of thousands of them were Jews."[90]

It was clear from the outset that Auschwitz had been the site of a tremendous crime and that the best way to use it as an indictment of National Socialism was to follow the example taken in Maidanek and establish the truth according to commonly accepted historical and judicial criteria of evidence. Therefore the Prosecutor's Office of the First Ukrainian Front immediately began a preliminary investigation. Like the investigation of Maidanek, it operated under the aegis of the Soviet State Extraordinary Commission for the Investigation of Fascist and Nazi Crimes. The investigators inspected the grounds of the camp, the pits containing human remains, and the ruins of the crematoria. They were assisted in the examination of the latter structures by Professor Roman Dawidowski, a specialist in heating and combustion technology from Cracow. They also studied the extermination process and the remaining loot. Physicians medically examined 2,819 former inmates and conducted autopsies on the corpses of 536 prisoners, and members of the Prosecutor's Office interviewed 200 of the remaining prisoners. They were fortunate in that they were able to interview three surviving members of the Sonderkommandos. Until the end, the Germans had kept some 100 Sonderkommandos around: thirty to run Crematorium V and seventy to clean out the incineration pits used in the summer of 1944. These 100 Sonderkommandos were marched out of the camp on January 18, but Alain Feinsilber (alias Stanislaw Jankowski), Schlomo Dragon, and Henryk Tauber were able to escape, and the last two returned in time to Oswiecim to give evidence to the Soviets. Dragon also remembered the location where his fellow Sonderkommando Salmen Gradowski had buried a journal, written in Yiddish, in an aluminum canteen.[91] The canteen was dug up in the presence of the members of the prosecutor's office. It contained an 81-leaf notebook and a letter, dated September 6, 1944. Significant parts of the journal, which he had begun before his transport to Auschwitz, had become unintelligible. However, the letter was preserved perfectly. It mentioned that the Germans had begun to obliterate the traces of the killings. "Everywhere, where there was much ash, they ordered to have it ground fine and to cart it away to the Vistula and to let it flow with the current." Gradowski implored the reader to search every inch of soil. "Tens of documents are buried under it, mine and those of other persons, which will throw light on everything that was happening here. Great quantities of teeth are also buried here. It was we, the Kommando workers, who expressly have strewn them all over the terrain, as many as we could, so that the world should find material traces of the millions of murdered people." Gradowski ended with the announcement of a planned revolt. "That day is approaching. It may happen today or tomorrow. I am writing these words in a moment of the greatest danger and excitement."[92] The uprising occurred one month after Gradowski wrote his letter, on October 7, 1944. Gradowski was one of the leaders of the revolt. The uprising failed. The Germans captured and tortured Gradowski and crushed his skull.[93]

The notebook that accompanied the letter contained a detailed description of Gradowski's deportation to Auschwitz. He described how tension mounted in the train when it passed Bialystok on its way to Warsaw. "Everyone plunged again into an atmosphere of absolute despondency. The sadness grew with every kilometre and with every kilometre the emptiness became greater. What happened? Here we are approaching the ill-famed station of Treblinka,[94] so tragic for the Jews, where, according to information which had filtered through to us, the majority of Poles and Jews from abroad were swallowed up and wiped out."[95] The train passed two women who made a gesture across their throat. Then the train began to slow down, and it stopped. "Two thousand five hundred persons held their breaths. Teeth were chattering with fright and hearts were beating like mad." Then the train whistle blew, and the train began moving again. "A fresh surge of hopeful thoughts has mastered everyone." The deportees once again believed that the atrocity stories they had heard concerned a single horrible event, "but not of mass phenomena. You can therefore notice now how everybody has plucked up his courage, deeming they were taken to live, perhaps to live a hard life, but still a life."[96] In the end, their optimism proved without foundation. After a grueling journey, the train stopped in Auschwitz, and the passengers were subjected to selection. The Germans ordered men and women to line up separately. "Nobody stirs from the spot, not being able to believe that which is unbelievable. It is not possible for something unreal to become real, a fact." Yet they were quickly beaten into obedience. "The strength of indissoluble family ties was still felt. Here are two persons standing, the husband on one side, the wife and the child on the other. Older people are standing, an old father and opposite the mother, weak already. Brothers are standing there, looking in the direction of their dear sisters. Nobody knows what is going to happen next."[97] Men who tried to cross over to the women's line were beat-

(Top) The Auschwitz branch of the Soviet State Extraordinary Commission for the Investigation of Fascist and Nazi Crimes, 1945. Courtesy Archive Auschwitz-Birkenau State Museum, Oswiecim.

(Left) Soviet soldiers interviewing survivors, 1945. Courtesy Archive Auschwitz-Birkenau State Museum, Oswiecim.

en up and driven back. The separation killed all the hope that had sustained them throughout their ordeal in the ghetto and the transit camp at Kielbasin. "The thought of staying together with the family, this opiate, which had kept up their spirits on the journey, has all at once stopped to act."[98] Lorries came up to transport the old people, the women, and the children. Gradowski was admitted into the camp. "Everyone is meditating on where his family is. . . . All are standing helpless, worried, full of despair, lonesome, unhappy, broken." Older inmates come in to ask about the size of the transport. "We are unable to grasp the meaning of such questions. Of what significance is [the list] of these numbers?" When the new arrivals asked what happened to those taken in the lorries, they were told that they had been killed.[99]

Remarkable as the discovery of Gradowski's journal was, and the other gruesome discoveries the Soviet commission made, the Soviets chose not to use the camp as a major destination for foreign journalists. In August 1944, nothing much was happening on the front—in fact, the Soviet armies had halted their advance in order to allow the Germans to crush the Warsaw uprising—and not only were many correspondents available to visit Maidanek, but the concentration camp also provided a convenient decoy to detract Western attention from the Soviet betrayal of the Polish underground army. Auschwitz was liberated just before the Yalta Conference. Exactly at the time that news of the liberation of Auschwitz reached Moscow, the Allied leaders were gathered in the Crimea, and most Western correspondents were there to cover the world-historical gathering. The

Gradowski's letter, his notebook, and the container that preserved them, 1945. Courtesy Archive Auschwitz-Birkenau State Museum, Oswiecim.

moment the conference was over, they returned to the front to report on the enormous offensive which was to end with the conquest of Berlin. There was too much to cover, and the liberation of "another Maidanek" several weeks earlier was not merely "old news" but was also of considerable less interest than, for example, the conquest of the industrial area of Upper Silesia, the siege of Breslau, the surrender of Danzig, or the crossing of the Oder River.

Only in April, in the very last weeks of the war, did the concentration camps return to the front pages of the press. With the liberation of Bergen-Belsen by British troops and the liberation of Ohrdruf, Buchenwald, and Dachau by the American army, for the first time large groups of Western observers confronted the horrors of the camps, and within days pictures of mountains of emaciated corpses and starved inmates filled the newspapers and airwaves. The BBC program *War Report* aired Richard Dimbleby's report from Bergen-Belsen on April 19. He reported his experience as he entered a barrack: "I picked my way over corpse after corpse in the gloom, until I heard one voice raised above the gentle undulating moaning. I found a girl, she was a living skeleton, impossible to gauge her age for she had practically no hair left, and her face was only a yellow parchment sheet with two holes in it for eyes." Outside he found many bodies, "all naked, all so thin that their yellow skin glistened like stretched rubber on their bones. Some of the poor starved creatures whose bodies were there looked so utterly unreal and inhuman that I could have imagined that they never lived at all."[100]

To the Allies, the discovery of the camps proved a final justification of their war effort. In 1940, Churchill had proclaimed that a Nazi victory would bring "a new Dark Age made more sinister by perverted science." The liberation of the camps proved that Churchill had not exaggerated the danger. And even though Auschwitz had been liberated by the Russians, the English and Americans heard many stories about that camp. Many of the surviving inmates in Belsen and Buchenwald had arrived there relatively recently, having been evacuated in January from Auschwitz. As journalists began to interview the survivors, they heard again and again that Belsen and Buchenwald had not been the worst. "The worst camps were those at Auschwitz, in Silesia, and Lublin, Poland where many of Buchenwald residents had been at one time or another,"[101] American journalist Helen Kirkpatrick noted. A correspondent of the Polish Telegraph Agency, who had witnessed the liberation of Buchenwald, also cabled to his head office in London that, for all its apparent horrors, "Buchenwald is not among the worst of the concentration camps. It was a camp of slow death, of death by exhaustion, sickness and hunger." And he quoted one of the liberated prisoners, who had also been an inmate in Auschwitz, that "by comparison with Oswiecim, Buchenwald was a paradise."[102] American intelligence officer Saul K. Padover, who visited the camp shortly after liberation, recorded how he met among the prisoners a Polish high school teacher from Kattowitz who had been imprisoned in Auschwitz. "As he talked he became hysterical and I had to put my hand on his shoulders to restrain him. 'I saw them murder the Jews. God Almighty, do you know what it means to see human beings burned to death? They were God's children, like us. God's children, like everybody, except the Germans.'"[103]

On April 20, Radio Luxembourg's German-language "Story of the Day," prepared by a small group of German exiles serving the American

Mass grave in Bergen-Belsen. The man in the foreground is the camp doctor, Fritz Klein. Imperial War Museum, courtesy USHMM Photo Archives.

army, carried an interview with an Auschwitz survivor who had been evacuated earlier that year, first to Buchenwald and finally to Ohrdruf. He told that "every day some transports arrived in Auschwitz, each of between 2,000 and 3,000 people," and described the procedure of selection in some detail: men and women were separated, and "each of these two groups was again subdivided into two." In the one group were those above fifty years old and those deemed to be unfit for work. In the other group were the younger and stronger people. "Those who belonged to the group of over 50-year-olds—and to this group also belonged the small children and mothers who did not want to be separated from their children—were immediately killed." Four crematoria served as killing stations. "Those condemned to death were led into these crematoria, had to undress themselves, and were gassed in a hall that was hermetically sealed. Then the corpses were incinerated in the same crematorium."[104]

The name "Auschwitz" turned up again and again. Members of the British Parliament, who had visited Buchenwald by invitation of General Eisenhower, were quoted in *The Times* of April 28 as saying that many prisoners told them that conditions in other camps, particularly those in Eastern Europe, were far worse than at Buchenwald. "The worst camp of all was said by many to be at Auschwitz; these men all insisted on showing us their Auschwitz camp numbers, tattooed in blue on their left forearms."[105]

As the British Members of Parliament drafted their report, a special intelligence team of the Psychological Warfare Division of the Supreme Headquarters Allied Expeditionary Forces, headed by Lieutenant Albert G. Rosenberg, questioned former inmates in an effort to document the atrocities. They were assisted by a group of prisoners, headed by Austrian journalist and economist Dr. Eugen Kogon—the same Kogon who was to become the focus of Stäglich's scorn thirty years later. The team interviewed some 150 people and in the process gathered a number of important testimonies about Auschwitz and other extermination camps in the East. It is important to note that at the time that Rosenberg, Kogon, and their colleagues took these testimonies, the Soviet commission had not yet published its results. One of the witnesses was 15-year-old Janda Weiss, who had been deported to Birkenau a year earlier with a transport of 1,500 Jews from Theresienstadt. He was one of the 98 people of the family camp who was spared when the Theresienstadt Jews were gassed. As a kitchen helper, he visited the barracks where the Sonderkommandos were housed. "These comrades told me about the horrors of the crematorium, where I would later work."

> I will now describe the crematoriums and the transports. At the station 2,000 people got off the trains. They had to throw away all their luggage. Afterward the men and women were divided into two groups, at which the larger boys were assigned to the group with the men. Then the great devourer of Jews, Mengele, drove by in a car, seeking out the strongest from each transport. They numbered around thirty out of 2,000. The remainder were led away by SS Technical Sergeant Moll, the officer of the crematorium. The elderly were loaded onto dump trucks and then dumped into burning trenches while still alive. The remainder were led into the gas chambers. Meanwhile new transports were arriving.
>
> In front of the gas chamber was a dressing room. On its walls

was written in all languages: "Put shoes into the cubbyholes and tie them together so you will not lose them. After the showers you will receive hot coffee." Here the poor victims undressed themselves and went into the chamber. There were three columns for the ventilators, through which the gas poured in. A special work detail with truncheons drove the people into the chamber. When the room was full, small children were thrown in through a window. Moll grabbed infants by their little legs and smashed their skulls against the wall. Then the gas was let into the chamber. The lungs of the victims slowly burst, and after three minutes a loud clamoring could be heard. Then the chamber was opened, and those who still showed signs of life were beaten to death.

The prisoners of the special work details (*Sonderkommandos*) then pulled the corpses out, took their rings off, and cut their hair, which was gathered up, put in sacks, and shipped to factories. Then they arranged the corpses in piles of ten each. After Moll had counted them, they were taken to the ovens, or if the crematoriums were insufficient, thrown into fire trenches.[106]

Kogon was to refer to Weiss's testimony in his book. As Kogon had never been in Auschwitz, Stäglich felt free, as we have seen at the beginning of this chapter, to reject Weiss's testimony. But when we consider the evidentiary value of Weiss's statement following Stäglich's hermeneutical rules, we must conclude that it should be taken seriously. He made specific allegations and he provided specific details, such as the name of the man in charge of the crematoria (Moll) and details of the undressing room and the gassing apparatus. Weiss's testimony did not contain contradictions, nor did it contain improbable allegations.[107]

German Jew Walter Blass testified that Jews were subjected to selection on other occasions after their arrival. This procedure was a regular occurrence for those imprisoned in the camp. "Selections occurred at irregular intervals, sometimes after two or three months, then after four to five months, then again, as in January 1944, twice within two weeks." At such a selection, "Jews had to undress completely and were quickly observed front to rear. Then, according to whim, they were sent to the right to record the prisoner number tattooed on the arm; that meant the death sentence. Or they were sent to the left, that is, back to the barracks; that meant a prolongation of life." Those who were sent to the right were locked in specially guarded barracks. "Often they remained there for two to three days, usually without food, since they were already considered to be 'disposed of.'"[108]

The interest in the camps generated by Belsen and Buchenwald and the various references appearing in the Western press to Auschwitz offered the Polish government-in-exile a good opportunity to present the atrocities of Auschwitz to the Western public. The first substantial report to appear after the liberation of Auschwitz was entitled "Polish Women in German Concentration Camps," and it was published in the May 1, 1945, issue of the *Polish Fortnightly Review*. The article consisted of two eyewitness testimonies, some statistics, and a note on medical experiments in the women's camp. The first testimony was entitled "An Eyewitnesses's Account of the Women's Camp at Oswiecim-Brzezinka (Birkenau)—Autumn, 1943, to Spring, 1944," and like all the other articles published in the *Polish Fortnightly Review,* it was anonymous. It is, however, clear that it was written shortly after the beginning of the Hungarian Action. The introduction testified to the authenticity of the account. "Instead of making the picture more glaring, I shall try to tone it down, to make it more credible. For the reality I have to write about is so horrible that it is difficult to believe it. Yet it is reality, and believe my words as you would believe someone returned from the dead."[109] The report began with some figures. At the time the author escaped, the serial numbers of new inmates surpassed 80,000; some 65,000 of this group had died. Most of the dead were Jewish women. Then the account discussed the conditions of work, the food, the distinguishing marks of various categories of prisoners sewn on the inmate uniforms, the camp administration, a description of the physical layout of the camp itself, and the crematoria, which were "intended for the living rather than the dead." Daily trains from all over Europe brought men, women, and children. "The scenes which take place there defy all powers of description," the report continued.

> It is terrible to think, terrible to watch when lorries pass through the Lagerstrasse, carrying four thousand children under ten years of age (children from the ghetto in Terezin in Bohemia) to their death. Some of them are weeping and calling "mummy," others were laughing at the passers by and waving their hands. Fifteen minutes later not one of them was left alive, and the gas-stupefied little bodies were burning in the horrible furnaces. But who will believe that this is true? Yet I swear that it was so, calling on the living and the dead as my witnesses.[110]

The second account dealt only with the living conditions in Birkenau, and it was followed by a table showing the monthly gassing rate of registered inmates in the women's camp for 1943. The average number was a little over 1,600 persons per month.[111]

On May 5, units of the American army liberated a concentration camp at Gunskirchen, a satellite camp of Mauthausen. A few days earlier, the SS had marched 17,000 inmates from Mauthausen to Gunskirchen. Conditions were so bad that only 5,400 were alive when the Americans arrived. One of them was 15-year-old Czech Jew Yehuda Bacon. Deported to Theresienstadt in 1942, Bacon and his family had been transported in December 1943 with almost 2,500 others to Auschwitz. The transport was not subjected to selection; instead, it was imprisoned in the so-called Czech family camp in section B IIb of Birkenau. When, after six months, the SS liquidated the Czech family camp, Yehuda Bacon survived three consecutive selections and was admitted to the men's camp. There he became a member of the so-called Rollwagenkommando (cart commando), a group of twenty boys who pulled a cart that transported goods between the various sections of Birkenau. During the Eichmann Trial, Bacon explained the purpose of this job during his examination-in-chief.

> [Attorney General Hausner]: "Who gave you orders where the cart should go?"

> [Yehuda Bacon]: "The Blockälteste (block elder) always went with us and he knew what we had to do. Our tasks were quite varied: Sometimes we had to collect papers, sometimes we had to transfer blankets, sometimes we had to go to the women's camp to which other people did not have access. With the *Rollwagenkommando* we went through all the camps of Birkenau, A, B, C, D, E and F, as well as the crematorium."

(Top) View of Crematorium 3, drawn by Yehuda Bacon, 1945. The drawing shows the outside staircase to the basement to facilitate access to the gas chamber. This outside staircase was included during the completion of the building. The drawing also shows the roof of the gas chamber (top left), with the covers of the gas columns. Courtesy Yad Vashem and Yehuda Bacon.

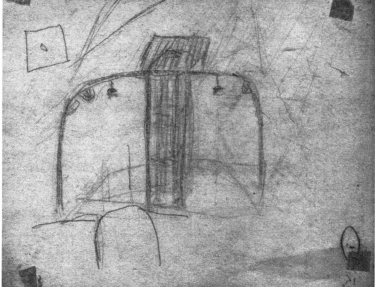

(Middle) View of the gas chamber of Crematorium 3, drawn by Yehuda Bacon, 1945. Bacon's attempt to draw an axonometric representation of the gas chambers shows the hollow gas column in the center, with its wooden cover. Bacon made a second drawing of the plan of the wooden cover in the top left corner of the drawing. He also showed the fake shower heads and the lights with their wire-mesh protective covers. A keen observer, he correctly remembered the barrel-vault-like appearance of the ceiling of the gas chamber, caused by the ventilation ducts located against the ceiling. Courtesy Yad Vashem and Yehuda Bacon.

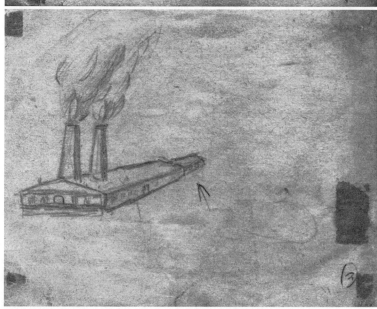

(Bottom) View of Crematorium 4, drawn by Yehuda Bacon, 1945. Bacon produced a remarkably correct representation of Crematorium 4, with its lower annex housing the gas chambers. Courtesy Yad Vashem and Yehuda Bacon.

Q.: "You went into the crematorium?"

A.: "Yes."

Q.: "Did you see the crematorium from the inside?"

A.: "Yes. We had to take wooden logs that were in the vicinity of the crematorium for the fire. Sometimes these had to be taken for regular heating in the camps. And when we finished our work and it was cold, the Kapo of the Sonderkommando took pity on us and said: 'Well, children, outside it is cold, warm yourselves in the gas chambers! There is nobody there'."

Q.: "And you went to warm yourselves inside the gas chambers?"

A.: "Yes. Sometimes we went to warm ourselves in the *Kleidungs-kammer,* sometimes in the gas chambers. It sometimes happened that when we came to the crematorium, we were told: 'You cannot enter now—there are people inside.' Sometimes, it was in crematorium 3, after they had been burned, we took the ashes, and in winter the ashes were to be used for the road."

Q.: "Did you use human ashes to spread on the roads?"

A.: "Yes."

Q.: "For what purpose?"

A.: "So that people could walk on the road and not slip."[112]

Bacon correctly referred to gas chambers in the plural because at the time that he visited the basement of the crematorium, the large room that had been designed as Morgue 1 had been subdivided in two rooms.

During his testimony, Bacon did not mention that he had also seen the roof of the underground gas chambers. As he wandered one day through the compound of Crematorium 3, he climbed up the low rise that marks the gas chambers and had a close look at one of the four little chimneys on that plateau. He removed one of the wooden covers and looked down into the central pipe, which was riddled with little holes; it was one of the four gas columns.[113]

Bacon stayed in Auschwitz until January 18, 1945, when he joined the death march to a small concentration camp in Blechhammer, from which he was transported by train to Mauthausen. When the Americans approached that camp, Bacon was sent to Gunskirchen, where he was finally liberated on May 5.

Upon his liberation an American soldier took pity on Bacon and had him admitted to a hospital in Steyr, where he recovered from typhus. After a month, he traveled to Vienna, crossing from the American into the Russian zones. In Vienna, he was taken in by a Czech family until his repatriation a few weeks later by truck to Prague. In Prague, he was sent to a children's home. In Vienna and Prague, Bacon began to draw what he had seen in Auschwitz. Three of these drawings are important as evidence about the gas chambers. Bacon submitted two of them as evidence to the District Court in Jerusalem. One drawing showed Crematorium 4 or 5 (in Bacon's numbering, 3 and 4).

[Attorney General Hausner]: "What do you have before you now, in this picture?" [*Hands a picture to the witness.*]

[Yehuda Bacon]: "Crematoria 3 and 4—they were built in a different style—they were older."

Q.: "Are these the ones you mentioned in your earlier testimony?"

A.: "Yes."

Q.: "At the end there is a small structure. What is that?"

A.: "Here, there were two gas chambers, on the extreme right-hand side."

Attorney general: "I submit this to the Court."

[Presiding Judge Landau]: "What does the arrow signify?"

A.: "The arrow points to the gas chambers, to the small structure containing the gas chambers."[114]

The drawing is important because its allows us to gauge the precision of Bacon's memory. The building Bacon drew matches the blueprints and the few surviving photos of Crematoria 4 and 5. Bacon correctly remembered the building as a large, higher shed with two tall chimneys on one side and a smaller, lower shed—the gas chambers—attached to the other side.

A second drawing, a bird's-eye view of Crematorium 2, confirms Bacon's ability to remember both the general shape and arrangement of a building as well as particular architectural details. Significantly, he correctly depicted in the top left corner of the drawing, at the back side of the crematorium, the roof of the gas chamber, with four squares indicating the four chimneys that connected to the gas columns below.

In a third drawing, Bacon made a section of the gas chamber in which he had been allowed to warm himself. This drawing was admitted as evidence in the Eichmann Trial and gave rise to the following discussion during Bacon's examination-in-chief.

[Attorney General Hausner]: "What are you holding in your hand now?"

[Yehuda Bacon]: "This is a view of the gas chambers and also Nos. 1 and 2 which were underground, and what one saw above. They looked like water sprinklers; I was curious and examined them closely. I saw there were no holes in them, this was just a sham; at first sight it seemed to be an actual shower-head.

Above there were lights covered with wire, and in each gas chamber there were two pipes leading from the ceiling to the floor, and around them were four iron columns surrounded by strong wire. When the operation was over and the people were forced inside, the SS opened some device above, like a drainage pipe, and through it introduced Zyklon B."

[Presiding Judge Landau]: "Did the gas remain in the middle of the chamber and spread from there?"

A.: "Yes."

[Judge Raveh]: "Is that what we see in the centre of the picture?"

A.: "Yes, there were two of these in each gas chamber in crematoria Nos. 1 and 2—that is to say, there were four; their dimensions were 40×40 centimetres; below were the ventilators and also holes for cleaning with water. Afterwards, when they dismantled the crematoria, we saw the ventilators separately."

[Presiding Judge Landau]: "Were these air vents?"

A.: "Yes. There were several openings. One opening was for the purpose of ventilation and one for washing the floor."

[Presiding Judge Landau]: "This drawing of the gas chamber will be marked T/1320."

[Attorney General Hausner]: "In order to make it quite clear, Mr. Bacon, what purpose did this ventilation serve?"

A.: "The ventilation made it possible for other people to enter at once."

Q.: "To ventilate the chamber after the killing?"

A.: "Yes. The bodies were removed from the chamber, there was a lift there—actually it consisted only of boards $2^{1}/_{2} \times 1^{1}/_{2}$ metres. I saw the lift on which they transferred the bodies to the top floor of that crematorium, from where there were rails of small trains with waggons, and they conveyed the bodies to the incinerators. I also saw the incinerators, and I remember that members of the Sonderkommando also showed me the crate in which they collected the gold teeth, which were melted down into gold bars."[115]

Bacon's drawing is certainly not a work of art. But as a piece of evidence about the machinery of death, it converges in essential aspects with evidence given in the spring and summer of 1945 by former inmates such as David Olère, Henry Tauber, and Michael Kula.

One day after Bacon's liberation, American troops rescued 43-year-old painter David Olère in the concentration camp at Ebensee, twenty-five miles south of Gunskirchen. Born in Warsaw, Olère had moved to Paris in 1923, where he found work making posters and designing film sets. He had been arrested in February 1943 and deported to Auschwitz on March 2 of that year. He was assigned to the Sonderkommandos of Crematorium 3, but he worked as an artist making paintings for the SS.[116] Olère lived in the attic of Crematorium 3 and was able to observe both the building and its operation. After his liberation, Olère returned home to Paris. There he began to draw his memories: over fifty sketches, done in 1945 and 1946. Many of them were purchased by the Bet Lohamei Haghettaot Museum in Israel. These sketches remained unknown until they were first exhibited in 1976. They provide a very important visual record of the design and operation of the gas chamber and the incinerators of Crematorium 3, and they were made before information about that building was published. The first two architectural sketches that are of great importance are pen drawings dated 1945 and 1946, which are "cleaned-up" versions of pencil sketches made in 1945. One of them, done in 1945, provides a plan of Crematorium 3; the second, done in 1946, a section.[117] The plan is a composite of the basement level with the underground undressing room and the gas chamber which jutted out beyond the footprint of the building (left), and the ground floor and the incineration room with its fifteen cremation ovens, the chimney, the incinerator for identity papers, the coke store, and the SS guard rooms. Arrows indicate the functional relationship between the various rooms: from the undressing room (1) people went through the

Plan of Crematorium 3, drawn by David Olère, 1945. Olère provided the drawing with a numbered key to identify the parts, and the following legend: One of the five triple-muffle ovens (0); undressing room (1); basement vestibule where the SS controlled the entry of the inmates into the gas chamber (2); gas chamber (3); corpse lift (4); room with five three-muffle ovens (5); room with waste incinerator (6); central chimney (7); storage for documents to be burned (8); guard room for the SS (9); the four openings to introduce Zyklon B (10); coke store (11); small truck to transport coke (12); entry to the basement for the SS (13). A vertical dotted line separates Olère's drawing in two parts. The left side (nos. 1, 3, 4, 10, 13) shows the plan of the basement of Crematorium 3; the right side (nos. 0, 5, 9, 11, 12) shows the plan of the main floor, with exception of the autopsy rooms, which are located above the two vestibules in the basement (no. 2) and the unnumbered space adjacent to the SS entrance to the basement. Courtesy Bet Lohamei Haghettaot Museum.

vestibule (2) to the gas chamber (3) to be killed. SS men overseeing the operation could enter the basement by a separate stairway connecting to the yard (13). After the gassing, Sonderkommandos moved the bodies to the elevator (4), which ascended to open into the incineration room (5), where other Sonderkommandos filled the fifteen incineration muffles of the ovens (0). The coke was brought with a truck running on rails from the coke store (11) to the back of the ovens (0). Through five underground flues the smoke left the ovens to the massive chimney (7). Olère's plan is fully corroborated by the plans that were found by the Russians in the building of the Central Construction Office, which will be discussed below. One detail of particular importance which cannot be found on the blueprints recovered from the Auschwitz building archive is the staggered arrangement of the four hollow wire-mesh columns (marked 10) in the gas chamber (marked 3) through which the Zyklon B was inserted into the room. As we will see below, there are various eyewitness accounts of these hollow columns, but they do not appear in the original blueprints because they were only added to the building shortly before completion. Olère's staggered arrangement is confirmed by air photos of Birkenau taken by the Americans on August 25, 1944, and can be explained by assuming that these wire-mesh columns were located on the west side of the first and fifth structural columns, which supported the roof of the gas chamber, and on the east side of the third and seventh structural columns.

The corresponding section, drawn in 1946, is a complex drawing that shows much information in an economical manner. At the underground level Olère depicted the undressing room to the west or left (marked A) with the staircase on the extreme left that provided the principal access to this space. Because the undressing room was not equipped with a ventilation system built into the walls, it was equipped with metal ventilation

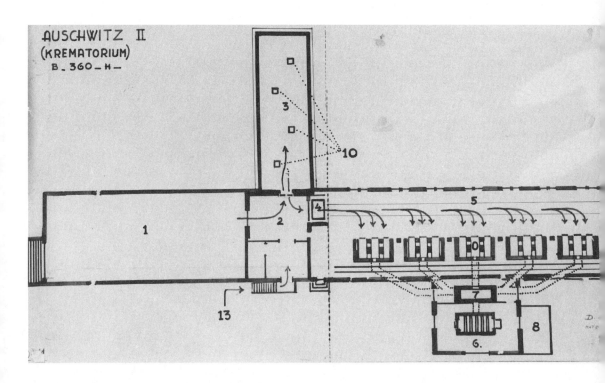

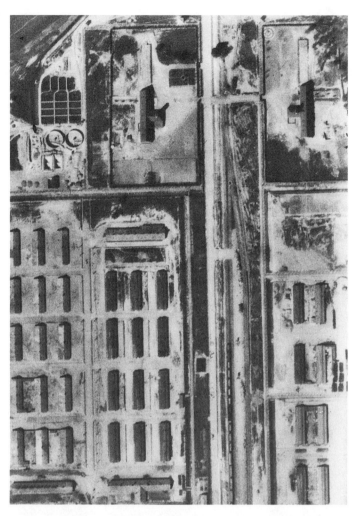

(Top) Aerial photo of the southwestern part of Birkenau, taken August 25, 1944. RG373-Can ON 24507-exp 3185. Courtesy National Archives, Washington, D.C.

(Bottom) Detail of aerial photo of Crematoria 2 and 3, taken August 25, 1944. RG373-Can ON 24507-exp 3185. Courtesy National Archives, Washington, D.C.

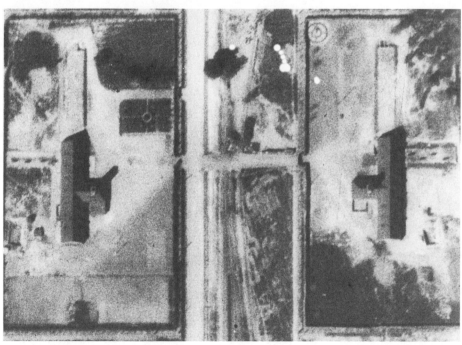

ducts that were suspended from the ceiling. Olère also depicts the benches and the clothing hooks. To the east or right of the undressing room is the vestibule with the corpse elevator (C) to the ground floor and the gas chamber (D). In order to represent the gas chamber, which projected outward to the north of the building at the back and would have been hidden by the vestibule, Olère defied convention and turned it 90° from a south-north to a west-east axis, so that it is depicted under the incineration room (which had no basement). The most important information contained in this part of the drawing are the four hollow wire-mesh columns (E). For the section of the incineration hall, Olère turned the five triple-muffle ovens 180° so that the muffles are visible. The forced-air blowers on the side of each furnace and the coke truck that supplied the back of the furnaces with coke are also important details. The corpses were loaded from the front.

In a number of other sketches, Olère provided additional information about Crematorium 3. One drawing from 1945 shows Crematorium 3

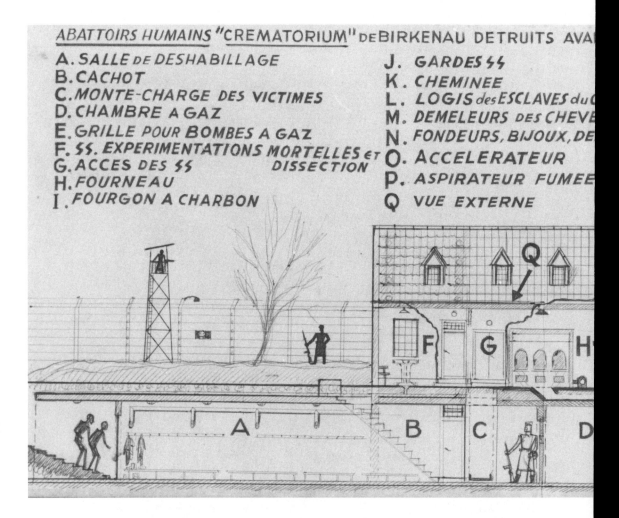

from the outside and people filing into the compound from the road along the tracks, moving toward the end of the undressing room. A second sketch, dated 1946, shows the interior of the undressing room, with the benches, hooks, and the ventilation system. A third drawing shows the interior of the gas chamber with Sonderkommandos collecting gold teeth and the hair of the women. One of the hollow wire-mesh columns is depicted in the back. Finally, a fourth drawing shows the incineration hall with, at the back, the corpse elevator that connects the basement level to the ground floor. The information in all of these drawings was to be corroborated in the testimony of the Sonderkommando Henryk Tauber (see below) and the blueprints found in the Central Construction Office (see below). None of these drawings could have been made on the basis of published material, because it was simply not available at the time.

Two other drawings are of interest. One, dated 1945, shows Bunker 2—a peasant cottage that was transformed into a gas chamber in 1942, taken out of commission in 1943, and brought back into operation during

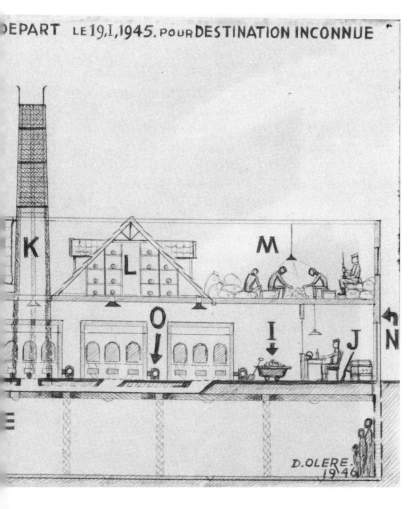

Section of Crematorium 3, drawn by David Olère, 1946. Olère provided the drawing with a lettered key to identify the parts and a legend. To facilitate comparison, I have also included, where relevant, the number that Olère used to indicate that same building part in his drawing of the plan for Crematorium 3 reproduced above. Olère represented the gas chamber (D / 3), which projected outward to the north of the building at the back and would have been hidden by the vestibule, under the incineration room (which had no basement). Olère's key: undressing room (A / 1); cell (B); corpse elevator (C / 4); gas chamber (D / 3); [metal] grate [columns] for gas bombs (E / 10); SS: lethal experiments and dissection (F); entry for SS (G); incinerator (H / 0); coke truck (I / 12); SS guards (J / 9); chimney (K / 7); quarters of the crematorium slaves (L); hair disentanglers (M); casters, jewels, teeth, gold (N); forced air ventilator (O); smoke extractor (P); outside view (Q). Courtesy Bet Lohamei Haghettaot Museum.

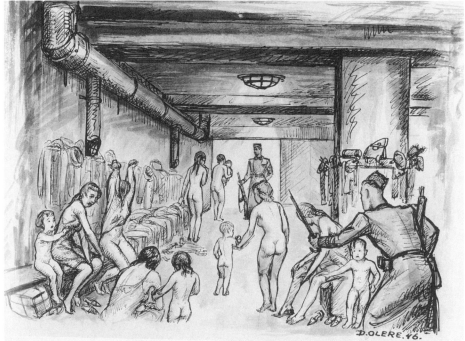

*View of Crematorium 3, drawn
by David Olère, 1945. Courtesy
Bet Lohamei Haghettaot
Museum.*

*Undressing room of
Crematorium 3, drawn by David
Olère, 1946. Courtesy Bet
Lohamei Haghettaot Museum.*

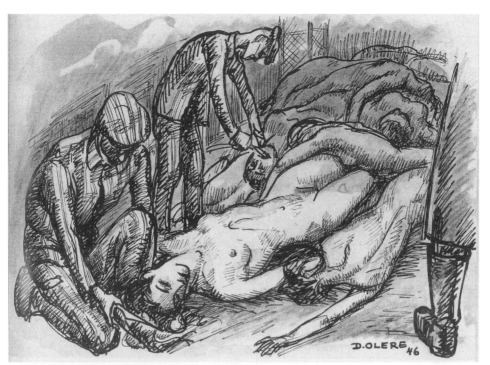

Collecting gold teeth and hair in the gas chamber, drawn by David Olère, 1946. Courtesy Olère family.

Incineration room of Crematorium 3, drawn by David Olère, 1945. Courtesy Bet Lohamei Haghettaot Museum.

Intentional Evidence • 179

the Hungarian Action. The drawing shows not only Bunker 2 but also the undressing barrack in its correct position vis-à-vis the cottage. Of particular interest is the small window in the side of the cottage with the heavy wooden shutter. This was the opening through which the SS introduced the Zyklon B into the room. The same way of introducing the gas was adopted in Crematoria 4 and 5, and not only do the plans, elevations, and photographs of the crematoria show these openings, but three of these shutters still survive and are presently stored in the coke room of Crematorium 1. Even in its details, Olère's drawing is supported by surviving material evidence.

The second drawing depicts the execution of women and children at the edge of an incineration pit behind Crematorium 5. It shows, to the left, Crematorium 5 depicted (again archaeologically correct), with the higher

Bunker 2, drawn by David Olère, 1945. Courtesy Olère family.

shed with the incineration rooms and the two chimneys to the far end and, closer to the main scene, the lower wing with the gas chambers. Olère again depicted one of the small windows with the heavy wooden shutters. Drawn from memory, the elevation of the gas chamber is not perfect: the short side contained in reality a door and two of these Zyklon B insertion points. But in its essentials Olère's representation is correct: the crematorium was a higher shed with two chimneys to which was attached a lower wing with small highly placed windows closed with heavy shutters.

On the same day that the Americans liberated Olère, May 6, 1945, the Soviet State Extraordinary Commission for the Investigation of Fascist and Nazi Crimes issued its findings, which were made available to the press a day later by the Soviet news agency Tass. The Soviet Embassy in Washington, D.C., published the English version of the whole report on May 29, 1945, under the lengthy title "Statement of the Extraordinary State Com-

*Crematorium 5 and its cremation
pit, 1945. Courtesy Olère family.*

mittee for the Ascertaining and Investigation of Crimes Committed by the
German-fascist Invaders and Their Associates in the Oswiecim Death
Camp." The report began with the statement that, on the basis of the interviews with the former inmates, study of German documents found, and
inspection of the remains of the crematoria, the commission had come to
the conclusion that some 4 million people had been killed at Auschwitz. "In
the degree of premeditation, technical organization, and mass scale and
cruelty of murder, the Oswiecim camp leaves far behind all German camps
known hitherto." Quoting German minutes of a meeting at the Auschwitz
architecture office held in August 1942, the Soviet report stated that the
Germans called the gas chambers "special purpose baths."

> On the entrance to the "bath" was written "For Disinfection,"
> and at the exit "Entrance to the baths." People earmarked for
> annihilation thus unsuspectingly entered the premises for disin-
> fection, undressed and from there were herded into the special
> purpose bath—that is, into the gas chambers where they were
> wiped out by cyclone poison.
> Special hospitals, surgical wings, histological laboratories
> and other installations were established in the camp not to heal
> people, but to kill them. German professors and doctors carried
> out wholesale experiments on perfectly healthy men, women and
> children in these institutions. They conducted experiments in
> sterilizing women and castrating men and boys, in infecting large

numbers of people with cancer, typhus and malaria, conducting observations upon them; they tested the action of poisons on them.[118]

Following these introductory paragraphs, the report presented the issues raised in greater detail. First of all, it provided a short account of the development of the camp, in which it gave prominence to the role of the firm Topf & Sons, suppliers of incineration equipment. The report mentioned that the Soviets had recovered a large correspondence between Topf and the camp administration, and it printed two letters as evidence. A page-long description of the gas chambers and incinerators followed. The report estimated that the Germans were able to kill and burn between 10,000 and 12,000 people per day—that is between 8,000 and 10,000 arriving deportees and between 2,000 and 3,000 inmates. It quoted surviving Sonderkommandos Dragon and Tauber and repeated the assertion that the crematoria could incinerate between 10,000 and 12,000 corpses per day.

The next parts of the report considered various issues:

1. The medical experiments.

2. The constant arrivals of transports from all over Europe—between three to five trains a day, each carrying between 1,500 and 3,000 deportees. The Germans selected from each train between 300 and 500 for work, and killed the remainder.

3. The exploitation of labor at IG Farben in such a way that people were completely expendable in a terrible "moving belt of death."

4. The murder of hundreds of thousands of children.

5. The liquidation of intellectuals and scientists from all over Europe.

6. The mass plunder of possessions of the deportees: the report included an accurate accounting of the remaining loot found in the camp—348,820 men's suits, 836,255 women's coats and dresses, 5,525 women's shoes, 38,000 men's shoes, 13,964 carpets, and so on—apart from seven railway wagons filled with another 514,843 garments ready for shipment to Germany and 293 bags with women's hair weighing 7,000 kilos, which probably belonged to 140,000 women.

The penultimate section of the report dealt with the German attempt to obliterate the traces of their crimes by destroying all documents concerning the number of people put to death in the Auschwitz camp. Yet the commission determined, on the basis of the remains of the crematoria, the testimonies of prisoners and other witnesses, and various documents, that millions of people were annihilated, poisoned, and burned at Auschwitz. Most important in their determination of the number of victims was their assessment of the capacity of the crematoria. Crematorium 1, so it was estimated, had had a monthly incineration capacity of 9,000 corpses. Having been in operation for 24 months, it was assumed that it had had a burning capacity of 216,000 bodies. Crematoria 2 and 3 were estimated to each have had a monthly capacity of 90,000 corpses. As they had been in operation for 19 and 18 months, respectively, they would have been able to incinerate together a total of 3,330,000 corpses. Crematoria 4 and 5 were estimated at 45,000 bodies per month, and as they had been in function for

17 and 18 months, respectively, they had together over that time a cremation capacity of 1,575,000 bodies. In total, the five crematoria would have been able to burn, at least in theory, 5,121,000 bodies. Added to that was an extra capacity provided by the pyres. Yet, "making allowances for possible undercapacity operation of the crematoriums and stoppages," the technical experts concluded that the total victim count was probably 4 million people.[119]

The Soviet investigation done by the Prosecution Office of the First Ukrainian Front had been short, and hurried, because the Army Group to which it belonged was at the time involved in heavy fighting: the conquest of Silesia, the siege of Breslau, and the final "Battle for Berlin" had a substantially higher priority than a forensic investigation in what quickly became the army rear. Yet, compared to the Polevoi account, the new report heralded an important step forward, and Polevoi's description of an extermination machine that consisted of an "electric conveyor belt connected to a slow moving conveyor feeding a blast furnace" was relegated to the dustbin of history. In general, the description of the operation of the camp and the life of the inmates was to be confirmed by the more careful investigations of the ensuing years.

Yet the report contained one very monumental error: the assertion that at least 4 million people had been murdered at Auschwitz. This figure was based on what was an admittedly quick and crude calculation of the supposed incineration capacity of the crematoria. Yet there were also other factors that influenced this assessment. Most important of all, the forensic investigation in Auschwitz was done in the wake of the publication of the Maidanek report, and according to the latter the Germans had killed about 1.5 million people in Maidanek. As we have seen, it would be two years before this figure was revised downward to 360,000 victims. In 1945, Maidanek provided the measuring stick by which to estimate the number of victims of Auschwitz, and in every aspect the latter camp was considerably larger. The six completed compounds of Maidanek held 144 barracks; the main compounds of Birkenau held more than twice that number, to which could be added the camp at Auschwitz I, the camp at Monowitz, and the many satellite camps. In Maidanek, the crematorium had five ovens; the four crematoria in Birkenau had nine times as many. Given these statistics, the commission, without any substantial data about the number of transports that had arrived at the camp, was inclined to see the number of victims as a multiple of that of Maidanek.

The response to the revelation was limited. There were many other things on people's minds. In the West, the main news concerned the collapse and official surrender of the German Reich, the chaos everywhere, and the political rearrangement of Europe. As far as the concentration camps were concerned, attention remained focused on the camps liberated by the English and the Americans—most specifically Bergen-Belsen and Dachau. While striking visual material from these camps and the deeply emotional observations of journalists and soldiers continued to remain directly available to the media, the English-language version of the Soviet report contained only one small picture showing a close-up of the bodies of Auschwitz victims.

While contemporaries did not pay attention to the Statement of the Extraordinary State Committee, and historians tend to ignore it because it was the product of a hasty investigation which was to be followed by a much more substantial Polish forensic investigation, a negationist such as Crowell gave it extraordinary significance because it crystallized, in his view, the "canonical" Holocaust story. He wrote, "The Soviet Special Commission on Auschwitz is probably the most important document ever issued on the gas extermination claim. Indeed, it is somewhat shocking to see the extent to which the claim is traced back to this slim and insubstantial brochure. But at the time it established not only the fact of the gas extermination claim but also the implementation of that alleged policy at the largest of all the concentration camps."[120] Having credited the Soviet report with a significance it did not have at the time, Crowell had no trouble using it as a straw man to make his case. Because it was so remarkably different from Polevoi's article and showed similarities with the War Refugee Board report, Crowell immediately assumed that an alleged original "Soviet Auschwitz narrative," which he assumed was created by Polevoi, was edited to make it conform to the War Refugee Board.[121] In other words, the difference between Polevoi and the Statement of the Extraordinary State Committee pointed at the fabrication of the Auschwitz narrative. He did not consider the possibility that the cause of the similarities between the War Refugee Board Report and the Soviet report was the fact that both referred to the same historical reality. In the world of intertextuality, such a logical assumption is, of course, irrelevant. But in historiographical practice, it is a first assumption one must make.

Important parts of the Soviet report would later be confirmed by eyewitnesses. In his attempt to neutralize these independent corroborations of the eyewitness testimony of survivors, Crowell used the fallacy of false cause when he argued that because the Soviets had been wrong in their conclusion that 4 million people had been killed in Auschwitz, any witness statement that provided that figure must have been inspired by the Soviet figure.

> The fact that the eyewitness testimonies and confessions in the postwar period correspond to the Soviet Special Commission could be taken as simple corroboration of the Soviet report, except that it has now been recognized that the Soviet report was wrong, in particular on its totally arbitrary calculation of four million victims (current estimates hold one million or less). That figure derived from the Soviet calculation of cremation capacities. It did not derive from testimony. On the other hand, we have several testimonies and confessions which support it. But since the figure is wrong, it follows that the testimonies and confessions which support the calculation were influenced by the report.
>
> If a witness or a confessor makes statements that corroborate statements in an official and widely publicized report, that witness may be viewed as independently verifying the truth, although the absence of material and documentary support would still leave the matter in doubt. But when the witness or confessor corroborates statements and the statements are false, then one can presume that the witness and confessor statements were simple derivatives of the reports. To put it another way, several testimonies may converge on a truth, but several testimonies cannot converge on a falsehood: in such a case one is dealing either with statements derived from a common erroneous source or a kind of mass hysteria determined by the authority of an erroneous source.[122]

Crowell did not consider the fact that the Sonderkommandos had given the Soviet investigators the figure of 4 million, while a calculation of the incineration capacity of the crematoria had initially generated a figure of 5.1 million. But Crowell did not limit himself to discrediting the witnesses by employing the fallacy of *non causa pro causa;* he also used the fallacy of composition to conclude by assuming that if indeed witnesses had taken the number of 4 million victims from the Soviet report, then all their testimony would be tainted. In fact, he argued that because allegations of mass gassings had been widely disseminated since 1942 and had assumed official status by the fall of 1944, "it would have been impossible to obtain 'blind' testimony or an untainted confession." Crowell did not mention that those who gave testimony had most often been isolated from the world between 1942 and 1944, imprisoned in Auschwitz. And he concluded that "only statements that provided high levels of corroborative detail would be really probative, yet that is precisely what was never offered. Eyewitness testimonies and confessions made the gravest errors, whenever they strayed into details."[123] As we will see, such testimonies with high levels of corroborative detail were offered at the time. Only by committing the fallacy of special pleading, by remaining silent about the testimonies of Germans such as Pery Broad and Jewish Sonderkommandos such as Shlomo Dragon and Henryk Tauber, could Crowell conclude that the Soviet report and eyewitness statements became quickly linked in some infernal loop in which the one corroborated the other and the relation between cause and effect was obscured. "Thus a version of the gassing claim, what we would call the Canonical Holocaust, evolved almost entirely through oral testimonies that built upon the basis of a report that had no substance. Meanwhile, the damning newsreels of Belsen would be manipulated and juxtaposed from camp to camp according to the whim of the prevailing culture, and provide the unanswerable ground to the claim."[124]

Let us turn our back on Crowell's manipulation of the evidence and look at the facts. In May 1945, serious forensic investigations at Auschwitz acquired momentum. The camp became one of the chief objects of study by the Polish Central Commission for the Investigation of German Crimes in Poland. The commission, fashioned after the model of the Soviet Extraordinary State Commission, was given responsibility for producing a full account of all the Nazi crimes in Poland. Judging its work by today's standards, one must admit that it tried to establish historical truth with remarkable scholarly professionalism and following due legal form. In the foreword to the publication of the first reports, the commission took justifiable pride in the fact that they had worked "according to the principles which are valid in all judicial proceedings—i.e. impartiality, proper caution in collecting evidence, and careful verification of witnesses' statements." As to the reports themselves, the commission stated that "only data of unquestioned evidential value were considered fit for publication."[125]

Jan Sehn, 1945. Courtesy Archive Auschwitz-Birkenau State Museum, Oswiecim.

In Auschwitz, the highly competent and scrupulous Judge Dr. Jan Sehn of the Cracow court led on behalf of the commission a very thorough year-long forensic and historical investigation in Auschwitz. In this process, he and his colleagues questioned and re-questioned many witnesses, including the surviving Sonderkommandos Dragon and Tauber, who had already testified for the Soviet-Polish commission, and Alain Feinsilber (alias Stanislaw Jankowski), who had only been able to return to Poland after the Soviet-Polish commission had completed its work.

Jankowski was the first Sonderkommando to testify before Sehn's commission. On April 16, he was questioned in Cracow by Sehn's deputy, Edward Pechalski. Jankowski explained that he fought in Spain on the

Stanislaw Jankowski, 1980s. Courtesy Archive Auschwitz-Birkenau State Museum, Oswiecim.

Republican side and that after the fall of Barcelona he had crossed into France, where he had been interned. After the German invasion, he escaped and ended up in Paris, where he was arrested as a Jew and interned in Drancy, to be deported to Auschwitz in March 1942. After an initial stay in Birkenau he was transferred to Auschwitz, where he worked in a carpentry shop. In November 1942, Jankowski was detailed to work in Crematorium 1. At that time, the gas chamber of Crematorium 1 was only sporadically used for killing people, having reverted back to its original function as a morgue. "The only gassing I knew about had taken place in November or December 1942. Over three hundred and ninety persons were then gassed, all of them Jews of various nationalities, employed in the Sonderkommando at Birkenau." As Jankowski witnessed, in late 1942 the Germans began to periodically kill the Sonderkommandos involved in the operation of the bunkers and crematoria in Birkenau. This happened initially in the gas chamber of Crematorium 1 in Auschwitz, which was done with the help of a special group of Sonderkommandos who were not involved in the genocide taking place in Birkenau. When Crematorium 1 was taken out of commission in 1943, the practice evolved that the first task of the newly appointed Sonderkommandos in Birkenau was to kill and incinerate their predecessors. Jankowski described how the gassing took place in the morgue, or Leichenhalle.

> We got the order to clear the *Leichenhalle* which was to be used for a larger transport. As there were many corpses collected in the mortuary at that time, we worked two days and two nights and cremated all corpses. I remember that after the mortuary had been cleared on Wednesday at about 11 A.M. those three hundred and ninety odd from Birkenau were brought into the yard under a strong escort of SS men (two SS men for every five prisoners). We, Jews, were told to leave the mortuary and to go to the coke store. When we were permitted to return to the yard after some time, we found there only the clothes of those prisoners. Then we were ordered to pass to the *Leichenhalle* where we found the corpses. After writing down the camp numbers of the gassed prisoners we had to carry the corpses to the cremators.[126]

In July 1943, Jankowski was transferred to Birkenau to join the squad of 120 prisoners that operated Crematorium 5. According to Jankowski, Crematoria 2 and 3 each had an incineration capacity of 2,500 corpses, while Crematoria 4 and 5 could burn 1,500 each. He described how old and sick people and "pregnant women and children" were selected to be killed. "All those who went straight to be gassed at Birkenau were not registered, both old people and women, children, above all, also all those who professed to be ill. The number of those who were not registered in the camp and who were cremated in the cremators at any rate surpassed many times the number of prisoners with camp numbers."[127] Later in his deposition, Jankowski came back to the very important fact that only those admitted to the camp received numbers. "No camp numbers were given and no registering was effected both in the cases of all those who went straight to the gas from transports and of those who for some considerations were not liquidated at once but, being beforehand destined for cremation, awaited their turn to come in special places of isolation."[128]

According to Jankowski, the zenith of killing occurred during the Hungarian Action.

The unloading ramp was situated opposite crematoria 2 and 3, more or less halfway between camps C and D. At that time about 18,000 Hungarians were daily murdered at Birkenau. Circa 30% of the then arriving transports, which kept coming one after another all day long, were selected to be put in the camp. They were registered in series A and B. The rest were gassed and cremated in the crematoria ovens. If the number of persons to be gassed was not sufficiently large, they would be shot and burned in pits. It was a rule to use the gas chamber for groups of more than 200 persons, as it was not worth while to put the gas chamber in action for a smaller number of persons.[129]

Jankowski was largely right in the last assertion: during the Hungarian Action, the practice evolved of shooting those deportees who were unable to walk to the crematoria at the pits. Throughout the killing operations, the Auschwitz SS always faced the problem of how to manage the circumstance that the arriving deportees were of different mobility. When the selections took place at the so-called Judenrampe outside of Birkenau, those who were selected to live would walk to the camp, while those who could not were loaded in trucks and brought to the bunkers or crematoria. When the rail spur was completed that connected Birkenau with the main railway line in early 1944, this procedure had to change because there was little room in the confined situation within the camp for trucks to operate. Most who were condemned to die could walk the relatively short distance from the place of selection to the crematoria. Because there was no transport available for those who could not, a situation arose in which those who had walked to the crematoria would have to wait a long time for those who were lame and crippled to catch up. Such a delay would disturb the efficiency of the killing operation and produce greater anxiety, hence the SS decided not to wait for those who were unable to join the main body of those deportees to be gassed and to begin gassing those who were able to walk to the crematoria immediately after they had undressed themselves. From this evolved the practice of shooting those who were left behind.

Jankowski's statements provided a solid basis for Sehn's investigation. They were to be corroborated in the testimonies and confessions taken in the two years that followed. On May 10, Sehn took the testimony of Dragon concerning the operation of Bunker 2, the gas chamber in the grove of birch forests that had been the site of most of the mass killings in the second half of 1942 and the first months of 1943. As we have seen earlier, Dragon became a Sonderkommando in December 1942, when he was put to work at Bunker 2 hauling the bodies of those killed from the gas chambers into the yard. "After having removed all the bodies from the cottage, we had to clean it thoroughly, wash the floor with water, spread it with sawdust, and whitewash the walls. The interior of the cottage was divided into four rooms by partition walls. One, in which one could house 1200 naked people, the second with a capacity of 700, the third of 400, and the fourth with a capacity of between 200 and 250."[130] Dragon told how he was later transferred to Crematorium 5, where he worked in the garden and was employed cutting lumber in the adjacent forest. During the Hungarian Action he was once more employed to remove bodies from the gas chambers of Crematorium 5. These rooms, which were attached in an annex to the main building itself, resembled in many ways the arrangement of Bunker 2. The procedure was similar, with an SS soldier throwing Zyklon B crystals through a little window located in the outer wall of the gas chambers. But in this case the window was so high that one needed a small ladder to reach it. After the gassing, Moll opened the doors of the gas

Shlomo Dragon, 1980s. Courtesy Archive Auschwitz-Birkenau State Museum, Oswiecim.

chambers. "We put on our gas masks and pulled the bodies out of the various rooms through a short corridor into the undressing room and from there, once more through a short corridor, to the ovens. In the first vestibule, the one with the entrance doors, the barbers shaved the heads, in the second the dentists removed the teeth. In front of the ovens we put the bodies on an iron stretcher, which then were inserted into the ovens by means of iron rolls fixed to the ovens." Dragon explained how they filled every oven with three corpses. They had to load the oven quickly, because by the time the third corpse was put in, the first had already started to burn and rise, which caused problems when inserting the third corpse. "We handled the stretcher in such a way that two inmates lifted the side that was farthest away from the oven and one [lifted] the end that was inserted first into the oven. After we moved the stretcher in one of the inmates held the corpse back with a long iron pole. We called it a rake with its end turned. The two others then pulled the stretcher out from under the dead."[131] According to Dragon, cremation lasted for fifteen to twenty minutes, and after that time they just opened the door and inserted new bodies. In a three-month period during the summer of 1944, the ovens were worked in two shifts, one from 6:30 A.M. to 6:30 P.M., and one from 6:30 P.M. to 6:30 A.M.

Remains at the site corroborated Dragon's account, and on orders of Jan Sehn, the local engineer, M. Nosal, himself an ex-inmate of the camp, drew up detailed drawings that showed the layout of Bunker 2, the site plan with the undressing barracks, Bunker 2, the tracks, and the four incineration pits. Dragon was precise and reliable when he talked about what he had witnessed in person, and none of the details he told were part of the Soviet report.

One week after examining Dragon, Sehn interrogated 28-year-old former Sonderkommando Henry Tauber. Dragon had been able to provide evidence about Bunker 2 and Crematoria 4 and 5, but Tauber had worked in Crematorium 2. Tauber was very hesitant to estimate how many people had been gassed. "At present, I am incapable of giving the exact number of all the people gassed and incinerated in the Krematorien and the pits." Yet in the end he was prepared to state that during the period that he worked at the crematoria (February 1943 to October 1944), 2 million people had been gassed. And he added that "during my time in Auschwitz, I was able to talk to various prisoners who had worked in the Krematorien and the bunkers before my arrival. They told me that I was not among the first to do this work, and that before I came another 2 million people had already been gassed in Bunkers 1 and 2 and Krematorium 1." And he concluded that, "adding up, the total number of people gassed in Auschwitz amounted to about 4 million."[132] Tauber made a clear distinction between what he accepted on the basis of his own observations and what he accepted on hearsay and showed himself to be a reliable witness. Indeed, his testimony proved very important: his very long and very detailed account of the operation of Crematorium 1 (where he worked from early February 1943 until March 4), Crematorium 2, and Crematorium 4 is almost wholly corroborated by the German blueprints of the buildings.

Tauber told that he arrived in Auschwitz on January 19, 1943, and that initially he was billeted in sector BIb. At the beginning of February, Tauber and nineteen other inmates were transferred to the main camp to work in Crematorium 1. After a pep talk by an SS man who told them that they better get accustomed to some unpleasant work, the group was brought to the "bunker" or the morgue/gas chamber, which was filled with

Henryk Tauber, 1945. Courtesy Archive Auschwitz-Birkenau State Museum, Oswiecim.

hundreds of corpses. They dragged these corpses to the furnace room. There they were instructed to load a truck that ran on rails with the corpses. Tauber provided an extraordinarily detailed description of the equipment, the procedure, and its problems.

> Its strong frame was in the form of a box, and to make it heavier we weighted it with stones and scrap metal. The upper part was extended by a metal slide over two meters long. We put five corpses on this: first we put two with the legs towards the furnace and the belly upwards, then two more the other way round but still with the belly upwards, and finally we put the fifth one with the legs towards the furnace and the back upwards. The arms of this last one hung down and seemed to embrace the other bodies below. The weight of such a load sometimes exceeded that of the ballast, and in order to prevent the trolley from tipping up and spilling the corpses we had to support the slide by slipping a plank underneath it. Once the slide was loaded, we pushed it into the muffle. Once the corpses were introduced into the furnace, we held them there by means of a metal box that slid on top of the charging slide, while other prisoners pulled the trolley back, leaving the corpses behind. There was a handle at the end of the slide for gripping and pulling back the sliding box. Then we closed the door. In crematorium 1, there were three two-muffle furnaces, as I have already mentioned. Each muffle could incinerate five human bodies. Thirty corpses could be incinerated at the same time in this crematorium. At the time when I was working there, the incineration of such a charge took up to an hour and a half, because they were the bodies of very thin people, real skeletons, which burned very slowly. I know from the experience gained by observing cremation in Krematorien 2 and 3 that the bodies of fat people burn very much faster. The process of incineration is accelerated by the combustion of human fat which thus produces additional heat.[133]

Tauber went on to describe the layout of Crematorium 1 in early 1943. At the back of the incineration room were a coke storage room and a (by 1943 obsolete) storeroom for urns. On inspection of the building in 1945, Tauber noted that the arrangement had changed: the door that in 1945 connected the "bunker" (morgue/gas chamber) and the furnace room was obviously a new addition. "When I was working in crematorium 1, that door did not exist." The only entrance to the furnace room had been through the vestibule. He was right: the new door was added in 1945. That same vestibule gave access to a storeroom, which at times was used as an undressing room.

> The men from small transports, brought by truck, used to undress there. When I was working at crematorium 1, they were shot in the bunker of the crematorium (the part of the building where they gassed people known as the "bunker"). Such transports arrived once or twice a week and comprised 30 to 40 people. They were of different nationalities. During the executions, we, the members of the *Sonderkommando*, were shut up in the coke store. Then we would find the bodies of the shot people in the bunker. All the corpses had a firearm wound in the neck. The executions were always carried out by the same SS man from the

Political Section, accompanied by another SS from the same Section who made out the death certificates for those shot.[134]

Tauber's account was confirmed at that same time by SS man Pery Broad, who in an English prisoner-of-war camp told his interrogators that the morgue served not only as a gas chamber but also as the site of executions by shooting. "The right-hand man of the camp leader, *SS-Hauptscharführer* Palitzsch, did the shooting. He killed one person after another with a practised shot in the back of the neck."[135]

One of the odd things Tauber noted while he was at work in Crematorium 1 was that his group was actually designated "Kommando Krem-

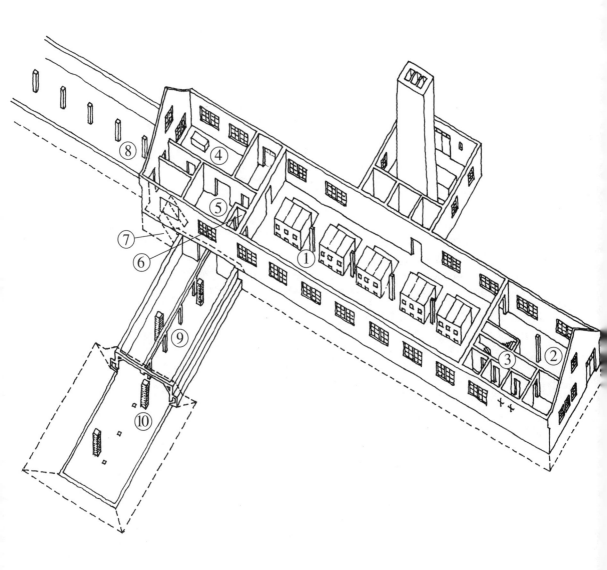

atorium II." On March 4, everything became clear when the whole group was sent to Birkenau to operate Crematorium 2. "We had been sent there for one month's practical training in crematorium 1 in order to prepare us for working in crematorium 2."

Crematorium 2 had a basement where there was an undressing room and a bunker, or in other words a gas chamber (Leichen-keller/corpse cellar). To go from one cellar to the other, there was a corridor in which there came from the exterior a [double] stairway and a slide for throwing the bodies that were brought to the camp to be incinerated in the crematorium. People went through the door of the undressing room into the corridor, then from there through a door on the right into the gas chamber. A second stairway running from the grounds of the crematorium gave access to the corridor. To the left of this stairway, in the corner, there was a little room where hair, spectacles and other effects were stored. On the right there was another small room used as a store for cans of Zyclon-B. In the right corner of the corridor, on the wall facing the door from the undressing room, there was a lift to transport the corpses. People went from the crematorium yard to the undressing room via a stairway, surrounded by iron rails. Over the door there was a sign with the inscription "*Zum Baden und Desinfektion*" (to bath and disinfection), written in several languages. In the undressing room, there were wooden benches and numbered clothes hooks along the walls. There were no windows and the lights were on all the time. The undressing room also had water taps and drains for the waste water. From the undressing room people went into the corridor through a door above which was hung a sign marked "*Zum Bade,*" repeated in several languages. I remember the [Russian] word "*banya*" was there too. From the corridor they went through the door on the right into the gas chamber. It was a wooden door, made of two layers of short pieces of wood arranged like parquet. Between these layers there was a single sheet of material sealing the edges of the door and the rabbets of the frame were also fitted with sealing strips of felt. At about head height for an average man this door had a round glass peephole. On the other side of the door, i.e. on the gas chamber side, this opening was protected by a hemispherical grid. This grid was fitted because the people in the gas chamber, feeling they were going to die, used to break the glass of the peep-hole. But the grid still did not provide sufficient protection and similar incidents recurred. The opening was blocked with a piece of metal or wood. The people going to be gassed and those in the gas chamber damaged the electrical installations, tearing the cables out and damaging the ventilation equipment. The door was closed hermetically from the corridor side by means of iron bars which were screwed tight. The roof of the gas chamber was supported by concrete pillars running down the middle of its length. On either side of these pillars there were four others, two on each side. The sides of these pillars, which went up through the roof, were of heavy wire mesh. Inside this grid, there was another finer mesh and inside that a third of very fine mesh. Inside this last mesh cage there was a removable can that was pulled out with a wire to recover the pellets from which the gas had evaporated.

(Opposite page) Crematorium 2. In order to facilitate comparison, the legend contains, where relevant, the letters and numbers used in Olère's drawings for Crematorium 3, which was the mirror image of Crematorium 2. Legend: incineration room (1; Olère 5); coke store (2; Olère 11); stairs to the attic where the Sonderkommandos lived (3); autopsy room (4; Olère F); room where corpses that were to be dissected were cleaned (5; Olère F); elevator connecting main floor to basement (6; Olère C / 4); stair and corpse slide originally planned (7); Morgue 2, designated as undressing room from December 1942 on (8; Olère A / 1); Morgue 1, designated as gas chamber from December 1942 on (9; Olère D / 3); ventilation system originally built into the wall of Morgue 1 (10). The roof of Morgue 1 is supported by nine concrete pillars. The perforated metal columns that allowed Zyklon B to be introduced into the space were close to the first, third, fifth, and seventh pillars (Olère E / 10). Each of these four metal columns connected at the ceiling to a short shaft that penetrated through the concrete roof of the morgue to four hatches closed by wooden covers. Axonometric reconstruction by Marc Downing.

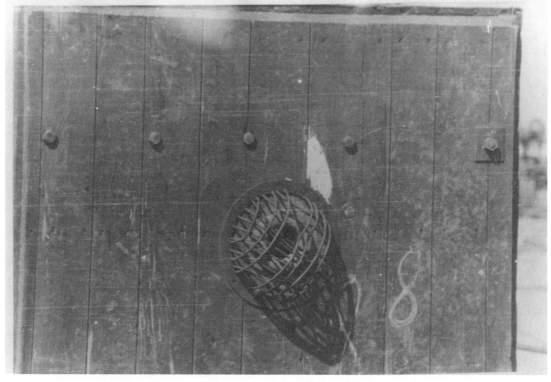

Besides that, in the gas chamber there were electric wires running along the two sides of the main beam supported by the central concrete pillars. The ventilation was installed in the walls of the gas chamber. Communication between the room and the ventilation installation proper was through small holes along the top and bottom of the side walls. The lower openings were protected by a kind of muzzle, the upper ones by whitewashed perforated metal plates.

The ventilation system of the gas chamber was coupled to the ventilation ducts installed in the undressing room. This ventilation system, which also served the dissection room, was driven by electric motors in the roof space of the crematorium.

The water tap was in the corridor and a rubber hose was run from it to wash the floor of the gas chamber. At the end of 1943, the gas chamber was divided in two by a brick wall to make it possible to gas smaller transports. In the dividing wall there was a door identical to that between the corridor and the original gas chamber. Small transports were gassed in the chamber furthest from the entrance from the corridor.[136]

All of Tauber's testimony up to this point can be confirmed in the blueprints or by means of other documents in the archive of the Auschwitz Central Construction Office. Only the division of the gas chamber of Crematorium 2 into two spaces cannot be traced in the archive. Negationists use this to refute the validity of the whole of Tauber's testimony. Daniel Bennahmias's memoirs of his imprisonment in Auschwitz provide independent confirmation, however. He stated that after some time, the gas chamber of Crematorium 2 was divided into two spaces, with a smaller one at the back. "The plan for the newly restructured Crematorium II entailed gassing smaller groups in the farther end of the gas chamber and larger groups in the remaining area. This was more or less what happened, but exceptions did occur. These exceptions had to do with the erratic pattern of the transports' arrival. This, if the smaller chamber was occupied and a larger transport arrived, the larger chamber might have been used for any number of persons. As new transports arrived, however, the smaller chamber was 'tended to' when there was time, but the larger functioned at all times. Despite the foregoing, the system still proved its efficiency because there were fewer people to process and a smaller area to clean. After splitting the chamber in this way, and employing the technique described, it was not unusual for the smaller of the two chambers to remain sealed and intact with its complement of people for as long as four or five days or longer. When the door finally was opened, the Sonderkommando was assaulted by an overwhelming stench and the ghastly sight of putrid flesh."[137]

Let us return to Tauber's description of the extermination installation:

The undressing room and the gas chamber were covered first with a concrete slab then with a layer of soil sown with grass. There were four small chimneys, the openings through which the gas was thrown in, that rose above the gas chamber. These openings were closed by concrete covers with two handles.

Over the undressing room, the ground was higher than the level of the yard and perfectly flat. The ventilation ducts led to the pipes and the chimneys located in the part of the building above the corridor and undressing room. I would point out that at first the undressing room had neither benches nor clothes hooks and

(Opposite top left) Outside of a gas-tight door found by the Russians in the Auschwitz building material yard in 1945. The movable bars on the left side show that this is the outside of the door; the hinges on the right side show that this side of the door opened outward. The proportions of this door suggest that it is not the door used in Crematorium 2, but one used in Crematorium 4 or 5, which would explain the difference between the arrangement of the wooden planks as described by Tauber and the door that was found. This discrepancy is important, as it suggests that Tauber described a door he remembered, and not a door that was presented to him during his interrogation. Courtesy Archive Auschwitz-Birkenau State Museum, Oswiecim.

(Opposite top right) Inside of a gas-tight door found by the Russians in the Auschwitz building material yard in 1945. The gas-tight seal surrounding the door is clearly visible, as is the hemispherical grid protecting the peephole. Courtesy Archive Auschwitz-Birkenau State Museum, Oswiecim.

(Opposite bottom) The hemispherical grid protecting the peephole on the inside of a gas-tight door. Courtesy Archive Auschwitz-Birkenau State Museum, Oswiecim.

Crematorium 2, gas chamber (no. 9 in axonometric reconstruction, above). The drawing shows the gas chamber before it was divided into two parts. Four of the seven concrete pillars and four of the wire-mesh gassing columns are visible. The ventilation openings of the air-extraction system can be seen at the bottom of the walls. The ventilation openings of the aeration system are located in the large triangular duct located at the intersection of the side walls and the ceiling. Drawing by Marc Downing.

there were no showers in the gas chamber. These fittings were not installed until autumn 1943 in order to camouflage the undressing room and gas chamber as a bathing and disinfestation facility. The showers were fitted to small blocks of wood sealed into the concrete roof of the gas chamber. There were no pipes connected to these showers, from which no water ever flowed.

As I have already said, there was a lift in the corridor or rather a goods hoist. A temporary hoist was installed pending delivery of the electric lift to carry the corpses to the ground floor.[138]

It is important to note that Tauber's description of the basement level of Crematorium 2 is fully corroborated by the surviving blueprints of the crematorium.

Tauber also gave a detailed description of the ground floor—an account that is likewise confirmed by the architectural drawings. The lift, he told Sehn, had two exits at this level. One led to the autopsy rooms, the other into the large furnace hall with its five triple-muffle ovens. "It was possible to put five human corpses in each muffle, which was closed by an iron door bearing the inscription 'Topf.' Beneath each muffle, there was a space for a bin to collect the ashes, also closed by an iron door made by the same firm." Behind the furnaces were the pits with the fireboxes and the coke storage. To the back of the incineration hall were rooms reserved for the SS, the chief capo, and the doctor. "A stairway led up to the roof space, where there was a dormitory for the men working in the *Sonderkommando* and, at the end, the electric motors for the lift and the ventilation system."

Facing the entrance gate to the crematorium grounds, in the centre of the building, was a wing in which rubbish was burnt in an incinerator. It was called "*Müllverbrennung.*" It was separate, reached by going down a stairway. It was surrounded by an iron platform and was coal fired. The entrance to the waste incinerator wing faced the crematorium access gate. This wing had, in addition to its entrance door with a transom window over it, two windows, one on the right and one on the left of the entrance. In the left corner of the entrance, there was an opening through which, from a walled-off area on the outside, the objects to be burned were passed inside. The incineration hearth for these things was to the left of the entrance and the firebox on the right. I would point out that it was in this particular furnace that the documents of the Political Section of the camp were always burned. From time to time, the SS would bring whole truckloads of papers, documents and files that had to be burned under their control. During the incineration of these papers, I noticed great stacks of records of dead people and death notices. We were not able to take any of these documents because we were operating under the close and direct surveillance of the SS. Behind the waste incinerator, at the end of the wing, was a chimney for all the cremation furnaces and the incinerator. At first, there were around this chimney three electric motors used for the draught. Because of the heat given off and the proximity of the incinerator, these motors often broke down. There was even a fire on one occasion. Because of these problems, they were later removed and the smoke flues of the cremation furnaces were connected directly to the chimney. A door allowed passage between the waste incinerator wing and the part where the chimney was. This part being slightly higher, it was reached by a few steps. After the motors were removed, some wash basins for the Sonderkommando were installed next to the chimney. . . . In the roof space above the waste incinerator wing, the hair cut from the victims was dried, tossed and put in sacks which were subsequently taken away by truck.[139]

Tauber continued with a very detailed account of the incineration equipment and procedures.

As I have already said, there were five furnaces in crematorium 2, each with three muffles for cremating the corpses and heated by two coke-fired hearths. The fire flues of these hearths came out above the ash boxes of the two side muffles. Thus the flames went first round the two side muffles then heated the centre one, from where the combustion gases were led out below the furnace, between the two firing hearths. Thanks to this arrangement, the incineration process for the corpses in the side muffles differed from that of the centre muffle. The corpses of "*Müselmanns*" or of wasted people with no fat burned rapidly in the side muffles and slowly in the centre one. Conversely, the corpses of people gassed directly on arrival, not being wasted, burned better in the centre muffle. During the incineration of such corpses, we used the coke only to light the fire of the furnace initially, for fatty corpses burned of their own accord thanks to the combustion of the body fat. On occasion, when coke was in short supply, we would put some straw and wood in the ash bins under the muffles, and once the fat of the corpse began to burn the other corpses would catch light themselves. There were no iron components inside the muffle. The bars were of chamotte,[140] for iron would have melted in the furnace, which reached 1,000 to 1,200° Celsius. These chamotte bars were arranged crosswise. The dimensions of the door and the opening of the muffles were smaller than the inside of the muffle itself, which was 2 meters long, 80 centimeters wide and about 1 meter high. Generally speaking, we burned 4 or 5 corpses at a time in one muffle, but sometimes we charged a greater number of corpses. It was possible to charge up to 8 "*Müselmanns.*" Such big charges were incinerated without the knowledge of the head of the crematorium during air raid warnings in order to attract the attention of airmen by having a bigger fire emerging from the chimney. We imagined that in that way it might be possible to change our fate. The iron components, in particular fire bars, still to be found in the camp, were from the fireboxes. Crematorium 2 had fire bars of heavy angle iron. Crematoria 4 and 5 were fitted with fire bars in the form of a lance, or rather were like swords with handles.[141]

After the description of the installation, Tauber recalled how on the first day, March 4, they operated the ovens in the presence of observers from the Political Section, representatives of the Berlin headquarters, and engineers of Topf—a visit also recorded by Vrba and Wetzlar. For this occasion, the Political Department had taken care to provide forty-five bodies of well-fed victims who had recently been killed in Bunker 2.

> Via the lift and the door leading to the furnace room, we took out the bodies and placed them two or three at a time on trolleys of the type I described for crematorium 1 and charged them into the different muffles. As soon as all the muffles of the five furnaces had been charged, the members of the commission began to observe the operation, watch in hand. They opened the muffle doors, looked at their watches, expressed surprise at the slowness of the cremation process. In view of the fact that the furnaces were not yet hot enough, even though we had been firing them since the morning, and because they were brand new, the incineration of this charge took about 40 minutes.[142]

Tauber went on to explain that later on incineration became more efficient and they could incinerate two loads per hour. In fact, the Sonderkommandos tried to overload the muffles, because this would allow them some free time.

> According to the regulations, we were supposed to charge the muffles every half hour. Ober Capo August explained to us that, according to the calculations and plans for this crematorium, 5 to 7 minutes was allowed to burn one corpse in a muffle. In principle, he did not let us put more than three corpses in one muffle. Because with that quantity we were obliged to work without interruption, for as soon as the last muffle was charged, the contents of the first had been consumed. In order to be able to

take a pause during the work, we would charge 4 or 5 corpses in each muffle. The incineration of such a charge took longer, and after charging the last muffle, we had few minutes' break until the first one was again available. We took advantage of this free time to wash the floor of the furnace room, as a result of which the air became a little cooler.[143]

After this first incineration, the Sonderkommandos kept the fires burning, but there were no corpses to burn until mid-March, when trucks began to arrive carrying people who had been selected at the Judenrampe outside of Birkenau.

> They were herded towards a hut erected perpendicular to the crematorium building, towards the entrance gate of crematorium II. The people entered through the door facing the gate and went down by the stairway to the right of the waste incinerator wing. At that time, this hut served as an undressing room. It was used for this purpose only for a week or so, then it was dismantled. After this hut was removed, the people were herded towards the basement area of the crematorium via a stairway leading to the underground undressing room, already described. After we had waited for two hours, we were let out and ordered to go to the gas chamber. We found heaps of naked bodies, doubled up. They were pinkish, and in places red. Some were covered with greenish marks and saliva ran from their mouths. Others were bleeding from the nose. There was excrement on many of them. I remember that a great number had their eyes open and were hanging on to one another. The bodies were most crushed together round the door. By contrast, there were less around the wire mesh columns. The location of the bodies indicated that the people had tried to get away from the columns and get to the door. It was very hot in the gas chamber and so suffocating as to be unbearable. Later on, we became convinced that many people died of suffocation, due to lack of air, just before the gassing. They fell to the floor and were trampled on by the others. They were not sitting, like the majority, but stretched out on the floor, under the others. It was obvious that they had succumbed first and that they had been trampled on. Once the people were in the gas chamber, the door was closed and the air was pumped out. The gas chamber ventilation could work in this way, thanks to a system that could both extract and blow.[144]

Tauber recorded that the Sonderkommandos wore gas masks when removing the bodies to the corridor, where a barber cut off the women's hair before the corpses were loaded on the lift for transport to the ground floor. There two dentists pulled out the gold fillings and false teeth.

> They also removed the rings and earrings. The teeth were thrown into a box marked "*Zahnarztstation.*" As for the jewels, they were put into another box with no label other than a number. The dentists, recruited from among the prisoners, looked into all the mouths except those of the children. When the jaws were too tightly clamped, they pulled them apart with the pincers used to extract the teeth.[145]

Tauber worked in Crematorium 2 until mid-April, incinerating the remains of Greek, French, and Dutch convoys. "I cannot say how many people were gassed during this period. We worked in two shifts, a day shift and a night shift. On average, we incinerated 2500 corpses a day."[146]

Tauber was a careful witness, clearly distinguishing between what he had seen himself and what he had not. At this time he did not witness how the people were herded into the undressing room and from there into the gas chamber because, when they arrived at the crematorium, all but two of the Sonderkommandos were locked up in the coke storage room—the remaining two were in the furnace room keeping the fires going. Finally he was detailed to that job, and this allowed him to witness the outside of the gassing procedure.

> Through the window of the incineration room, I observed how the Zyklon was poured into the gas chamber. Each transport was followed by a vehicle with Red Cross markings which entered the yard of the crematorium, carrying the camp doctor, Mengele, accompanied by *Rottenführer* Scheimetz. They took the cans of Zyklon from the car and put them beside the small chimneys used to introduce the Zyklon into the gas chamber. There, Scheimetz opened them with a special cold chisel and a hammer, then poured the contents into the gas chamber. Then he closed the orifice with a concrete cover. As there were four similar chimneys, Scheimetz poured into each the contents of one of the smallest cans of Zyklon, which had yellow labels pasted right round them. Before opening the cans, Scheimetz put on a gasmask which he wore while opening the cans and pouring in the product. There were also other SS who performed this operation, but I have forgotten their names. They were specially designated for it and belonged to the "*Gesundheitswesen.*" A camp doctor was present at each gassing. If I have mentioned Mengele, that is because I met him very often during my work. In addition to him, there were other doctors present during the gassings, like König, Thilo and a young, tall, slight doctor whose name I do not recall.[147]

Unlike the practice at Crematorium 1, the Sonderkommandos operating Crematorium 2 soon abandoned the use of trolleys for transporting and inserting the corpses into the muffles. They were replaced by metal stretchers that were loaded according to procedure:

> The procedure was to put the first corpse with the feet towards the muffle, back down and face up. Then, a second corpse was placed on top, again face up, but head towards the muffle. This method was used so that the legs of the upper corpse blocked that below and did not get in the way when the corpses were introduced into the furnace. Two prisoners loaded the stretchers. One end of the stretcher was put in front of the muffle, below the bar, alongside which stood two prisoners. While the corpses were being loaded on the stretcher, one of these opened the door of the muffle and the other positioned the rollers. Then, they lifted the stretcher and put it on the rollers, while a fifth prisoner, positioned at the handles at the other end of the stretcher, lifted it at the same time as them and pushed it into the muffle. As soon as the corpses were inside, a sixth prisoner held them there with a fire iron while the fifth withdrew the stretcher. The sixth man also had to cool the stretcher as it came out of the furnace by pouring over it water in which soap had been dissolved so that the next load of corpses

would slide easily on the metal of the stretcher without sticking to it. The same procedure was used for the following charge destined to be incinerated in the same muffle. We had to work fast, for the corpses put in first soon started to burn, and their arms and legs rose up. If we were slow, it was difficult to charge the second pair of corpses. During the introduction of these other two corpses, I was able to observe the cremation process. It appeared that the trunk of the body rose and the arms stretched towards the sky before contracting. The same thing happened with the legs. The bodies became covered in blisters. Gassed bodies that had remained in the store room for two days were swollen, and in the fire their diaphragm burst and their intestines poured out. I was also able to observe how cremation proceeded while I was moving the corpses in the furnace with a fire iron, to accelerate the combustion. After each charging, the SS head of the Kommando checked to make sure that the furnaces were properly filled. We had to open each muffle for him and at that moment we could see what was happening inside. We burned the bodies of children with those of adults. First we put in two adults, then as many children as the muffle could contain. It was sometimes as many as five or six. We used this procedure so that the bodies of children would not be placed directly on the grid bars, which were relatively far apart. In this way we prevented the children from falling through into the ash bin. Women's bodies burned much better and more quickly than those of men. For this reason, when a charge was burning badly, we would introduce a woman's body to accelerate the combustion.[148]

Tauber remembered that the ovens needed little coke when they had been in use for some time. "The furnaces burned thanks to the embers produced by the combustion of the corpses."

So, during the incineration of fat bodies, the fires were generally extinguished. When this type of body was charged into a hot furnace, fat immediately began to flow into the ash bin, where it caught fire and started the combustion of the body. When "Müselmanner" were being cremated, it was necessary to constantly refuel the fireboxes. The shift boss wrote in a notebook the number of corpses incinerated per charge and the head of the Kommando, an SS man, checked these entries. After an entire transport had been cremated, he took away the notebook.[149]

Tauber continued his testimony with detailed reports on the various personalities that operated the crematoria.

In April 1943, he was transferred to the newly completed Crematorium 4. It was of a different design. Instead of having five triple-muffle ovens, this crematorium had one double-four-muffle furnace. As in the case of his account of Crematorium 2, Tauber's description of Crematorium 4 is fully corroborated by a surviving blueprint.

The muffles were in pairs on each side. One firebox heated two muffles, which together made up half of a furnace. Each furnace had its own chimney. The undressing room and the gas chambers were installed on the ground floor, and the part of the building where they were located was not so high as the furnace room so

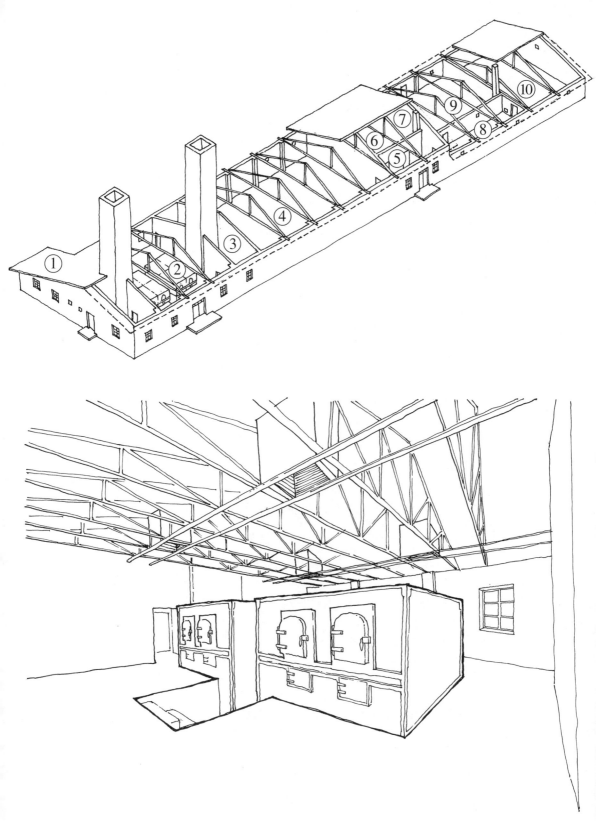

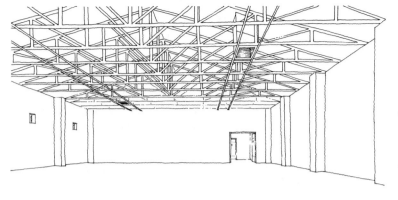

(Opposite top) Crematorium 4, axonometric. Coke storage (1); incineration room with the double-four-muffle oven and the two chimneys (2); room where gold teeth were removed from the corpses (3); undressing room (4); vestibule (5); doctor's room (6); Sonderkommando room (7); first gas chamber (8); second gas chamber (9); third gas chamber (10). Drawing by Marc Downing.

(Opposite bottom) Crematorium 4, incineration hall (no. 2 in axonometric above). Each oven consisted of two units of two pairs of back-to-back muffles. The stoking pit was located between the two units. Drawing by Marc Downing.

(Top) Crematorium 4, undressing room (no. 4 in axonometric above). The view is taken from the vestibule, or, as Tauber calls it, the corridor that separated the undressing room from the gas chambers. Drawing by Marc Downing.

(Bottom) Crematorium 4, vestibule or corridor (no. 5 in axonometric above). The view is toward the gas chambers. The door to the yard is to the right. Drawing by Marc Downing.

that it had the appearance of an annex to the crematorium. The boiler room was separated from the undressing room by a narrow corridor with four internal doors, allowing passage between the two rooms. The undressing room was illuminated by four small barred windows giving on the exterior. Another door led to a corridor whose entrance door opened onto the yard of the crematorium. This entrance was flanked by two windows.

Opposite the entrance door in the corridor, there was a door that opened on a room with a window which was the kitchen for the SS working in the crematorium, a kitchen where the dishes were prepared by members of the Sonderkommando. This room was next to that of the Sonderkommando prisoners. . . . The third door in the corridor led to a corridor with a barred window and a door leading to the crematorium yard.

From this corridor, the door on the right gave access to the first of the gas chambers and that opposite to the smallest of the chambers, communicating by another door with the biggest.

This corridor, and the three following rooms were used as chambers for gassing people. All had gas-tight doors, and also windows that had bars on the inside and were closed by gas-tight shutters on the outside. These small windows, which could be reached by the hand of a man standing outside, were used for throwing the contents of cans of Zyklon-B into the gas chambers full of people. The gas chambers were about two meters high and had an electric lighting installation on the walls but they had no ventilation system, which obliged the Sonderkommando who were removing the bodies to wear gasmasks. The corpses were dragged along the floor into the access corridor, where the barbers cut off the hair and then into the undressing room, which also served, in this kind of crematorium, as a store room for the corpses. It was a big hall where the bodies were put while the gas chambers were being cleaned up. Then they were taken through the narrow corridor between the undressing room and the furnace room, where at each end a dentist tore out the gold teeth. In the furnace room, there was the room of the head of the *Kommando* and beside it another one for the rest of the SS.

This was followed by a narrow corridor, which originally led to the east yard of crematorium 4, the SS washroom and WC and the coke store. The building was entirely brick-built, with a wooden roof, covered with asbestos sheets and roofing felt. The yards of all the crematoriums were separated from the outside world by a thick enclosure of wicker and a hedge to which straw hurdles were attached.

In the yard, there were watchtowers, where SS armed with machine guns kept guard. Furthermore, the whole area was surrounded by electrified barbed wire and the yards were lit by powerful lamps. In May 1944, the SS ordered us to dig five pits in the yard of crematorium 5, between the building itself and the drainage ditch, five pits which were used later for incinerating the corpses of gassed people from the Hungarian transports. Although a track for the trolleys was laid between the building and the pits, we never used it because the SS considered it to be inconvenient, so we had to drag the corpses straight from the gas chambers to the pits. At the same time, the old Bunker 2, with its incineration pits, was also made ready for re-use. I never worked there. It was realized that the pits burned the corpses better, so the crematoria closed down one after the other after the pits came into operation. The first to be stopped was crematorium 4, apparently in June 1944, then, in October 1944, I think, crematoria 2 and 3. Crematorium 5 kept going until the Germans fled. Towards the end, it was used to incinerate the bodies of prisoners who died naturally or were executed. Gassing ceased in October 1944.[150]

Tauber recalled how after the gassing stopped the Germans began to dismantle the equipment. "The parts were taken to the goods platform and loaded onto trains."[151]

(Opposite top) Crematorium 4, first gas chamber (no. 8 in axonometric above). The view is from the corridor toward the second gas chamber at the left and the third gas chamber at the far end. Two of the small windows that can be closed with gas-tight shutters are visible. At the far end of the first gas chamber, next to the door to the third gas chamber, one can see the opening giving access to the stove in the third gas chamber. Drawing by Marc Downing.

(Opposite bottom) Crematorium 4, third gas chamber (no. 10 in axonometric above). The view is from the outside door toward the stove and the door that connects to the first gas chamber. Drawing by Marc Downing.

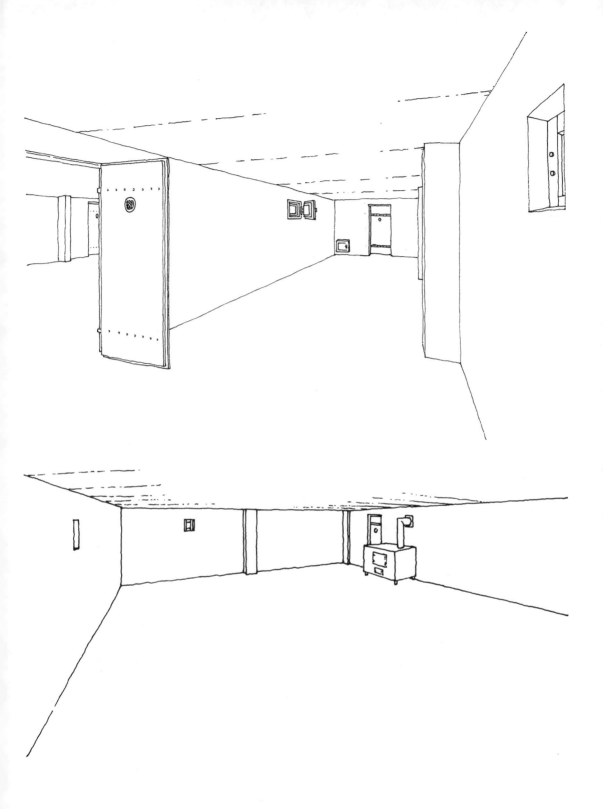

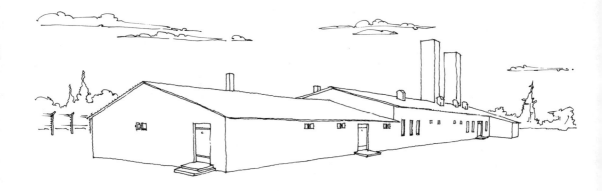

Crematorium 4, exterior from the west. The lower part contains the three gas chambers. The door closest gives access to the third gas chamber; the other door to the second gas chamber. Drawing by Marc Downing.

With Tauber, Sehn had found an almost ideal witness. Even Stäglich ought to have been impressed by his testimony, if he had known it. Tauber's statement was extremely specific, it did not contain contradictions, and it did not contain improbable allegations. In fact, negationists have not been able to discredit him as a witness. Spanish negationist Enrique Aynat Eknes did try to insinuate that Tauber could not be trusted because "this testimony is in agreement with the official thesis."[152] In other words, it must have been scripted somewhere else. But in his attempt to discredit Tauber, he could come up with only two arguments.

> It contains a contradiction where he states that he was assigned to the Sonderkommando of crematorium II on 4 March 1943, inasmuch as this crematorium was not turned over to the camp administration until the 31st day of that month. H. Tauber further declared: "Between these two rooms [the disrobing room and the gas chamber] there was a corridor to which there was access from the outside by way of few stairs, and a chute down which they flung the cadavers coming from the camp, to convey them to the crematories." This chute for cadavers establishes at least that the Germans had designed the crematoriums *also* for the incineration of prisoners who died from natural causes or epidemics, since, as we shall see, the "circuit" followed by those destined for extermination in the gas chambers was different. The tacit acknowledgement of the mixed use of the crematoriums that is derived from Tauber's statement is per se disturbing for the credibility of the official doctrine. It is difficult to accept that the Germans had established a "circuit" for the cremation of the deceased from non-criminal causes which interfered with that followed by the victims of the gas chambers. It would have been much simpler to take the ones who died from natural causes

directly to the crematory furnaces, avoiding their passage through the crowded basement of the crematorium.[153]

Is there a contradiction between Tauber's claim that he had been assigned to the Sonderkommandos of Crematorium 2 on March 4, 1943, while documents showed that Crematorium 2 was only turned over to the camp administration on March 31? There is not. The official transfer of the crematorium occurred when the building had been fully completed and after tests of the incinerators had been completed. These tests had been initiated on March 5, when corpses of people who had died outside the crematorium were incinerated, and were continued on March 13, when not only the ovens but also the gas chamber was tried out. Both operations required a team of Sonderkommandos. Only when the crematorium was deemed fully operational was it signed over to the camp authorities. As a result, there is no contradiction between the fact that Tauber was assigned to the Sonderkommandos of Crematorium 2 on March 4 and the official transfer of the building more than three weeks later.

Eknes claimed that Tauber stated that "there was a corridor to which there was access from the outside by way of few stairs, and a chute down which they flung the cadavers coming from the camp, to convey them to the crematories." The translation made by Dorota Ryszka and Adam Rutkowski, used by Pressac and consequently by myself, reads that "there was a corridor, in which there came from the exterior a stairway and a slide for throwing the bodies that were brought to the camp to be incinerated in the crematorium." Thus, while Eknes made a claim about a *practice* (of throwing corpses into the basement of Crematorium 2), Tauber referred to the *intention* of the slide—an intention that preceded the transformation of Morgue 1 into a gas chamber. It is unclear to what extent that intention was actually realized during the operation of Crematorium 2. What is clear is that even if the slide was used, there is no necessary contradiction with the use of the basement as an extermination installation. Eknes claimed that "it is difficult to accept that the Germans had established a 'circuit' for the cremation of the deceased from non-criminal causes which interfered with that followed by the victims of the gas chambers. It would have been much simpler to take the ones who died from natural causes directly to the crematory furnaces, avoiding their passage through the crowded basement of the crematorium." He assumed, therefore, that there were two continuous processes, represented by two "circuits" that ought not interfere with each other. Yet the basement of Crematorium 2 was not constantly crowded. Especially before the Hungarian Action, there were many days that no gassings took place, and there was ample time and space for corpses of inmates who had died in the camp to be brought to the basement of the crematorium, where their numbers would be registered in the death books and their gold teeth, if they had any, would be removed.

Given Eknes's difficulty in discrediting Tauber's testimony, it is not surprising that negationists preferred to bury it in silence. Yet we do well to attach the highest evidentiary value to it, and not only because of its internal consistency. Tauber's statements were largely corroborated by the contemporary testimonies of Jankowski and Dragon and by the later memoirs of Filip Müller. The surviving blueprints also corroborated many of the details, and the ruins corroborated some others. The only piece of his testimony for which there was no corroboration in the drawings are the metal columns in the gas chamber of Crematorium 2. Attached to the four structural concrete columns, which supported the roof, these columns allowed for the introduction of the Zyklon B. They were retroactively fitted into the space but do not appear on the blueprints which, with one exception, were all drawn before the decision was made to use Leichenkeller 1 as a gas chamber. Yet their existence is independently confirmed in eyewitness accounts of the gas chamber, the drawings made by David Olère (see below), and the following testimony of Michael Kula, who manufactured these columns.

On June 11, Sehn interviewed 32-year-old former inmate Michael Kula. The Roman Catholic Kula, a mechanic by training who was a resident of the neighboring town of Trzebinia before his incarceration in Auschwitz, had been brought to the camp on August 15, 1940. In his testimony he gave an account of how, exactly on the evening of the first anniversary of his arrival, the Germans initiated experiments to gas 250 inmates with Zyklon B in the basement of Block 11. He had been able to witness some of it, because he had the afternoon off on the 15th of August, in honor of the Feast of Assumption. The killing had taken two days, and only on the night of the 16th did the nurses of the lazaret retrieve the corpses to take them out of the camp. Kula was able to witness this from a window of the dental station in Block 21. Right in front of Kula's observation point a cart loaded with corpses broke down, and many fell on the ground. "I saw then that they were greenish. The nurses told me that the corpses were cracked, and the skin came off. In many cases they had bitten fingers and necks."[154]

Kula worked in the metal workshop of the camp and had forged many of the metal pieces for the crematoria. For Crematorium I, for example, he and his colleagues had made the trucks for inserting the corpses into the ovens, the tracks, and the iron framework that braced the brickwork of the ovens. They had also made "the supporting framework for the fire boxes and the ventilation pipes from the gas chamber. In addition to that we did small repairs in that room."[155] Kula gave a detailed account of the work done for the crematoria at Birkenau. This included the iron braces for all the ovens, all the scaffolds, the tools for retrieving the corpses, the metalwork of the doors, and the hooks, the shovels and all that was necessary to run the ovens and the pit incinerations. His most important testimony concerned the construction of the four wire-mesh columns in the large gas chambers of Crematoria 2 and 3. As we have seen, Tauber had described them as three structures of ever finer mesh. Within the innermost column there was a removable can to pull after the gassing with the Zyklon "crystals," that is, the porous silica pellets that had absorbed the hydrocyanide. Kula, who had made these columns, provided some technical specifications.

> Among other things the metal workshop made the false showers intended for the gas chambers, as well as the wire-mesh columns for the introduction of the contents of the tins with Zyklon into the gas chambers. These columns were around 3 meters high, and they were 70 centimetres square in plan. Such a column consisted of 6 wire screens which were built the one within the other. The inner screen was made from 3 millimeter thick wire, fastened to iron corner posts of 50 by 10 millimeters. Such iron corner posts were on each corner of the column and connected on the top in the same manner. The openings of the wire mesh were 45 millimeters square. The second screen was made in the same manner, and constructed within the column at 150 millimeters distance from the first. The openings of the second were around 25 millimeters square. In the corners these screens were connected to each other

by iron posts. The third part of this column could be moved. It was an empty column with a square footprint of around 150 millimeters made of sheet zinc. At the top it was closed by a metal sheet, and at the bottom with a square base. At a distance of 25 millimetres from the sides of this columns were soldered tin corners supported by tin brackets. On these corners were mounted a thin mesh with openings of about one millimeter square. This mesh ended at the bottom of the column and from here ran in the [collection cup] of the screen a tin frame until the top of the column. The contents of a Zyklon tin were thrown from the top on the distributor, which allowed for a equal distribution of the Zyklon to all four sides of the column. After the evaporation of the gas the whole middle column was taken out. The ventilation system of the gas chamber was installed in the side walls of the gas chambers. The ventilation openings were hidden by zinc covers, provided with round openings.[156]

The wire-mesh columns were totally dismantled after the cessation of gassings and before the demolition of the crematoria, and no remains were found. Yet the dismantling crews were not able to remove the ventilation system because it was a structural part of the walls; consequently, they forgot to remove the zinc covers mentioned by Kula. They were dislocated when the demolition squads dynamited the gas chambers, but six of them were retrieved in the rubble of Crematorium 2 and sent for analysis to the forensic laboratory in Cracow. The laboratory report noted that they were covered with a thin, white-colored, and strongly smelling deposit. The laboratory retrieved 7.2 grams of the deposit and dissolved it in water. Sulphuric acid was added to this solution, and the resulting gas was absorbed in an absorbent material. This was divided in two and subjected to two different tests, each of which revealed the presence of hydrocyanide.[157]

Sehn and Dawidowski did more than study the remains of the bunkers and the crematoria, interview witnesses, and send material for chemical analysis. They also studied the plans for the crematoria. These plans were part of the archive of the Zentralbauleitung der Waffen SS und Polizei, Auschwitz O/S (Central Building Authority of the Waffen-SS and the Police, Auschwitz in Upper Silesia), located in a compound of barracks at some distance from the main camp. When the Germans burned the archives of the camp Kommandantur prior to their evacuation from Auschwitz in January 1945, they overlooked the archive of the building office that had been closed some months earlier, and as a result the materials in this archive were found more or less intact. The Soviet commission paid scant attention to the massive amount of paperwork. It was up to the Poles to fully exploit the evidentiary value of this source.[158]

Building at the concentration camp had been subject to normal civilian procedures as well as to the wartime superstructure of special permissions, and as a result multiple copies of many documents survive with the comments and signatures of the individual bureaucrats or businessmen to whom they were sent. The result was that Sehn and Dawidowski found a broad paper trail that included tens of thousands of different items such as plans, budgets, letters, telegrams, contractors' bids, financial negotiations, work site labor reports, requests for material allocations, and the minutes of meetings held in the Building Office among the architects themselves with camp officials and with high-ranking dignitaries from Berlin.

Comparing the results of the site visits with the blueprints and the

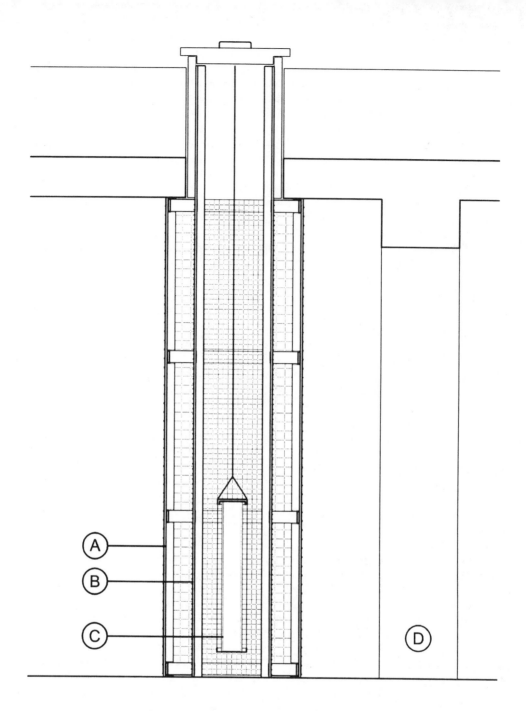

Reconstruction of a gas column based on the testimony of Tauber and Kula. The column consists of three structures: a fixed outer column to provide structural stability (A), a fixed inner column (B), and a movable part (C). The movable part contained a cup at the bottom. The Zyklon would be inserted into the cup, and the movable part would be inserted into the gas chamber. After the victims had died, the SS could remove the movable part with the cup containing the still degassing Zyklon. Also depicted is a structural column supporting the roof of the gas chamber (D). Drawing by Scott Barker.

other documentation that had been recovered, Roman Dawidowski wrote a (roughly) 10,000-word-long expert report on the technology of mass extermination in Auschwitz.[159] Dawidowski's text was never published as a whole, but Sehn summarized its most important conclusions in the official account of the operation of the camp published by the Central Commission in 1946. The relative obscurity of the Dawidowski report is troublesome, as it erroneously suggests that the Poles did not do their homework in the postwar years. To be sure: today we know more about the construction of Auschwitz and the crematoria than Dawidowski did. Yet, given the short time available to him and the general chaos in postwar Poland, it is still quite remarkable that most of his observations and conclusions have been confirmed over time.

Study of the archives quickly revealed that the creation of the crematoria and the gas chambers was less straightforward than the language used by the Soviet experts and the journalists suggested: the development of Auschwitz as a "factory of death" followed a twisted course. Correspondence suggested, for example, that the Germans had an important change of mind in early 1942. Originally, they had planned to construct a large crematorium with five triple-muffle ovens in Auschwitz and two small crematoria with two triple-muffle ovens in Birkenau. At the end of February, the chief of construction in the SS, Hans Kammler, decided in consultation with the Auschwitz Zentralbauleitung to erect the large crematorium with five triple incinerators in Birkenau. Dawidowski did not know the exact circumstances for this change in plan, but he correctly inferred that it had to do with the adaptation of Birkenau into an extermination camp.[160]

As he studied the blueprints and the correspondence, Dawidowski discovered that the role of the crematoria in the Final Solution was veiled in innocuous-sounding code words. Whenever they were designated as extermination installations, the crematoria were referred to as *Spezialeinrichtungen* (special installations) for the *Sonderbehandlung* (special treatment) of inmates. The latter term referred to killing.[161] Dawidowski also found that the architects only once made a direct reference to the underground gas chambers of Crematoria 2 and 3 as *Vergasungskeller* (gassing cellars) and only once to the adjacent space as *Auskleideraum* (undressing room). In general they designated the gas chamber of Crematoria 2 and 3 as Leichenhalle (morgue), Halle (hall), Leichenkeller 1, L-Keller 1, or Keller 1, while the undressing room was Leichenkeller 2 or simply Keller 2. Given all the other evidence he had found, Dawidowski was not particularly fascinated by the document with the reference to the *Vergasungskeller,* and he did not find it necessary to quote it. Yet more recently negationists have argued that this document is the "only" evidence for the genocidal use of the crematoria and have spent considerable effort to challenge the commonsense interpretation that the word *Vergasungskeller* refers to a homicidal gas chamber. Therefore it is good to print the letter in full.

29 January 1943

To the Chief Amtsgruppe C, SS-Brigadeführer and General-Major of the Waffen-SS, Dr. Ing. Kammler.
Subject: Crematorium II, condition of the building.

The crematorium has been completed—save for minor constructional work—by the use of all the forces available, in spite of

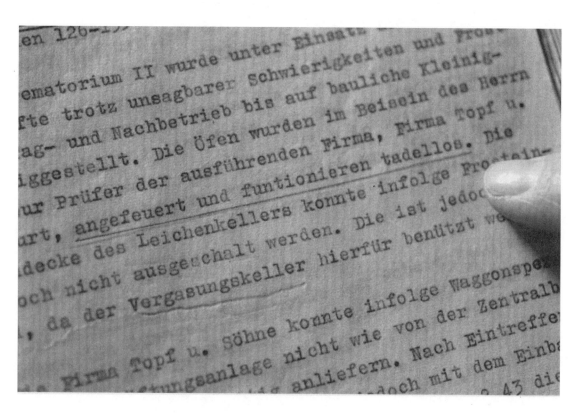

unspeakable difficulties, the severe cold, and in 24 hour shifts. The fires were started in the ovens in the presence of Senior Engineer Prüfer, representative of the contractors of the firm of Topf and Sons, Erfurt, and they are working most satisfactorily. The planks from the concrete ceiling of the cellar used as a mortuary could not yet be removed on account of the frost. This is, however, not very important, as the gassing cellar [*Vergasungskeller*] can be used for that purpose.

The firm of Topf and Sons was not able to start deliveries of the installation in time for aeration and ventilation as had been requested by the Central Building Management because of restrictions on use of railroad cars. As soon as the installation for aeration and ventilation arrive, the installing will start so that the complete installation may be expected to be ready for use 20 February 1943.

We enclose a report of the testing engineer of the firm Topf and Sons, Erfurt.

The Chief of the Central Construction Management,
Waffen-SS and Police Auschwitz,
SS-Hauptsturmführer

[Bischoff]

Distribution:
1—SS Ustuf Janisch and Kirschneck
1—Filing office (file crematorium)

Certified true copy:

[signature] SS-Ustuf (F)

Cross-referencing this letter with blueprints of the basement of Crematorium 2, Dawidowski concluded that the designation "*Vergasungskeller*" applied to Morgue 1. He noted that the blueprints showed that the section of this morgue differed from that of Morgue 2 in that the former was equipped with two built-in ventilation ducts on each side. Correspondence explained that these ventilation ducts were connected to a ventilator driven by a 3.5-horsepower electric motor and that the space was also equipped with a separate system for introducing warm air into it—an arrangement that made no sense if the space was used as a morgue (because corpses must be stored cold) but which made a lot of sense if the space was used as a Zyklon B gas chamber (because hydrogen cyanide, which has a boiling point of around 27° Celsius, works much faster when used in a preheated space—an issue Dawidowski was to discuss at length later in his report).[162] Eyewitness testimonies, the blueprints, and the correspondence corroborated each other.

Not all of Dawidowski's observations were equally valid. For example, he stressed the fact that the location of the crematoria was determined by the desire to achieve maximum camouflage, both to the outside world and to the victims, who had to be fooled until the very end. In fact, the issue of camouflage only seems to have become of concern after the crematoria were completed and does not seem to have determined their original location.[163] Dawidowski also showed an unusual interest in an issue that seems rather arcane in hindsight: the fact that both the design and the operation procedures of the crematoria in Birkenau violated the Ger-

(Opposite top) Reconstruction of the killing installation of Crematorium 2 made in 1945. To the left are the stairs leading to the entrance (wchód) of the underground undressing room (rozbieralnia), which connects to the gas chamber (komora gazowa). The Zyklon B was introduced through four poison introduction devices (wsyp trucizny). Courtesy Archive Auschwitz-Birkenau State Museum, Oswiecim.

(Opposite bottom) Detail of letter of Karl Bischoff to Hans Kammler, January 29, 1943. Courtesy Nubar Alexanian.

man Law on Cremation promulgated on May 15, 1934. Contrary to the stipulations of the law, which decreed that crematoria should be dignified in appearance, the Auschwitz crematoria had a factory-like appearance. More serious than the question of aesthetics, the design of the Auschwitz incinerators violated the very important principle that only one corpse ought to be incinerated at a time, and that the ashes of the deceased ought to be identifiable and collected in an urn. The ovens designed by Topf did not heed the law: they had three (Crematoria 2 and 3) or eight muffles (Crematoria 4 and 5), and because up to five corpses could be incinerated in every muffle at the same time, it was unavoidable that the ashes were mixed. Finally, Dawidowski complained that the SS did not obey the law in its demand that the wishes of the persons or their immediate family about burial or cremation were to be honored. "It is clear that the prisoners who had been given registration numbers, or the millions who were brought straight from the station to the gas chambers, were not asked before their murder if they wished that their corpses would be incinerated, or buried. Nor was their family asked, as stipulated by German law (§2)."[164] Dawidowski's outrage about this issue seems oddly misplaced, yet it does remind us of the fact that, even in 1945, the reality of the camps was still largely unimaginable.

On the basis of the documents, Dawidowski reconstructed the development of the crematoria in its relation to the growth of the camp. The construction of Crematorium 1 dated from 1940, and it was equipped with two double-muffle ovens. Dawidowski noted that the oven was initially heated by gasses created through the burning of coke. Once they had reached the ideal incineration temperature, the corpses were inserted. From that moment onward, the remains provided the most important fuel. He calculated that the original daily capacity of the crematorium was 200 corpses. After the addition of a third double-muffle oven in 1941 and the modification of the flues, the capacity rose to 350. This capacity was necessary, because the mortality in the camp had risen to up to 390 people per day at times. Causes of death were the general violence, starvation, exhaustion; murder by means of phenol injections; and executions by rifle. According to Dawidowski, Zyklon B was first used as a killing agent in August 1941. Initially, rooms in the basement of Block 11 were used as gas chambers. Later, the SS adapted the morgue of the crematorium for that purpose.[165]

When transports of Jews began to arrive in 1942, the gas chamber of the crematorium in Auschwitz proved inappropriate, and the SS transformed two buildings in Birkenau, the cottages of farmers Wiechuja and Harmata, into gas chambers. In his description of these extermination installations—Bunkers 1 and 2—Dawidowski relied on Dragon's testimony and the remains of the buildings because he had not found any documents or blueprints describing the two buildings. In fact, none were ever found. It seems that the two cottages were transformed without much fuss.

From a description of the bunkers, Dawidowski went on to a lengthy description of the chemical properties of Zyklon B and the unusual form in which the agent was shipped to Auschwitz. Violating three decrees, the Zyklon B used in Auschwitz did not even come with a warning label. Because the hydrogen cyanide contained in the Zyklon grains evaporated more easily when the environment was warmer, Dawidowski noted that the gas chambers were either preheated with portable stoves or, in the case

Inspection by Jan Sehn (in center, wearing a striped tie) of the entrance to the ruined undressing room of Crematorium 2. Courtesy Archive Auschwitz-Birkenau State Museum, Oswiecim.

of Crematoria 2 and 3, by warm air generated by the ovens. And he presented the results of the laboratory analysis of the six zinc covers found in Crematorium 2 and the bags of hair, which confirmed the presence of hydrogen cyanide.[166]

Initially the SS buried the corpses of those killed in the bunkers in large mass graves. On the basis of the testimony of Kula, Dawidowski came to the conclusion that in 1942 these corpses had begun to smell terribly. In response, the SS ordered the opening of the mass graves and the destruction of the remains with the help of flame-throwers. (As we have seen before, the War Refugee Report described this episode in great detail.) This, so he argued, had triggered the decision to equip the camp with virtual "death factories": crematoria equipped with gas chambers and powerful incinerators.

In this case negotiations were undertaken with the largest crematorium construction firm in Germany, J. A. Topf and Sons in Erfurt. This firm proposed projects and the SS headquarters in Berlin accepted them (letter of 3.8.1942 No. 11450/Bi/Ha). The latter demanded the completion of the crematoria at the beginning of 1943 (letter of the Firm Topf of 22.12.1942 No. 20420/42, as well as letter from Berlin of 18.12.1942 No. Geh./42/Er/Z). In the course of 1942 the Firm Topf began with the construction of two very large crematoria, designated in Birkenau with numbers 2 and 3. At the same time that firm transported to Auschwitz, to ensure a faster progress of construction, parts of crematoria ovens intended by the SS for Mogilev, and built in Birkenau two more, somewhat smaller crematoria, designated with the numbers 4 and 5. All this haste explains that the crematoria, built by the same firm, represented two different types, the [first] type of the similar crematoria 2 and 3, and the second type of crematoria 4 and 5.[167]

Later research, comparing the design and construction schedules of the various crematoria, was to show that the difference between the two types of crematoria derived from the fact that the type used in Crematoria 2 and 3 was developed before the transformation of Auschwitz into an extermination camp, while Crematoria 4 and 5 were designed from the very beginning to serve the Final Solution.

Dawidowski provided a detailed description of the technical equipment and interior arrangement of the crematoria, giving special attention to the killing installations, providing at every point cross-references to the blueprints and the correspondence. Dawidowski noted that the plans for the basement of Crematorium 2 provided for a room indicated as *Goldarb.[eiters]* (Goldworkers)—the space where the dental gold removed from the dead was melted. In the case of the two adjacent spaces, the undressing room designated as Morgue 2 and the gas chamber designated as Morgue 1, "these spaces formed a unit that was carefully planned with the sole aim for the mass extermination of people using poison gas."[168] The gas chambers of Crematoria 4 and 5 had been aboveground, and they were of various sizes.

The report continued with a lengthy description of the killing procedures in the various crematoria, based on the testimonies of Dragon and Tauber. This was followed by Dawidowski's calculations of the incineration capacity of the ovens. He assumed that each muffle could incinerate up to five corpses simultaneously and that the average cremation duration was between twenty-five and thirty minutes. On the basis of these figures, he came to an hourly incineration rate of 175 corpses for Crematoria 2 and 3 and a daily capacity of 2,500 persons for each crematorium—a reduction of 16 percent from the figure estimated by the Soviet-Polish commission shortly after the liberation of the camp, but a figure that was a little over 60 percent higher than the official capacity calculated by Topf of 1,440 corpses per day. According to Dawidowski, Crematoria 4 and 5 had an incineration capacity of 1,500 corpses per day—a figure that was equal to the assumed capacity of the gas chambers, equal to the earlier Soviet estimate, and around double the official German figure of 768 corpses per day.[169] During the Hungarian Action, however, actual incineration capacity exceeded the total capacity of the crematoria of 8,000 corpses per day. Two incineration pits created in the spring of 1944 had a capacity of 5,000

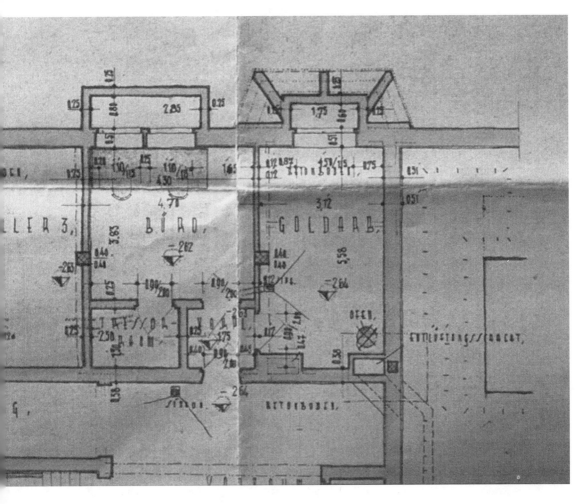

Detail of modified plan of Crematorium 2, spring 1942. Courtesy Nubar Alexanian.

corpses each, which brought the total incineration capacity at Birkenau to 18,000—a figure far below the (theoretically) maximum killing rate of 60,000 people in all the gas chambers.

In his conclusion, Dawidowski summarized the results: Crematoria 2, 3, 4 and 5 were purposefully designed and built as extermination installations following an industrialized system of mass production. "One finds a planned sequence of living and dead material from the entrance to the undressing room to the ovens," and the factory also allowed for the production of "secondary products, such as dental gold." A final development in German perversity was the attempt to use the heat generated in the ovens to warm water. Throughout the history of the camp, the SS was engaged with "intensive, yes even feverish attempts to improve the gassing action, as also to make it more efficient and more economically. In this effort local initiatives were in competition with the headquarters in Berlin."[170]

Dawidowski's report was not without flaws, but it did mean an enormous step forward compared to the Soviet report. The report studied the remains of the crematoria in relation to the testimonies of Dragon, Tauber, and Kula and cross-referenced them with the documents in the archive of the Central Construction Office; it put the history of the extermination installations at Auschwitz on a solid historical basis. If we may quarrel today with some of Dawidowski's conclusions about the capacity of the crematoria or the motivations for the design changes between various crematoria types, we must also acknowledge that subsequent discoveries and the confessions of Kommandant Höss, made after Dawidowski had done his work, largely corroborated the Dawidowski report.

The Central Commission accepted Dawidowski's conclusions and integrated them in the first report on the history of the camp, written by Jan Sehn and published in 1946. For better or for worse, Sehn's history became the foundation of all subsequent histories of Auschwitz. "For better," because in what it describes, the text is both responsible and accurate. "For worse," because Sehn presented the history in such a manner that he subtly suppressed the contingency of the camp's history in order to stress what he assumed was the universality of its impact. The beginning of Sehn's narrative stresses the fact of Auschwitz's isolation from the rest of the world. "The small, provincial Polish town of Oswiecim is situated far from the main railway centres and the more important lines of communication," Sehn claimed. It set the tone for a theme that was to continue all through the text: the Germans chose Oswiecim as a location for an extermination camp because the site offered isolation and camouflage. Yet, even more important, the site was unhealthy. "Oswiecim and its surrounding[s] are not only damp but also abound with malaria and other diseases, which endanger man's life."[171] Sehn argued that "the choice of Oswiecim for a place of punishment was not accidental," but that "the German authorities used the climate and geographical character of Oswiecim with premeditation in their criminal design."[172] Sehn saw a direct causal link between geography, geology, and the creation of Birkenau, which he described in a following chapter. Sehn had no doubt that the original designation of Birkenau as a prisoner-of-war camp was mere camouflage to hide a more sinister purpose. One of the clues which led him to this conclusion was the fact that the building office created to design and oversee the construction of the camp was called *Sonderbauleitung,* which was rather ominous because correspondence clearly stated that the camp was meant *Durchführung der Sonderbehandlung* ("to carry out special treatment")—a purpose that was realized when the trains that started arriving were designated as *Sondertransporte* (Special Transports) and when their passengers were led to a *Badeanstalt für Sonderaktion* (Bathing Establishment for Special Action). Sehn emphasized that all these terms that began with the adjective *sonder* (special) "were concealing the mass murder of millions of people, and that the special camp constructed for the carrying on of this Sonderbehandlung was already by assumption a huge extermination camp (Vernichtungslager)." Therefore the German government, "as [were] those who carried out orders on the spot at Auschwitz[,] [was] conscious of the purpose of the camp, and did everything to enable this camp to fulfil completely its mission of extermination of the conquered nations of Europe with the Slav nations and the Jews in first order of importance."[173]

Let there be no confusion: Birkenau became the largest extermination center in Europe. But does this mean that it was meant to become that center? Sehn felt the need to introduce from the very beginning of his narrative a sense of foreboding: Oswiecim had been a place avoided by life for thousands of years, and the fact that the building office that constructed Birkenau was called a *Sonderbauleitung* seemed to point to the camp's future use as a center of *Sonderbehandlung*. It is here, however, that Sehn's inexperience as a writer and a professional historian caught up with him. He did not negotiate the paradox that underlies every historical narrative: that while in everyday life—even in Auschwitz—each moment unfolds with no certainty of outcome, "history" is based on a known conclusion that charges an otherwise tedious chronicle with portent and pregnancy. Yet, in criticizing Sehn, one must also remember that he wrote his account without the aid of the confessions of memoirs of Rudolf Höss, which only became available later in 1946 and 1947. Without any sources that provided a possibility to reconstruct the changing motivations of the SS in Auschwitz, the blueprints and correspondence of the Central Construction Office *could* be plausibly interpreted as pointing to a unified development following an unchanging purpose—that is, as long as one forgot the beginning of Dawidowski's report that suggested a change of mind in the beginning of 1942, when Kammler decided to cancel two small incinerators in Birkenau and build there a large crematorium originally planned for the main camp.

Whatever its flaws in describing the origin and development of the camp, Sehn's history of Auschwitz provided much useful information on the arrangement and administration of the camp, the housing conditions, the life and death of the prisoners, the medical experiments, the selections within the camp, and selections of Jews on arrival.

The report ended with a discussion, largely based on Dawidowski's forensic report, of the gas chambers, the crematoria, and the attempts to wipe out the traces of the crime. Sehn mentioned that after the first experimental gassings in Block 11, a gas chamber was created near Crematorium 1 and, after that, in the fall of 1941, in two peasant cottages in the Birkenau forest.

> In the summer of 1942 it was decided to extend enormously gassing operations and to improve them technically, entrusting the construction of huge crematoria to the firm of J. A. Topf and Sons at Erfurt (ms. of Aug. 3, 1942, No. 11450/42/Bi/H). This was done just after SS. Reichsführer Himmler's visit of inspection. The construction began immediately, and in the early months of 1943 four huge modern crematoria were ready for the use of the camp authorities; their fundamental and essential part consisted of a set of gaschambers of a type unknown before. These crematoria were distinguished by the numbers 2, 3, 4 and 5. Crematoria 2 and 3 had underground areas, called on the construction drawing Nos. 932 and 933 of Jan. 28, *Leichenkeller* 1 and 2, both of which were intended for the gassing of human beings. Cellar 2 had an area of 400 sq. meters (480 sq. yards) and was 2.3 meters high. Cellar 1 had an area of 210 sq. meters and was 2.4 meters (7 ft. 9 in.) high. In crematoria 4 and 5 chambers were built on the surface, each having an extent of 580 sq. meters (694 sq. yards), which were officially called Badeanstalt für Sonderaktion ("Baths for Special Action") (*Aktenvermerk* of Aug 21, 1942, No. 12115/42). From the specifications of the central building board of Feb. 19, May 6, 1943 and Apr. 6, 1943 it appears that both cellar No.

1 in crematoria 2 and 3 and the Badenanstalten in crematoria 4 and 5 had gas-tight doors with grated observation windows of unbreakable 8 mm glass. The true purpose of all these rooms variously described is revealed by Bischoff's letter of Jan. 29, 1943, to the Chief of the Official Group C. Kammler, 22250/43, in which he called them gas-chambers (*Vergasungskeller*).[174]

Sehn followed with a description of the gassing procedure.

After undressing they were driven through a corridor to the actual gas chamber (Leichenkeller 1), which had previously been heated with the aid of portable coke braziers. This heating was necessary for the better evaporation of the hydrogen cyanide. By beating them with rods and setting dogs on them about 2000 victims were packed into a space of 210 sq. metres (250 sq. yds.).

From the ceiling of this chamber, the better to deceive the victims, hung imitation shower-bays, from which water never poured. After the gas-tight doors had been [c]losed the air was pumped out and through four special openings in the ceiling the contents of cans of cyclon, producing cyanide hydrogen gas, were poured in.

The contents of the cans fell down a cylindrical shaft constructed of four corner pieces covered with wire mesh-work of varying density. In the case of the surface gas-chambers in crematoria 4 and 5, the contents of the cans of cyclon were poured in through openings in the side-walls.[175]

Both the cruel regime and the gas chambers produced many corpses. Initially they were buried in mass graves, but as the War Refugee Board report had already described, the mass graves created an ecological problem. Following Dawidowski's assessment, Sehn argued that the problems caused by the mass burials necessitated the construction of the four new crematoria.

Together, therefore, the four new crematoria had 46 retorts, each with a capacity of 3–5 corpses. The burning of one retort load lasted about half an hour, and as the cleaning of the fireplaces took about an hour per day, so all the four crematoria could burn about 12,000 corpses in 24 hours, which would give 4,380,000 a year.[176]

It is unclear why Sehn chose to change Dawidowski's assessment that the capacity of the four crematoria in Birkenau was 8,000 per day. Sehn's calculations do not make sense: even if we assume a load of 5 corpses per muffle and an incineration time of 30 minutes, and an operation period of 23 hours per day, we come to a capacity of "only" $(46 \times 5 \times 2 \times 23) = 10,580$ corpses per day.

The report continued with a description of how in the summer of 1944, during the Hungarian Action, even the crematoria could not cope, and how the practice of open-pit burning was reintroduced. It then went on to address the total number of victims:

On the basis of calculations made by experts of the Investigation Technical Commission under the guidance of Prof. Dawidowski it was stated during the inquiry that the installations for disposing of corpses in pits and crematoria could have burnt more than 5 million bodies during the period in which they were active.

As is well known, the Soviet Legal and Medicinal Commission, which arrived at Auschwitz immediately after the flight of the Germans, has stated that the number of prisoners murdered exceeded 4,000,000.[177]

Finally, Sehn dealt with the obliteration of the evidence. The Germans not only removed documents and killed prisoners who knew too much, they also destroyed the crematoria.

As early as May, 1944, the old crematorium at Auschwitz was transformed into an air-raid shelter. Crematorium 4 was burnt on Oct. 7, 1944, during a fire which broke out when the members of the *Sonderkommando* tried to avoid being gassed. The technical installations at crematoria 2 and 3 were dismantled in November, 1944, and part of them sent up to the camp at Gross Rosen, and the buildings were blown up. Crematorium 5 was burnt and its walls blown up in the night of Jan. 20, 1945.[178]

In conclusion, Sehn reiterated once more that Auschwitz was an extermination camp which "already at its foundation was designed by the Nazi authorities as a place of execution for millions of people."[179]

Using the findings of the Central Commission and cross-referencing them with their own experiences, Czech former inmates Ota Kraus and Erick Schön/Kulka published in 1946 their *Tovarna Na Smrt* (*Factory of Death*).[180] Both Kraus and Schön had been employed in Auschwitz as locksmiths, and as such they had been able to move throughout the camp. Their book was a generally careful and well-organized account of the operation of the camp, and the chapter entitled "Masinerie smrto" ("Machinery of Death") calmly presented the terrible facts without recourse to histrionics.

Kraus and Kulka located the beginning of mass destruction by gas in the spring of 1942 with the killing of 700 Slovak Jews in Crematorium 1. According to them, Crematorium 1 was only an experimental killing station. Once the Germans had devised a workable method there, "work was started at Birkenau on the construction of four large crematoria complete with gas chambers."[181] On their completion, Crematorium 1 was closed down. The program of extermination overtook the schedule of the architects, however, and therefore the SS was forced to adopt a stopgap solution and adapt two cottages into gas chambers. After a description of Bunkers 1 and 2, Kraus and Kulka described the gassing operation and the disposal of the corpses in mass graves.

After a few months, although the corpses were covered with chlorine, lime and earth, an intolerable stench began to hang around the entire neighbourhood. Deadly bacteria were found in springs and wells, and there was a severe danger of epidemics.

To meet this problem, the Sonderkommando was increased in size. Day and night, working in two shifts, the prisoners in the squad dug up decaying corpses, took them away on narrow-gauge trucks and burnt them in heaps in the immediate vicinity.

The work of exhuming and burning 50,000 corpses lasted almost till December 1942.

After this experience the Nazis stopped burying their victims and cremated them instead.

Such were the emergency methods used for destroying people

at Birkenau in the early days. They continued in use until February, 1943, when the crematoria were completed and brought into use—first Crematorium I, and then the others.[182]

Kraus and Kulka stressed that these new crematoria were ultramodern "factories of corpses."[183] Their book reproduced the blueprints of the crematoria which, as they claimed, inmate architect Vera Foltynova had removed from the architectural office in August 1944. Foltynova had given the plans to Kraus and Kulka, who in turn had been able to smuggle the plans out of the camp and send them on their way to Czechoslovakia "because at that time we assumed that both the crematoria and ourselves would be liquidated as witnesses to German crimes."[184]

> At first sight the crematoria—one-storey buildings in the German style, with steep roofs, barred windows and dormer windows—presented the appearance of large bakeries.
>
> The space around them was enclosed by high tension barbed wire and was always well kept. The roads were sprayed with sand, and well-tended flowers bloomed in the beds on the lawn. The underground gas chambers, projecting some 50 cm. above ground level, formed a grassy terrace.
>
> A person coming to the crematoria for the first time could have no idea what these industrial buildings were actually for.
>
> Crematoria I and II were close to the camp itself and were visible from all sides. Crematoria III and IV, on the other hand, were hidden in a little wood; tall pine trees and birches concealed the tragedies that befell millions. This place was called Brzezinka, from which the name Birkenau is derived.[185]

Kraus and Kulka followed with a description of the interior arrangement of the basement of Crematoria 2 and 3 (I and II in their numbering system).

> At Crematoria I and II there were two underground rooms. The larger of these was an undressing room and was occasionally used as a mortuary; the other was a gas chamber.
>
> The whitewashed undressing-room had square concrete pillars, about 4 meter[s] apart. Along the walls and round the pillars there were benches, with coat-hooks surmounted by numbers. A pipe with a number of water taps ran the entire length of one of the walls.
>
> There were notices in several languages:

KEEP CALM!
KEEP THIS PLACE CLEAN AND TIDY!

And arrows pointing to the doors bearing the words:

DISINFECTION
BATHROOM

> The gas chamber was somewhat shorter than the undressing-room and looked like a communal bathroom. The showers in the roof, of course, never held water. Water taps were placed along the walls. Between the concrete pillars were two iron pillars, 30 cm × 30 cm, covered in thickly plaited wire. These pillars passed through the concrete ceiling to the grassy terrace mentioned above; here they terminated in airtight trap-doors into which the

SS men fed the cyclon gas. The purpose of the plaited wire was to prevent any interference with the cyclon crystals. These pillars were a later addition to the gas chamber and hence do not appear in the plan.

Each of the gas chambers at Crematoria I and II was capable of accommodating up to 2,000 people at a time.

At the entrance to the gas chamber was a lift, behind double doors, for transporting the corpses to the furnace rooms on the ground-floor, with their 15 three-stage furnaces.

At the bottom stage air was [brought] in by electric fans, at the middle the fuel was burnt, and at the top of corpses were placed, two or three at a time, on the stout fire-clay grate. The furnaces had cast-iron doors which were opened by means of a pulley.

There was also a dissecting-room on the ground-floor where the prisoner-doctors in the Sonderkommando carried out various experiments and post mortems under the supervision of SS doctors.[186]

One of the great services of Kraus and Kulka's book was that it was the first to provide reliable plans of Auschwitz and Birkenau. For example, their description of the crematoria was accompanied by a foldout sheet with a set of three annotated plans showing the basement of Crematorium 3, the first floor of the same building, and the plan of Crematorium 4.[187] They also provided two photographs of a model of Crematorium 3, which showed the underground gas chamber, the incineration hall with the five triple-muffle ovens, and the living quarters of the Sonderkommandos in the attic.[188] Kraus and Kulka provided lengthy descriptions of the arrival procedures both before and after the completion of the spur line that connected Birkenau to the main railway lines. Before the spring of 1944, transports arrived at a special ramp outside the camp adjacent to the railway corridor, and were greeted by the SS and inmates of the so-called Canada Squad who had orders to take care of all the deportees' belongings.

As the men got out of the trucks, they were separated from women and children. Then an SS doctor and SS officer, after a superficial examination of each man, would show by a jerk of the thumb whether they were to go to the right or left—life or death.

Children were assigned to death, and women who did not want to be separated from their children went with them. Of the remaining women only those from sixteen to thirty who were young and healthy were selected for the camp; the rest were sent to the gas chambers. Of the men some 15 to 20% were classified fit for work.

People destined for the gas chambers were loaded on to waiting lorries. Those classified as fit for work had to walk to the camps on foot, but before they left they were given the option of going on the lorries, if they thought they could not walk—which meant death in the gas chambers.

We shall never forget the sight of those long convoys of fast-moving lorries, packed full of people. We were unable to give them the last word or sign to show them where they were heading—but they were really better off if they did not know.

One of the most cynical touches in the whole affair was the

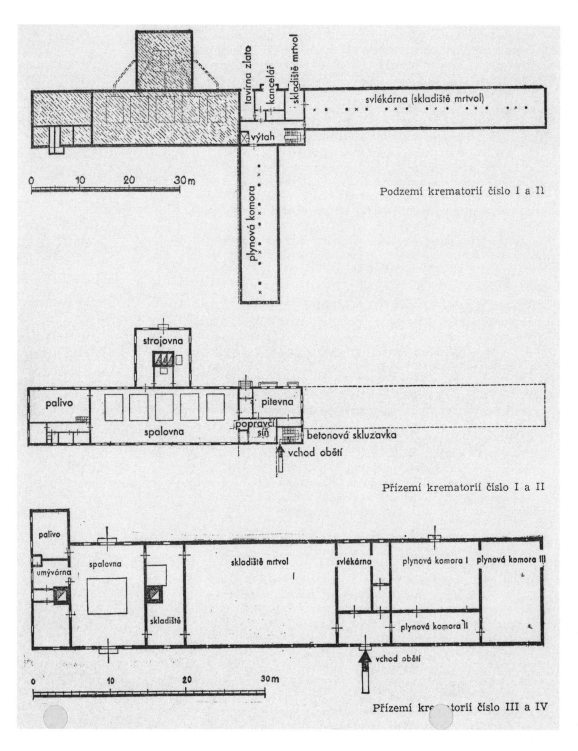

Plans of the crematoria as published in Kraus and Kulka,
Tovarna Na Smrt *(1946).*

use of an ambulance, marked with the Red Cross. The vehicle waited at the ramp, to give the impression that it was performing the normal function of an ambulance, and then moved off at the tail of the convoy. But instead of medicines and patients it carried tins of deadly cyclon B crystals for the gas chambers.[189]

Well written and filled with observations based on personal experience, Kraus and Kulka's *Factory of Death* was to become a classic, going through many and increasingly expanded editions in Czech and other languages.

Four

Confessions and Trials

By the end of 1945, the major elements of the wartime history of Auschwitz had been established on the basis of on-site inspections, the testimony of witnesses, and study of the crematoria files in the archive of the Zentralbauleitung. Yet the Poles had not been able to interview any of the men who had constructed and run the camp, who could give some insight into the aims that had shaped the development of the camp. One document that became available to the Poles in late 1945, the testimony of SS-Unterscharführer Pery Broad, was both extremely important as corroborating evidence and quite informative. Broad, who served in the Political Department (the "camp Gestapo") at Auschwitz, wrote it shortly after the German capitulation while he was in British captivity. By all accounts, he wrote the report voluntarily while working in the camp as a translator for the British counterintelligence unit. In 1964, during the Frankfurt Auschwitz Trial, Broad's British superior Cornelis van het Kaar testified that in the beginning of June 1945, Broad approached him and told him the history of Auschwitz. Van het Kaar told him to write everything down: "Especially write about the daily life there."[1] Broad created six copies of his report. One of them was given to van het Kaar's superior, Hermann Rothmann, who provided it to the Frankfurt court for Broad's trial. Examined during the trial under oath, Rothmann declared that Broad had written it by himself and that the report roughly covered what Broad had told him in person.[2] Broad admitted, after some hesitation, that the report was his and that the only part of the report he did not recognize as his own was the various numbers it mentioned.[3]

The Broad report, which was of independent origin, corroborated important elements of the picture that had begun to emerge in Sehn's investigation and added important new descriptions. Perhaps most important was Broad's recollection of the first gassings in Crematorium 1, which was located adjacent to his own office in the barrack that housed the camp's Political Department.

Pery Broad, 1960. Courtesy Archive Auschwitz-Birkenau State Museum, Oswiecim.

> From the first company of the *SS-Totenkopfsturmbannes*, stationed in the Auschwitz concentration camp, *SS-Hauptscharführer* Vaupel selected six particularly trustworthy men. Among them were those who had been members of the black General SS for years. They had to report to *SS-Hauptscharführer* Hössler. After their arrival Hössler cautioned them to preserve the utmost secrecy as to what they would see in the next few minutes. Otherwise death would be their lot.
>
> The task of the six men was to keep all roads and streets completely closed around the area near the Auschwitz crematorium. Nobody should be allowed to pass there, regardless of rank. The offices in the building from which the crematorium was visible were evacuated. No inmate of the SS garrison hospital was allowed to come near the windows of the first floor which looked onto the roof of the nearby crematorium and the yard of that gloomy place.
>
> Everything was made ready and Hössler himself made sure that no uncalled-for persons would enter the closed area. Then a sad procession walked along the streets of the camp. It had started at the railway siding, located between the garrison storehouse and the German Armaments Factory (the siding branched off from the main railway line, which led to the camp). There, at the ramp, cattle vans were being unloaded, and people who had arrived in them were slowly marching towards their unknown destination. All of them had large, yellow Jewish stars on their miserable clothes. Their worn faces showed that they had suffered many a hardship. The majority were elderly people. From their conversation one could gather that up to their unexpected transportation they had been employed in factories, that they were willing to go on working and to be as useful as they could. A few guards without guns, but with pistols well hidden in their pockets, escorted the procession to the crematorium. The SS-men promised the people, who were beginning to feel more hopeful, that they would be employed at suitable work, according to their preoccupations. Explicit instructions how to behave were given the SS-men by Hössler. Previously the guards had always treated new arrivals very roughly, trying with blows to make them stand in ranks "at arm's length," but there were no uncivil words just now! The more fiendish the whole plan!
>
> Both sides of the big entrance gate to the crematorium were wide open. Suspecting nothing the column marched in, in lines of five persons, and stood in the yard. There were three or four hundred of them. Somewhat nervously the SS guard at the entrance waited for the last man to enter the yard. Quickly he shut the gate and bolted it. Grabner and Hössler were standing on the

roof of the crematorium. Grabner spoke to the Jews, who unsuspectingly awaited their fate, "You will now bathe and be disinfected, we don't want any epidemics in the camp. Then you will be brought to your barracks, where you'll get some hot soup. You will be employed in accordance with your professional qualifications. Now undress and put your clothes in front of you on the ground."

They willingly followed these instructions, given them in a friendly, warm-hearted voice. Some looked forward to the soup, others were glad that the nerve-racking uncertainty as to their immediate future was over and that their worst expectations were not realized. All felt relieved after their days full of anxiety.

Grabner and Hössler continued from the roof to give friendly advice, which had a calming effect upon the people. "Put your shoes close to your clothes bundle, so that you can find them after the bath." "Is the water warm? Of course, warm showers." "What is your trade? A shoemaker? We need them urgently. Report to me immediately after!"

Such words dispelled any last doubts or lingering suspicions. The first lines entered the mortuary through the hall. Everything was extremely tidy. But the special smell made some of them uneasy. They looked in vain for showers or water pipes fixed to the ceiling. The hall meanwhile was getting packed. Several SS-men had entered with them, full of jokes and small talk. They unobtrusively kept their eyes on the entrance. As soon as the last person had entered they disappeared without much ado. Suddenly the door was closed. It had been made tight with rubber and secured with iron fittings. Those inside heard the heavy bolts being secured. They were screwed to with screws, making the door air-tight. A deadly paralyzing terror spread among the victims. They started to beat upon the door, in helpless rage and despair they hammered on it with their fists. Derisive laughter was their only reply. Somebody shouted through the door, "Don't get burned, while you make your bath!" Several victims noticed that covers had been removed from the six holes in the ceiling. They uttered a loud cry of terror when they saw a head in a gas mask at one opening. The "disinfectors" were at work. One of them was *SS-Unterscharführer* Teuer, decorated with the Cross of War Merit. With a chisel and a hammer they opened a few innocuous-looking tins which bore the inscription "Cyclon, to be used against vermin. "Attention, poison! To be opened by trained personnel only!" The tins were filled to the brim with blue granules the size of peas.

Immediately after opening the tins, their contents was thrown into the holes which were quickly covered.

Meanwhile Grabner gave a sign to the driver of a lorry, which had stopped close to the crematorium. The driver started the engine and its deafening noise was louder than the death cries of the hundreds of people inside, being gassed to death. Grabner looked with the interest of a scientist at the second hand of his wrist watch. Cyclon acted swiftly. It consists of hydrocyanic acid in solid form. As soon as the tin was emptied, the prussic acid escaped from the granules. One of the men, who participated in the bestial gassing, could not refrain from lifting, for a fraction of a second, the cover of one of the vents and from spitting into the hall. Some two minutes later the screams became less loud and only an indistinct groaning was heard. The majority of the victims had already lost consciousness. Two minutes more and Grabner stopped looking at his watch.

It was over. There was complete silence. The lorry had driven away. The guards were called off, and the cleaning squad started to sort out the clothes, so tidily put down in the yard of the crematorium.

Busy SS-men and civilians working in the camp were again passing the mound, on whose artificial slopes young trees swayed peacefully in the wind. Very few knew what terrible event had taken place there only a few minutes before and what sight the mortuary below the greenery would present.

Some time later, when the ventilators had extracted the gas, the prisoners working in the crematorium opened the door to the mortuary. The corpses, their mouths wide open, were leaning on one another. They were especially closely packed near to the door, where in their deadly fright they had crowded to force it. The prisoners of the crematorium squad worked like robots, apathetically and without a trace of emotion. It was difficult to tug the corpses from the mortuary, as their twisted limbs had grown stiff with the gas. Thick smoke clouds poured from the chimney.— This is how it began in 1942![4]

Broad's testimony was important, but as any observer will notice, not without problems. Broad showed some literary ambition in his account, and his flowery and sentimental descriptions clashed with the evidentiary import of his recollections.

According to Broad, the main motivation to build the four new crematoria in Birkenau was the difficulties the Germans had in keeping the killings at Bunkers 1 and 2 secret. The inhabitants of Wola, located at the opposite shore of the Vistula, had been able to observe the proceedings.[5] The burning pyres produced a terrible stench and colored the sky red at night. "It was by reason of the unmistakable sweet smell and the nightly flames that the neighbourhood of Auschwitz learnt about the goings-on in the camp of death," Broad wrote.[6] The completion of four new crematoria, which ended the need to incinerate the corpses on large pyres, allowed the Germans to restore secrecy. Broad's description of the crematoria was rather precise. "Two of them had underground gas chambers, in each of which 4,000 people could be killed at the same time. The other two smaller crematoria had two gas chambers partitioned into three sections, built on the ground floors." He mentioned that all the crematoria were equipped with undressing rooms. Those of Crematoria 2 and 3 were underground: "Stone stairs, about two metres wide, led down to them." The stairs can still be observed. As to the incineration capacity, he mentioned that Crematoria 2 and 3 had fifteen ovens each, "and each oven was equipped to hold four or five corpses."[7] It is important to remember that Broad provided this information independently of Tauber.

Because he had worked in an administrative capacity in the Political Department of the camp (the in-house Gestapo office), Broad was able to provide some valuable information regarding record-keeping.

When information was requested by the Reich Main Security Office concerning a past transport, as a rule nothing could be ascertained. Former transport lists were destroyed. Nobody could learn anything in Auschwitz about the fate of a given person. The person asked for "is not and never has been detained in camp," or "he is not in the files"—these were the usual formulas given in reply. At present, after the evacuation of Auschwitz and the burning of all papers and records, the fate of millions of people is completely obscure. No transport or arrival lists are in existence any more.[8]

Broad was called as one of the witnesses in the trial of Bruno Tesch, Joachim Drosihn, and Karl Weinbacher. Tesch had been the owner of the firm of Tesch and Stabenow, which had supplied Zyklon B—the commercially sold fumigation product that had hydrogen cyanide as its active agent—to Auschwitz and other camps; Weinbacher had been a manager in the firm and Droshin the chief technician. According to the indictment, the defendants had known since 1942 that Zyklon B was used not only for its normal fumigation purposes but also to kill human beings. Nevertheless Tesch and his subordinates had continued to supply the product. According to the prosecution, "Knowingly to supply a commodity to a branch of state which is using that commodity for the mass murder of Allied civilian nationals is a war crime, and the people who did it were war criminals for putting the means to commit the actual crime into the hands of those who actually carried it out."[9]

During the trial, Broad testified on behalf of the prosecution. He testified that he had witnessed a gassing at Crematorium 1 from 40 to 45 meters away.

Q.: "Will you tell us what you saw in connection with exterminations at the old crematorium?"

A.: "The installation at the crematorium was the following. The roof was plain, and there were six holes of the diameter of ten centimetres. Through these holes, after the tins had been opened, the gas was poured in."

Q.: "How many people were they putting in at a time in the old crematorium?"

A.: "At the time when I observed it, there were about 300 or 400 or there might have been even 500."

Q.: "How long did the gassing take to finish the 500 off?"

A.: "One could hear the screaming of the people who were killed in the crematorium for about two or three minutes."

Q.: "Did you later get to know more about the gassing operations?"

A.: "Yes; later on I got to know the name of that particular gas; it was Zyklon."

Q.: "Did you ever see any gassings at the new crematoriums at Birkenau?"

A.: "I have seen those gassing actions from a rather bigger distance."

Q.: "At Birkenau?"

A.: "Yes."

Q.: "How many gas crematoriums were there at Birkenau?"

A.: "There were four crematoriums at Birkenau."

Q.: "How many people a day were they gassing at Birkenau?"

A.: "In the months of March and April 1944 about 10,000."

Q.: "Per day?"

A.: "Yes, per day."[10]

Broad was asked to identify the labels of the Zyklon B cans and then to explain who the victims were. He estimated the total number of victims at between 2.5 and 3 million. Then he described the gassing and incineration procedures at the crematoria and the renewed use of pyres in 1944 when the killing exceeded the incineration capacity of the ovens.

Q.: "Who were the men who actually did the gassing? What type of man was that in the camp?"

A.: "They were called disinfectors."

Q.: "Will you tell us about these disinfectors shortly?"

A.: "They were under the orders of the doctor and their duties comprised, apart from killing human beings, also the disinfection and the delousing of the internees' clothes."

Q.: "How was that delousing and disinfection carried out?"

A.: "In airtight rooms. The clothing was dealt with in the same way as the human beings."

Q.: "Will you look at this extract from this report and tell me if you know anything about it? Who wrote that report, which is set out there in inverted commas?"

A.: "I myself."

Q.: "The disinfectors are at work. . . . With an iron rod and hammer they open a couple of harmless looking tin boxes, the directions read 'Cyclon [sic], vermin destroyer, Warning, Poisonous.' The boxes are filled with small pellets which look like blue peas. As soon as the box is opened the contents are shaken out through an aperture in the roof. Then another box is emptied in the next aperture, and so on. And in each case the cover is carefully replaced on the aperture. . . . Cyclon works quickly, it consists of a cyanic compound in a modified form. When the pellets are shaken out of the box they give off prussic acid gas (Blausauregas). . . . After about two minutes the shrieks die down and change to a low moaning. Most of the men have already lost consciousness. After a further two minutes . . . it is all over. Deadly quiet reigns. . . . The corpses are piled together, their mouths stretched open. . . . It is difficult to heave the interlaced corpses out of the chamber as the gas is stiffening all their limbs. Is that based on your experience?"

A.: "Yes."[11]

The Broad report has been available to researchers of Auschwitz since their discovery or compilation in 1945. A second, and important, document, created in the summer of 1945, was to remain hidden in the Public Record Office until it was released for study in 1992. Ironically, the first to see it was David Irving.[12] Irving, however, initially chose not to go public with his discovery of the five accounts about Auschwitz created shortly after the war by Höss's one-time deputy Hans Aumeier. Seeking to make the best from a very bad situation, he buried his attack on Aumeier's statement in a footnote in his 1996 book on the Nuremberg Trials: "Aumeier was initially as incoherent as Höss under interrogation by the British in Norway and England. The memoirs and manuscripts which he pencilled in the Kensington interrogation center commanded by Lieut.-Col. Scotland also displayed an increasing precision with each week that passed. The final manuscript (or fair copy) signed by Aumeier was pencilled in British Army style with all proper names in block letters."[13] In other words, Irving suggested that Aumeier wrote down what his captors told him to.

SS-Hauptsturmführer (Captain) Hans Aumeier became Lagerführer (Camp Leader) of Auschwitz in early 1942, and as such he was responsible for the day-to-day operation of the *Schutzhaftlager* (literally "Protective Custody Camp"), the inmate compound of the concentration camp. He remained in that function until the end of that year, and therefore oversaw the transformation of Auschwitz from a "normal" concentration camp into a camp that, among other functions, also served as an extermination camp for Jews. Aumeier was not very effective, and in early 1943 he was transferred to run a concentration camp in Estonia. His superior Höss did not miss him. He described Aumeier as a man with narrow views, without much foresight, and without initiative, and noted that his increasing responsibilities had made him nervous and careless. "He began to smoke and drink more and more. He became increasingly irresponsible and was literally 'bowled over' by this complex operation. He could not control this huge operation anymore. He tried to swim, but he was carried along by the current of events."[14] Despite (or perhaps because of) his limited abilities, Aumeier ended up running a concentration camp in Norway. Arrested after the German capitulation in May 1945, he was initially interrogated in Norway. In a first account written by Aumeier, dated June 29, 1945, he stated that during his tenure as Lagerführer 3,000 to 3,500 prisoners died in Auschwitz. He denied any knowledge of gas chambers.[15]

A month later, Aumeier admitted that gas chambers had been in operation in Auschwitz and that they were used for the killing of Jews. He knew of three or four gassings in Crematorium 1. "These always occurred in the evening hours. In the morgue were two to three air vents[,] and medical orderlies, wearing gas masks, shook blue [cyanide] gas into these. We were not allowed to come close, and only the next day the bunker [gas chamber] was opened." The main killing site however, was Birkenau. Aumeier gave quite a precise description of the first gas chambers in the birch forest.

> In Birkenau, close to the burial sites, two empty houses were equipped by the construction office with gas chambers. One house had two chambers, the other four. These houses were designated as bunkers 1 and 2. Each chamber accommodated about 50 to 150 people. At the end of January or February [1942], the first gassings were undertaken. The Kommando was called SK [*Sonderkommando*], and the camp commandant had put it under direct authority of *Untersturmführer* Grabner and

Hans Aumeier, 1945. Courtesy Archive Auschwitz-Birkenau State Museum, Oswiecim.

was again led and brought into action by [. . .] H[öss]ler. The area was surrounded by notices and marked as a security zone, and moreover encircled by eight guard posts from the Kommando.

From that moment onwards the camp doctors sorted from the arriving transports immediately the inmates, and those who were destined to be gassed. They had instructions to select for gassing those crippled by illness, those over 55 years of age who could not work, and children up to 11 or 12 years.[16]

Crowell has tried to interpret the Aumeier statement as a proof that gassings in Auschwitz were an ad hoc strategy for controlling epidemics and those incapable of working. "This is much better than those accounts that insist that gassing was introduced as part of the 'Final Solution' and that it was applied immediately to all Jewish internees."[17] A master in the creation of straw men, Crowell misrepresented what historians have said about the Final Solution. No one has ever suggested that upon the decision to enact the so-called Final Solution all Jewish internees were immediately gassed. Furthermore, he ignores Aumeier's statement that "[f]rom that moment onwards the camp doctors sorted from the arriving transports immediately the inmates, and those who were destined to be gassed. They had instructions to select for gassing those crippled by illness, those over 55 years of age who could not work, and children up to 11 or 12 years." If these selections were not part of the "Final Solution," what were they part of?

Let us return to Aumeier.

Near bunkers 1 and 2 two barracks were built, and in this one inmates had to undress, and there they were told that they were to be deloused and bathed. Then they were brought to the chambers. Air vents were set in the side walls of these chambers.

In the same manner as described above, gassings took place under control of the doctor. The bunker was always opened the next day. On the next day gold teeth would be broken out of the corpses under supervision of a dentist or a medical orderly, and after that the corpses were burned in trenches in a manner described above.

At the same time doctors also selected seriously ill Jewish prisoners in the sick wards of the camp, and from time to time led to the gassing. It must have been around the middle of April 1943 that crematorium I [2] in Birkenau was completed and brought into operation. In the basement of the crematorium (I believe it had eight ovens) had been built a concrete bunker that had place for between 600 to 800 people. In front of the crematorium was also built a hut for undressing.

Aumeier refers here to Crematorium 2, but he is confused when he thinks that it contained eight ovens. Crematoria 4 and 5 were equipped with double-four-muffle ovens (which add up to eight muffle ovens); Crematoria 2 and 3 had five triple-muffle ovens. He is, however, correct in his description of the underground gas chamber and the presence of the undressing hut, which was in operation in the spring of 1943 before Morgue 2 had been completed as an undressing room.

Gassing occurred likewise through air vents from above. The Bunker had a system to introduce fresh air, so that after gassings the bunker could be opened after five to eight hours. The corpses were then brought with an elevator directly to the ovens for incineration.

Additionally it is worth to mention that valuables were taken from the Jews and were sent by the administration to the SS-Wirtschafts-verwaltungshauptamt. After delousing, the clothes were partly issued in the [Auschwitz] camps, and partly sent to other camps.

At the beginning of May 1943 crematorium II (5 ovens) was completed and alternately gassings also took place there. Its gas chamber was smaller and held perhaps 400 to 500 people. It did not have a system to bring in fresh air, and gassings happened by means of air vents in the side walls.[18]

At the time of my transfer crematorium III was still under construction and not ready. It was roughly planned on the same model as crematorium II (5 ovens).

It is clear that when Aumeier mentions Crematorium I, the first to be completed, he uses the terminology that described the crematoria of Birkenau as I, II, III, and IV. When he mentions the second crematorium to be completed, he labels it for that reason crematorium II, but its official designation was actually Crematorium 4 (or III in the alternate classification). When he mentions crematorium III, the number he assigns it can be attributed to the fact that it was indeed the third crematorium to be completed or that this crematorium was officially known as Crematorium 3. His idiosyncratic numbering system probably resulted from the fact that when he left the camp in the middle of 1943, he had not become accustomed to what became the official system.

Aumeier continues: "My estimate is that during my tenure between 15,000 and 18,000 Jewish prisoners were gassed."[19] His statement is important. While there are many errors, especially with regard to dates or the number of Jews gassed, he is basically correct in his description of Bunkers 1 and 2 and the gas chambers in Crematoria 2 and 4. Although it is less detailed, Aumeier's confession provides important independent corroboration of Broad's account, the statements made in Poland by surviving Sonderkommandos, and the forensic investigations done by Roman Dawidowski. Aumeier was to elaborate further on his statement in the months that followed, providing more details about the gassing operation. In these statements he stressed again, on various occasions, that "there was a Reichsführer-SS order to this effect which banned all written reports, counts, statistics, or the like in this context"[20] and that "no lists were kept of those gassed and those were also not recorded by name from the transports. As already mentioned, it was forbidden to make notes or lists about it."[21]

In the months immediately after the end of the war in Europe, Broad's report and Aumeier's explanations provided important additional evidence about the history of Auschwitz as an extermination camp. Yet the immediate impact of these documents was small. This was not the case with the so-called Belsen Trial, held by a British military tribunal in the fall of 1945 in the German city of Lüneburg to try the captured SS personnel of Bergen-Belsen. The trial did more than merely generate valuable evidence; it also focused attention on Auschwitz, because most of the defendants had, at one time or another, worked in Auschwitz before being transferred to Bergen-Belsen. Kommandant Josef Kramer, for example, had also served as Lagerführer of Birkenau during the Hungarian Action. Hence there were two distinct charges upon which the accused were arraigned. The first concerned the criminal and inexcusable neglect that characterized SS rule in Belsen, and the second focused on the carefully designed and executed policy of extermination in Auschwitz.

In the opening speech for the prosecution, Colonel T. M. Backhouse stated that he was to provide evidence to show that the conditions in Bergen-Belsen and Auschwitz were caused not only by criminal neglect but also by deliberate starvation and ill-treatment and that in Auschwitz "there was deliberate killing of thousands and probably millions of people."[22] The first witness for the prosecution to testify on the conditions at Auschwitz was Polish-Jewish physician Dr. Ada Bimko. She arrived in Auschwitz in August 1943 with 5,000 other Jews from Sosnowitz. Of this transport, 4,500 were sent directly to the crematorium. "My father, mother, brother, husband and small son of six years of age were included in that number."[23]

Some of the defendants in the Lüneburg Trial. Josef Kramer (no. 1) served as Kommandant at Bergen-Belsen and Fritz Klein (no. 2) served as camp doctor. Imperial War Museum, courtesy USHMM Photo Archives.

Dr. Bimko testified that she had seen one of the gas chambers. While she did not identify which crematorium she visited, it seems that she visited Crematorium 5. In her original deposition, she discussed the circumstances that made the visit possible. The women who had been waiting in Block 25, the holding pen in the women's camp for those selected for the gas chambers, would be ordered to undress and leave their clothes behind there. Occasionally they were allowed to cover their bodies with hospital blankets. Attached to the hospital in the women's camp, Dr. Bimko was responsible for recovering the blankets which the naked prisoners used after having undressed in Block 25. "I took the opportunity, as I always wanted to see with my own eyes this ill-famed gas chamber, and I went in." One day, she arranged with an SS-Unterscharführer who belonged to the medical staff to see the crematorium. He gave her a little tour. The gas chamber was square and resembled a shower-bath. "There were many sprays all over the ceiling in rows which were parallel. All these people who went into this room were issued with a towel and a cake of soap so that they should have the impression that they were going to have a bath, but for anybody who looked at the floor it was quite clear that it was not so, because there were no drains." She never saw the incineration room. "I believe the crematorium was in the same building," she stated, "but I myself did not see the stove."[24] But she did see something few others would ever see: the ductwork of the ventilation system installed above the gas chambers. Her SS guide told her, erroneously, that the ducts which extracted the poison *from* the gas chambers served the opposite purpose, namely to force the hydrogen cyanide *into* the gas chambers, and he wrongly identified the cylindrical drums that contained the ventilators as gas cylinders. Not in a position to challenge his explanation, Bimko accepted it for what it was.[25]

One of the other witnesses for the prosecution was Dr. Charles Sigismund Bendel, a Romanian-Jewish physician living in Paris. Arrested in November 1943, he had been taken first to the transit camp at Drancy and from there to Auschwitz. At the end of February 1944, Bendel was detailed as a doctor to the Romani camp in Birkenau, where he witnessed Dr. Mengele's medical experiments on twins.

> [Colonel T. M. Backhouse]: "In June, 1944, was your employment changed?"
>
> [Bendel]: "Indeed, it was changed. Dr. Mengele gave me the honour to attach me to the crematorium. The men who worked there were called Sonderkommando, a Special Kommando numbering 900. They were all deported people. Just as there existed a Sonderkommando amongst the prisoners so there was a Sonderkommando also amongst the S.S. They enjoyed special privileges, for instance, in alcohol, and were completely separated from the other S.S. There were about fifteen S.S. in this Sonderkommando, three for each crematorium. The prisoners amongst the Sonderkommando lived in the camp in two blocks which were always locked, and were not allowed to leave them. Some of S.S. of the Sonderkommando were on night duties and others did their duty in rotas. They were always relieved by the others. At first I lived in the camp with the other prisoners, but later on in the crematorium itself. The first time I started work there was in August, 1944. No one was gassed on that occasion, but 150 political prisoners, Russians and Poles, were led one by one to the graves and there they were shot. Two days later, when I was attached to the day group, I saw a gas chamber in action. On that occasion it was the ghetto at Lodz—80,000 people were gassed."
>
> Q.: "Would you describe just what happened that day?"
>
> A.: "I came at seven o'clock in the morning with the others and saw white smoke still rising from the trenches, which indicated that a whole transport had been liquidated or finished off during the night. In Crematorium No. 4 the result which was achieved by burning was apparently not sufficient. The work was not going on

quickly enough, so behind the crematorium they dug three large trenches 12 metres long and 6 metres wide. After a bit it was found that the results achieved even in these three big trenches were not quick enough, so in the middle of these big trenches they built two canals through which the human fat or grease should seep so that work could be continued in a quicker way. The capacity of these trenches was almost fantastic. Crematorium No. 4 was able to burn 1000 people during the day, but this system of trenches was able to deal with the same number in one hour."

Q.: "Will you describe the day's work?"

A.: "At eleven o'clock in the morning the chief of the Political Department arrived on his motor cycle to tell us, as always, that a new transport had arrived. The trenches which I described before had to be prepared. They had to be cleaned out. Wood had to be put in and petrol sprayed over so that it would burn quicker. About twelve o'clock the new transport arrived, consisting of some 800 to 1000 people. These people had to undress themselves in the court of the crematorium and were promised a bath and hot coffee afterwards. They were given orders to put their things on one side and all the valuables on the other. Then they entered a big hall and were told to wait until the gas arrived. Five or ten minutes later the gas arrived, and the strongest insult to a doctor and to the idea of the Red Cross was that it came in a Red Cross ambulance. Then the door was opened and the people were crowded into the gas chambers which gave the impression that the roof was falling on their heads, as it was so low. With blows from different kinds of sticks they were forced to go in and stay there, because when they realized that they were going to their death they tried to come out again. Finally, they succeeded in locking the doors. One heard cries and shouts and they started to fight against each other, knocking on the walls. This went on for two minutes and then there was complete silence. Five minutes later the doors were opened, but it was quite impossible to go in for another twenty minutes. Then the Special Kommandos started work. When the doors were opened a crowd of bodies fell out because they were compressed so much. They were quite contracted, and it was almost impossible to separate one from the other. One got the impression that they fought terribly against death. Anybody who has ever seen a gas chamber filled to the height of one and a half metres with corpses will never forget it. At this moment the proper work of the Sonderkommandos starts. They have to drag out the bodies which are still warm and covered with blood, but before they are thrown into the ditches they have still to pass through the hands of the barber and the dentist, because the barber cuts the hair off and the dentist has to take out all the teeth. Now it is proper hell which is starting. The Sonderkommando tries to work as fast as possible. They drag the corpses by their wrists in furious haste. People who had human faces before, I cannot recognize again. They are like devils. A barrister from Salonica, an electrical engineer from Budapest—they are no longer human beings because, even during the work, blows from sticks and rubber truncheons are being showered over them. During the time this is going on they continue to shoot people in front of these ditches, people who could not be got into the gas chambers because they were overcrowded. After an hour and a half the whole work has been done and a new transport has been dealt with in Crematorium No. 4.[26]

Under cross-examination by Captain L .S. W. Cranfield, one of the lawyers for the defense, Bendel gave more details about the arrival procedures of the selected deportees at the crematoria.

[Cranfield]: "When a party arrived for the gas chamber, was it brought down by one of the doctors?"

A.: "No. There was one S.S. in front and one at the back. That is all."

Q.: "Did these parties usually arrive in trucks?"

A.: "It varied—some prisoners arrived marching; on the other hand, sick people arrived in trucks. These trucks were so constructed that they could be tipped over, and the drivers found amusement in doing so, and throwing the people out."[27]

Perhaps the most important witness was the Kommandant of Bergen-Belsen, Josef Kramer. Initially, during the pretrial interrogations, the former Lagerführer of Birkenau had maintained that there had been no gas chambers in Auschwitz.[28] Yet he changed his story when the prosecution was able to present him with proof that he had constructed and operated a gas chamber during his tenure as Kommandant of the camp at Natzweiler-Struthof. Confronted with this material, Kramer decided that it was better to confess to the existence of gas chambers in both Natzweiler-Struthof and Auschwitz but to deny any direct responsibility. In the case of Auschwitz, where he served as Lagerführer of Birkenau, his denial of direct authority over the crematoria was, probably, justified. The crematoria were located outside the prisoner compound and were under the direct responsibility of the Political Department and the Kommandant.

Josef Kramer after his arrest, 1945. Hadassah [Ada] Bimko-Rosensaft, courtesy USHMM Photo Archives.

The first time I saw a gas chamber proper was at Auschwitz. It was attached to the crematorium. The complete building containing the crematorium and gas chamber was situated in camp No. 2 (Birkenau), of which I was in command. I visited the building on my first inspection of the camp after being there for three days, but for the first eight days I was there it was not working. After eight days the first transport, from which gas chamber victims were selected, arrived, and at that time I received a written order from Hoess, who commanded the whole of Auschwitz camp, that although the gas chamber and crematorium were situated in my part of the camp, I had no jurisdiction over it whatever. Orders in regard to the gas chamber were, in fact, always given by Hoess, and I am firmly convinced that he received such orders from Berlin. I believe that had I been in Hoess's position and received such orders, I would have carried them out, because even if I had protested it would only have resulted in my being taken prisoner myself. My feelings about orders in regard to the gas chamber were to be slightly surprised, and wonder to myself whether such action was really right.[29]

Kramer testified on Monday, October 8. Major T. C. M. Winwood, his counsel, first examined the discrepancy between Kramer's two depositions.

Q.: "Will you explain to the Court how it is that, in the first statement you made, you said the allegations referring to gas chambers, mass executions, whipping and cruelty were untrue, whereas in your second statement you said they were true?"

A.: "There are two reasons for that. The first is that in the first statement I was told that the prisoners alleged that these gas chambers were under my command, and the second and main reason was that Pohl, who spoke to me, took my word of honour that I should be silent and should not tell anybody at all about the existence of the gas chambers. When I made my first statement I felt still bound by this word of honour which I had given. When I made the second statement in prison, in Celle, these persons to whom I felt bound in honour—Adolf Hitler and Reichsführer Himmler—were no longer alive and I thought then that I was no longer bound."[30]

During cross-examination, Colonel Backhouse once more confronted Kramer with the issue of the conflicting statements.

Q.: "Do you believe in God?"

A.: "Yes."

Q.: "You remember the oath which you took when you first went into the witness box. Do you realize that to lie after you have taken that oath is deliberate perjury?"

A.: "Yes."

Q.: "In the first statement you made at Diest did you make precisely the same oath before you signed your statement?"

A.: "I am not sure whether it was before or after."

Q.: "I put it to you that you took precisely the same oath that you took in this court before you made your statement and that you lied and knew you were lying when you made that statement in which you said that there were no gas chambers at Auschwitz at all."

A.: "I have already said that, at that time, I felt still bound to my word of honour on that subject."[31]

When he was examined by his counsel, Kramer gave a description of who was responsible for what, carefully distancing himself from the whole issue.

Q.: "Did Kommandant Hoess say anything to you about the gas chambers?"

A.: "I received a written order from him that I had nothing to do with either the gas chambers or the incoming transports. The Political Department which was in every camp had a card index system of prisoners and was responsible for personal documents and for any sort of transports or incoming prisoners. At Auschwitz the Political Department was also responsible for all the selections from incoming transports for the gas chamber. In the crematorium the S.S. and prisoners—Sonderkommando—were under the command of the Kommandant of Auschwitz, Hoess. As the place where transports generally arrived was in the middle of my own camp I was sometimes present at their arrival. The people who took part in supervising and who were responsible for the security were partly from Auschwitz No. 1, and partly from my own camp at Birkenau, but the selection of these people who had to supervise was done by the Kommandant of Auschwitz No. 1. The actual selections of the internees were made only by the doctors. Those who were selected for the gas chambers went to the different crematoria, those who were found to be fit for work came into two different parts of my camp, because the idea was that in a few days they were to be re-transferred to different parts of Germany for work."

Q.: "Did you yourself ever take part in the selections?"

A.: "No, I never took part, nor did the other S.S. members of my staff. I do not know exactly who the doctors got their orders from, but I think it was probably from Dr. Wirths, the senior doctor of the camp. The doctors lived together in Auschwitz No. 1 where the headquarters were."

Q.: "What did you personally think about the whole gas chamber business?"

A.: "I asked myself, 'Is it really right about these persons who go to the gas chambers, and whether that person who signed for the first time these orders will be able to answer for it?' I did not know what the purpose of the gas chamber was."[32]

Mrs. Rosina Kramer testified on behalf of the defense of her husband. During cross-examination, Colonel Backhouse asked if she knew about the gassings. "Everybody in Auschwitz knew about them," she replied.[33]

One of the main defendants was Dr. Fritz Klein, an ethnic German from Rumania who had been drafted into the SS. As a physician, he participated in many selections. In his initial deposition he gave a very concise description of his responsibility, or lack thereof.

When transports arrived at Auschwitz it was the doctor's job to pick out those who were unfit or unable to work. These included children, old people and the sick. I have seen the gas chambers and crematoria at Auschwitz, and I knew that those I selected were to go to the gas chamber. But I only acted on orders given me by Dr. Wirths. I cannot say from whom Dr. Wirths received his orders and I have never seen any orders in writing relating to the gassing of prisoners. All orders given to me were given verbally.[34]

Under examination by his counsel, Major Winwood, Dr. Klein discussed the selection in greater detail.

Q.: "Will you tell us what happened on selections?"

A.: "Dr. Wirths, when the first transport arrived, gave me orders to divide it into two parts, those who were fit to work and those who were not fit, that is those who, because of their age, could not work, who were too weak, whose health was not very good, and also children up to the age of fifteen. The selecting was done exclusively by doctors. One looked at the person and, if she looked ill, asked a few questions, but if the person was healthy then it was decided immediately."

Q.: "What happened to those people who were selected as capable of work?"

A.: "The doctor had only to make the decision. What happened to them afterwards was nothing to do with him."

Q.: "What happened to those people whom the doctors selected as unfit for work?"

A.: "The doctor had to make a selection but had no influence on what was going to happen. I have heard, and I know, that part of them were sent to the gas chambers and the crematoria."[35]

Later on Klein admitted that he had visited a gas chamber when it was not in operation. Asked his opinion about "this gas chamber business," he answered that he did not approve, and added "I did not protest because that was no use at all."[36]

The third important defendant was Franz Hoessler, who in 1944 had served as Lagerführer at Auschwitz I. In his deposition, he admitted to the existence and use of the gas chambers.

Everyone in the camp knew about the gas chamber at Auschwitz, but at no time did I take part in the selection of prisoners who were to go to the gas chamber and then be cremated. Whilst I was there selection of prisoners for the gas chamber was done by Dr. Klein, Dr. Mengele and other young doctors whose names I do not know. I have attended these parades, but my job was merely to keep order. Often women were paraded naked in front of the doctors and persons selected by the doctors were sent to the gas chamber. I learnt this through conversation with the doctors. I think those selected were mostly those who were not in good health and could not work. When transports of prisoners arrived the prisoners were taken from the train and marched to the camp. On arrival they were paraded in front of the doctors I have mentioned, and persons were selected for the gas chamber, the remainder being sent to the concentration camp. I have also attended these parades, but only when I have been Orderly Lagerführer, as this was part of his duties. Train-loads of 2000 and 3000 arrived at the camp and often as many as 800 went to the gas chamber. The doctors were always responsible for these selections.

Whilst I was at Auschwitz the Kommandant, until June, 1944, was Hoess and he was succeeded by Baer. I made many complaints to Hoess about the way people were being sent to the gas chamber, but I was told it was not my business. The camp was inspected once a year by Himmler and also Obergruppenführer Glücks and Obergruppenführer Pohl from Berlin.

Himmler knew people at Auschwitz were gassed because it was he who gave the orders that this would be done. These orders could only have come from the top. Hitler must also have known that this was going on as he was the head of the country."[37]

Under examination by his counsel, Major A. S. Munro, Hoessler went into greater detail.

Q.: "Did you have to attend selections for the gas chambers?"

A.: "Yes, I attended these selections because I had to guard the

Franz Hoessler after his arrest, 1945. Imperial War Museum, courtesy USHMM Photo Archives.

prisoners. I did not make selections myself, and there were no selections without doctors."

Q.: "What did you think when you were told to attend a selection parade for the first time?"

A.: "When they told me for the first time, in summer 1943, I did not know even what it meant. I only thought I had to see that the people got out of their wagons and came into the camp."

Q.: "Did you later learn the real purpose of these parades?"

A.: "Yes, I heard about it and did not think that that was right. Once when Hoess arrived in his car I asked him if it was all right what was going on, and he just told me to do my duty. I received the order to go on selection parade personally and verbally from Hoess."

Q.: "Will you explain exactly what happened when transports arrived in the camp?"

A.: "The transport train arrived at the platform in the camp. It was my duty to guard the unloading of the train and to put the S.S. sentries like a chain around the transport. The next job was to divide the prisoners into two groups, the women to the left, the men to the right. Then the doctors arrived, and they selected the people. The people who had been inspected by the doctors and found to be fit for work were put on one side, the men and the women. The people who were found to be unfit for work had to go into the trucks, and they were driven off in the direction of the crematorium."[38]

Within the difficult circumstances of the time, the Belsen Trial was conducted with due regard to proper procedure. Some of the court-appointed defenders put up a spirited fight. For example, Major T. C. M. Winwood, counsel for Kramer, argued that really Heinrich Himmler was responsible, and that if anyone deserved the epithet "Beast of Belsen" it was the Reichsführer-SS, and not Kramer, who had the misfortune to have become the "Scapegoat of Belsen."[39] And the fact that the latter had volunteered to work in a concentration camp should not be held against him, certainly not by an English court, because the British held a patent on concentration camps.[40] After having explained why one should not judge the Germans too harshly for confining Jews to camps, Winwood proceeded effortlessly to put the blame for the conditions within the camps on the inmates. Like prisoner-of-war camps, inmate officials ran the camps. "The type of internee who came to these concentration camps was low, and had very little idea of doing what they were told, so that the control of these internees was a great problem."[41] Rassinier could not have agreed more.

Major L. S. W. Cranfield did his best to assault the credibility of witnesses and to create reasonable doubt about the operation of Auschwitz as an extermination camp. The summary of his closing speech reads in many ways as the founding document of negationism. "The court had first of all to decide what were the facts about the selections for the gas chamber at Auschwitz and what actually had happened," Cranfield argued. How did people know that those who had been selected ended up in the gas chambers?

From the evidence it appeared that the usual grounds for inferring people had been gassed was that they disappeared, but the same thing would have happened if they had been sent away to a factory or to another camp. With regard to Block 25, it might well have been that that block was used as a staging block for any party that was to leave the camp after a selection. When parties had been chosen they would obviously have to be segregated until they got away. Witnesses had spoken about people staying in Block 25 for days. If the authorities had decided to have a gas chamber selection they would not have done that unless they knew that the gas chamber was ready to take the people selected. Would they have selected 1000 people for the gas chamber and put them in Block 25 and kept them there for three days?[42]

Thus Cranfield began the search for the alternative explanations that, as we will see in the next chapter, would become a hallmark of negationist reasoning.

Cranfield also tried another route. In his opening speech for defendants Irma Grese and three others, Cranfield argued that the concentration camps were prisons under German law and that their inmates were legally imprisoned. He admitted that even if the camps had been legally established, the defendants should have refused to obey their superiors because they should have known that they were participating in a crime against humanity. "I answer that by saying that the accused can only judge what is a crime against humanity by their own environment," Cranfield retorted. "What is alleged to have been done in these concentration camps was to the accused nothing else than common form in Europe."[43]

Obviously, Cranfield's reasoning was less than satisfactory, and therefore Colonel Smith, sometime professor of international law at London University, was added to the defense team to help them deal with the legality of the indictment from the perspective of international law. Smith first of all argued that what happened in the concentration camps was not a war crime because it did not involve an offense against the legitimate conduct of the operations of war.

> This policy of concentration camps was started by Hitler within a few weeks of his ascension to power in early 1933. It was continued with ever increasing intensity throughout the whole time of peace, and it would have continued after the war if the Germans had won the war. It was part of a national German policy, a policy which we are all agreed is detestable, primarily the degradation and ultimate extermination of the Jewish race. More than that, in addition to the unfortunate Jewish race the Germans regarded as their inferiors the Slavonic races, who were treated with scarcely less severity. So I would like to submit to the Court, and as strongly as I can, that we are dealing here with incidents which occur, it is true, in time of war, but which have no logical connection with the war whatever—a policy which was begun in peace as a peace-time policy and was intended to be carried on as a permanent and long-term policy.[44]

As a result, Cranfield argued, it was inappropriate to indict the defendants with a war crime and try them before a military court.

Colonel Smith even maintained that the orders that had been given to build and operate the gas chambers were legal within the admittedly unusual legal structure of the Third Reich and that Kramer could therefore not be tried because he merely had obeyed the law. Smith observed that

Hitler had become the law by the mid-1930s, that he had chosen to delegate some of his powers to Himmler, and that Himmler had placed his instruments of power—the Gestapo, the concentration camps—outside the control of the courts. "Apply that to the most important thing in the charges, the gas chamber at Auschwitz," Smith asked. "If you ask me to produce a law legalizing the gas chambers at Auschwitz and Belsen, of course I could not do it," Smith admitted. But this did not matter, he argued. All that mattered was that Himmler had said "Have a gas chamber." His order was sufficient.

> What it leads to is this. In the case of the average German it was impossible to have the kind of conflict which might arise in England, where a man might question the order of his superior officer and say: "You cannot give me that order under the Army Act," and so on. An order as an order is perfectly legal, and where there is a conflict between internal law and the international law the individual must always obey the law.[45]

Because Kramer and his colleagues had not built the gas chambers on their own initiative, and because they had sent people there on orders of others which, ultimately, came from Hitler, Kramer could not be held accountable under international law.

Observers who followed the trial were in fact quite troubled by the amount of leeway given to the defense. "Impatience over the Belsen trials seems to be growing, and ought to be," the British weekly *The Spectator* reported as early as October 5. While it was proper that the accused should be adequately defended, there were limits. "It would almost appear as if the relevant authorities were determined to get Kramer and his Kramerish colleagues acquitted at any price," wrote Norman Bentwich, the representative of Jewish relief organizations at the Belsen Trial.[46] More than a month later, public opinion had not changed much. "The Belsen trial is at last reaching its end, and justice will at last be done," observed Bentwich.

> The general verdict that is passed on its protracted hearing is that, while it was an example of British administration of justice, conducted with dignity and with every regard for the accused, it involved an efflorescence of legal procedure. The twelve defending officers put all the forty-five accused persons into the box to tell a long story; and people began to believe the wisecrack, that was passed around Luneburg in the first week of the trial, that they would save their clients from the gallows by boring them to death.[47]

The prosecution rested its case on November 13, 1945. Colonel Backhouse made it clear that he had no doubts about the historical record.

> There is only one general picture of Auschwitz. Here was a camp in Poland, in a place where even the S.S. objected to being posted, and you have seen the type of place it was from the film supplied by the Russian government and heard what went on there from a variety of people. Can the Court have the slightest doubt, first of all, about the gas chamber or the selections which were made? It is freely admitted that there were in the camp Birkenau five gas chambers attached to the crematoria, and that when they were really busy the latter could not keep up, so that they had in addition to dig pits where bodies were thrown and burned by oil or petrol being poured upon them. People were gassed night and

day. We have been told that these gas chambers could carry 1000 people at each gassing and that during some periods people were saved up until there were 1000 in order to save wasting gas. In the busy period the Sonderkommando was working so that there was a gassing every hour and they were working in double shifts day and night. You have heard that utterly foul picture painted by Dr. Bendel. Can you have any doubt about it? The persons who were being put into these gas chambers were not people who had committed any crime or offence, they were not people who had been submitted to any trial; they were pure and simply persons who were no longer fit to work for the Reich, and although Kramer would not admit it to me in cross-examination, when it was put to him in reexamination he said: "It was a doctrine of my party to destroy the Jewish race." Whatever other places may also have been used in the course of this destruction, in Auschwitz alone literally millions of people were gassed for no other reasons than that they were Jews. The people who were gassed were the old, the weak, the pregnant women, and children under 14. Those were the people who were being selected and put into these gas chambers and quite blatantly murdered. No one could for a moment believe that that was anything but murder and an obvious crime against humanity.[48]

Given all the hesitation the Russian report—the only one available at the time of the Belsen Trial—had shown in even mentioning the word "Jew," Backhouse's closing speech was a remarkably straightforward and honest assessment of who had been the principal victims of the gas chambers. And these were not, as Kramer had suggested, "the dregs of the ghettos" without whom the world was better off. "This is manifestly untrue from the evidence," Backhouse asserted. "The people who were going through this gas chamber were going through without regard to class or ability; without regard to anything at all except for the fact of their religion, their race, or that they could work no longer as slaves."[49]

Conforming with customs of military justice, the judge advocate—lawyer C. L. Stirling—provided a summary of the arguments, laying out the legal issues and the questions the court should consider. One of those was the question of whether the crime set out in the charge sheet had been established. "Rightly or wrongly (it is, of course, for you to decide whether or not you accept it) in my view there is a tremendous general body of evidence going to establish that at Auschwitz the staff responsible for the well-being of internees were taking part in these gassings."[50] At the end of his summation, Stirling reminded the court of their duty.

You are about, in the next few minutes, to go to the peace and quiet of your own room to decide the fate of these men and women in the light of evidence. When you go I would ask you to take with you the words of Lord Sankey in the famous case of *Woolmington v. The Director of Public Prosecutions*, 1935 A.C. 462, a case that is known throughout the length and breadth of every English court. "Throughout the web of the English Criminal Law one golden thread is always to be seen, that is the duty of the prosecution to prove the prisoner's guilt. If at the end of and on the whole of the case there is a reasonable doubt created by the evidence given by either the prosecution or the prisoner, the prosecution has not made out the case and the prisoner is entitled to an acquittal no matter what the charge or where the trial." The principle that the Prosecution must prove the guilt of the prisoner is part of the common law of England, and no attempt to whittle it down can be entertained, and no attempt has been made in this case by the Prosecution to whittle it down.[51]

The court withdrew and returned with thirty guilty verdicts and fourteen acquittals. Of the thirty guilty verdicts, ten included a conviction for having committed a war crime in Auschwitz. Kramer, Klein, and Hössler were among those convicted. They were sentenced to death.

The proceedings of the Belsen Trial were published in 1949, and in the introduction, the editor, Raymond Phillips, observed that at some future date, the trial would perhaps be remembered "for the achievement of the British Legal System in refusing to be stampeded into the wild justice of revenge." Confronted with charges that had aroused "the resentment and horror of humanity," the court had brought "a cool, calm, dispassionate and unhurried determination."[52] I agree with Phillips. On reading and rereading the proceedings, one is not left with the sense that there were many, if any, loose ends. The prosecution did establish that the crime happened, that gas chambers operated in Auschwitz, and that many of the accused shared a responsibility for it.

For the first time in the West, people entrusted with judicial authority had to pass formal judgment on the evidence from Auschwitz according to traditional and proven methods. At the conclusion of the trial, the editors of *The Spectator,* who had shown so much criticism for the proceedings before, finally admitted that all the attention to judicial form had served an important purpose.

> There has been much criticism of the proceedings, chiefly directed to their length and the pains taken to ensure that justice shall be done and shall be seen to be done. Now the trial is over, such criticism seems very near praise. The trial has served a valuable purpose in exposing in detail some of the horrible crimes which were common form in the Germany of the concentration camps and in ensuring that they met with the strictest justice. One of the most interesting features was that the accused, who were capable of such inhuman cruelty, presented no appearance of abnormality and regarded their crimes as honourable services to their fatherland.[53]

With the Belsen Trial, the gas chambers at Auschwitz formally entered the historical record as what Colonel Backhouse rightly identified as "a war crime which has never been equalled."[54] It is therefore not surprising that negationists credit the trial as the occasion that the Allies transformed a lie into truth. "It was at this British Military Tribunal that much of the 'Holocaust' dogma and wartime tales of German bestiality were chiselled into the United Nations 'Behistan Rock' to justify forever the United Nations acts vis-a-vis Germany," William B. Lindsey wrote in the *Journal of Historical Review.*

> This was done by parading before the Tribunal a nondescript chorus of Yiddish voices, each chorus member seeking to gain for himself, for varied reasons, the prestigious role of a latter-day Judith or Esther, a Samson or Mordecai, and each seeking to outdo his predecessor on the witness stand with a horror tale of abuse and privation—naturally all unsubstantiated. It was here that the first United Nations prosecutor sought to establish legal credence and respectability for the earlier rumors of German

bestiality and particularly the unsubstantiated allegations that 4,000,000 Jews had been killed at Auschwitz-Birkenau. It was here that physicians Ada Bimko and Charles Bendel made their bows on the front pages of the world's newspapers before figuring in the tribunal trying Dr. Tesch and Herr Weinbacher—and after that disappearing, but leaving behind a legacy of falsehood and confusion which became, nevertheless, a part of the unquestioned, unchallengeable litany of the "Holocaust credo."[55]

The venom that the Belsen Trial generates in negationist circles is deserved, because it indeed brought Auschwitz into the public domain. The publication of the Soviet report in May had little impact in the end because it was, after all, just another report. In the Belsen Trial, the reality of the German regime at Auschwitz was for the first time given a face: Kramer, presented in the press as the "Beast of Belsen," was depicted in caricatures as a shambling gorilla thirsty for blood.

On August 8, 1945, the four Great Powers signed an accord to establish an international military tribunal in Nuremberg that was to prosecute and punish leading war criminals. The tribunal was initially given jurisdiction over three types of crimes: 1) crimes against peace; 2) war crimes; and 3) crimes against humanity. The last included the extermination, enslavement, and deportation of civilians and persecution on political, racial, or religious grounds. The tribunal charged twenty-two political and military leaders of the Third Reich, including Ernst Kaltenbrunner, who was chief of the Reich Security Main Office after January 30, 1943—the central agency charged with the coordination of the so-called Final Solution of the Jewish Problem. Of all the defendants, Kaltenbrunner was the only SS official and had had as such the most business with Auschwitz. But even so, Kaltenbrunner had relatively little significance in the history of the camp: the main architect of the camp's history and its transformation from a regular concentration camp into an extermination camp, Reichsführer-SS Heinrich Himmler, was dead, as was his aide Reinhard Heydrich. As a result, the wartime history of Auschwitz had little *direct* bearing on the proceedings against the defendants. Only in the case against Kaltenbrunner was there an explicit connection between the camp and a defendant's direct responsibility. And, as we will see, it was in the case against Kaltenbrunner that the most important testimony was to occur.

The first time that the role of Auschwitz was highlighted at the Nuremberg military tribunal was on January 3, 1946, in the testimony of Dieter Wisliceny, who had been an aide to Eichmann. Wisliceny told the court about his involvement in 1942 with the deportation of Slovak Jews as forced labor to Auschwitz and of his involvement in early 1943 with the preparations for the deportation of more than 50,000 Saloniki Jews in between 20 and 25 transports of between 2,000 and 2,500 people each to Auschwitz.[56]

[Lt. Col. Brookhart]: "And what was the ultimate disposition of the Jews sent to Auschwitz from Greece?"

[Wisliceny]: "They were without exception destined for the so-called final solution."[57]

Wisliceny also testified that he had participated in the deportation of some 450,000 Jews from Hungary.

Q.: "What became of the Jews to whom you have already referred—approximately 450,000?"

A.: "They were, without exception, taken to Auschwitz and brought to the final solution."

Q.: "Do you mean they were killed?"

A.: "Yes, with the exception of perhaps 25 to 30 percent who were used for labor purposes. I here refer to a previously mentioned conversation on this matter between Hoess and Eichmann in Budapest."[58]

Later that January, Auschwitz took center stage, for a short time, in the presentation of the French case against the defendants. It was appropriate that the French should raise the issue, as they had suffered under Nazi rule and 69,000 French citizens had been deported to Auschwitz. Interestingly, the French described the world of the camps as the center of a conspiracy against *civilization* itself—the very civilization of which France had been such a staunch defender. Chief Prosecutor François de Menthon defined "the organized and vast criminality" of National Socialism as a denial of "all spiritual, rational, and moral values by which the nations have tried, for thousands of years, to improve human conditions." Its aim, he said, was to "plunge humanity back into barbarism, no longer the natural and spontaneous barbarism of primitive nations, but into a diabolical barbarism, conscious of itself and utilizing for its ends all material means put at the disposal of mankind by contemporary science." Indeed, to de Menthon, the defendants did not stand accused because of war crimes committed "in the excitement of combat" or "under the influence of a mad passion" or out of "a warlike anger" or out of "an avenging resentment" but "as a result of cold calculation, of perfectly conscious methods, of a pre-existing doctrine."[59]

Given this approach, the concentration camps were important evidence of the German assault against civilization. Three witnesses described life and death in Mauthausen, and two testified about conditions in Buchenwald. On January 28, 1946, Marie Claude Vaillant-Couturier, deputy of the Constituent Assembly and Knight in the Legion of Honor, provided a long, precise, and important testimony on the situation in Auschwitz. Vaillant-Couturier—a gentile—had been a member of the resistance, and she was arrested in 1942 and deported to Auschwitz in 1943. Examined by Deputy Prosecutor Charles Dubost, she provided a detailed account of the atrocious conditions in the women's camp at Birkenau, the sterilization of women, the killing of babies born of women who had arrived pregnant, and so on.

[Dubost]: "What do you know about the convoy of Jews which arrived from Romainville about the same time as yourself?"

[Vaillant-Couturier]: "When we left Romainville the Jewesses who were there at the same time as ourselves were left behind. They were sent to Drancy and subsequently arrived at Auschwitz, where we found them again 3 weeks later, 3 weeks after our arrival. Of the original 3,000 only 125 actually came to the camp; the others were immediately sent to the gas chambers. Of these 125 not one was left alive at the end of 1 month.

The transports operated as follows:

When we first arrived, whenever a convoy of Jews came, a selection was made; first the old men and women, then the mothers and the children were put into the trucks together with the sick or those whose constitution appeared to be delicate. They took in only the young women and girls as well as the young men who were sent to the men's camp.

Generally speaking, of a convoy of about 1,000 to 1,500, seldom more than 250—and this figure really was the maximum—actually reached the camp. The rest were immediately sent to the gas chamber.

At this selection also, they picked out women in good health between the ages of 20 and 30, who were sent to the experimental block; and young girls and slightly older women, or those who had not been selected for that purpose, were sent to the camp where, like ourselves, they were tattooed and shaved.

There was also, in the spring of 1944, a special block for twins. It was during the time when large convoys of Hungarian Jews—about 700,000—arrived. Dr. Mengele, who was carrying out the experiments, kept back from each convoy twin children and twins in general, regardless of their age, so long as both were present. So we had both babies and adults on the floor at that block. Apart from blood tests and measuring I do not know what was done to them."

Q.: "Were you an eye witness of the selections on the arrival of the convoys?"

A.: "Yes, because when we worked at the sewing block in 1944, the block where we lived directly faced the stopping place of the trains. The system had been improved. Instead of making the selection at the place where they arrived, a side line now took the train practically right up to the gas chamber; and the stopping place, about 100 meters from the gas chamber, was right opposite our block though, of course, separated from us by two rows of barbed wire. Consequently, we saw the unsealing of the cars and the soldiers letting men, women, and children out of them. We then witnessed heart-rending scenes; old couples forced to part from each other, mothers made to abandon their young daughters, since the latter were sent to the camp, whereas mothers and children were sent to the gas chambers. All these people were unaware of the fate awaiting them. They were merely upset at being separated, but they did not know that they were going to their death. To render their welcome more pleasant at this time—June-July 1944—an orchestra composed of internees, all young and pretty girls dressed in little white blouses and navy blue skirts, played during the selection, at the arrival of the trains, gay tunes such as "The Merry Widow," the "Barcarolle" from "The Tales of Hoffman," and so forth. They were then informed that this was a labor camp and since they were not brought into the camp they saw only the small platform surrounded by flowering plants. Naturally, they could not realize what was in store for them. Those selected for the gas chamber, that is, the old people, mothers, and children, were escorted to a red-brick building."

Q.: "These were not given an identification number?"

A.: "No."

Q.: "They were not tattooed?"

A.: "No. They were not even counted."

Q.: "You were tattooed?"

A.: "Yes, look. [*The witness showed her arm.*] They were taken to a red brick building, which bore the letters 'Baden,' that is to say 'Baths.' There, to begin with, they were made to undress and given a towel before they went into the so-called shower room. Later on, at the time of the large convoys from Hungary, they had no more time left to play-act or pretend; they were brutally undressed, and I know these details as I knew a little Jewess from France who lived with her family at the 'Republique' district."

Q.: "In Paris?"

A.: "In Paris. She was called 'little Marie' and was the only one, the sole survivor of a family of nine. Her mother and her seven brothers and sisters had been gassed on arrival. When I met her she was employed to undress the babies before they were taken into the gas chamber. Once the people were undressed they took them into a room which was somewhat like a shower room, and gas capsules were thrown through an opening in the ceiling. An SS man would watch the effect produced through a porthole. At the end of 5 or 7 minutes, when the gas had completed its work, he gave the signal to open the doors; and men with gas masks—they too were internees—went into the room and removed the corpses. They told us that the internees must have suffered before dying, because they were closely clinging to one another and it was very difficult to separate them.

After that a special squad would come to pull out gold teeth and dentures; and again, when the bodies had been reduced to ashes, they would sift them in an attempt to recover the gold."[60]

By the time Dubost finished his presentation of the evidence of the concentration camps, there were few doubts left that the French prosecution had achieved its aim. Judge Sir Norman Birkett noted in his diary that "the evidence is building up a most terrible and convincing case of complete horror and inhumanity in the concentration camps." And he added that one did not need much more. "The case has been proved over and over again."[61]

Despite the excellent job the French prosecutors had done in presenting the evidence on Auschwitz, the Russian prosecutors did not see any reason not to confront the court once more with that camp. On February 27, 1946, they presented Severina Shmaglevskaya, a Polish inmate in Auschwitz, with the single aim of receiving testimony about the attitude of the SS.

[Mr. Counsellor Smirnov]: "Tell me, Witness, did you yourself see the children being taken to gas chambers?"

[Shmaglevskaya]: "I worked very close to the railway which led to the crematory. Sometimes in the morning I passed near the building the Germans used as a latrine, and from there I could secretly watch the transport. I saw many children among the Jews brought to the concentration camp. Sometimes a family had several children. The Tribunal is probably aware of the fact that in front of the crematory they were all sorted out."

Q.: "Selection was made by the doctors?"

A.: "Not always by doctors: sometimes by SS men."

Q.: "And doctors with them?"

A.: "Yes, sometimes, by doctors too. During such a sorting, the youngest and healthiest Jewish women in very small numbers entered the camp. Women carrying children in their arms or in carriages, or those who had larger children, were sent into the crematory with their children. The children were separated from their parents in front of the crematory and were led separately into gas chambers.

At that time, when the greatest number of Jews were exterminated in the gas chambers, an order was issued that the children were to be thrown into the crematory ovens or the crematory ditches without previous asphyxiation with gas."

Q.: "How should we understand that? Were they thrown into the ovens alive or were they killed by other means before they were burned?"

A.: "The children were thrown in alive. Their cries could be heard all over the camp. It is hard to say how many there were."

Q.: "Nevertheless, there was some reason why this was done. Was it because the gas chambers were overworked?"

A.: "It is very difficult to answer this question. We don't know whether they wanted to economize on the gas or whether there was no room in the gas chambers.

I should also add that it is impossible to determine the number of these children—like that of the Jews—because they were driven directly to the crematory, were not registered, were not tattooed, and very often were not even counted. We, the internees, often tried to ascertain the number of people who perished in gas chambers; but our estimates of the number of children executed could only be based on the number of children's prams which were brought to the storerooms. Sometimes there were hundreds of these carriages, but sometimes they sent thousands."

Q.: "In one day?"

A.: "Not always the same. There were days when the gas chambers worked from early morning until late at night."[62]

That same day the prison psychologist at the Nuremberg Trial, Gustave M. Gilbert, noted in his diary that Karl Doenitz's lawyer, Otto Kranzbuehler, had asked Doenitz "Didn't *anybody* know *anything* about *any* of these things?" Doenitz had just shaken his head, shrugging sadly. Gilbert went over to Alfred Jodl to ask him if it was possible that nobody knew anything about the camps.

"Of course, somebody knew about it," Jodl said quietly. "There was a whole chain-of-command from the Chief of the RSHA down to the people who executed those commands."

I then walked over to Kaltenbrunner. "I suppose you didn't know anything about these things either."

"Of course not," he whispered. "The people who did are all dead.—Hitler, Himmler, Bormann, Heydrich, Eichmann—"

"Did those few people have the sole knowledge and responsibility for the murder of millions of people and the burning of children alive?"

"Well, no—the people who actually participated in it did. But I had nothing to do with it."

"Even as Chief of the RSHA?"

"Concentration camps were not my responsibility. I never found out anything about any of this."[63]

By the end of February, no one felt that there was a need for more testimony about Auschwitz in the trial. The French and Russian prosecutors rightly assumed they had made their point, and the lawyers for the defendants felt no inclination to call attention to the camp. Then, on March 11, 1946, everything changed: British soldiers found Auschwitz Kommandant Rudolf Höss, who had been in hiding since the end of the war.

By his own account, initially the British treated Höss roughly.[64] At the end of March, his treatment improved, and he was flown to Nuremberg to serve as a defense witness for Kaltenbrunner. As we have seen, Kaltenbrunner maintained that he had nothing to do with Auschwitz—"Concentration camps were not my responsibility. I never found out anything about any of this"—and Kaltenbrunner's lawyer Kurt Kauffmann believed that Höss could confirm Kaltenbrunner's claims in the matter of Auschwitz. In Nuremberg, Höss was interrogated. At a certain moment he was asked if he could confirm that Jews had started to arrive in great numbers in 1942. Höss did, and then gave a detailed list of the numbers: 250,000 from Poland, 65,000 from Greece, 100,000 from Germany, 90,000 from Holland, 110,000 from France, 90,000 from Slovakia, 20,000 from Belgium and 400,000 from Hungary. The conversation continued as follows:

Q.: "Now you just told us that you had facilities for 130,000. If you add all those figures they amount to a much greater number than 130,000. How could you accommodate all those people?"

A.: "They were not supposed to be employed in work there, but they were supposed to be exterminated."[65]

On April 5, Höss was given an affidavit which he corrected and ultimately signed. In this text, which I quoted at greater length in Chapter 1, he admitted that he had overseen the extermination, "by gassing and burning," of at least two and a half million human beings—mostly Jews.

When I set up the extermination building at Auschwitz I, I used Cyclon B, which was crystallized Prussic Acid we dropped into the death chamber from a small opening. It took from 3 to 15 minutes to kill the people in the death chamber depending upon climatic conditions. We knew when the people were dead because their screaming stopped. We usually waited about one-half hour before we opened the doors and removed the bodies. After the bodies were removed our special commandos took off the rings and extracted the gold from the teeth of the corpses.[66]

On Monday, April 15, Höss was called to the witness stand. Examined by Kaltenbrunner's lawyer Kauffmann, Höss tried to serve Kaltenbrunner's case as best as he could, and he confirmed that Kaltenbrunner had never inspected the camp.[67] Kauffmann's examination did not help Kaltenbrunner's case. American prosecutor Colonel John Harlan Amen's cross-examination proved damaging for all the defendants. Initially Amen asked Höss a few simple questions about the practice of high German functionaries of visiting the camps and, more specifically, about Kaltenbrunner's connection to Auschwitz. Then he turned to the affidavit and asked if Höss had signed it voluntarily. Höss answered in the affirmative.[68]

Höss's testimony created great gloom among the accused. Dr. Gilbert noted in his diary that the former governor-general of Poland, Hans Frank, told him that "that was the low point of the entire Trial—to hear a man say out of his own mouth that he exterminated 2½ million people in cold blood. That is something that people will talk about for a thousand years."[69] Gilbert, however, was not surprised by Höss's willingness to testify. He had gotten to know him during two visits. On April 9, Gilbert visited Höss in his cell.

> He readily confirmed that approximately 2½ million Jews had been exterminated under his direction. The exterminations began in the summer of 1941. In compliance with Goering's scepticism, I asked Hoess how it was technically possible to exterminate 2½ million people. "Technically?" he asked. "That wasn't so hard— it would not have been hard to exterminate even greater numbers." In answer to my rather naïve questions as to how many people could be done away with in an hour, etc., he explained that one must figure it on a daily 24-hour basis, and it was possible to exterminate up to 10,000 in one 24-hour period. He explained that there were actually 6 extermination chambers. The 2 big ones could accommodate as many as 2,000 in each and the 4 smaller ones up to 1500, making a total capacity of 10,000 a day. I tried to figure out how this was done, but he corrected me. "No, you don't figure it right. The killing itself took the least time. You could dispose of 2,000 in a half hour, but it was the burning that took all the time. The killing was easy; you didn't even need guards to drive them into the chambers; they just went in expecting to take showers and, instead of water, we turned on poison gas. The whole thing went very quickly." He related all of this in a quiet, apathetic, matter-of-fact tone of voice.[70]

Asked by Gilbert to provide more detail, Höss wrote later that month a short memorandum which Gilbert did not publish at the time, but which he presented during the Eichmann Trial to the District Court of Jerusalem. It gave a detailed description of the arrival, selection, and killing of the deportees.

> The freight trains with the Jews destined for extermination moved along a special railroad installation which had been laid down especially for this purpose right up to the extermination installations. Notification of these trains was given in advance by Obersturmbannführer Eichmann of the RSHA, and they were allocated consecutive numbers, together with letters of the alphabet, in order to prevent a mix-up with transports of other prisoners. Each cable relating to these transports bore the reference: "In accordance with the specified directives, and are to be subjected to special treatment." These trains consisted of closed freight cars and contained, on the average, about 2,000 persons. When the trains arrived at the aforementioned ramp, the accompanying railway personnel and the accompanying guard—members of the Security or Order Police—had to leave the area. Only the transport commander who had delivered it remained until it had been

Rudolf Höss in Polish captivity, 1946. Courtesy Archive Auschwitz-Birkenau State Museum, Oswiecim.

completely handed over, and the numbers checked, to the duty officer of the camp. After the trains were off-loaded and the numbers determined (lists by names were not drawn up), all the people had to file past two SS duty doctors, and in the course of this, those who were fit for work were separated from those who were unfit. On the average about twenty-five percent were found to be fit for work. These were marched off immediately into the camp, in order to change their clothes and be received there. All the luggage remained on the ramp and, after those unfit for work had also been sent off, it was brought to the store of personal effects, to be sorted out. Those unfit for work were classified according to sex—men, women, and children—and marched off to the nearest available extermination installation. Those unable to walk and women with small children were transported there on trucks. When they arrived, all of them had to strip naked in rooms which gave the impression of being delousing installations. The permanent labour unit of prisoners who worked in these installations—and who were also housed there and did not come into contact with other inmates of the camp—helped with the undressing and coaxed the hesitant to hurry up, so that the others would not have to wait so long.

They were also told to take note where they put away their clothes, so that they would be able to find them again immediately after taking their bath. All this was done on purpose, in order to dispel any fears which might arise. After they had taken off their clothes, they were taken into a nearby room—the gas chamber itself. It had been prepared to look like a washroom—that is to say, showers and pipes were installed throughout, water drainage channels, etc. The moment the entire transport had entered the chamber, the door was closed, and simultaneously the gas was forced in from above through a special aperture. It was Zyklon "B" gas, cyanide acid in the form of crystals, which vaporized immediately, that is to say, it took effect immediately upon coming into contact with oxygen. The people were dazed already on taking their first breath, and the process of killing took from thirteen to fifteen minutes, depending upon the weather conditions and the number of people locked up within. Thereafter, nothing moved any more. Thirty minutes after the gas had been released and had entered the chambers, they would be opened, and the transfer of the bodies to the crematoria would commence. Throughout all these years, I never came across a single case of a person coming out of the gas chambers while still alive. While the bodies were taken out, the women's hair was still cut, and gold teeth and rings [were] removed by prisoner dentists who were employed in this unit.

In Birkenau there were five installations—two large crematoria, each of which had a capacity for receiving 2,000 persons in the course of 24 hours. That is to say, it was possible in one gas chamber to put to death up to 2,500 persons; in five double ovens heated with coke, it was possible to burn at most 2,000 bodies within 24 hours; two smaller installations could eliminate about 1,500 people, with four bigger double ovens to each of them. Furthermore, there was also an open-air installation—that is, an old farmhouse was sealed and turned into a gas chamber, which could also contain 1,500 persons at one and the same time. The incineration was carried out there in an open pit on wood, and this was practically limitless. In my estimation, it was possible to burn there, in 24 hours, up to 8,000 persons in this way. Hence it was possible to exterminate and eliminate up to 10,000 people within 24 hours in the installations described above. As far as I am aware, this number was attained only once in 1944, when delays occurred in the arrival of trains, and consequently five transports arrived together on one day. The ashes of the burnt bodies were ground into dust, which was poured into the Vistula in remote places and swept away with the current.

On the basis of the figure of 2.5 million, which is the number of people who—according to Eichmann—were brought to Auschwitz for extermination, it may be said that on average, two transports arrived daily, with a combined total of 4,000 persons, of whom twenty-five percent were fit for work, the balance of 3,000 were to be exterminated. The intervals in the various operations can be computed together at nine months. Thus there remain 27 months, with 90,000 people each month—a total of 2,430,000 people. This is a calculation of the technical potential. I have to keep to the figure mentioned by Eichmann, for he was the only SS officer who was allowed to keep records concerning these liquidation operations, according to the orders of the Reichsführer-SS. All other units which took part in any way had to destroy all records immediately. Eichmann mentioned this number in my presence when he was called upon, in April 1945, to present a report to the Reichsführer-SS. I had no records whatsoever. But, to the best of my knowledge, this number appears to me much too high. If I calculate the total of the mass operations which I still remember, and still make allowance for a certain percentage of error, I arrive, in my calculation, at a total of 1.5 million at the most for the period from the beginning of 1941 to the end of 1944. But these are my computations which I cannot verify.
Nuremberg, 24 April 1946 (Signed) Rudolf Höss

(At the bottom of the document): Hungary—400,000; Slovakia—90,000; Greece—65,000; Holland—90,000; France—110,000; Belgium—20,000; the region of the Generalgouvernement and Upper Silesia—250,000; Germany and Terezin—100,000. Total—1,125,000.[71]

Gilbert noted that Höss had little remorse. "One gets the general impression of a man who is intellectually normal but with schizoid apathy, insensitivity and lack of empathy that could hardly be more extreme in a frank psychotic."[72]

Höss's Nuremberg testimony marked an important development in the historiography of Auschwitz. Until Höss took the stand, information had been based on the testimony of survivors, on the testimony of members of the camp's lower personnel and middle management, on a document collection that was only comprehensive where it concerned the construction of the camp, and on the inspection of the site itself. It had become clear by 1946 that the history of the camp was complex, but there was little insight into why and how the camp had evolved. In Poland, Jan Sehn was ready not only to prosecute Höss for war crimes, but he was also very anxious to interview him as an eyewitness to history, as only the former commandant would be able to answer most of the outstanding questions concerning the evolving purpose of Auschwitz. Sehn got his chance when, at the request of the Polish government, Höss was extradited to Poland.

After Höss's arrival in Poland on May 25, 1946, Sehn and psychologist Professor Stanislaw Batawia, who had been assigned the task of creating a psychological profile of Höss, set out to establish a working relationship with him. Knowing quite well that he had no chance of acquittal, Höss decided to cooperate, and at their suggestion he wrote thirty-four shorter (the shortest is one paragraph long) and longer (the longest is 114 densely written pages long) documents. The first essay Höss drafted was a roughly 9,000-word statement on the role of Auschwitz in the Holocaust entitled "The Final Solution of the Jewish Question in Concentration Camp Auschwitz." In this essay, and in accordance with earlier statements made in Nuremberg, Höss claimed that Himmler had made the decision to transform Auschwitz into an extermination camp for Jews in the summer of 1941. There is no independent corroboration of Höss's account of his conversation with Himmler, so one can come to only tentative conclusions about the value of Höss's account of the decision to make Auschwitz into a final destination for European Jewry. However, what is fully corroborated by many other witnesses—both Germans such as Broad and Aumeier as well as others—is the bulk of Höss's testimony. The first experimentation with the use of Zyklon B as a killing agent occurred in the fall of 1941. Initially rooms in the basement of Block 11 were used as primitive gas chambers. As it was difficult to ventilate these spaces, the morgue of Crematorium 1 was adapted for the purpose: "The doors were made airtight, and we knocked some holes in the ceiling through which we could throw in the gas crystals."[73] Finally Höss ordered the transformation of some peasant cottages into gas chambers. They were designated as "bunkers."

> The Jews had to undress at the bunker and were told that they would have to go into the delousing rooms. All of the rooms—there were five of them—were filled at the same time. The airtight doors were screwed tight, and the contents of the gas crystal canisters emptied into the rooms through special hatches.
>
> After half an hour the doors were opened and the bodies were pulled out. Each room had two doors. They were then moved using small carts on special tracks to the ditches. The clothing was brought by trucks to the sorting place. All of the work was done by a special contingent of Jews. They had to help those who were about to die with the undressing, the filling up of the bunkers, the clearing of the bunkers, removal of the bodies, as well as digging the mass graves and, finally, covering the graves with earth. These Jews were housed separately from the other prisoners and, according to Eichmann's orders, they themselves were to be killed after each large extermination action.[74]

As Höss mentioned, initially the corpses of those murdered were buried. Then in the summer of 1942, a decision was taken to change the manner of corpse disposal. The occasion was the well-documented two-day visit by Himmler.

> During his visit in the summer of 1942, Himmler very carefully observed the entire process of annihilation. He began with the unloading at the ramps and completed the inspection as Bunker 2 was being cleared of bodies. At that time there were no open-pit

burnings. He did not complain about anything, but he didn't say anything about it either. Accompanying him were District Leader Bracht and SS General Schmauser. Shortly after Himmler's visit, SS Colonel Blobel from Eichmann's office arrived and brought Himmler's order, which stated that all the mass graves were to be opened and all the bodies cremated. It further stated that all the ashes were to be disposed of in such a way that later on there would be no way to determine the number of those cremated.

Blobel had already conducted various experiments in Kulmhof [Chelmno], which tried to burn the bodies in various ways. He was ordered by Eichmann to show me the installations. I drove with Hössler to Chelmno for an inspection.[75]

As Höss was to explain elsewhere, the most important reason for the change in corpse disposal was the fact that the enormous mass graves putrified the water supply at the camp and the surrounding area.

As late as the summer of 1942 the corpses were still buried in mass graves. Not until the end of the summer did we start burning them. At first we put two thousand bodies on a large pile of wood. Then we opened up the mass graves and burned the new bodies on top of the old ones from the earlier burials. At first we poured waste oil over the bodies. Later on we used methanol. The burning went on continuously—all day and all night. By the end of November all the mass graves were cleared. The number of buried bodies in the mass graves was 107,000. This number contains not only the first Jewish transports which were gassed when we started the burnings, but also the bodies of the prisoners who died in the main Auschwitz camp during the winter of 1941–42 because the crematory was out of order. The prisoners who died at Birkenau are included in that number.[76]

The open-air cremations attracted attention to the killings, and therefore Höss did everything to get the four new crematoria completed. The large ones, with a capacity of 2,000 corpses per day, "both had underground undressing rooms and underground gas chambers in which the air could be completely ventilated. The bodies were taken to the ovens on the floor above by an elevator." Höss remembered the small crematoria, with a capacity of 1,500 bodies per day, as cheap constructions. "They were built above ground and the ovens were not as solidly constructed."[77]

Höss gave a detailed description of the killing procedure in which he expanded considerably on the information that he had given in his Nuremberg affidavit. In his testimony, he was anxious to stress that the victims suffered little, a fact contradicted by witnesses such as Dr. Bendel.

The extermination process in Auschwitz took place as follows: Jews selected for gassing were taken as quietly as possible to the crematories. The men were already separated from the women. In the undressing chamber, prisoners of the Sonderkommandos, who were specially chosen for this purpose, would tell them in their own language that they were going to be bathed and deloused, and that they must leave their clothing neatly together, and, above all, remember where they put them, so that they would be able to find them quickly after the delousing. The Sonderkommando had the greatest interest in seeing that the operation proceeded smoothly and quickly. After undressing, the Jews went into the gas chamber, which was furnished with showers and water pipes and gave a realistic impression of a bath house.

The women went in first with their children, followed by the men, who were always fewer in number. This part of the operation nearly always went smoothly since the Sonderkommando would always calm those who showed any anxiety or perhaps who had even some clue as to their fate. As an additional precaution, the Sonderkommando and an SS soldier always stayed in the chamber until the very last moment.

The door would be screwed shut and the waiting disinfection squads would immediately pour the gas [crystals] into the vents in the ceiling of the gas chamber down an air shaft which went to the floor. This ensured the rapid distribution of the gas. The process could be observed through the peep hole in the door. Those who were standing next to the air shaft were killed immediately. I can state that about one-third died immediately. The remainder staggered about and began to scream and struggle for air. The screaming, however, soon changed to gasping and in a few moments everyone lay still. After twenty minutes at most no movement could be detected. The time required for the gas to take effect varied according to weather conditions and depended on whether it was damp or dry, cold or warm. It also depended on the quality of the gas, which was never exactly the same, and on the composition of the transports, which might contain a higher proportion of healthy Jews, or the old and the sick, or children. The victims became unconscious after a few minutes, according to the distance from the air shaft. Those who screamed and those who were old, sick or weak, or the small children died quicker than those who were healthy and young.

The door was opened half an hour after the gas was thrown in and the ventilation system was turned on. Work was immediately started to remove the corpses. There was no noticeable change in the bodies and no sign of convulsions or discoloration. Only after the bodies had been left lying for some time—several hours—did the usual death stains appear where they were laid. Seldom did it occur that they were soiled with feces. There were no signs of wounds of any kind. The faces were not contorted.

The Sonderkommando now set about removing the gold teeth and cutting the hair from the women. After this, the bodies were taken up by an elevator and laid in front of the ovens, which had meanwhile been fired up. Depending on the size of the bodies, up to three corpses could be put in through one oven door at the same time. The time required for cremation also depended on the number of bodies in each retort, but on average it took twenty minutes. As previously stated, Crematories 2 and 3 could cremate two thousand bodies in twenty-four hours, but a higher number was not possible without causing damage to the installations. Crematories 4 and 5 should have been able to cremate 1,500 bodies in twenty-four hours, but as far as I know this figure was never reached.[78]

Because the crematoria ovens failed at times, Höss ordered that the possibility of open-air cremations should remain available. During the Hungarian Action, when the daily number of gassed Jews far exceeded the official incineration capacity of the crematoria, open-air pyres took care of the excess.[79]

The killing frenzy that characterized the Hungarian Action marked the nadir in the history of Auschwitz. At other times there were few killings. As a result, one could not calculate the total number of victims using the Soviet method of using the total incineration capacity of Auschwitz over its history as a point of departure—a method that had led the Soviet State Extraordinary Commission for the Investigation of Fascist and Nazi Crimes to speculate that more than 4 million people had been murdered in Auschwitz. Höss explicitly rejected the Soviet number and also the figure of 2.5 million victims which he had initially mentioned during his Nuremberg interrogations. Questioned by Sehn, he confirmed that the number of victims had been most likely less than 1.2 million persons—a conclusion he had first reached in the document he wrote that described the technology of the Final Solution, drawn up in April at the request of Gilbert. "I regard the number of 2.5 million as far too high. Even Auschwitz had limits to its destructive capabilities."[80]

Höss completed his essay on the use of Auschwitz as a killing installation for Jews in November 1946. In the month that followed, he wrote at the invitation of Sehn thirty-two shorter essays on various aspects of the SS and its men. In some of the biographical essays he touched on various aspects of the killing operations at Auschwitz. For example, in his portrait of Dr. Gravits, the surgeon-general of the SS, Höss discussed the role of the SS Hygiene Institute and its leader Dr. Mugrowski in obtaining the cyanide used in the gas chambers.

> If I remember correctly, the Cyclon B gas was manufactured by the Tesch and Stabenow firm until 1942 in Hamburg. This was the gas used for disinfection and also for the extermination of the Jews. It was procured by the administration from Tesch and Stabenow. From 1942, all poison gas was purchased for the SS by a central authority. Mugrowski was in charge of the Hygienic Department and he alone was responsible for the shipments of the gas. So he was the one who continually had to get the gas for the extermination of the Jews. Tesch and Stabenow was able to deliver the needed amounts of gas by railroad on time until 1943. But after 1943 the increasing Allied air raids made this impossible. Consequently, Auschwitz was forced a few times to use trucks to get the gas from the manufacturing plant in Dessau.[81]

A number of the permission slips to dispatch a truck from Auschwitz to Dessau, signed by Höss's adjudant, Mulka, survived the war and were submitted as evidence in the Frankfurt Auschwitz Trial (1963–1964). During cross-examination of Mulka, the presiding judge asked him about these slips.

> [Chairman]: "Accused Mulka, have you signed permissions for trips to Dessau?"

> [Mulka]: "I only remember one occasion. A permission was signed by Glücks and at the left bottom counter-signed by me. It concerned a disinfection means."

> Q.: "Here it reads 'For the Resettlement of the Jews' and 'In confirmation of the copy Mulka.' You knew what the resettlement of the Jews meant?"

> A.: "Yes, that was known to me."

> Q.: "And what were those materials for the resettlement of the Jews?"

A. (quietly): "Yes, raw materials."

Q.: "All right then. That was thus Zyklon-B."

A. (even more quietly): "Yes, Zyklon-B."[82]

Let us return to Höss's essay on the SS Hygienic Institute. In this same account, Höss remarked on the use of the ambulances to transport the gas to the gas chambers.

> The ambulances were for use by the garrison doctor, and he was authorized to issue orders for their use. Because there was a constant shortage of trucks in Auschwitz, the garrison doctor had no choice but to use the ambulances for shipments to other camps. It gradually became the custom that all necessary trips for the garrison doctor were carried out with the ambulances. So, not only the sick were driven from camp to camp, but the dead also. Medicines, bandages, and surgical equipment were all transported in the same ambulances. The doctors and the medics drove them to their duties on the ramp and to the gas chambers. The Jews who could not walk were driven from the ramp to the gas chambers in ambulances. If no trucks were available, the standby ambulances were used. Because the medics were the ones who threw the gas into the gas chambers, they would be driven with their cans of gas to the gas chambers using the ambulances when no other trucks were available. They just hitchhiked a ride with the doctors who were going there anyway.
>
> As time went by the ambulances were used for all kinds of purposes because no other trucks were available. No one ever gave a thought that they were profaning the symbol of the Red Cross when the ambulances drove to the gas chambers loaded with those who were to be gassed and the gas itself. No doctor ever objected to this. Even the ever-sensitive Dr. Wirths never brought the subject up with me, and I myself never gave it a thought either.[83]

In a separate report on the institutional structure of Auschwitz, Höss once again discussed the role of Dr. Wirths and his colleagues in the Holocaust.

> Aside from the customary medical duties, the SS doctors of Auschwitz pursued the following activities:
> 1. According to Himmler's guidelines, they had to select males and females from the incoming transports of Jews who were able to work.
> 2. The doctors had to be present during the extermination process in the gas chambers to supervise the prescribed application of the poison gas Cyclon B by using the disinfection fixtures. Furthermore they had to make certain after the gas chambers were opened that the extermination process had been completely carried out.
> 3. The dentists continuously had to conduct spot checks to make certain that the prisoner dentists of the Sonderkommando pulled all the gold teeth from the gassed and dropped them into a special security container. Furthermore they had to supervise the melting of the gold teeth and their safekeeping until delivery to the proper SS branch was made.[84]

In a long essay on Heinrich Himmler and his role in the development of Auschwitz, Höss provided much detail about Himmler's crucial two-day visit to Auschwitz of July 17 and 18. Höss recorded that the Reichsführer-SS was briefed on the progress of the design of the settlement and the IG Farben complex and that he visited the Stammlager, Birkenau, and the various agricultural and industrial operations in the camp's Zone of Interests. As a special treat, he witnessed the first day of the complete extermination process of a transport of Dutch Jews which had just arrived. "He also looked on for a while during a selection of those who would work and those who would die without any complaint on his part. Himmler made no comment about the extermination process. He just looked in total silence."[85] The next morning Himmler told Höss that "Eichmann's program will continue and will be accelerated every month from now on. See to it that you move ahead with the completion of Birkenau. The Gypsies are to be exterminated. With the same relentlessness you will exterminate those Jews who are unable to work."[86]

As he was completing his essays, Höss faced justice. On January 11, 1947, Höss testified in Cracow before Judge Jan Sehn and Edward Pechalski, Vice Prosecutor of the Court of Appeal in Cracow, about the structure and operation of concentration camps in general and Auschwitz in particular.[87] After a lengthy description of the way the camps operated as an instrument of political terror within Germany, Höss stated that after the war began, the role of the camps expanded to include political opponents from the conquered countries. "All of them were treated as enemies of the German State. Accordingly, the camps were organised so that most of these enemies were to die in them. Neither Himmler nor any of his helpers ever said it clearly. Yet they used to create such living conditions for prisoners in the camps that this order, unspoken officially, was practically fully executed in the camps."[88] Above and beyond the normal task of imprisoning political opponents, Auschwitz had been given an extra function: "It became the place of mass destruction of Jews of all nationalities and from all countries conquered by the Third Reich."

> This second role of the Auschwitz camp I have described in details in my essay where I call the camp a place of destruction [*Vernichtungsanstalt*] in connection with its function within the action to exterminate the Jews [*Judenvernichtungsaktion*]. During the war waged by the Third Reich this extermination action expanded according to the following stages. In the first period of the war *Einsatzkommandos* consisting of RSHA officers and police members followed German armies. These *Einsatzkommandos* were commanded by SS-Brigadeführer Ohlendorf and were to clean occupied area from hostile elements. Therefore their first victims were Jews, who were gathered into groups and exterminated on the spot. The next stage were actions carried out in Poznan by the Higher SS and Police Leader von Alvensleben and in Lublin and, after the war with Russia began, in the adjacent eastern districts by the SS and Police Commander Globocnik. Both Alvensleben and Globocnik set up extermination places for Jews that were subordinated to them: Alvensleben in Chelmno (Kulmhof) and in Grudziaz, and Globocnik in Sobibor, Belzec, Treblinka, and Lublin.[89]

According to Höss, an important advantage of these extermination camps over the shootings by the Einsatzgruppen was the possibility of recovering and exploiting the personal property of the victims. "[Globocnik] used to deliver valuables looted in the progress of the action to Himmler." Because camps operated by von Alvensleben and Globocnik had no excess capacity to deal with the Jews from countries other than Poland, "Himmler summoned me in the summer of 1941 and ordered me to prepare in Oswiecim instruments of destruction that could be used in this action."

I took up this task, details of my activities in this field I have described in my essay I have submitted and in the essay about Eichmann's activity. I request to enclose this essay to the current report. The second function, conducting the action of extermination of Jews in the Auschwitz camp, I fulfilled in this camp on the basis of Himmler's verbal order, at the same time fulfilling officially functions of the SS Garrison Commander and the Commandant of the camp in Auschwitz. I held these positions since May 1940 till the end of November 1943.

On the 1st of December 1943 I was transferred from Auschwitz to the post of the chief of the DI office at the Main Economic-Administrative Office of the SS [SS-WVHA] in Berlin-Oranienburg. It was the political department of the SS-WVHA. As the chief of the department I took care of all matters concerning the concentration camps of interest to the RSHA. After I left the commandant's post in Auschwitz, the extermination of the Jews continued to be carried out in that camp. It was directed by my successor on the post of the garrison chief and camp commandant, SS-Obersturmbannführer Arthur Liebehenschel, who held this position until the beginning of June 1944. Under his management the liquidation of Jews coming in transports proceeded inefficiently. Therefore, in the beginning of June 1944, Pohl sent me to Auschwitz to improve the action and adjust it to the plan set by RSHA. In 1944 I directed this action in June, July and August. In this period of time, because of seniority I was officially the garrison chief in Auschwitz. Baer was already the commandant of Auschwitz I, Kramer of Auschwitz II, and Schwartz of Auschwitz III. I finally left Auschwitz at the end of August 1944. Kramer, as the commandant of the camp Auschwitz II where instruments of destruction were concentrated, co-operated with me in the June to August period in the action of exterminating the Jews. After my final departure Kramer continued the action until November 1944, when Himmler forbade further extermination of Jews. He issued this ban as a result of negotiations with the Jewish representatives, among them were envoys of the Zionists leader Weissmann. Becher in Budapest, in Switzerland and Turkey carried out the negotiations. They were based on the idea the Jews were to deliver various goods in exchange for Jews the Germans kept. Because foreign Jews' representatives demanded immediate stop to the destruction actions, the German side prolonged the negotiations as much as possible to win some time and annihilate as many Jews as possible. Only in November 1944, Himmler finally acceded to the condition given by the Jewish representatives, that is, to immediately stop the action.[90]

In his testimony, Höss addressed the question of the number of victims.

One man, Eichmann, had all notes concerning the number of Jews destroyed in the action I have described. I cannot give figures for Auschwitz because I did not use to record them. I was acting in accordance with Himmler's order. Just before the breakdown of the Reich in April 1945, I was present when Eichmann gave a report to Glücks on the number of Jews destroyed and killed. I remember precisely that Eichmann gave a figure of 2½ million for Auschwitz. In the same report he said to Glücks that in the course of anti-Jewish action in Auschwitz, some 25 to 30 percent of all newcomers were selected as fit for work, and were not annihilated immediately. I stress that all arriving Jews selected as fit for work, and kept in the camp, were registered and included in camp evidential number series. However I cannot explain if they were numbered only in A and B series or in the general male and female series as well. As I recall, Jewish numbering series A and B were introduced only in 1943. I suppose Jews who came previously were numbered in the general series. Hungarian Jews, Polish Jews from Upper Silesia and the General Government, French Jews, German Jews and Jews from Theresienstadt, Dutch, Slovakian, and Greek Jews, and smaller groups of Jews of various other nationalities such as Yugoslavia and Russia were annihilated in mass actions in Auschwitz. I mentioned the nationalities in order of number of victims. The largest quota of registered prisoners who were imprisoned in the camp, and not brought to the camp for extermination, were Aryan Poles. Reich Germans and Czechs were the next largest categories. There were smaller numbers of Yugoslavs, French, Belgians, Germans, Italians, Latvians, Russians, Lithuanians and Spanish in the Auschwitz camp. Moreover there was a number of Jews with fake passports issued to them by representatives of various South American and other countries from all over the world. I can give neither the general number of prisoners numbered in all series nor the highest figures in each series. I cannot give the figure of victims from among numbered prisoners.[91]

Höss testified that he did everything he confessed he did out of a sense of duty toward his superiors. Yet he confessed that he had often felt doubts.

Many times in the course of action of mass destruction of Jews I wondered if some Providence exists and if yes, how it is possible such things may happen. Nevertheless I was present everywhere, both at the coming transports reception and at gassing in gas chambers and corpses cremation, trying to set an example to my subordinates and avoid accusation of requiring something I run away from myself.[92]

At the end of his testimony, Höss summarized his life and activities. He admitted that "since the summer of 1941 I prepared, and since January 1942 I directed the action of mass killing of Jews in extermination installations of the concentration camp in Auschwitz. During my activity in Auschwitz millions of people died there, and I am unable to establish their exact number."[93]

Höss testified in German, which was translated into Polish. The Polish text was retranslated into German and approved by Höss. "The whole content of the protocol before me has been translated into German. The record presents my deposition both literally as well as to its meaning. In endorsement, I personally sign the protocol."[94]

When he was cross-examined during his trial, Höss went into greater detail about many of the issues he had discussed in his deposition on the Final Solution.

[Höss]: "On the basis of those reports, Reichsführer-SS Himmler ordered that I was to personally carry out this action in Auschwitz. In his program Eichmann had envisioned a schedule of four trains every day. This was, however, not feasible despite the development of all existing installations. For that reason, I personally travelled to Eichmann in Budapest to annul this order. We solved the matter as follows: one day two trains, and the next day three trains were to leave for Auschwitz. I remember precisely that the schedule, negotiated with the railway authorities in Budapest, anticipated a total of 111 of such trains. Nevertheless, when the first transports arrived in Auschwitz, Eichmann came also in order to find out if it wouldn't be possible to send more trains: the Reichsführer-SS demanded that the Hungarian action was to be accelerated."

[Prosecutor Siewierski]: "Let the defendant explain it more clearly: after your return to Auschwitz, did you give any orders of technical nature to speed up the gassing and incineration of Jews?"

A.: "I remember that we accelerated the expansion of the railway station inside the camp with its siding consisting of three tracks. Furthermore we reactivated the open-air cremation site known as installation 5. We also reinforced the squads who were to sort the luggage of the deportees. It took between four and five hours to unload a train—people and all their luggage—and there was no way to do it faster. People could be dealt with within this time, but the luggage was accumulating in such quantities that this forced us to abandon the idea to increase the number of transports. Even as we added another 1,000 additional inmates to the squads sorting the luggage, there was no way to speed up the action. We had not enough space to store all these things, and this is why we failed in our effort to faster send out of the camp all the clothing and belongings these people had brought to Auschwitz. No improvements could be made to the crematoria. After eight to ten hours of operation the crematoria were unfit for further use. It was impossible to operate them continuously. As Eichmann had mentioned that we should expect by the end of the year 1944 and in 1945 more transports, we planned a larger crematorium. It was to be a huge, circular brick furnace, to be built underground. Due to lack of time, it was never designed."

Q.: "When the defendant came to supervise the action, did you consider Moll—the chief of the crematoria—to be the right man in the right place, or did the defendant have to give further orders?"

A.: "When I came to Auschwitz, Moll worked in some satellite camp. I withdrew him from that camp, and assigned him to the cremating kommando—the one burning prisoners in the open air. The previous chief could not handle it."

Q.: "And Moll could?"

A.: "Yes. He proved capable."[95]

Given Höss's full confession, it was no surprise that the court convicted him for mass murder. Remarkably, however, the court did not accept the number of 4 million victims mentioned in the Soviet Report that was assumed in the indictment. In its judgment, the court stated that Höss had been responsible for the deaths of "300,000 persons imprisoned in the camp as prisoners and listed in the camp register"; responsible for the killing of "an indeterminate number [of victims], but certainly no less than 2,500,000, mostly Jews, brought in transports from various European countries for the purpose of immediate extermination, and therefore not officially registered"; and responsible for the murder of "at least 12,000 Soviet prisoners of war."[96] It condemned him to death by hanging.

As he waited for his execution, Höss wrote a 224-page detailed autobiography that expanded on his earlier statements on the gassings and placed them within the context of the larger history of Auschwitz. It did not, however, add substantial new information.

Is Höss's testimony credible? Let us apply Stäglich's test to it. First of all, Stäglich stated that "as evidence for the alleged gassing of the Jews, reports that do not contain specific details about it, but are limited to quite vague allegations of this type—as is usually the case—must be rejected at once."[97] It is obvious that Höss provided plenty of details. Stäglich also stated that "only statements free of contradictions, which do not stand in contradiction to other circumstances and facts, may lay claim to credibility." Höss produced much written text and he gave a number of testimonies, and from Rassinier onward negationists have tried to find contradictions in Höss's testimony. Rassinier, for example, made a lot of the fact that Höss made contradictory estimates about the number of victims and that his own estimates contradicted the estimate of the Polish court that tried Höss ("2,912,000 persons") and the estimate of those who put the victim total at 4 million.

> In reply to the question put by Dr. Kaufmann, Kaltenbrunner's legal counsel at Nuremberg, "Did Eichmann tell you in fact that more than 2,000,000 Jews were destroyed at Auschwitz camp?" Höss answered, "Yes, that is right." (T. XI, p. 409.) Behind the scenes he is supposed to have told American psychologist Gustave Gilbert that "every day two trains brought in 3,000 persons, for 27 months" (therefore, for the whole length of the period of deportation, from March 1942 to July 1944). "So that makes a total of about 2,500,000 people." (Statement of Professor Gilbert before the Jerusalem Tribunal in judgment on Eichmann, May 30, 1961.) But when it came to giving details about these 2,500,000 people he wrote in the Le Commandant d'Auschwitz parle (p. 239, French ed.): "As for me, I never knew the total number, and had no way of determining it. I can only remember the number in the most important cases, often pointed out to me by Eichmann or one of his deputies.

A page from Höss's autobiography, 1946. Courtesy Archive Auschwitz-Birkenau State Museum, Oswiecim.

From Upper Silesia, or Poland in general:	250,000
From Germany, or Theresienstadt:	100,000
Holland:	95,000
Belgium:	20,000
France:	10,000
Greece:	65,000
Hungary:	400,000
Slovakia:	90,000
TOTAL:	1,130,000

The figures concerning cases of less importance are not graven in my memory, but they were insignificant compared with the above. I think the figure of 2,500,000 much too high."[98]

Rassinier's text is riddled with mistakes, misinterpretations, and falsifications, but I will not answer it here in detail, as I have already dealt with the origin of the confusion in Chapter 2. The contradiction that Rassinier noted between the figures of 2.5 million and 1.1 million did not exist. Höss clearly stated that he took Eichmann's figure of 2.5 million deportees as a point of departure and that he agreed that this number of victims could indeed have been achieved with an average of 90,000 victims over 27 months. But he also had stated that the number of $(27 \times 90,000) = 2,430,000$ should only be seen as "a calculation of the technical potential," and that he believed that the number had been 1.1 million. Quoting partially and out of context, Rassinier gave the false impression that Höss came to one conclusion in one place and another elsewhere—in short, that Höss was an unreliable witness. In fact, Höss showed a remarkable consistency in his computations—especially so if one remembers that he did the two calculations Rassinier quoted at different periods and without the opportunity to compare them. *The contradiction does not exist, except in Rassinier's mind.*

Rassinier did not give up attacking the credibility of Höss by identifying contradictions.

> We are concerned here with the witness Hoess, not the general statistics. And about those two trains that for 27 months brought 3,000 people to Auschwitz everyday, witness Hoess does not seem very certain. On this subject I invite the reader to think about these three propositions:
> 1. "As far as I can remember the convoys arriving at Auschwitz never carried more than 1,000 prisoners." (p. 220)
> 2. "Following some delays in communication, five convoys a day, instead of the expected three, arrived." (p. 236)
> 3. "In the extermination of Hungarian Jews, convoys were arriving at the rate of 15,000 persons a day." (p. 239)
> From which it appears that under certain circumstances five trains per day of 1,000 persons each delivered a total of 15,000 persons.[99]

So let us follow Rassinier's proposal, and consider these three propositions. First of all, let us establish their context. The first quote appears in a discussion of the early transports of Upper Silesian Jews to Auschwitz.

> I am unable to recall when the destruction of the Jews began— probably in September 1941, or perhaps not until January 1942. At first we dealt with the Jews from Upper Silesia. These Jews were arrested by the Gestapo from Katowice and transported via the Auschwitz-Dziediez railroad and unloaded there. As far as I can recall, *these* transports never numbered more than a thousand persons. (Emphasis added.)[100]

Comparison of the German original and the English translation shows that the latter has some problems, but on a crucial point it is correct: when Höss discusses the size of the transports, he only refers to those early transports. "These transports never numbered more than a thousand persons." He does not refer to other transports. In fact, the use of the demonstrative adjective "these" and the double adverb "never . . . more" suggest that other—that is, later—transports were larger. By changing "these transports" to "the transports," Rassinier distorted Höss's text.

A misrepresentation of a different kind occurs when he quotes Höss as saying that "following some delays in communication, five convoys a day, instead of the expected three, arrived." The context of this sentence, in the translation of Andrew Pollinger, is as follows:

> The highest total figure of people gassed and cremated in twenty-four hours was slightly more than nine thousand. This figure was reached in the summer of 1944, during the action in Hungary, using all installations except Crematory [IV]. On that day five trains arrived because of delays on the rail lines, instead of three, as was expected, and in addition the railroad cars were more crowded than usual.[101]

Rassinier was quite brazen with his third quotation: "In the extermination of Hungarian Jews, convoys were arriving at the rate of 15,000 persons a day." It does not appear in the original. He seems to have made it up. In conclusion, Rassinier suggests a discrepancy between three figures that does not exist. The two that could be traced back applied both to specific, and what proved to be atypical, situations—one at the (hesitant) beginning of the history of Auschwitz as a site of the Shoah and one extraordinary situation during its peak.

In the next paragraph Rassinier, who has shown poor exegetic skills, provided an example of his mathematical skills.

> To the Tribunal on April 15, 1946, Hoess had stated that these trains carried 2,000 persons each (T. XI, p. 412). To Professor Gustave Gilbert he said that they contained 1,500 each, and in his book, he comes down to 1,000. What is certain [is] that for the period given none of these estimates on the capacity of the trains corresponds to a total of 1,130,000. The last one is the closest to the truth with an exaggeration of only 300,000. Since Mr. Raul Hilberg takes under consideration six "killing centres," an exaggeration of 300,000 for each one would yield a total exaggeration of nearly 2,000,000 persons and, out of six million a total exaggeration of that magnitude is quite important.[102]

I will not comment on the easy way Rassinier was able to bring back to life, at the end of this paragraph, almost 2 million Jews with a stroke of the pen. Of greater interest is his statement about the capacity of the trains and his conclusions. First of all, there is the contradiction between the numbers. As we have seen, Höss mentioned the figure of 1,000 in relation to the transports of early 1942 from the surrounding region of Upper Silesia. The figure of 2,000 that he mentioned on April 15, 1946, referred to "the whole period up until 1944."

> [Dr. Kaufmann]: "And then the railway transports arrived. During what period did these transports arrive and about how many people, roughly, were in such a transport?"

> [Höss]: "During the whole period up until 1944 certain operations were carried out at irregular intervals in the different countries, so that one cannot speak of a continuous flow of incoming transports. It was always a matter of 4 to 6 weeks. During those 4 to 6 weeks two to three trains, containing about 2,000 persons each, arrived daily.[103]

Again, although Höss was specific and made historically important distinctions, Rassinier chose to lump things together. He also was incompetent as an accountant when he stated that there is no way one could reach, on the basis of trains with between 1,000 and 2,000 Jews, a total number of 1,130,000 arriving deportees. Yet a simple calculation shows otherwise. Let us take as our basis the statement that the deportations occurred over a period of 27 months (a figure which Rassinier endorsed a little earlier). This is a little over 800 days. This means that, *on average,* Auschwitz would have received 1,412 deportees per day. This is the average of the three figures Rassinier quoted—that is, the total number of 1,130,000 deportees could have been easily reached if one train of 1,500 people per day arrived at the camp over a period of 27 months. But, as Höss wrote, during many actions the average rate was between two and three trains per day, and during the Hungarian Action the normal rate was three trains per day. How could Rassinier state with such conviction that "for the period given none of these estimates on the capacity of the trains corresponds to a total of 1,130,000"?

In the next paragraph Rassinier showed his general ignorance of the meaning of the documents of the Zentralbauleitung found in Auschwitz at the time of the liberation.

> The same observation holds for the soundness of [Hoess's] testimony. "In the middle of spring, 1942, hundreds of human beings perished in the gas chambers." (p. 178.) But, as we have seen, Document No. 4401 establishes beyond any doubt that the so-called "gas chambers" were not ordered for Auschwitz until August 8, 1942 and Document No. 4463 establishes that they were not actually installed until February 20, 1943. At Nuremberg, Hoess had already stated in his deposition that "in 1942, Himmler came to visit the camp and was present at an execution from beginning to end," (T. XI, p. 413); no one called his attention to the fact that even if it were possible that Himmler had gone to Auschwitz in 1942, it was not possible for him to have been present at an execution, since the gas chambers had not been constructed yet. And, furthermore, we know that it would have been unlikely for Himmler to have been present at an execution because as we learned after the war from his physician, Dr. Kersten, he could not bear the sight of an execution.[104]

Two documents that relate to the construction of the four new crematoria equipped with gas chambers in no way preclude the existence of other gas chambers in Auschwitz. In fact, Bunker 1 had been in operation since March of that year and Bunker 2 since July. These were the converted farmhouses and, in fact, Höss mentions them as the place of execution in the paragraph preceding the sentence Rassinier chose to quote. He also mentioned them more obliquely in the sentence itself that Rassinier chose to quote only partly, suppressing among other things not only the location but also Höss's sickeningly sentimental attempt at poetry. "In the spring of 1942 hundreds of people in the full bloom of life walked beneath the budding fruit trees of the farm into the gas chamber to their death, most often without a hint of what was going to happen to them."[105] ("*Im Frühjahr 1942 gingen Hunderte von blühenden Menschen unter den blühenden Obstbäumen des Bauerngehöftes, meist nichtsahnend, in die Gaskammern, in den Tod.*"[106]) It is significant in this context that Rassinier uses the definite article "the" when he mentions the gas chambers: "It was not possible for him to have been present at an execution, since *the* gas chambers had not been constructed yet. (My emphasis.)" The definite article "the" suggests there was only one set of gas chambers at the site that came into operation in 1943. In fact, there were many different gas chambers, some of which were used for longer periods and some for a shorter time, some of which were spaces converted from other uses and some of which were designed as gas chambers.

Then there is Rassinier's treatment of Himmler's visit. Höss provided a few short accounts of this visit in his autobiography and in his essay on the Final Solution.[107] In the latter text, the account reads as follows.

> During his visit in the summer of 1942, Himmler very carefully observed the entire process of annihilation. He began with the unloading at the ramps and completed the inspection as Bunker 2 was being cleared of bodies. At that time there were no open-pit burnings. He did not complain about anything, but he didn't say anything about it either. Accompanying him were District Leader Bracht and SS General Schmauser. Shortly after Himmler's visit, SS Colonel Blobel from Eichmann's office arrived and brought Himmler's order, which stated that all the mass graves were to be opened and all the bodies cremated. It further stated that all the ashes were to be disposed of in such a way that later on there would be no way to determine the number of those cremated.[108]

In his biographical essay on Himmler, Höss provided a very long (four pages) and very detailed account of this visit. It included Himmler's response to the killings.

> After inspecting Birkenau, Himmler witnessed the complete extermination process of a transport of Jews which had just arrived. He also looked on for a while during a selection of those who would work and those who would die without any complaint on his part. Himmler made no comment about the extermination process. He just looked in total silence. I noticed that he very quietly watched the officers, the NCOs and me several times during the process.[109]

It is obvious that Himmler was more of a "man" than both Kersten and Rassinier assumed.

Another attempt by Rassinier to discredit Höss also falls flat.

> Hoess' comments concerning the capacity of the gas chambers and the crematories also are grossly contradictory. For example, he says on one page that: *The maximum figure for the number of people gassed or incinerated every 24 hours was a little more than 9,000 for* all *the installations* (p. 236). But, then, he says a few pages later: *As I have already said, Crematories I and II could incinerate about 2,000 bodies in 24 hours; it was not possible to exceed this if one wanted to avoid damage. Installations III and IV were supposed to incinerate 1,500 corpses in 24 hours. But, as far as I know, these figures were never reached.* (p. 245). How can one fail to deduce from these flagrant contradictions that here is a document which was fabricated hastily after the event by illiterates?[110]

So let's look again at what Höss really says. For the record: with Anlage II (Installation II) Hoess points at Bunker 2. As we have already seen, Bunker 2 was a peasant cottage west of Birkenau that had been transformed into a gas chamber in the summer of 1942. It was taken out of commission after the completion of the crematoria in 1943 but brought back into operation during the Hungarian Action in 1944 and renamed as

Bunker 5. Outside Bunker 2/5 were large burning pits where bodies were cremated in the open. The remains of these pits, together with the ashes, are still visible today.

> Installation II, later designated as Open Air Installation or Bunker V, was in operation until the very end, especially as a standby in case of breakdowns in crematoria I to IV. In the case of actions with train transports arriving shortly after each other daytime gassings were conducted at V, and nightly arriving transports at I to IV. *The cremation possibility at V was practically unlimited as long it was still possible to burn both by day and night.* Because of enemy air activity it was not possible anymore from 1944 onwards to burn at night. The highest total figure of gassings and cremations within 24 hours was a little over 9,000 at all locations except at III in the summer of 1944 during the Hungarian Action, as due to train delays five instead of the expected three trains arrived within 24 hours, and these were also more heavily loaded. (My emphasis)[111]

In other words, there is no contradiction. The open-air cremation pits at Bunker 5 account for the much higher figure. By partially quoting the paragraph, Rassinier either incompetently or malevolently tried to change the record.

Elsewhere Rassinier was just sloppy.

> Finally, a careful analysis of the following language reveals a pearl: *Toward the end of 1942, all the mass graves were cleaned [crematory ovens had not been built yet, and incineration was done in mass graves]. The number of cadavers buried there exceeded 107,000. This figure [as Rudolph Hoess explains farther on] includes not only convoys of Jews gassed from the beginning, until the moment when they went on to incineration, but also the cadavers of all the prisoners who died in Auschwitz-Birkenau camp* (p. 231). From this statement one infers that in nearly three years 107,000 persons died. I say "in nearly three years" because the two phrases "toward the end of 1942" and "until the moment when they went on to incineration," are paradoxical, since the cremations could not have begun, according to the official thesis, before February 20, 1943. Therefore, for the two to be concomitant, which is called for here, it is absolutely necessary that both should have occurred on this last date. Since the camp was opened on June 14, 1940, one has to speak of almost three years. Hence the cremation of 107,000 cadavers before February 1943 must mean that all of the rest were cremated at a later date. Taking into account that between February 1943 and October 1944 (the official end of the exterminations) there are 17 months and that, as the Kasztner Report tells us, for 8 or 9 months (the autumn of 1943 to May 1944) the gas chambers at Auschwitz were out of order and not working, it remains to be established how many persons more than 107,000 could have been "incinerated," from February 1943 to October 1944, when the camp was equipped with four crematoria ovens of 15 burners each. I would be very astonished if a cremation expert, given these facts, should reply that it was possible to cremate the million bodies that are claimed by Mr. Raul Hilberg, or even the 900,000 of the Institute of Jewish Affairs.[112]

Rassinier began his argument with a quote from Höss's report. Let us carefully examine this quote in its proper context. In the preceding paragraphs, Höss recorded the beginning of the extermination of Jews in Bunker I, describing the procedure in some detail.

> During the spring of 1942 we were still dealing with small police actions. But during the summer the transports became more numerous and we were forced to build another extermination site. The farm west of crematoria 4 and 5, which were built later, was chosen and prepared. Five barracks were built, two near Bunker 1, and three near Bunker 2. Bunker 2 was the larger one. It held about 1,200 people. As late as the summer of 1942 the corpses were still buried in mass graves. Not until the end of the summer did we start burning them. At first we put two thousand bodies on a large pile of wood. Then we opened up the mass graves and burned the new bodies on top of the old ones from the earlier burials. At first we poured waste oil over the bodies. Later on we used methanol. The burning went on continuously—all day and all night. By the end of November all the mass graves were cleared. The number of buried bodies in the mass graves was 107,000. This number contains not only the first Jewish transports which were gassed when we started the burnings, but also the bodies of the prisoners who died in the main Auschwitz camp during the winter of 1941–42 because the crematory was out of order. The prisoners who died at Birkenau [Auschwitz 2] are included in that number.[113]

Examination of the text shows the flaws in Rassinier's comments. Let's look at them sentence by sentence. "From this statement one infers that in nearly three years 107,000 persons died." In fact, this inference is wrong. All the statement says is that 107,000 people were buried in mass graves until the onset of the incinerations on the pyres; that is, until the end of the summer of 1942. *It does not even include those people who arrived after the end of the summer to be killed and cremated immediately upon death without having been buried first in a mass grave*. It only includes those who were killed and initially buried without the intention of later cremation.

The largest group of these people were Jews who had arrived mostly after the spring of 1942—the transports in the spring were still classified as "small police actions." So these were people who were killed in the camp between, let's say, June and September—that is, three months and not three years. Added to that were two smaller groups—inmates who had died in Auschwitz I in the winter of 1941/1942 when the crematorium there was in repair and the prisoners who had died in Birkenau since its opening in the beginning of March 1942. Ignorant of the context, Rassinier's following sentence is incorrect. "I say 'in nearly three years' because the two phrases 'toward the end of 1942' and 'until the moment when they went on to incineration,' are paradoxical, since the cremations could not have begun, according to the official thesis, before February 20, 1943." The paradox does not exist, because it is absolutely clear that Höss refers in his "*bis zu Beginn der Verbrennungen* [until the beginning of the incineration]" to the open-air incinerations discussed earlier in the same paragraph and not to the in-house incinerations in the crematoria mentioned ten paragraphs later. Because these open-air incinerations began at the end of the summer, they could very well have ended by the end of November 1942.

As a result, Rassinier's conclusion that between June 1940 and February 1943 only (!) 107,000 people were cremated is unfounded: it only applies to three distinct groups of murdered people which represent, according to current data, about half of the total mortality of Auschwitz in 1942. Furthermore, these cremations took place in very primitive circumstances; hence, any attempt to extrapolate from the number of 107,000 the number of total cremations in Auschwitz is inappropriate, given the fact that in early 1943 four new crematoria with 46 ovens became available. Official figures of the Central Construction Office mentioned a total cremation capacity of 4,756 corpses per day. Yet Rassinier has no qualms about trying to suggest that there should be some balance between the (false) figure of 107,000 corpses cremated before February 1943 and the total amount of cremations between February 1943 and October 1944.

> Since the camp was opened on June 14, 1940, one has to speak of almost three years. Hence the cremation of 107,000 cadavers before February 1943 must mean that *all of the rest* were cremated at a later date. Taking into account that between February 1943 and October 1944 (the official end of the exterminations) there are 17 months and that, as the Kasztner Report tells us, for 8 or 9 months (the autumn of 1943 to May 1944) the gas chambers at Auschwitz were out of order and not working, it remains to be established how many persons more than 107,000 could have been "incinerated," from February 1943 to October 1944, when the camp was equipped with four crematoria ovens of 15 burners each. I would be very astonished if a cremation expert, given these facts, should reply that it was possible to cremate the million bodies that are claimed by Mr. Raul Hilberg, or even the 900,000 of the Institute of Jewish Affairs. (My emphasis)[114]

With "all of the rest" I assume that Rassinier means the other 900,000 (Hilberg) or 800,000 corpses (Institute of Jewish Affairs).

Negationists have not been successful in attacking Höss's credibility by pointing out contradictions. They have, however, done their best to show that Höss's testimony did not fulfil Stäglich's third demand: "Finally, to have probative value, a statement must contain nothing improbable, something that may seem obvious to most people, but—as we shall see— is not always the case with reports about the Birkenau crematoria."[115] American negationist Arthur R. Butz proposed a broad definition of "the improbable." Butz assumed that procedures or structures have only one meaning or purpose and that if we find that they have more than one—that is, one "routine" meaning or purpose and one "extraordinary" meaning or purpose—the latter will be a fictional significance grafted on the factual one or, in other words, an improbable meaning.

> This is the basic structure of the Auschwitz extermination legend. It is shown here that every real fact contained in the story had (not could have had, but had) a relatively routine significance, having nothing to do with the exterminations of a people. Thus those who claim extermination must advance a thesis involving a dual interpretation of the facts, but by then the impartial reader, in consideration of what has just been noted, should be on my side; the need for a dual interpretation of fact, the trademark of the hoax, has emerged.[116]

Butz rightly noted that people had to undress when subjected to delousing; that Zyklon was used for delousing purposes; that morgues were used to store corpses; that crematoria incinerated the corpses of people who had died as the result of starvation, exhaustion, mistreatment, or because of natural causes; and that chemical factories create stench. He therefore jumped to the conclusion that the author of the hoax intelligently created a fiction in which people had to undress when subjected to gassing, that Zyklon was used for killing purposes, that morgues were used as gas chambers, that crematoria incinerated the corpses of people who had been murdered in the gas chambers, and that the cremations created a stench. In other words, the hoax criminalized "routine" activities. What Butz did not consider was that people had to undress both when subjected to delousing *and* when subjected to gassing; that Zyklon was used for delousing purposes *and* for killing purposes; that some morgues were used to store corpses *and* others as gas chambers; that crematoria incinerated the corpses of people who had died as the result of starvation, exhaustion, mistreatment, or because of natural causes, *and* that they incinerated the corpses of people who had been murdered in the gas chambers; and that both chemical factories *and* crematoria create stench. And what Butz did not consider either is the rather simple explanation, proven to be true, that the various procedures or structures historically had two meanings or purposes because the second one evolved from, or was grafted onto, the first. For example, Zyklon was used in the camp for delousing purposes, but when searching for a simple, effective, and cheap killing agent for humans, the SS discovered that hydrogen cyanide not only killed lice, it *also* killed people, and at much lower concentrations than needed to kill lice. When the Auschwitz crematoria were being built, they were *also* designed to function as killing stations. The well-ventilated morgues *also* functioned well as gas chambers with some minor adaptations. In other words, contingency marked the development of the camp, and, as in all cases where contingency rules, things designed to do one thing ended up doing something else *also*.

So let's look in some detail at the substance of Butz's attempt to discredit Höss. He began with an analysis of the Höss affidavit of April 5, 1946.

> I commanded Auschwitz until 1 December, 1943, and estimate that at least 2,500,000 victims were executed and exterminated there by gassing and burning, and at least another half million succumbed to starvation and disease, making a total dead of about 3,000,000. This figure represents about 70 or 80 percent of all persons sent to Auschwitz as prisoners, the remainder having been selected and used for slave labor in the concentration camp industries.[117]

Butz commented rather tamely that "it would have been helpful in putting things into slightly better focus and perspective if Hoess had briefly indicated what the nature of the 'concentration camp industries' at Auschwitz was, and the enormous importance this industry had for the Germans."[118] He did not go into detail about why this would have been helpful but assumed that the reader would remember an earlier discussion in which he claimed that because Auschwitz was the site of many industries that used the slave labor of the camp, it could not *also* have been a center of extermination. As for the number of two and half million people Höss claimed to have gassed in Auschwitz, Butz repeated Rassinier's argument that a year later Höss mentioned a figure of 1,135,000 people murdered. And he continued as follows:

> The lowest figure to be claimed by those who claim that gassings took place is 750,000. The Russians claimed 4,000,000, includ-

ing some killed by "injections, ill treatment, etc," but the highest figure claimed seems to be 7,000,000.[119]

Butz left his readers to draw their own conclusions, but his suggestion is clear: when the lowest and highest estimate differ a whole order of magnitude, there is no reason to trust any of them.

> Mass executions by gassing commenced during the summer 1941 and continued until fall 1944. I personally supervised executions at Auschwitz until the first of December 1943 and know by reason of my continued duties in the Inspectorate of Concentration Camps WVHA that these mass executions continued as stated above.[120]

Butz suggested that this was improbable because Höss had stated elsewhere that when Himmler ordered him to transform Auschwitz into an extermination camp in 1941, Inspector of the Concentration Camps Glücks was not to know about it. Thus, how could Höss have known about the exterminations after he had left the camp to take up a post at Glücks's inspectorate?[121] Butz did not consider the probability that Himmler's order of secrecy vis-à-vis Glücks in 1941 made sense in a context of the initial preparation for the Final Solution and had become obsolete by 1943, when the genocide of the Jews had been under way for more than a year.

Commenting on Höss's statement that "when I set up the extermination building at Auschwitz I, I used Cyclon B," Butz noted that because the Auschwitz SS normally used "liberal quantities" of Zyklon to kill the lice that caused epidemics, it was improbable that it would have been used to kill humans. "Here we have, on a major point, the main attribute of a hoax as we begin to examine the details of the Auschwitz extermination claims: the fact requiring a dual interpretation."[122] Having noted the "dual interpretation," Butz did not find it necessary anymore to engage and refute Höss's graphic description of the gassing procedure itself. By implication, the gassing procedure was now a phantasm because Zyklon was also used to kill lice. Butz felt that a particularly powerful example of the improbability that Zyklon was used to kill people could be found in Höss's statement that in 1943 a large group of Jews from Theresienstadt was initially not subjected to selection but was lodged in family groups in Birkenau. "Since these people were put into 'quarantine' it is certain that their quarters had been disinfected with the Zyklon just prior to their moving in," Butz speculated. And then he noted with indignation: "Now we are asked to believe that the Germans planned to kill them with the same chemical product later on!"[123] And one wonders, why not? But for Butz it did not make any sense at all.

> The part of the Auschwitz legend touching on the Theresienstadt Jews is obvious nonsense even without contrary evidence, however. It is not believable that the Germans would quarter for six months at Birkenau each of three distinct groups of people of a category for which there exists an extermination program at Birkenau. The dual role of the Zyklon in this story merely effects passage from the nonsensical to the incomparably absurd.[124]

Then Butz turned to the issue of selections.

> With the "selections" we are offered another fact for dual interpretation. There is no doubt that the extensive industrial and other activities required "selections" of people for various con-

ventional purposes. We are then asked to add an "extermination" purpose to these activities.[125]

Having no doubts as to the real meaning of the word *selection*, Butz failed to provide evidence for the selections "for various conventional purposes," nor did he feel obliged to engage Höss's testimony on this issue, or the many other testimonies that corroborate it. The only thing that mattered was that the word "selection" could be interpreted in two different ways, which "proves" that the idea of selection as a part of the process of extermination is a fabrication.

Finally, Butz engaged Höss's statement that "we were required to carry out these exterminations in secrecy but of course the foul and nauseating stench from the continuous burning of bodies permeated the entire area and all of the people living in the surrounding communities knew that exterminations were going on at Auschwitz." Butz admitted that this subject "is a big one," and then proceeded to argue that the crematoria in Auschwitz only served the "routine" purpose of incinerating corpses and did not serve as extermination installations. His first argument was that the crematoria were already planned before Himmler ordered any extermination program in the summer of 1942.

> It is claimed that the new crematoria were intended for extermination of Jews but we have suggested a more routine purpose in the preceding chapter. Let us review their history. The construction was well into the preliminary stages of planning and ordering early in 1942 and this fact, in itself, makes it difficult, to say the least, to believe that they were related to any extermination program ordered by Himmler in the summer of 1942. The construction plans for four structures containing crematory furnaces are dated 28 January 1942.[126]

This is a nice try, but this reasoning is first of all wrong, in that the designs of only two of the crematoria were dated January 1942, while the others dated from the summer of 1942. Second, Butz did not take into account the possibility, proven in the late 1980s to be historical fact, that the designs of the two earlier crematoria were modified later in order to accommodate gas chambers. Again, he was not prepared to admit the possibility that the SS had changed its mind.

Robert Faurisson also attempted to show that what Höss had said was improbable, if not impossible. Faurisson juxtaposed two of Höss's statements.

> The door was opened a half an hour after the gas was thrown in and the ventilation system was turned on. Work was immediately started to remove the corpses.[127]

> They dragged the bodies from the gas chambers, removed the gold teeth, cut off the hair, then dragged the bodies to the pits or to the ovens. On top of that, they had to maintain the fires in the pits, pour off the accumulated fat, and poke holes into the burning mountain of bodies, so that more oxygen could enter. All these jobs they performed with an indifferent coolness, just as if this was an everyday affair. While dragging the bodies, they ate or smoked. Even the gruesome job of burning the bodies dug up after being in mass graves for a long time did not prevent them from eating.[128]

Closely reading this first passage, Faurisson noted the adverb "immediately." In other words, work began immediately after the ventilation began; that means when the room was still highly toxic. This was very dangerous. It was evident, Faurisson argued, that the Sonderkommandos could have entered the space only if they were equipped with gas masks.[129] The second statement by Höss seemed, however, to preclude this possibility because it recorded that Sonderkommandos dragged bodies while eating and smoking. This meant that they could not have been wearing gas masks. In short, there was an inexplicable contradiction between the extreme toxicity of the gas chamber and the behavior of the Sonderkommandos. Adding to his collection of "contradictions" the official instruction manual of Zyklon B, which stipulated that spaces that had been fumigated with the agent should air out for at least twenty hours, Faurisson came to the conclusion that Höss obviously did not know what he was writing about and that his testimony was worthless.[130]

Yet on examination, it is clear that his "Ajax method" did not do the texts justice. The second quotation taken from Höss occurs in the middle of a paragraph that deals with the "strange" behavior of the Sonderkommandos. It did not discuss the extermination procedure in any logical order. When Höss mentioned that the Sonderkommandos ate or smoked while dragging bodies, he did not say "while dragging bodies from the gas chambers." In fact, there was a lot of body-dragging in Auschwitz: in Crematoria 2 and 3, bodies were dragged along the incineration halls from the elevator doors to the ovens; in Crematoria 4 and 5, bodies were dragged not only from the gas chambers to the morgue but also from the morgue to the incineration room; and in the case of the open-air burning of the buried corpses in the late summer and fall of 1942, bodies were dragged from the opened mass graves to the incineration pits. At no time did the Sonderkommandos need a gas mask for this awful job. Faurisson also misrepresented the Zyklon B instruction manual. The rule that spaces needed to be aired for twenty hours after application of Zyklon B applies to rooms without any special ventilation system. The situation in the gas chambers was different. With its powerful ventilation system and with the fact that most of the hydrogen cyanide was absorbed by the victims' bodies, the time could be reduced to twenty minutes.

Given Stäglich's criteria and the inability of major negationists such as Rassinier, Butz, and Faurisson to successfully challenge Höss's testimony, there is only one way to sow doubt about its authenticity. That is to claim that all of it was a fabrication from the very beginning. This is, in fact, the approach Irving chose to make. In his *Nuremberg: The Last Battle* (1996), Irving did more than just misconstrue and misrepresent the evidence given by Vaillant-Couturier and in the diary of Judge Biddle. Irving also consistently tried to destroy the credibility of Höss's testimony, without ever asking if it contained any credible parts. Irving made much of the fact that Höss's first confession was given in a situation of duress.

> This confession, which subsequently came to be submitted to the Nuremberg tribunal as document NO-1210, had taken three days of torture, as his captor, Sergeant Bernard Clarke himself would describe, to obtain. It contained numerous perhaps deliberate errors, for instance the identification by Höss of an extermination camp at "Wolzek near Lublin," in addition to those at "Belzek" and "Tublinka," all spelt thus. Wolzek has never existed, and the two other camps, Belzec and Treblinka, were not in existence at the time that Höss testified to.[131]

Irving was right in that Höss's first confession was obtained when the witness was denied sleep for three days, but he did not mention that although this confession was submitted to the tribunal, it was never used in court. Instead, the tribunal heard on April 15, 1946, extracts from the affidavit which he signed on April 5, 1946, after a few days of civilized interrogation in the witness wing of the Nuremberg prison.[132] On the witness stand, Höss confirmed that the affidavit was true and that he had signed it voluntarily.[133] When asked if he understood the English of the affidavit, Höss declared that he understood "English as it is written above," that "the above statements are true," and that "this declaration is made by me voluntarily and without compulsion."[134]

Irving chose not to quote this affidavit, which was probably the most important piece of evidence about Auschwitz to be presented during the Nuremberg proceedings, and which was publicly confirmed by Höss in court; instead, Irving spent much energy discrediting it.

> On April 5 the Americans placed before him a three-page affidavit, which they themselves had drafted and typed, for his signature. Written in English throughout, it contained the admission by Höss that he had "gassed" 2.5 million people in Auschwitz in addition to the half million who had died there of diseases.
>
> "We have prepared an affidavit written in English—," they began by informing their prisoner; whereupon, according to the verbatim transcript, the witness (Höss) "read through" the statement that followed and replied that he had read it and understood it.
>
> "Yes," continues the transcript, "I understand everything that I read."
>
> In reality Höss could not understand English. It merits passing comment that this English affidavit by Höss was *not* in fact signed at any point by him, although the Nuremberg interrogating officers and interpreter all presigned the document as witnesses to his "signature."
>
> Not for three days was Höss shown a German translation of the English affidavit ("which you signed"); the transcript of this new conversation on April 8 shows Höss belatedly insisting on changes to the text. An anonymous hand interpolated entire lines, while other lines were deleted by a stroke of the pen; there are no initials in the margin to endorse such changes, but Höss signed this entire German document in its new form on each page ("after reading over the statement"). It included the following curiously worded statement typed in English at its foot: "I understand English as it is written above. The above statements are true; this declaration is made by me voluntarily and without compulsion."[135]

The fundamental premise that guided Irving's attack on the credibility of the affidavit is the assumption that Höss could not read English. He also used this argument when he wrote, a little further, that Höss confirmed in court the passages of his affidavit that had been read in English. Yet Höss did know English. In his autobiography, written in a Polish jail, Höss recalled how he learned English during his imprisonment in the 1920s for his participation in the Parchimer Vehme murder.

> After this low, this breakdown, my life in prison passed without particular incident. I became more and more calm and clear-

thinking. In my free time I eagerly studied English. I even had textbooks sent to me. Later I had them regularly send me books and magazines in English, so that in about a year I learned this language without anyone helping me. This was a terrific discipline for my mind.[136]

If Irving had been right about the issue of Höss's lack of foreign-language abilities, one could have made the case that there were real problems with the affidavit he endorsed in court. Now all that remains are a few small quibbles about the lack of initials to confirm some insertions—objections that are of no significance in the context of the repeated willingness of Höss to confirm the affidavit as his own.

Irving, who invoked the diary of Dr. Gustave Gilbert, the Nuremberg prison psychologist, whenever it suited his exculpatory cause, found no reason to quote Gilbert's record of his conversations with Höss. This diary is a historically important and reliable source, a fact that was well established during the Eichmann Trial, when the court questioned Gilbert on the manner in which he had compiled the diary. The reason for Gilbert's appearance in Jerusalem was that Höss had made a number of observations on Eichmann's role in the Final Solution, and as Höss could not be cross-examined (having been executed fourteen years earlier), Gilbert's account of Höss's testimony became quite important. On May 29 and 30, 1961, in the 55th and 57th sessions of that trial, Gilbert testified. He was asked when and how he made his notes.

> [Gilbert]: "I made very extensive notes after every conversation—but not in their presence. I recorded the summary of our conversations with extensive verbatim quotations, and compiled this in my own diary; and the defendants were unaware of this until the end of the trial."[137]

The next day, under cross-examination by Eichmann's lawyer, Robert Servatius, the issue was revisited.

> [Servatius]: "The value of a diary assuredly depends on whether the entries were recorded immediately or at a later time. Were these entries recorded the same days as the date they bear?"

> [Gilbert]: [*replies in German*] "They were always taken down on the same day and then dictated to my secretary."

> Q.: "Did you supplement or revise them later, or has everything remained as it was originally recorded?"

> A.: "I would rather carry on in English."

> [Presiding Judge Landau]: "Please do."

> [Gilbert]: [*in English*] "In dictating the notes to my secretary, I took advantage of the trial manuscripts and any additional facts that I recalled in the meantime. But this dictation usually took place the next day. There was no long time between the conversation and the actual dictation of notes for the diary."

> [Servatius]: "Do you want your diary to be regarded as an authoritative and scientific account?"

> [Gilbert]: "The diary comprises the original raw data for later scientific evaluation. So, to answer your question about expert evaluation, that really takes place in the second book, in which I

evaluate all of the factual data which I collected, and on that basis make my expert evaluation of the Nazi system and its leaders, including Hitler."

Q.: "For evaluating material, it is assuredly important whether a report has been written *sine ira et studio* (without wrath and excessive eagerness)—the concept will surely be known to you—in other words, without preconceptions, without bias. Was that how this diary was written?"

A.: "Yes, I had the advantage of American ignorance of the Nazi system, except for a little briefing as a military intelligence officer; I also had the advantage of being completely uninformed and incredulous about the events that we are discussing today, and I had to be convinced, more and more, about what actually took place. It took me a year to get the whole picture."[138]

The Israeli court accepted the evidentiary value of the Gilbert diary—the same diary that Irving quoted whenever it suited him. Irving found no use for the extraordinary account of Gilbert's conversation with Höss on April 9, 1946, in which the latter had discussed the technical problems of genocide: "The killing itself took the least time. You could dispose of 2,000 in a half hour, but it was the burning that took all the time." And Gilbert had noted that "he [Höss] related all of this in a quiet, apathetic, matter-of-fact tone of voice."[139]

In his diary, Gilbert explicitly raised the question of whether Höss's statements could be trusted. He noted that, during one of his visits to Höss, the latter remarked that, as a psychologist, Gilbert undoubtedly would want to know if he was normal. Höss declared that he was normal. "Even while I was doing this extermination work, I led a normal family life, and so on." When Gilbert asked him if the Jews who were killed deserved such a fate, Höss replied that this was an unrealistic question because it showed a great ignorance of the world of the SS. "Don't you see, we SS men were not supposed to think about these things; it never even occurred to us. —And besides, it was something already taken for granted that the Jews were to blame for everything."[140] Höss admitted that the work was unpleasant. "But Himmler had ordered it and had even explained the necessity and I really never gave much thought to whether it was wrong. It just seemed a necessity."

> In all of the discussions Hoess is quite matter-of-fact and apathetic, shows some belated interest in the enormity of his crime, but gives the impression that it never would have occurred to him if somebody hadn't asked him. There is too much apathy to leave any suggestion of remorse and even the prospect of hanging does not unduly distress him.[141]

In Jerusalem, the court revisited the issue because, having admitted Höss's statement that indicted Eichmann as evidence, Attorney General Gideon Hausner could not examine him and Eichmann's lawyer Robert Servatius could not cross-examine him. Remarkably, the latter, who had served in Nuremberg as counsel to Fritz Sauckel, did confirm that the accused willingly and without coercion cooperated with Gilbert. He noted also that "subsequently the accused men held conversations amongst themselves, in which they made sarcastic references to their discussions with the witness, and they even voiced a kind of mocking comment on the 'soul examiner.'"[142] Servatius therefore accepted that the diary could be entered in evidence, but said that Gilbert should limit his comments to it. The court agreed, and it asked Gilbert to comment on Höss's mental state when he gave his public and private testimony.

> [Attorney General Hausner]: "I take it that, as a psychologist, you certainly understand that sometimes there is a state of mind of the accused which tends to drag down other people, as it were, and to incriminate them?"

> [Gilbert]: "Yes, I certainly understand that. It's one of the common guilt defences."

> Q.: "Would you say that Rudolf Höss was in that particular state of mind when you were speaking to him?"

> A.: "No, definitely not. As I said before, he was a man who was just automatically telling the facts as he knew them. It apparently meant nothing to him that he had murdered millions of people, he had no hesitation in describing everything in detail, and without any attempt to share blame, or to prepare a defence or anything, quite spontaneously—certainly not with any urging on my part— the name of Eichmann came into his statements again and again and again, and finally I realized that this man was a key figure in the extermination programme. May I amplify a little further? By contrast, I saw that Kaltenbrunner was a liar. When he tried to disclaim knowledge of the atrocities and shove the blame onto someone else, I could see—and got corroboration from actual statements from the others—that this was outright perjury, false testimony, outright lies. So I was aware at all times that it is possible that any of these men might be lying, but Höss definitely was not."[143]

It is clear that Irving's description of the way the Holocaust in general, and Auschwitz in particular, figured in the Nuremberg Trial has no value. A historian would have considered all the evidence at hand; Irving only chose to (mis)quote whatever suited his preconceived notions.

Höss was not the only SS official tried in Poland for war crimes committed in Auschwitz. Eight months after the Höss trial the Supreme National Tribunal began proceedings in Cracow against forty former SS men who had served for a longer or shorter time in Auschwitz. The trial did not add much new information about the way Auschwitz had operated. The bulk of the evidence the prosecutors presented consisted of material collected by Sehn and, of course, Höss's confessions. One new piece of evidence was introduced in the case against Dr. Johann Paul Kremer, who was a *Dozent* of anatomy at the University of Münster and who served for a few months as a camp doctor in 1942. The evidence was his wartime diary. As it has attracted much attention from both Holocaust historians and negationists, I included a discussion of it in two places of my report.

Kremer had volunteered as a member of the General SS in 1935, and he had been detailed to Auschwitz in August 1942 to replace a physician who had fallen ill. He served there until November 20. An avid diarist since he was sixteen, Kremer recorded his impressions at the time. Kremer was not part of the overall command structure, and while he was on temporary duty in Auschwitz he showed remarkably little curiosity about the historic events he witnessed and, in a subordinate role, helped to shape. Yet this very lack of engagement is the reason why the diary is of great historic interest. One of the remarkable aspects of the Holocaust was that it was conceived, initiated, executed, and completed by ordinary men who had learned to kill as part of their ordinary activities.

Kremer's diary was found when he was arrested and it was immediately recognized as an important piece of evidence of the atrocities committed in Auschwitz. Here are a few excerpts:

> August 30, 1942. Departure from Prague 8.15 A.M. through Böhmisch Trübau, Olmütz, Prerau, Oderberg. Arrival at Concentration Camp Auschwitz at 5.36 P.M. Quarantine in camp on account of numerous contagious diseases (typhus, malaria, dysentery). Received to secret order through garrison physician Hauptsturmführer [Kurt] Uhlenbrock and accommodation in a room (no. 26) in the Waffen-SS club-house [Home].

> August 31, 1942. Tropical climate with 28° Centigrade in the shade, dust and innumerable flies! Excellent food in the Home. This evening, for instance, we had sour duck livers for 0.40 RM, with stuffed tomatoes, tomato salad, etc. Water is infected, so we drink seltzer-water which is served free (mattoni). First inoculation against typhus. Had photo taken for the camp identity card.

> September 1, 1942. Have ordered SS officer's cap, sword-belt and brace from Berlin by letter. In the afternoon was present at the gassing of a block with Cyclon B against lice.

> September 2, 1942. Was present for the first time at a special action at 3 A.M. By comparison Dante's inferno seems almost a comedy. Auschwitz is justly called an extermination camp![144]

After his arrest, Kremer was extradited to Poland, and he became one of the defendants in the Auschwitz Trial held before the Supreme National Tribunal in Cracow in November and December 1947. During his pretrial interrogation Kremer was asked to elucidate the various entries of his diary. On August 18, 1947, he stated that "by September 2, 1942, at 3 A.M. I had already been assigned to take part in the action of gassing people."

Johann Paul Kremer, 1945. Courtesy Archive Auschwitz-Birkenau State Museum, Oswiecim.

> These mass murders took place in small cottages situated outside the Birkenau camp in a wood. The cottages were called "bunkers" in the SS-men's slang. All SS physicians on duty in the camp took turns to participate in the gassings, which were called *Sonderaktion* [special action]. My part as a physician at the gassing consisted in remaining in readiness near the bunker. I was brought there by car. I sat in front with the driver and an SS hospital orderly sat in the back of the car with oxygen apparatus to revive SS-men, employed in the gassing, in case any of them should succumb to the poisonous fumes. When the transport with people who were destined to be gassed arrived at the railway ramp, the SS officers selected from among the new arrivals persons fit to work, while the rest—old people, all children, women with children in their arms and other persons not deemed fit to work— were loaded onto lorries and driven to the gas chambers. I used to follow behind the transport till we reached the bunker. There people were driven into the barrack huts where the victims undressed and then went naked to the gas chambers. Very often no incidents occurred, as the SS-men kept the people quiet, maintaining that they were to bathe and be deloused. After driving all of them into the gas chamber the door was closed and an SS-man in a gas mask threw the contents of a Cyclon tin through an opening in the side wall. The shouting and screaming of the victim[s] could

be heard through that opening and it was clear that they were fighting for their lives. These shouts were heard for a very short while. I should say for some minutes, but I am unable to give the exact length of time.[145]

Three days later Kremer witnessed another gassing and dutifully recorded it in his diary.

September 5, 1942. At noon was present at a special action in the women's camp (Moslems)—the most horrible of all horrors. Hschf Thilo, military surgeon, was right when he said to me today that we are located here in the anus mundi. In the evening at about 8 P.M. another special action with a draft from Holland. Men compete to take part in such actions as they get additional rations—$^1/_5$ litre vodka, 5 cigarettes, 100 grammes of sausage and bread. Today and tomorrow (Sunday) on duty.[146]

In Poland, Kremer again gave a full explanation of this entry. On July 17, 1947, he testified that "the action of gassing emaciated women from the women's camp was particularly unpleasant."

Such individuals were generally called *Muselmänner* [Moslems]. I remember taking part in the gassing of such women in daylight. I am unable to state how numerous that group was. When I came to the bunker they sat clothed on the ground. As the clothes were in fact worn out camp clothes, they were not let into the undressing barracks but undressed in the open. I could deduce from the behaviour of these women that they realized what was awaiting them. They begged the SS-men to be allowed to live, they wept, but all of them were driven into the gas chamber and gassed. Being an anatomist I had seen many horrors, had dealt with corpses, but what I then saw was not to be compared with anything ever seen before. It was under the influence of these impressions that I noted in my diary, under the date of September 5, 1942, "The most horrible of all horrors. Haupsturmführer Thilo was right when he said to me today that we are located here in the anus mundi." I used this expression because I could not imagine anything more sickening and more horrible.[147]

Yet by the next day Kremer was sufficiently recovered to enjoy an "excellent" Sunday dinner consisting of "tomato soup, one half chicken with potatoes and red cabbage (20 grammes of fat), dessert and magnificent vanilla ice-cream."[148]

Three more entries are of interest. The first one is of October 3.

October 3, 1942. Today I preserved fresh material from the human liver, spleen and pancreas, also lice from persons infected with typhus, in pure alcohol. Whole streets at Auschwitz are down with typhus. I therefore took the first inoculation against abdominal typhus. Obersturmbannführer Schwarz ill with typhus![149]

During his trial, Kremer commented at length on the first sentence of this entry.

In my diary I mentioned in several entries the taking, for research purposes, of fresh human material. It was like this: I had been for an extensive period interested in investigating the changes devel-

Von Berlin schriftlich Führermütze, Koppel und Rosenträger angefordert. Nachmittags bei der Vergasung eines Blocks mit <u>Zyclon B</u> gegen die Läuse.

Zum 1. Male draußen um 3 Uhr früh bei einer Sonderaktion zugegen. Im Vergleich hierzu erscheint mir das Dante'sche Inferno fast wie eine Komödie. Umsonst wird Auschwitz nicht das Lager der Vernichtung genannt!

Zum 1. Male an der hier im Lager jeden befallenden Durchfällen mit Erbrechen und Koliken anfallsweise Schwersten erkrankt. Da ich keinen Tropfen Wasser getrunken, kann es hieran nicht liegen. Auch das Brot kann es nicht schuld sein, da auch solche erkranken, die nur Weißbrot (Zwieback) zu sich genommen haben. Höchstwahrscheinlich liegt's an dem ungesunden kontinentalen und sehr trockenen Tropenklima mit seinen Staub- und Ungeziefermassen (Fliegen).

Gegen die Durchfälle: 1 Tag Schleimsuppe und Pfeffermünztee, dann Diät für eine Woche : Zwieback, dazu Kohle und kaum albin. Schon erhebliche Besserung.

Heutemittag bei einer Sonderaktion aus dem F. K. L. (Muselmänner): das Schrecklichste der Schrecken. Hschf. Thilo* hat Recht, wenn er mir *Truppenarzt. heute sagte, wir befänden uns hier am anus mundi. Abends gegen 8 Uhr wieder bei einer Sonderaktion aus Holland. Wegen der dabei abfallenden Sonderverpflegung, bestehend aus einem fünftel Liter Schnaps, 5 Cigaretten, 100 g Wurst und Brot, drängen sich die Männer zu solchen Aktionen. Heute und morgen (Sonntag) Dienst.

oping in the human organism as a result of starvation. At Auschwitz I mentioned this to Wirths who said that I would be able to get completely fresh material for my research from those prisoners who were killed by phenol injections. To choose suitable specimens I used to visit the last block on the right [Block 28], where prisoners who acted as doctors presented the patients to the SS physician and described the illness of the patient. The SS physician decided then—taking into consideration the prisoner's chances of recovery—whether he should be treated in the hospital, perhaps as an outpatient, or be liquidated. Those placed by the SS physician in the latter group were led away by the SS orderlies. The SS physician primarily designated for liquidation those prisoners whose diagnosis was *Allgemeine Körperschwäche* [general bodily exhaustion]. I used to observe such prisoners and if one of them aroused my interest, owing to his advanced state of emaciation, I asked the orderly to reserve the given patient for me and let me know when he would be killed with an injection. At the time fixed by the orderly the patients selected by me were again brought to the last block, and were put into a room on the other side of the corridor opposite the room where the examinations, during which the patient had been selected, had taken place. The patient was put upon the dissecting table while he was still alive. I then approached the table and put several questions to the man as to such details which pertained to my research. For instance, I asked what his weight had been before the arrest, how much weight he had lost since then, whether he took any medicines, etc. When I had collected my information the orderly approached the patient and killed him with an injection in the vicinity of the heart. As far as I knew only phenol injections were used. Death was instantaneous after the injection. I myself never made any lethal injections.[150]

The second entry is from October 12.

October 12, 1942. The second inoculation against typhus; strong reaction in the evening (fever). In spite of this was present at night at another special action with a draft from Holland (1,600 persons). Horrible scene in front of the last bunker! (Hössler!) This was the 10th special action.[151]

On July 18, 1947, Kremer elucidated this entry as follows:

In connection with the gassing described by me in the diary under the date of October 12, 1942, I have to explain that around 1,600 Dutchmen were then gassed. This is an approximate figure which I noted down after hearing it mentioned by others. This action was conducted by the SS officer Hössler. I remember how he tried to drive the whole group into one bunker. He was successful except for one man, whom it was not possible by any means to squeeze inside the bunker. This man was killed by Hössler with a pistol shot. I therefore wrote in my diary about horrible scenes in front of the last bunker, and I mentioned Hössler's name in connection with this incident.[152]

Finally, there is the entry for October 18.

October 18, 1942. In wet and cold weather was on this Sunday morning present at the 11th special action (from Holland). Terrible scenes when 3 women begged merely to have their lives spared.[153]

Again, Kremer explained this entry during his trial.

> During the special action, described by me in my diary under the date of October 18, 1942, three women from Holland refused to enter the gas chamber and begged for their lives. They were young and healthy women, but their begging was to no avail. The SS-men, taking part in the action, shot them on the spot.[154]

The diary provided little new information about the wartime history of Auschwitz, and in the Cracow trial its major function was to provide a structure for Kremer's interrogation. However, decades later it was recognized as a very important and rare document, because unlike the Broad report and Höss's writings, it provided a piece of eyewitness testimony of various "actions" written within hours after the event, and with no other intention than to serve as a private document to be seen by no one but the author. It is therefore a particularly honest document, and as such it presents a big problem for negationists.

In the 1970s, Faurisson decided to tackle and neutralize the evidentiary value of the Kremer diary. In a 50-page essay entitled "Professor of Medicine Johann Paul Kremer Faces the Horrors Caused by Typhus in Auschwitz during September and October 1942,"[155] Faurisson tried to show that Kremer's diary proved not that Auschwitz had been a place where Germans murdered Jews; rather, he argued it merely proved that Auschwitz was a place where epidemics killed people. In other words, the diary proved that Auschwitz may have been a place where many people died, but it was not a factory of death. Thus Kremer, the apparent witness for the prosecution, became the witness for the defense—of the Nazis, that is.

Faurisson's article began with a 2-page introduction about the prevalence of exanthematous typhus during the Second World War and the German inability to suppress it. "Neither the Germans nor the English killed in Bergen-Belsen; typhus killed: first and foremost typhus, but also other related epidemics caused by malnutrition."[156] I will forego the task of analyzing Faurisson's exculpating language, with the suggested equivalence between the inability of the German jailers to stop the epidemic in a concentration camp of their making and the inability of the English liberators to immediately stop the ravaging effects of the disease after they had taken over the camp. Instead, I will concentrate on Faurisson's textual analysis of Kremer's diary. The first observation one can make is that Faurisson's approach was wrought with contradiction. Following his own principles of textual exegesis, Faurisson completely discarded any testimony given in Cracow—that is, any external evidence given by the author of the diary that helped to elucidate his own text. Yet, at the same time, Faurisson was happy to provide an exegesis of various diary entries to establish that Dr. Kremer was first of all a decent scientist. For example, on January 13, 1943, Kremer wrote that the Nazis had gagged science. "The situation in Germany today is no better than in the times when Galileo was forced to recant and when science was threatened by tortures and the stake. Where, for Heaven's sake, is this situation going to lead us in the twentieth century!!! I could almost feel ashamed to be a German."[157] Faurisson happily quoted these lines as a character reference but remarkably failed to provide the context for Kremer's observation on the state of science in Germany: his failure to obtain a well-paid academic chair which meant that, at the age of fifty-nine, he would remain stuck at the bottom end of the academic hierarchy.[158] Given this context, it is clear that, without any further corroboration, his rant cannot be taken as convincing evidence for his integrity as a scientist.

Having constructed Kremer's moral universe, Faurisson ventured to reconstruct the circumstances of his time in Auschwitz. Kremer had arrived in Auschwitz in the midst of a typhus epidemic. After quoting the various references in Kremer's diary to typhus, Faurisson tried to "neutralize" Kremer's entries that mentioned outright murder. The most problematic one was, of course, the entry of September 2 which mentioned that he attended "a special action at 3 A.M. By comparison Dante's inferno seems almost a comedy. Auschwitz is justly called an extermination camp!"[159] Considering the original German, Faurisson attempted to turn the meaning of the entry from the obvious to the opposite.

> *Zum 1. Male draussen um 3 Uhr früh bei einer Sonderaktion zugegen. Im Vergleich hierzu erscheint mir das Dante'sche Inferno fas wie eine Komödie. Umsonst wird Auschwitz nicht das Lager der Vernichtung genannt.*[160]

Faurisson noted that the adverb "*draussen*" ("outside") and the personal pronoun "*mir*" ("to me") were of crucial significance. Furthermore Kremer identified Auschwitz as "*das lager der Vernichtung*" ("the camp of extermination") and not as "an extermination camp." Hence he translated the entry as follows:

> September 2, 1942. Was present for the first time **outside** at a special action at 3 A.M. By comparison Dante's inferno seems **to me** almost a comedy. Auschwitz is justly called **the camp of extermination!**

All of this made a tremendous difference, according to Faurisson. "Special Actions," so he claimed, were usually interpreted as gassings. Yet Kremer said that he participated in a special action that took place outside. Hence it could not refer to a gassing, since the Germans gassed people inside.[161] Then there was the issue of the term "*Vernichtung*" and the fact that Kremer called Auschwitz "the camp of extermination." This, Faurisson claimed, did not refer to what legend knows as "an extermination camp" but to "a camp in which extermination occurs."

To understand the entry of September 2, Faurisson claimed, it was necessary to put it in the context of the entries of September 1 and September 3.

> September 1, 1942. Have ordered SS officer's cap, sword-belt and brace from Berlin by letter. In the afternoon was present at the gassing of a block with Cyclon B against lice.
> September 2, 1942. Was present for the first time at a special action at 3 A.M. By comparison Dante's inferno seems almost a comedy. Auschwitz is justly called an extermination camp!
> September 3, 1942. Was for the first time taken ill with the diarrhoea which attacks everybody in the camp here. Vomiting and colic-like paroxysmal pains. Water did not cause it as I had not drunk any. Neither was it the bread. People who take white bread only (diet) also fall ill. Most probably it is the unhealthy tropical climate, very dry and tropically hot, with clouds of dust and insects (flies).[162]

This context made it clear, Faurisson argued, that the entry of September 2 should be considered within the context of the epidemic, referred to obliquely in the entry of September 1 as the delousing of a barrack with Zyklon B, which kills the primary hosts of the typhus virus: lice. There is a description of the effects of illness in the entry of September 3. Thus the entry of September 2 ought be read as referring to an event related to the epidemic. Noting that Kremer had not provided the potentially incriminating term *Sonderaktion* within quotation marks, Faurisson observed that this was absolutely appropriate because the term *Sonderaktion* routinely occurred in German military vocabulary.

> The real work of professor of medicine Johann Paul Kremer at Auschwitz is his laboratory research on all kinds of diseases, especially typhus. But at times he is also asked to participate in special actions: assist in taking charge of a transport, in solving some difficulty, at the sorting of the ill in the hospital wards, and so on. I believe to know that, in the French army, all extra efforts, which are not really covered within one's normal duties, carry the pompous name *"mission exceptionelle"* (special mission), the word "mission" denoting a "task" without necessarily implying an idea of movement. At three o'clock in the morning, Dr. Kremer is asked for a special action that takes place "outside" (*draussen*), which means that there are also special actions that take place "inside" (*drinnen*). It is a pity that we cannot precisely establish what this action was, but we know it was horrible, at least in his eyes. . . . One always claims that this special action concerned the arrival of a convoy from Drancy. That is not impossible. In fact, a convoy from Drancy arrived in Auschwitz on September 2, 1942. One should verify the hour of arrival. It is not difficult to imagine the arrival of those people who were not affected by the epidemic in a camp that has fallen prey to typhus. The task of the doctor was not only to separate those fit to work from those who are unfit. . . . It is also necessary to find billets for the arrivals in the barracks in the camp. Or always, or almost always, there are at the place of arrival ill people and people who are on the verge of death. One should imagine the crowding. To assist with that for many hours, sometimes in the middle of the night, sometimes at dawn, sometimes during the day, that must have been Dantesque. One may imagine the terrible anxiety of those who arrive in that hell. . . . After the war, in a similar fashion, the German populations deported from the East, who were discreetly referred to as "displaced persons," were also crammed in overpopulated camps ravaged by epidemics.[163]

Thus ends Faurisson's "debunking" of Kremer's diary entry of September 2. The only other trump card he has not shown yet, but which he will produce close to the end of his essay, is the final "proof" that with the words "Dante's Inferno" he referred to a hell caused by typhus. After all, in a letter he wrote back home on October 21, he announced that he did not know for certain but that he expected "to be back in Münster before December 1, so that I will have definitively turned my back to this hell Auschwitz, where now not only typhus and so on reigns, but also typhoid fever."[164] And Faurisson triumphantly exclaimed:

> Here then that "inferno of Dante" of his entry of 2 September 1942! Professor of medicine Johann Paul Kremer has seen the horrors of a massive epidemic *destroying* in Auschwitz both prisoners and guards: he has never seen the monstrous gassing operations meant to exterminate human beings.[165]

So much for the application of the "Ajax method" to history.

I will not deal with his attempt to negate the plain meaning of some of the other entries; instead, I will move straight to the entry of October 12.

> October 12, 1942. The second inoculation against typhus; strong reaction in the evening (fever). In spite of this was present at night at another special action with a draft from Holland (1,600 persons). Horrible scene in front of the last bunker! (Hössler!) This was the 10th special action.[166]

> *2. Schutzimpfung gegen Typhus; danach abends starke Allgemeinreaktion (Fieber). Trotzdem in der Nacht noch bei einer Sonderaktion aus Holland (1600 personen) zugegen. Schauerliche Szene vor dem letzten Bunker (Hössler)! Das war die 10. Sonderaktion.*[167]

Faurisson attached great significance to the fact that the German text did say "*Sonderaktion aus Holland (1600 Personen).*" It is, admittedly, rather awkward in German: "Special Action from Holland (1600 persons)." To make it grammatically correct one needs to add between "Special Action" and "from" something like "of a draft" or "of a group of people." Yet this commonsense interpretation of Kremer's shorthand notation did not satisfy Faurisson's sense of the possible. He brazenly proposed that the preposition "*aus*" referred to the German nouns of "*Auswahl*" or "*Auslehse,*" synonyms of "*Selektion,*" selection. The verb "to choose from" is "*auswählen*" or "*auslesen*" in German. On the basis of this tenuous link he proposed that the text referred to "a simple medical selection (to separate those fit for work and those unfit for work; or also, in that situation, the sick and the healthy; or the contagious and the not-contagious) enacted on a group of 1,600 people."[168]

After much thought, the logic of Faurisson's interpretation still eludes me, even if it was not without precedent: in 1949, in the Kravchenko trial, historian Jean Bruhat had employed this kind of philological reasoning to whitewash the Soviet regime. "The Purges of the Bolshevik Party," he testified, "present absolutely no mystery."

> Every Soviet citizen who joins the Bolshevik Party knows that by entering it, he undertakes a certain number of responsibilities. And no one compels him to be a member of the Bolshevik Party. Among other obligations, he must accept this one, which is to account publicly at any moment for his activity. That is what is called a Purge.[169]

Faurisson had no difficulty neutralizing the obvious reading of the sentence "Horrible scene in front of the last bunker!" by arguing that it referred to the situation at either Bunker 1 or Bunker 2 in Birkenau, the converted cottages that served as gas chambers until the completion of the four new crematoria in the spring of 1943. Completely ignoring the fact that both the SS and the inmates referred in common parlance to those extermination installations as "bunkers," Faurisson stated that the true meaning of the sentence must be obvious to "anyone who knows the topography of the Auschwitz camp." And with that he led us to a place more than two miles away from Bunkers 1 and 2.

> The "last bunker" cannot be but the bunker at the end of the camp, the famous bunker no. 11 that houses the prison of the camp, very far from the place where the deportees disembarked (the railway platforms that also served as the place of selection).

It is in front of that bunker (exactly between bunker 10 and 11) that the place of executions was located.[170]

The problem, of course, is that while Faurisson may have claimed to know the topography of the camp, he showed himself wholly ignorant of the nomenclature. The buildings he referred to, the camp prison and the adjacent barrack with the execution place in between, are, were, and always have been known as "Block 11" and "Block 10," not "Bunker 11" and "Bunker 10." The noun "bunker" referred in camp jargon either to the two cottages (1 and 2, or perhaps "the first" and "the last") that served as gas chambers or, after the completion of Crematoria 2, 3, 4 and 5, it referred to their gas chambers. In the latter instance, this was because these gas chambers took over the function of the "bunkers."

Of course, Faurisson would not look at external evidence to guide his interpretation. Yet if he had chosen to do so, he could, for example, have found in the testimony of Shlomo Dragon a precise description of the situation at the "last bunker."

> We were taken into a forest where there was a brick cottage covered with thatch; its windows were bricked in. On the doors to the interior of the cottage was a metal plate with the inscription "Hochspannung—Lebensgefahr" ("High Voltage—Danger"). Two wooden barracks were at 30 or 40 meters distance. On the other side of the cottage were four pits 30 meters long, 7 meters wide and 3 meters deep. The edges of these pits were burned and blackened. . . . I was detailed with 11 others in a group which, as we learned later, was to remove the bodies from this cottage. We were all given masks, and were led through the door into the cottage. Moll opened the door, and only then could we see that the cottage was full of naked corpses of both sexes and all ages. Moll ordered us to remove these corpses from the cottage through the door to the yard.[171]

Dragon testified that sometimes he was assigned to help undress ill people. At those times he witnessed how, after all had been driven into the cottage, the doors were closed, and how SS-Rottenführer Steinmetz collected a tin of Zyklon B from a Red Cross van, donned a gas mask, opened it, threw it through one of the windows, closed the window, and carried the tin back to the van.[172]

If Faurisson missed Dragon's account, he certainly should have been able to consult the account of Pery Broad, as it had been published by the time he began his investigation. The Broad report corroborated Dragon's account of the Birkenau extermination installations, those "innocuous looking farmhouses, the 'bunkers' as those gas chambers were generally called."[173] Fearful of external evidence, Faurisson stayed away from Dragon and Broad and the many other testimonies that describe the operation of the bunkers in excruciating detail. Ignorant of context, he soldiered on, with his only compass the linguistic insights offered by his "Ajax method." Persistence paid off. After many years of work, he finally was able in late 1978 to make his epochal announcement in *Le Monde* that Kremer's testimony had always been wrongly interpreted.

> The physician Johann Paul Kremer's diary should be quoted correctly. It will thus be observed that when he speaks about the horrors of Auschwitz, it is an allusion to the typhus epidemic of September–October 1942. On October 3, he wrote: "At Ausch-

witz, whole streets have been annihilated by typhus." He himself
would contract what he calls "the Auschwitz disease." Germans
would die of it. The sorting out of the ill from the healthy was the
"selection" or one of the forms of the "special action" performed
by the physician. The sorting out took place either within buildings or outdoors. Never did he write that Auschwitz was a
Vernichtungslager, that is, according to a terminology developed
by the Allies after the war, an "extermination camp" (by which
we are to understand a camp endowed with a gas chamber). In
reality, what he wrote was: "It is not for nothing that Auschwitz
is called the camp of annihilation (*das Lager der Venichtung*)." In
the etymological sense of the word, typhus annihilates those
whom it strikes. Another seriously mistaken quotation: for the
date of September 2, 1942, Kremer's manuscript reads: "This
morning, I was present, outdoors, for the first time, at a special
action." Historians and magistrates customarily suppress the
word "outdoors (*draussen*)" in order to have Kremer say that the
action took place in a "gas chamber." Finally, the atrocious scenes
in front of the "last bunker" (this was the courtyard of Bunker 11)
were executions of prisoners sentenced to death, executions the
physician was obliged to attend. Among those sentenced were
three women who had arrived in a convoy from Holland.[174]

This passage received the reply it deserved in Pierre Vidal-Naquet's
brilliant essay "Un Eichmann de papier" ("A Paper Eichmann"). Vidal-
Naquet characterized Faurisson's method as "the Art of Not Reading
Texts," and in his comment on Faurisson's interpretation of Kremer's diary, Vidal-Naquet amply demonstrated that, unlike Faurisson, he understood the art of reading texts. For example, about Faurisson's discussion of
the all-important distinction between *Vernichtungslager* and *das Lager der
Vernichtung,* Vidal-Naquet wrote that "the fact that Auschwitz was the
Lager der Vernichtung has no relation to typhus epidemics."

> Indeed, Faurisson, who is so concerned with precision when it
> comes to translation, did not perceive that Kremer, in speaking of
> typhus, did not use the verb *vernichten.* He wrote on October 3,
> "In Auschwitz whole streets have been stricken down by typhus
> (*In Auschwitz liegen ganze Strassenzüge an Typhus darnieder*)."
> The difference in verbs (*darniederliegen* instead of *vernichten*) is
> significant, and Faurisson allowed himself to be fooled by the
> translation of the Polish publisher. Finally, a detail which I men-
> tion to show how Faurisson reads texts: it is false that Kremer had
> typhus and that what he called the Auschwitz illness is typhus.
> The indications in the diary for September 3, 4 and 14, show
> clearly that the Auschwitz illness is diarrhea with a moderate
> fever (37.8 degrees C. on September 14). Kremer was, in fact,
> vaccinated against (exanthematic) typhus and against typhoid
> fever. Faurisson's interpretation is thus not admissible, and the
> explanation—so dear to those revisionists, like Butz, prepared to
> admit that there was a lot of dying in Auschwitz—of the death
> rates at Auschwitz by typhus stands condemned along with it.
> One must return to what is to be learned from the camp archives
> and from Kremer's confessions: that the "special actions" corre-
> spond to the arrival of convoys of deportees (who were, as a rule,
> duly registered in the camp archives); that deportees not enrolled

in the camp were gassed in the bunkers of Birkenau (small houses located in the forest); that those suffering from illnesses in the camp (and specifically from typhus) as well as male and female "Muslims" were also gassed; and that at the last moment, there were occasionally painful scenes, such as that of October 18, 1942, with three "young and healthy" Dutch women who "did not want to enter the gas chamber and cried to save their lives" and who were shot, scenes that disturbed the SS-imposed order.

When Kremer spoke of *the* camp of annihilation, he was not, it is true, referring to a juridico-administrative concept, which did not figure, as is also true, on the official rolls of the Third Reich. He was simply speaking about what he saw. On the level he most cherishes, that of philological precision and accurate translation, Faurisson's interpretation is incoherent; on the level of intellectual ethics and scientific probity, it is bogus.[175]

Despite Vidal-Naquet's sensible response, just enough people were convinced by Faurisson's arguments to enable the "Faurisson Affair" to take off, which in turn created the causal chain that was to bring Leuchter to the crematoria in Auschwitz, Irving to the District Court in Toronto, and myself to the Royal Courts of Justice in London.

In the foregoing pages I reviewed a negationist attempt to "turn" an eyewitness. The only reason, of course, that Faurisson had any hope of success was the fact that Kremer had died by the time the French scholar began the hermeneutical attack on his diary. If Kremer had lived and been confronted with Faurisson's interpretation, the German physician, who would have been 90 years old in 1978, would probably not have understood what Faurisson was up to, and if he did, he would have tried to stay out of it. But when pressed by journalists, he would probably have referred them to his Cracow testimony. In other words, if Kremer had lived, his explanation of his diary would have had greater authority than the conclusion Faurisson reached through the application of his "Ajax method" to the text, and Kremer would have been considered an eyewitness no different from Höss or Broad or, for that matter, Dragon or Tauber. The only reason that Faurisson had any hope of pulling off his feat of interpretation were the facts that Kremer was dead and that his eyewitness testimony was, in fact, a wartime document that could be interpreted as a piece of "non-intentional" evidence. While the diary was a record of Kremer's observations as an eyewitness, it was not meant to serve as testimony. Only his death had changed the epistemological status of the diary.

Negationists prefer dead texts over live witnesses because the SS men who were tried for their participation in the exterminations in Auschwitz generally lived up to their own pasts. In 1978, the year that Faurisson made his findings about Kremer public, journalist Ebbo Demnant interviewed in a German prison Josef Klehr, a former SS guard in Auschwitz. At one point in the interview, Demnant confronted Klehr with the negationist argument that in Auschwitz Jews were never gassed. Klehr had heard about such arguments.

Jews never gassed? No? Yes, I have already been asked about that. . . . Three elderly ladies come to visit us here. That is such an official society. They always want to support us a little bit, to give us a present on our birthdays, and so on, and one of them asked me once if people were gassed in Auschwitz? I said—I will tell you openly and honestly, but if it were someone else, I would have answered that I did not know. But because it is you, I will tell you precisely, that people were gassed. And anyone who maintains that there are no gassing. . . . Yes, I don't understand him, he must be crazy or on the wrong. . . . When you are three, four years in Auschwitz and experienced everything, then I cannot get myself to lie about it and say that no gassings were conducted.[176]

Ten years later, German filmmaker Bernhard Frankfurter interviewed Hans-Wilhelm Münch, a former SS doctor in Auschwitz who was acquitted by the Cracow tribunal. Münch described the selections and gassings in detail. When asked about the negationist argument that Auschwitz is a hoax, Münch responded wearily.

When someone tells that Auschwitz is a lie, that it is a hoax, I feel hesitation to say much to him. I say, the facts are so firmly determined, that one cannot have any doubt at all, and I stop talking to that person because it has no use. One knows that anyone who clings to such things, which are published somewhere, is a malevolent person who has some personal interest to want to bury in silence things that cannot be buried in silence.[177]

In my report, I did not present the evidence given by Klehr or the other defendants in the Auschwitz Trial at Frankfurt (1961–1964) or Münch's descriptions of Auschwitz. My aim was to provide a reconstruction of how knowledge of Auschwitz had emerged, and 1947 was a good date to stop. It was clear that Crowell's version that gassing claims arose from a combination of delusion and censorship is not credible. Auschwitz was not the product of intertextuality. It was not a hystory, but history. In my report, I made clear that limiting my account to a five-year period (1942–1947) did not imply that no important "intentional" evidence emerged after 1947. To the contrary: after having recovered from their camp experience, many survivors would write down their memoirs, and some of them would provide details about the killing procedures not known before. In addition, the Eichmann trial in Jerusalem (1961), the Auschwitz Trial in Frankfurt, and the Dejaco-Ertl trial in Vienna (1971) generated important historical material. But there is no doubt that with the memoirs of Höss the historiographical "house" Höss built in Auschwitz acquired a roof that made it, at least metaphorically, rainproof. While construction continued, and still continues, the changes made in our understanding of the history of Auschwitz have been, in essence, no more than the historiographical equivalents of building some additions (most of the studies published in the *Hefte von Auschwitz* fall in this category), upgrading the kitchens and bathrooms (Pressac's work may be considered here), and laying out a new garden (our own *Auschwitz: 1270 to the Present*).

In other words, as far as eyewitness evidence is concerned, I wrote that it was not necessary to look beyond 1947. In my conclusion of this part of the report, I stated that by early 1947, there was a massive amount of evidence of the use of the camp as a site for mass extermination.

This evidence had become slowly available during the war as the result of reports by escaped inmates, had become more substantial through the eyewitness accounts by former Auschwitz inmates immediately after their liberation in Auschwitz and other concentration camps, and was confirmed in the Polish forensic investigations undertaken in 1945 and 1946. Finally, this evidence was corroborated by confessions of leading German personnel employed at Auschwitz during its years of operation.

It is, in other words, highly implausible that knowledge about Auschwitz was a wartime fabrication by British propagandists. Instead, the material brought together in Part Two shows that knowledge about Auschwitz emerged cumulatively from a convergence of independent accounts, acquiring an epistemological status located somewhere in the realm framed on the one hand by a judgment that knows a fact "beyond reasonable doubt," and on the other hand by the always receding horizon that promises unqualified certainty. In short, it has become possible, on the basis of the material presented and discussed so far, to assert as "moral certainty" the statement that Auschwitz was an extermination camp where the Germans killed around one million people with the help of gas chambers.

It was clear that, apart from making an attempt to discredit Vaillant-Couturier and Höss, Irving had not engaged this evidence before making statements such as the one that Auschwitz was "baloney" and "a legend." At the lecture he gave in Calgary in September 1991, he addressed eyewitness testimony straight on.

> And all the old stories are coming about, out again, about the eyewitnesses and all the vilification is starting again. And how do you explain the hundreds of thousands of eye-witnesses in Auschwitz? And I say, "Well, the existence of hundred of thousands of eye-witnesses from Auschwitz is in itself proof that there was no dedicated programme to kill them all." And anyway, as for eye-witnesses I'm inclined to go along with the Russian proverb, recently quoted by Julian Barnes, the novelist in a novel that he published called *Talking it Over*. And he quotes the Russian proverb which is: "He lies like an eye-witness, he lies like an eye-witness."[178]

A few minutes later he came back to the subject when he mentioned that the Austrian police had issued an arrest warrant against him for having said that "the eye-witnesses to the gassings in Auschwitz are an interesting case for the psychiatrists."

> I'm not implying that they've got a mental problem, I'm implying that it's an interesting psychological phenomenon that people over a period of years begin kidding themselves that they have seen something. And the more they come to have taken part in a traumatic experience themselves, the more they are persuaded that they were right centre stage. They are the bride at every funeral and the corpse at every wedding, I think somebody once said.[179]

Having refused to give serious consideration to the testimonies of Dragon, Tauber, Broad, and Höss, it is clear that Rampton was not out of line when, on January 19, 2000, he reminded Irving that "a man in your position does not enter the arena waving flags and blowing trumpets unless he has taken the trouble to verify in advance what it is that he is proposing to say, particularly when what he is proposing to say is something of great sensitivity and importance to millions of people throughout the world."

Five

"Witnesses Despite Themselves"

When I began writing my expert opinion, I realized that while Irving might try to attack the credibility of the testimonies given by eyewitnesses after the war, the major engagement would concern what Bloch had labeled "non-intentional evidence," or the "evidence of witnesses despite themselves."[1] I expected that during my cross-examination Irving would try to argue on the basis of analysis of the remaining ruins of the crematoria, wartime German documents, English radio intercepts, and aerial photos taken by American bombers that the position he had adopted in a Toronto courtroom in 1988 was perfectly reasonable and that therefore his endorsement and publication of the Leuchter Report could not be seen as a proof of Lipstadt's charge that, familiar with historical evidence, he had manipulated it until it conformed with his ideological leanings and political agenda.[2] First of all, the crumbling concrete, the traces of cyanide, the archival documentation (including both documents and photographs) of the construction process, the SS messages about the mortality in Auschwitz, and the reconnaissance shots would be the focus of attention because they provided the raw material for the negationist case that Auschwitz had not been an extermination camp. This would be understandable because the negationists could not rely on eyewitness evidence to make their case. To be sure, two Germans had come forward in the 1970s claiming that they could offer eyewitness evidence that Auschwitz could not have been an extermination camp. One of them was, as we have seen, Wilhlem Stäglich. While he served with an anti-aircraft battery unit near Auschwitz, he had visited the main camp a few times; he reported that "on none of these visits did I see gassing installations, crematoria, instruments of torture, or similar horrors."[3] A second witness, Thies Christophersen, had served for a short time at one of the agricultural satellite camps of Auschwitz. In 1973, Christophersen published a booklet entitled *Die Auschwitz Lüge* (*The Auschwitz Lie*). "I was in Auschwitz from January to December 1944," Christophersen wrote. "After the war I heard about the alleged mass murders of Jews and I was quite taken aback. Despite all the testimony submitted and all the reports in the media, I know such atrocities were never committed."[4] His certainty derived from the fact that his wife was allowed to visit him. "Had Auschwitz been the death factory it is reputed to have been, such visits would certainly not have been permitted."[5] When confronted with the argument that the killings took place in Birkenau, Christophersen recalled that he had once visited Birkenau. "This camp I did not like," he admitted. "It was overcrowded and the people there did not make a good impression on me. Everything looked neglected and grubby. I also saw families with children. It hurt to see them, but I was told that the authorities felt it kinder not to separate children from their parents when the latter were interned." And he knew everything about selections, because he had conducted such selections himself—to find workers for his farm. "This 'selection' was later completely misinterpreted," he claimed. "The purpose was to give the inmates something to do and they themselves wanted to be occupied. Selecting them meant no more than to inquire about their inclinations, their capabilities, and their physical state of health with regard to the work they were to do."[6] When he heard rumors about crematoria, Christophersen asked his Polish maid Olga about them. "She could not tell me anything either." Then he asked his colleagues, but they responded with "a shrug of the shoulder and 'don't pay any attention to those rumors.'"[7] That settled the issue.

Negationists hailed Christophersen's account as "one of the most important documents for a re-appraisal of Auschwitz," because it added to the "mounting collection of evidence" that showed that "the giant industrial complex of Auschwitz" had not been "a place of 'mass extermination.'"[8] But for all their praise, the fact remained that one or two Germans who had come in contact only with peripheral functions of Auschwitz and who claimed that they had not seen any extermination installations did not even begin to challenge the preponderance of eyewitness evidence claiming that such installations had existed and operated. Apart from that, the testimonies of Stäglich and Christophersen were unlikely to change the minds of serious historians who are taught to avoid the fallacy of negative proof—which means that a factual proposition (for example "Auschwitz was not an extermination camp . . .") cannot be proven merely by negative evidence (". . . because both Mr. Stäglich and Mr. Christophersen did not see killings taking place").

With regard to eyewitnesses, the obvious choice for negationists was to dismiss all eyewitness evidence as irrelevant and turn to the brick, cyanide traces, documents, and photos that cannot protest attempts to manipulate, misconstrue, and falsify. In each of these instances of "non-intentional" evidence, they have had only two choices. The first was to commit the fallacy of negative proof. Irving took this road when he claimed on various occasions that it was clear that Auschwitz was not purposefully operated as an extermination camp because there are no official German wartime documents that prove that Auschwitz was purposefully conceived and operated as an extermination camp. To some extent, Leuchter used the same approach when he claimed that the morgues of the crematoria did not function as gas chambers because there are only negligible traces of cyanide in the walls. Neither argument is legitimate because every historian knows that most evidence does not survive and that the reconstruction of any historical event is based on accidentally preserved relics, which, in this case, may or may not be a document or significant traces of cyanide. Because the variety of historical evidence is infinite, one should not expect that a particular historical question can be proved only by one particular piece of evidence. This explains why the issue of negative evidence is so problematic.

The other option for negationists is to follow Faurisson's "turning" of Kremer's diary, described in the last chapter, and argue that what seem to be clear-cut German wartime documents that attest to the presence and operation of homicidal gas chambers have, in fact, a more innocent meaning. In the case of Auschwitz, the most important wartime documents available to us come from the archive of the Auschwitz Central Construction Office. When the Germans burned the archives of the camp Kommandantur prior to their evacuation from Auschwitz in January 1945, the archive of the construction office, some three hundred yards away from the Kommandantur, was overlooked and remained intact. The reason that the SS forgot it was simple: the construction office had been closed for some time and no one was left in the building, so no one warned the men charged with the destruction of the evidence that the office contained much architectural material that could be incriminating. And so the building archive survived.

Construction at Auschwitz, both in the concentration camp and in the town, was subject to normal civilian procedures as well as to the wartime superstructure of special permissions. Multiple copies of many documents survive with the comments and signatures of the individual bureaucrats or businessmen to whom they were sent. The Building Office generated a wide paper trail: plans, budgets, letters, telegrams, contractors' bids, financial negotiations, worksite labor reports, requests for allocations of material, and the minutes of meetings held in the Building Office among the architects themselves, with camp officials, and with high-ranking dignitaries from Berlin.

As a source of historical material, the archives of the Central Construction Office are very important. But it is also important to remember that during the war the architects who produced the documents that are part of that archive were told to apply self-censorship when writing things down that related to the genocide in the camp. On January 21, 1972, architect Fritz Ertl, who had been employed at the Auschwitz Construction Office until early 1943, testified in court in Vienna about the genocidal use of the crematoria. The first time that he was informed about the use of Auschwitz in the Final Solution was in the summer of 1942.

Fritz Ertl. Courtesy Berlin Document Center.

Then I talked with an employee of the Political Department who was in private life a judge. He then told me something. Normally one would not have dared to talk while on duty, because one had to fear to be punished for that. . . . This judge has enlightened me. That must have been in the summer of 1942. He came from Hamburg and later fell on the front. Auschwitz, so he told me, is an extermination camp. Many people were to be executed, that means condemned by courts-martial. Then he indicated through reference to the Jewish Problem that larger exterminations were to come. He counseled me to find ways to quickly get out. He himself left somewhat later, and fell in Russia. This statement was for me a warning, I was shocked and enraged. This conversation took place at the time that construction began of the crematoria. This I used as an occasion to ask for a transfer. Bischoff yelled at me and told me that he was not prepared to consider this.[9]

A little later Ertl commented that the new crematoria were necessary "because of the special actions."[10] When asked if he knew what the word "special measures" meant, Ertl told the court that he knew the significance.[11] Then Ertl commented on a letter that had already attracted the attention of Professor Dawidowski in 1945, which was submitted under number NO-4473 as evidence in the Nuremberg Trials. The letter was written on January 29, 1943, by the Chief Architect of the camp, Karl Bischoff, to his superior, the Chief of the SS Building Department in Berlin, Hans Kammler. It concerned the progress of construction of Crematorium 2. In an earlier letter, Bischoff had promised that the crematorium would be completed on January 31. Now he had to break the news to his boss that he would not been able to deliver on his promise.

29 January 1943

Karl Bischoff. Courtesy Berlin Document Center.

To the Chief Amtsgruppe C, SS-Brigadeführer and General-Major of the Waffen-SS, Dr. Ing. Kammler.
Subject: Crematorium II, condition of the building.

The crematorium has been completed—save for minor constructional work—by the use of all the forces available, in spite of unspeakable difficulties, the severe cold, and in 24 hour shifts. The fires were started in the ovens in the presence of Senior Engineer Prüfer, representative of the contractors of the firm of Topf and Sons, Erfurt, and they are working most satisfactorily. The planks from the concrete ceiling of the cellar used as a mortuary could not yet be removed on account of the frost. This is, however, not very important, as the gassing cellar [*Vergasungskeller*] can be used for that purpose.

The firm of Topf and Sons was not able to start deliveries of the installation in time for aeration and ventilation as had been requested by the Central Building Management because of restrictions in the use of railroad cars. As soon as the installation for aeration and ventilation arrive, the installing will start so that the complete installation may be expected to be ready for use 20 February 1943.

We enclose a report of the testing engineer of the firm Topf and Sons, Erfurt:

The Chief of the Central Construction Management,
Waffen-SS and Police Auschwitz,
SS-Hauptsturmführer

[Bischoff]

Distribution: 1 - SS Ustuf Janisch and Kirschneck
1 - Filing office (file crematorium)

Certified true copy:

[signature] SS-Ustuf (F)

To Dawidowski, and anyone else who has considered the letter in its historical context, the meaning of the text is quite clear when one compares it with a plan of the basement of Crematorium 2. The basement plan shows two large spaces indicated as "Leichenkeller," or morgues. Originally designed as spaces to store corpses, the smaller of the two morgues, Leichenkeller 1, was transformed during its construction into a gas chamber. The second morgue, Leichenkeller 2, initially was meant to function both as a morgue and an undressing room, but it quickly was fully committed to the latter purpose. The letter thus mentions that there are problems with completing Leichenkeller 2 and that therefore the gas chamber—formerly Leichenkeller 1—would have to serve (temporarily) its original purpose and store corpses.

Historiographically, Bischoff's letter is important because it violated the general policy in the architectural office in the camp never to use the term "gas chamber" in documents or blueprints. The letter was drawn up hastily in response to an urgent request from Berlin for information on the progress of construction, and Bischoff did not notice the "slip." When the letter was archived in the crematorium dossier of the Auschwitz Zentralbauleitung, however, someone did, and marked the forbidden word "*Vergasungskeller*" with a red pencil, writing on the top of the letter the words "SS-Ustuf (F) Kirschneck!" It was clear that Kirschneck was responsible for the slip and should be told of it.[12]

In his testimony given on January 21, 1972, Ertl was confronted with the letter. He said that he had not seen it.

> At this time I was not anymore in Auschwitz. In my personnel dossier it is recorded that I left Auschwitz on January 25, 1943. I did not get a copy of this letter.
>
> The only names it is copied to are "Janisch" and "Kirschneck."
>
> In this letter one talked quite openly, which is clear from the use "gassing basement."
>
> The reference sign is "Bischoff." I can imagine that he has written this himself. I had received the order of Bischoff that I could never write the word "gassing." I always had to circumscribe it.
>
> *Concerning the question of the chairman of the court if Bischoff had directly told Ertl that he could not write that, or if this order had come from higher up, the accused Ertl gave the following statement:*
>
> I believe that Bischoff pointed out to me, that the word "gassing" should not appear. It is also possible that once such an order has come from higher up. I can't remember that now. However, because this word "gassing" was always circumscribed, with "special action" or "special measure," I am convinced that this was ordered. I am surprised that Bischoff used this word "gassing basement" himself. Because higher up always used the word "special action," I also used it so. I adopted that term.[13]

An important document in the archive confirms Ertl's statement about Bischoff's policy to use camouflage language. On August 19, 1942, Ertl chaired a meeting in which members of the Central Construction Office discussed with Engineer Kurt Prüfer of Topf & Sons the creation of four crematoria in Birkenau. Item 2 mentioned the construction of two triple-oven incinerators near the "bathhouses for special actions"—"*Badeanstalten für Sonderaktionen.*"[14] These were the gas chambers also known as

38

Bftgb.Nr. 13 115/42/Er/Ha.

Aktenvermerk

Betr.: Anwesenheit von Obering. Prüfer der Fa. Topf u. Söhne Erfurt, bezüglich Ausbau der Einäscherungsanlagen in K.G.L. Auschwitz

Vormerk: Herr Ing. Prüfer sprach am 19.8.1942 um 14,oo Uhr bei hiesiger Dienststelle vor, um über den Einbau von 5 Stück 3 Muffel-Einäscherungsöfen in Krematorium des K.G.L. und Neuanlage von 2 Stück 3 Muffelöfen in einfacher Bauweise lt. Plan Nr. D 59 - 570 und Nr. D 59 399 die erforderlichen Einzelheiten zu besprechen.

Hierbei wurde folgendes festgelegt:

1.) Spätestens 26. - 27. August trifft der Monteur Molik aus Buchenwald hier ein, der Monteur Koch in ca. 14 Tagen. Mit dem Aufbau der 5 Stück 3 Muffelöfen in K.G.L. wird sofort begonnen. Die Fa. Köhler-Myslowitz führt die Ausmauerung der Öfen und Fuchse sowie die Errichtung des Schornsteines lt. Plänen und Angaben der Fa. Topf u. Söhne durch.

2.) Bezüglich Aufstellung von je 2 Dreimuffelöfen bei den "Badeanstalten für Sonderaktionen" wurde von Ing. Prüfer vorgeschlagen, die Öfen aus einer bereits fertiggestellten Lieferung nach Mogilew abzuzweigen und wurde sogleich der Dienststellenleiter welcher beim SS-Wirtschafts-Verwaltungshauptamt in Berlin anwesend war, hiervon tel. in Kenntnis gesetzt und gebeten, das weitere veranlassen zu wollen.

3.) Bezüglich Errichtung eines 2. Krematoriums mit 5 Dreimuffelöfen, sowie Be- und Entlüftungsanlagen muß erst das Ergebnis der bereits laufenden Verhandlungen mit dem Reichssicherheitshauptamt bezgl. Zuteilung von Kontingenten abgewartet werden.

- 2 -

(13)

Bunkers 1 and 2. Ertl testified in court that when he wrote down the words "bathhouses for special actions" he knew exactly what this euphemism meant. "I knew at the time, that this concerned gassing spaces."[15]

In October 1990, Irving discussed Bischoff's letter in a speech entitled "The Controversy on Auschwitz and the Dangers of Censorship." He recalled that when he had testified two years earlier in Toronto, Crown Attorney Pearson had presented him with this letter.

> One of these documents was thrown on the wall in the courtroom at Toronto where I was giving evidence. And I have to admit I had not seen the document before, and I was a bit flabbergasted, but I looked at the document and the prosecuting counsel said, "Mr. Irving, how do you explain this?" It is a letter written by the architect's office in Auschwitz to a firm of construction engineers saying they are having difficulty completing the concrete ceiling, which is going to be put in, the slab over the mortuary, before winter sets in and therefore they could perhaps use another room which they identified as the *Vergasungskeller*, a gassing cellar, if you want to translate it that way. And the prosecuting counsel said to me, "Mr. Irving, how do you explain that?" And I said straight away, "Well let me point out to you as a German linguist, and I have known German fluently for the last thirty or forty years, the word '*vergasen*' has various meanings like a lot of words in German have various meanings. '*Vergasen*' can mean to gas somebody. It can also mean to gasify, as in a carburetor." A carburetor in a motor car in Germany is *Vergaser*. And a crematorium would have a kind of carbureting system. Quite definitely, because you need very high temperatures to cremate. And this is quite definitely a document connected with the cremation process. And when the prosecuting counsel appeared a bit fazed by this particular suggestion, I said to him suddenly, I said, "Excuse me, can we have that document back on the screen again? Because I want to look at something, and point it out to the jury." And he put it back onto the screen. And I said, "There you are. I will tell you what is most significant in that document is not what it says, but what it does not say. We are being told by you, by the prosecution, this is a document concerning the gassing of millions of Jews, which was the most secret operation in the Third Reich apparently. So secret that almost nothing exists about it. Certainly nothing in the archives. Top secret. And yet here is a document that bears no kind of security classification at all." In short that was the proof that the document was totally innocuous. In fact it was of janitorial level I would say. Of janitorial level. Broom cupboard level.[16]

Like so many other statements he has made, Irving's account of his testimony about Bischoff's letter of January 29, 1943, is a mixture of fact and fiction. Irving stated in the lecture that he had never seen the document before. Yet the transcripts of the court proceedings reveal that Irving told Pearson that "I am familiar with the document and I was familiar with the document before I came to Toronto."[17] When asked by Pearson if he had any reason to question the authenticity of the letter, Irving answered he had not. Pearson never challenged Irving to explain to him the occurrence of the word *Vergasungskeller*. The twice-repeated "Mr. Irving, how do you explain this?" does not appear in the record. Instead, Pearson asked Irving if he thought the English translation was correct.

Memorandum of a meeting held at the Auschwitz Central Construction Office, August 19, 1942. Courtesy Archive Auschwitz-Birkenau State Museum, Oswiecim. (opposite page)

[Irving]: "It is a satisfactory translation apart from one sentence where—which is quite clearly the operative sentence, which says —I would translate it as 'This is, however unimportant, as the *Vergasungskeller.*'"

[Pearson]: "Let's put it up on the overhead to see what we're talking about. First of all, is this the original German?"

A.: "It is the same document."

Q.: "Document January 29th, 1943?"

A.: "It is the same document and I am referring to this sentence here, 'Die ist jedoch unbedeutend, da der *Vergasungskeller* hierfür benutzt werden kann.' I translate as 'This is, however, unimportant as the *Vergasungskeller* can be used for this,' and the German word *Vergasungskeller* is a noun coming from the German verb *Vergas[en],* and the German verb *Vergas[en],* like many German words, has different translations, some of them completely different in meaning from each other."

Q.: "All right."

A.: "It can mean gassing, it can mean '[carburetion],' as in the sense of a carburetor on a car and this is the meaning which I don't find, the alternative meaning in the translation of the document, the possibility that it refers not to gassing but to the 'carburetion' process in some kind of oil fire heater, so when we are looking at a *Vergasungskeller,* I think it is tendentious to translate it as gas chamber. I mentioned on Friday that a German—"

Q.: "What do you mean by tendentious?"

A.: "Tendentious? I think it is trying to arrive at an impression. It is giving possibly a deliberately wrong translation of the word. It is a possible translation but it is an unlikely translation because if a German was going to write the word 'gas chamber,' he would not write '*Vergasungskeller.*' He would write '*Gasungskeller.*'"[18]

This misrepresentation of the exchange between himself and Pearson suggests that Irving was dramatizing the event in order to depict himself as the champion who defeated another attack by the enemy. The rest of his account does not reflect the record. While Irving indeed asked Pearson to put the document back on the projection screen, he did not point out that the document was more significant for what it did not say, more significant for not containing the designation "(top) secret." Instead, Irving argued that because the letter referred in the reference line to a crematorium and because a crematorium is meant to incinerate corpses, by implication everything in the letter would refer to construction of elements required for the process of cremation alone.

[Pearson]: "Right, all right. So you agree that that translation, subject to the proviso that you've entered, is an accurate translation."

[Irving]: "Yes. I would draw attention to the translation of the first line. I'm sorry, you've removed the document. Could you possibly return it?"

Q.: "In English?"

A.: "The German document. I would draw attention to this line here, "*Betr.: Krematorium II. Bauzustand.*" That means this document is "Re: Krematorium No. II, construction status.""

Q.: "Right."

A.: "In other words this entire document refers to Krematorium No. 2, not to any other building or any other installation. Purely to the crematorium. I think that needs possibly to be underlined. I think this justifies me in suggesting that if we're looking for which of the alternative translations to look for this key word underlined here, *Vergasungskeller,* it is some piece of equipment to do with a crematorium process and not to do with any other process."

Q.: "What's the *Leichenkeller*?"

A.: "I beg your pardon?"

Q.: "What's—"

A.: "A *Leichenkeller,* a morgue."

Q.: "And that's in the crematorium complex, isn't it?"

A.: "It would indeed be."

Q.: "Right. And are you familiar with the plan of Crematorium 2 and 3 at Birkenau?"

A.: "If I could project one on the screen and we could look at it, that would answer your questions no doubt."

Q.: "Are you familiar?"

A.: "I'm sure you would have projected one on the screen if it would help us."

Q.: "You can't tell us what Crematorium 2 is, can you?"

A.: "I know what a crematorium is. And this document concerns a crematorium."

Q.: "And the only reason you say that is because it refers to Crematorium 2."

A.: "It says at the top quite specifically 're: Crematorium No. II, construction stage.'"

Q.: "And if Crematorium 2 referred to a complex which had within it undressing rooms, a *Leichenkeller* or gas chamber and a crematorium and all those three were referred to as Crematorium 2, it wouldn't be referring to just the crematorium part, would it?"

A.: "I'm sure if you had a plan suggesting that you would show it to the jury and that would save us a lot of time examining alternative translations of words."[19]

It is clear that Irving totally misrepresented the exchange in his lecture. Instead of addressing the issue that the document was not marked "(top) secret," he raised an altogether different issue: the fact that it referred to the construction of a crematorium and that hence nothing in this letter could apply to a gas chamber. Pearson, however, was not so easily caught. As he cross-examined Irving, he was able to make clear not only that Irving had no idea about the actual layout of the crematorium, but he was also able to make the simple point that in official correspondence a crematorium equipped with gas chambers would still be referred to as "crematorium." Thus, while Irving pretended to have brought new light to the issue, he in fact was shown to be uninformed about its meaning and context.

So much for Irving's credibility as an eyewitness. Let us now consider his qualities as a linguist. In his lecture, Irving claimed that as a "German linguist," he knew that the verb "*vergasen*" could mean not only "to gas somebody" but also "to gasify, as in a carburetor"—a translation which led to his speculation that the noun *Vergasungskeller* would have referred to "a kind of carbureting system" for the ovens. In his Toronto testimony, Irving declared that "if a German was going to write the word 'gas chamber,' he would not write '*Vergasungskeller.*' He would write '*Gasungskeller.*'" This was simply wrong. Wartime German documents show that the adjective *Vergasungs-* was commonly used to qualify means or procedures used in the gassing of people. For example, in the notorious letter of October 25, 1941, which Advisor for Jewish Affairs in the Ostministerium Dr. Erhard Wetzel drafted for Alfred Rosenberg, Wetzel mentions that "Oberdienstleiter Brack of the Führer's Chancellery has agreed to assist in the construction of the necessary buildings and gassing apparatus [*Vergasungsapparate*]. . . . In the present situation, there are no objections to getting rid of Jews who are unable to work with the Brack remedy."[20] The "gassing apparatus" was a gas van. In his memoirs, written after the war, Adolf Eichmann was to call these gas chambers on wheels "gassing cars" [*Vergasungswagen*].[21] And both Walther Dejaco and Fritz Ertl, testifying during their trial in 1972, used the term gassing spaces—*Vergasungsräume* —to denote gas chambers. For example, in his testimony given on January 19, 1972, Dejaco denied that he had transformed the morgue of crematorium 1 into a "gassing space."

> I have certainly not inserted a wall in crematorium 1. With this work I had, as I have already made clear, nothing to do. I did not know anything about the gassing space [*Vergasungsraum*]. I have not inserted any wall. . . . I did not know what went on behind my back. At this time one was of course very much concerned, that no one would know what was happening in Auschwitz. Therefore the Kommandantur will have done such work as the insertion of a wall in the crematorium or the purchase of the incineration ovens and the installation of gassing spaces [*Vergasungsräume*] on its own initiative. After all, no one should know what happened there.[22]

Ertl commented on January 21, 1972, that when he wrote in his report of August 19, 1942, about the so-called bathhouses for special actions— *Badeanstalten für Sonderaktionen,* he "knew at the time, that this concerned gassing spaces [*Vergasungsräume*]."[23] And if negative proof is worth anything, may it be noted that I have never found an example of Germans using the adjective *Gasung-* in the context of a discussion on the killing of people in gas chambers. Hence Irving's argument is incorrect. While indeed the word *Gaskammer* is more common when referring to a (homicidal) gas chamber, the common use of the adjective *Vergasungs-* in conjunction with a noun in the context of discussion on the gassing of people fully explains why Kirschneck, who had drafted the letter for Bischoff, would have formed the composite neologism *Vergasungskeller* when referring to a basement that was to function as a gas chamber.

In his lecture, Irving may have given the impression that his superior knowledge of German had allowed him to trump Pearson. But in fact, without mentioning his source, Irving had presented the court with one of the classic negationist attempts to discredit an important piece of documentary evidence. Irving's claim that the word *Vergasungskeller* referred to some carburetion process originated not in his own knowledge of German but in his digestion of Butz's *The Hoax of the Twentieth Century*. Butz was the first to argue that the noun *Vergasungskeller* did not refer to a gas chamber or, more precisely, gassing cellar, but to a carburetion room. He developed his theory in response to paragraph 7 of Höss's Nuremberg affidavit, in which Höss bragged how the Auschwitz "extermination plants" were superior to the killing installations of Treblinka. This allowed Butz to introduce Bischoff's letter, referred to by its Nuremberg number NO-4473.

The final subject in paragraph 7 is the gas chambers which, except for Hoess' early sealed-up huts, are supposed to have been integrated into the crematoria buildings. Reitlinger and Hilberg take different approaches to making this claim. Reitlinger interprets NO-4473, whose translation as it appears in the NMT volume is presented above (p. 116), as evidence for a gas chamber in crematorium II. This is a result of a mistranslation.

The crematoria at Auschwitz are frequently referred to as "gas ovens" but this is hardly informative since, with the exception of electric cremators which enjoyed a brief existence during the Thirties, all modern crematoria consist of "gas ovens"; a fuel-air mixture, which may be considered a "gas," is introduced into the oven to start, control, and finish the burning. The fuel used may be "gas"; town gas or some sort of liquefied gas is popular. Such a cremator is termed "gas-fired" on account of the use of gas as a fuel. Other types are "oil-fired" and "coke (or coal)-fired," but all are 'gas ovens" since in all three cases it is a fuel-air mixture which is injected, under pressure, into the oven.

The customary German word for the concept in question here is "*Gaskammer,*" but the word in NO-4473 which was translated "gas chamber" is "*Vergasungskeller,*" which Reitlinger also mistranslates as "gassing cellar."

Now the word *Vergasung* has two meanings. The primary meaning (and the only one in a technical context) is gasification, carburetion or vaporization, i.e. turning something into a gas, not applying gas to something. A *Vergaser* is a carburetor and, while *Vergasung* always means gasification in a technical context, it usually means, specifically, carburetion in such a context. . . .

The translation "gassing cellar" is thus not absolutely incorrect; it is just over-hasty and presumptuous. A "gas oven" requires some sort of gasification or carburetion. In the case of the gas fired-ovens of Utting and Rogers in 1932: "*Burners set in the crown and sole of the furnace are fed by a mixture of air and gas under pressure; the mixture is regulated by fans, housed in a separate building. Separate control of both air and gas provides better regulation of the furnace temperature.*"

That building is just a big carburetor. Oil-fired crematoria are so similar in design that most gas-fired ovens can be easily adapted for use with oil.

The ovens at Birkenau seem to have been coke or coal-fired, and with this type there is an extra stage of fuel processing due to the initially solid state of the fuel. The two most common methods of producing fuel gasses from coal to coke are, first, by passing air through a bed of burning coke to produce "coke oven gas" and second, by passing steam through the coke to produce "water gas." The first coke cremators employed what amounted to coke oven gas. Processes for generating such gases are termed "*Vergasung*" in German, as well as processes of mixing them with air. . . .

In any case it is obvious that the crematoria at Auschwitz required equipment for doing *Vergasung* in order to inject a fuel-air mixture into the ovens and the translation of NO-4473 should be revised, possibly to "gas generation cellar." I have confirmed this interpretation of the "*Vergasungskeller*" with technically competent sources in Germany. The reasons for installing such equipment in special separate rooms or even buildings are most probably the considerable noise that must be made by the fans and, in coal-fired ovens, the heat of burning coal.

The primary meaning of the word *Vergasung* is of necessity applicable to document NO-4473. It is written in a technical context; it is a letter from the chief of the Auschwitz construction management to the head of the SS engineering group. It makes reference to a process, *Vergasung*, which is standard with all crematoria, and the wording of the letter is such that it is implied that it would normally be peculiar to find bodies in the *Vergasungskeller*, since bodies are normally stored in what is correctly translated as the "cellar used as a mortuary."

Document NO-4473 tends, in fact, like so many prosecution documents, to rejection of the prosecution's claim when it is properly understood. We see that in crematorium II there were at least two cellars, a *Leichenkeller* and a *Vergasungskeller*, and that neither was a "gas chamber."[24]

Before we continue with Butz's argument that the term *Vergasungskeller* could refer to a carburetion room, it is good to remember one of the classic historiographical fallacies graduate students in history learn to avoid: the fallacy of the possible proof. David Hackett Fischer described this fallacy as the attempt "to demonstrate that a factual statement is true or false by establishing the possibility of its truth or falsity."

"One of the greatest fallacies of evidence," a logician has observed, "is the disposition to dwell on the actual possibility of its being false; a possibility which must exist when it is not demonstrative. Counsel can bewilder juries in this way till they almost doubt their own senses." This tactic may indeed prove to be forensically effective in an Anglo-American court of law, but it never proves a point at issue. Valid empirical proof requires not merely the establishment of possibility, but of probability. Moreover, it demands a balanced estimate of probabilities pro and con. If historians, like lawyers, must respect the doctrine of reasonable doubt, they must equally be able to recognize an unreasonable doubt when they see one.[25]

As we will see, the word *Vergasungskeller* has generated a host of possible proofs, none of which are probable.

Nowhere in the whole correspondence between the makers of the ovens, Topf, and the SS and nowhere in the technical specifications of the ovens is there any mention of a carburetion room. Nothing in the blue-prints supports Butz's contention: none of the two large underground spaces is in any way connected to the ovens in such a way that they could function as carburetion rooms. It is sufficient to note that Butz himself, in 1992, was forced to publicly distance himself from this misinterpretation of the word *Vergasungskeller*. The occasion was the publication of Pressac's tome *Auschwitz: Technique and Operation of the Gas Chambers* (1989)—a book that made available in published form a massive amount of archival material concerning the construction of the gas chambers and the crematoria which were used in the 1945/1946 forensic investigation at Auschwitz and which were presented again during the trial of the Auschwitz architects Walther Dejaco and Fritz Ertl but had since been forgotten. Pressac refuted Butz's argument that the *Vergasungskeller* had been a carburetion room. Remarkably enough, Butz reconsidered the issue in light of Pressac's refutation and acknowledged that he had been wrong.

> I interpreted the *Vergasungskeller* mentioned in the 1943 document as a place where coke or coal was converted into a combustible gas, mixed with air, and then introduced under pressure into the cremation ovens.
>
> While this interpretation is not "technically worthless," Pressac shows that it is not correct in this instance. His proof consists of (1) many engineering drawings of Crematorium 2, in various stages of design, which show no such facility, and (2) engineering drawings of, and other data on, typical Topf company crematory ovens, which show that they were not of the design I assumed, and which used as fuel coke supplied directly behind the ovens.[26]

Having admitted that his original interpretation did not hold up, Butz had to produce another challenge to the commonsense interpretation of Bischoff's letter that the two underground rooms were a mortuary and a gas chamber and that due to the delay in completion of the mortuary, the gas chamber was going to be temporarily used as a mortuary.

> As noted by others, Pressac is in the strange position of claiming that a room consistently designated *Leichenkeller* 1 on all engineering drawings was to be used only temporarily as a *Leichenkeller,* either instead of normally as a gas chamber, or simultaneously as a gas chamber and a morgue. In the latter case the unsuspecting victims must presumably stand on the corpses. In the former case (the only interpretation worth considering), the implied delay in the use of the building for extermination was "unimportant," a major contradiction if one claims, as Pressac does, that the primary role of the building was for mass gassing.[27]

The adjective "unimportant" now acquired great importance. In the letter, it clearly referred to the delay in the removal of the formwork for the reinforced concrete ceiling of Morgue 2, which prevented the room from being used at short notice as a storage place for corpses. In other words, it applied to a temporary situation. We must remember that the ovens were not yet to be operational for another month and a half! During that time, no gassing should start, and so for that month and a half the gas chamber could easily be used as a morgue.

But Butz was undeterred.

> Because the document confirms that in January 1943 the Germans were working, under great pressure, to make this installation operational as an ordinary crematorium, I regard it as further evidence against the claim that it had been decided in the summer of 1942 that the primary purpose of these crematoria was extermination by lethal gassing. The use of the *Vergasungskeller* as a morgue not only did not interfere with bringing Crematorium II into operational status, it advanced it. Here I am arguing, in passing, for a focus on what the document says rather than on the term *Vergasungskeller* mentioned in it.[28]

Of course, the primary purpose of the crematoria always was incineration and not gassing because, as Höss observed in his conversation with Dr. Gilbert, and experience in Auschwitz and the other camps taught, incineration capacity and not gassing capacity was the bottleneck. Gassing could be done in simple sealed rooms, as the experience with the bunkers amply demonstrated. In fact, Butz admitted this in 1976, when he wrote that "the limit on the rate at which people could have been exterminated in a program of the type alleged is not determined by the rate at which people could have been gassed and the gas chambers ventilated, but by the rate at which bodies could have been cremated."[29] Yet in 1992 he chose to forget his earlier assessment.

Butz continued as follows:

> In any case, Pressac's logic in interpreting the *Vergasungskeller* as a gas chamber depends entirely on the assumption that there was a gas chamber in Crematorium 2. Without that assumption we have the following situation:
>
> (1) One (and apparently only one) document concerned exclusively with the operational status of Crematorium II makes reference to a *Vergasungskeller* to be temporarily used, in support of the Crematorium, as a morgue and not for its intended or normal function,
>
> (2) In the many engineering drawings of the crematoria that Pressac has examined, there is no mention of a *Vergasungskeller, Gaskammer,* or anything similar, and
>
> (3) Nothing in those engineering drawings implies or calls for something describable as a *Vergasungskeller.* For example the cremation ovens have been shown to be of a design not calling for such a facility.
>
> The appropriate conclusion, I believe, is that the *Vergasungskeller* was not in Crematorium 2 at all. I assume that it was somewhere in the vicinity, but in the light of the current knowledge the only basis for inferring that it was in the Crematorium building is an assumption that there was a gas chamber there. In the absence of the massive documentation presented by Pressac, it

seemed logical to assume that the *Vergasungskeller* was located in Crematorium II. I made just that assumption in writing my book, and the assumption seemed confirmed for me by the observation that crematorium technology could call for such a facility. However Pressac has shown, without realizing it, that the *Vergasungskeller* was not in Crematorium II because it did not appear on the many engineering plans, and is not implied or called for by anything that appears on those plans. Only an unfounded or arbitrary prior assumption can place it there.

If the *Vergasungskeller* was not in Crematorium II, then the questions of what and where it was are only of limited importance. It suffices, I believe, to show that the term could have applied to operations that transpired, or may have transpired, elsewhere in the camp.[30]

Butz's argument began with the observation that "Pressac's logic in interpreting the *Vergasungskeller* as a gas chamber depends entirely on the assumption that there was a gas chamber in Crematorium 2." Is this an unwarranted assumption? According to Butz it was, but given the fact that there are many eyewitness testimonies that place a gas chamber in the basement of Crematorium 2, that assumption is a valid point of departure. If one posits as a hypothesis, based on the eyewitness testimonies, that Morgue 1 was a gas chamber, then many different pieces of evidence fall into place, such as the fact that this morgue was designed to be heated and that construction documents refer to a "gasdoor" with a "spy-hole of double 8 mm glass with a rubber seal and metal fitting" for that space, or that the other large underground space (Morgue 2) is referred to as an undressing basement. The hypothesis that "*Vergasungskeller*" referred to Morgue 1 of Crematorium 2, and that this space was used as a gas chamber, can therefore be tested and confirmed. This is what Pressac did, and this is what Dawidowski had done forty years earlier. Consequently, the burden of proof was on Butz to show that the assumption was wrong. And indeed, in his original argument, he did accept this principle and tried to show how the general assumption was invalid and that the "alleged" gas chamber in Crematorium 2 had been, in all probability, a carburetion chamber.

The three points of Butz's argument do not support the conclusion that "the *Vergasungskeller* was not in Crematorium 2." It is obvious why he wanted to relocate it elsewhere: as long as it remained likely that the *Vergasungskeller* was in Crematorium 2, and more specifically in the basement of this building, the only possible conclusion that remains is that Bischoff designated Morgue 1 as such. The question then remained: If it was not a homicidal gas chamber, then what was it? The logic of Bischoff's letter suggests that if the *Vergasungskeller* was not in the crematorium, it must have been very close, or at least at a reasonable distance. However there is no trace of any basement space close to the crematorium or, for that matter, anywhere in Birkenau!

Butz went to search for the *Vergasungskeller* in the wider environment of Auschwitz. It is worthwhile to quote his journey, in which he allowed his imagination to run wild, in full.

If the *Vergasungskeller* was not in Crematorium 2, then the questions of what and where it was are only of limited importance. It suffices, I believe, to show that the term could have applied to operations that transpired, or may have transpired, elsewhere in the camp.

To give my favored interpretation first, it is unlikely that the town of Auschwitz had preexisting means for production and/or distribution of fuel or town gas sufficient for the needs of the huge complex of camps we call "Auschwitz." Such needs could have been for cooking, heating, or incineration of waste, and so forth. On account of the paucity of natural gas, but abundance of coal in Europe, the Germans had extensively developed the gasification of coal. In the Auschwitz region coal was particularly abundant, so processes of coal or coke gasification were suited for the conditions there.

In offering my earlier interpretation of the Vergasungskeller as a fuel gas generator for the crematorium ovens I wrote: "The two most common methods of producing fuel gases from coal or coke are, first, by passing air through a bed of burning coke to produce 'coke oven gas' and second, by passing steam through the coke to produce 'water gas.'" I now offer almost the same interpretation, but modified so that the specific location of the Vergasungskeller is no longer known, and the gas generated is for general application and not specifically for cremation. This seems entirely justified by the engineering plans that indicate no Vergasungskeller in the crematoria, by the great likelihood that the camp required fuel gas, and in view of the easy availability of coal there.[31]

Butz proved unable to point at any structure in or adjacent to the camp designed as a plant for coal or coke gasification. In fact, there was none. In order for his assumption to warrant any discussion, he should have at least suggested where this building could have been! There is more, however. Butz assumed "the likelihood" of the camp having been supplied by gas. It would not have been too difficult to establish a certain level of certainty in this matter. Inspection of the site, the buildings, and the engineering plans would have shown him that the infrastructure to pipe gas to the camp and its buildings was neither designed nor constructed.

Yet Butz did not limit himself to the chimera of his "favored" or "preferred" suggestion. He also dreamed up some others:

It has already been remarked that fuel gas generated in the camp could have been used, among other things, in waste incineration. That is, the fuel gas could have served as the auxiliary fuel. There is also a second sense in which "Vergasung" can apply to waste incineration, because the technology views the waste as a combustible fuel being turned into gases. Incineration (or Verbrennung) is actually a special case of gasification (or Vergasung) in which all combustibles are oxidized to the highest degree possible, for example, producing carbon dioxide (CO_2) instead of carbon monoxide (CO, a combustible gas, in which case it would be said that Vergasung had taken place). Since perfect incineration does not exist in this sense, the line between Verbrennung and Vergasung can be blurred. What is termed waste gasification, or Müllvergasung in ordinary technical German, was developed as a practical process only after the war. It appears that during the war Vergasung could have been used in the waste incineration context only in the sense of one of many specific processes taking place inside a plant viewed as performing Müllverbrennung. Thus this second sense of application of "Vergasung" to waste incineration does not seem to apply, and it is very unlikely that at Auschwitz any waste incinerator would have been spoken of as performing *Vergasung*.

This possibility is nevertheless worth mentioning. There was a waste incinerator in what I would call the chimney housing behind the cremation ovens in Crematorium II. The effluent gases from the incinerator combined with the effluent of the ovens in sharing the chimney and the suction type forced draft system. I do not believe that the "*Vergasungskeller*" was this chimney housing because, apart from the reasons already given, it was not referred to as such on the drawings, and seems to have had insufficient free space to serve as a plausible temporary substitute for the huge *Leichenkeller* 2. All the same, it is at least worth noting that "*Vergasung*" could apply as an inclusive description of the two processes (cremation and waste incineration) involved there. However I do not consider a waste incineration interpretation of the *Vergasungskeller* a likely possibility.[32]

It is unnecessary to comment on these two paragraphs of a book that is claimed on its jacket to be "unsurpassed as the standard scholarly refutation of the Holocaust extermination story," and which in a German negationist review of the literature is still celebrated as the "revisionist standard work."[33] Perhaps all we need to do to comment on Butz's vaporous yes/no/yes/no argument is to add the observation that the word "*Vergasungskeller*" indicates a basement space, and the incineration room in the chimney housing was aboveground.

Butz finally arrived at a third possibility, which was as preposterous as his previous conjectures:

In the vicinity of the crematoria at Birkenau there were three sewage treatment plants (*Kläranlagen*) in various stages of completion. Sewage treatment amounts basically to the acceleration of the natural processes in which bacteria metabolize solid waste into gases and inoffensive solids (sludge), and to the disposal or use of these products. There are several senses in which *Vergasung* could arise.[34]

Butz proceeded to discuss the possible use of the term "*Vergasung*" in the processes of aeration and chlorination of sewage, in spontaneous methane production from sewage, sewer gasification, and sludge incineration. Yet all his speculations were to no avail, as he had to admit himself.

I have not located the Vergasungskeller in the sewage plants. Rather, I have listed five senses in which generation of, or treatment with, a gas comes up in sewage technology. I have not found the term "*Vergasungskeller*" or "*Vergasungskammer*" in the German literature on wastewater treatment, but that is not necessary. The document in question [i.e., Bischoff's letter of January 29, 1943] was not written by a sewage engineer; it was written by a construction engineer for the information of another construction engineer, and the author never imagined that half a century later people would be poring over his hurried note. Nevertheless, I still favour the first interpretation offered, namely that the *Vergasungskeller* was a generator of fuel or town gas intended for general use.

Only the study of complete engineering plans for the camp could settle this question.[35]

Mr. Butz may rest assured that in none of the plans for the sewage treatment plant, which have all been preserved, are there any spaces, and to be more specific basement spaces, for the aeration or chlorination of sewage, the removal of methane, the removal of sewer gas, or the incineration of sludge. Nor do the engineering plans of the camp indicate any space, certainly not belowground, that could have served any such function.[36]

Butz obviously did not really believe the arguments he had proposed in 1992, because in 1997 he came back to the issue. He promised to offer an interpretation "more plausible than any earlier offered by me or anybody else."[37] The *Vergasungskeller* had been a gas shelter! "We should view all three cellars in Crematorium 2 as emergency air-raid shelters, with only one being provided with the additional measures to make it effective as a gas shelter."[38] Butz derived this last interpretation from one proposed eighteen years earlier by Stäglich, who had also tried to neutralize the evidentiary significance of Bischoff's letter.

> Dr. Butz gives a convincing explanation of the function of this part of the crematoria. Except for electrically powered units, which do not figure in the Auschwitz controversy, all crematoria, including those which use coal, coke, or wood as fuel, are fired with gas. According to his research, the space in which the primary fuel is converted into combustible gas before being fed into the hearth is known in German as the "Vergasungsraum" or "Vergasungskeller." Hence these terms have nothing whatsoever to do with the "gassing" of human beings.[39]

Yet obviously Stäglich did not fully trust Butz, and after first endorsing Butz's interpretation, he added his own suggestion, namely that the *Vergasungskeller* was a gas chamber after all; not one to kill people, but one to kill lice.

> Another plausible explanation is that this room was intended for the fumigation of clothing and other personal effects, a common practice in all concentration camps. The proprietary hydrocyanic fumigant Zyklon B used for this purpose is supposed to have been used for the 'extermination of Jews' as well. Never has there been any question that these "Vergasungskeller" were used as "gas chambers" for exterminating Jews.[40]

Stäglich's alternative is characterized by a total ignorance of the circumstances. First of all, the rooms designed for fumigation of clothing and other objects with Zyklon B have never been referred to as *Vergasungskeller*. They were either called simply gas chambers [*Gaskammer*], or standard gas chambers [*Normalgaskammer*], or delousing rooms [*Entlausungskammer*]. The only time the noun *Vergasungskeller* appears is in the letter of January 29. Furthermore, these delousing gas chambers were always constructed in such a way that they had two doors: one entrance and one exit. The entrance door opened to the *unreine* (unclean) side, the exit door opened to the *reine* (clean) side. This arrangement conformed not only to common sense, but also to specific SS regulations issued by the SS construction bureau in 1941, and it determined the design of the special delousing facilities constructed in Auschwitz and Birkenau.[41] The SS built a very large delousing installation, the so-called central sauna, right between Crematoria 3 and 4. It was constructed following the guidelines issued by the SS construction bureau. One wonders why the SS would have erected the central sauna if the crematoria already provided such ample delousing capacity. Even at Auschwitz there was a limit to the need for delousing installations.

Stäglich continued his attack on the commonsense interpretation that the *Vergasungskeller* referred to the homicidal gas chamber of Crematorium 2 with the observation that this was impossible because the letter implies that the morgue and the gassing basement were two different spaces. The traditional interpretation held that the gassing took place in the morgue. He did not consider the possibility that Crematorium 2 had two morgues, that one of them could not be used because of the delay in construction, and that therefore the other morgue, referred to as gassing basement, was to be temporarily used to store corpses. Yet Stäglich rushed to his conclusion:

> Since Bischoff's letter of January 29, 1943 is the only known document from the Auschwitz camp files in which the word "Vergasung" is used in connection with the crematoria, one should now realize that there is no documentary evidence for the allegation that chambers for killing people by means of lethal gas were part of the crematoria.[42]

Stäglich may have been right that Bischoff's letter of January 29 was "the only known document from the Auschwitz camp files in which the word 'Vergasung' is used in connection with the crematoria," but this does not mean that there are not other documents that show similar violations of the general rule not to use language that directly referred to gassing, gas chambers, and so on. Most of these other examples that were less obvious occurred in the records kept by the contractors of the crematoria. For example, in the daily timesheets kept by the contractor Riedel and Son from Bielitz (Bielsko-Biala), we read that on February 28 the foreman fitted gas-tight windows [*gasdichter Fenster*] in an unspecified space of Crematorium 4.[43] Two days later, he jotted down that he had "covered the ground with hard fill, tamped [it] down, and concreted the floor in the gas chamber [*Gaskammer*].[44] Then, on various occasions, the fitter Messing of the crematoria-oven manufacturer Topf & Sons mentioned in the timesheets for his work on Crematoria 2 and 3 that he had been working in the ventilation system of the "undressing basement" [*Auskleidekeller*],[45] a space obviously located next to the basement used, according to Bischoff's letter of January 29, 1943, as a gassing basement [*Vergasungskeller*].

All of these "slips" were made in error. Certain "slips," however, could not be avoided. Sometimes the Central Construction Office had to be specific in order to get exactly what they wanted. For example, on February 26, 1943, at 6:20 P.M., SS-Untersturmführer Pollok sent a cable, cosigned by SS-Untersturmführer Kirschneck and Jährling, to Topf with the following message: "Send immediately 10 gas detectors [*Gasprüfer*] as discussed. Send your invoice later."[46] Faurisson responded to the discovery of the order for the gas detectors with the argument that this order should not surprise anyone. According to him, the gas detectors were meant to detect carbon monoxide and carbon dioxide. "The firm Topf & Sons, manufacturers for crematory ovens, routinely supplied detectors for CO and CO_2." Faurisson added, "Why try to convince us that this type of company, on receipt of an order for 'gas detectors,' would have understood by way of telepathy that in this case it was to supply detectors for HCN (and not CO

Record of cable sent February 26, 1943, ordering 10 gas detectors. Courtesy Nubar Alexanian.

and CO_2) and . . . that it would be in a position to furnish an item that it didn't manufacture?"[47] This convinced the negationists for some time. Then Jean-Claude Pressac found Topf's response, dated March 2, 1943, to the order of the gas detectors.

> Re: Crematorium, Gas detectors.
> We acknowledge receipt of your telegram specifying "Immediately send ten gas detectors as agreed, price quote to follow."
> We hereby inform you that two weeks ago we inquired, of five different companies, concerning the residual prussic acid detection devices sought by you. We have received negative responses from three companies and two have not yet answered.
> When we receive information on this matter, we shall immediately contact you, in order to put you in touch with a company that makes these devices.[48]

Faurisson's initial "attack" had failed. Then he regrouped and explained that it was to be expected that the Central Construction Office would have ordered HCN gas detectors because Morgue 1, the gassing cellar, was used as a delousing room.[49] Yet this explanation did not satisfy Butz. He rightly noticed that if the gas detectors had indeed been used for normal delousing operations, the SS Central Construction Office would not have ordered them from the furnace maker Topf but from the Degesch company, the firm that normally supplied delousing equipment.[50] So how to explain the gas detectors without assuming the use of Morgue 1 as a gas chamber? Butz, as may be expected, came up with a very ingenious solution. He noticed a waste incinerator in the plans for Crematoria 2 and 3, located close to the chimney.

HCN release was possible in the waste incinerator, which shared the chimney with the crematory ovens. Many materials may release HCN when burned. Among these are many fabrics, a highly relevant observation because the waste incinerator was most likely used to incinerate used camp fabrics (such as inmate uniforms, bed linen, and mattresses).[51] For example, Nylon and wool can release HCN when burned, a fact that has been known since the Thirties.[52]

Thus began Butz's speculation that because cloth that had become popular in wartime Germany had a high rayon content, the camp uniforms were also made from rayon. He had to admit that rayon itself did not produce hydrocyanide when burned because it had no nitrogen in its chemical composition. Yet he was not going to be stopped by this.

The burning of rayon can generate HCN gas if the rayon is impregnated with, but not chemically bound to, compounds of ammonia, which supply the necessary nitrogen. . . . Ammonium compounds are added to many fabrics to make them flame retardant (this is sometimes called "fireproofing," but that cannot be done literally with ordinary fabrics). . . .

While I do not have a document that says so, I consider it very plausible that many concentration camp fabrics were treated with flame retardants for security reasons, that is, to limit the effects of fires started by inmates. This would have been particularly the case with bed linens and mattress fillings. Thus I am proposing the possibility that fabrics used in the camps, destined to be disposed of by incineration, were known to present a danger of evolution of HCN in such incineration.[53]

Not only is there no evidence that the Germans fireproofed the inmate uniforms and their (non-existent) bed linens and (non-existent) mattresses, it is even more highly implausible that they would have cared to do so.

At the end of his highly original and also highly implausible interpretation of the purpose of the gas detectors, Butz offered some general observations on the problems revisionists have in dealing with the kind of evidence Faurisson and he had tried to interpret.

The revisionists may not be able to immediately offer correct replies to the defenders of the [extermination] legend. This appears to me to have been the case with the Topf letter. I don't believe Faurisson's immediate replies (which I would also have made) were correct. In fact nobody could be relied on to be correct under the circumstances and on the time schedule involved. A comparison: there is much building activity at Northwestern University now. Does anybody believe that, 50 years from now, perhaps after some cataclysm, anybody could reliably interpret individual documents that were records of this construction? Of course not. Nobody could do that, and nobody could infallibly interpret every Auschwitz document from the period 1941–1945. Indeed, the hypothesis I have advanced here may be wrong, even though I have had a few years to consider the solitary document in question.[54]

But is it necessary to be "infallible"? A good architectural historian can create a fair and useful reconstruction of a building's design, construction, and subsequent history without having to be "infallible."

That is why one mostly considers documents not in isolation, but with reference to other documents. For example, we know that more or less at the time that the gas detectors were ordered, the Central Construction Office also ordered a gas door with a peephole for the crematorium—an order which does not square with the assumption that the gas detectors were related to anticipated problems with hydrocyanide development in the waste incinerator. The letter in question was sent by Bischoff on March 31, 1943, to the German Armament Works.

Letter from Karl Bischoff to the German Armament Works, March 31, 1943. Courtesy Archive Auschwitz-Birkenau State Museum, Oswiecim. (opposite page)

> In the letter mentioned above informs you that you must make three gas-tight doors [*gasdichte Türe*][55] according to the order of January 1, 1943 for BW 30b and 30c,[56] following exactly the size and construction of those already delivered.
>
> At this occasion we remind you of another order of March 6, 1943 for the delivery of a gasdoor 100/192 [*Gastür 100/192*] for morgue 1 of crematorium 3, Bw 30a, which must be equipped exactly in the form and size of the basement door of crematorium 2, located opposite, to be made with a spy-hole of double 8 mm glass with a rubber seal and metal fitting. This order must be considered as very urgent.[57]

It is obvious that the contents of this letter square with those of Bischoff's letter of January 29, 1943. Morgue 1 of Crematorium 2 and Morgue 1 of Crematorium 3 are both equipped with a gas door with a spyhole. This morgue is labeled "gassing basement" in the letter from January 29. Yet Stäglich decided otherwise. He asked, cynically, "Could this be the famous peep-hole through which the SS physicians who allegedly supervised the 'gassing' of inmates are said to have observed the death-throes of the victims?" His answer was not surprising: "Probably not."

> Like the other documents of its kind, it really proves nothing. At that time, gas-tight doors were not uncommon, since every cellar had to double as an air raid shelter. The peep-holes in these doors were a source of light and a means of observing the outside. . . . Air raid shelters had to be secure not only against explosives, but against gas as well. Considering that Birkenau had no other fortified places, it would only have been common sense to make the cellars of the crematoria into air raid shelters.[58]

Stäglich's speculation did not consider the facts on the ground. First of all, if, as he assumed, Morgue 1 was used as a mortuary, then the problem arises about the protocol during an air raid. Would the living join the putrefying dead for the duration of the alarm? Furthermore, the design of the structure does not indicate an air-raid shelter. The concrete columns are strong enough to support the roof but not strong enough to withstand a bomb. In fact, when the gas chamber of Crematorium 1 was adapted into an air-raid shelter in 1944, the room was subdivided for that very reason into many small rooms divided by heavy walls to support the reinforced roof. And if the provision of gas-tight doors for a basement space may be explained with reference to air-raid precautions, what about the twelve gas-tight shutters ordered for the lightly built aboveground rooms of Crematoria 4 and 5? Finally, the location: unlike Crematorium 1, which was located next to the SS hospital and the Kommandantur, Crematoria 2 and 3 were very far from any location where SS were present in sufficient numbers to warrant such a facility. The alleged air-raid shelters at Crematoria 2 and 3 were more than a mile away from the SS quarters.

31. März 1943.

49

26171 /43/Ki./Schul.

Betrifft: Auftrag 2261/8o/17 vom 18.1.43 Bw 3o b
Bezug: Dort. Schreiben vom 24.3.43, Nr.6o56 - 43 -
Anlagen: keine.

Fa.
Deutsche Ausrüstungswerke
G.m.b.H.

Werk A u s c h w i t z /O.S.

          Es wird auf o.a. Schreiben mitgeteilt, dass
drei gasdichte Türme gemäss des Auftrages vom 18.1.43
für das Bw 3o b und 3o c auszuführen sind, genau nach
den Ausmaßen und der Art der bisher angelieferten
Türme.

          Bei dieser Gelegenheit wird an einen weiteren
Auftrag vom 6.3.43 über Lieferung einer Gastür loo/192
für Leichenkeller I des Krematoriums III, Bw 3o a , er-
innert, die genau nach Art und Maß der Kellertür des ge-
genüberliegenden Krematoriums II mit Guckloch aus doppelte
8 - mm - Glas mit Gummidichtung und Beschlag auszuführen ist. Dieser Auftrag ist als besonders dringend
anzusehen.

          Die mit Auftrag vom 23.1.43 für Bw 3o bestellte
Bodenabschlusstür, sowie 1 Stück Bleidrahmentür braucht
nicht ausgeführt werden, dieser Auftrag ist hinfällig.

          Die vorbereiteten lo ebm Brennholz werden bei
nächster Gelegenheit abgeholt.

                    Der Leiter der Zentralbauleitung
                 der Waffen - ∭ und Polizei Auschwitz

                    ∭ - Sturmbannführer.

Verteiler:
Registratur, Akt BW 3o
Z.A. Teichmann
Baultg. K.L. - ∭ - Ustuf. Kirschneck

Yet once proposed, Stäglich's suggestion took on a life of its own, like one of Showalter's "hystories." For Samuel Crowell, the assumption that the gas chambers were really air-raid shelters is of cardinal importance to his thesis that the gas chambers were a hystory. According to Crowell, the Germans suffered from a deep anxiety about poison gas—a direct result of the gas attacks of the First World War and the Italian use of gas in the Abyssinian War. After giving several literary references, Crowell concluded that "the culture was primed for accusations of poison gas usage."[59] In response, the Germans "invested hundreds of millions of dollars in the preparation of air raid shelters." These were not only to protect against blasts but also against gas. Crowell wrote, "As a result, special air-raid shelter doors were developed, usually made of steel. The doors would feature a round peephole covered with a perforated steel plate to prevent breakage, the peephole meant to facilitate visual inspection without having to break the gas-tight seal by opening the door."[60] Crowell assumed that these civil defense measures were also applied to concentration camps:

> Each of the Birkenau crematoria was equipped with a gas-tight bomb shelter, and . . . these shelters also included decontamination facilities in the form of showers and baths. In this respect it is important to note that the Crematorium at the base camp was known to have been used as an air raid shelter, although its poison gas protection features have rarely been commented on.

We should emphasize that all of the material and documentary evidence, when placed in a larger context, points to gas tight air raid and anti-gas shelters, although it is likely that at least

Plan for the transformation of the morgue and adjacent rooms into an air-raid shelter, Crematorium 1, September 1944. Courtesy Archive Auschwitz-Birkenau State Museum, Oswiecim.

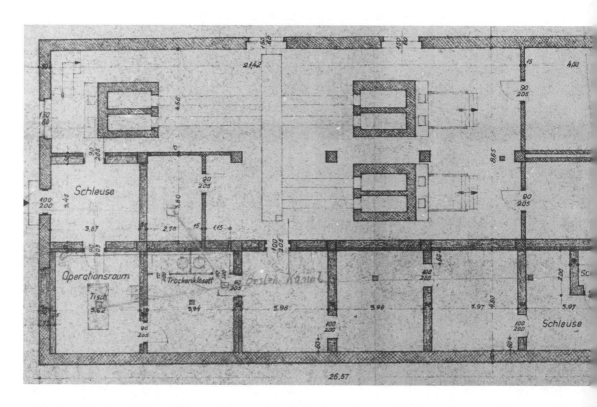

two of the traces—the gas detectors, and possibly the term "*Vergasungskeller*"—are rooted in other benign procedures, including disinfection. There is no material or documentary support for the claim that these spaces were designed, let alone used, as extermination gas chambers.[61]

More to the point: *there is not a shred of evidence to support Crowell's claim that those spaces were designed, let alone used, as air-raid shelters.* In a footnote to this section, Crowell went into greater detail about the many possible functions of the air-raid shelter/gassing basement/morgue. "It is conceivable that part of it was intended for the disinfecting or delousing of clothing of the dead or the corpse handlers," Crowell observed, "but in that case it is doubtful that the entire *Keller* would have been set aside for that purpose: then the use of the word would be an example of metonymy, and the facility itself could well have been used for a variety of purposes: disinfecting corpse handlers, *ad hoc* disinfection and delousing of camp arrivals, and decontamination."[62]

Crowell's argument, made both in the main body of his text and in the footnote, does not make any sense. As we have seen above, the architectural layout of the basement of Crematoria 2 and 3 does not follow the strict division between the unclean and clean sides that were characteristic of delousing facilities, and there is absolutely no indication anywhere in either the plans of these spaces or in the correspondence that these spaces were designed to support the delousing of the clothing of the dead, the disinfecting of corpse handlers, ad hoc disinfection and delousing of camp arrivals, or decontamination. Of course, in theory anything is possible, but only a few things are probable, and historians take the probable and not the possible as the point of departure for their musings. Furthermore, the design of the two morgues does not support the claim that they were meant as air-raid shelters. As we have seen above, when the Germans designated Crematorium 1 as a shelter for those working and recovering in the SS hospital in Auschwitz I, they subdivided the space into small interconnected cells separated by sturdy walls that gave extra support to the roof. There is absolutely no evidence that such a structural modification was ever contemplated or executed for the basement spaces of Crematoria 2 and 3. The location of the alleged air-raid shelters in the crematoria more than a mile from the SS camp does not make any sense. The Moscow archives house a substantial body of archival material concerning the building of air-raid shelters. None of the documents refer to any air-raid shelters in the Birkenau crematoria, and at no point did the SS consider the issue of air-raid shelters before the fall of 1943. While the air-raid–shelter file was created in 1942, the only item in the first year of its existence was a "cold call" from a shelter manufacturer seeking business. The Auschwitz Central Construction Office did not respond. Finally, and most important: sufficient mutually corroborating evidence of different origin converges on the conclusion that Morgue 1 of Crematorium 2 and Morgue 1 of Crematorium 3 were used as gas chambers.

It is important to observe that even if Crowell had been able to make a plausible case that the basement spaces of Crematoria 2 and 3 had been used as air-raid shelters, he would still have faced the problem of explaining the aboveground gas chambers of Crematoria 4 and 5. The plans, elevations, and sections of these spaces have all been preserved, and none shows any indication that these spaces could have offered any protection during an air raid. Apart from that, these spaces in no way follow the standard layout for delousing facilities.

Finally, Crowell offered a contorted argument in which he argued that because all the "non-intentional" evidence of gas chambers in Auschwitz can be explained in the language of civil air defense and disinfection literature, one may safely infer that "there is no longer any documentary or material evidence that mass gassings took place at all." This argument is an obvious example of a non sequitur, as is Crowell's assertion that because Dawidowski and Sehn misinterpreted those documents that attested to the presence of air-raid shelters in the crematoria, one may infer that "there was never any merit to the extermination gassing claim in the first place." And he concluded that "shown in their proper context, these documents, now clearly seen as having been misused, bring us face to face with the possibility of a deliberate Polish and Soviet communist fraud."[63] Because to Crowell the air-raid shelter origin of the gas chambers was obvious, failure to consider the possibility could only be explained as an attempt "to suppress the issue of air raid shelters *per se,* because otherwise it most certainly would have been (and would be!) a valuable addition to our knowledge of the Holocaust."[64] The problem with Crowell's theorizing, of course, is that Dawidowski and Sehn had no reason to consider the possibility that the gas-tight features pointed toward air-raid shelters because there was no reason to do so. Information derived from many different sources—both intentional and non-intentional evidence—pointed clearly at the use of *Leichenkeller 1* in Crematoria 2 and 3 as gas chambers, and not one source suggested that these spaces had been used as air-raid shelters.

The negationists claim to be revisionist historians, but they have yet to produce a history that offers a credible, "revised" explanation of the events in question. Until Crowell's piece appeared, Rassinier and his disciples had an exclusively nihilist agenda. They attacked the inherited account on the unproven assumption of some general conspiracy, but they had not been able, or willing, to even begin writing a single piece of investigative journalism (let alone produce one product of serious revisionist historiography) that gives us the origin and development of this conspiracy—the reason why and how it seized on, of all places, those very "ordinary" Auschwitz concentration camps as the fulcrum of its effort to hoodwink both gentiles and Jews—to leverage the international community in general and defraud the Germans and the Palestinians in particular. Crowell's article attempts to create a plausible narrative that could have begun, at least superficially, to engage with issues of relevancy and causation. But one cannot but judge Crowell's attempt an utter failure. The hypothesis that air-raid shelters explain the "myth" of the gas chambers does not stand up to serious criticism. Not only do his claims make little sense, but his hypothesis is without any value because he did not submit it to an essential test: if Auschwitz was equipped with substantial gas-tight civil defense measures within its crematoria, then one should be able to deduce that other concentration camps had similar equipment. If they did not, the hypothesis should account for the departure from concentration camp policy at Auschwitz. Crowell did not test his hypothesis, and therefore it cannot be verified. He has not offered a single scrap of evidence that confirms the entailed consequent of the hypothesis. Hence, for all his effort, his hypothesis that the gas chambers can be explained as substantial gas-tight civil defense measures is without any value.

Irving did not seem to be bothered by all of this. Not only did he offer a link between his Web site and Crowell's essay, but he also posted another Crowell piece, which he introduced as follows:

New Documents on Air Raid Shelters at Auschwitz Camp

Brief Introduction

AMERICAN WRITER "Samuel Crowell" [*pseudonym*], author of *Technique and Operation of German Anti-Gas Shelters in WW2*, published in German translation in Germar Rudolf's journal *Vierteljahreshefte für freie Geschichtsforschung* [VffG/ VHO@aol.com] submitted three documents recently obtained from the archives of the former Soviet special state archives (the "trophy") archives. [For Crowell's other writings, see http:// www.codoh.com/inconshr123.html.] These bear on his thesis that the gas-tight doors found at the Auschwitz site (a facsimile of which is displayed at the Holocaust Memorial Museum at Washington, D.C.) were nothing more sinister than the remains of air-raid shelters; all such shelters were fitted with gas-tight doors, in anticipation of Allied poison-gas attacks.

What the documents do not state explicitly, in our opinion, is whether the shelters were for prisoners, the camp guards, or both. Focal Point Publications.[65]

The three letters that Crowell obtained from Moscow with the help of an anonymous donor indeed concern the creation of air-raid shelters. Two of the documents date from late 1943 and concern problems in the production and delivery of 176 prefabricated concrete arches that were installed over small one- and two-person trenches that were created at regular intervals around the perimeter of Birkenau in order to provide shelter for the SS men guarding the camp in case of an air raid. These small shelters, which are still to be seen all around the perimeter of the camp, were not gas-tight; they were completely open toward the prisoner compound so that the guards could continue to cover the part of the perimeter assigned to them with their machine guns. Both the letters of October 25 and November 5, 1943, clearly refer to these small open shelters, and neither letter contains any reference to a gas-tight shelter.

The third letter dates from November 16, 1944. By the late fall of 1944, Allied air raids in the Auschwitz area had become commonplace, and the Soviet army had advanced to within sixty miles of Auschwitz. The Central Construction Office was ordered to create several larger shelters for a maximum of fifty men each and one smaller shelter with room for twenty persons and an emergency operation room. These were to accommodate SS personnel and were to be built in the large SS compound at Birkenau—primarily in the eastern section of the SS camp to service the SS hospital. The design for the shelter for fifty men, which survives in the archive of the Central Construction Office, consisted of a C-shaped trench covered with sixty-six of the same kind of prefabricated concrete arches as had been used for the small one- to two-person shelters designed a year earlier. But now the arches were interconnected to make four interconnected bombproof corridors, each 1.5 meters wide. Each corridor was designed to accommodate fifteen men in theory, but as the letter indicates, the Berlin headquarters wanted to lower the maximum accommodation from sixty to fifty people. The blueprints show four small toilet spaces attached to the four corridors that make up the main shelter and four entrances. At each of the four entrances, the architects projected a small vestibule identified as *"Gasschleuße"* (gas locks). The second design shows a trench shelter reinforced with masonry walls, covered with a concrete

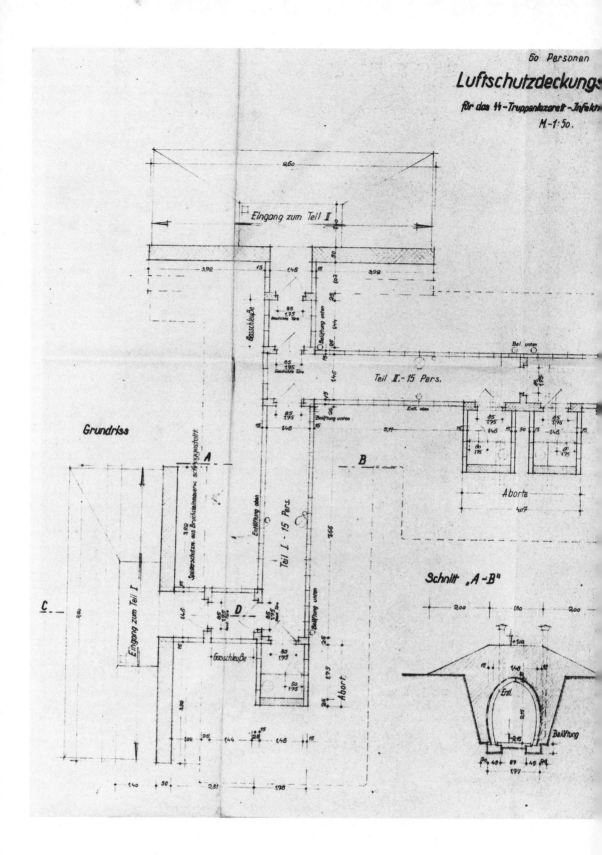

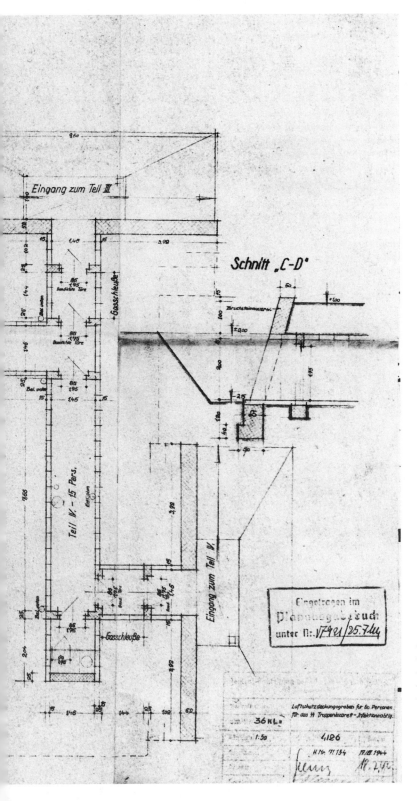

Design for an air-raid shelter for 50 persons, Auschwitz, November 1944. Courtesy Archive Auschwitz-Birkenau State Museum, Oswiecim.

roof. Like the other design, it is equipped with a gas lock. These air-raid shelters were indeed gas tight. It is interesting to note, however, that the architects achieved their goal of producing a gas-tight shelter by means of a lock that was designated as a gas-lock in the drawings.[66] None of the blueprints of the crematoria show a space identified as a *"Gasschleuße"*—another indication that Crowell's hypothesis does not hold. None of the designs for Morgue 1 of Crematoria 2 and 3 show the required emergency exit—every air-raid shelter was required to have an alternative exit. None of these designs show the required strength of the walls and roofs or the required 80-centimeter-thick earth covering.[67] The designs for the two air-raid shelters designed for the SS compound in Birkenau follow the norms published in Neufert's 1944 edition of his *Bau-Entwurfslehre*—a fact that should not surprise us; this book was owned by the SS Central Construction Office in Auschwitz.

In his comments on the letter, which took the form of nine points, Crowell assumed that the letters of late 1943 and the letter of November 1944 referred to exactly the same kind of shelter.

> #3 The three documents give us some idea of scope and cost. We know we are talking about trench shelters, because these usually hold about 50 people (letter of November 11, 1944) and are built for the prisoners ("Defending," Part 2). We must be discussing at least 176 such shelters, so as I interpret the "Bogenstücke." . . . [68]

The blueprint BW 14 makes it clear that the shelter was to accommodate SS men, and the suggestion that there were 176 such shelters is simply absurd. The shelter BW 14 uses sixty-six of the prefabricated concrete arches, and the letter of October 25, 1943 mentions the delivery of only 176 pieces, barely enough to make only three of these shelters. But, as we have seen, in 1943 the goal was to create many small shelters to serve the SS men who guarded the periphery of the camp, not large shelters.

In points 5 to 7 Crowell presents a remarkable example of false analogy:

> #5 The German civil defense philosophy was that Luftschutz-kreisen were designed to be fully integrated; in other words, you did not build just a few shelters for a few people, you endeavored to build shelters for everyone ("Defending," Part 1). The presence of these trench shelters, in other words, strongly implies that fixed structures were also equipped with air raid shelters.
> #6 To put it another way, the presence of these trench shelters strongly argues that the crematoria were also equipped with their own air raid/gas shelters, because that accords with German LS policy.
> #7 Since #6 is the argument of "Technique," we can safely argue that each crematorium had such air raid/gas shelters. But in that case, where were the gas chambers?[69]

While it is true that the German civil defense system was based on the principle that in theory all citizens were to have equal access to air-raid shelters, one cannot argue that this philosophy also applied to the concentration camps, and it certainly did not apply to (Jewish) inmates imprisoned in those camps. On November 9, 1943, during the first meeting held in the Central Construction Office to discuss the construction of air-raid shelters in the camp, the decision was taken that shelters would be provided only for SS men and civilian workers who lived in the camp area. "It is impossible to create splinter protection trenches for the inmates of the main camp or the prisoner of war camp [Birkenau] because of the alignment of the streets, the drainage trenches and the high occupancy of the building sections."[70] In the summer of 1944, the decision that no shelters would be built in the main camp or Birkenau was reconfirmed.[71] And no shelters were built for the inmates, either in the main camp, in Birkenau, or in the satellite camp that provided labor for the construction of the IG Farben Buna plant.

Shortly after his return from Auschwitz-Monowitz, Primo Levi recorded that the inmates were not allowed to seek shelter when the bombings of the IG Farben Buna plant began in August 1944.

> Entry to the reinforced shelters was forbidden to us. When the earth began to tremble, we dragged ourselves, stunned and limping, through the corrosive fumes of the smoke bombs to the vast waste areas, sordid and sterile, closed within the boundary of the Buna: there we lay inert, piled up on top of each other like dead men, but still aware of the momentary pleasure of our bodies resting. We looked with indifferent eyes at the smoke and flames breaking out around us: in moments of quiet, full of the distant menacing roar that every European knows, we picked from the ground the stunted chicory leaves and dandelions, trampled on a hundred times, and chewed them slowly in silence.
>
> When the alarm was over, we returned from all parts to our posts, a silent innumerable flock, accustomed to the anger of men and things; and continued that work of ours, as hated as ever, now even more obviously useless and restless.[72]

Thus the presence of a few shelters for SS men does not imply the presence of shelters for the inmates. And certainly it does not lead to the conclusion that the crematoria were equipped with shelters. After all, if the narrow, uncomfortable concrete-reinforced trenches were good enough for the SS, why would the inmates have deserved better? Crowell assumed that "fixed structures were also equipped with air raid shelters." It is up to him to show evidence for this. The only "fixed structure" in Auschwitz that was retroactively fitted with an air-raid shelter was Crematorium 1. Located next to the SS hospital of Auschwitz I, it was meant to serve sick SS men. No other buildings were so equipped. This can be easily determined by means of even a cursory glance at the blueprints preserved in the Auschwitz-Birkenau State Museum in Oswiecim, or by visiting the remaining "fixed structures." So therefore the reasoning that

1. There are trench shelters in Auschwitz *therefore*
2. the "fixed structures" in Auschwitz are equipped with shelters *therefore*
3. the crematoria are equipped with shelters *therefore*
4. the crematoria did not contain gas chambers

fails.

In my report, I paid considerable attention to the air-raid shelter madness because I assumed that Irving would bring it up in the trial. I was right. Many times Irving invoked variations of Crowell's thesis. One particular exchange was very memorable. It occurred on January 24, 2000, the eighth day of the trial. The occasion was Rampton's introduction of a Polish forensic report from 1945 that mentioned the presence of traces of cyanide on ventilator gratings taken from Morgue 1 of Crematorium 2.

[Irving]: "I do not think I have any problem with this document at all. I will concede that they found in the ventilator grating taken from mortuary No. 1 of crematorium 2 remains of cyanide."

[Rampton]: "Yes. How do you account for that, Mr Irving?"

A.: "Because that particular room was used as Vergasungskeller, as a gassing cellar."

Q.: "Yes. Gassing what?"

A.: "I think the evidence is clear that it was used as a gassing cellar for fumigating objects or cadavers."

Q.: "Fumigating cadavers?"

A.: "Yes."

Q.: "What makes you say that?"

A.: "That is what that room was for. That is what mortuaries are for. In mortuaries you put cadavers."

Q.: "That is news to me, Mr Irving. What is the evidence for that?"

A.: "I beg your pardon?"

Q.: "What is the evidence that they used that for gassing corpses?"

A.: "That is what it was built for."

[Justice Gray]: "I am sorry, this seems a crude question, but what is the point of gassing a corpse?"

A.: "Because they came in heavily infested with the typhus bearing lice that had killed them."

[Rampton]: "So why would it need a gas type door with a peep hole with double eight millimetre thick glass and a metal grill on it?"

A.: "Well, I think you will have to show us the evidence for this."

Q.: "I will do."

A.: "And the evidence that this door was intended for that particular room and the evidence it was possible to obtain doors without the peep holes and the evidence that the room was not intended to be used for other purposes too."

Q.: "No, Mr Irving. You see, I do not have to prove anything. I am testing your, I have to say, slightly bizarre suggestion that you put Zyklon B into a room where the people are already dead. You tell me, 'Oh, well, that is because they wanted to delouse the corpses'. Then I asked you, 'Why then does it need a gas type door with a peep hole and a metal protection on it?'"

A.: "Because at this time in the war most of Germany was coming under the, it was feeling the weight of Royal Air Force bomber commands forays. We were bombing all over Eastern Europe. Our bombing raids were extending further and further into Central Europe. You will see from the Auschwitz construction department files an increasing concern about the need to build bomb tight shelters and gas tight shelters because of the danger of gas attack."

Q.: "Now it is an air raid shelter, is it?"

A.: "I beg your pardon?"

Q.: "In early 1943, Mr Irving, the first bombing raid anywhere near Auschwitz was not until late '44?"

A.: "Mr Rampton, if the court so pleases, I will tomorrow produce to you an index of all the documents in the Auschwitz construction department files from late 1942 onwards dealing with the necessity to build air raid shelters, gas tight air raid shelters and other similar constructions on the Auschwitz compound and on the Birkenau compound for precisely the reasons that I have mentioned."

Q.: "It is either a cellar for gassing corpses, is it, Mr Irving, or else it is an air raid shelter?"

A.: "Did I say either or?"

Q.: "Both. . . ."[73]

This almost surreal exchange does not need any comment. The only point that deserves some elaboration is Irving's claim that the index of the air-raid shelter files from the Central Construction Office would prove that gas-tight air-raid shelters were a major concern from late 1942 onward. In fact, a little later that same day, he came back to that issue.

[Irving]: "My Lord, I do not know whether it is better to do it from here or from the witness stand. Just before the adjournment we were talking about the danger of air raids. I told your Lordship that I would bring evidence tomorrow. In fact, by chance—"

[Mr. Justice Gray]: "May I interrupt you? Why do you not go back and then you can give the evidence that I think you were wanting to give before the adjournment about air raids in 1943."

A.: "By chance I have two copies of a three page extract I did from the US Holocaust Memorial Museum's catalogue of the Moscow records of the Auschwitz construction office, and I did this three-page extract purely relating to records on the air raid precautions in Auschwitz camp. I have given a copy to Mr Rampton, which I also have by chance. It contains files, for example, 1943 to 1944, on means of defence against bombs."

[Mr. Justice Gray]: "Are these Russian bombers?"

A.: "No."

Q.: "Western?"

A.: "It is a good question, my Lord."

Q.: "I think it might have been."

A.: "It could have been either. They did have Soviet air raids on Berlin, certainly."

Q.: "Anyway, it says, does it, that there were air raids going on in 1943?"

A.: "It actually goes back to August 1942, my Lord, the various files, detailed instructions on how to build air raid shelters and protect buildings against incendiary bombs, equipping of bunker, down at the bottom of the page more exchanges of notes and memos about various camp construction projects, many having to do with providing air-raid shelters."

Q.: "Yes. I think that is probably enough."

A.: "There are quite a lot of files relating to plans for air-raid shelter, estimates and accounts for construction of bomb shelters and so on. It was very much in the air, if I could put it like that, from August 1942 onwards."[74]

In his closing speech of March 15, Irving came back to this issue. "The captured Bauleitung records of Auschwitz housed in Moscow confirm that from mid 1942 onwards they began to consider the construction at the camp of shelters, splinter trenches, and other ARP, Air Raid Precaution, measures."[75]

Given the importance he attached to the Moscow files, it is necessary to look at these in some more detail. The "Preliminary Finding Aid" of the microfilmed Moscow holdings of Auschwitz Zentralbauleitung, issued by the United States Holocaust Memorial Museum in Washington, D.C., indicates that in Record Group (RG) 11.001M.03 of the Museum, which concerns the microfilmed collection of the Moscow holdings of the Auschwitz Zentralbauleitung, reel 47 contains eight files under a heading "Bombshelter." They are numbered with the Moscow numbers 502—1 - 400–407.

[502—1 -] 400 Corr. with firm "Geyneman & K-o" re supply of construction materials for construction of a bombshelter. 1942, 5 pp

[502—1 -] 401 Corr. with Silisian construction inspectorate and other higher institutions re provision of bomb and gas shelters. (Includes blueprints) 1940–44, 241 pp

[502—1 -] 402 Idem, 1944, 54 pp

[502—1 -] 403 Plan and report for an air-raid shelter for 35 persons, near building No. 24, 1944, 1p

[502—1 -] 404 Explanatory letter re air-raid shelter in the building of the Komandatura, 1944, 5 pp

[502—1 -] 405 Estimates and accounts for construction of bombshelters (with blueprints), 1944, 63 pp

[502—1 -] 406 Blueprints of bombshelters in the KL and accounts with the firm Polner, 1944, 118 pp

[502—1 -] 407 Corr. with the construction directorate and firms re provision of materials (cement, iron, lime etc.) for the air-raid shelters. Reports on work on them; accounts. 1944, 295 pp[76]

Irving stated that these files showed considerable interest in air-raid shelter construction from 1942 onward, and therefore we can limit ourselves to a consideration of files 400 and 401, the only two that contain material from before 1944. (Air-raid shelter construction in 1944 is obviously irrelevant to the negationist argument that Morgue 1 of Crematoria 2 and 3 was an air-raid shelter, as these spaces were designed in 1942 and completed in 1943.) None of the documents included in file 502—1 - 400 mention any crematorium or morgue, or a plan to convert a morgue of any crematorium into an air-raid shelter. Similarly, none of the documents dated from December 31, 1943, or earlier included in file 502—1 - 401 mention any crematorium or morgue, or a plan to convert a morgue of any crematorium into an air-raid shelter. Furthermore, none of the documents included in file 502—1 - 400 mention any intended or executed construction of an air-raid shelter in any of the Auschwitz camps. Similarly, none of the documents dated from December 31, 1943, or earlier included in file 502—1 - 401 mention any intended or executed construction of an air-raid shelter in any of the Auschwitz camps before November 1943.

Having considered the negative evidence, let us look at the positive evidence. What do these files contain? File 502—1 - 400, which gave Irving the reason to think that air-raid shelter construction was an issue at Auschwitz as early as 1942, is in fact a "cold call" by the building material supply firm Heinemann & Co from Berlin. It is a standard letter following a boilerplate model obviously sent to many organizations by a business hungry for orders. The letter is (wrongly) addressed to the SS-Neubau-leitung Auschwitz O/S (in fact, the construction office was at that time already known as SS-Zentralbauleitung). It is dated January 27, 1942, and it reads as follows:

> Re: air-raid protection shelter trench for work camps, factories, public areas etc.
>
> With reference to the decree of the Reich Marshal [Goering] concerning air-raid protection we present you with the enclosed
>
> Description and drawing* of air raid protection tunnel frame made from concrete, which can be delivered immediately from our yard at a suburban railway station in Berlin by railway or road truck. These air-raid protection tunnel frames can be used both below as well as above grade.
>
> The assembly of these ready-made slabs is very simple. These concrete frames have often stood the test.
>
> For the first erection we will make available a master installer for the costs involved.
>
> These air-raid protection tunnel frames have been approved by the board of the reich air-raid protection society.
>
> We would very much welcome your order, and are available to you at any time.
>
> Heil Hitler!
>
> Heinemann & Co.
> Building Materials.
>
> enclosed:
> 1 description
>
> *drawing will be sent on request.[77]

The enclosed document is three pages long and contains the offer listing the cost per stretching meter (64.20 RM), the cost of an entrance (139.20 RM) and so on.[78]

The letter from Heinemann & Co was received at Auschwitz on January 29, 1942. The Auschwitz Zentralbauleitung did not bother to reply. No further letters were received from this firm.

The documents included in file 502—1 - 401 that date from December 31, 1943, or earlier do not indicate any plans or attempts to construct air-raid shelters in Auschwitz before the end of 1943. Most of the documents in this file were circular letters issued by SS headquarters instructing local SS units how to prepare for air attacks. The file makes clear that the only issue of concern in Auschwitz before November 1943 was the problem of enabling the camp to adhere to blackout rules and the creation of fire precautionary measures, including the installation and maintenance of fire extinguishers in various buildings, and the creation of fire ponds to serve as water reserves in case of an attack with incendiary bombs.

The only document in the files that dates from 1943 and that indicates a concern for shelters is a memorandum of a meeting held on November 9, 1943. Two representatives of the regional air-raid protection authority [*Luftgaukommando VIII*] visited the camp to see what kind of preparations had been made to protect SS men and civilian workers and prevent the escape of inmates during air raids. The meeting was attended by senior members of the Auschwitz SS. Points 1 and 2 of the agenda dealt with measures to produce a blackout. Points 3 and 4 do mention the beginning of construction.

> 3. For the protection in case of possible attacks of SS men of the guard units or the administration who are not on duty, and of [civilian] workers who live in the camp area, the construction of splinter protection trenches following the existing rules has been planned, and the *Zentralbauleitung* has begun their construction by means of the making and installation of the [prefabricated] concrete elements.

> 4. It is impossible to create splinter protection trenches for the inmates of the main camp or the prisoner of war camp [Birkenau] because of the alignment of the streets, the drainage trenches and the high occupancy of the building sections [sub-camps]. Therefore, to create special security, a second security belt was created.

> 5. The creation of a splinter protected operation room in the basement of the hospital was begun.[79]

The rest of the memorandum concerned measures to prevent the escape of inmates in case of an air raid.

It is clear that the evidence of the archives does not support Irving's statement that "the captured Bauleitung records of Auschwitz housed in Moscow confirm that from mid 1942 onwards they began to consider the construction at the camp of shelters, splinter trenches, and other ARP, Air Raid Precaution, measures." To the contrary: the evidence makes clear that air-raid shelters were not a concern before November 1943. When this evidence is combined with the negative evidence that crematoria are mentioned in none of the air-raid shelter files, it is clear that the Moscow files do not support any suggestion that Morgue 1 of Crematoria 2 and 3, which was planned in 1942 and constructed in the fall of 1942 and the winter of 1942/1943, was intended as an air-raid shelter. The only thing the Moscow files demonstrate is that Trevor-Roper was justified in accusing Irving of seizing "small but dubious particle[s] of 'evidence'" to build upon it "a large general conclusion," while disregarding "more substantial evidence and probability against it."[80]

I would like to discuss one more document, which I found in 1993. When I began work on the history of Auschwitz, using, among other sources, the archive of the Central Construction Office, I did not set out to discover more "slips." As far as I was concerned, the point had been made. Yet as I worked my way through the material, I did encounter one slip that had not been noticed before. The document was written on the very same day that Bischoff referred to the *Vergasungskeller* in his letter to Kammler. In this case, the document is a minute of a meeting between SS-Unterscharführer Swoboda and AEG Engineer Tomitschek. The document was countersigned by Bischoff.

Auschwitz, 29.1.1943

Memorandum

re: Electricity Supply and Installation of the KL [*Konzentrationslager*, or Auschwitz] and KGL [*Kriegsgefangenenlager*, or Birkenau]

Conference held on 29.1.43 between the Central Construction Office Auschwitz and AEG-Kattowitz, present:
     Engineer Tomitschek—AEG and
     SS-Unterscharführer Swoboda—Central Construction Office
AEG informs that it has not yet received valid iron and metal certificates in response to its iron and metal request, which were partly already filed in November 1942. Therefore it was not possible for this firm to begin construction on the ordered parts of the installation. There is a great likelihood that, due to the continued delay in the allotment of these requests, delivery will take much longer.
     As a result of this, it is not possible to complete the installation and electricity supply of crematorium 2 in the Prisoner of War Camp [Birkenau] by January 31, 1943. It is only possible to complete the crematorium for operation earliest by February 15, 1943 using materials that are in stock for other building projects. This operation can only involve a limited use of the available machines (whereby is made possible burning with simultaneous Special Treatment), because the main electricity supply to the crematorium is not capable to carry its power consumption. Yet similarly the iron and metal certificates for the overhead line necessary for this have not been issued yet.
     Because of this, it is absolutely impossible to supply crematorium 3 with electricity.

Tomitschek.	Swoboda
Representative of AEG	SS-Unterscharführer

Taken note of
Bischoff.[81]

It is important to know the context of this letter: throughout January regular transports were arriving in Auschwitz, and the bunkers were hardly able to keep up. In fact, Eichmann was forced to divert trains destined for Auschwitz to Sobibor and Treblinka. Completion of the crematoria was of the greatest urgency. But in fact, construction had fallen two months behind schedule. Unexpected problems in the electricity supply to the buildings caused additional delays. When the SS architects modified the basement plan of Crematoria 2 and 3 to include a gas chamber, they increased the anticipated electricity consumption of the building. The ventilation system was now intended to simultaneously extract the Zyklon B from the gas chamber and fan the flames of the incinerators. They had tgb.: 44/86/43/Swo/Lm   Auschwitz, am 29.1.1943

A k t e n v e r m e r k

Betr.: Stromversorgung und Installation des KL und KGL.

    Besprechung am 29.1.43 zwischen Zentralbauleitung
Auschwitz und AEG-Kattowitz, Anwesende:
        Ing. Tomitschek - AEG und
        4-Uscha. Swoboda - Zentralbauleitung.
    Die AEG teilt mit, dass ihr auf ihre Eisen- und Metall-
anforderung, welche teilweise schon im November 1942 ausge-
schrieben wurden, bisher noch keine gültigen Eisen- und Metallscheine zur Verfügung gestellt wurden. Es war dieser Firma
aus diesem Grunde bisher nicht möglich, die bestellten
Anlagenteile in Arbeit zu nehmen. Es besteht die grosse Ge-
fahr, dass durch weitere Verzögerung in der Kontingentierung
dieser Aufträge die Liefertermine wesentlich verlängert werden.
    Aus diesem Grunde ist es auch nicht möglich, die In-
stallation und Stromversorgung des Krematoriums II im KGL
bis 31.1.43 fertigzustellen. Das Krematorium kann lediglich
aus lagernden, für andere Bauten bestimmten Materialien so-
weit fertiggestellt werden, dass eine Inbetriebsetzung frühe-
stens am 15.2.43 erfolgen kann. Diese Inbetriebsetzung kann
sich jedoch nur auf beschränkten Gebrauch der vorhandenen
Maschinen erstrecken (wobei eine Verbrennung mit gleichzeitiger
Sonderbehandlung möglich gemacht wird), da die zum Krematorium führende Zuleitung für dessen Leistungsverbrauch zu
schwach ist. Für das hierfür erforderliche Freileitungs-
material sind ebenfalls noch keine Eisen- und Metallscheine
zugewiesen worden.
    Eine Stromversorgung des Krematoriums III ist aus
vorgenannten Gründen derzeit überhaupt nicht möglich.

Vertreter der AEG
z.K.g.:

4-Hauptsturmführer   4-Unterscharführer contacted AEG, the contractor for the electrical systems, but due to rationing AEG had been unable to get the heavy-duty wiring and circuit breakers the system required. As a result, Crematorium 2 was to be supplied with a temporary electrical system; nothing at all was available for use in Crematorium 3. The AEG representative in Kattowitz, Engineer Tomitschek, warned the Auschwitz Building Office that the capacity of the temporary system would not allow for simultaneous "special treatment" and incineration. The SS did not heed his warning: when Crematorium 2 was finally handed over to the camp authorities, they immediately began to work the ovens at full capacity, against Tomitschek's advice. The electrical system caught fire. Both the forced-draft system that fanned the incinerator flames and the ventilation system to extract the Zyklon B from the gas chamber were damaged.

I provided the historic context of this document because, like any other document, it is mute when taken by itself. Like any other piece of evidence, it must be placed where it belongs, and this requires knowledge of what was going on at the time, at the building site in Birkenau, in the architect's office and, in this case, in Greece. Considering the context, it was obvious that the AEG document came into existence when it became clear there would be a delay in the completion of the crematoria, which was partly caused by the slow arrival of rationed electrical equipment, and when it also became clear that this delay would conflict with Eichmann's schedule of deportations. Our understanding of this context is based on other evidence, such as the notorious letter dated January 29, 1943, in which Bischoff reported to Kammler on the progress of construction of Crematorium 2, which contained the information that "the planks from the concrete ceiling of the cellar used as a mortuary could not yet be removed on account of the frost. This is, however, not very important, as the gassing cellar (*Vergasungskeller*) can be used for that purpose."[82]

I discussed the letter in a BBC Horizon documentary entitled "Blueprints of Genocide." This generated a response by the negationist *Journal of Historical Review*. "During a dramatic high point of the broadcast, van Pelt is shown holding a document while stating: 'It says very clearly, "You will be able to kill and you will be able to burn simultaneously in this building [Crematory 2]."'" This document, which is not shown to viewers, is actually a simple memorandum of January 29, 1943, not even marked 'Secret,' about . . . electricity supply." After judging my accidental reversion of the word order of "killing" and "burning" as deceitful, it noted the way I rendered "*Sonderbehandlung*" as "kill."

> Commenting on this misrepresentation, Robert Faurisson has written that "the word 'Sonderbehandlung' could mean, by its place in the phrase, anything except to kill because this 'special treatment' was simultaneous with burning." Moreover, as Faurisson further noted, it is obvious that if Fleming, or anyone, had actually discovered a wartime German document that clearly says what Holocaust historians have been seeking for decades, it would be publicized everywhere as a discovery of the greatest historical importance. (See R. Faurisson, "A KGB Novelist: Gerald Fleming," Adelaide Institute on-line newsletter [Australia], Dec. 1996, pp. 23–25.)[83]

Memorandum of a meeting held at the Auschwitz Central Construction Office, January 29, 1943. Courtesy Osobyi Archive, Moscow. (opposite page)

Let us begin with the negationist challenge that the document is "not even marked 'Secret,'" a common negationist argument to attack the validity of most pieces of evidence. Their argument is that because the so-called Final Solution of the Jewish Problem occurred "in secret," all documents that relate to it should be marked as "Secret." This argument suffers from the fallacy of division, which arises when one argues from the properties of a whole (the general secrecy of the "Final Solution") to the properties of the constituent parts of that whole (a discussion about the electricity supply to a crematorium equipped with gas chambers). There is, of course, no reason to assume that what is true of the whole is true of all the parts and that evidence for the existence of a largely secret operation cannot be derived from parts of that operation that were not secret. None of the documents in the Auschwitz building archive deal directly with the Holocaust; they all deal with the construction of buildings. Insofar as secrecy was an issue, it seems that everyone involved in the killing of Jews in Auschwitz signed a general statement in which they promised secrecy. Hans Aumeier testified in his statement of July 25, 1945, that after witnessing the gassing, Höss told him "that the whole affair was a secret Reich matter, and that because of our oath of allegiance we would be condemned to death by the Reichsführer SS if we were to talk about it to others. We had to sign a declaration to this effect, which was given for safekeeping by the camp commandant." And he added that "all the men who later had something to do with the commando were instructed by Untersturmführer Grabner, and also had to sign such a declaration in his presence."[84]

The negationist attack on the document continued with the observation that Robert Faurisson has written that "the word 'Sonderbehandlung' could mean, by its place in the phrase, anything except to kill because this 'special treatment' was simultaneous with burning." In other words, Faurisson argues with his usual literal-mindedness that because the adjective "simultaneous" means "at the same time," it is impossible that the noun *Sonderbehandlung* could refer to killing because one first kills and then burns the body. The problem with Faurisson's observation is that it ignores the context of the clause "whereby is made possible burning with simultaneous Special Treatment." If it were an instruction for the Sonderkommandos on how to kill and incinerate the victims, Faurisson would have a point, but it is not. The context is a discussion about the electricity supply to the crematorium. The problem which Tomitschek and Swoboda discussed was rooted in the circumstance that electricity was necessary to operate the ventilation system of the gas chambers. Yet, at the same time that this ventilation system was to extract the hydrogen cyanide from the gas chamber, the crematorium also needed electricity to operate the forced-air system to heat the incinerators as they were readied to cremate the remains of the people killed in the gas chambers. In other words, there was an overlap in the electricity consumption of the gas chamber and the ovens, the former still using electricity *after the killing had occurred,* the latter using electricity *before the incineration could commence.*

Then there is Faurisson's implicit argument that the context of the letter does not count. I will review the reasons for Faurisson's refusal to consider the context below. Here it is important to note that a basic rule in the interpretation of historical evidence is that any piece of evidence depends upon the context from which it is taken. David Hackett Fischer observed in his *Historians' Fallacies* that "no historical statement-in-evidence floats freely outside of time and space. None applies abstractly and universally."[85] Faurisson did not choose to consider the context and hence did not apply historical criticism to the text of the memorandum.

Finally there is Faurisson's last argument: that if "Fleming, or anyone, had actually discovered a wartime German document that clearly says what Holocaust historians have been seeking for decades, it would be publicized everywhere as a discovery of the greatest historical importance." In other words, the fact that I did not choose to publicize my discovery "everywhere," trumpeting it as "a discovery of the greatest historical importance," suggests that this document probably does not exist, because if it did, it would have been "what Holocaust historians have been seeking for decades." When I came upon the Tomitschek/Swoboda memorandum in 1993, I was pleased to find another small piece of a large puzzle but in no way thought it to be "of the greatest historical importance." I did not find any reason in the past, nor do I today, to set my research agenda according to Faurisson's wishes. In 1979, he proposed in a letter to *Le Monde* that he wanted a public debate on "the problem of the gas chambers." Faurisson rejected the premise that there was a "superabundance of proofs that attest to the existence of 'gas chambers'" and proposed that someone supply him "with a proof, one single precise proof of the actual existence of one 'gas chamber,' one single 'gas chamber.'" And he concluded his challenge with the exhortation: "Let us examine this proof together, in public."[86]

No single piece of evidence can "prove" the existence of any historical event. From a historian's point of view, Faurisson's challenge is absurd. No piece of evidence is conclusive by itself. Historians reconstruct the past by cross-referencing different pieces of evidence, each of different evidential value. Negationists such as Faurisson and Irving seem unable to assimilate this principle; they continue to throw challenges to academic historians to produce "one single proof." As we saw in Chapter 1, a literary analysis of a text as a verbal icon, as an autonomous verbal structure, that forecloses any appeal to history, biography, or cultural context may make sense when applied to poems, but it does not make sense to apply this methodology to a historical document. Faurisson's "Ajax method" cannot be applied to the study of practical messages, which are successful *if and only if* we correctly infer the intention. The hastily written Tomitschek/Swoboda memorandum is completely unintelligible as a historical source if one does not know the historical context, which includes the speed with which the SS tried to complete the crematoria, the difficulty they had obtaining allocations for building materials, the meaning of the word *Sonderbehandlung,* the need to fire up the ovens before they were used, and so on.

Enough about "single proofs" that in the case of Auschwitz seem destined to appear in "slips." The real historical importance of the archives of the Central Construction office is *not* that they prove independent of other evidence that Auschwitz was an extermination camp. Insofar as the issue of "proof" is relevant, the archives are important because they provide additional evidence of a "non-intentional" nature that allows us to interpret and cross-examine the "intentional" evidence given by important and informative witnesses such as Tauber and Höss. While the negationists have tried to abuse these architectural documents to narrow down the amount of admissible evidence with their insistence that nothing is relevant except the wartime document, we consider them as a means to increase the amount of evidence. For example, when we consider the blueprints of Crematorium 2 and use them to reconstruct this building, it becomes possible to follow Tauber's narrative sentence by sentence. Or when one considers the blueprints of Crematorium 4, one can study not only the logical arrangement of the building—with its sequence of three gas chambers (with stoves to heat the rooms during the winter), the vestibule and the room containing the fuel supply for the stoves in the gas chambers, the large morgue, and the cremation section with the anteroom, the incinera-

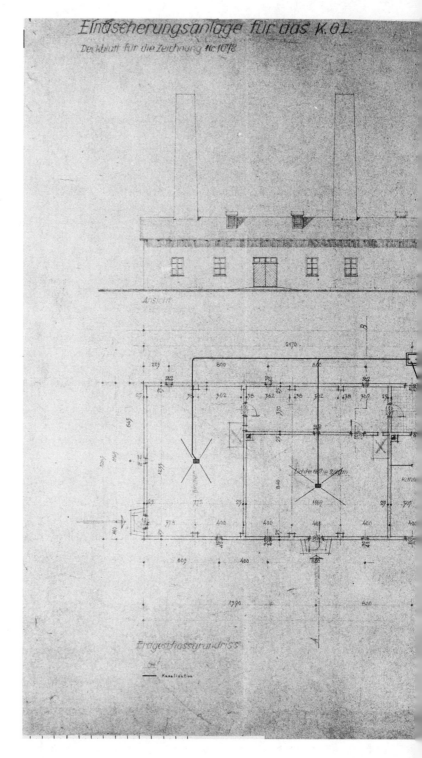

Plan and elevation of Crematorium 4, 1943. In the plan, the three gas chambers are depicted at the left, while in the elevation they are to be seen at the right. The three small windows in the low wing containing the gas chambers are the apertures through which the Zyklon B was inserted into the gas chambers. Courtesy Archive Auschwitz-Birkenau State Museum, Oswiecim.

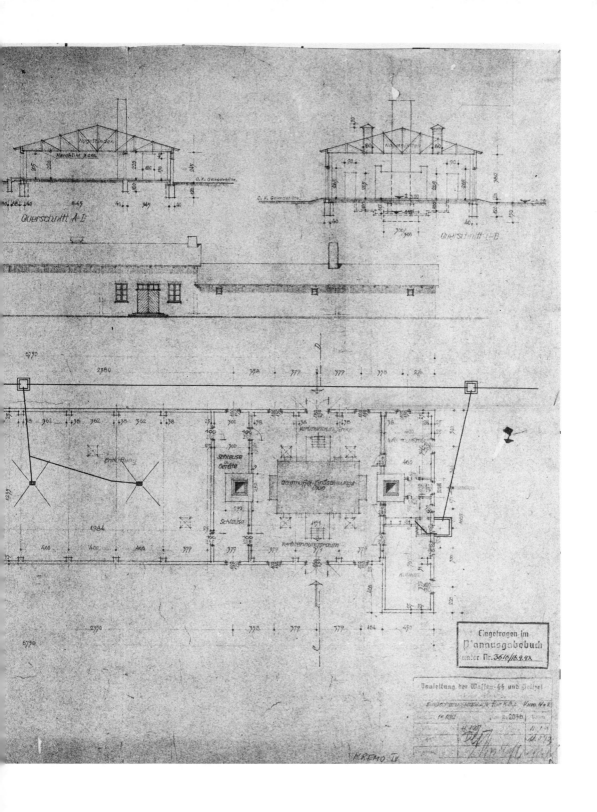

Querschnitt A-B

Querschnitt C-D

Eingetragen im
Plannusgabebuch
unter Nr. 3616//6.9.43.

KREMO IV

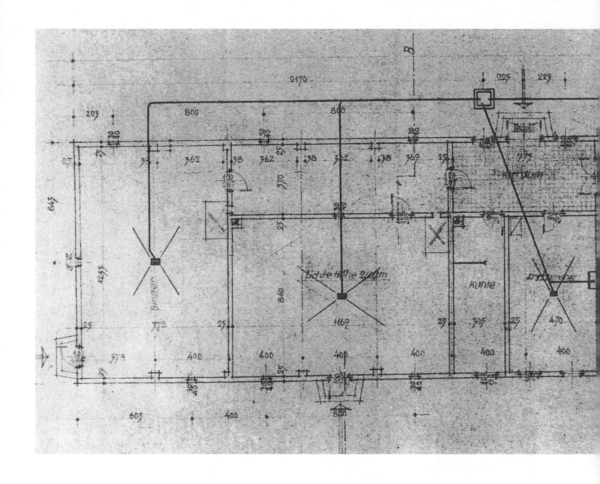

Detail of the plan of Crematorium 4, showing the three gas chambers. Visible are the two stoves, marked with a cross, included to preheat the gas chambers. Courtesy Archive Auschwitz-Birkenau State Museum, Oswiecim.

tion room with the eight-muffle oven, the coke room with the fuel that supplied the 8-muffle incineration oven, and a small office—but also square this with the remaining fragments of the building and eyewitness statements. For example, in the former coke storeroom of Crematorium 1, the Auschwitz-Birkenau State Museum preserves some of the gas-tight shutters from Crematorium 4. The shutters measure 30 cm by 40 cm and are marked with the inventory numbers PMO-II-5-64/1, PMO-II-5-64/2, and PMO-II-5-64/3. In the plan they are indicated as having a size of 30 cm by 40 cm. In an order dated February 13, 1943 they are mentioned as "12 pieces gas-tight doors of 30/40 cm"—"*12 St. Gasdichte Türen cca 30/40 cm.*" And on the back of the same order one finds a note from the camp workshop, dated February 24, requesting materials to construct these twelve shutters. Once again they are identified as "*12 st. gasdichte Türen cca 30/40 cm.*"[87] Obviously, the plan, the bill, and the relics coincide. As we have seen, David Olère depicted these gas-tight shutters in his drawings of Crematorium 5 and Bunker 2. And then there are eyewitness statements of the way these gas-tight doors functioned. Let us quote, once more, part of Tauber's recollections of Crematorium 4. We begin in a room labeled in the plan as "*Vorraum*"—vestibule.

> Opposite the entrance door in the corridor, there was a door that opened on a room with a window which was the kitchen for the SS working in the crematorium, a kitchen where the dishes were prepared by members of the Sonderkommando. This room was

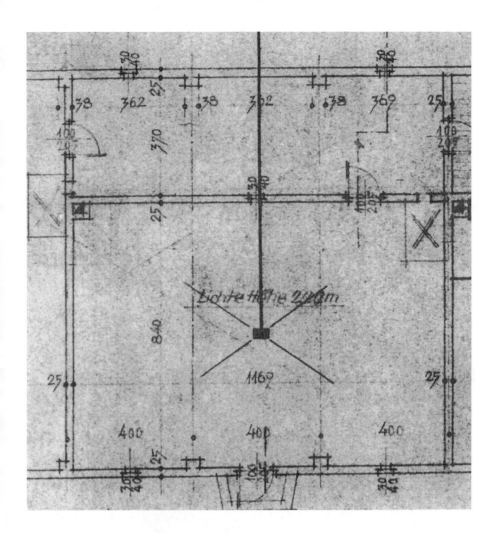

Detail of one of the three gas chambers. The size of the apertures through which Zyklon B was inserted in the room is clearly marked as 30 cm by 40 cm. Courtesy Archive Auschwitz-Birkenau State Museum, Oswiecim.

Shutter measuring 30 cm by 40 cm found at Crematorium 5 and stored in the coke room of Crematorium 1. Photo by Omer Arbel, 1999.

Order of 13 February 1942 for Crematoria 4 and 5 issued by the Auschwitz Central Construction Office to the Deutsche Ausrüstung Werke. The order is for the "Production of 12 gas-tight doors approximately 30/40 cm exactly like those already made in the inmates' woodworking shop, with bolt and catch" (Anfertigung von 12 Stück gasdichten Türen ca 30/40 cm genau wie bereits angefertigte in der Häftlingstischlerei mit Riegel u. Verschluss). Courtesy Archive Auschwitz-Birkenau State Museum, Oswiecim. (opposite page)

next to that of the Sonderkommando prisoners. . . . The third door in the corridor led to a corridor with a barred window and a door leading to the crematorium yard.

From this corridor, the door on the right gave access to the first of the gas chambers and that opposite to the smallest of the chambers, communicating by another door with the biggest.

This corridor, and the three following rooms were used as chambers for gassing people. All had gas-tight doors, and also windows that had bars on the inside and were closed by gas-tight shutters on the outside. These small windows, which could be reached by the hand of a man standing outside, were used for throwing the contents of cans of Zyklon-B into the gas chambers full of people. The gas chambers were about two meters high and had an electric lighting installation on the walls but they had no ventilation system, which obliged the Sonderkommando who were removing the bodies to wear gasmasks. The corpses were dragged along the floor into the access corridor, where the barbers cut off the hair and then into the undressing room, which also served, in this kind of crematorium, as a store room for the corpses. It was a big hall where the bodies were put while the gas chambers were being cleaned up. Then they were taken through the narrow corridor between the undressing room and the furnace room, where at each end a dentist tore out the gold teeth. In the furnace room, there was the room of the head of the Kommando and beside it another one for the rest of the SS.[88]

Thus the blueprints help to corroborate eyewitness evidence. They do not, and should not, take the place of it.

Zentral-Bauleitung
der Waffen-SS und Polizei
Auschwitz O/S.

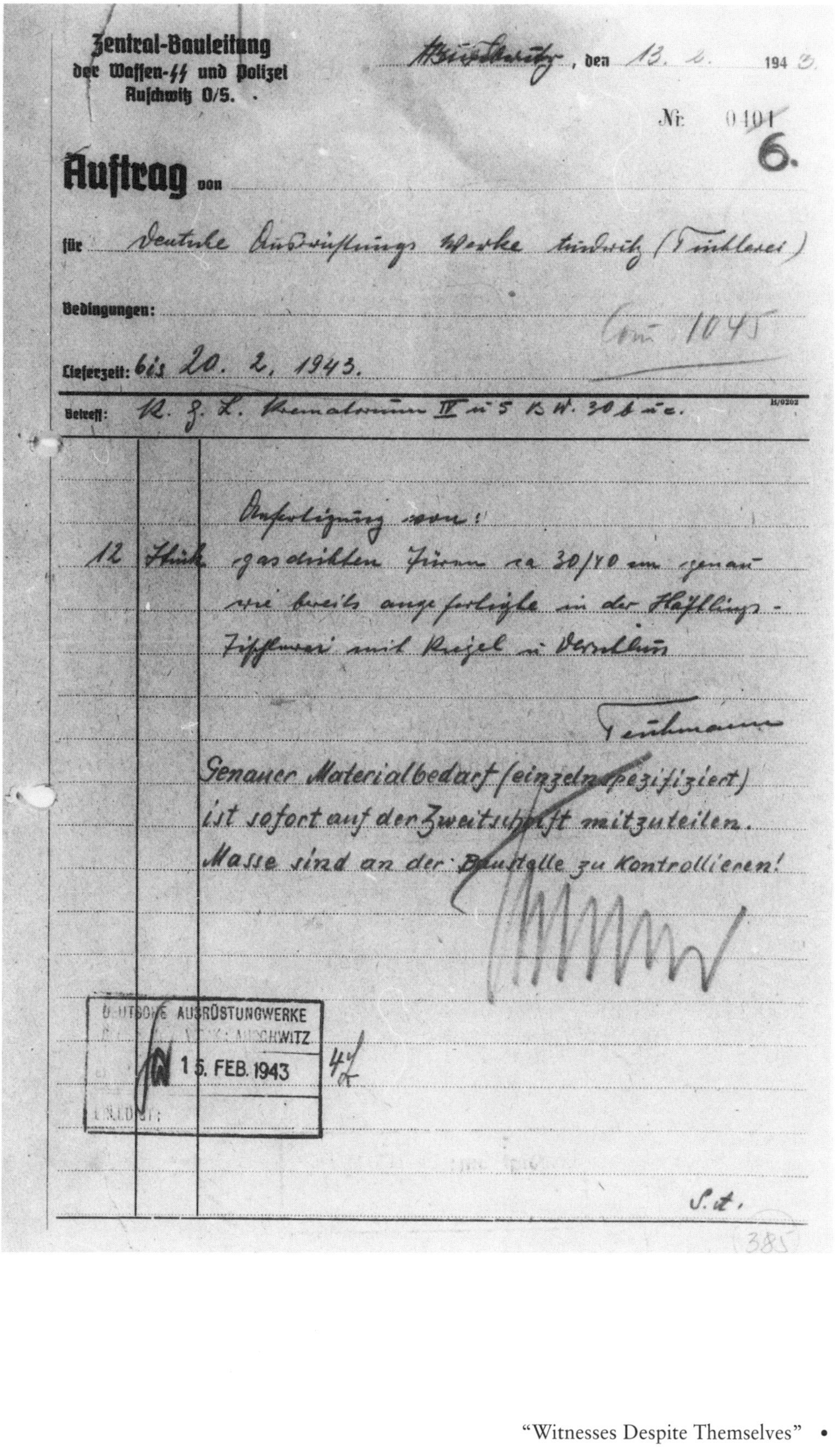

Auschwitz, den 13. 2. 1943

Nr. 0101 6.

Auftrag von

für Deutsche Ausrüstungswerke Auschwitz (Tischlerei)

Bedingungen: Kom. 1045

Lieferzeit: bis 20. 2. 1943.

Betreff: KL. u. KL. Krematorium IV u. V BW. 30 b u. c.

H/0202

Anfertigung von:

12 Stück gasdichten Türen ca 30/40 cm genau wie bereits angefertigte in der Häftlings-Schlosserei mit Riegel u. Verschluss

Teuchmann

Genauer Materialbedarf (einzeln spezifiziert) ist sofort auf der Zweitschrift mitzuteilen. Masse sind an der Baustelle zu Kontrollieren!

DEUTSCHE AUSRÜSTUNGWERKE
... AUSCHWITZ
15. FEB. 1943
ERLEDIGT:

S.t.

(385)

Photo of Crematorium 2, taken from the south, December 1942. The gas chamber can be seen just to the right of the locomotive's smokestack. The concrete roof is not yet covered with dirt, and therefore the tops of three of the four gas insertion columns can be seen. Courtesy Archive Auschwitz-Birkenau State Museum, Oswiecim.

The same applies to, for example, photos of the crematoria. During the construction of the camp, the Central Construction office documented the progress of construction photographically. All these photos were assembled in the so-called Bauleitung Album, which survived the war. One of the photos shows the back of Crematorium 2 shortly before its completion. One can see the basement space known in the plans as Morgue 1 projecting outward from the long side of the building. It is not yet covered with earth, and as a result one can easily see (just right of the smokestack of the locomotive in the foreground) the more or less cubical tops of three of the four wire-mesh Zyklon B insertion columns made by Kula, drawn by Olère, and described by Tauber. Again, by itself the photograph would not be conclusive evidence, but in combination with eyewitness evidence it proves the existence of these columns beyond reasonable doubt.

Yet sometimes study of the plans and photos helps us to reconstruct important elements in the development of Auschwitz as an extermination camp for which there is no eyewitness evidence. For example: all the evidence points to the fact that the Germans changed the purpose of Crematorium 2 between its first inception in the fall of 1941 and its final completion in the spring of 1943. At the time of the original design this crematorium was meant to incinerate the corpses of inmates who had died as the result of the "ordinary" violence of concentration camp existence and the "ordinary" mortality that results from seasonal infectious diseases such as typhus and typhoid fever. By the time it was completed, Crematorium 2, Crematorium 3, and two other crematoria (4 and 5) were meant to serve the original function and also incinerate the corpses of deportees who had arrived in Auschwitz to be immediately selected for the gas chambers and killed. On the basis of ample evidence, we know that by the time of their completion, Crematoria 2, 3, 4, and 5 were equipped with homicidal gas chambers and that they were used to kill the vast majority of deportees. Yet how and when did the intended purpose of the buildings change?

The blueprints and the correspondence that goes with them offer evidence that allows us to understand some aspect of the changing purpose of the crematoria. I will discuss three variables: the information the blueprints give us about the evolution of the projected inmate population, the incineration capacity (calculated per month of 30 days), and the morgue capacity (calculated in terms of morgue units per month of 30 days, in which each unit is one corpse-day: which means that a morgue with a capacity of 100 corpses has a capacity of $100 \times 30 = 3000$ morgue units per month). The period under consideration stretches from the fall of 1941 to the spring of 1943.

The basis for the calculation of the capacity of the crematoria is a wartime German document. Dated June 28, 1943, the letter reads as follows:

28 June, 1943.

Concerns: the completion of crematorium 3.

Reference: none

To the SS-Administrative and Economic Head Office,
department C,
SS-Brigadeführer and General Major Dr. Ing. Kammler
Berlin—Lichterfelde—West
Unter den Eichen 120–135.

Report the completion of crematorium 3 at 26 June 1943. Therewith all the crematoria ordered have been completed.

Capacity of the now available crematoria per 24 hours:
1. old crematorium 1
    3×2 muffle ovens   340 persons
2. new crematorium 2 in KGL
    5×3 muffle ovens   1,440 persons
3. new crematorium 3
    5×3 muffle ovens   1,440 persons
4. new crematorium 4
    8 muffle oven   768 persons
5. new crematorium 5
    8 muffle oven   768 persons

Total per 24 hours   4,756 persons

The leader of the Central Building Administration of the Waffen SS and Police Auschwitz,

Signed: [Bischoff]
SS-Sturmbannführer.

Cc: dossier—Janisch
dossier—Kirschnek
file KGL BW 30.[89]

31550/Ja./Ne.-

Betr.: Fertigstellung d. Krematoriums III

Bezug: ohne

Anl.: -/-

An das

SS-Wirtschafts-Verwaltungs-
hauptamt, Amtsgruppenchef C
SS-Brigadeführer u. Generalmajor
Dr.-Ing. K a m m l e r
Berlin- Lichterfelde - West.

Unter den Eichen 126 - 135

      Melde die Fertigstellung des Krematoriums III mit dem
26.6.1943.Mithin sind sämtliche befohlenen Krematorien fertiggestellt.

      Leistung der nunmehr vorhandenen Krematorien
         bei einer 24 stündigen Arbeitszeit :

1.) altes Krematorium I		
3 x 2 Muffelöfen	340	Personen
2.) neues Krematorium i.K.G.L. II		
5 x 3 Muffelöfen	1440	Personen
3.) neues Krematorium III		
5 x 3 Muffelöfen	1440	Personen
4.) neues Krematorium IV.		
8 Muffelofen	768	Personen
5.) neues Krematorium V.	768	Personen
8 Muffelofen		
Insges. bei 24 stündiger Arbeitszeit	4756	Personen

Verteiler:
Akt - ~~Jantzen~~ Bauen,
" - Kirschnek
Registratur K.G.L. BW. 30

Der Leiter der Zentralbauleitung
der Waffen-SS und Polizei Auschwitz

SS-Sturmbannführer.

Two questions must be asked before we continue. First, is there any reason to doubt the authenticity of this letter, and, second, are the figures credible? During the proceedings in the Royal Courts of Justice, Irving accepted every document I had used in my expert opinion as genuine except this one. He had no choice but to challenge it, because if it was authentic, it would prove very damaging for his case.

Irving argued that the document was a forgery. But if it was, who would have made it? Obviously the Russians, Irving argued. If they had done so, with what purpose? Obviously to embarrass the Germans, he claimed. It is an unlikely scenario. "It may in general be said that no one ever forged evidence to deceive historians," the prominent historian Geoffrey Rudolph Elton wrote in his *Practice of History* (1967). "The intention, nearly always, is to deceive contemporaries, and mostly in a court of law."[90] The problem with the scenario that the Soviets had forged the letter to stress the diabolical project of the Germans through inflation of the incineration capacity in Auschwitz is that the figures in the official "Statement of the Extraordinary State Committee for the Ascertaining and Investigation of Crimes Committed by the German-fascist Invaders and Their Associates in the Oswiecim Death Camp," issued in May 1945, were much higher than the figures in Bischoff's letter.

This report assumed that Crematorium 1 was able to reduce 300 corpses per day, Crematoria 2 and 3 a total of 3,000 corpses per day each, and Crematoria 4 and 5 a total of 1,500 corpses each. In other words, the Soviet report assumed more than double the actual incineration capacity. If some Soviet agency had taken the trouble to forge one document, one would expect that they would have wanted to back up their own figures—especially as Bischoff's numbers would only add up to a total possible incineration of 2.6 million corpses over the life span of the crematoria (1: 24 months; 2: 19 months; 3: 18 months; 4: 17 months; 5: 18 months). This figure was much lower than the assumed 4 million victims. It is highly implausible that the Soviets would have created a document that would only support 50 percent of their own estimate, which had been basic in their determination that 4 million people died at Auschwitz.

It is also important to note that the Soviet Report of May 1945 gave prominence to the role of the firm Topf & Sons, suppliers of incineration equipment. It mentioned that the Soviets had recovered a large correspondence between Topf and the camp administration, and it printed two letters as evidence, one sent by Topf to the Central Construction Office on February 12, 1943, confirming, among other things, "two electric lifts for hoisting corpses and one temporary lift for corpses" and a letter from the Central Construction Office to Topf dated August 21, 1942, dealing with the construction of ovens near the "Bathhouses for Special Actions." The Soviet Report did not mention the letter of June 28, 1943. But we know that the Soviet State Extraordinary Commission for the Investigation of Fascist and Nazi Crimes did know about this document: the Moscow copy of this document is accompanied by a Russian translation made by a person identified as "Wolynskaja." This translation is dated April 28, 1945. Why would the Soviets forge a document and then suppress it?

The second question is whether the figures are right. In his discussion of this document, Stäglich rejected it out of hand. "The sheer punctiliousness of the accounting—right down to the very last corpse—is suspicious, for cremation is a complicated technical process, involving so many variables that the incineration capacity of a crematorium is not always the same."[91] Be that as it may, the way Bischoff came to his numbers is not difficult to establish. Crematoria 2 and 3 each had 15 muffles, and it is clear that Bischoff established a capacity of 1,440 corpses per day on the assumption that each muffle could reduce 96 corpses per day, or 4 corpses per muffle per hour. Crematoria 4 and 5 each had 8 muffles, and with a capacity of 96 corpses per muffle per day, Bischoff arrived at a figure of 768 corpses per crematorium. The old crematorium had a lower capacity of 57 corpses per muffle per day because the ovens were of an older design and construction. Of course, these numbers are averages and included downtime for cleaning and so on.

The question is now if Auschwitz Crematoria 2, 3, 4, and 5 could have incinerated four corpses per muffle per hour. If one followed normal civilian practice, *in which it is absolutely essential to preserve the identity of the remains from the beginning of incineration to the final gathering of the ashes,* Bischoff's figures would indeed be absurd. It would be impossible to insert a body in the muffle, cremate it, and remove the remaining bones and ashes within fifteen minutes. But the situation changes radically when the identity of the remains ceases to be important. First of all, if the size of the muffle permits, it becomes possible to insert more than one corpse at the same time. Furthermore, it becomes feasible to create something of a continuous process, in which, after initial heating of the incinerators, the burner can be turned off, thus making full use of the phenomenon that at the right temperature the body will combust and consume itself without any further application of an external source of energy.

In his testimony, Tauber gave an extensive description of the incineration procedures and implicitly confirmed the validity of Bischoff's figures. According to him, each muffle in Crematorium 1 could incinerate five bodies. "At the time when I was working there, the incineration of such a charge took up to an hour and a half, because they were the bodies of very thin people, real skeletons, which burned very slowly."[92] If we take Tauber's figures, it would take 17 hours to incinerate the 340 corpses mentioned in the letter of June 28, 1943.

Tauber provided a very detailed account of the incineration procedure in Crematorium 2. As we have seen in Chapter 3, he discussed how the Sonderkommandos developed a whole science based on the observation that the incineration process for the corpses in the side muffles differed from that of the center muffle. The corpses of "*Müselmanns,*" or of wasted people with no fat, burned rapidly in the side muffles and slowly in the center one. Conversely, the corpses of people gassed directly on arrival, because they were not wasted, burned better in the center muffle. "As the retort was almost 7' long, 2'8" wide and about 3'4" high, one could normally load it with four or five corpses. But sometimes we charged a greater number of corpses. It was possible to charge up to 8 '*Müselmanns.'*"[93] During the trial runs of the ovens of Crematorium 2, observers from the Political Section, representatives of the Berlin headquarters, and engineers from Topf timed the process. Each muffle was loaded with three corpses for the occasion.

> As soon as all the muffles of the five furnaces had been charged, the members of the commission began to observe the operation, watch in hand. They opened the muffle doors, looked at their watches, expressed surprise at the slowness of the cremation process. In view of the fact that the furnaces were not yet hot enough, even though we had been firing them since the morning, and because they were brand new, the incineration of this charge took about 40 minutes.[94]

The ovens of Crematorium 2, shortly before their completion, January 1943. Courtesy Archive Auschwitz-Birkenau State Museum, Oswiecim. (following pages)

Tauber went on to explain that later on incineration became more efficient, and they could incinerate two loads per hour. In fact, the Sonderkommandos tried to overload the muffles, because this would allow them some free time.

> According to the regulations, we were supposed to charge the muffles every half hour. Ober Capo August explained to us that, according to the calculations and plans for this crematorium, 5 to 7 minutes was allowed to burn one corpse in a muffle. In principle, he did not let us put more than three corpses in one muffle. Because with that quantity we were obliged to work without interruption, for as soon as the last muffle was charged, the contents of the first had been consumed. In order to be able to take a pause during the work, we would charge 4 or 5 corpses in each muffle. The incineration of such a charge took longer, and after charging the last muffle, we had a few minutes' break until the first one was again available. We took advantage of this free time to wash the floor of the furnace room, as a result of which the air became a little cooler.[95]

According to Tauber's testimony, the incinerators of Crematorium 2 should have burned, according to the regulations, $(15 \times 2 \times 3) = 90$ bodies per hour. This would mean that the official daily capacity of 1,440 would be reached in 16 hours of operation $(90 \times 16 = 1,440)$.

Höss confirmed Tauber's account. In 1946, he wrote while in Polish captivity that "the two large crematories were built in the winter of 1942–43 and brought into service in the spring of 1943."

> Each had five ovens with three doors [retorts] per oven and could cremate about two thousand bodies in less than twenty-four hours. Technical difficulties made it impossible to increase the capacity. Attempts to do this caused severe damage to the installations. . . .
>
> The two smaller crematories [4 and 5] were capable of burning about 1,500 bodies in twenty-four hours, according to the calculations made by the construction company called Topf of Erfurt.[96]

A few pages later, in a different context, Höss returned to the issue of the incineration capacity of the crematoria.

> Depending on the size of the bodies, up to three corpses could be put in through one oven door at the same time. The time required for cremation also depended on the number of bodies in each retort, but on average it took twenty minutes. As previously stated, Crematories 2 and 3 could cremate two thousand bodies in twenty-four hours, but a higher number was not possible without causing damage to the installations. Crematories 4 and 5 should have been able to cremate 1,500 bodies in twenty-four hours, but as far as I know this figure was never reached.[97]

A final indication that the testimony of Tauber and Höss may be trusted, and that the Topf ovens had a capacity in the range listed by Bischoff, can be found in the patent application T 58240 Kl. 24 for a "Continuous Operation Corpse Incineration Furnace for Intensive Use," filed by Topf on November 5, 1942. In the first paragraph, the application referred to the situation in the camps in the East.

In the gathering camps in the occupied territories in the East with their high mortality rate, as they are affected by the war and its consequences, it has become impossible to bury the great number of deceased inmates. This is the result of both the lack of space and personnel and the immediate and longterm danger to that immediate and farther surroundings that is caused by the burial of the dead who often succumbed to infectious diseases.

Therefore there is a need to quickly, safely and hygienically dispose of the constantly great number of corpses. In that process it will, of course, be impossible, to operate according to the legal stipulations that are valid in the territory of the Reich. Thus it will be impossible to reduce to ashes only one corpse at a time, and the process cannot be done without extra heating. Instead it will be necessary to incinerate continuously and simultaneously many corpses, and during the duration of the incineration the flames and the gasses of the fire will have to engage the corpses to be incinerated directly. It will be impossible to separate the ashes of the simultaneously incinerated, and the ashes can only be handled together. Therefore one should not really talk in the depicted disposition of corpses of "incineration," but it really concerns here corpse burning.

To realize such corpse burning—following the principles sketched above—a number of multi-muffle ovens were installed in some of those camps, which according to their design are loaded and operated periodically. Because of this these ovens do not fully satisfy, because the burning does not proceed quickly enough to dispose of in the shortest possible time the great number of corpses that are constantly presented.[98]

It is clear that the ovens referred to in the last paragraphs are the multi-muffle ovens supplied by Topf to Auschwitz.

The patent application describes the continuous cremation furnace as a structure in which the corpses are inserted at the top, and as they slowly slide down a system of inclined grids, they are quickly reduced to ashes. It does not provide data about the capacity of the furnace, but in 1985, the consulting engineers Klaus and Christel Kunz made, in consultation with Rolf Decker, manager of incinerator production at the Ruppmann company in Stuttgart, an engineering assessment of Topf's continuous-cremation furnace. They assumed that the furnace could be initially loaded with fifty corpses and that in the upper part of the furnace the bodies would dry out through evaporation; after falling into the second part, these corpses would be burned while the first part of the furnace was being reloaded. After falling into the third part of the furnace, the remains would be completely reduced to ashes.

On the basis of the plan one may only theoretically calculate the capacity and duration, because exact data can only be determined through practical trials. Nevertheless it is quite conceivable to introduce, when the object is appropriately dimensioned, some 50 corpses on the shelf, assuming it has a length of 25 meters. The process of evaporation in position should take some 15 minutes, so that at a continuous operation one could arrive at an incineration capacity of around 4,800 corpses per 24 hours.

Pre-heating of such an oven should take at least two days. After this preheating the oven will not need any more fuel due to the heat produced by the corpses. It will be able to maintain its necessary high temperature through self-heating. But to enable it to maintain a constant temperature, it would be necessary to introduce at the same time so-called well-fed and so-called emaciated corpses, because one can only guarantee continuous high temperatures through the emission of human fat. When only emaciated corpses are incinerated, it will be necessary to add heat continuously. The results of this would be that the installation could be damaged because of the thus created temperatures and one would expect shorter or longer breakdowns.[99]

The report ended with the assertion that after some initial experience it should be possible to increase the initial load from 50 to 100 corpses. This would increase the loading rhythm from every 15 to every 20 minutes, and as a result the daily capacity would increase from $(50 \times {}^{60}/_{15} \times 24) = 4,800$ corpses to, at least theoretically, $(100 \times {}^{60}/_{20} \times 24) = 7,200$ corpses. It is unclear whether the incinerator would ever have worked. What is important, however, is that both the text of the patent application and the design of the incinerator make the incineration process described in Tauber's testimony not merely plausible but, indeed, probable.

The only possible challenge to Bischoff's figure is a recently discovered note from Topf engineer Kurt Prüfer to the SS, dated September 8, 1942. Prüfer calculated the daily incineration capacity of the three double-muffle ovens of Crematorium 1 as 250 corpses, the five triple-muffle ovens of Crematoria 2 and 3 as 800 corpses each, and the eight-muffle ovens of Crematoria 4 and 5 as 400 corpses each. In short, according to Prüfer, the daily incineration capacity was to be 2,650 corpses, or 55 percent of Bischoff's number.[100] While much lower than the official daily capacity of 4,756 corpses per day, the crematoria would still have been able to easily incinerate the corpses of the 1.1 million people who were killed in Auschwitz. (If Prüfer's conservative estimate was right, and if we disregard the use of incineration pyres, the total incineration capacity of the crematoria over the period of their existence would have been 1.4 million corpses.) When considering Prüfer's figures, it must be remembered that, because the contracts were already signed, it was in his interest to provide very conservative numbers, because the Topf firm was to be accountable for the functioning of the ovens. We should keep Prüfer's figures in mind but may cautiously proceed on the basis of Bischoff's letter of June 28, 1943.

Graph showing the projected inmate population of Auschwitz, the projected incineration capacity per month, and the projected morgue capacity, September 1941 to December 1943. Drawn by Jesse Dormody and Andrew Haydon. (opposite page)

As I observed before, I aimed to obtain some insight into the changing purpose of the crematoria by measuring and comparing the evolution of the projected inmate population, of the incineration capacity (calculated per month of 30 days), and of the morgue capacity (calculated in terms of morgue units per month of 30 days, in which each unit is one corpse-day, which means that a morgue with a capacity of 100 corpses has a capacity of $100 \times 30 = 3,000$ morgue units per month). I calculated, on the basis of German data, that every 120 cu ft. of morgue space accommodated 1 corpse. The results are depicted on page 351. They show that in September 1941, the SS planned for 30,000 inmates, an incineration capacity of 10,000 corpses per month (Crematorium 1: 10,000), and a morgue capacity of 1,200 morgue units (Crematorium 1: 5,000 cu ft.). In October 1941 the projected size of the camp had increased to 120,000 inmates, the incineration capacity had risen to 40,000 corpses per month (Crematorium 2: 40,000), and the morgue capacity to 12,000 morgue units (Crematorium 2: 50,000 cu ft.). As I have shown elsewhere, the proportion of 120,000 inmates to an incineration capacity of 40,000 corpses per month was in line

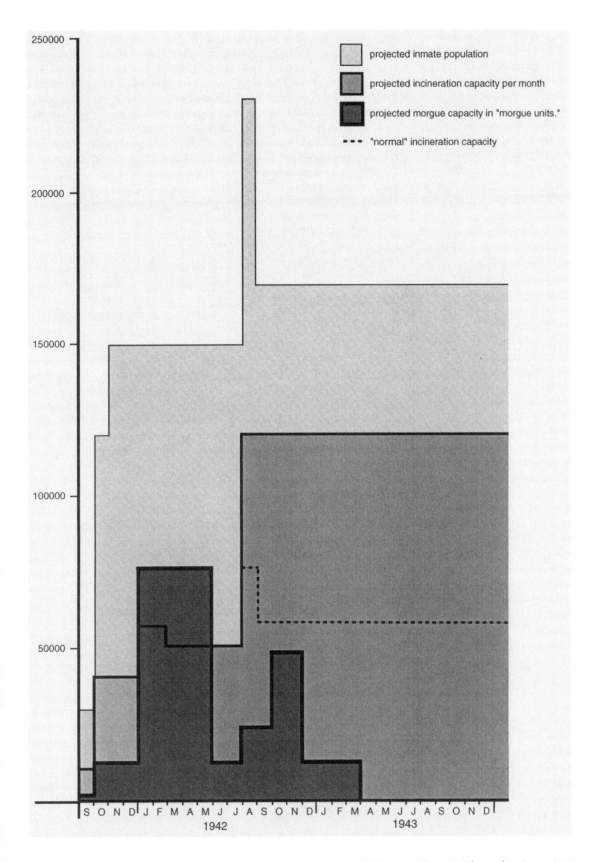

with that of Dachau and Buchenwald. In January 1942, the numbers were 150,000 inmates, 57,000 corpses per month (Crematorium 2: 40,0000; two auxiliary crematoria in Birkenau: 8,500 each), and 75,600 morgue units (300,000 cu ft.). In May 1942, the figures were 150,000 inmates, 50,000 corpses per month (Crematorium 1: 10,000; Crematorium 2: 40,000), and 80,600 morgue units (305,000 cu ft). In July 1942, Himmler visited Auschwitz and ordered that the camp become an important link in the so-called Final Solution of the Jewish Problem. The new purpose is reflected in the figures. By the end of August 1942, the SS planned for 230,000 inmates and had ordered crematoria with a total incineration capacity of 120,000 corpses per month (Crematorium 2: 40,000, Crematorium 3: 40,000; Crematorium 4: 20,000; Crematorium 5: 20,000), but they had reduced the anticipated morgue capacity to 24,000 morgue units (100,000 cu ft.). By October 1942, the total anticipated inmate population had dropped to 170,000 inmates, but the projected incineration capacity remained at 120,000 corpses per month (Crematorium 2: 40,000, Crematorium 3: 40,000; Crematorium 4: 20,000; Crematorium 5: 20,000). Morgue capacity was increased to 48,000 morgue units (200,000 cu ft.). It is clear that compared to other concentration camps such as Dachau and Buchenwald, which could incinerate the population of their own camps in three months, Auschwitz was now to have a dramatic incineration overcapacity of ([120,000 × 3] - 170,000 =) 190,000 corpses per three months, or more than 60,000 corpses per month, or more than 2,000 corpses per day. Where were those 2,000 anticipated corpses per day to come from? In January 1943 the numbers were 170,000 inmates, 120,000 corpses per month (Crematorium 2: 40,000, Crematorium 3: 40,000; Crematorium 4: 20,000; Crematorium 5: 20,000) and 12,000 morgue units (50,000 cu ft), and finally in May 1943: 170,000 inmates, 120,000 corpses per month (Crematorium 2: 40,000, Crematorium 3: 40,000; Crematorium 4: 20,000; Crematorium 5: 20,000), and no morgue units.

If Auschwitz, as negationists have maintained, was a "normal" concentration camp comparable to Dachau and Sachsenhausen—that is, a camp not dedicated to systematic extermination of large transports—then one should expect an incineration and morgue capacity comparable to those "normal" concentration camps. If Auschwitz was more lethal than other concentration camps because of the greater prevalence of infectious diseases, then one should expect perhaps a higher incineration capacity, but also a very much higher morgue capacity to provide a buffer between the seasonally fluctuating discrepancy between incineration capacity and mortality. But, as we have seen, morgue capacity actually dropped from August 1942 onward. It seems, therefore, that the numbers suggest that Auschwitz was an extermination camp in which most people were murdered "on command." This accounts for a high incineration capacity and a low morgue capacity, because the administrators of the killing process were in a position to send only as many people to the gas chambers as the crematoria could handle—assuming that the corpses of those killed would be incinerated within the next twenty-four hours.

Until now I have dealt with German wartime documents. But there are other categories of non-intentional evidence. One genre of this kind of evidence that has been the object of some discussion in the last twenty years are the aerial photos taken by British Mosquito reconnaissance airplanes and American planes that bombed Auschwitz on five dates in 1944. I already gave a short introduction to this evidence in Chapter 2. Interest in the photos was generated by a 19-page report entitled *The Holocaust*

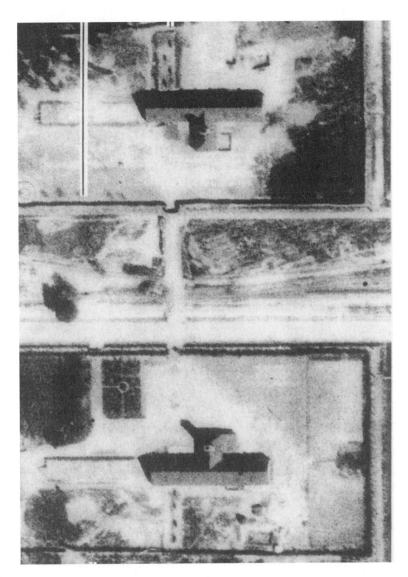

Aerial photo of Crematoria 2 and 3, taken on August 25, 1944. RG373-Can ON 24507-exp 3185. Courtesy National Archives, Washington, D.C.

Revisited: A Retrospective Analysis of the Auschwitz-Birkenau Extermination Complex written by Dino A. Brugioni and Robert G. Poirier and issued by the CIA. Brugioni and Poirier claimed that these aerial photos provided evidence of extermination activities. For example, in the photo taken on August 25, 1944, one could see trains at the station in Birkenau with prisoners being marched to Crematorium 2. "On the roof of the subsurface gas chambers, we can see the vents used to insert the Zyklon-B gas crystals," Brugioni and Poirier wrote.[101] Yet their reading was not convincing: the group of people alleged to be walking toward the crematorium were still at a large distance from the crematorium and would not have necessarily ended up there.

The original CIA analysis was based on the study of analog enlargements. With new digital technologies it became possible, however, to revisit the issue of the evidentiary value of the photos. As I wrote earlier, in 1996,

Dr. Nevin Bryant of NASA's Jet Propulsion Laboratory in Pasadena, one of the world leaders in the analysis of aerial and satellite images, agreed to analyze the photos with his computers, enhancing the data with software programs used by NASA. The most important results were that the four shaded markings on the roofs of Morgue 1 of both Crematorium 2 and Crematorium 3 did belong to the original negative and were not added later on. Furthermore, Dr. Bryant discovered a long line of people moving into the compound of Crematorium 5 by comparing various consecutive exposures taken on May 31, 1944.[102] Danuta Czech's Kalendarium records that on May 31, 1944, two transports arrived from Hungary and that from the first one 100 Jews were selected for work. "The remaining people are killed in the gas chambers." And of the second transport, 2,000 Jews were admitted to the camp. "The remaining people are killed in the gas chambers."[103] Why would the Germans have moved a large group of people into the compound of Crematorium 5, which was off limits to inmates, if not to kill them?

The most important evidence provided by the air photos is, however, rather simple and does not need digital technology to be revealed. As I discussed in Chapter 3, one of the important eyewitnesses of the killing installations in Auschwitz was French painter David Olère. In 1945, he created a plan of Crematorium 3 in which he indicated the position of the four gas columns in the gas chamber. He showed them in a staggered arrangement. When he drew this plan, he could not have had access to the photos the Allies had made only a year earlier. These photos show the position of the small chimneys that capped the gas columns to be exactly as Olère drew them. In other words, the photos corroborated an essential piece of eyewitness evidence and confirmed the existence of the gas columns.

Which brings us to a final and most problematic category of "nonintentional" evidence: the traces of hydrogen cyanide (HCN) in the brickwork. As we have seen, the Leuchter Report claimed that the low residue of cyanide in the brickwork of the gas chambers proved that they had not been used to kill people. Measurements done by respected Polish forensic scientist Professor Jan Markiewicz, director of the Institute of Forensic Research in Cracow, confirmed the presence of cyanide ions (CN^-) in the brickwork.[104] Of samples taken in the delousing shed BW5a, the highest measured concentration was 840 µg CN^- per kg. (A µg is a microgram, or 1/1,000,000 gram. One kg equals one billion µg.) Of samples taken in the gas chamber of Crematorium 1, the highest measured concentration was 292 µg CN^- per kg; of samples taken in the gas chamber of Crematorium 2, the highest measured concentration was 640 µg CN^- per kg; of samples taken in the gas chamber of Crematorium 4, the highest measured concentration was 500 µg CN^- per kg, and of samples taken in the gas chamber of Crematorium 5, the highest measured concentration was 248 µg CN^- per kg. In the case of Crematoria 4 and 5, the samples had been exposed to the weather for years. In samples taken in dwelling spaces in Block 3 and Block 8, which had been fumigated with hydrogen cyanide once, no traces of CN^- were found. When we read these figures, two things must be kept in mind. First of all, the concentration of hydrogen cyanide needed to kill lice is twenty times the concentration necessary to kill humans, and lice need to be exposed much longer to cyanide than humans for death to occur. Hence, one would not expect comparable concentrations of CN^- in the walls of delousing rooms and those of homicidal gas chambers. Second, conditions for the preservation of hydrogen cyanide in homicidal gas chambers would have been far worse than in fumigation gas chambers: as they breathed, the victims would have introduced carbon dioxide into the gas chamber. After several minutes, the concentration of carbon dioxide would have been ten times the concentration of hydrogen cyanide.[105] This is important because carbon dioxide affects the preservation of hydrogen cyanide.

Testing over a month, Markiewicz found that the samples that had been exposed to hydrogen cyanide only showed an average decrease of 56 percent, while the samples that had been exposed to the combination of carbon dioxide and hydrogen cyanide showed a loss of 73 percent. "In as many as four samples that loss ranged from 97% to 100%."[106] In other words, the conditions in homicidal gas chambers for the preservation of hydrogen cyanide were much worse than in delousing chambers. Hence Markiewicz's results positively demonstrate that the alleged gas chambers were used to kill people.

Or better, they show that Leuchter's conclusions ought not to be taken seriously. As we have seen, Irving openly joined the negationist ranks when he first endorsed and later published the Leuchter Report. If it had not been for that, he would not have figured in Lipstadt's book, and there would have been no libel case. Not long after I agreed to write an expert opinion, I realized that the Leuchter Report would become a main battleground. If I could show that, as Rampton would later put it, the Leuchter Report was "a piece of so-called research which is not worth the paper it is written on,"[107] then we would have a strong case with which to justify Lipstadt's allegation that "familiar with historical evidence, [Irving] bends it until it conforms with his ideological leanings and political agenda.[108]

From the very beginning, Irving had ignored the engineering part of the Leuchter Report and only concentrated on the samples. For example, in a press statement issued by Focal Point announcing publication of the Leuchter Report, Irving wrote that "scientists, using the same ultra-modern equipment and methods that detected the centuries-old fraud of the Turin Shroud, have established that there is no significant trace of any poison residues in the 'gas chambers' of Auschwitz."[109] In his introduction to the Leuchter Report, Irving challenged anyone to explain to him "why there is no significant trace of any cyanide compound in the building which they have always identified as the former gas chambers. Forensic chemistry is, I repeat, an exact science."[110]

But I believed that I was to consider the report as a whole, not just the chemical analysis. As I read the transcripts of the 1988 Zündel Trial, it became clear that Leuchter did not attach too much significance to his samples. When Crown Attorney Pearson asked him "What percentage of your conclusions is based on these conclusions you draw from the cyanide traces?," Leuchter answered: "Ten percent."

[Pearson]: "What other—what are the other foundations for your conclusion?"

[Leuchter]: "The other foundations are that the facilities that I looked at were physically not designed and could not have been operations as gas chambers."

Q.: "And what do you rely on for that conclusion?"

A.: "I rely on my knowledge of gas chamber construction and design."

Q.: "So you rely on your knowledge and experience as somebody constructing gas chambers in the United States for the purposes of executing one person as humanly as possible with as less danger to other people as possible."

A.: "Partially."

Q.: "Well, that's your only experience, isn't it?"

A.: "It's my only experience at constructing gas chambers. I don't believe anyone has had any experience constructing larger gas chambers that took more than two people. But, the—"

Q.: "Did you read the testimony of the commandant of Auschwitz, Rudolf Höss?"

A.: "I did."

Q.: "Okay. So, you've told us about your experience and you said that the hydrogen traces account for ten percent of your conclusion. What percent of your conclusion is your experience in the construction of modern gas chambers?"

A.: "Twenty, maybe thirty percent."

Q.: "Okay. What else is there then, please?"

A.: "Good engineering design in terms of building structure, air moving equipment, plumbing equipment that would be utilized to handle the air and mechanical equipment that would be utilized to introduce gas and gas carriers into a structure."

Q.: "And what percentage of your opinion is based on that?"

A.: "Fifty or sixty percent."

Q.: "And that is all based on the assumption that the physical plant presently at that location in Poland is what was there in 1942, '43, '44 and '45. Is that right?"

A.: "That is correct."[111]

Given the fact that Leuchter himself based 90 percent of his conclusion on considerations of engineering, I felt that I ought to concentrate on his observations as an engineer. It was, of course, more convenient: many of his engineering conclusions were based on observations about design and technology that could be verified in the archives. While I was not an engineer, I knew the documentation and would be able to identify those arguments that were based on false historical premises—premises such as Leuchter's assumption that "the physical plant presently at that location in Poland is what was there in 1942, '43, '44 and '45."

Leuchter claimed that he used a seven-step approach to research and write his report.

1. A general background study of the available material.

2. An on-site inspection and forensic examination of the facilities in question which included the taking of physical data (measurements and construction information) and a considered removal of physical sample material (brick and mortar) which was returned to the United States for chemical analysis.

3. A consideration of recorded and visual (on-site) logistic data.

4. A compilation of the acquired data.

5. An analysis of the acquired information and comparison of this information with known and proven design, procedural and logistic information and requirements for the design, fabrication and operation of actual gas chambers and crematories.

6. A consideration of the chemical analysis of the materials acquired on site.

7. Conclusions based on the acquired evidence.[112]

In a section entitled "Synopsis and Findings," Leuchter summarized the results of his seven-step approach as follows:

> After a study of the available literature, examination and evaluation of the existing facilities at Auschwitz, Birkenau and Majdanek, with expert knowledge of the design criteria for gas chamber operation, an investigation of crematory technology and an inspection of modern crematories, the author finds no evidence that any of the facilities normally alleged to be execution gas chambers were ever used as such, and finds, further, that because of the design and fabrication of these facilities, they could not have been utilized for execution gas chambers.
>
> Additionally, an evaluation of the crematory facilities produced conclusive evidence that contradicts the alleged volume of corpses cremated in the generally alleged time frame. It is, therefore, the best engineering opinion of the author that none of the facilities examined were ever utilized for the execution of human beings and that the crematories could not have supported the alleged work load attributed to them.[113]

The study of the "available literature" was not very impressive. During his testimony during the trial, he told the court that he reviewed some parts of Hilberg's *Destruction of the European Jews,* a Degesch document on how to handle Zyklon B which had been submitted as evidence in the Nuremberg Trials (NT-9912), a DuPont flyer on safety when handling its own brand of hydrocyanide, and some negationist literature, among which was the article by William C. Lindsey on the trial of Bruno Tesch, an article by a certain Friedrich Paul Berg on German delousing chambers, and Arthur Butz's *The Hoax of the Twentieth Century.*[114] In other words, he had gone to Auschwitz with very little preparation.

As I considered ways to organize my analysis, I found a passage in Leuchter's report that contained his main observations about the gas chambers.

> Bunkers 1 and 2 are described in Auschwitz State Museum literature as converted farm houses with several chambers and windows sealed. These do not exist in their original condition and were not inspected. Kremas 1, 2, 3, 4 and 5 are described historically and on inspection were verified to have been converted mortuaries or morgues connected and housed in the same facility as crematories. The on-site inspection of these structures indicated extremely poor and dangerous design for these facilities if they were to have served as execution gas chambers. There is no provision for gasketed doors, windows or vents; the structures are not coated with tar or other sealant to prevent leakage or absorption of gas. The adjacent crematories are a potential danger of explosion. The exposed porous brick and mortar would accumulate the HCN and make these facilities dangerous to

humans for several years. Krema I is adjacent to the S.S. Hospital at Auschwitz and has floor drains connected to the main sewer of the camp—which would allow gas into every building at the facility. There were no exhaust systems to vent the gas after usage and no heaters or dispersal mechanism for the Zyklon B gas to be introduced or evaporated. The Zyklon B was supposedly dropped through roof vents and put in through windows—not allowing for the even distribution of gas or pellets. The facilities are always damp and not heated. As stated earlier, dampness and Zyklon B are not compatible. The chambers are too small to physically contain the occupants claimed and the doors all open inward, a situation which would inhibit removal of the bodies. With the gas chambers fully packed with occupants, there would be no circulation of the HCN within the room. Additionally, if the gas eventually did fill the chamber over a lengthy time period, those throwing Zyklon B in the roof vents and verifying the death of the occupants would die themselves from exposure to HCN. None of the alleged gas chambers were constructed in accordance with the design for delousing chambers which were effectively operating for years in a safe manner. None of these chambers were constructed in accordance with the known and proven designs of facilities operational in the United States at that time. It seems unusual that the presumed designers of these alleged gas chambers never consulted or considered the United States technology, the only country then executing prisoners with gas.[115]

I decided to organize my discussion of Leuchter by subjecting every sentence of this central statement to a discussion. The result was shattering.

"Kremas 1, 2, 3, 4 and 5 are described historically and on inspection were verified to have been converted mortuaries or morgues connected and housed in the same facility as crematories."

The sentence did not make any sense. I presumed that Leuchter meant to write "[The alleged gas chambers of] Kremas 1, 2, 3, 4 and 5 are described historically and on inspection were verified to have been converted mortuaries or morgues connected and housed in the same facility as crematories." If this is what he meant, and I could not imagine any other possible explanation for why he wrote what he wrote, it became important to ask how he had determined "on inspection" that all these alleged gas chambers had been morgues. While he could have done so safely in Crematorium 1, where the space is still available for inspection, and while he could have inferred from the underground position of the alleged gas chambers of Crematoria 2 and 3 that they most likely were designed as morgues, and while he would have found evidence in the blueprints provided by Faurisson that these places had indeed been designated as morgues (*Leichenkeller*), he could not have come to that conclusion by studying the remains of Crematoria 4 and 5. First of all, virtually nothing is left of these structures except concrete slabs and some low walls reconstructed after the war, and the blueprints of these buildings do not show any designation of gas chambers as morgues. So it is unclear what evidence he used to verify the intended functions of Crematoria 4 and 5.

"The on-site inspection of these structures indicated extremely poor and dangerous design for these facilities if they were to have served as execution gas chambers," Leuchter claimed. "There is no provision for gasketed doors, windows or vents; the structures are not coated with tar or other sealant to prevent leakage or absorption of gas." I could not grasp how Leuchter, on the basis of the remains of the crematoria, could have come to this statement. With the exception of Crematorium 1, the other four crematoria are merely rubble, a fact which Leuchter admitted in cross-examination and which he also observed in the paper he presented at the Ninth International Revisionist Conference in 1989.[116] Simply stated, there is simply not enough evidence remaining to establish if the gasketed doors, windows, or vents were or were not there. There is, however, enough left to see that the walls were plastered: in 1990, the forensic scientists of the Institute of Forensic Research in Cracow used plaster samples from the gas chambers of Crematoria 2 and 3 as the basis for their analysis of residual cyanide. Yet, undeterred by all of this, Leuchter had no qualms about his claim that, on the basis of the few remains of the gas chamber of Crematorium 2, the walls of that room had been rough, unsealed brick and mortar and that those walls had never been coated.[117] This was important because, if the wall had been coated with tar or plastered, the bricks that remained would have been protected from the hydrogen cyanide and it would have been impossible for a chemical reaction to occur between the hydrogen cyanide and the brick and mortar.[118] But because he, or at least Faurisson, had aimed to establish that the absence of residual cyanide in the bricks pointed to the fact that no hydrogen cyanide had been used in those rooms, he had to postulate a priori that the bricks in the walls had not been exposed. However, the remains of the rooms did not support such an assumption.

Remains of Crematorium 4, 1999. Photo by Omer Arbel.

"The adjacent crematories are a potential danger of explosion," Leuchter observed. His reasoning was based on the fact that hydrogen cyanide is combustible, and because the gas chambers were located not too far from the incineration ovens, there ought to have been a danger for explosion. Yet during cross-examination Leuchter had to admit that hydrogen cyanide becomes combustible at 60,000 parts per million and is lethal at 300 parts per million, that is at 0.5 percent of the combustion point.

Q.: "And I want to ask you about your answer to me. I said it takes a higher concentration of hydrogen cyanide to exterminate insects than it does to kill human beings. You said no. We go to the Degesch manual and it says that it requires twenty times as much to kill beetles as to kill rats and it takes three times as much to kill rats [as] it does to kill humans."

A.: "Maybe it depends upon the insects. Most of the work that I've been looking at, they've been killing lice and ticks. And their recommendation for general fumigation purposes is three thousand per million."

Q.: "What is twenty times 833 parts per million?"

A.: "What is twenty times 833 parts per million?"

Remains of Crematorium 5, 1999. Photo by Omer Arbel.

Remains of the west wall of the gas chamber of Crematorium 2, 1999. The remains of a cement coating are clearly visible. Photo by Omer Arbel.

Q.: "Right."

A.: "16,600."

Q.: "16,600. So what Degesch are saying, the people who make the product, is that if you want to kill beetles, you should have a concentration of—of what, sir?"

A.: "16,600, apparently."

Q.: "Right. And it takes three hundred parts per million to kill a human being in a matter of minutes?"

A.: "Or more."

Q.: "In a matter of minutes."

A.: "Twenty minutes, fifteen minutes, yes."

Q.: "Right. And here they're talking about a time of exposure from 2 to 72 hours, right?"

A.: "Right."

Q.: "Now, you gave us as a conclusion about the danger of explosion, didn't you?"

A.: "Yes."

Q.: "This was a big factor in your mind, this possibility of explosion. Did you look at the Degesch manual when it talked about inflammability?"

A.: "I'm looking at it now, counsellor."

Q.: "Page five?"

A.: "Yes."

Q.: "'*Liquid HCN,*' that is hydrocyanic acid, right?"

A.: "Correct."

Q.: "'. . . *burns like alcohol. Gaseous [H]CN forms an explosive mixture with air under certain conditions. The lower explosion limit, however, lies far above the concentration used in practical fumigation work.*' So, they tell us that if we're going to exterminate beetles, we have to have a concentration of 16,600 and they tell us if we have a concentration of 16,600, the lower explosion limit lies far above that concentration."

A.: "The lower explosion limit is six per cent."

Q.: "And what's six percent?"

A.: "Six thousand."

Q.: "Isn't it sixty thousand, sir?"

A.: "Correct. Sixty thousand."

Q.: "Sixty thousand parts per million of air. Right?"

A.: "Correct, but you must understand that at the Zyklon-B material, when the gas is being given off, you have a percentage per volume of air of ninety to one hundred per cent. That means you have almost pure hydrogen cyanide at the carrier."

Q.: "At the point where the Zyklon-B is vapourizing, I agree, you have a ninety-nine per cent concentration level. But how far did you tell us these ovens were from the chamber we are talking about?"

A.: "150, 160 feet."

Q.: "And doesn't gas diffuse, sir?"

A.: "It may or it may not."

Q.: "And what would its concentration be 150 or 160 feet away?"

A.: "I have no idea and no one could answer that question for you."

Q.: "Right, you don't know, do you?"

A.: "Most people would tell you it's very dangerous."[119]

Pearson effectively and publicly demolished Leuchter's argument that there would have been a danger of explosion, because the concentration used in the gas chambers was around 300 parts per million, that is, at 0.5 percent of the combustion level. Irving, who was to testify the following day, was in the audience and watched it all. The exchange obviously did not leave an impression on him. But the issue was to follow him relentlessly. A year later, after publishing the Leuchter Report, he was reminded of Leuchter's fallacy by David A. Crabtree, who wrote in his critique of Leuchter that "the fatal percentage of gas is so far below the flammability or explosive limit that it could not have ignited or exploded."[120]

"The exposed porous brick and mortar would accumulate the HCN," Leuchter wrote in his report, "and make these facilities dangerous to humans for several years." Yet in the trial he admitted that hydrogen cyanide had only a very short life—a few days at best, and that the only way it could remain in the walls was if the cyanide were to combine with iron present in brick or mortar to make the harmless pigment ferro-ferri cyanide, also known as Prussian blue.[121]

"Krema I is adjacent to the S.S. Hospital at Auschwitz," Leuchter observed, and he continued to assert that it "has floor drains connected to the main sewer of the camp—which would allow gas into every building at the facility." He was right in observing a floor drain in the former gas chamber of Crematorium 1. Yet there was no way in which he could positively determine if, first of all, this drain was "connected" to the main sewer of the camp and, second, if the wartime camp possessed a "main sewer" at all: the main survey of the Polish military base that was to become the Stammlager, drawn up in December 1939, indicates that the water supply was by means of outside pumps while outside latrines served the soldiers' needs.[122] Projecting expectations about the usual infrastructure of American military installations to Polish military barracks in the 1930s does not show much historic sense. But even if the drain was connected to a main sewer, it is highly unlikely that the hydrogen cyanide would have been able to travel from the gas chamber to other buildings. Hydrogen cyanide is very soluble in water. The water would dilute the hydrogen cyanide to such a degree that it would become a harmless solution to be dumped into the Sola River. Once dissolved in the water, the hydrogen cyanide would not evaporate again to (possibly) penetrate into other buildings.

"There were no exhaust systems to vent the gas after usage," Leuchter observed. Prompted by Christie, Leuchter repeated this, according to him, crucial piece of evidence at various points during his testimony. Discussing Crematorium 2, he stated that he did not find any means by which to ventilate the alleged gas chamber.

> [Christie]: "In this on-site inspection, did you find any roof vent capabilities as indicated on the various drawings that were given?"
>
> [Leuchter]: "There was no ventilation capability for this facility at all. The door to the facility, the one door, as you can see, goes into the main area of the building, and it should be remembered that morgue 2 and morgue 1 and morgue 3 were all [under]-ground. They were in actuality a basement for the building. They were floor level and they were ground level and with no structure above them. To the right of the building where it says 'Crematory', that was a structure that was ground up and was one and a half storeys with a stack for the furnaces. Now, these—both facilities, as I said, were underground. This was underground. There was only one door going to the morgue at that time and absolutely no way of getting air into the facility. There was a second door down at this end with a stairway, and in my opinion

there will be no way of adequately ventilating this building and it would take a very long time since the only way you could allow the gas to come out would be through the stairway. Since there were no other apertures, it wouldn't even make sense to put an exhaust fan in because there would be no way of getting air into the building, because there was no air intake at any point in the facility."[123]

Without a proper ventilation system, the basement of Crematorium 2 could not have been used as a homicidal gas chamber.

[Christie]: "And can you tell us why you hold that opinion?"

[Leuchter]: "Yes, essentially for the same reasons that I felt that the mortuary at Krema I was not an execution gas chamber. The building was not sealed with tar or pitch in any manner. There was no ventilation system. There was no means at all for introducing the Zyklon B gas. There was a story in something I read in some of the available literature that there was a hollow column that the materials would drop through. All of the columns were solid reinforced concrete."[124]

During cross-examination, when Pearson confronted Leuchter with a letter written by the leader of the Auschwitz Zentralbauleitung, Karl Bischoff,

Section of Morgue 1 of Crematorium 2. The ventilation ducts marked Belüftung *(against ceiling) and* Entlüftungskanal *(near ground) are clearly visible. Courtesy Archive Auschwitz-Birkenau State Museum, Oswiecim.*

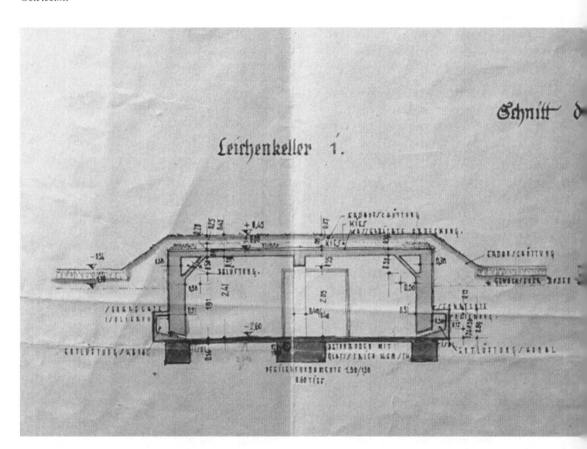

which mentioned that Topf would proceed with "the installation in time for aeration [*Belüftung*] and ventilation [*Entlüftung*]" immediately when transport became available, Leuchter wrongly concluded that "this ventilation system was, in fact, the blower for the furnace. It had nothing to do with ventilating the alleged gas chamber area. Since Topf made it, we know they manufactured furnace equipment, crematory equipment."[125] Yet the plans of the crematoria show that built into the walls of the gas chamber were ducts indicated in the drawings as "*Belüftung*" and "*Entlüftungskanal.*" The remains of this system can still be seen in the ruined east wall of the gas chamber of Crematorium 3. Ignoring important evidence, and refusing to examine the blueprints in relation to the correspondence and the remains of the crematoria, Leuchter had jumped to the wrong conclusion. There was a ventilation system.

The question remains, of course, whether that ventilation system was powerful enough to remove the gas relatively quickly, allowing the process of incineration to begin. As we have seen in Chapter 1, Faurisson claimed in his paper "The Mechanics of Gassing" that for the gassing to have occurred as eyewitnesses such as Kommandant Höss testified, the gas chambers ought to have been equipped with a fan "with magical powers."

> It becomes, therefore, apparent that in the absence of a magical fan capable of instantly expelling a gas that is "difficult to ventilate, since it adheres strongly to surfaces," the "human slaughterhouse" called a "gas chamber" would have been inaccessible for nearly a full day. Its walls, floors, ceiling would have retained portions of a gas which was highly poisonous to man.[126]

Thus, assuming an extremely toxic environment with cyanide dripping off the walls, the presence of a very powerful ventilation system became a sine qua non for the underground gas chambers of Crematoria 2 and 3 to have functioned. And according to Faurisson and his followers, such a very powerful ventilation system did not exist.

However, Richard Green and Jamie McCarthy have shown that the ventilation system of the crematoria was able to quickly remove the gas.[127] The gas chambers of Crematoria 2 and 3 were 30 m long by 7 m wide and 2.4 m high, which resulted in a volume of 504 cu m.[128] They were equipped with a ventilation system with both intake and exhaust fans that were capable of cycling 8000 cu m through the room each hour.[129] In other words, the system was able to create $8,000 \div 504 = 15.8$ air exchanges per hour. What does this mean if the ventilators were turned on after a gassing and the concentration of HCN (hydrogen cyanide) was, for example, a lethal-for-humans 1,000 ppm (parts per million)? A rough guideline is that the concentration in the gas chamber is cut to slightly more than one-third for each room replacement of air. Using an industrial hygiene calculator that can be downloaded from the Web site of the American Conference of Governmental Industrial Hygienists, one can come to more precise results.[130] The mathematical equation used is

$$C(t) = C_0 \, e^{-9.94t}$$

in which $C(t)$ is the concentration of HCN at time t in hours, and C_0 is the initial concentration. The tables give not only the concentration after 10, 20, 30, 40, and 50 minutes of ventilation but also the mean concentration to which a person is exposed who stays in that room for 15 minutes after entering it at the moment that the ventilation begins and after 10, 20, 30, 40, and 50 minutes.

Table 5.1

Concentration of 1,000 ppm HCN over Time

Time in minutes	NCH concentration in ppm	Mean concentration after 15 minutes exposure in ppm
0	1,000	380
10	191	73
20	36	14
30	7	3
40	1	—
50	—	—

If we take an initial concentration of 10,000 ppm, the results are as follows:

Table 5.2

Concentration of 10,000 ppm HCN over Time

Time in minutes	NCH concentration in ppm	Mean concentration after 15 minutes exposure in ppm
0	10,000	3,805
10	1,908	726
20	364	138
30	70	26
40	13	5
50	2	1

What do these numbers mean? DuPont provides standards that allow us to interpret these figures:

2–5 ppm Odor threshold

4–7 ppm OSHA exposure limit, 15 minute time weighted average

20–40 ppm Slight symptoms after several hours

45–54 ppm Tolerated for $\frac{1}{2}$ to 1 hour without significant immediate or delayed effects

100–200 ppm Fatal within $\frac{1}{2}$ to 1 hour

300 ppm Rapidly fatal (if no treatment)[131]

Of course, the SS did not care about safety standards, as they did not care about the health of the slave workers. But even so, it is clear that with an initial concentration of HCN of 1,000 ppm it would have been safe to enter the gas chamber after 30 minutes of ventilation, and with a concentration of 10,000 ppm, one would have had to wait 10 minutes longer. The fan that ventilated the gas chamber of Crematoria 2 and 3 was certainly not a magical fan, but it was sufficient for the Germans' needs.

If Leuchter had spent a little more time in Auschwitz and if he had consulted the archive of the camp, he would have been able to find independent confirmation of the existence of the ventilation system in Tauber's testimony.

Remains of a ventilation duct in the east wall of the gas chamber of Crematorium 3, 1999. Photo by Omer Arbel.

Besides that, in the gas chamber there were electric wires running along the two sides of the main beam supported by the central concrete pillars. The ventilation was installed in the walls of the gas chamber. Communication between the room and the ventilation installation proper was through small holes along the top and bottom of the side walls. The lower openings were protected by a kind of muzzle, the upper ones by whitewashed perforated metal plates.

The ventilation system of the gas chamber was coupled to the ventilation ducts installed in the undressing room. This ventilation system, which also served the dissection room, was driven by electric motors in the roof space of the crematorium.[132]

But Leuchter never even thought about cross-referencing his own observations, the German blueprints, and the testimonies of eyewitnesses. He could, for example, have found some use for the statements of well-known Israeli artist Yehuda Bacon during the Eichmann trial that were quoted in Chapter 3.

Leuchter did not consult the records of the Eichmann trial or, for that matter, testimony given at other trials. During the cross-examination Pearson asked Leuchter why he did not consult any witnesses when he did his investigation.

> [Leuchter]: "I don't know who I would speak to, sir, because I would submit that the person that I should speak to would have to be someone who was operating the chamber. If I am to believe

the literature, these people all died in the operation of the chamber."

Q.: "How about some of the people that cleared the bodies out of the chambers?"

A.: "Well, from what I've been able to determine from most of the literature, these people are expendable and probably all deceased and were deceased shortly after the operation of the facility."[133]

The SS men who were involved in the gassings were not "expendable," and Leuchter could have found some interesting testimony about the operation of the gas chambers from, for example, a well-known witness such as Pery Broad or a more obscure SS man such as Hans Stark. Like Broad, Stark had been employed in the Auschwitz Political Department, better known as the "Camp Gestapo." During the Frankfurt Auschwitz Trial, Stark provided useful evidence about the procedures in the Political Department and the various ways of execution. One of these was gassing in Crematorium 1.

> As early as autumn 1941 gassings were carried out in a room in the small crematorium which had been prepared for this purpose. The room held 200–250 people, had a higher-than-average ceiling, no windows and only a specially insulated door, with bolts like those of an airtight door. There were no pipes or the like which would lead the prisoners to believe that it was perhaps a shower room. In the ceiling there were openings of about 35 cm in diameter at some distance from each other. The room had a flat roof which allowed daylight in through the openings. It was through these openings that Zyklon B in granular form would be poured.[134]

Stark participated in some of those gassings. Sometimes his job was to check the numbers.

> About 200–250 Jewish men, women and children of all ages were standing at the crematorium. There may also have been babies there. There were a great many SS members present, though I could not say what their names were, plus the camp commandant, the Schutzhaftlagerführer, several Blockführer, Grabner and also other members of the Political Department. Nothing was said to the Jews. They were merely ordered to enter the gas-chamber, the door of which was open. While the Jews were going into the room, medical orderlies prepared for the gassing. Earth had been piled up against one of the external walls of the gassing room to ceiling height so that the medical orderlies could get on the roof of the room. After all the Jews were in the chamber the door was bolted and the medical orderlies poured Zyklon B through the openings.[135]

One time Stark was ordered to pour Zyklon B into the room because only one medical orderly had shown up. It was essential, he claimed, that Zyklon B be poured simultaneously through both openings.

> This gassing was also a transport of 200–250 Jews, once again men, women and children. As the Zyklon B—as already mentioned—was in granular form, it trickled down over the people as it was being poured in. They then started to cry out terribly for

they now knew what was happening to them. I did not look through the opening because it had to be closed as soon as the Zyklon B had been poured in. After a few minutes there was silence. After some time had passed, it may have been ten or fifteen minutes, the gas-chamber was opened. The dead lay higgledy-piggledy all over the place. It was a dreadful sight.[136]

Stark described the procedure at Crematorium 1. Leuchter could have profited from Tauber's testimony to help him understand the slightly different arrangement at Crematorium 2.

The contents of a can of Zyklon B found in Maidanek, 1944. Main Commission for the Prosecution of Crimes against the Polish Nation, courtesy USHMM Photo Archives.

Crematorium 2 had a basement where there was an undressing room and a bunker, or in other words a gas chamber. . . . The roof of the gas chamber was supported by concrete pillars running down the middle of its length. On either side of these pillars there were four others, two on each side. The sides of these pillars, which went up through the roof, were of heavy wire mesh. Inside this grid, there was another finer mesh and inside that a third of very fine mesh. Inside this last mesh cage there was a removable can that was pulled out with a wire to recover the pellets from which the gas had evaporated.[137]

These wire-mesh columns had been made in the camp metal workshop. As we saw in Chapter 3, one of the inmates employed there, Pole Michael Kula, testified immediately after the war that he had made various metal parts for the Birkenau crematoria, including the four wire-mesh columns in the large gas chambers of Crematoria 2 and 3. Tauber described the three structures of ever finer mesh. Within the innermost column there was a removable can to pull after the gassing with the Zyklon "crystals," that is, the porous silica pellets that had absorbed the hydrocyanide.

These wire mesh columns do not appear in the blueprints of the crematoria, nor do the holes in the roof that allowed the SS to introduce the Zyklon B into those columns. The reason for this is easily explained: they became part of the building's equipment relatively late in the construction process (November/December 1942), some ten months after the basic set of blueprints that formed the basis of construction had been completed (January 1942). The architects of the crematoria worked with great economy: for example, no special set of blueprints was made for Crematorium 3, a building that was a mirror image of Crematorium 2. Nor did they add to the blueprints the changes that were made in the design as construction progressed. For example, the elevations of Crematorium 2 in the set of blueprints that formed the basis of all work (drawings 935–938 and drawings 1173–1174) and a set of supplementary drawings (drawings 2136, 2197) do not show the two chimneys that served the ventilation system of the crematorium. These two ventilation chimneys were built, as photos clearly show. Thus, a very important part of Crematoria 2 and 3, clearly visible on wartime photos taken of these buildings, did not exist if we would allow the blueprints to be the only arbiter of what was and what was not constructed.

Furthermore, it is important to note that the set of drawings that survived is far from complete. The archives in Oswiecim and Moscow contain remarkably few working drawings, which in any case were produced by the contractors. In November and December 1942, when I believe the wire mesh columns were designed, Crematoria 2 and 3 were under construction, and at that time working drawings were the major tool of communication between architect and contractor. Changes would have been made in the working drawings. The archive of the Auschwitz-Birkenau State Museum contains a list with sixteen Huta working drawings for Crematorium 2 which all carry the general number 7015/IV. One of these drawings concerns the "Reinforcement for the ceiling over morgue 1."[138] It was drawn on October 22, 1942, and it was given the number 7015/IV—109/6. It is likely that this working drawing was the instrument to make modifications that introduced the holes and possibly the gas columns. It is important to note that shortly before the liquidation of the camp, the Auschwitz Zentralbauleiting requested Huta to send all working drawings back, both originals and copies.[139] The only possible explanation is that the architects wanted to remove incriminating evidence. The working drawing of the roof of Morgue 1, which most likely would have contained the change involving the wire-mesh column, drawing 7015/IV—109/6, was returned, but it did not survive.

The wire-mesh columns did not survive, either. It was relatively easy to dismantle these columns after the SS stopped gassing people at Auschwitz and before they demolished the crematoria, which explains why Leuchter did not find any remains.

These columns were connected to small holes that penetrated the concrete ceiling of the gas chamber, which opened to four small "chimneys," for lack of a better word. These are visible in one of the photos of Crematorium 2 taken by the SS during construction and in the aerial photos taken by the Americans in 1944, and they have been described by, among others, Tauber.

> The undressing room and the gas chamber were covered first with a concrete slab then with a layer of soil sown with grass. There were four small chimneys, the openings through which the gas was thrown in, that rose above the gas chamber. These openings were closed by concrete covers with two handles.[140]

As we have seen, Tauber also witnessed the way the Germans inserted the Zyklon B through these small chimneys.

> Through the window of the incineration room, I observed how the Zyklon was poured into the gas chamber. Each transport was followed by a vehicle with Red Cross markings which entered the yard of the crematorium, carrying the camp doctor, Mengele, accompanied by Rottenführer Scheimetz. They took the cans of Zyklon from the car and put them beside the small chimneys used to introduce the Zyklon into the gas chamber. There, Scheimetz opened them with a special cold chisel and a hammer, then poured the contents into the gas chamber. Then he closed the orifice with a concrete cover.[141]

After having quoted Tauber, I wrote five sentences which came to haunt me during my cross-examination in the Royal Courts of Justice. *Today, these four small holes that connected the wiremesh columns and the chimneys cannot be observed in the ruined remains of the concrete slab. Yet does this mean they were never there? We know that after the cessation of the gassings in the Fall of 1944 all the gassing equipment was removed, which implies both the wire-mesh columns and the chimneys. What would have remained would have been the four narrow holes in the slab. While there is not certainty in this particular matter, it would have been logical to attach at the location where the columns had been some formwork at the bottom of the gas chamber ceiling, and pour some concrete in the holes, and thus restore the slab.* In the next chapter, I will come back to these words.

"The Zyklon B was supposedly dropped through roof vents and put in through windows," Leuchter observed, "not allowing for the even distribution of gas or pellets." Leuchter attached great importance to the even distribution of the gas, and this could not be obtained by inserting the Zyklon at only some points. In cross-examination he was challenged on this assumption, which also led Leuchter to conclude elsewhere in the report that, on the basis of his calculation of the ideal air-flow requirement, a gas chamber of 2,500 square feet could hold only 278 people.

[Pearson]: "Some of the calculations that you made were based on the executed person occupying nine square feet?"

[Leuchter]: "That's correct."

Q.: "How do you calculate that measurement?"

A.: "The space required is determined by what's necessary for air circulation and those figures are normally used by all air moving engineers throughout the world."

Q.: "So once again, we're talking about figures that you would use in the United States in 1988 to conduct the execution of a condemned person. Is that right?"

A.: "Yeah, or in 1810. It doesn't matter when it is, the requirements for moving air have stayed the same."

Q.: "But would you agree with me that if you want the person to die quickly, if you put a premium on executing the person quickly, you want to have as much flow of air as possible. If you're not really concerned about how long it takes, the amount of time it takes for the air to flow, it isn't as important. Would you agree?"

A.: "Within reason."[142]

Unlike the state of Missouri, which stipulates in one of its statutes that an execution by gas should occur as quickly as possible, the SS were not bound by any statute or protocol to ease the suffering of their victims.

"The facilities are always damp and not heated." It was essential to Leuchter's argument that the temperature in the gas chambers while they were being operated was low. "We know that the facilities in question were operated at low temperatures," he testified in court. "We know that there would have been a considerable amount of condensation of liquid hydrogen cyanide on the walls, floor and ceiling of these facilities."[143] Leuchter was even prepared to testify that "these facilities were operated at zero degrees fahrenheit or near zero temperatures and perhaps below that."[144] It is not clear what evidence Leuchter used to come to this conclusion. In fact, there is ample evidence that the gas chambers were heated. As we have seen, one piece of anecdotal evidence was given by Yehuda Bacon during the Eichmann trial.

Q.: "Did you see the crematorium from the inside?"

A.: "Yes. We had to take wooden logs that were in the vicinity of the crematorium for the fire. Sometimes these had to be taken for regular heating in the camps. And when we finished our work and it was cold, the Kapo of the Sonderkommando took pity on us and said: 'Well, children, outside it is cold, warm yourselves in the gas chambers! There is nobody there'."

Q.: "And you went to warm yourselves inside the gas chambers?"

A.: "Yes. Sometimes we went to warm ourselves in the *Kleidungskammer*, sometimes in the gas chambers."[145]

There are also German documents that attest to the fact that the gas chamber was heated, a fact which, as I have pointed out above, strongly suggests that that room was *not* intended to be used as a morgue anymore. The most important is a letter the chief architect of Auschwitz, Karl Bischoff, sent to Topf on March 6, 1943. In it, Bischoff discussed the heating of Morgue 1 of Crematorium 2.

Letter from Karl Bischoff to Topf and Sons, March 6, 1943. Courtesy Archive Auschwitz-Birkenau State Museum, Oswiecim. (opposite page)

> In accordance with your proposal, the department agrees that morgue 1 will be preheated with the air coming from the rooms with the 3 installations to generate the forced-draught. The supply and installation of the necessary ductwork and ventilators most follow as soon as possible. As you indicate in your letter, the work should begin this week.[146]

Both Bacon's testimony and Bischoff's letter demolished Leuchter's argument that the gas chamber of Crematorium 2, and by implication the gas chamber of Crematorium 3, was not heated.

"As stated earlier, dampness and Zyklon B are not compatible." For once, I had no complaint with Leuchter's assertion, yet it had become irrelevant.

"The chambers are too small to physically contain the occupants claimed and the doors all open inward, a situation which would inhibit removal of the bodies." Surviving Sonderkommandos and Höss claimed that the gas chambers of Crematoria 2 and 3, which were 210 square meters each, held up to 2,000 people at a time. This meant some nine to ten people per square meter. Leuchter categorically refused to accept the possibility that 2,000 people could be crammed in such a space, but during cross-examination he had to admit that he could not back up his judgment.

[Pearson]: "Have you ever put 2,000 people into a room?"

[Leuchter] "No. But I'm sure I couldn't get them into that room."

Q.: "You've never done it, you have not conducted any experiments but you're sure. Is that what you're saying?"

A.: "That's what I'm saying. I don't believe anyone else has either."[147]

After I wrote my analysis of the Leuchter Report, I found an interesting fact: German legislation determining the number of people that may occupy the aisle in streetcars assumes that one person of 65 kilos occupies 0.125 square meters, or eight people per square meter. Thus, following German standards, the gas chamber of Crematorium 1 could have given space to 618 people at a time, and the gas chambers of Crematoria 2 and 3, which were about 200 square meters each, would have been able to hold 1,600 people per gas chamber—that is, a total number of people that exceeds by 10 percent the official incineration rate of these crematoria of 1,440 people per day. The three gas chambers of Crematoria 4 and 5 were also more than adequate for the job: the two larger ones were about 95

Krema II u. III.

Auschwitz, am 6.3.1943

PANSTWOWE MUZEUM W OSWIĘCIMIU
ARCHIWUM
BW 30/25

Bftgb.: 24365/43/Ja/Lm

Betr.: Kla Auschwitz, Krem. II und III KGL, BW 30 u. 30 a
Bezug: Dort. Schreiben vom 22.2.43 D.IV. Prf.
Anlg.: - - -

Firma
T o p f und S ö h n e
E r f u r t

Auf Grund Ihres Vorschlages erklärt sich die Dienststelle einverstanden, dass der Keller 1 mit der Abluft aus den Räumen der 3 Saugzuganlagen vorgewärmt wird. Die Anlieferung und der Einbau der hierfür benötigten Rohrleitungen und des Druckluftgebläses muss schnellstens erfolgen. Wie Sie in o.a. Schreiben angeben, sollte die Ausführung noch in dieser Woche geschehen. Um Hergabe eines spezifizierten Kostenangebotes 3-fach für Lieferung und Einbau wird gebeten.

Desgleichen wird um Einsendung eines Nachtragsangebotes für die Umänderung der Entlüftungsanlage für den Auskleideraum gebeten.

Nach Eingang dieser Angebote wird Ihnen schriftlich Auftrag erteilt.

Der Leiter der Zentralbauleitung
der Waffen-SS und Polizei Auschwitz

SS-Sturmbannführer

Verteiler:
1 Bault. KL u.Landw.
2 Registr. KGL BW 30 u.30 a
1 Sachbearb.

7.

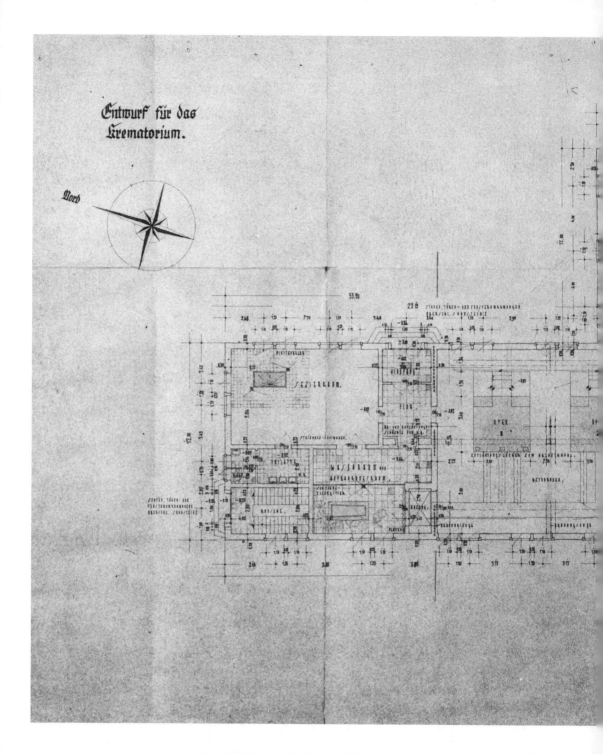

Detail of the plan of the ground floor of Crematorium 2. The three forced draft ventilators (marked Saugzuganlagen) *can be seen adjacent to the chimney. Courtesy Archive Auschwitz-Birkenau State Museum, Oswiecim.*

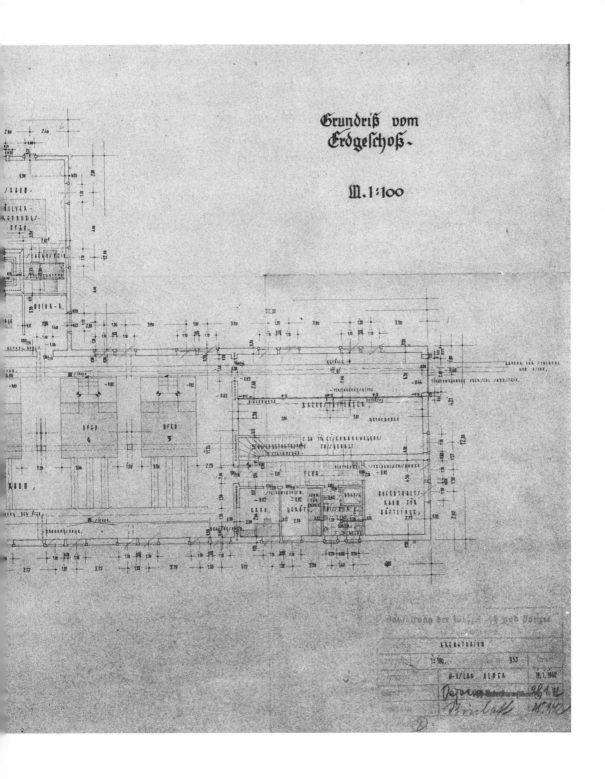

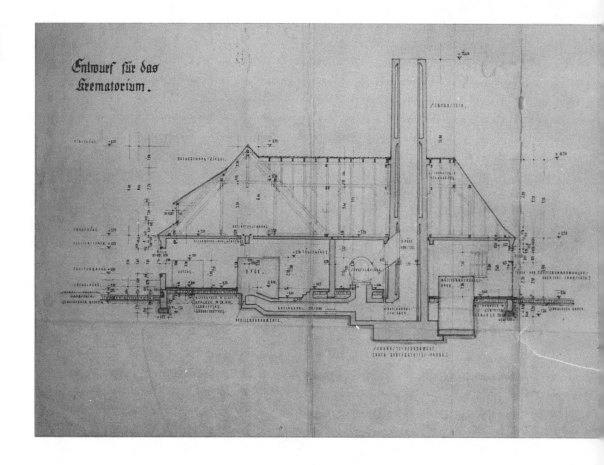

square meters each, allowing for 760 victims each—which comes close to the official incineration capacity of 756 corpses per day—and the smaller one of about 40 square meters could still accommodate 320 people.[148]

To my delight, I found that even negationists had informed Irving that Leuchter's data were wrong. In his letter to Irving, David Crabtree wrote that he had special trouble with Leuchter's assumption that the gas chambers could only be packed at a density of one "executee" per nine square feet.

> Mention is made of chambers too small to contain the occupants claimed, or attributed. This statement appears to be based on the assumption that executees were evenly spaced at 3 foot intervals, as per the reference to 9 square feet in col I, this page. An assumption is an assumption, and is not necessarily wrong. However, this one is comparable with a popular cocktail party. Surely the popular conception of the holocaust is more like the Tokyo underground at rush hour, or even the Guinness Book of Record figures for how many people get to fill a telephone kiosk or a Volkswagen beetle. 1.5 square feet per person seems more likely, given the alleged conditions. The number of executees per day should be therefore 6 times those used by the author. He can do this without interfering with his argument. He just makes it more acceptable. Even if the executees were allowed 9 square feet each

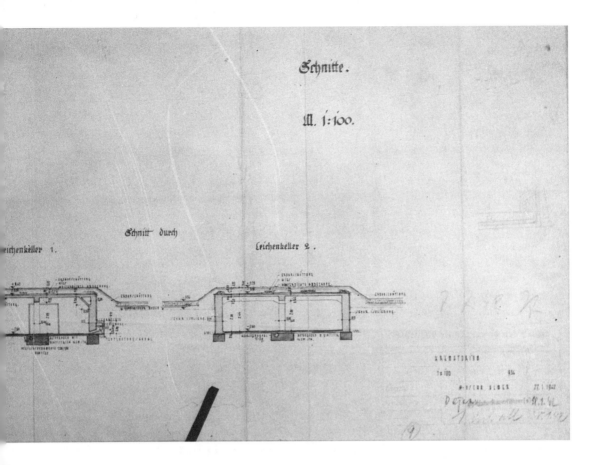

Section of Crematorium 2. The five triple-muffle incinerators (left) and the one trash incinerator (right) are connected to the chimney with underground flues. Adjacent to the chimney can be seen one of the three forced draft ventilators (each ventilator is connected to two flues). Each of these ventilators was placed in a small room, which was to become very hot when the crematorium was in operation. Bischoff's letter of March 6, 1943 proposed to recycle the heat of these rooms into Morgue 1—obviously to facilitate the evaporation of the hydrogen cyanide from the Zyklon B pellets. To the right are the sections of the gas chamber and the undressing room. Courtesy Archive Auschwitz-Birkenau State Museum, Oswiecim.

to be executed in, they would not use the space, as they would crowd themselves as densely as possible away from any perceived poison source, and towards any possible escape route.

Proposal—that the calculated output of corpses be increased accordingly. It is still not enough to support the holocaust figures. And the chemical evidence is in any case overwhelming, that it never happened.[149]

So much for the first part of the sentence. The second part—"the doors all open inward, a situation which would inhibit removal of the bodies"—could also be proven wrong. There is no evidence in the rubble of Crematoria 2 to 5 to come to any judgment about whether the doors opened one way or another. The blueprints that have been preserved in the archive of the Auschwitz-Birkenau State Museum in Oswiecim, however, directly and convincingly refute Leuchter's assertion. Drawing BW (B) 30/12, which shows Walther Dejaco's drawing for the modification of the entrance to the basement of Crematoria 2 and 3, shows that the doors to the gas chamber, indicated here as "L.[eichen] Keller 1" swing to the outside; drawing BW (B) 30b, which shows Walther Dejaco's design for Crematorium 4, shows that the doors to the gas chambers, located on the left of the plan but depicted on the right of the elevation, open again to the outside.

"With the gas chambers fully packed with occupants, there would be no circulation of the HCN within the room." It is undoubtedly true that

Krematorium im K.G.L.

Deckblatt zu Zeichnung № 932 u. 933,
Verlegung des Kellerzuganges an die Strassenseite.

Kellergeschoss

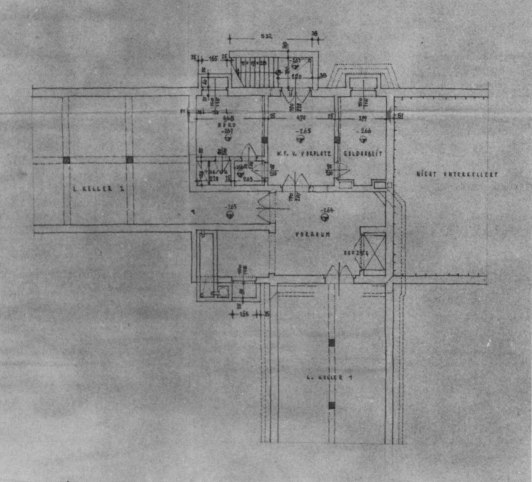

packing the gas chamber with people did not aid the rapid circulation of the hydrogen cyanide. Yet the design of the hollow, perforated columns did help to allow the gas to reach the higher reaches of the gas chamber, where the air was not displaced by the bodies, and where the heavy panting of 2,000 panicking people, or less, would—so one would assume—cause some circulation.

"Additionally, if the gas eventually did fill the chamber over a lengthy time period, those throwing Zyklon B in the roof vents and verifying the death of the occupants would die themselves from exposure to HCN." This seemed an odd sentence, as the adverb "eventually" suggests that even Leuchter assumed that it would take some time before the gas would reach the roof vents. Nevertheless, during his testimony Leuchter repeated his assertion that the SS men dropping the Zyklon B through the roof vents would face real danger. "The gas would come back up while they were doing this and probably kill all of the personnel operating the facility."[150] Pearson did not accept this reasoning and forced Leuchter to address this issue once more during cross-examination.

[Pearson]: "Now, hydrogen cyanide is slightly lighter than air?"

[Leuchter]: "That's correct."

Q.: "It means it rises slowly?"

A.: "Very slowly."

Q.: "Very slowly. So this stuff you told us about people on the roof who dropped the gas down and how they would be committing suicide, it would take a matter of minutes before the gas got to them, wouldn't it?"

A.: "Unquestionably."

Q.: "So, if they closed the vent and got off the roof, there would be nothing to concern them, would there?"

A.: "If they got off the roof. But at some point they have to do an inspection to determine whether the parties are deceased."

Q.: "They send in the Sonderkommandos to do that, sir, and they don't care what happens to them."

A.: "Right, all right."[151]

In fact, for this purpose the doors of the gas chambers were equipped with spyholes. Again, Tauber's testimony was rather specific on this point.

It was a wooden door, made of two layers of short pieces of wood arranged like parquet. Between these layers there was a single sheet of material sealing the edges of the door and the rabbets of the frame were also fitted with sealing strips of felt. At about head height for an average man this door had a round glass peephole. On the other side of the door, i.e. on the gas chamber side, this opening was protected by a hemispherical grid. This grid was fitted because the people in the gas chamber, feeling they were going to die, used to break the glass of the peep-hole. But the grid still did not provide sufficient protection and similar incidents recurred.[152]

Modified plan of the basement of Crematorium 2, December 1942. Courtesy Archive Auschwitz-Birkenau State Museum, Oswiecim. (opposite page)

Also, experience helped in guessing when it was time to turn on the ventilators. After a few gassings the men operating the gas chambers knew how long it took how many people to die as the result of how much hydrogen cyanide.

"None of the alleged gas chambers were constructed in accordance with the design for delousing chambers which were effectively operating for years in a safe manner." I questioned Leuchter's assumption that the Germans would have bothered to use the design of delousing chambers for their gas chambers. First of all, the delousing chambers were designed to operate with very high concentrations of hydrogen cyanide—between forty and seventy times the concentration the Germans used to kill humans in Birkenau—and these concentrations were applied for several hours. Second, the delousing chambers were, as Leuchter observed, designed in such a way that they guaranteed the highest possible safety for their users while allowing for the greatest possible efficiency in the quick loading and unloading of the chamber. The issue of safety was of lesser importance in the gas chambers, because the Sonderkommandos who entered the room were expendable. Furthermore, in the case of the gas chamber, efficiency in filling the room with living people and retrieving their bodies afterward was less important. But in the case of the delousing chambers, the rate-delimiting factor was the technology of the room itself; in the case of the gas chambers it was the cremation process which invariably went considerably slower than the gassing. In other words, the delousing rooms were designed to operate more or less continuously with high doses of hydrogen cyanide and relatively short periods of downtime in between, while the gas chambers were designed to operate for very short times with low doses of hydrogen cyanide while remaining idle for extended periods of time.

"None of these chambers were constructed in accordance with the known and proven designs of facilities operational in the United States at that time. It seems unusual that the presumed designers of these alleged gas chambers never consulted or considered the United States technology, the only country then executing prisoners with gas." It is obvious that, in late 1941 or early 1942, a letter from Kommandant Höss to the warden of, let's say, the Missouri State Penitentiary in Jefferson City, Missouri, which had been equipped with a state-of-the-art hydrogen cyanide gas chamber in 1939, would not have elicited a steady stream of collegial advice about the design and operation of gas chambers. Furthermore, it is not clear why Höss would have bothered to consult with others, as became clear in Leuchter's cross-examination.

> [Pearson]: "Would you agree with me that the gassing process itself is not a very difficult or complex process? The difficulty arises in constructing chambers which meet the requirements of safety and humane execution."
>
> [Leuchter]: "That's probably true, yes."[153]

The fallacy of Leuchter's reasoning, which went back to Faurisson, was the assumption that American gas chambers would be comparable with German gas chambers. First, American gas chambers were designed to provide for a quick and, given the circumstances, "humane" execution that not only satisfied the sense of decency of the witnesses (who, seated in an adjacent room equipped with air-sickness bags, could see all through a glass window) but also preempted a possible constitutional challenge on the grounds of "cruel and unusual" punishment. Everything was designed to introduce the gas immediately after the execution command was given and to ensure that the concentration of gas in the room quickly reached such a level that death followed immediately. Related to the necessary "constitutionality" of the American gas chambers and the irrelevance of this notion in the case of the Auschwitz killing installations is the fact that the former are, in a sense, only the last station in a long, ritualized path that takes the condemned a week to travel and that both provides a sense of legality and removes any possibility of individual accountability. Michael Lesy wrote in *The Forbidden Zone* that "since there's no holy law to protect them, prison officials rely on a system of divided responsibilities."

> Procedures are so fragmented that no single person remains re-sponsible. All actions are mediated by others or shared with others. Everything is done by administrative decree and court order, conveyed from person to person, down a chain of com-mand and obedience: "I-did-what-I-did-because-he-did-what-he-did." By the time a death sentence is carried out, it's impossible to accuse any particular person of anything. In Georgia, murderers die, but no one man ever kills them.[154]

The whole ritual develops on the understanding that it may be stopped, even a second before the final command, because of a last-minute stay of execution. The situation in Auschwitz could not have been more different.

Having considered every word of the paragraph devoted to the Ausch-witz gas chambers in the section entitled "Design and Procedures at the Alleged Execution Gas Chambers," I felt that I had firmly unmasked Leuchter's engineering opinion concerning the crematoria at Auschwitz as uninformed. In an early draft, I reproduced the passage once more, show-ing all the sentences that could be challenged on factual grounds in a cross-out mode.

> Bunkers 1 and 2 are described in Auschwitz State Museum litera-ture as converted farm houses with several chambers and win-dows sealed. These do not exist in their original condition and were not inspected. ~~Kremas 1, 2, 3, 4 and 5 are described histori-cally and on inspection were verified to have been converted mortuaries or morgues connected and housed in the same facility as crematories. The on-site inspection of these structures indi-cated extremely poor and dangerous design for these facilities if they were to have served as execution gas chambers. There is no provision for gasketed doors, windows or vents; the structures are not coated with tar or other sealant to prevent leakage or absorption of gas. The adjacent crematories are a potential dan-ger of explosion. The exposed porous brick and mortar would accumulate the HCN and make these facilities dangerous to humans for several years. Krema I is adjacent to the S.S. Hospital at Auschwitz and has floor drains connected to the main sewer of the camp—which would allow gas into every building at the fa-cility. There were no exhaust systems to vent the gas after usage and no heaters or dispersal mechanism for the Zyklon B gas to be introduced or evaporated. The Zyklon B was supposedly dropped through roof vents and put in through windows—not allowing for the even distribution of gas or pellets. The facilities are always damp and not heated.~~ As stated earlier, dampness and Zyklon B are not compatible. ~~The chambers are too small to physically contain the occupants claimed and the doors all open inward, a~~

*When considering the numbers
mentioned on the opposite page,
it is good to remember that they
concern people who were
murdered because they were
considered as mere figures.
Auschwitz-Birkenau, 1944.
Courtesy Yad Vashem.*

~~situation which would inhibit removal of the bodies. With the gas
chambers fully packed with occupants, there would be no circulation of the HCN within the room. Additionally, if the gas
eventually did fill the chamber over a lengthy time period, those
throwing Zyklon B in the roof vents and verifying the death of the
occupants would die themselves from exposure to HCN. None of
the alleged gas chambers were constructed in accordance with the
design for delousing chambers which were effectively operating
for years in a safe manner. None of these chambers were constructed in accordance with the known and proven designs of
facilities operational in the United States at that time. It seems
unusual that the presumed designers of these alleged gas chambers never consulted or considered the United States technology,
the only country then executing prisoners with gas.~~

On reading my report, a friend counseled against such a presentation, and
I did not include it in the final draft.

Having compared Leuchter's forensic observations with the historical
record, I turned to his mathematics. Despite the fact that Leuchter ada-
mantly asserted that the Auschwitz "facilities" could not have worked as
gas chambers, he was in the end prepared to calculate how many people
could have been killed in these spaces. "The alleged gas chamber in each of
Kremas 2 and 3 had an area of 2500 sq. ft. This would accommodate 278

people based on the 9 square foot theory."[155] Leuchter assumed that it would take a week to ventilate the room because he had not found evidence of a ventilation system, and so, with a stroke of the pen, the daily extermination capacity became a weekly one. Crematoria 2 and 3 had been in operation for a total of 84 and 72 weeks respectively, and thus Leuchter came to a maximum extermination capacity of 23,352 persons for Crematorium 2 and 20,016 persons for Crematorium 3. Using a similar approach, he concluded that the gas chambers of Crematorium 4 could kill 209 people daily/weekly and those of Crematorium 5 could kill 570 on a daily/weekly basis. As each of them had been in operation for 80 weeks, the maximum extermination capacity for Crematorium 4 had been 16,720 people, and Crematorium 5 had been able to gas a total of 45,600 people in Leuchter's calculations.[156] This gave a total of 105,688—a number that did not include the 6,768 people who could have been killed in Crematorium 1, or the people killed in Bunkers 1 and 2—gassing installations for which Leuchter did not provide any data.

It was not difficult to establish that Leuchter's numbers were wrong. I refused to assume that the gas chambers could be used only once a week, and I arrived at a subtotal of $7 \times 105,688 = 739,816$. Then I assumed instead of a density of one person per nine square feet a more realistic figure of one person per two square feet, and I arrived at a killing capacity of above 3.3 million victims for the four crematoria of Birkenau as they operated from the spring of 1943 to the fall of 1944. Then when I added to this the killing capacity of Crematorium 1 and Bunkers 1 and 2 (Bunker 1 some 500 square feet, which leads to a killing capacity of at least 250 people per day; Bunker 2 had some 650 square feet of usable space, which leads to a capacity of 320 people per day; Bunker 1 was at least 6 months in operation and Bunker 2 at least 14 months, which adds another 180,000 to the total killing capacity of the camp), the figure became even higher, rising to at least 3.5 million people.

Leuchter not only studied the technology of the gas chambers; he also was prepared to act as an expert witness for the construction of incinerators. He wrote, in his unique style, that "a consideration of crematories, both old and new, must be made to determine the functionability of the German Kremas at accomplishing their attributed tasks."[157] It is important to note that, during cross-examination, Leuchter had to admit that he had no expert knowledge of crematories.

[Pearson]: "Now, you devote in your report, one, two, three, four, five, six—seven paragraphs to gas chambers and you devote one, two, three, four, five, six, seven, eight, nine, ten, eleven, twelve, thirteen, fourteen, fifteen, sixteen, seventeen—seventeen sections or paragraphs to crematoriums."

[Leuchter]: "I'm not sure that is entirely true, counsellor, because there's information interspersed throughout this as necessary. You're simply going by the section headings and I would submit if you would read each section in each paragraph, you would see that the two are intertwined and there is information contained on gas chambers throughout."

Q.: "Well, unfortunately I haven't been given an opportunity to read it so you'll have to bear with me. I'm just going by the headings. What expertise do you have with designing crematoriums?"

A.: "Nothing in design, sir."

Q.: "All right. Do you operate a crematorium?"

A.: "No."

Q.: "What experience do you have with crematoriums?"

A.: "I made a determination before and after I began this project to apprise myself of crematorium design and operation. I consulted with a number of the crematorium manufacturers, I received data from these manufacturers on instruments that are used for cremation, and likewise, I visited two crematories and I watched the entire operation several times and the cremation of a number of corpses from the start of putting the corpses into the retort, until the bones were crushed and the ashes were put into the urn."

Q.: "You said both before and after you were retained. What made you look into this before you were retained?"

A.: "There's a misunderstanding there, counsellor. What I said before and after I went to Poland."

Q.: "All right. Sorry. So once again, we're talking about knowledge that you picked up since February when you were retained, I will suggest on a part-time basis or while you were working on one of a number of projects that your company was engaged in. Is that right?"

A.: "Most likely, yes."

Q.: "And I suggest, sir, that that really doesn't give you the expertise required to give opinions and extrapolate with respect to crematoriums."

A.: "Only to the extent, sir, that it is common and expected of an engineer that's dealing with any given problem to investigate the problem and then to investigate procedures relative to that problem."

Q.: "Sir, you went to school in Massachusetts?"

A.: "I did."

Q.: "Do they give degrees of engineering in Massachusetts?"

A.: "Some schools do."

Q.: "For instance, does MIT give out degrees in engineering?"

A.: "It does."

Q.: "You don't have a degree in engineering, do you?"

A.: "No, I do not."[158]

Consequently, the court rejected Leuchter's qualifications as an expert witness about the design and construction of crematories.

Leuchter's lack of expertise did not prevent either Zündel or Irving from including Leuchter's observations on the Auschwitz crematoria and his conclusions regarding the total incineration capacity of these installations for the period that they were in operation. After a short historical introduction, in which Leuchter observed that Orthodox Judaism forbade cremation, he reviewed modern practices.

> Earlier retorts were simply a drying or baking kiln and simply dried the human remains. Modern retorts of brick-lined steel actually blow fire from a nozzle onto the remains setting them afire, causing combustion and rapid burning. . . .
>
> These modern retorts or crematories burn at a temperature of 2000+°F, with an afterburner temperature of 1600°F. This high temperature causes the body to combust and consume itself, allowing for the burner to be shut down. . . . At 2000°F or more with a 2500 cfm blowered air supply from the outside, modern retorts will cremate one corpse in 1.25 hours. Theoretically, this is 19.2 in a 24 hour period. Factory recommendations for normal operation and sustained use allow for three (3) or less cremations per day. Older oil, coal and coke furnaces with forced air (but no direct flame application) normally took 3.5 to 4 hours for each corpse. Theoretically, this could allow for 6.8 corpses in a 24 hour time period at a maximum. Normal operation permits a maximum of three (3) cremations in a 24 hour time period. These computations are based on 1 corpse per retort per cremation.[159]

This led Leuchter to the conclusion that with 3 furnaces with 2 muffles each, Crematorium 1 would have had a theoretical incineration rate of (6 × 6.8) = 40.8 corpses per day, and a "real-time" rate of (6 × 3) = 18 corpses per day. Crematoria 2 and 3 could have incinerated then "theoretically" (15 × 6.8) = 102 and practically (15 × 3) = 45 corpses per day, and Crematoria 4 and 5 respectively (8 × 6.8) = 54.4 and (8 × 3) = 24. This resulted in a combined daily incineration capacity in Auschwitz of 353.6 (theoretical) or 156 (practical). These numbers led Leuchter to infer that, over the history of the crematoria which operated over a minimum of 72 weeks (Crematoria 1 and 3) and a maximum of 84 weeks (Crematorium 2), the total number of cremations would have been 193,576 (theoretical) and 85,092 (practical).[160]

As with his calculations for the gas chambers, Leuchter operated in a make-believe universe, in which he consulted neither German documents nor the testimony of witnesses. Leuchter claimed that before his journey to Poland, he had studied Raul Hilberg's *The Destruction of the European Jews*. In note 110 of Chapter 9, "Killing Center Operations," Hilberg mentioned a letter written by the Auschwitz Zentralbauleitung.[161] It is Bischoff's letter of June 28, 1943, which provided Kammler with the incineration capacities of the crematoria: Crematorium 1: 340 persons; Crematoria 2 and 3: 1,440 persons each; Crematoria 4 and 5: 768 persons each. Total per 24 hours: 4,756 persons.[162] In his cross-examination, Pearson confronted Leuchter with Hilberg's reference.

> [Pearson]: "Now, that document suggests that there is a capacity in a twenty-four hour period of 4,756 persons in the crematoriums?"
>
> [Leuchter]: "Yes."
>
> Q.: "That's quite different from your report, isn't it?"
>
> A.: "It is."
>
> Q.: "Have you looked at that document before?"

A.: "I have never seen that document before."[163]

I have already established the credibility of the document and its figures above, and so I will be brief here. A wartime German document states that the daily incineration capacity of the crematoria came close to 4,500 corpses per day, two independent testimonies corroborate this range of cremation capacity, and a wartime patent application by the makers of the ovens corroborates the incineration procedure described in these testimonies. There is little reason to dwell much longer on Leuchter's assertion that the theoretical incineration rate was a whole order of magnitude smaller and that the practical incineration rate was 156 corpses per day, a little over 3 percent of the official German rate.

Finally I turned to the dreaded issue of the samples. As we have seen, Leuchter did not find them too important, but because their alleged evidentiary value impressed Irving, Faurisson, and so many others, it was necessary to consider them in some detail.

I investigated the assumptions that led Leuchter to assume that there would be residual cyanide, in the form of ferro-ferri-cyanide, in the walls of the Auschwitz gas chambers. At the second Zündel trial, Leuchter admitted that one should not expect any residual cyanide in the walls of American gas chambers.

[Pearson]: "You'd agree with me that the purpose of a ventilation fan is to remove the gas from the—the place where the gas is at."

[Leuchter]: "That is true."

Q.: "And it will have a bearing on what traces are present at some later date. Isn't that right?"

A.: "That's very true."

Q.: "Very true."

A.: "Yes."

Q.: "Now, with respect to the delousing chamber, if there was no ventilation at all, we could expect high levels of cyanide traces, couldn't we?"

A.: "It depends upon how—the system was used. That's partially true, yes."

Q.: "Well, if there's no ventilation at all and there's no way for the gas to get out, then we would expect high levels of cyanide traces, wouldn't we?"

A.: "Again, counsellor, it depends upon the ventilation system."

Q.: "I'm saying no ventilation system."

A.: "Probably."

Q.: "All right. Now, if, on the other hand, the location is extremely well ventilated to get all the gas out, I suppose that's the optimum, if the ventilation system works perfectly, and would you agree with me that it's very difficult to reach perfection with respect to ventilation?"

A.: "I do."

Q.: "Although that's basically one of your engineering tasks with these modern gas chambers you produce, isn't it?"

A.: "Yes, it is."

Q.: "Do you expect that forty-five years from now, people will be able to find cyanide traces in your gas chambers?"

A.: "No, I do not."[164]

He continued to explain that good ventilation, heating the room so that the hydrogen cyanide would not condense on the walls, and coating the walls with epoxy or some other sealant prevented the formation of residual cyanide such as ferro-ferri-cyanide in the walls of modern gas chambers.

Leuchter wrongly assumed that the Auschwitz gas chambers were not ventilated. Furthermore, he wrongly hypothesized that the gas chambers operated at very low temperatures and that therefore there would have been "a considerable amount of condensation of liquid hydrogen cyanide on the walls, floor and ceiling of these facilities."[165] He wrongly inferred from the ruins of Crematoria 2, 3, 4, and 5 that the walls of the gas chambers had not been coated and that therefore the liquid hydrogen cyanide could have reacted with the iron in the bricks and mortar to form ferro-ferri-cyanide. Then he wrongly reasoned that, in accordance with American practice, the Germans had used a high concentration of 3,600 parts of hydrogen cyanide per million parts of air—the concentration used in United States gas chambers to ensure that the condemned will die a quick death—while in fact the Germans used a concentration of 300 parts per million to kill their victims.[166] Nor did he consider the amount of hydrogen cyanide that would be absorbed by the bodies of the victims. Finally, he did not take into account the effects of changes in the situation of the gas chambers in the last forty-five years. For example, the gas chamber of Crematorium 1 was abandoned in 1943 and was transformed into an air-raid shelter in 1944, undergoing substantial modifications in the process. Then, after the war, it was once more changed to provide a museological reconstruction of the original gas chamber. Leuchter assumed that the layer of plaster from which he took his samples was the same that had coated the walls in 1942. There is little to no evidence to support that premise. Then he took no account of the fact that the gas chambers of Crematoria 2 and 3 had been purposefully demolished in 1944, that their remains had been exposed to the elements for forty-five years, and that the walls had been washed with acid rain—a fact of some importance because, contrary to Leuchter's belief, ferro-ferri-cyanide is not stable under all conditions but tends to slowly dissolve in an acidic environment. Finally, he did not know that the low brick walls that mark the plan of Crematoria 4 and 5 were rebuilt after the war using bricks from the original buildings, but not necessarily in the right position. In other words, the walls that now define the outlines of the gas chamber could have been rebuilt using bricks originally used for the construction of the incineration rooms or the coke storage rooms.

On the basis of wrong assumptions, Leuchter expected that one would find relatively high residual cyanide in the walls of the gas chambers if they had been indeed used for genocidal purposes. When he did not, he immediately jumped to the conclusion that those spaces had not been used as gas chambers. He was strengthened in his conviction by a few "control samples" he took from rooms that had been used as hydrogen cyanide delousing chambers. These samples showed a very high degree of ferro-ferri-cyanide—something that did not surprise anyone, as the walls of these delousing rooms showed large Prussian blue stains. Leuchter wrongly assumed that the delousing rooms had been exposed to much lower quantities of gas than the homicidal gas chambers—in fact, the opposite is true, and while the delousing chambers operated more or less nonstop, the homicidal gas chambers operated only for very short times—and drew his "shattering" conclusion.

> One would have expected higher cyanide detection in the samples taken from the alleged gas chambers (because of the greater amount of gas allegedly utilized there) than that found in the control sample. Since the contrary is true, one must conclude that these facilities were not execution gas chambers, when coupled with all the other evidence gained on inspection.[167]

As we have seen, "all the other evidence gained on inspection" was less than it purported it to be.

Again, as in the case of Leuchter's discussion of the capacity of the gas chambers, after writing my critique of Leuchter's report I found some interesting material on the issue of the samples in Irving's discovery. As I described in Chapter 1, in the late fall or early winter of 1989 Irving received a very tough critique of the Leuchter Report. The author noted that the basis of Leuchter's assumption, the idea that it would be possible to gauge the Germans' use of hydrocyanic gas as a killing agent in Auschwitz by contemporary American practices, was invalid. In American gas chambers, inmates were killed with 3,200 ppm, the effect of which the critique describes as "one-gulp-and-you're-dead."[168] A concentration of 300 ppm brought about "rapid and immediate death." Given the fact that there were accounts that it took people up to 30 minutes to expire, concentrations at Auschwitz could have been as low as 100 ppm.

> A supplementary factor is that in a US judicial execution chamber the victim is strapped, fully dressed, into a chair. Gas ingestion is thus by inhalation. According to literature the victims of the alleged gas chambers were herded bare-arse naked into the facility having been made to run from the undressing rooms to the chambers. The victims were thus gasping for breath while immersed in a toxic atmosphere. Since HCN can access the body by skin absorption as well as by inhalation, this greatly increased the effectiveness of the low concentrations of gas and makes the use of 100 ppm fully credible. The result makes a dramatic difference to the whole report.[169]

Because the gas chambers were operated with a low (but lethal) hydrocyanide concentration of 100 ppm, there was no danger of explosion. More important, at such a low concentration the major issue (for Leuchter and Faurisson) of ventilation ceased to be a point. The author of the critique did not know that the underground gas chambers of Crematoria 2 and 3 were equipped with a ventilation system which, as we have already seen, made Leuchter's opinion about the impossibility of using these rooms as gas chambers moot. But the smaller aboveground gas chambers of Crematoria 4 and 5 did not have a separate ventilation system, only doors that opened directly to the outside. It is therefore interesting to note his comments on the issue of ventilation.

> Leuchter claims that at least a week would be needed to ventilate the chambers prior to removing the bodies and cleansing. This is based on US industrial safety standards, a complete lack of ventilation and the 3200 ppm concentration. The use of 100 ppm dramatically reduces the time needed to reduce concentration. It is obvious that the German guards would not have applied 1989 US industrial safety standards to the slave labour reputedly used to clear the chambers. The volume of one chamber is quoted as 7657 ft^3. A swept volume of 120 ft^3/min would be needed to completely change this in one hour equating to a flow rate of 0.5 ft^3/sec. A current of this speed is hardly distinguishable from still air. Assuming 1 hour is left for ventilation the result would be a residual gas concentration of 15–25 ppm within the chamber. The symptoms in crews used to clear/clean the chamber would, after prolonged exposure, be headaches, nausea, reddening of eyes, giddiness and weakness. These are exactly the symptoms experienced by survivors of the work teams reputedly used for this purpose and previously assumed to be a psychosomatic result of the horror of the experience. This is a further case of Leuchter's own work actually verifying Holocaust accounts.[170]

As a result, it would have been possible to use the gas chambers twice a day instead of once a week. This immediately increased the possible death rate of the gas chambers from a little over 100,000 to close to 1.5 million people. Added to that was the fact that Leuchter's assumption that the gas chambers were loaded with victims at a density of one per nine square feet was obviously wrong. The author of the critique assumed a density of at least one person per six square feet, which brought the possible death toll to 2.2 million people.[171]

Then the critique addressed the assumption that had informed Leuchter's sampling technique.

> The 100 ppm operating concentration discredits his sample technique. Obviously if the gas concentration was 100 ppm, the residue concentration in the walls cannot be greater. The samples were exposed to a damp, cold environment for 40 years. Leaching and chemical breakdown would be such that even the stablest complexes would be degraded. To find 6 ppm under such circumstances is remarkable. The control sample was from a delouser used several times per day at 3200 ppm and A SMALL, SELF-CONTAINED UNIT COMPLETELY ENCLOSED AND SHELTERED. To consider this a control is exceptionally bad technique and discredits the entire sample programme. I repeat at 100 ppm initial I would expect NO DETECTABLE CONCENTRATION in an exposed sample.[172]

The word "important" is written in the photocopy of the critique in Irving's handwriting. The report's final conclusion went farther than even I had dared to go:

> The evidence of the Leuchter Report, when taken in the context of the times and in full consideration of all other evidence is consistent with that other evidence and together strongly supports both

the fact and the scale of the massacres in the gas chambers of Birkenau provided that assumption is made that the gas chambers operated at relatively low toxic concentrations.[173]

As I wrote my critique of Leuchter, my experience with Errol Morris proved useful. In order to prepare for the filming in Poland, I had carefully studied the videotapes which were made of his trip to Poland, which clearly show that Leuchter took incorrect samples for the analysis of cyanide content. When Alpha Laboratories analyzed the cyanide content of the samples, they provided the measurements of the total cyanide concentration in each of the samples. They did not measure the concentration of cyanide on the outer surface of the samples. As Dr. Jim Roth, who had analyzed the samples in 1988, explained to Morris, "Hindsight being 20/20, the test was not the correct one to have used for the analysis."[174] Roth explained that cyanide will react on the surface of brick or plaster, penetrating the material not more than 10 microns, or 0.01 mm, or one-tenth the thickness of a human hair (one micron equals $\frac{1}{1,000,000}$ of a meter, or 0.000039 inch). In other words, if one wants to analyze the cyanide concentration in a brick sample, one should take a representative sample of the surface that is 10 microns thick, and no more. Yet, as Roth remembered, "[Leuchter] presented us with rock samples anywhere from the size of your thumb up to half the size of your fist. We broke them up with a hammer so that we could get a sub-sample; we placed it in a flask, add concentrated sulfuric acid. It undergoes a reaction that produces a red-colored solution. It is the intensity of this red color that we can relate with cyanide concentration."[175] Roth explained that his laboratory analysis could not make up for faulty sampling technique. If the sample was not representative, the results would be meaningless. Because the cyanide did not penetrate the brick more than 10 microns, the cyanide concentration would be diluted only 10 times when the sample is 100 microns (or 0.1 mm or 0.0039 inches) thick, but it would be diluted 1,000 times when the sample is 10 mm (or 0.39 inches) thick. Leuchter did not carefully slice the surface of the materials he was sampling. In fact, as the videotapes clearly showed, he hacked into the walls and took samples that included at least 1,000 layers of material that could not have reacted with the cyanide. As Roth remarked, "I might have had the back side of the brick, not the front side of the brick, but I didn't know which side was up and which was down. That's the point: Which was the exposed surface? I didn't even have any idea. That is like analyzing paint on a wall by analyzing the timber that's behind it." In conclusion, Roth stated that "I don't think the Leuchter results have any meaning."[176] Indeed, the only conclusion one may legitimately draw from Leuchter's sampling is that the very fact that Alpha Laboratories found any residual cyanide at all is extremely significant. In fact, Leuchter's samples most likely proved the use of Morgue 1 of Crematoria 2 and 3 as a gas chamber.

This brought me then to consider the legitimate forensic studies which were undertaken at the Auschwitz crematoria by Polish scientists in the early 1990s. When the first news about the Zündel trial and Leuchter's testimony reached the Auschwitz Museum, its director Kazimierz Smolen wrote to highly experienced and respected Polish forensic scientist Professor Jan Markiewicz, director of the Institute of Forensic Research in Cracow, with the request that he take samples from the wall plaster of the gas chambers and analyze them for the presence of hydrogen cyanide. Smolen did not inform Markiewicz about the existence of the Leuchter

Report. Markiewicz responded that he thought "the chances of detecting hydrogen cyanide in such samples as nearly none."[177] Nevertheless, he dispatched two of his employees to the camp, who took twenty-two samples on February 20, 1990: ten from rooms in Block 3 of the Auschwitz Stammlager that had served as delousing rooms, five from the ruins of the gas chamber of Crematorium 2 and 3, and one sample each from Crematorium 5 and Crematorium 1. No samples were taken from Crematorium 4—it was left alone since all the walls had been reconstructed after the war. The results showed traces of hydrocyanic compounds in seven samples taken from Block 3 and in one sample taken from a remaining pillar of the gas chamber of Crematorium 2.

The letter that Markiewicz sent to the museum was leaked to the revisionists, and in the newsletter of the Institute for Historical Review much was made of it. Mark Weber, associate editor of the *Journal of Historical Review,* then wrote to Markiewicz and asked him to comment on the relevance of his own findings for the Leuchter Report. Markiewicz responded in a letter dated June 7, 1991, in which he observed that the initial research had been a little too hasty.

> Now, in the light of letters and publications coming to us from different countries, I have arrived at the conclusion that our investigations aiming at the confirmation, if possible, of the use of cyanic preparations in the rooms that survived whole or only in the form of ruins, were rather preliminary in nature and incomplete. We are bent on widening and deepening these investigations and have already been preparing for them. It is only now when suitable materials from literature have become accessible to us that we see the purpose and sense of such studies. Naturally, we shall publish their results and make them accessible to you and your Institute.[178]

The Institute for Historical Review did not wait, however, for the new report. Immediately after receiving Markiewicz's letter they published an article entitled "An Official Polish Report on the Auschwitz 'Gas Chambers': Krakow Forensic Institute Bolsters Leuchter's Findings." It claimed that Polish scientists had "replicated Leuchter's findings and implicitly corroborated his conclusions." Wrongly arguing that the whole of the gas chamber of Crematorium 2 was protected from the elements by the collapsed concrete ceiling "and is otherwise in its original condition," the author of the article found it worth noting that the Cracow scientists had not responded to the "compelling reasons given by Leuchter for doubting the orthodox extermination story." For example, they had not engaged him on his engineering considerations—a fact which should not have surprised them because Markiewicz had written in his letter to Weber that they had not known about the Leuchter Report when they took their samples or wrote their report. The main text of the article ended with the following comment:

> Auschwitz State Museum officials initiated this investigation rather obviously hoping that the Institute's report would discredit Leuchter's findings and corroborate the orthodox extermination account. And just as obviously, if the Institute's report had, in fact, discredited the American engineer's conclusions, the Auschwitz State Museum would certainly have wasted no time in giving it maximum publicity.

Although neither the Auschwitz State Museum nor the Krakow Institute has (so far) made this September 1990 report public, Revisionists were nevertheless able to obtain a copy of the original document. Professor Robert Faurisson in France and Fred Leuchter in the United States were quick to cite the "Polish Leuchter Report" as corroboration of the Revisionist view of the Auschwitz extermination story.

Having rudely awakened to the realities of negationism, Markiewicz and his people decided to move with greater care. In the final report, which they published in 1994, they discussed Leuchter's investigations and their own early sampling and its results.

When the dispute on the Leuchter Report arose, we undertook a closer study of the problem, availing ourselves, among other publications, of J.C. Pressac's comprehensive work. In consequence, we decided to start considerably more extensive and conscientiously planned researches. To carry them out, the Management of the Auschwitz Museum appointed their competent workers, Dr. F. Piper (custodian) and Mr. W. Smerk (engineer) to join the commission, in which they co-worked with the authors of the present paper, representing the Institute of Forensic Research. Under this collaboration, the Museum workers were providing us on the spot with exhaustive information concerning the facilities to be examined and—as regards the ruins—a detailed topography of the gas chambers we were concerned with. And so they made it possible for us to take proper samples for analysis. We tried to take samples—if at all possible—from the places best sheltered and least exposed to rainfall, including—also as far as possible—fragments from the upper parts of the chambers (hydrogen cyanide is lighter than air) and also of the concrete floors, with which the gas from the spilled Zyklon B came into contact at rather high concentrations.

Samples, about 1–2 g in weight, were taken by chipping pieces from bricks and concrete or scraping off, particularly in the case of plaster and also mortar. The materials taken were secured in plastic containers marked with serial numbers. All these activities were recorded and documented with photographs. Work connected with them took the commission two days. The laboratory analysis of the material collected was conducted—to ensure full objectivity—by another group of institute workers. They started with preliminary work: samples were comminuted by grinding them by hand in an agate mortar, their pH was determined at 6 to 7 in nearly all samples. Next the samples were subjected to preliminary spectrophotometric analysis in the infrared region, using a Digilab FTS-15 spectrophotometer. It was found that the bands of cyanide groups occurred in the region of $2000–2200\ cm^{-1}$ in the spectra of a dozen samples or so. However, the method did not prove to be sensitive enough and was given up in quantitative determinations. It was determined, using the spectographical method, that the main elements which made up the samples were: calcium, silicon, magnesium, aluminium and iron. Moreover, titanium was found present in many samples. From among other metals in some samples there were also barium, zinc, sodium, manganese and from non-metals boron.

The undertaking of chemical analysis had to be preceded by careful consideration. The revisionists focussed their attention almost exclusively on Prussian blue, which is of intense dark-blue colour characterized by exceptional fastness. This dye occurs, especially in the form of stains, on the outer bricks of the walls of the former bath-delousing house in the area of the Birkenau camp. It is hard to imagine the chemical reactions and physico-chemical processes that could have led to the formation of Prussian blue in that place. Brick, unlike other building materials, very feebly absorbs hydrogen cyanide, it sometimes does not even absorb it at all. Besides, iron occurring in it is at the third oxidation state, whereas bivalent iron ions are indispensable for the formation of the $[Fe(Cn)_6]^{-4}$ ion, which is the precursor of Prussian blue. This ion is, besides, sensitive to the sunlight.

[...]

We decided therefore to determine the cyanide ions using a method that does not indice the breakdown of the composed ferrum cyanide complex (this is the blue under discussion) and which we had tested before on an appropriate standard sample. To isolate cyanide compounds from the materials examined in the form of hydrogen cyanide we used the techniques of micro-diffusion in special Conway-type chambers. The sample under examination was placed in the internal part of the chamber and next acidified with 10% sulfuric acid solution and allowed to remain at open room temperature (about 20°C) for 24 hrs. The separated hydrogen cyanide underwent a quantitative absorption by the lye solution present in the outer part of the chamber. When the diffusion was brought to an end, a sample of lye solution was taken and the pyridine-pyrazolone reaction carried out by Epstein's method. The intensity of the polymethene dye obtained was measured spectrophotometrically at a wavelength equal to 630 nm. The calibration curve was constructed previously and standards with a known CN^- content were introduced into each series of determinations to check the curve and the course of determination. Each sample of materials examined was analysed three times. If the result obtained was positive, it was verified by repeating the analysis. Having applied this method for many years, we have opportunities to find its high sensitivity, specificity and precision. Under present circumstances we established the lower limit of determinability of cyanide ions at a level of 3–4µg CN^- in 1 kg of the sample.

The results of analyses are presented in Tables 5.1 through 5.4. They unequivocally show that the cyanide compounds occur in all the facilities that, according to the source data, were in contact with them. On the other hand, they do not occur in dwelling accommodations, which was shown by means of the control samples. The concentrations of cyanide compounds in the samples collected from one and the same room or building shows great differences. This indicates that the conditions that favour the formation of stable compounds as a result of the reaction of hydrogen cyanide with the components of the walls, occur locally. In this connection it takes quite a larger number of samples from a given facility to give us a chance to come upon this sort of local accumulation of cyanide compounds.[179]

Table 5.3

Extant Concentrations of Cyanide in Gas Chambers at Auschwitz

Cellars of Block 11 Used as Experimental Gas Chambers in 1941

Sample no.	13	14	15
Concentration of CN⁻ (µg/kg)	28	20	0
	24	16	0
	24	16	0

Crematorium 1

Sample No.	16	17	18	19	20	21	22
Concentration of CN⁻ (µg/kg)	28	76	0	0	288	0	80
	28	80	0	0	292	0	80
	28	80	0	0	288	0	80

Crematorium 2

Sample No.	25	26	27	28	29	30	31
Concentration of CN⁻ (µg/kg)	640	28	0	8	20	168	296
	592	28	0	8	16	156	288
	620	28	0	8	16	168	292

Crematorium 3

Sample No.	32	33	34	35	36	37	38
Concentration of CN⁻ (µg/kg)	68	12	12	16	12	16	56
	68	8	12	12	8	16	52
	68	8	8	16	8	16	56

Crematorium 4

Sample No.	39	40	41	42	43
Concentration of CN⁻ (µg/kg)	40	36	500	trace	16
	44	32	496	0	12
	44	36	496	0	12

Crematorium 5

Sample No.	46	47	48	49	50	51	52
Concentration of CN⁻ (µg/kg)	244	36	92	12	116	56	0
	248	28	96	12	120	60	0
	232	32	96	12	116	60	0

Source: Compiled from Jan Markiewicz, Wojciech Gubala, and Jerzy Labedz, "A Study of the Cyanide Compounds Content in the Walls of the Gas Chambers in the Former Auschwitz and Birkenau Concentration Camps," *Z Zagadnien Nauk Sadowych* (*Problems of Forensic Science*) 30 (1994): 19–27.

Samples 1 to 8 were taken from fumigation chambers in Blocks 1 and 3 in the Stammlager and showed concentrations of CN⁻ that went in one instance (sample 6) as high as 900 μg/kg. Samples 9 to 12 were taken from dwelling spaces in Block 3 and 8 and all showed a total absence of CN⁻. These rooms were known to have been fumigated with hydrogen cyanide only once. Samples 13 to 52 were taken from places which served as homicidal gas chambers. Samples 13 to 22 were taken in Auschwitz 1. As I considered Roth's observations, I was sorry that the report does not mention the thickness of the samples; again, the knowledge that cyanide only reacts on the surface of brick remains an important fact of consideration. Therefore I did not like to assign more than relative significance to the Polish measurements. Yet, even so, they seemed important in their own right, because they clearly show the presence of cyanide in the walls of the gas chambers, confirming the "alleged" use of these spaces as killing installations.

Finally samples 53 to 59 were taken from the same delousing building, BW5a, from which Leuchter had obtained his control samples. Samples 53 to 55 were taken from the dark-blue stains on the outer side of the building wall, sample 56 was mortar taken from the outer side of the building wall, samples 57 and 58 were plaster taken from dark blue stains on the inner side of the building wall, and sample 59 was plaster taken from white walls inside the building.

The forensic team also conducted various other tests to study the absorptive behavior of various materials. In the first test, the scientists exposed fresh plaster, fresh mortar, new brick, and old brick, both in dry and wet forms, to a high concentration of hydrogen cyanide (2 percent) for 48 hours. The results of this test, which simulated the conditions that existed in a fumigation room, showed that the various materials absorbed the hydrogen cyanide with very different rates.

In a second test, the team added carbon dioxide to the hydrogen cyanide, introducing the two gases in a rate of 5 parts CO_2 to one part HCN. This test simulated the conditions that existed in homicidal gas chambers.

Table 5.4

Summary of Markiewicz's Forensic Sampling at Auschwitz

Building	300–1,000 μg CN⁻/kg	100–300 μg CN⁻/kg	0–100 μg CN⁻/kg	0 μg CN⁻/kg
BW5a	XXX	X	XXXX	—
Crematorium 1	—	X	XXX	XXX
Crematorium 2	X	XX	XXX	X
Crematorium 3	—	—	XXXXXXX	—
Crematorium 4	X	—	XXX	X
Crematorium 5	—	XX	XXXX	X

Source: Compiled from Jan Markiewicz, Wojciech Gubala, and Jerzy Labedz, "A Study of the Cyanide Compounds Content in the Walls of the Gas Chambers in the Former Auschwitz and Birkenau Concentration Camps," *Z Zagadnien Nauk Sadowych* (*Problems of Forensic Science*) 30 (1994): 19–27.

In their reasoning the revisionists did not take into consideration certain circumstances, namely, the simultaneous action of cyanides and carbon dioxide on the chamber walls. In the air exhaled by man carbon dioxide constitutes 3.5% by volume. Breathing for 1 minute, he takes in and next exhales 15–20 dm^3 of air, comprising on the average 950 cm^3 CO_2; consequently, 1000 people breathe out about 950 dm^3 of carbon dioxide. And so it can be estimated that, if the victims stayed in the chamber for 5 minutes before they die, they exhaled 4.75 m^3 of carbon dioxide during that period. This is at least 1% of the capacity, e.g. of the gas chamber of Crematorium 2 at Birkenau, the capacity of which was about 500 m^3, whereas the concentration of hydrogen cyanide virtually did not exceed 0.1% by volume (death occurs soon at as low HCN concentrations as 0.03% by volume).[180]

After having been exposed to the CO_2 and HCN mixture, the samples were aired for 48 hours in the open air at a temperature of about 10 to 15°C and then subjected to analysis.

While in the tests that simulated the situation in the fumigation rooms, the CN^- content was higher in the wetted materials, in the tests that simulated the condition in the homicidal gas chambers, the results were reversed, that is, that the CN^- content was lower in the wetted content. "It seems that here a tendency is revealed towards the competitive action of carbon dioxide, which dissolved in water," Markiewicz's report explained. And it added that "in this series of tests fresh plaster showed an exceptionally high affinity to hydrogen cyanide."[181]

The samples of both tests were analyzed again one month later. In the samples that had been exposed to hydrogen cyanide only, the average decrease was 56 percent, while in the samples that had been exposed to the combination of carbon dioxide and hydrogen cyanide, the loss was 73 percent. "In as many as four samples that loss ranged from 97% to 100%."[182] This was an important result, because the negationists had claimed that conditions for the preservation of HCN in homicidal gas chambers should have been better than in fumigation gas chambers. In fact, it was opposite.

Finally Markiewicz's team tested the way water elutes cyanide ions. Taking two plaster samples of 0.5 grams each that had been fumigated with hydrogen cyanide, they flushed them with one liter of clean de-ionized water. The first sample showed a loss in concentration of HCN in µg/kg of 82.5 percent (160 vs. 28), the second of 90.7 percent (1200 vs. 112). This test is important because the remains of the gas chambers of Crematoria 2 to 5 have been exposed to the elements since the end of the war, and "it can be estimated, on the basis of climatological records, that in these last 45 years or so they have been rinsed rather thoroughly by a column of water at least 35 m in height(!)."[183]

The conclusion of what one should call the Markiewicz Report was straightforward and, as far as the Leuchter Report was concerned, shattering.

The present study shows that in spite of the passage of a considerable period of time (over 45 years) in the walls of the facilities which once were in contact with hydrogen cyanide the vestigial amounts of the combinations of this constituent of Zyklon B had been preserved. This is also true of the ruins of the former gas chambers. The cyanide compounds occur in the building materi-

Table 5.5

Extant Traces of Cyanide in Delousing Shed BW5a at Auschwitz

Sample no.	53	53a	54	55	56	57	58	59
Concentration	24	224	36	736	4	840	348	28
of CN⁻ (μg/kg)	20	248	28	740	0	792	324	28
	24	228	32	640	0	840	348	28

Table 5.6

Residues of Cyanide in Various Materials after Exposure to 2 Percent Cyanide

Material	Fresh Plaster		Fresh Mortar		New Brick		Old Brick	
Condition	Dry	Wetted	Dry	Wetted	Dry	Wetted	Dry	Wetted
CN⁻ (μg/kg)	24	480	176	2,700	4	52	20	0

Source: Compiled from Jan Markiewicz, Wojciech Gubala, and Jerzy Labedz, "A Study of the Cyanide Compounds Content in the Walls of the Gas Chambers in the Former Auschwitz and Birkenau Concentration Camps," *Z Zagadnien Nauk Sadowych* (*Problems of Forensic Science*) 30 (1994): 19–27.

Table 5.7

**Residues of Cyanide in Various Materials after Exposure to a Mixture of
2 Percent Cyanide and 10 Percent Carbon Dioxide**

Material	Fresh Plaster		Old Mortar		Fresh Mortar		New Brick		Old Brick	
Condition	Dry	Wetted	Dry	Wetted	Dry	Wetted	Dry	Wetted	Dry	Wetted
CN⁻ (μg/kg)	5,920	1,280	1,000	244	492	388	52	36	24	60

Source: Compiled from Jan Markiewicz, Wojciech Gubala, and Jerzy Labedz, "A Study of the Cyanide Compounds Content in the Walls of the Gas Chambers in the Former Auschwitz and Birkenau Concentration Camps," *Z Zagadnien Nauk Sadowych* (*Problems of Forensic Science*) 30 (1994): 19–27.

als only locally, in the places where the conditions arose for their formation and persistence for such a long time.

In his reasoning Leuchter claims that the vestigial amounts of cyanide combinations detected by him in the materials from the chamber ruins are residues left after fumigations carried out in the Camp, "once, long ago" (Item 14.004 of the Report). This is refuted by the negative results of the examination of the control samples from living quarters, which are said to have been subjected to a single gassing, and the fact that in the period of fumigation of the Camp in connection with a typhoid epidemic in mid-1942 there were still no crematoria in the Birkenau camp. The first crematorium (Crematorium 2) was put to use as late as 15 March 1943 and the others several months later.[184]

Of course, at the time of the second Zündel trial, the Markiewicz report did not exist. Yet at that time it was clear to the court, at least, that Leuchter's methodology and data simply did not meet the judicial requirements for admissible evidence. While this impressed the jury and the judge, it did not impress Irving, who hailed the Leuchter Report as an important breakthrough.

Six
Auschwitz at the Irving Trial

On Thursday, June 10, 1999, I arrived in Oswiecim, accompanied by my friend and research assistant, Omer Arbel. We had just come from the weekly LOT Polish Airlines Toronto-to-Cracow flight to spend a day in the camp before meeting Deborah Lipstadt, barristers Richard Rampton QC and Heather Rogers, and solicitors Veronica Byrne of Mishcon de Reya and Mark Bateman of Davenport Lyons. During a two-day visit, I was to familiarize the lawyers with the layout of the camp and the archival documents, and Arbel was to create a written and photographic record of our inspection.

The trip to Oswiecim was a direct reflection of the significance Auschwitz had acquired in the preparation of the case. Three months earlier, I had met Rampton and Rogers for the first time at a large meeting of experts and lawyers convened by Mishcon de Reya. The date of the trial had just been set to begin on January 11, 2000, and the court had established a deadline in April for the submission of the expert reports. Things had begun to move. Drafts of all the expert reports had been circulated, and at the meeting historians Richard Evans (Irving's historiography), Christopher Browning (implementation of the Final Solution), Peter Longerich (Hitler's role in the Final Solution), Wolfgang Benz (numbers of victims), political scientists Roger Eatwell and I (Irving's political extremism in Great Britain), Hajo Funke (Irving's political extremism in Germany), and Brian Levin (Irving's political extremism in the United States) were to exchange views on all the reports to identify and, if possible, achieve consensus about any possible contradictions.

But there was also a second aim for the meeting. With a firm court date, the solicitors for Penguin and Lipstadt had engaged as lead counsel Richard Rampton QC. Sage and sharp-witted, Rampton was widely known for his flair for quickly mastering the most esoteric details of technical and historical issues, remarkable even for a barrister. Given the complexity of the historical material that was to be central to the case, he was the obvious choice. His junior counsel was the meticulous and level-headed Heather Rogers. As Rampton and Rogers were to conduct the defense in court—later Solicitor Anthony Julius of Mishcon de Reya was to join Rampton as a second junior counsel—they needed to know the historical evidence in the expert reports by heart. The meeting was to begin that process of assimilation.

And it did. The meeting of the experts not only proved to be the beginning of a close collaboration between Rampton, Rogers, and me, but it also began that kind of fellowship which offers a refuge of humanness in a world marked by a crime such as the Holocaust and the madness of its negation. Having become friends, I asked Rampton and Rogers to make the effort to go to Oswiecim. I told them that it was important for them to get a firsthand knowledge of the documentary evidence in the archives, of the collections, and of the prima facie evidence of the enormous site itself. I did not tell them my second and more important aim. The trial was caused by one man's need to incessantly mock the history of that place and the fate of those who had been brought there. From the evidence I had seen, it was clear to me that he had used Auschwitz in order to further his political ambitions, commercial aims, and psychological needs. It was unavoidable that in the trial Irving would try to score points by using Auschwitz and that in turn Rampton and Rogers would be forced to do the same. I knew I could not prevent Auschwitz from becoming a pawn in a complex judicial game. Yet I hoped that if Rampton and Rogers were to tread on sacred ground, they would at least know that they were encroaching on something that ought to have remained outside of the courtroom, a cursed reality that ought to have been left alone. I believed that a legal victory on Auschwitz would still mark a defeat of sorts, since the battle of Auschwitz ought not to have been fought to begin with. I wanted them to see Auschwitz.

And so we found ourselves in Oswiecim in June. We spent half a day in the archives, discussing the blueprints for Crematoria 2 and 4, cross-referencing them with letters such as that of Bischoff of March 6, 1943, which proposed to preheat Morgue 1 with hot air. We looked at the evidence of the modifications in the basement of Crematorium 2 to accommodate a genocidal purpose. In the case of the single plan of Crematorium 4, I pointed out the gas chambers with the small openings measuring 30 by 40 centimeters and compared them with the corresponding order of February 13, 1943, which concerned the construction of twelve "gas-tight doors of 30/40 cm." Later that day, we inspected three of these gas-tight shutters of that size, marked with the inventory numbers PMO-II-5-64/1, PMO-II-5-64/2, and PMO-II-5-64/3, in the storeroom of Crematorium 1. We looked at them carefully, and not only did we positively establish that they were gas tight, with a double, tight-fitting wooden seal, but also that they could be screwed tight from the outside with a butterfly nut—a clear indication that they could not have been gas-tight shutters of an air-raid shelter. In any case, the blueprint had made clear that the rooms equipped with the "gas-tight doors of 30/40 cm" could not have been air-raid shelters because their walls and roof were of very light construction.

We reviewed a collection of written construction documents, including the work sheets of Topf that referred to work done on an "Undressing
Basement" ["*Auskleidekeller*"] in Crematorium 2 and the inventory of
Crematorium 2 that mentioned not only the presence of 4 "wire mesh
introduction devices" ["*Drahtnetzeinschiebvorrichtugen*"] in Morgue 1 of
Crematorium 2—the gas columns constructed by Kula—but also 4 "wood-
en covers" ["*Holzblenden*"], which obviously referred to the covers for
the four chimneys that capped the wire-mesh columns. Furthermore, we
looked at the correspondence between the Central Construction Office in
Auschwitz and outside agencies such as the Berlin headquarters, Topf &
Sons, and other firms. We found the order for 10 gas detectors and
Bischoff's letter to the German Armament Works ordering "three gas-tight
doors." Finally, we looked at the notorious letter written by Bischoff on
January 29, 1943, that mentioned a gassing basement [*Vergasungskeller*].

Following the visit to the archives, we began our inspection of the
camp, and for a day and a half I not only pointed out all the important
places but also tried to locate the various negationist hobbyhorses within
the landscape. Thus, we paid a lot of attention to the small air-raid shelters
made of three prefabricated concrete arches, each providing shelter for one
SS man guarding the perimeter of the camp, and considered the transformation of Crematorium 1 into an air-raid shelter in situ. We looked at all
the places where Leuchter had taken his samples and compared his observations on the remains of the crematoria with the evidence before our eyes.
We went on the roof of Morgue 1 of Crematorium 2, where we inspected
the ruined concrete slab. The situation at that place was exactly the
opposite to that of Crematorium 4: in the latter building, the walls of the

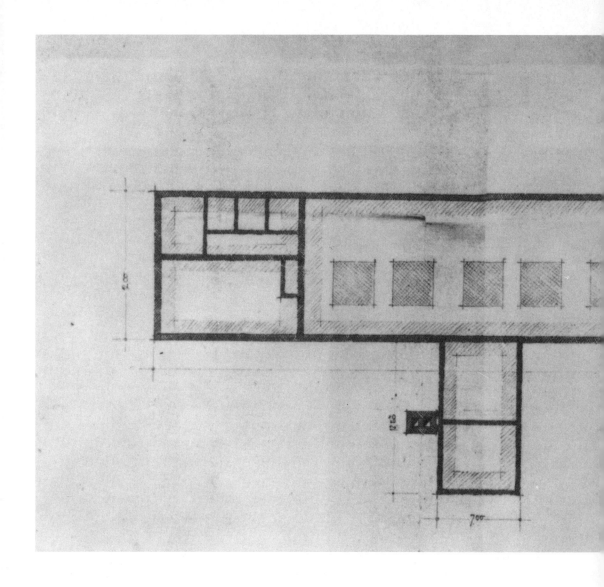

*Basement in the first plan of
Crematorium 2, October 1941.
The door to Morgue 1 opens
inward. Also the slide and the
adjacent stairways are clearly
visible. Courtesy Osobyi Archive,
Moscow.*

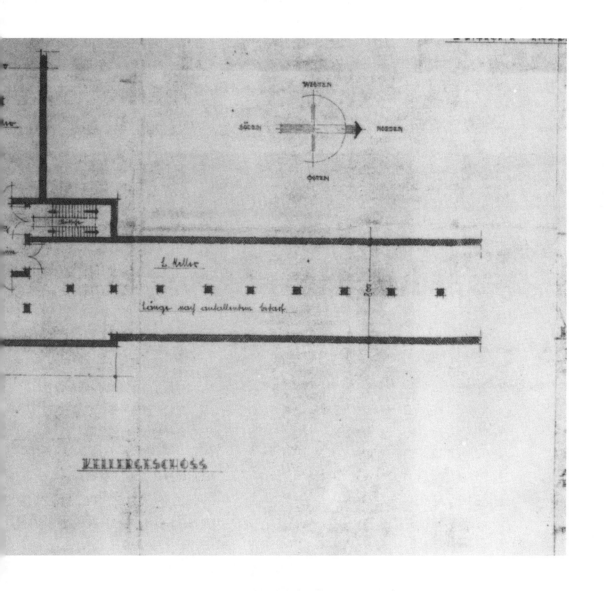

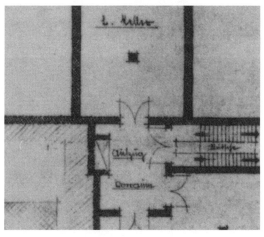

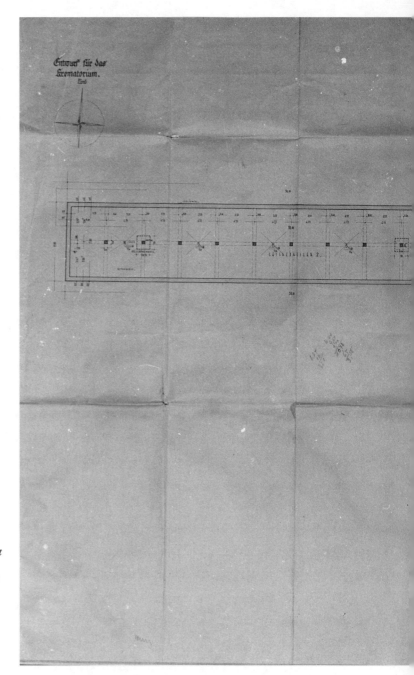

Basement in the second plan of Crematorium 2, January 1942. The arrangement of the basement follows the layout of the plan of October 1941. Courtesy Archive Auschwitz-Birkenau State Museum, Oswiecim.

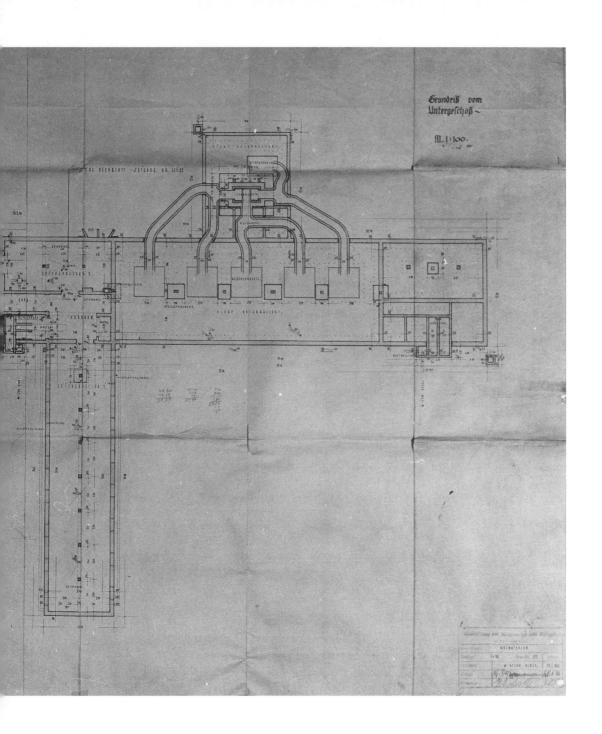

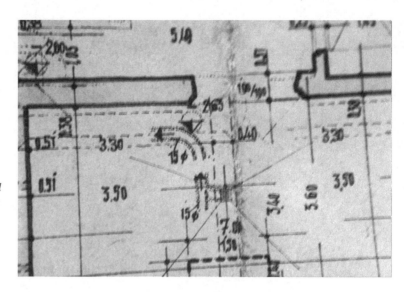

Detail of basement in the second plan of Crematorium 2, January 1942. While it is difficult to see, as the architect rubbed out the lines showing the door panels, it is still possible to determine that in this plan the doors to Morgue 1 open inward. Also the slide and the adjacent stairways are clearly visible. Courtesy Archive Auschwitz-Birkenau State Museum, Oswiecim.

gas chambers had almost completely disappeared, but the gas-tight shutters that had covered the small windows that allowed for the introduction of Zyklon B had been preserved. In the case of Crematorium 2, the roof that had contained the holes that allowed for the introduction of Zyklon B into the wire-mesh columns below still existed, but the gas-tight wooden covers [*Holzblenden*] which had covered the little chimneys that capped the holes had been lost, and the chimneys and the gas columns were not there. I reminded Rampton and the others that after the cessation of the gassings in the fall of 1944, all the wire-mesh columns and chimneys had been removed. They had not been part of the building's structure, and because they had been added shortly before its completion, they were easily removed. I surmised that four narrow holes would have remained in the slab and assumed that the Germans would have backfilled the holes with concrete. The condition of the roof made it impossible to either prove or disprove this assumption.

Rampton asked me to review the evidence for the existence of the holes. I reminded him of Kula's and Tauber's testimony, the aerial photos taken by the Americans in 1944, and, most important, Olère's drawing of Crematorium 3, which showed the arrangement of the holes in a pattern identical to the one visible in the aerial photos. Arbel asked if the fact that the holes could not be observed posed a problem. Rampton replied that he was satisfied that they had existed. He quoted Sherlock Holmes's maxim that "when you have excluded the impossible, whatever remains, however improbable, must be truth."[1] The convergence of both intentional and non-intentional evidence showed that Morgue 1 had been a gas chamber, and all alternative explanations to account for the designation of the space as a *Vergasungskeller,* the gas-tight door, and the presence of cyanide remains in the walls could be rejected on empirical or logical grounds. Therefore, the unavoidable conclusion was that Morgue 1 indeed had functioned as a gas chamber. Similarly, the convergence of evidence showed that the Zyklon B had been introduced into Morgue 1 through the roof, and as there was no way one could explain the similarity of the pattern of black spots on the roof of Morgue 1 of Crematorium 3, photographed in 1944, and the

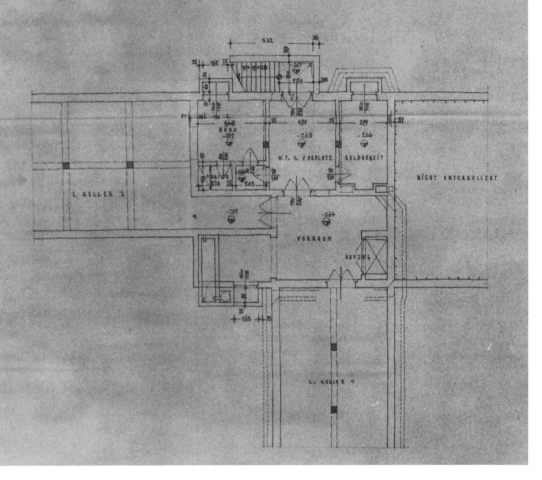

Detail of basement in the final modification of Crematorium 2, December 1942. The doors to Morgue 1 now open outward. The slide with the adjacent stairways has disappeared. A new outside stairway is now projected on the side of the crematorium that faces the railway tracks. Courtesy Archive Auschwitz-Birkenau State Museum, Oswiecim.

Small air-raid shelter near Crematorium 1, 1999. Photo by Omer Arbel.

pattern of the gas columns as drawn by Olère in 1945 except by assuming that both referred to the same fact, the conclusion must be that the holes had existed, even if it was impossible to identify their presence and location in the remains of the slab covering Morgue 1 of Crematorium 3 (which was totally fragmented) or in the remains of its counterpart at Crematorium 2. This settled the issue at the time.

Throughout our inspection of Birkenau, Rampton fired questions. For example, after observing that the Germans did not bother to blow up delousing buildings or the one crematorium that had been converted into an air-raid shelter (Crematorium 1), he asked: "Why did the Germans go to the trouble to blow up Morgue 1 of Crematorium 2 if it had been merely an air-raid shelter or a delousing establishment?" And so he went on,

Richard Rampton, the author, and Deborah Lipstadt inspecting the remains of Crematorium 4, 1999. Photo by Omer Arbel.

asking me to provide him with a possible negationist answer to each of his queries. Lipstadt was not amused, and she shared her exasperation. She felt that it was blasphemous to raise these issues at the ruins. Rampton responded perhaps a little too sharply that he was in Auschwitz to prepare a case, not on a pilgrimage. Yet it was clear that the place touched him more than he was willing to admit at that time to either Lipstadt or the rest of the group. He became increasingly anguished and angry—indignant because of what had happened there and infuriated at those who sought to negate that it had happened. In fact, at the close of the first day in the camp he told me that if he were to stay much longer he would be too enraged to conduct the case.

Two weeks after we left Oswiecim, lawyers of Mishcon and Davenport Lyons handed the expert reports of Evans, Browning, Longerich, and myself to Irving. That same day, July 30, 1999, his Web site announced: "Identities of Lipstadt's courtroom experts revealed: Debate-dodgers now obliged to face questions." The statement generously described us as "reputable historians of the highest calibre" and mentioned that "Mr Irving has had words of high praise for Pelt's recent book *Auschwitz: 1270 to the Present*, in which a chapter is largely devoted to exposing the gaschambers on display to tourists at Auschwitz (as opposed to Birkenau) as being a regrettable post-war fraud." Remarkably enough, Irving only served one expert report on the defense. Written by Kevin Macdonald, professor of psychology at California State University-Long Beach, it argued that "the attacks made on David Irving by Deborah Lipstadt and

Gas-tight shutters, 1999. Photo by Omer Arbel.

Jewish organizations should be viewed in the long-term context of Jewish-gentile interactions."[2] In other words, it dealt with the supposed Jewish conspiracy against Irving, and as such did not concern my area of expertise. Initially I was somewhat surprised that Irving had not engaged "Crowell" to write him a report to attack the evidence on Auschwitz. Then I remembered that he probably would like to keep room to maneuver and that it would be very difficult to shift and change position when pinned down by an explicitly negationist "expert" report.

As the trial approached, Rampton, Rogers, and I worked hard to distill from my report a case to be presented in court. It was clear that our

Mark Bateman, Richard Rampton, the author, and Deborah Lipstadt discussing the problem of the holes, 1999. Photo by Omer Arbel.

main purpose was to impress on the judge that while not all eyewitness evidence was reliable, and while parts of the documentary evidence could be interpreted in more than one way, the totality of the available evidence ought to persuade any objective and reasonable historian that Auschwitz was not merely one of the many concentration or labor camps established by the Nazi regime but that it also served as a death or extermination camp where hundreds of thousands of Jews were systematically put to death in gas chambers by means of hydrogen cyanide. We expected that Irving would argue that there is no convincing evidence that gas chambers were in existence at the time in Auschwitz and that there is no evidence that such chambers were commissioned. Furthermore, we expected that he would argue that there is no convincing evidence that any Jew at Auschwitz lost his or her life as a result of being gassed. Therefore we would have to prove that Irving's denial of the genocidal use of the gas chambers disregarded the historical evidence and that his overnight adoption of the negationist position after reading the Leuchter Report could only be explained as the expression of his own extremist ideological views: no careful and responsible historian would have adopted Leuchter's conclusions because it ought to be clear to anyone reading it that Leuchter's conclusions were fatally flawed because of his totally mistaken premise that a far higher concentration of cyanide would be required to kill people in the gas chambers than would be required for the purpose of delousing clothing. In fact, it was the other way around: while high levels of cyanide are required for delousing purposes, lower concentrations suffice for the purpose of killing human beings. If Irving had read the report carefully, he would have known this.

He would have picked up the fundamental fallacy of the Leuchter Report and realized that many of Leuchter's reasons for denying the existence of the killing chambers were invalid. For example, Leuchter had argued that the ventilation system of the chambers would have been wholly inadequate. But if the concentration required was much lower than he assumed, it follows that the ventilation requirements would be correspondingly reduced. Similarly, Leuchter's argument that the high concentration of cyanide required to kill humans would have created a high risk of toxic contamination of the sewers would be invalidated if the concentration required was a fraction of that assumed by Leuchter. Also, the need for elaborate safety precautions would be radically reduced.

To press our case and destroy Irving's position before he entered the courtroom, Rampton prepared a set of so-called interrogatories on the basis of the expert reports—a kind of written cross-examination. In the case of Holocaust denial, the interrogatories contained 113 questions, and of those, 104 concentrated on Leuchter. The goal was not only to show to Irving that his position regarding Leuchter was untenable but also to find out what he really meant when he claimed to still stand by Leuchter.

The initial questions were to establish if Irving agreed that when he referred to "the Holocaust," he used the expression in its generally accepted sense, that is to say, "the systematic mass murder of millions of people, in particular Jews, by the Nazis during the Second World War." Furthermore, he was asked if he had repeatedly asserted that the Holocaust is a myth which has no basis in historical fact, that the most important element in the creation and maintenance of this "myth" has been the assertion that the Nazis killed millions of Jews in gas chambers at Auschwitz-Birkenau, that there were in fact no homicidal gas chambers at Auschwitz, and, finally, that there are no authentic German wartime documents referring to (homicidal) gas chambers or gassings. Then Rampton confronted Irving with Bischoff's letter of January 29, 1943, which mentioned a gassing cellar, and a timesheet of the contractor Riedel & Sohn for March 2, 1943, which mentioned a gas chamber. After asking if Irving agreed that these were authentic wartime German documents, he asked if Irving agreed "that a competent historian conversant with the relevant historical, archaeological and scientific evidence would conclude that these references were references to homicidal gas chambers?"[3]

The most important purpose of the interrogatories was, however, to establish that the Leuchter Report was worthless as evidence and that Irving had known this all along. After asking if Irving agreed that the Leuchter Report had been the principal foundation for his assertions that there were no homicidal gas chambers used at Auschwitz and that the Holocaust is a myth, Rampton discussed ten major fallacies of the Leuchter Report. These concerned safety, the original purpose of Crematoria 4 and 5, the preheating of the gas chambers, the capacity of the gas chambers, Leuchter's theoretical execution rates for the gas chambers in Crematorium 2 and Crematorium 3, the entrance doors to the alleged gas chambers, the incineration capacity, the concentration of hydrogen cyanide used for the alleged gassings, the dispersal of the gas within the gas chambers, and the cyanide traces in the remains of the crematoria. If Irving had given careful consideration to Leuchter's propositions, he ought to have recognized these fallacies. They are precisely argued and bring analysis of the Leuchter Report to a new level; all fifty-four pages of the interrogatories deserve publication. Considerations of economy force me to concentrate on those questions that concern the samples—which Irving had accepted as decisive evidence that there had been no gassings in Auschwitz. Rampton covered this issue in points 8 (the concentration of HCN used for the alleged gassings) and 10 (cyanide traces in the remains of the crematoria).

3.8 The concentration of HCN used for the alleged gassings

Questions

81. Do you agree that the concentration of HCN used would have a direct and, according to the actual concentration, more or less significant bearing on the following issues:

a) the amount of gas (as a proportion of air) left in the chamber after inhalation and absorption by the victims;

b) the degree of risk (if any) to camp personnel engaged in carrying out the gassings and in emptying the chamber of corpses after a gassing;

c) the need for an efficient (or any) ventilation system;

d) the degree of risk (if any) of explosion;

e) the degree of risk (if any) from dissolved HCN in the sewers;

f) the amounts of HCN which might penetrate plaster, mortar or brick; and hence;

g) the degree of risk (if any) which the presence of cyanide compounds in those materials might present to humans; and

h) the amounts of cyanide compounds which might be found in the remains of the crematoria after 40 years or more, particularly if they have been exposed to the elements during that time?

82. If you do not agree with any of the foregoing propositions, please state the reasons why do you not.

Please refer to:

a) The Leuchter Report, page 12

TOXIC EFFECTS
OF HCN GAS

Medical tests show that a concentration of hydrogen cyanide gas in an amount of 300 ppm in air is rapidly fatal. Generally for execution purposes a concentration of 3,200 ppm is used to ensure rapid death

b) Leuchter's testimony, 9203-4:

Q: "Okay. So, your calculation was based on a figure of thirty-six hundred parts [of gas] per million parts of air. Is that right?"

A: "That is correct."

Q: "But you'll agree with me that Zyklon-B like any other hydrogen cyanide, is lethal for humans at three hundred parts per million in air. Isn't that correct?"

A: "Over a given time period, yes."

Q: "Well, in a matter of minutes?"

A: "A matter of minutes. Ten or fifteen, yes."

Q: "Well, in half an hour, a concentration of one hundred and fifty parts per million is lethal, isn't it?"

A: "Certainly."

c) Leuchter's testimony, 9250:

Q: "Right. And it takes three hundred parts per million to kill a human being in a matter of minutes?"

A: "Or more."

Q: "In a matter of minutes?"

A: "Twenty minutes, fifteen minutes, yes."

d) The recollections of Rudolf Höss as quoted on pages 305 and 316–7 of van Pelt:

The moment the entire transport had entered the chamber, the door was closed, and simultaneously the gas was forced in from above through a special aperture. It was Zyklon "B" gas, cyanide acid in the form of crystals, which vaporized immediately, that is to say, it took effect immediately upon coming into contact with oxygen. The people were dazed already on taking their first breath, and the process of killing took from thirteen to fifteen minutes, depending upon the weather conditions and the number of people locked up within. Thereafter, nothing moved any more. Thirty minutes after the gas had been released and had entered the chambers, they would be opened, and the transfer of the bodies to the crematoria would commence.

After twenty minutes at most no movement could be detected. The time required for the gas to take effect varied according to weather conditions and depended on whether it was damp or dry, cold or warm. It also depended on the quality of the gas, which was never exactly the same, and on the composition of the transports, which might contain a higher proportion of healthy Jews, or the old and the sick, or children. The victims became unconscious after a few minutes, according to the distance from the air shaft. Those who screamed and those who were old, sick or weak, or the small children died quicker than those who were healthy and young.

The door was opened half an hour after the gas was thrown in and the ventilation system was turned on. Work was immediately started to remove the corpses.

e) Leuchter's testimony, 8964:

Q: "You must have an opinion whether hydrogen cyanide is an effective means of exterminating people."

A: "I do."

Q: "Is it?"

A: "It is effective and also very expensive."

Q: "And when you say effective, that is because it is very lethal?"

A: "That is correct."

Questions (3.8: the concentration of HCN)

83. Given that, as Leuchter acknowledged, HCN at a concentration of 300 ppm is fatal to human beings in 20 minutes or less and, further, that as Leuchter stated, HCN is very expensive, do you agree that the Nazis would have been likely to have used as low a concentration as was sufficient for their purposes?

84. Do you therefore also agree that Leuchter's assumption that the Nazis would have used a concentration similar to that used for the legal execution of a single person in the USA and more than ten times greater than they needed is absurd?

85. Do you agree that the recollections of Rudolf Höss set out at (d) above, taken with the testimony of Leuchter set out at (b) and (c) above, suggest that the concentration of HCN used by the Nazis was *in fact* about 300 ppm?

86. Do you agree that Leuchter's assumption of a concentration of 3200 (or 3600) ppm was unsupported by any relevant evidence and contrary to the available evidence?

87. In the light of the foregoing, do you agree that Leuchter's estimates and conclusions in relation to the issues listed at 81(b)–(h) above are seriously undermined?

88. If you do not agree with any of the foregoing propositions, please state the reasons why you do not.[4]

Rampton had slowly forced Irving into a tight corner from which he could not escape: either he had to accept that he had all too hastily accepted Leuchter's flawed conclusions in 1988—which would immediately raise the question of why he had done so—or, if he was not prepared to do so, he risked looking like a gullible fool.

I will pass over questions 89 to 91, which deal with Leuchter's claims concerning the dispersal of the gas within the gas chambers, and move straight to the questions concerning cyanide in the remains of the crematoria.

3.10 Cyanide in the remains of the crematoria

Please refer to:

a) The Leuchter Report, page 15:

> The control sample was removed from a delousing chamber in a location where cyanide was known to have been used and was apparently present as blue staining. Chemical testing of the control sample No. 32 showed a cyanide content of 1,050 mg/kg, a very heavy concentration.

The conditions at areas from which these samples were taken are identical with those of the control sample: cold, dark and wet. Only Kremas IV and V differed, in the respect that these locations had sunlight (the buildings have been torn down) and sunlight may hasten the destruction of uncomplexed cyanide. The cyanide combines with iron in the mortar and brick and becomes ferric-ferro cyanide or prussian blue pigment, a very stable iron-cyanide complex. The locations from which the analysed samples were removed are set out in Table III.

It is notable that almost all the samples were negative and that the few that were positive were very close to the detection level (1 mg/kp [sic]): 6.7 mg/kp [sic] at Krema III: 7.9 mg/kp [sic] at Krema I. The absence of any consequential readings at any of the tested locations as compared with the control sample reading of 1,050 mg/kp [sic] supports the evidence that these facilities were not execution gas chambers. The small quantities detected would indicate that at some point these buildings were deloused with Zyklon B—as were all the buildings at these facilities. Additionally, the areas of blue staining show a high iron content, indicating ferric-ferro cyanide, no longer hydrogen cyanide.

One would have expected higher cyanide detection in the samples taken from the alleged gas chambers (because of the greater amount of gas allegedly utilized there) than that found in the control sample. Since the contrary is true, one must conclude that these facilities were not execution gas chambers, when coupled with all the other evidence gained on inspection.

b) Appendix III to the Leuchter Report (translation of Nuremberg document no. NI-9912), at page 24:

IX. THE STRENGTH OF THE GAS AND THE TIME REQUIRED FOR IT TO TAKE EFFECT DEPENDS ON:

• The type of vermin.

• The temperature.

• The amount of furniture in the rooms.

• The imperviousness of the building.

For inside temperatures of more than 5 degrees Centigrade, it is customary to use 8 g. prussic acid per cbm.

Time needed to take effect: 16 hours, unless there are special circumstances such as a closed-in type of building, which requires less time. If the weather is warm it is possible to reduce this to a minimum of 6 hours. The period is to be extended to at least 32 hours if the temperature is below 5 degrees Centigrade.

The strength and time as above are to be applied in the case of: bugs, lice, fleas, etc. with eggs, larvae and chrysalises.

c) Appendix XII to the Leuchter Report (the Degesch Manual), at page 4:

HYDROCYANIC ACID

———

1 ppm = 0.0012 g/m^3

d) The statements by Leuchter in his report and his testimony which are set out at 3.8(a), (b) and (c) (following question 82) above.

e) The videotape of "Mr Death: The Rise and Fall of Fred A. Leuchter Jr" and the statement by Dr Jim Roth, the chemist who analysed Leuchter's samples in 1988 as follows (1 hour, 7 minutes, 30 seconds):

I don't think the Leuchter results have any meaning.

There is nothing in any of our data that says those surfaces were exposed or not.

Hindsight being 20/20, the test was not the correct one to have been used for the analysis.

[Leuchter] presented us with rock samples anywhere from the size of your thumb up to half the size of your fist. We broke them up with a hammer so that we could get a sub-sample; placed it in a flask; add concentrated sulphuric acid; and it undergoes a reaction that produces a red-coloured solution. It is the intensity of this red colour that we can relate with cyanide concentration.

You have to look at what happens to cyanide when it reacts with a wall. Where does it go? How far does it go? Cyanide is a surface reaction it's probably not going to penetrate more than 10 microns, a human hair is 100 microns in diameter.

Crush this sample up: I have just diluted that sample ten thousand, a hundred thousand times. If you are gonna go look for it, you are going to look on the surface only. There's no reason to go deep because it is not going to be there.

Which was the exposed surface? I didn't even have any idea. That is like analyzing paint on a wall by analyzing the timber that's behind it.

f) The videotape which is a film of Leuchter taking the samples in Auschwitz Birkenau.

Questions (3.10: cyanide remains)

92. Do you agree that the information set out at (b) and (c) above means that, in favourable conditions and over a minimum period of 6 hours, the concentration of HCN required for killing lice in a delousing facility is about 6,666 ppm (on the basis that 1 g/m^3 gives a concentration of about 833 ppm)?

93. Do you therefore agree that Leuchter's assertion in the last paragraph of (a) above that the material taken from the alleged gas chambers would be expected to reveal a higher (emphasis added) concentration of cyanide than material taken from a delousing facility ("the control sample") is precisely contrary to the evidence appended to his report and to the statements made by him in his report and in his testimony which are referred to at (d) above?

94. If you do not agree with either of the foregoing propositions, please state the reasons why you do not.

95. Do you agree that:

a) based on the statements by Roth in (e) above, if the cyanide cannot penetrate into the brick for more than 10 microns, it is unavoidable that the cyanide concentration will be diluted 10 times when the sample is 100 microns or 0.1 mm thick?

b) the videotapes show that Leuchter did not carefully slice or scrape the surface of the materials that he was sampling?

c) in fact the samples he took counted at least a thousand of layers of material that could not have reacted with the cyanide?

96. If you do not agree with any of the propositions set out in question 95 above, please state the reasons why you do not.

Please refer to:

Pages 198–9 of van Pelt, which refer to the report of 15 December 1945 of the Forensic Laboratory at Cracow.

Questions (3.10: cyanide remains—continued)

97. Do you accept that tests carried out by the laboratory on the zinc ventilation covers retrieved from the rubble of KII revealed the presence of cyanide?

98. Do you also accept that tests carried out by the same laboratory on quantities of human hair found in bags at Birkenau also revealed the presence of cyanide?

Please refer to:

Jan Markiewicz, Wojciech Gubala, Jerzy Labedz *"A Study of the Cyanide Compounds Content in the Walls of the Gas Chambers in the Former Auschwitz and Birkenau Concentration Camps"* Z Zagadnien Nauk Sadowych/Problems of Forensic Science, vol. 30 (1994), 27:

The present study shows that in spite of the passage of a considerable period of time (over 45 years) in the walls of the facilities which were once in contact with hydrogen cyanide the vestigial amounts of the combinations of this constituent of Zyklon B had been preserved. This is also true of the ruins of the former gas chambers. The cyanide compounds occur in the building materials only locally, in the places where the conditions arose for the formation and persistence for such a long time.

In his reasoning Leuchter claims [in his report] that the vestigial amounts of cyanide combinations detected by him in the materials from the chamber ruins are residues left after fumigations carried out in the camp "once, long ago" (Item 14,004 of the Report). This is refuted by the negative results of the examination of the control samples from living quarters, which are said to have been subjected to a single gassing and the fact that in the period of fumigation of the camp in connection with a typhoid epidemic in mid-1942 there were still no crematoria in the Birkenau camp. The first crematorium (Crematorium 2) was put to use as late as 15th March 1943 and the others several months later.

Questions (3.10: cyanide remains—continued further)

99. Have you read this report or otherwise became aware of its contents and conclusions?

100. Do you see any reason to doubt the accuracy of its findings?

101. If so, please state what they are.

Please refer to:

The last paragraph on page 542, the whole of page 543 and the first two paragraphs on page 544 (to the end of the quotation from the Leuchter Report) of van Pelt.

Questions (3.10: cyanide remains—continued)

102. Do you disagree with any of the criticisms of the Leuchter Report there made?

103. If you do, please give your reasons for doing so.

104. In the light of the foregoing material, do you agree that the fact that:

> a) the Forensic Laboratory in Cracow in 1945;
>
> b) Dr Jim Roth in 1988; and
>
> c) Professor Markiewicz in 1994;
>
> all found traces of cyanide in material taken from the remains of the alleged gas chambers studied by Leuchter is persuasive evidence that those buildings were indeed gas chambers?

105. If you do not agree, please give the reasons why you do not.

106. Do you, in any event, agree that Leuchter's study of this issue, and the conclusions he drew in the course of it, are in their methodology, their logic and their failure to give due consideration to the available evidence, so flawed as to be worthless?

107. If you do not agree, please state the reasons why you do not.[5]

Irving had no choice: either he had to accept that the Leuchter Report was worthless or he would have to provide some obviously fatuous justifications that would not impress a judge.

The concluding questions completed Rampton's demolition of Leuchter:

4. Leuchter—Conclusion

108. Do you agree that any serious investigation, whether historical, archaeological or scientific, and whether general or particular, into the question whether there were homicidal gas chambers
used at Auschwitz-Birkenau requires that the investigator should:

> a) have such expertise or experience as is required by the
> nature and extent of his investigation;

> b) consider all the available evidence, giving each piece of
> evidence such weight as it merits in the light of all the other
> evidence; and

> c) avoid reaching firm conclusions on the basis of assumptions
> unless those assumptions are validated by the evidence?

109. Do you agree that Leuchter failed on all those counts?

110. If so, do you agree that the Leuchter Report, as a contribution to the question whether there were homicidal gas chambers
used at Auschwitz-Birkenau, is worthless?

111. If you do not agree with any of the foregoing propositions,
please state the reasons why not (by reference, where appropriate,
to earlier answers).

112. If you do agree, please state whether, and, if so, why, you still
adhere to the proposition that there were no homicidal gas chambers used at Auschwitz-Birkenau.[6]

The interrogatories were served in October 1999. Irving did not reply.
Thus, the interrogatories became the basis of Rampton's cross-examination of Irving on Leuchter in court.

Rampton and Rogers not only pressed Irving into a corner, they also
used the time before the commencement of the trial to refashion the
pleadings of the defendants. The arguments of the original "Defence of
Second Defendant" had become largely obsolete, thanks to the work of the
experts. Using their reports, the barristers comprehensively reorganized
the defense. Drafted in its final form by Rogers, the new "Defendants'
Statement of Case" was a kind of road map that connected, by means of a
systematic series of maps of increasingly smaller scale, the general issue of
the case to the detailed arguments derived from the expert reports. The
"Defendants' Statement of Case" included seven sections, covering: 1) the
Holocaust and Holocaust denial (10 pages); 2) Auschwitz (26 pages); 3)
Leuchter (18 pages); 4) historiography (32 pages); 5) Dresden, Hitler's
adjutants and Nazi anti-Semitism (16 pages); 6) right-wing extremism (22
pages); and 7) Irving's alleged misuse of archival material in Moscow (5
pages).

Rogers's point of departure, contained in Section 1, was the most basic
question: "What is the Holocaust?" Her answer was simple and straightforward:

"The Holocaust" denotes the attempt during the Second World
War by Nazi Germany, led by Hitler, to exterminate the Jewish
population in Europe, which attempt succeeded to the extent of
murdering between 5 and 6 million Jews in a variety of ways, including mass gassings in camps built for the purpose.[7]

This definition was important, because Irving had often claimed that he was not a Holocaust denier because all the suffering of "innocent" civilians in the Second World War marked a Holocaust, and he did not negate this suffering.

Having circumscribed the Holocaust, Rogers identified four propositions that were the core of Holocaust denial: 1) the numbers of Jewish victims are much lower than usually claimed; 2) the gas chambers did not play an important part, or even any part, in whatever killing took place; 3) there was no systematic program of extermination; 4) the Holocaust is a myth invented by Allied propaganda and exploited by Jews. Rogers then undertook a systematic review of Irving's negationism. She observed that, with regard to the numbers, Irving "consistently understated the number of Jews killed in the Holocaust—both generally and with specific reference to those killed in Auschwitz" and that his estimates were not based on proper evidence or research.[8] With regard to the gas chambers, Irving "has claimed since 1988 that there were no gas chambers at Auschwitz; that not a single Jew was killed in a gas chamber at Auschwitz; and (more generally) that the gas chambers were a lie, a fiction, or a legend (that is, that there were no gas chambers at all)," and that "his claims to that effect fly in the face of extensive evidence to the contrary, of which he is aware."[9] Addressing Irving's refusal to accept the systematic nature of the extermination, Rogers mentioned Irving's assertions that the Einsatzgruppen killings "were unauthorised atrocities, for which the Nazi regime was not responsible," and that Irving had claimed "that there was no systematic policy of extermination of the Jews on the part of the Nazi regime."[10] Finally she laid out Irving's claims that the evidence of the Holocaust was the result of a fabrication concocted by the British Psychological Warfare Executive and that "all eyewitness evidence to the existence and/or operation of gas chambers is to be disbelieved and that all eyewitnesses should be psychiatrically examined."[11] For each of these four allegations, Rogers provided proof that Irving had made those claims.

Then Rogers turned to a more detailed refutation of Irving's position. Section 2, Auschwitz, summarized the conclusions of my report and reorganized the evidence I had presented.

Summary of case

P claims that there were no homicidal gas chambers at Auschwitz and that not a single person was killed in a gas chamber there. Those claims fly in the face of a mass of evidence that Auschwitz was an extermination camp where around one million people were killed, largely by the use of gas chambers (Van Pelt page 333).

P made those claims without carrying out any or any proper investigation or research. His claims take no account of the overwhelming evidence that:

i) Auschwitz was equipped with homicidal gas chambers, which were systematically used (see Van Pelt page 769);

ii) Auschwitz functioned as an extermination camp for Jews between summer 1942 and autumn 1944 (see Van Pelt pages 769–770);

iii) Most Jews were murdered on arrival at Auschwitz (see Van Pelt page 770);

iv) That about 1 million Jews were victims of Auschwitz (see Van Pelt pages 770–771).

Further, P's claim that the gas chambers "lie" was a piece of atrocity propaganda, invented by the British PWE, and that all eye-witness evidence is to be disbelieved are highly implausible. The mass of evidence (referred to below) emerged gradually and cumulatively from a convergence of independent sources (see Van Pelt 333). The evidence became slowly available during the war, became more substantial through eye-witness accounts by former inmates, and was confirmed by Polish forensic examination in 1945–1946 and confessions of leading German personnel. There is also powerful corroborative "non-intentional" evidence from contemporary documents.[12]

This summary of case was followed by a detailed classification of evidence. Rogers chose to distinguish no less than twenty different categories. Some of them contained many different items, others only one. Altogether, the twenty classes formed a formidable arsenal of facts available to wage war on the claim that no evidence existed for the existence and genocidal operation of the Auschwitz gas chambers.

1. Evidence available before the end of 1944. . . .

2. Evidence gathered during the investigation under the aegis of the Soviet State Extraordinary Commission. . . .

3. Evidence gathered by the Polish Central Commission for Investigation of German Crimes in Poland 1945–1947, in a year long investigation under Jan Sehn. . . .

4. Drawings by David Olère, a Frenchman, who worked as a Sonderkommando in crematorium 3 at Auschwitz. . . .

5. The memoirs of Filip Müller, a Sonderkommando in crematorium 1 in Auschwitz. . . .

6. The memoirs of Ota Kraus and Erich Kulka, two Czech inmates of Auschwitz, employed as locksmiths. . . .

7. Other evidence obtained after the liberation of the camps. . . .

8. The diary kept by Dr Johann Paul Kremer, an SS physician, which included a record of his work at Auschwitz, which included references to "special actions". . . .

9. The eyewitness testimony of Pery Broad, an SS officer, who testified (amongst other matters) to gassings in Auschwitz and the burning of corpses. . . .

10. The eyewitness testimony of Hans Aumeier, an SS officer and one-time deputy to Höss (commandant of Auschwitz). . . .

11. Evidence from the "Belsen Trial," the trial of Josef Kramer (Lagerführer of Birkenau during the Hungarian Action in the summer of 1944) and others in Lüneburg in 1945. . . .

12. Evidence from the Nuremberg Trials. . . .

13. Evidence from the Eichmann trial (Jerusalem in 1961). . . .

14. Evidence from the trials of Mulka and others in Frankfurt in 1963–1965. . . .

15. Evidence from the trials of Walther Dejaco and Fritz Ertl, architects at Auschwitz, in Vienna in 1972. . . .

16. Documentary evidence, in particular, from the records of the Construction Office at Auschwitz, which was not destroyed. . . .

17. Aerial photographs, taken by Allied forces in 1944. These show shaded markings on the roof of morgue 1 (gas chamber) of crematoria 2 and 3, supporting eyewitness evidence that there were vents in the roof of the gas chamber, through which Zyklon-B was inserted into the gas chambers;

18. Three surviving reports made by the head of the labour allocation of the inmates at Auschwitz to his superiors in Berlin, which show that a percentage of the arrivals was selected "fit for work," while the rest "unfit for work" were subjected to "special treatment" or "specially lodged". . . .

19. Evidence from serious scholarly investigation of the numbers of deaths in Auschwitz. . . .

20. "A Study of the Cyanide Compounds Content in the Walls of the Gas Chambers in the Former Auschwitz and Birkenau Concentration Camps" (1994) by Jan Markiewicz, Wojciech Gubula [sic] and Jerzy Labedz. This analysis of samples from areas of Auschwitz show (amongst other things) the presence of cyanide in the walls of the gas chambers, confirming the use of these areas as killing installations.[13]

Rogers chose to subdivide many of these classes. For example, category 16, on documentary evidence, listed 12 subcategories, some containing one piece of evidence, and others many.

i) Note of 19 August 1942 of a meeting at Auschwitz of construction staff and Topf & Sons, which mentioned the construction of ovens near the "bathhouses for special actions" ("Badeanstalten für Sonderaktionen"). . . .

ii) Note of a talk given by Oswald Pohl, business administrator of the SS, to senior SS personnel during his visit to Auschwitz on 23 September 1942. . . .

iii) Documents containing "slips," that is, some reference to gas chambers or gassings. . . .

iv) Plans and blueprints for and photographs of the crematoria built at Auschwitz. . . .

v) Other material evidence found at Auschwitz, including personal possessions stored in a part of the camp known as "Canada". . . .

vi) Patent application by Topf & Sons dated 5 November 1942. . . .

vii) Memorandum of 27 November 1942, written by Wolther, concerning ventilation of the crematoria at Auschwitz. . . .

viii) Memorandum of 29 January 1943, signed by Ing Prüfer of Topf & Sons, which concerned aeration and ventilation for crematorium 2.

ix) A letter of 6 March 1943 from Bischoff to Topf concerning the pre-heating of morgue 1 in crematoria 2 and 3. . . .

x) Letter dated 28 June 1943 from the Auschwitz Zentralbau-leitung to Ing Kammler in Berlin, concerning the capacity of the crematoria at Auschwitz. . . .

xi) A plan relating to the ventilation system of crematorium 1 at Auschwitz.

xii) A note dated 22 January 1943 from an SS Doctor at Auschwitz to the Kommandantur detailing his requirements for the dissecting rooms in the new crematoria being built at Birkenau (K2 and 3) and asking for the provision of an undressing room in the basement of each of those installations. . . .[14]

Categories 16 (iii) and 16 (iv) each contained many documents.

iii) Documents containing "slips," that is, some reference to gas chambers or gassings. These include:

a) Letter of 29 January 1943, concerning the construction of Crematorium 2, which refers to a "gassing cellar". . . .

b) Memorandum of meeting on 29 January 1943, which refers to the possibility of simultaneous burning and special treatment. . . .

c) Order of 13 February 1943 for 30 cm by 40 cm gas-tight doors. . . .

d) Timesheet for construction worker at Auschwitz for 28 February 1943, referring to fitting "Gastight windows" in crematorium 4. . . .

e) Timesheet for construction worker at Auschwitz for 2 March 1943 referring to concreting the floor "in the gas chamber". . . .

f) Timesheets for a fitter from Topf & Sons (manufacturer of crematoria-ovens) working on crematoria 2 and 3, referring to work on the ventilation system of the "undressing basement". . . .

g) A cable of 26 February 1943, asking Topf & Sons (manufacturers of crematoria ovens) for 10 gas detectors. . . .

h) A letter dated 31 March 1943 from Bischoff (senior architect at Auschwitz) to the German Armament Works, stating that it must make "three gastight doors" ("*drei gasdichte Türme*") according to an order of 1.1.43 for crematoria 4 and 5; also reminder of another order of 6.3.43, for the delivery of a "gasdoor" ("*Gastür*") for morgue 1 of crematorium 3, in the same form and size as the equivalent door in crematorium 2, to have a spy-hole of double 8mm glass, with a rubber seal and metal fitting which order "must be considered as very urgent." . . .[15]

iv) Plans and blueprints for and photographs of the crematoria built at Auschwitz. . . . Amongst other matters:

a) Blueprints of the ground plan of the basement of crematorium 2. . . .

b) Cross-section drawing of Leichenkeller 1 of crematorium 2. . . .

c) A plan . . . which shows 30/40 cm shutters; as were ordered on 13th February 1943 (see above); as drawn by David Olère (see above); as confirmed by eyewitness evidence (Tauber) and as now stored in the Auschwitz museum.

d) Two plans. . . .

e) The ground-plans of crematoria 4 and 5 (which show, amongst other things, drains and stoves for heating). . . .

f) The plan . . . which shows that the chimney at crematorium 1 is attached to the building below the ground.

g) Photographs of a gas-tight door, with peephole. . . .

h) Photographs of rectangular galvanised metal sheets, with round holes. . . .

i) Photographs of gas-tight shutters. . . .

j) Photographs of gas-tight shutters taken by Omer Arbel at Auschwitz, 12 June 1999.[16]

The result was impressive, especially to me. Taking my narrative, she had articulated the considerable evidentiary basis and classified the sources in a rational and convenient manner. In creating what earlier generations would have named a *Regesta* of sources, she had given new validity to my argument that the "convergence of evidence" unequivocally supported the historical record.

The "Defendants' Statement of Case" also included a long section on the Leuchter Report, which it described as the basis of Irving's claim that there were no homicidal gas chambers in Auschwitz, or anywhere else for that matter. In twenty-two separate arguments that covered twenty-one pages, Rogers reorganized, with the help of Rampton's interrogatories, my analysis of the Leuchter Report in a scathing attack. Her conclusion was clear.

22.1 There was never any proper reason to rely upon the Leuchter Report as "evidence" (still less, compelling evidence) in connection with gas chambers at Auschwitz: RVPp584–587.

22.2 That the Leuchter Report did not constitute evidence (still less, compelling evidence) was further demonstrated by the critiques P received and by the Markiewicz Report: see above and RVPp556–557.

22.3 P was full aware of the fact that the Leuchter Report did not constitute proper evidence. His decision to rely upon it to support his "conversion" to the view that there were no homicidal gas chambers in Auschwitz was not the act of an historian or scholar, but demonstrates his commitment to the cause of Holocaust denial.[17]

With the new "Defendants' Statement of Case," supported as it was by various expert reports, the prospects for victory looked good. Yet the road to victory was uncertain. As I prepared for my cross-examination by Irving, which I expected to focus on the non-intentional evidence, I realized that it would be difficult to answer with clarity the various challenges I expected because of the nature of that evidence. It was likely that he would discuss the blueprints and the ruins of the crematoria. I did not expect the judge to be conversant with the conventions of architectural drawings or with the layout of the remains of the crematoria. I decided to prepare a fallback position if confusion were to arise about the plans, and asked two of my ex-students at the University of Waterloo School of Architecture, Jed Braithwaite and Wayne Austin, to prepare a set of reconstructions of the crematoria, based on the blueprints. These images would allow for easy correlation between the drawings, the wartime appearance of those buildings, and the ruins.

By mid-December everything seemed to be ready for the trial, and I prepared for some time in my life that did not include Auschwitz. Things worked out differently: on December 19, 1999, Irving informed the solicitors of Penguin and Lipstadt that he would cross-examine me "in detail about Zyklon B deliveries and consumption rates for the various camps including Oranienburg, Sachsenhausen, Auschwitz; and that it would be useful if [van Pelt] would bone up on the quantities needed to delouse buildings (i.e. how many kilograms per thousand cubic meters) and clothing (i.e. how many grams per outfit)."[18] Having been given a warning, I decided that it made sense to "bone up" on Zyklon B use. While Irving did not announce the material he was going to introduce as evidence, it was likely, given the specific reference to Oranienburg, that he would introduce the invoices from the firm of Degesch to SS-Obersturmführer Kurt Gerstein, covering the period February to May 1944, for deliveries of Zyklon B to the concentration camps of Oranienburg and Auschwitz. These invoices had been submitted as evidence in the Nuremberg Trial. I therefore wrote a supplement to my expert opinion to put these invoices in their historical context and to discuss in more general terms what we know about deliveries of Zyklon B to concentration camps in general and Auschwitz in particular and the conclusions that can be drawn from that knowledge.

As far as the invoices were concerned, I reconstructed Irving's argument as one based on the following crude syllogism:

> In early 1944 Oranienburg and Auschwitz received the same quantity of Zyklon B.
>
> In Oranienburg no people were gassed with Zyklon B.
>
> Therefore in Auschwitz no people were gassed with Zyklon B.

Or one could make the syllogism more refined by creating a combination of three syllogisms:

> In early 1944 the concentration camps at Auschwitz was 1.5 times as large as the concentration camps at Oranienburg/Sachsenhausen (90,000 vs. 60,000).
>
> Zyklon B for delousing purposes was allocated on a basis proportionate to the inmate population.
>
> Therefore Auschwitz should have been supplied with 1.5 times the Zyklon B sent to Oranienburg.
>
> In the Spring of 1944 Oranienburg and Auschwitz received the same quantity of Zyklon B.
>
> Auschwitz should have received 1.5 times the amount of Zyklon B sent to Oranienburg.

Therefore Auschwitz was undersupplied with Zyklon B.

In Oranienburg Zyklon B was not used for homicidal purposes.

Compared to Oranienburg, Auschwitz was undersupplied with Zyklon B.

Therefore in Auschwitz Zyklon B was not used for homicidal purposes.

This would make some sense if we knew that the invoices represented a relic of typical shipments to the concentration camps and that they could therefore be taken as the basis for the kind of statistical speculations embodied in the proposed syllogisms. Yet after a lengthy consideration of the provenance of the invoices, I came to the conclusion that the purchase of these 158 boxes each containing 30 500-gram tins of Zyklon B was not part of the usual supply of Zyklon B to those camps, and "that the extraordinary character of these shipments forbids us to draw any conclusions from these invoices concerning the regular shipments of Zyklon B to Auschwitz and other places."[19]

As Irving had raised the issue of Zyklon B deliveries, I thought that it would be good to study the matter further. Data that had emerged in the war crimes trial of the distributors of Zyklon B—Dr. Bruno Tesch, Karl Weinbacher, and Dr. Joachim Drosihn, who had run the pest-control company Tesch und Stabenow (TeSta)—that was held from March 1 to March 8, 1946, in Hamburg made it clear that in 1942 TeSta had supplied 9,131.6 kg Zyklon B to various concentration camps. Of this amount, 7,500 kg (or 82 percent of all Zyklon B supplied to the camps) went to Auschwitz. In 1943, TeSta supplied 18,302.9 kg to the camps. Again Auschwitz was the largest recipient, with 12,000 kg Zyklon-B (or 65 percent of all Zyklon B supplied to the camps).[20]

Taking these and other figures that emerged in the TeSta trial as my basis, I made a whole series of detailed calculations, concentrating on 1943 as a year that typhus in Auschwitz was very much under control. My conclusion was that of the 12,000 kg Zyklon B delivered to Auschwitz in that year, a maximum 9,000 kg could have been used for "ordinary" delousing procedures (2,730 kg would have been used for the delousing of clothing, blankets, and other items in use by the prisoners, while some 6,270 kg could have been used for the delousing of barracks). This would mean that all the rest of the Zyklon-B shipped to Auschwitz in 1943 (3,000 kg) would have been available for purposes above and beyond those engaged in at other camps. I calculated that 400 kg of Zyklon B would have been used for the delousing of the clothing of the deportees in the delousing chamber in Canada I before shipment to the Volksdeutsche Mittelstelle (VoMi) for redistribution among the ethnic Germans. I also calculated that a maximum of 940 kg could have been used for the occasional delousing of the railway freight carriages before their dispatch back to origin. I concluded that at least 1,660 kg of Zyklon B was unaccounted for, and I asked the obvious question: How many people could be killed by such an amount? The German Health Institution of the Protectorate of Bohemia and Moravia in Prague calculated that 70 mg of Zyklon B is sufficient to kill one person.[21] This meant that, in theory, the surplus of 1,660 kg of Zyklon B, if used with 100 percent efficiency, could have killed (1,660 x 14,000) = 23.2 million people. But, of course, the efficiency was much lower. Pery Broad testified that the SS used two 1-kg tins to kill 2,000 people, or 1 kg per 1000 people. It is important to note that in his report written before the war ended, Kurt Gerstein mentioned that "I have with me invoices for 2,175 kilos, but in truth the amount involved was around 8,500 kilos, enough to kill eight million people."[22] In assuming that 8,500 kg of Zyklon B would be sufficient to kill 8 million people, Gerstein used the same ratio as Broad. This implies that 1,660 kg of Zyklon B could have killed 1.6 million people. When he testified in Hamburg, Dr. Bendel stated that a 1-kg tin was good for the murder of 500 people, which means that 1,660 kg of Zyklon B was sufficient to murder 830,000 people. I concluded that in 1943 Auschwitz had a surplus of Zyklon B of between three to six times what was necessary to kill the 250,000 people murdered in Auschwitz that year.

Researching and writing this 32-page supplementary report entitled "Deliveries of Zyklon B to Auschwitz and Consumption Rates of Zyklon B in Auschwitz and Other Camps" proved useful, and the results were handed to Irving before the beginning of the trial. During the trial, Irving still contended that the Zyklon B deliveries were for the purpose of fumigating the camp and the clothes of the inmates. A large quantity of the cyanide was needed to combat the typhus outbreak in the summer of 1942. However, he did not subject my supplementary report to cross-examination. In the end, Justice Gray decided that while "the quantities of Zyklon-B delivered to the camp may arguably be explained by the need to fumigate clothes and other objects," that contention did not challenge the considerable "cumulative effect of the documentary evidence for the genocidal operation of gas chambers at Auschwitz."[23]

Stores of Zyklon B found in Maidanek, 1944. Main Commission for the Prosecution of Crimes against the Polish Nation, courtesy USHMM Photo Archives.

On January 11, 2000, Justice Gray opened the proceedings in Courtroom 37 of the Royal Courts of Justice in London. Auschwitz came up in the very first minute of the trial, when the schedule became subject of a tug-

David Irving entering the Royal Courts of Justice in London. Courtesy The Times.

of-war between Rampton and Irving. Rampton proposed that they treat Auschwitz separately, and Irving agreed, because it was "the most complicated to prepare."[24] But there the agreement ended. Rampton wanted it early in the trial, Irving at the end. One of the reasons Irving gave was that he had only just received the bundles which I had provided with the photocopied sources for each of my footnotes. It came to 6,000 pages of material, and Irving rightly argued that he needed time to study them. Yet he also proved willing to accommodate me. "I am perfectly prepared to have Professor van Pelt come over in the middle of whatever else is going on and we can take him as a separate entity. He is certainly an extremely interesting witness to be heard."[25]

In Irving's opening speech, Auschwitz came up in context of a discussion of the conviction that followed an address he gave on April 21, 1990, in Munich. He claimed that in this speech he had said "We now know that the gas chamber shown to the tourists in Auschwitz is a fake built by the Poles after the war, just like the one established by the Americans at Dachau." After mentioning that his remark was true—"the Poles admitted it in January 1995"—Irving told the court that "we shall hear, indeed, from the Defence's own expert witnesses, though perhaps the admission will have to be bludgeoned out of them, that the gas chamber shown to the tourists at Auschwitz was indeed built by the Polish communists three years after the war was over." But that is all he wanted to say about the gas chambers in his opening speech; as an aside, he added that "by the time this trial is over we shall all be heartily sick of the debate which has little or no relevance, in my submission, to the issues that are pleaded."[26]

Irving claimed that the trial was not really about what happened to the Jews in the Second World War. "I submit that, harsh though it may seem, the court should take no interest in that tragedy." The only thing that mattered was "what happened over the last 32 years on my writing desk in my apartment off Grosvenor Square." According to Irving, the central issue was Lipstadt's accusation that Irving had manipulated and distorted the historical evidence, and therefore the defense had to prove not only that he had misrepresented what happened but that he knew what happened and that he "perversely and deliberately, for whatever purpose" had chosen to represent it differently. The history of the Holocaust was irrelevant. "In effect, this enquiry should not leave the four walls of my study," Irving stated. "It should look at the papers that lay before me and not before some other magnificently funded research or scholar, and at the manuscript that I then produced on the basis of my own limited sources."[27] Later in the same speech Irving changed his tune, when he argued that the historical facts did matter: in order to plea justification, the defense had to show "first that a particular thing happened or existed; second that I was aware of that particular thing as it happened or existed, at the time that I wrote about it from the records then before me; third, that I then wilfully manipulated the text or mistranslated or distorted it for the purposes that they imply."[28]

Justice Charles Gray. Universal Pictorial Press photo.

Irving's argument raised an important issue, because if it were to be accepted, Irving could always claim to have been a negligent historian. Justice Gray perceived Irving's strategy, and after Irving had concluded his speech, he asked Irving to clarify his own understanding of the task of the defense. To aid Irving, Justice Gray told him that the position of the defense was that the question of whether he knew about a particular fact was not important; what was important was the question of whether it was available to him. Irving responded that in that case, the issue was not the one that the defense had pleaded—namely, that he had manipulated evidence —but the issue under discussion was whether he had been a "rotten" or "lazy" or "indolent" historian. This could be so, or no, but it was irrelevant, Irving said. Rampton immediately replied that the position of the defense was not that Irving was indolent but that he deliberately perverted history: "He leapt on to the 'Sink the Auschwitz battleship' campaign without even opening the front of the file."[29]

Justice Gray did not rule that day on Irving's attempt to narrow the consideration of the evidence to the actual documents that had been on his writing desk in his apartment on Duke Street. Yet as the trial progressed, it became clear that Justice Gray did take a broader view. As a historian, Irving could be held accountable not only for what he had considered but also for what he ought to have considered.

The second day, at the opening of the proceedings, Irving launched into Auschwitz by showing a videoclip of a German newsreel from January 1948 which reported on the judgment in the Auschwitz Trial in Cracow. The commentator stated that "altogether nearly 300,000 people from the most different nations died in the Auschwitz concentration camp." According to Irving, this showed that over the years, "a broad band of opinion" had developed about the number of victims of the camp. This was relevant because in his own case the number of victims "is a matter of contention. We are told by the expert witnesses in this case that anybody who says the figure is less than is now commonly assumed is a 'Holocaust denier.'"[30] When Justice Gray observed that he could not attach too much evidentiary value to a newsreel, Irving responded that "if this was one of the documents before me at the time I wrote my book, my Lord, then I could hardly be accused of manipulation or distortion if I choose to rely on this document rather than on the evidence of someone like Rudolf Höss."[31] Justice Gray chose not to directly engage the obvious issue of why Irving would give greater weight to a 20-second newsclip produced in 1948 over the hundreds of pages written in 1946 by the very man who had created and operated the camp at Auschwitz. Instead, he proposed that Irving state his case on Auschwitz. Surprisingly, given the fact that he had chosen to bring Auschwitz into the court that day, Irving now resisted presenting his case on the camp, claiming that "our work on that is not complete."[32] He probably referred to a critique on my own expert opinion which, at that time, was still being written by a British architect working in New York. Irving's admitted inability to either present his evidence-in-chief on Auschwitz or face cross-examination on that topic irritated Justice Gray, who noted that Irving had had sufficient notice—in fact more than six months— to prepare for the issue of Auschwitz at the trial.[33]

Following these discussions about how to proceed with the case, Irving presented his evidence-in-chief—minus any evidence that related to Auschwitz. He reviewed Lipstadt's allegations and the damage they had caused. When Irving told the court that he did not deny that Jews had been murdered by Germans, Justice Gray asked him if he agreed that this murder was systematic. Irving responded that "if by using the word 'systematic' you are implying that the system, the Third Reich as such originated these massacres, then I have to quibble with that."[34] Justice Gray then asked for further clarification.

> [Justice Gray]: "Can I ask you a similar question: do you accept or deny totally that there was any systematic gassing of Jews in gas chambers, whether in Auschwitz or elsewhere? I know we are not dealing with Auschwitz, but think that this ought to be part of—"
>
> [Irving]: "Yes. I think that we can leave out the word 'systematic,' which is contentious. I do not deny that there was some kind of gassing at gas chambers in Birkenau. It is highly likely that there was."
>
> Q.: "—on a solely experimental basis—"
>
> A.: "That is the word I have used to give an indication of scale and to give an indication of the authority on which it was conducted."[35]

That same day Irving concluded his evidence-in-chief, and Rampton began his cross-examination. Auschwitz was not to be discussed, but it cropped up constantly. For example, at the beginning of his cross-examination, Rampton turned to the 1977 edition of *Hitler's War*. He asked Irving if that edition contained references to the Holocaust and if he referred in that edition to Auschwitz as an extermination camp. Irving acknowledged that this was true. Then Rampton asked if in the second edition of *Hitler's War* he defined Auschwitz as a slave labor camp. Again Irving agreed. Then Rampton confronted Irving with a statement he had made in Calgary in 1991. "For example, until 1988 . . . I believed that millions of people had been killed in factories of death. I believed in the gas chamber. I believed in all the paraphernalia of the modern Holocaust." When asked what those paraphernalia of the modern Holocaust were, Irving replied "the factories of death."[36] The designation "factory of death" was to acquire great importance in a kind of semantic game Irving was to play whenever convenient in the trial. Irving was to argue that a factory was a building purposefully designed for mass production of a certain product. At times he claimed that when he denied that Belzec or Sobibor or Treblinka or Auschwitz had been "factories of death," he only stated that these places had not been purposefully designed for mass murder. It must have seemed a smart strategy, because in the case of Belzec, Sobibor, and Treblinka there was no wartime documentary evidence proving that these camps had been designed as purposeful "factories of death," while in the case of Auschwitz it was clear that the camp and the two major crematoria, Crematoria 2 and 3, had not been designed with the aim to create an extermination camp. As Dwork and I had clearly shown in our book, the purpose of Auschwitz had changed from a more benign into a genocidal one. Thus, invoking his narrow definition of what constitutes a "factory of death," Irving could claim support in our work. Justice Gray was not impressed by Irving's sophistry.

Throughout the first day of cross-examination, Rampton tried to nail Irving down. He asked if Irving had stated during the launch of the second edition of *Hitler's War* that "the blood libel on the German people" was "the lie that the Germans had factories of death with gas chambers in which they liquidated millions of their opponents." Irving acknowledged that "that is an accurate transcription of what I said."[37] Rampton asked him how many Jews the Nazis deliberately killed. Repeating his opening statement that he was not a Holocaust expert, Irving refused to answer. "What I would now say would be a figure without any value whatsoever. . . . It would be a waste of this court's time for me to make an assessment."[38] Rampton did not give up. When he tried to establish what Irving denied, the latter responded that he did not believe that millions of people had been killed in the gas chambers. "A million people weigh 100,000 tonnes," he interjected. "We are talking of a major logistical problem here."[39] Pressed again, Irving stated that he denied that "any kind of multiples of millions of people were killed in the gas chambers at Birkenau."[40] When challenged on Sobibor, Treblinka, Belzec, and Chelmno, Irving refused to make any statement, claiming he was not an expert. Then Rampton turned again to the differences between the first and second editions of *Hitler's War*. When he reminded Irving that in the first edition he had accepted that Auschwitz was an extermination center, Irving responded with "Yes, a lazy acceptance which I now regret."[41] The cross-examination, which was only meant to establish Irving's position, quickly became a semantic word game that frustrated Rampton. When it proved impossible to get Irving to make a clear declaration of his position, he exclaimed that he was sorely tempted to turn to Auschwitz straightaway. Irving responded coolly: "I am looking forward to Auschwitz."[42]

Throughout the third and fourth days, Rampton and Irving worked to keep Auschwitz out of the courtroom. It must have been difficult, because Auschwitz was the pivot of the case, if only because of the importance of the Leuchter Report in Irving's conversion to negationism and his subsequent appearance in Lipstadt's *Denying the Holocaust*. On the fifth day, the stated resolve not to address Auschwitz until Irving was ready for it dissolved when Rampton confronted Irving with a passage from the 1991 edition of *Hitler's War.* "On July 19th 1942, the day after Himmler's tour of Auschwitz, he issued a written order to Krüger: 'I decree that the transfer of the entire Jewish population of the General Government is to be carried out and completed by December 31st 1942.'"

> Hitler might still be dreaming of Madagascar, but the head office of the Eastern Railroad at Krakow reported: "Since July 22 one trainload of 5,000 Jews has been running from Warsaw via Malkinia to Treblinka every day, and in addition a trainload of 5,000 Jews leaves Przemysl twice a week for Belsec."[43]

After reading this passage back to Irving, Rampton asked him "Why was it that one trainload a day of 5,000 Jews was going from Warsaw to Treblinka and one twice a week of 5,000 Jews to Belzec from the place which begins with P?" Irving responded: "The documents do not tell us." Rampton then produced a wartime German railway map of occupied Poland and traced the routes these trains had taken. It showed clearly the destination of those trains carrying hundreds of thousands of Jews to "three villages on the Russian border," and he asked Irving if he could explain this. Irving refused, arguing that it was irrelevant to the issues pleaded. Rampton replied that it was relevant, because the report of the head office of the Eastern Railroad revealed "the scale of the operation." Rampton added that he would demonstrate that "anybody who supposes that those hundreds of thousands of Jews were sent to these tiny little villages, what shall we say, in order to restore their health, is either mad or a liar." Which led Irving to reply that "during World War II large numbers of people were sent to Aldershot, which is also a tiny village, but I do not think anybody is alleging there were gas chambers at Aldershot."[44] Ignoring the fallacious parallel between Treblinka and Aldershot, Rampton continued with his argument that the scale of Jewish deportations to places where they could not have survived was sufficient proof that the killing of Jews was not some random action but a planned operation, and that as a responsible historian Irving should have drawn that conclusion. It was clear that Justice Gray agreed, and with that Irving had effectively lost his argument that the only relevant question was if he had misrepresented the papers laying before him. In his account of the transports of the Jews to Treblinka and Belzec, given in the 1991 edition of *Hitler's War,* Irving had not literally misquoted the report by the Head Office of the Eastern Railroad at Cracow, but he had failed to draw the only obvious conclusion, and hence he had not provided a fair representation of the evidence. While Irving's description of the report was literally true, it was also misleading for anyone who would read Irving's words as providing a fair description of the document because it excluded the predominant feature of that document—namely, that it concerned the transport of hundreds of thousands of Jews to nowhere. Irving had to admit as much when, after some more cross-examination, he had to concede that, on the balance of probabilities, Belzec, Sobibor, and Treblinka had been extermination camps.[45] But he held out that these camps had not operated as part of a general policy, because the killing in those camps did not show "that efficiency we come to associate with the German name."[46]

The discussion turned to Auschwitz when Rampton tried to show how, years earlier, Irving had made statements about Treblinka and Sobibor that extrapolated from his knowledge about Auschwitz. Irving had argued that if Auschwitz was not a killing station, "a dedicated factory of death, then, on the balance of probabilities, it is likely that these two were not dedicated factories of death either." Rampton countered with the observation that these camps could not be compared because they had had very different origins.

[Rampton]: "Why? Auschwitz started out as a huge grandiose scheme by Himmler, did it not, to provide a sort of fife for the SS in central or south Poland at which there would be vast factories and brilliant agricultural lands and experiments of that kind, without any thought of killing anybody at all except through hard work?"

[Irving]: "You are giving evidence on my part."

Q.: "That is right, is it not?"

A.: "That is absolutely right and I wish you were my counsel at this moment."

Q.: "That is how Auschwitz started out. Its origins were quite different from those of the three so-called Reinhardt camps?"

A.: "It now squares up to the chronology, Mr Rampton. We are told by your experts that Auschwitz had become a dedicated killing station by the end of 1941 or early 1942 at the latest, and yet apparently they also had found it necessary to establish other places to do killings too."

Q.: "Mr Irving, I am sorry—"

A.: "So that is what I mean by extrapolating. If you have a super mass production factory here, then why do you build these villages elsewhere?"

Q.: "If you read Professor van Pelt's report with any care you would know that that was complete nonsense, that the evolution of Auschwitz into a dedicated killing facility, in fact not Auschwitz, Birkenau, really began at the end of 1942. There were some gassings by the use of a cellar at Auschwitz, one, and by, two, converted farm houses during 1942."

A.: "But there was of course a huge rate of mortality at Auschwitz in the middle of 1942."

Q.: "We will get on to Auschwitz next week, but do not misrepresent what Professor van Pelt has said, unless you are sure of your ground, because it is not what he said."

A.: "You have brought up Auschwitz now and you are talking about dates and months, and when I try to pin you down on the huge mortality rate in the middle of 1942 you are saying let us talk about that next week."

Q.: "There was a typhus epidemic at Auschwitz in 1942."

A.: "So we are saying now that all the deaths in 1942 were from typhus?"

Q.: "Mr Irving, surely you can do better than that."

A.: "You just said it, Mr Rampton."

Q.: "I said there was a huge typhus epidemic in 1942."

A.: "The killings did not start until the end of 1942."

Q.: "I did not say that. At the same time people were being gassed in what are known as bunkers one and two, and that the conversion of the two planned crematoria at Birkenau into gas chambers took place in the late part of 1942 at the planning stage, and that they came into operation in early 1943."

A.: "With the cyanide being dropped in through the roof, right?"[47]

This was a first indication of what was to become Irving's main position: the fact that today the remains of the roof of Morgue 1 at Crematorium 2 show no sign of the wire-mesh columns through which the gas was introduced into the chamber below. Irving was to argue that if the columns had passed through the roof, the roof would to this day have four holes. As there were no traces of these holes, and as the chimneys do not appear in the blueprints for the construction of the crematoria, they never existed. However, Justice Gray had had enough of the way Auschwitz continued to crop up in other discussions, despite the agreement to exclude it for the time being. At the end of that day's proceeding, he told Irving and Rampton that he wanted it to be dealt with. "The sooner we have the argument the better."[48] Both parties agreed that Auschwitz would be on the agenda for Thursday, January 20.

At the moment that Justice Gray called the parties to engage Auschwitz directly, I was packing my bags. I had been asked to leave for Great Britain on Wednesday, January 19. The prospect was that Rampton would begin his cross-examination of Irving on Auschwitz on Monday, January 24. On that day I would have sufficiently recovered from jet lag to support Rampton, if necessary. Gray's decision to move Auschwitz to Thursday, January 20 meant that I would go straight from the plane to the courtroom. It was not an attractive scenario.

On Wednesday January 19, 2000, I left Toronto for London. That same day Irving made it clear that he looked forward to the Battle of Auschwitz. It was appropriate, he argued, "to hinge this case on Auschwitz rather than what I might call the lesser camps, where there is a great deal of uncertainty, whereas Auschwitz is really the battleship, the capital ship of this entire case."[49] According to Irving, Belzec, Sobibor, and Treblinka—camps in which a total of more than 1.5 million people were killed—were not really central. "These are the minor escorts, the corvettes and minesweepers, not the actual battleship which is Auschwitz itself."[50]

At the end of that Wednesday, Justice Gray asked Rampton to summarize what his case would be on Auschwitz, which was to be the subject of Irving's cross-examination the next day. Rampton replied that he did not intend to prove that Auschwitz had homicidal gas chambers. His main aim was to demonstrate that Irving, "on the back of a piece of so-called research which is not worth the paper it is written on jumped up and said he was perfectly certain that there were never any gas chambers at Auschwitz." He had repeated that statement in meetings of people who were likely to be anti-Semites, which gave his pronouncements a political dimension. "As an insight into Mr Irving's credentials as a so-called historian, it is extremely illuminating, and that is the whole of my argument."[51]

On Thursday, January 20, I arrived at Rampton's chambers at 9:30 A.M. I found him "ready for Auschwitz," as he said. He felt that the case was going well. The concessions Irving had made the day before about Belzec, Sobibor, and Treblinka were important, not because we had won him over, which for Rampton was irrelevant, but because it would allow him to argue at a later stage in the case that Irving's readiness to contradict earlier statements he had made about crucial aspects of the Holocaust was a clear proof of his willingness to make assertions about the Nazi era which are irreconcilable with the available evidence. Rampton did not believe that Justice Gray was impressed by Irving's assertion that he had made his concessions just to allow for the Battle of Auschwitz to begin. While Justice Gray obviously tried to speed up the proceedings, he was the last man to easily pass over the deaths of more than 1.5 million people for the sake of expediency. With his quick concessions and the way he had justified them, Irving had clearly damaged his own standing in court.

A little after ten we left the Middle Temple, crossed the Strand, and entered George Edmund Street's neo-Gothic masterpiece. We did not go to Courtroom 37, which had been abandoned because it could not contain the many people who wanted to attend the proceedings. Its replacement, Courtroom 73, proved paltry and disappointing. It did not have any of the splendor of the vaulted hall, the so-called *Salle Des Pas Pardus*, where we had entered. The only ornament was an elaborately carved Royal Coat of Arms behind the judge's bench. It appeared out of place. Yet, the almost shabby, if not sorry, setting seemed appropriate, given the silliness of Irving's legal suit.

Irving entered the room, a heavyset and tall man of military bearing with a florid face crowned by an impressive head of silver hair. Dressed in a well-tailored pin-striped suit, he looked at home in Courtroom 73. In strange contrast to his carefully considered appearance, he carried his papers in a cheap plastic shopping bag. As he walked to his table, I felt a strange and indeed unexpected response to him. From the moment that I had agreed to join the case, I had done so without hatred or contempt for him. Thanks to the discovery process, I had access to his dirty laundry, so to speak, and while it had proven very dirty indeed, it also had led to a certain (admittedly one-sided) intimacy with the man. And after I had completed my report, I had tried to imagine his character, because we would face each other in combat, and I could not afford to underestimate my opponent. I had studied the maritime metaphors he lived by, rented the 1960 movie *Sink the Bismarck,* and set out to analyze his mode of operation as the historiographical version of the smoke-bank tactics practiced by British warships when meeting a stronger opponent: hide in the safety of the smoke until ready to attack, leave the smoke to shoot, and return into the smoke cover before the enemy gunners have found their target. As he put his papers on the table, I realized that I knew more about him than anyone else in that room—more than I knew about many of my friends.

I left my seat, walked over to him, and introduced myself. Irving seemed surprised. Perhaps he had been a pariah too long. We exchanged some civilities, and then Irving showed me a poster-size aerial photo of the ruins of the crematoria. He told me that it had been recently taken by "one of our people" and that he would introduce it in court during my cross-examination. Either he lied, or he had been lied to: on the image, which was in fact not a photo but a print, one could clearly see crosses and Stars of David in the so-called field of ashes behind the ruins of Bunker 2. These had been removed in early 1998. After a few more pleasantries, I returned to our side where I was received with puzzled looks. Only Rogers smiled.

"Court rise!," called the usher, and in walked Justice Gray. A handsome man in his late 50s, he radiated an impatient energy and with his unaffected presence immediately transformed the prosaic surroundings of his bench into the appropriately unadorned workshop of history. That morning Donald Cameron Watt, emeritus professor of international history at the London School of Economics and Political Science, testified. Because Irving had collaborated with Cameron Watt in the 1960s, Irving had subpoenaed him to give evidence on his abilities as a historian, and Cameron Watt told the court that as the author of *Hitler's War,* Irving deserved to be taken seriously. "He is, after all, the only man of standing, on the basis of his other research, who puts the case for Hitler forward and it seems to me that it is mistaken to dismiss it." Yet Cameron Watt completely rejected Irving's assertion that Himmler could have organized the Holocaust behind Hitler's back. "He was a man who was almost incapable of originating anything himself unless he had what he thought was approval from above. . . . He was a man who was dependent on approval of those whom he idolised."[52]

Watching the examination-in-chief of Cameron Watt proved useful. On the invitation of Justice Gray, he sat in the witness box, and from there he made a less-than-impressive figure. He was seated at eye level with Irving, who was standing, but not at eye level with Justice Gray. I made the decision that, when my turn was to come, I would exploit the psychological advantage offered by the location of the witness box and stand: it would bring me eye-to-eye with Justice Gray, force Irving to look up to me, and allow me to look down on him.

After Cameron Watt stood down as a witness, it was time for Auschwitz. Before Rampton began his cross-examination on that topic, Irving pleaded once again that he could be judged only on the way he had handled documents on Auschwitz that he had actually seen and used and that the question of what documents he ought to have seen was irrelevant. He justified this argument by referring to the defendants' pleadings that he had been deceitful, which meant that he would have had to have had documents on Auschwitz before him at the time he wrote his books, and that he had "wilfully or perversely attached to those documents meanings that no reasonable man could say they could bear."[53] Irving added that, unable to prove deceit, Rampton was now throwing in negligence as well, although this had not been pleaded. Rampton immediately responded with a firm "No. . . . We are not." Irving replied that "if they are saying, in effect, Mr Irving is a rotten historian, he did not do his job properly. He spoke about Auschwitz, he wrote about Auschwitz and the Holocaust. He ought to have known better, then this is a plea of negligence." Because the defendants had not pleaded negligence before, Irving assumed that such an argument would make it necessary for them to amend their pleadings, and he warned that if they did so, "I would immediately ask your Lordship order that all the costs up to that point should be borne by the Defendants." As Justice Gray did not respond, Irving continued to argue that there was no purpose in considering what had happened in Auschwitz "if it was not known to me at the time I wrote the book." Justice Gray reformulated the argument proposed by Rampton: the issue was not whether the evidence about Auschwitz had been on Irving's desk, but whether it was available to him, "because if you knew it was there and you, as it were, put your telescope to your blind eye and ignored it, then that is as good as having seen it, and decided to suppress it, as they would put it."[54]

It was obvious that Justice Gray did not accept Irving's very narrow interpretation of what constituted deceit and that he would consider not only what Irving had seen but also what was available to him. Yet not realizing that Justice Gray seemed to have made up his mind on the issue, Irving tried to push his luck, and he repeated that with regard to the evidence on Auschwitz—"which will no doubt be of the utmost interest to everybody in this court, and at the expense of the person who pays the costs of this action, or persons"—Justice Gray should only consider relevant what fell within the ambit of "deceit," and not allow evidence for what could be considered "negligence." But by trying to establish a firm boundary between "deceit" and "negligence," Irving had opened a Pandora's box, because it allowed Justice Gray to ask a very obvious question. If Irving pleaded negligence in relationship to the Auschwitz evidence, then that very plea implied that he accepted now that there was more evidence and that he accepted that evidence. Justice Gray explained that if Irving was prepared to state this, Rampton could decide not to cross-examine Irving on the Auschwitz material. And Rampton agreed: he would be prepared to drop the whole Auschwitz issue if Irving would accept "that the Leuchter Report is indeed bunk and very easily detected bunk, because what a responsible historian cannot do, unless he is motivated by some sinister ulterior motive, is nail his colours to the mast, as he said he did, without critical review of the mast to which he is nailing his colours, namely the Leuchter Report. And that is exactly what he did."[55]

However, Irving was not prepared to accept the obvious implication of his negligence argument—namely, that it implied that he ought now accept that there was overwhelming evidence for the assertion that Auschwitz was an extermination camp equipped with homicidal gas chambers—and this made not only his cross-examination on Auschwitz unavoidable, but also mine. For a moment it had appeared that I could have flown back without actually being called as a witness—a prospect that was extremely attractive. I did not mind flying back that same weekend and resuming a life without Irving, without Leuchter, maybe even without Auschwitz. Yet Irving's refusal to accept the implications of the negligence argument—the fact that he had been wrong in endorsing Leuchter—suggested that the battle was on. Indeed, after lunch, Justice Gray ruled that it was legitimate for Rampton to deploy evidence about what had happened at Auschwitz, "even if it is Mr Irving's case that he was unaware of it at the time when he made his various pronouncements about Auschwitz around the world."

> In my judgement, such evidence is relevant and admissible to Mr Rampton's contention that Mr Irving deliberately disregarded such evidence because it did not fit in with his own political and ideological beliefs. This appears to me to constitute historiographical dishonesty of the kind which the Defendants are in this case alleging against Mr. Irving.[56]

With this, the battle for Auschwitz began. First Rampton and Irving went over how he met Leuchter in 1988. Irving said that he had looked at the Leuchter Report, "glanced at the summary at the beginning and . . . looked at the principal conclusions."[57] He did not read it but instead used his weekend to see the Niagara Falls, to which Rampton replied "If I may say so, a good deal more edifying than the Leuchter report." Then Rampton confronted Irving with his Toronto testimony and his volte-face. Asking Irving what had made him change his mind about the Holocaust, Irving replied "A few figures in a column of chemical tests. Percentages."[58] Rampton asked Irving if he thought it was sensible for a man in his position, who had gone all the way to Canada to give expert evidence on a different aspect of the case, to arrive at so certain a conclusion on the basis of one evening's reading of one part of a report made by a man who had no expertise in history. Irving responded that he accepted that he had been given genuine forensic analysis figures and that "any person with even a smattering of knowledge of chemical analysis, quantitative and qualitative, would have to accept that the story, as it had been preached so far, was untenable."[59]

Then Rampton began to work on Irving. "Did you notice that Mr Leuchter's conclusion that there were no homicidal gas chambers at Auschwitz was based in part upon the assumption that higher concentrations would have been needed to kill people than were needed to kill lice?"[60] Irving claimed he had not picked up the false premise of Leuchter's reasoning and that he had not bothered to verify Leuchter's science. Rampton then suggested that Irving's behavior could not be simply explained as negligence, but that it revealed an ulterior motive, that "venturing on to a territory of history, an area of history, of which he had absolutely no knowledge whatever, making world-shattering statements from the witness box in Canada without having done any research" suggested that he had "an ulterior motive for doing it."[61]

The rest of the afternoon was spent finding proof of those ulterior motives by going through Irving's lectures. Rampton concentrated on one talk Irving had given in Ottawa a few months after he gave testimony in the Zündel trial. In this lecture, he asked the audience to imagine "the omelette on their faces if we managed to unmask the other six million lie." When Rampton asked what Irving meant with the words "the other 6 million lie," Irving responded that he referred to "*Der Stern* spending $6 million on buying the Adolf Hitler diaries."

[Rampton]: "So this is what you call the Holocaust lie, is it not?"

[Irving]: "Well, it is obviously a play on words between $6 million and 6 million people, yes."[62]

Rampton read how Irving had told the audience that in speaking as he did he risked his reputation and his career and that he had told them that in Germany "it is now a criminal offence to challenge that six million lie. And I think that alone is proof sufficient that there is not documentary evidence to back the lie up." He pressed on, quoting Irving as having said that some negationists who had not used a scientific approach had damaged "our cause." When Rampton suggested that "our cause" was "the cause of like minded anti-Semitic Holocaust deniers," Irving replied that "I do not think there is the slightest hint of that in those lines." This prompted Justice Gray to ask: "Who else's cause would you be talking of?"[63]

After a quarrel about whether the charge of anti-Semitism was relevant or not, Rampton skillfully returned to the issue of negligence versus deception. He quoted from Irving's Ottawa speech his claim that, in response to the Leuchter Report, he had gone round the archives "with a completely open mind, looking for the evidence myself because, if Auschwitz, just to take that one cardinal tent pole of the case, itself was not an extermination factory, then what is the evidence that it was?" Rampton noted that Irving had not bothered to go to the Auschwitz archive, which elicited Irving's response that in 1988 "Poland was still behind the iron curtain. The wall had not come down. Am I making my point?"[64] Rampton reminded Irving that Jean-Claude Pressac had done his work in the Auschwitz archive in the mid-1980s, and then continued with the claim that Irving had lied when he claimed that he had gone round the archives.

[Irving]: "If I say I have been round the archives, I am not saying I have been round all available archives, including those in Poland

and elsewhere. I am saying I have been round the archives, which at that time is perfectly true. I might even have gone to the Public Records Office to see what they had."

[Rampton]: "You might have been round the archives of the Royal Botanical Gardens in Kew, for all I know."

A.: "I find that a cheap remark."

Q.: "Of course it is cheap, but this is a very cheap—"

A.: "Which you say is a matter of great sensitivity to the Jewish people."

Q.: "This is a very cheap fraud that you have perpetrated on the 50 or so people in this room because what you are telling me is that you have looked everywhere and all anybody can come up with is two or three documents."[65]

Justice Gray asked Irving which archives he had visited in order to find evidence about Auschwitz. Irving did not really remember but assumed that it would have been the German Federal Archives and the National Archives in Washington, "and possibly . . . the Hoover library in California." Rampton replied that he obviously had not searched "the archives of the entire world" for evidence about Auschwitz. In other words, he had deceived his audience. When Irving tried to argue that he had perhaps been negligent, Rampton replied that he had deliberately decided not to go to Auschwitz because he had not been interested in finding the truth. "If you were the slightest bit interested in the truth about Auschwitz, you would have gone there."[66]

That Thursday afternoon we left the court in good spirits, but we had little time to celebrate. On Monday, Rampton was to commence his cross-examination on the Leuchter Report, and it was absolutely necessary to have all the evidence at hand in easily manageable bundles. It had become obvious that Justice Gray was overwhelmed by the enormous amount of historical documents and that it was in our best interest to provide him with easy access to the evidence. Thus Rampton, Rogers, and I spent Friday and Saturday photocopying hundreds of wartime German documents, photos, and other evidentiary material, arranging them in the anticipated order of the cross-examination. There were to be no interruptions in the prosecution of the attack with all of us scrambling to find a document in one of the hundreds of thick files stored in the bookcases lining the walls of Courtroom 73. It was to be all at hand, in three times three binders, right on the desks of Justice Gray, Rampton, and Irving.

As we worked on the bundles, I logged on to the Web and found an interesting editorial on the trial written by Dennis Roddy and published by the *Pittsburgh Post Gazette*. Roddy summarized Irving's career as a man who had once been lauded as "a World War II historian of equal parts energy and promise" who now had become "a right-wing loose cannon." He described Irving's historical technique as one that "approximates a long wall coal mining machine: a crush-proof cab attached to an endless digging belt that simply ploughs through a likely seam, pulls it all loose, and lets everything collapse around it." Roddy's article also announced that Irving would provide new proofs that Auschwitz had no gas chambers, "evidence he'll unleash when he gets one of Lipstadt's expert witnesses on the stand. 'The battleship Auschwitz as the capital ship of the Holocaust legend will have sunk,' Irving assures me."[67]

On Monday, January 24, Irving presented the torpedo that was to sink the battleship Auschwitz. On entering the court, Irving gave the defense team a document containing twenty-nine typed pages and seven photocopied illustrations from *Auschwitz: 1270 to the Present*. It was an attack on my expert opinion, entitled "Critique of the Pelt Report by Robert Jan van Pelt, 1999, By **** ******, January, 2000." In the introduction, the anonymous author (who for the sake of convenience I will assume to be male) described himself as having studied architecture between 1974 and 1981 and having qualified as an architect in 1982. After practicing for nine years in London, he worked in Paris, Berlin, and New York.

> My experience is as a practicing qualified architect, with extensive experience in many countries of the design and construction of a large range of building types. I contrast my qualifications with those of Professor van Pelt, who is not an architect (and is not registered as such with the Stichting Bureau Architectenregister of The Netherlands). I do note that Professor van Pelt is a Professor of Architecture at a School of Architecture in Canada (Pelt, 1). I would point out that in all my years as a student of architecture and as an architect, I have never encountered a Professor of Architecture who was not an architect, although I understand that it is possible albeit rare in North America.[68]

I thought that it was rather brazen for a man who was unwilling to disclose his own identity and qualifications to launch such an ad hominem attack. It also seemed irrelevant, because I had never claimed to be an architect. I counted various non-architects among my colleagues who carried the title of professor of architecture, such as a distinguished structural engineer, a civil engineer, a furniture designer, and a poet. Obviously the University of Waterloo curriculum was more broadly based than the school the anonymous critic came from.

The next paragraph brought me great amusement, as it was obviously designed to protect Irving, who had no degree in history, from the possible implication of the proposition that I could not talk about architecture because I had not studied architecture.

> The title of architect is protected in the United Kingdom by statute, and it is similarly protected in most countries of the world. It is my view that it is fully justified that my professional title is so protected, because there can be grave physical consequences to unqualified and unregistered practice of the applied art and science of architecture. It is not my view that the title "historian" should be similarly protected and regulated, by the State or by anybody else, appointed by the State, or indeed appointed by themselves. An historian is a reporter of past events whose findings metaphorically stand or fall through the free interchange of ideas and information; buildings stand or fall for other more tangible reasons.[69]

The anonymous critic then went into a rant in which he argued that I wanted to disbar Irving from carrying the title of "historian"—something which I did not want to do. He concluded that "in his report, the Professor of Architecture, who is not an architect, frequently strays into my field of expertise as a registered architect, and uses 'heterologic' to come to the most absurd conclusions. He does this all for the process of disbarring an historian from a title which is not statutorily protected."[70]

I stopped reading when Rampton resumed his cross-examination of Irving, which quickly turned to the Leuchter Report. Rampton's purpose was to address not the objective value of the report but Irving's treatment of it in the light of the knowledge which he had and which is itself contained in the report. Irving had made his volte-face despite the fact that he either knew, or should have known, that the report was wrong: the gas densities were wrong and the amount of people who could have been killed in the gas chamber of Crematorium 2 was wrong. Irving admitted that he knew there were problems and that in his correspondence with other negationists he had challenged various aspects of the report. Rampton immediately retorted: "Have you ever made that statement publicly before today?" Irving replied: "No, because that was not the crucial element of the Leuchter Report on which I relied. The crucial element is the scientific findings."[71] Then Rampton confronted Irving with a letter he had written to Colin Beer, in which he had conceded that Leuchter's assumption that the SS had used a hydrogen cyanide concentration of 3,200 parts per million was untenable. When Rampton confronted Irving with the last paragraph of Beer's conclusions, which stated that once one assumed that the gas chambers had operated on relatively low toxic concentrations, the Leuchter Report "strongly supports both the fact and scale of the massacres in the gas chambers at Birkenau,"[72] Irving admitted that this was a key observation and that because a homicidal gas chamber used a much lower concentration, this did imply that first of all the need for a ventilation system was much reduced. He also admitted that it was a logical conclusion that the risk of contamination of water in the sewers would be much reduced, possibly to complete insignificance. Rampton pushed on.

> [Rampton]: "It would be a logical conclusion that the need for the people administering the poison gas to take what I might call strong security precautions, safety precautions, is much reduced, is it not?"
>
> [Irving]: "That would be a logical conclusion to your hypothesis, yes."
>
> Q.: "It means, does it not, Mr Irving, that the time which has to be waited before the Sonderkommandos can go in and get the bodies out, whether or not they are wearing gas masks, is much reduced, is it not?"
>
> A.: "This would be the logical conclusion of your hypothesis, yes."
>
> Q.: "Above all, it means this, does it not, that the discovery by Mr Leuchter of the small traces of cyanide compounds in material taken from the walls of the alleged gas chambers at crematorium 3 in Birkenau is entirely consistent with a low concentration having been used in the first place?"[73]

At that point Irving was reluctant to draw the obvious conclusion. But that did not matter to Rampton: as he told the court, after receiving the comments by Mr. Beer, he knew that Leuchter had completely reversed the significance of the concentration. "So the principal brick falls straight out of Fred Leuchter's report."[74]

Until that point, the cross-examination had yielded few surprises. Rampton followed the logical script developed in the interrogatories, and Irving tried to defend his earlier support of the Leuchter Report without appearing to be a credulous fool for having done so. As I sat in the courtroom, I remembered that in his opening speech Irving had suggested that a proper title for his libel action was "Pictures at an Execution," to which he had added the qualification "—my execution." The execution to which he referred was, of course, Lipstadt's alleged libel and the alleged public lynching that had followed the announcement by St. Martin's Press of the forthcoming publication of his biography of Goebbels. But whatever criticism he had met since 1993 paled with what he had to endure in court as Rampton skillfully transformed the plaintiff into a defendant, the accuser into the accused. But Irving showed that he still had some tricks up his sleeve. When Rampton confronted him with the results of a Polish forensic investigation of the ventilator gratings taken from Morgue 1 of Crematorium 2, which had revealed traces of cyanide, Irving admitted the validity of the document. Rampton challenged him to explain the presence of cyanide, and Irving responded: "Because that particular room was used as *Vergasungskeller,* as a gassing cellar." "Gassing what?," Rampton inquired. "I think the evidence is clear that it was used as a gassing cellar for fumigating objects or cadavers," Irving replied.

As Irving produced his stunning answer, I found its source in the anonymous critique that I had received minutes before the beginning of the proceedings. The architect had developed the following argument. Crematoria 2 and 3 were each equipped with autopsy rooms. They were carefully designed, and the anonymous critic assumed that they were to be used for autopsies meant to establish the cause of death of those to be incinerated. This explained, according to him, why the corpse chute had been removed. In my own report, I had concluded that the removal of the slide and the introduction of stairs as the way to gain access to the basement was a clear indication that its purpose had been changed. "Live human beings descend staircases. Dead bodies are dropped through a chute. The victims would walk to their death." Irving's advisor proposed that the practice of autopsies would explain why the chute was removed: it would damage bodies. "Damaged bodies would not cause a problem if they were immediately cremated, but would have caused complications if the corpse was selected for autopsy."[75] However, the problem with this explanation is that it does not address why the chute had been originally introduced and why chutes were built to give access to other morgues in concentration camps, such as Sachsenhausen. There the morgue was connected to an autopsy room.

The autopsy theory also explained why Morgue 1 had heating, the critic claimed. In our arguments, Bischoff's proposal to bring hot air from the ventilator room to Morgue 1 had been an indication that it was to be used as a gas chamber. The presence of a ventilation system was also important. The architect who critiqued my report disagreed. He quoted from Neufert the statement that "the temperature of the morgue [was] 2°, never below, as frost expands the corpses and can make them burst. This temperature must be maintained through central heating and cooling by continuous ventilation, especially in summer."[76] Therefore he concluded that Morgue 1 "was something more than a simple gathering space for corpses prior to their immediate cremation, as the intent was obviously to store corpses through careful environmental control for as long as possible." Again the use of the corpses for autopsies would explain this. Yet this did not explain why there was no trace of heating before the building was completed. Why was this suddenly so urgent in March 1943 when the design dated back to October 1941?

> As the large mortuary, *Leichenkeller 2,* was cool but had no heating, it would have been unsuitable in all conditions for the storage of the small percentage of bodies selected for autopsy. All

bodies would have been undressed in the large mortuary, *Leichen-keller 2*, where an initial inspection and selection would have been made as to whether to take the corpse to the more controlled environment of the small mortuary, *Leichenkeller 1*. As a primary function of autopsy would have been to determine whether the cause of death had been contagious (and one thinks primarily of typhus), the assumption can safely be made that the small mortuary, *Leichenkeller 1*, was envisaged as a repository for highly infectious and dangerously contagious corpses.[77]

This would also explain why Morgue 2 was referred to as undressing room, according to my critic:

The corpses would not be stripped naked in their barracks, nor where they fell, nor on the way to the crematorium. The corpse would have been undressed in the receiving mortuary, and we should not be surprised that it was occasionally referred to as an undressing room.[78]

All of this made clear why Morgue 1 would have been referred to as a gassing basement, he claimed:

It is perfectly obvious to an architect that the small mortuary, *Leichenkeller 1*, was a special mortuary. It is also perfectly obvious that it was intended to contain bodies dead from (or suspected of having died from) typhus, or similar contagious diseases. It also follows that those bodies would have had to have been disinfested of lice before they were brought into close proximity with any examining doctor investigating the actual cause of death. As the only way the Germans had of disinfesting anything was with the use of HCN gas, it is impossible to believe that the architects of the *Zentralbauleitung Auschwitz* (and indeed, Georg Werkmann, the original design architect) were unaware of the operational intention of disinfesting the space using *Zyklon B*.[79]

The doctors would have insisted that the morgue that was to store the corpses on which they were to perform autopsies would be regularly deloused, my critic argued. This practice would also have prevented spread of the disease because the lice would have left the corpses that were cooling in search of new hosts. Those delivering the bodies to Morgue 1 would have been at risk of picking up the lice and transferring them back to the rest of the camp. Also, those working the ovens had to be protected.

The unknown architect's argument is obviously absurd. It is not based on any evidence whatsoever. In the archive of the Central Construction Office there are many files dealing with the construction of delousing installations and delousing procedures, but there is none that suggests the delousing of corpses with Zyklon B. Also, I have never encountered any indication that such installations were ever considered or built anywhere else. The reason for this seems straightforward: one does not need to conduct autopsies to establish that typhus was the cause of death. The symptoms are very clear while the patient is still alive, and the corpses of those who have died from typhus show a characteristic rash on the back, chest, and abdomen and possibly gangrene on the fingers, genitals, nose, and ears. Obviously the unknown architect strayed in a statutorily protected field of expertise—namely medicine—to reach absurd conclusions. His speculation is also wholly unsupported by the evidence from eyewitnesses. No one has ever testified that the Auschwitz doctors were engaged in a serious enterprise to routinely establish the cause of death through autopsies. In fact, procedures in the Auschwitz autopsy room are well known, because one of the doctors who worked there, Hungarian pathologist Dr. Miklos Nyiszli, testified immediately after the war in Hungary and wrote his memoirs thereafter. He described at length the comparative dissections he undertook as part of Dr. Josef Mengele's research program on twins (research on twins that involves comparative dissection is difficult because under normal circumstances they die at different ages and different locations; in Auschwitz, twins could be killed at the same time, and therefore a comparative dissection was possible) and the dissections he did as part of Dr. Wolff's research program on dysentery. Nyiszli did not mention typhus. The only time that Nyiszli mentioned doing autopsies to establish if the patient had died from a contagious disease concerned the corpses of two women who were thought to have died of typhoid fever. If this cause of death could be confirmed, all those who shared the barrack of the two women were at risk of immediate liquidation. These women obviously had died before their bodies were covered with the small, rose-colored spots that are visible symptoms of the disease. Nyiszli established that the small intestines showed the ulcers typically caused by typhoid.[80] Even if autopsies were to have been routinely used to establish early instances of typhoid, it would not have been sufficient to delouse those corpses with Zyklon B, because typhoid is caused by a bacterium that enters the body by means of contaminated food or water; it is not louse-, flea-, or mite-born like epidemic typhus, endemic typhus, or scrub typhus.

The proposition of the anonymous architect was absurd. But if one was prepared to accept its absurd premise—namely, that doctors were busy establishing the cause of death of typhus victims through autopsies—then it showed at least some crazy logic. But Irving was insufficiently prepared to exploit that logic—for whatever it was worth. Rampton had no difficulty attacking the proposition that Morgue 1 had been used for gassing corpses and for clothes: if that had been the case, why didn't Leuchter find the same concentrations of hydrogen cyanide residue in those rooms as he did in the delousing facility? "Frankly, I do not know the answer to that," Irving responded. Rampton pressed on.

> Q.: "If they were used for gassing corpses, I wonder if you can help me to understand the point, because shortly after they were in the mortuary they went to be incinerated?"
>
> A.: "Yes."
>
> Q.: "What would be the point of gassing a corpse that was shortly going to be incinerated?"
>
> A.: "The corpses arrived fully clothed. Before they were cremated they were undressed, and various other bestialities were performed on them. I believe the gold teeth were taken out and other functions were performed. As the corpses cooled, the lice that may have been on the body crawled off the body because lice were seeking heat. As the body cooled, they crawled off so you had an infestation problem."
>
> Q.: "Where?"
>
> A.: "I am not sure saying this off the top of my head, Mr Rampton. I have taken advice on this."
>
> Q.: "Where would the infestation problem arise, Mr Irving?"

A.: "Anywhere between the place of death and the Leichenkeller."

Q.: "No. You were talking about gassing corpses in Leichenkeller 1, beside which is a lift straight up to the incineration chamber?"

A.: "Yes."

Q.: "Think about it. Why would you gas a corpse that was going straight up to be cremated?"[81]

Irving responded with an unconvincing "I thought I gave the explanation." Yet he did not mention what the premise was of the whole proposition that corpses would have to be deloused in Morgue 1: the assumption that doctors dissected them in the autopsy room. He did recover a little later, when Rampton asked:

[Rampton]: "I have one final question, to which I am sure I know the answer. In January 1942 an SS doctor at Auschwitz wrote an internal memo to the Kommandatur at Auschwitz, on the one hand making requests for the detailed provision for the dissection room in the new crematoria, and on the other hand requesting that there should be in the keller rooms, cellar rooms, of that edifice an undressing room. Why would the SS doctor want an undressing room next to the dissection room?"

[Irving]: "I have to admit that I am not very well versed in practice of morticians and pathologists, but I can well imagine that corpses which are infected would be undressed in one room, which would be regarded as a dirty room, and then cleaned, and then taken into the dissection room for dissection. This again is purely common-sense operating and not specific knowledge."

Q.: "It is in this bundle but I am not asking you to look at it now unless you actually want to. Your thesis is that the reference to an *Auskleideraum* in this document is to the undressing of people who are already dead. Is that right?"

A.: "I am not sure if you have read Neufert, which is the standard architects handbook in Germany over the last seven or eight decades. Both Professor Jan van Pelt and I have obtained a wartime copy of Neufert, one each, and the layout of mortuaries and crematoria is described in some detail in this architects handbook, and it does include an undressing room. So, in other words, this is nothing unusual in a properly designed mortuary."[82]

Irving's answer was guided by the critique written by the anonymous architect, who had observed that Neufert wrote that a crematorium in big cities should have a "special room for found bodies with room for their clothing, and also an autopsy room and doctor's room."[83] This room was to fulfil the functions of the forensic dissections on the corpses of "found bodies," that is, of those whose identities was not known and who were thought to have died an unnatural death. In other words, it was a special morgue connected to the dissection room. While it contained storage lockers so that the clothing that was removed from the corpses could be stored in that room, it was not an "undressing room," and it was not referred to as an "undressing room."

Whatever support Irving may have had from the anonymous document, he was on his own again when Rampton turned once again to the Leuchter Report, claiming that it is not worth the paper it is written on,

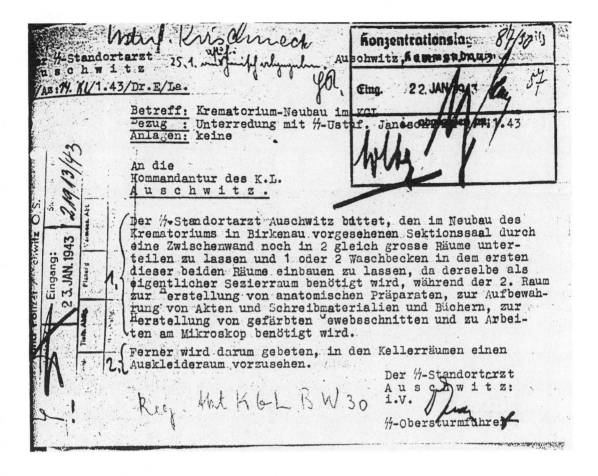

that he got the crucial concentration completely the wrong way round and therefore drew false conclusions from it, and that the true measurement of concentration is consistent with what Markiewicz found in 1994. "Your only way round that is to assert that these were indeed gas chambers, but not for killing people. Is that not right?" Irving replied that he stood by the Leuchter Report because the measurements were done not by Leuchter but by Dr. Roth. To which Rampton replied that these results were consistent with the kinds of concentrations in residue which you would expect in low-concentration homicidal gas chambers and in high-concentration delousing chambers.[84]

Rampton tried to get Irving to admit that the contemporaneous documentary evidence suggested that the crematoria had been equipped with homicidal gas chambers. Irving refused to do that. "From the Auschwitz archives and from the Moscow archives, historians have now retrieved many hundreds of thousands of pages of documents, and we are entitled to at least one explicit, non-ambiguous, non-reading between the lines, non-euphemism type of document which would gives us the clear smoking gun. That document does not exist." Rampton replied that Irving now demanded a document such as the order by Adolf Hitler for the beginning of the Final Solution, and he asked sarcastically: "Since it does not exist, it did not happen; is that right?"

[Rampton]: "Leaving aside the absence of an actual document saying, 'Now we must build some homicidal gas chambers at the order of SS-Reichführer Himmler—'"

[Irving]: "I try to avoid sarcasm like that. I try to look at it at a more serious and objective level."

Q.: "No, but, I am sorry, it does seem to me perhaps appropriate to use sarcasm in this area."

A.: "Sarcasm is the last resort of the scoundrel."

Q.: "Leaving that on one side, do you agree that otherwise the tendency of the surviving contemporaneous evidence—by this I include the remains of the buildings such as they are—is to suggest that, yes, indeed, these were homicidal gas chambers?"

A.: "The tendency of?"

Q.: "Surviving documentary evidence and the ruins is to suggest that these were, indeed, homicidal gas chambers?"

A.: "No, I do not agree [with] that."

Q.: "Why not?"

A.: "Because there are alternative explanations which are equally plausible."[85]

Which introduced once again a discussion on the alleged delousing function of the morgue. Rampton confronted Irving with Bischoff's order for gas-tight doors for Crematoria 4 and 5, which also included a reminder that the German Armament Works should finish a gas door for Morgue 1 of Crematorium 3, which ought to be identical to the door already produced for Morgue 1 of Crematorium 2, "with a peep hole with double eight millimetre glass with a rubber gasket and steel mounting." Irving then fell back on his third suggestion: that it was an air-raid shelter and that the door had been "a typical air raid steel door, a gas tight door, of the kind which was standard throughout Germany at that time." Rampton replied that it puzzled him that there was no emergency exit, which was an obligatory element of any air-raid shelter. And then there was the metal protection for the peephole on the inside of the door. Irving responded that all air-raid shelter doors were supplied with peepholes, all the gas-tight doors had peepholes. "It is rather like the ATM machines which have a little braille pad on them, whether or not it is even a drive-by ATM machine, it still has the braille pad on it, although, obviously, drivers are not blind, because that is the cheapest way to make ATM machines." Rampton replied that this was nonsense, as we were obviously not dealing with an assembly-line-produced door, but with a custom piece ordered by Bischoff from the workshop at Auschwitz. Irving then admitted that, indeed, it was on the face "a very incriminating and highly sinister and murderous document," but that appearances were wrong because it lacked a security classification. "There is no secret stamp on it. . . . This is a document of janitorial level which you are trying to hype up into a smoking gun." To which Rampton replied that because it was a document of janitorial level, one would not expect a security classification.[86]

As they were arguing about whether the morgues would have worked as air-raid shelters, Rampton observed that the morgues were too far from the SS barracks. "If this is for the SS, this air raid shelter, it is a terribly long

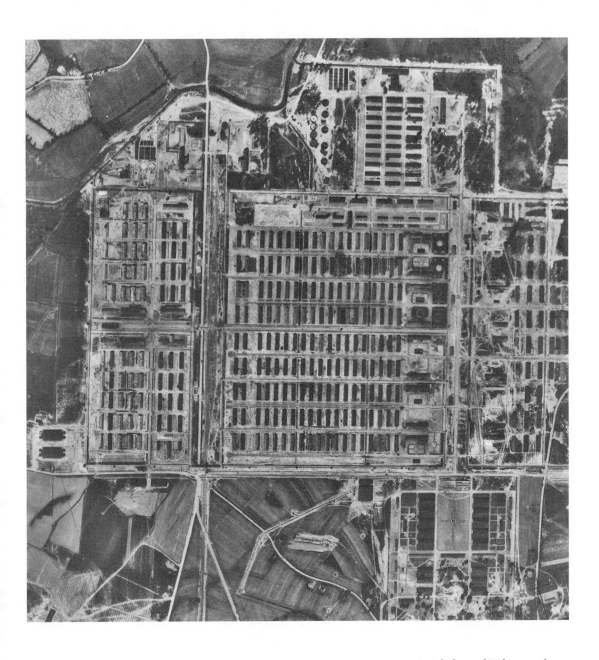

Aerial photo of Birkenau, taken on May 31, 1944. The crematoria with the alleged air-raid shelters are at the top left corner of the photo, while the SS barracks are arranged in two rows along the large square parade place at the bottom right corner of the photo. RG373-Can ON 22483-exp 3055. Courtesy National Archives, Washington, D.C.

PAŃSTWOWE MUZEUM W OŚWIĘCIMIU
A R C H I W U M

22957/43/Jäh/Pa.

Betr.: Krematorium III- K.G.L.-Auschwitz- O/S.
Bezug: Telegramm der Zentralbauleitung Auschwitz
       vom 1o.2.1943 - 2o,o5 Uhr.-
Anlg.: - - -

Firma

J.A. T o p f & S ö h n e
Maschinenfabrik

E r f u r t
Dreysestrasse 7/9

Mit c.a. Telegramm wurde der bereits getätigte Auftrag der gesamten Maschineneinrichtungen einschl.2 Stck.endgültigen e-
lektrischen Leichenaufzügen und 1 provisorischen,kurzfristig
lieferbaren Leichenaufzug,sowie einer praktischen Kohlenbe-
schickungs- und Aschentransportvorrichtung nochmals bestätigt.
Sie haben daher die Anlage K III kompl.zu liefern und zu er-
stellen.Es wird erwartet,dass nunmehr alles daran gesetzt wird,
damit die gesamten Maschinenteile sofort fertiggestellt werden
und zum Versand kommen.
Die Inbetriebnahme der Gesamtanlage muß bestimmt am 1o.April
1943 erfolgen.
Die Zentralbauleitung erwartet,daß Sie mit der Einhaltung des
Termins bei dieser Anlage die Scharten wieder auswetzen,welche
durch Nichterfüllen von Versprechungen und mehrmalige Schreiben,die nicht den Tatsachen entsprachen,bei den Lieferungen
der Öfen für Krem.II.K.G.L.entstanden.So schreiben Sie am
21.1.1943,daß die gesamten Materialien für die Be- und Entlüftungsanlage am 22.1.43 zum Versand kommen.Beim Eintreffen des
Waggons fehlten diese Teile,sodaß Ihr Monteur Messing nicht
weiter konnte.Am Telefon sagte Ihr Herr Prüfer,daß sämtliche
Materialien abgegangen seien.Bei nochmaliger Reklamierung wurde

- 2 -

Letter from Karl Bischoff to Topf and Sons, February 11, 1943. Courtesy Archive Auschwitz-Birkenau State Museum, Oswiecim.

von einem anderen Herrn mitgeteilt,daß die restlichen Materiali-
en noch nicht fertig seien.Zum Schluß waren dann die fertiggestellten Materialien angeblich im Lager gestapelt worden.
Jetzt geht ein Frachtbrief ein mit Versandanzeige vom 6.2.1943.
Nach Prüfung desselben und Rücksprache mit Ihrem Monteur wird
festgestellt,daß ein Gebläse Nr. 450 mit 3.5 PS-Motor wieder
fehlt und ausgerechnet das Gebläse für L.-Keller I,welches am
dringendsten benötigt wird. Außerdem 1 Motor 7,5 PS für das Ab-
luftgebläse Nr. 550 für L-Keller II.
Es wurde Ihnen dieserhalb wieder telegraphiert:"Absendet sofort
auf Versandanzeige 6.2.43 nicht angegebenes Gebläse 450
mit 3,5 PS-Motor für L-Keller I und Motor 7,5 PS für Abluftge-
bläse Nr.550 für L-Keller II, da andernfalls Anlage nicht in
Betrieb genommen werden kann.Drahtantwort."
Durch diese Vernachläßigungen Ihrerseits entstehen der Zentralbauleitung die größten Schwierigkeiten.Sie werden deshalb er-
sucht,sofort die fehlenden Materialien per Eilgut zum Versand
zu bringen,damit endlich die Anlage fertiggestellt wird.

Der Leiter der Zentralbauleitun
der Waffen-SS und Polizei Auschwitz

gez. Bischoff

SS-Sturmbannführer.

Verteiler:

1 Sachbearbeiter Jährling
1 SS-Ustuf.Janisch
1 SS-Ustuf.Kirschneck
1 Registratur (Akt:BW.30.-Krematorium)

F.d.R.d.A.
gez.Unterschrift
SS-Untersturmführer(F)

F.d.R.d.A.

way from the SS barracks, is it not? They would all be dead before they ever got there if there was a bombing raid. Have you thought about that? It is about two and a half miles." Irving replied that during the war they got air-raid warnings half an hour before the planes arrived. Rampton confronted Irving once again with the suggestion that it was absurd to have "a whole lot of heavily armed soldiers running two-and-a-half or three miles from the SS barracks to these cellars at the far end of the Birkenau camp," to which Irving replied that it made sense to adapt the only two underground buildings which had reinforced concrete roofs into shelters.

Then Rampton shifted the focus to a letter sent by Bischoff to Topf on February 11, 1943. It mentions the order for the corpse elevators for Crematorium 3, which was to be put into operation on April 10, 1943. Then the letter turns angry, with Bischoff complaining that despite repeated promises Topf had not delivered all the parts of the ventilation system. A delivery sent on January 22 did not include essential parts.

> Now a consignment note arrives with a date of February 6, 1943. After examination of this and a conversation with your fitter, it appears that *a No. 450 blower with a 3.5 horsepower motor is still missing, and it is precisely this blower destined for morgue 1 which we need most urgently.* Also a motor of 7.5 horsepower for the air extraction blower No. 550 [is still missing].
>
> We therefore cabled you once more: "Dispatch immediately blower 450 and 3.5 horsepower motor for morgue 1 and 7.5 horsepower motor for air extraction blower No. 550 for morgue 2, not appearing on dispatch note of February 6, 1943, because otherwise the installation cannot be brought into service. Reply by telegram."[87] [Bischoff's italics]

The obvious question to be asked was, of course, why the blower for the air-extraction system of Morgue 1 was needed "most urgently" ["*dringend-sten*"], why the blower for the air-extraction system of Morgue 2 was less urgent, and why failure to deliver these blowers in time would have the result that "the installation cannot be brought into service."

> [Justice Gray]: "You are probably familiar with it, are you not?"
>
> [Irving]: "Since yesterday, my Lord. Yes, it was delivered to me yesterday. I have asked all my colleagues around the world what the explanation for all this is and nobody has expressed very great alarm, except that I do draw attention, if I may, to the reference in the third and fourth lines to the provision eventually of two final permanent electric corpse elevators, or lifts, and one temporary corpse elevator which is to be installed as an improvisation."

When Justice Gray asked if the word *Leichenaufzug* meant corpse lift, Irving answered in the affirmative.

> [Irving]: "Yes, *Leichenaufzug*. They play quite an important part in the whole of the argument I shall develop when I come to get revenge on Professor van Pelt later on."
>
> [Justice Gray]: "That is not the right way of expressing yourself."
>
> A.: "Well, I have had to endure a public flogging now for three weeks."
>
> [Rampton]: "Well, Mr Irving, you brought this action, if I may call it that."

A.: "I am very much entitled to, yes."

Q.: "So you must expect to be flogged publicly. If the blows have been a little bit painful, I am sorry, but I am going to go on landing them. Look at the second page of this letter, will you?"

A.: "Yes."

Q.: "Am I right that, in effect, the whole of this letter is a frightful—I am going to use schoolboy language—blowing up administered by the people of Auschwitz, Bischoff, to the supplier because they are behind in their supplying?"

A.: "That is right, yes."

Q.: "And he is saying in the last paragraph but one, is he not: 'Unless this stuff turns up quickly,' and he is reciting a telegram he has already sent, 'we cannot get this thing off the ground, the whole installation'"?

A.: "Yes."

Q.: "The second paragraph from the end. That is right, is it not, and he uses the word in the previous paragraph "*dringendsten*" which means "most urgent," yes?"

A.: "Yes."

Q.: "Why the urgency if it is a mere air raid shelter or a delousing chamber?"[88]

Irving first suggested that a typhus epidemic was the cause for the urgency, then that the word *dringendsten* did not mean anything, and finally that they needed the ventilators because without them, the crematorium could not meet the building inspector's standard. Rampton, however, replied that the most likely explanation was simple: "'We want to start the big extermination programme in March, get on with it.'"

Toward the end of the afternoon, the anonymous critique of my report was mentioned in court. It appeared, for a moment, that Irving wanted to submit it as an expert report. Rampton commented "It has no name on it," implying that an anonymous report could not be accepted. Irving replied "You are not entitled to this man's name, with respect."

[Justice Gray]: "I am afraid that is a matter for me and I do not at the moment understand why you say that."

[Irving]: "This man is obviously in a leading position in the world of architecture and he is, frankly, frightened because he knows what the people backing the Defendants in this action are capable of doing to people of stature."

[Justice Gray]: "Hang on, are you proposing to call him to give evidence?"

A.: "No, I am not. He is purely a person who has advised me in private on some of the technical matters, the architectural matters, which are involved in this case, as the nature of correspondence."

[Justice Gray]: "Then, subject to Mr Rampton, I think you can put the propositions contained in whichever document you are talking about, because I do not think I have seen it, and I do not think there is any reason why I should compel his identity to be disclosed."[89]

By the end of the afternoon it had become clear that I would be on the stand the next day. I read through the anonymous architect's critique of my report and decided against answering every challenge. I believed that my grasp of the issues and my knowledge of the material was sufficient to deal with every item as it came along—if at all. As I read the document closely, I found a new installment of the *Vergasungskeller* saga. As we saw before, the anonymous architect did accept that it referred to a gas chamber, but a gas chamber for corpses. In his analysis of Bischoff's letter of January 29, 1943, the anonymous architect rejected my analysis of the fact that in the preserved copy, the word *Vergasungskeller* was underlined with red pencil and that someone had written with the same pencil "SS-Ustuf (F) Kirschneck!" on top. I had argued in my report that this indicated that Kirschneck, who had drafted the letter for Bischoff, was to have been reprimanded for the linguistic slip that violated Bischoff's own rule never to refer to gassing in building documents. The anonymous architect mocked this interpretation. "In all my years as an architect, I have never drafted a letter for anybody else, nor have I had another architect draft a letter for me to sign."

> That Bischoff (an important man) writes to Kammler (an even more important man) and gets Kirschneck (not a very important project architect) to draft his important letter, is frankly unbelievable. According to Van Pelt, Kirschneck, the drafter of Bischoff's letter, uses a forbidden word, and is reprimanded for having done so by an unknown member of the Central Building office.[90]

This would have been unlikely because it also implied criticism of Bischoff, my anonymous critic suggested. Instead, he theorized that the underlining was an instruction, in all possibility from Bischoff himself. It would have meant:

> Kirschneck! It has been agreed at the highest level that completion of *Leichenkeller 2* can be delayed, because *Leichenkeller 1* (the *Vergasungskeller*) will be immediately completed and ready for use as a mortuary. Make sure this happens![91]

The problem with this interpretation is, of course, that in the copy of the letter preserved in Auschwitz, *only* the word *Vergasungskeller* is underlined—that is, the very noun which the anonymous architect had to relegate in his "instruction" to a subordinate situation by means of parentheses. If Irving was to raise this matter in court, it would not be too difficult to create a riposte.

The critique was full of fantastic alternatives. For example, the anonymous architect suggested that Morgue 1 would have been too expensive a space to turn into a gas chamber:

> Had the camp authorities converted the underground mortuaries to a homicidal gassing facility, they would have been losing a very valuable resource, which they had taken great care and pains to design and build, at great expense of scarce skilled labour and material. The mortuaries were cooled by being underground, one was heated and ventilated, and they were 2.4m high, which is standard ceiling height of a modern European office. The underground complex made for very good mortuaries, perfect for their function, but would have made an extremely bad and inefficient

killing machine. To realize how inefficient it would have been, it is worth looking by way of contrast at the dedicated design of a Degesch *Entlausingskammer* (Delousing Chamber), which van Pelt shows in his book *Auschwitz: 1270 to the Present,* and which he entitles *Design of a Degesch Zyklon B gas chamber.* There is no doubt that the design would have worked just as efficiently as a homicidal gas chamber. The illustrated delousing chamber has a height of 1.9m, to save on use of *Zyklon B,* and the saving would have been significant, as a gas chamber of 2.4m (the height of *Leichenkeller 1*) would need 25% more gas to achieve the same concentration. The chamber is also at ground level, making loading and unloading as simple as possible. Doors on opposite walls make for efficient throughput, and are used to allow natural cross ventilation to clear the space of gas following the delousing procedure. . . . The *Entlausungskammer* was a very simple structure, which could have been built for a very small fraction of the cost of building the mortuaries at Crematorium 2. It would have worked far better as a homicidal gas chamber, and could have been built and fully operational in several weeks, as opposed to the many months it took to build the mortuaries.[92]

There was some merit to this argument, if only because the first gas chambers the Germans built in Birkenau—Bunkers 1 and 2—actually followed the pattern of the Degesch delousing chambers. And these gas chambers proved very efficient in the killing of more than 200,000 Jews. Yet in the end, the disposal of bodies, not the killing, proved to be the difficult part. In the case of Bunkers 1 and 2, this involved first burial and later burning in open trenches. Not only did these strategies for disposal create enormous technical difficulties but they also could not be camouflaged. This is why Crematoria 2 and 3 were so welcome to the SS, even if the decision to adapt Morgue 1 into a gas chamber forced the SS to rely on a space that had a somewhat greater volume than absolutely necessary, on mechanical instead of natural ventilation, and on an awkwardly located and somewhat small elevator to bring the corpses from the basement to the incineration room. In short, the critique of the anonymous architect only makes sense if one considers the problems of killing separately from those of incineration.

As expected, on Tuesday the 25th of January, I was called as a witness. At the last moment, Irving tried to prevent this by arguing that my appearance at that time had "driven a cart and horses right through my preparations for the major part of the case," and only after he was reminded by Rampton that he had agreed on the first day to "have Professor van Pelt come over in the middle of whatever else is going on," and only after Justice Gray had showed his irritation with the way Irving was already rewriting the history of what transpired in court did Irving accept that I be called.[93] When I was finally allowed to proceed to the witness box, Rampton asked Justice Gray if I could take the oath on my own Bible. Justice Gray agreed. As I ascended the steps, Justice Gray nodded to me and said: "Professor van Pelt, I assume it is the Dutch Protestant Bible?" I responded: "No, my Lord, the Jewish Tenach." For a moment, Justice Gray looked puzzled, and then he smiled.

Rampton began with a short examination-in-chief. He posed only a few questions on the forensic investigations of the presence of residual cyanide in the Auschwitz gas chambers. He asked me to consider a few of the measurements of Markiewicz's investigation which clearly showed that the highest measured amount of residual cyanide in the delousing shed BW5a (sample 57, which showed concentrations of 840, 792 and 840 μg CN⁻ per kg) had not been remarkably higher than the highest measured amount of residual cyanide in Morgue 1 of Crematorium 2 (sample 25, which showed concentrations of 640, 592, and 620 μg CN⁻ per kg). As everyone agreed that BW5a had been intensely used for Zyklon B delousings, the equivalence of the two samples suggested that Morgue 1 had also seen intensive use of Zyklon B.

Having concluded the exercise with the samples, Rampton ended the examination-in-chief. I had not been able to expound on any of the issues that I had addressed in my 770-page report. As far as Rampton was concerned, this was unnecessary because the judge had read my report, and because the only purpose of the report had been to convince the judge that Irving had ignored all the evidence concerning Auschwitz when he declared the gas chambers a lie, a re-presentation of the report's contents in court would only be a waste of everybody's time. I, however, felt somewhat cheated of the opportunity to show my learning in a systematic manner. Instead, my whole appearance would be limited to defenses against Irving's attacks.

Irving first welcomed me and complimented me on the Auschwitz book, telling me, "It is one of the few books that I have read from cover to cover and it was a book that I found very difficult to put down."

> [Irving]: "And you are now Professor of the History of Architecture at the University of Waterloo in Toronto?"
>
> [van Pelt]: "No. The issue of my appointment is kind of confusing. I am in the Department of Architecture and hence I am officially a Professor of Architecture. Your title as Professor depends on the department you are in. However, I teach in what we call the Cultural History stream, so normally, in order to prevent confusion in ordinary usage, I would call myself Professor of Cultural History because, both in my background, my PhD and my teaching duties, I teach cultural history in the architectural school. However, when I was advised about the way I had to create my curriculum vitae for this proceeding, I was told that I had to be extremely precise in the legal sense of what I was, so again I put in Professor of Architecture."
>
> [Justice Gray]: "So you are really a cultural historian?"
>
> A: "I am really a cultural historian."[94]

This answer energized Irving. He asked me if I knew that it was illegal in Great Britain to call oneself an architect unless one was registered with the professional body. I answered that this applied to most countries. It was clear that he was going to follow the script supplied by the anonymous architect.

> [Irving]: "Am I right in saying that you are not registered with the Bond van Nederlandse Architecten?"
>
> [van Pelt]: "I have never had any reason to do so since I never studied in an architectural school."
>
> Q.: "So you cannot legally pretend to be an architect, if I can put it like that?"
>
> A.: "No, I could be prosecuted."

Q.: "You could be prosecuted?"

A.: "Yes."

Q.: "Rather like Mr Leuchter was prosecuted in Massachusetts for pretending to be an engineer?"

A.: "Yes."[95]

The point of Irving's cross-examination was clear: my expertise as an architect was the same as Leuchter's expertise as an engineer, or, as he put it a little later, "if I am called a pseudo historian, then you are a pseudo architect, if I can put it like that?" My response was simple: "Yes, except I have never claimed to be either an architect or a pseudo architect." To which Irving replied that I left people with the impression that I was an expert on architecture, "and yet you have never studied it and you have never qualified and you are not registered as such."

[van Pelt]: "I must say that I probably would prefer to be called a professor of cultural history, but the fact of the matter is that the university has given me an appointment as professor of architecture. So—"

[Irving]: "But you are not giving evidence here on the culture of Auschwitz; you are giving evidence on the architecture of Auschwitz."

A.: "I am going to give evidence, I hope, on the history of Auschwitz—and the architectural documents are a very important historical source. I think we both agree on that. I think, as an historian, you can talk about various forms of evidence and architectural documents are one of these forms of evidence."[96]

At that moment Irving ceased his attack with the remark that it ought to be clear to Justice Gray that we were equally qualified, or unqualified, to talk about the architectural material.

This whole exchange did not impress Justice Gray, as he did in the end fully accept my expertise. Nor did it unsettle me, as I was perfectly comfortable with my qualifications for what I was doing. But it must have given Irving a great kick. After the trial, his *Action Report* was to describe this exchange as one of several "direct hits" Irving scored during the action. "Lipstadt's chief architectural witness admitted he was an unqualified unregistered charlatan, who would be arrested if he stepped outside the courtroom and called himself an 'architect.'"[97] Probably it gave Irving and his followers some amusement. It only showed to me that, once again, Irving confused history with propaganda.

Having followed the script, Irving soon introduced his own theme. If the anonymous architect had tried to expose me as an unqualified charlatan, Irving was to unmask me as a weak-kneed wimp.

[Irving]: "You were deeply moved to visit the actual location where these atrocities had occurred?"

[van Pelt]: "More than moved. I was frightened. I—"

Q.: "Ghosts of the dead were still all around?"

A.: "No, I do not believe in ghosts and I have never seen ghosts in Auschwitz, but it is an awesome place in many ways, and it is also an awesome responsibility one takes upon oneself when one starts to engage this place as an historian. For many years I felt I was not up to that task. It was only after very careful preparation that I finally decided to go there and to start work in Auschwitz. As with many things in life, it became easier to work on it as I was there, as you actually start confronting what the place is."[98]

As I gave my answer, I noticed a small smile on Justice Gray's face. It was obvious that he was amused by the way I had turned Irving's attack against himself. As my only goal was to preserve the credibility of myself and the authority of my expert report, I felt that I was on the right track.

Probably Irving realized this also, and he abandoned his attempt to reveal me as a maudlin milksop. He began to set what was soon to be revealed as his "trap."

> [Irving]: "Professor, just so that we can be completely clear about this and the record can be clear, you are describing Crematorium 2 as being the place where 500,000 people were killed or—"
>
> [van Pelt]: "Yes."
>
> Q.: "—give or take a few numbers."
>
> A.: "Yes."
>
> Q.: "And that this was the centre of the atrocity?"
>
> A.: "Yes."
>
> Q.: "So if I am to concentrate a large part of my investigation in this cross-examination on that one building and, in fact, on *Leichenkeller 1*, the one arm of the crematorium, this is not entirely unjustified if I am trying to establish that the factories of death did not exist as such?"
>
> A.: "No. I think that the obvious building to challenge would be Crematorium 2."[99]

I quickly realized I had made a big mistake in giving Irving the green light to concentrate his attack on Crematorium 2. As I browsed through the critique written by the anonymous architect, I had found a section which claimed that "the core question" concerning Auschwitz concentrated on Leichenkeller 1.

> The question of whether or not holes ever existed in the roof of *Leichenkeller 1* of Crematorium 2 is of the very first importance to anybody who looks for one of the indisputable facts about what happened there 56 years ago. For *Leichenkeller 1* to have been used as a homicidal gas chamber, it is absolutely beyond dispute that there had to be a practical method for an *SS-Rottenführer* from the Gesundheitswesen to introduce Zyklon B pellets to the space without being killed himself. The only practical method was for the pellets to be dropped through holes in the roof.[100]

In my expert opinion, I had written that these holes could not be observed today but that they had probably been backfilled when the gas chambers were dismantled in November 1944—two months before the destruction of the crematoria in January 1945. Invoking an argument that traces of those repairs should be visible today, the anonymous architect had argued that the fact that traces of the holes could not be observed today had profound implications.

Van Pelt tells us that the holes in the roof of *Leichenkeller 1* of Crematorium 2 cannot be observed. He asks rhetorically "Does this mean that they were never there?" The answer is a categoric, absolute, and undoubted "Yes." The fact that the traces of the holes cannot be observed means that the holes were never there.

Until the 18th century, any European could have stated that "All Swans are white." All known previous observations would have confirmed the statement and all empirical data would have induced the generally accepted truth that "all swans are white." When Australia was discovered, and the first European saw a black swan for the first time, what had been generally accepted as inviolable truth was thereafter seen as a conjecture that had been refuted. All swans are not white. Some swans are black.

The lack of holes in the roof has exactly the same effect on the theory of homicidal gassings in *Leichenkeller 1* as the observation of the first black swan had on the one-time generally accepted theory of the universal whiteness of all swans. The theory of homicidal gassings in *Leichenkeller 1* is refuted.[101]

When I had read this argument, I had not paid particular attention to it. First of all, it was based on a false analogy. The problem of identifying traces of holes in a ruined slab has no relationship whatsoever with the discovery of the first black swan, because in the one case we deal with negative evidence (no holes) and in the other case with positive evidence (black swans). In the one case we deal with an assertion about an empirically established particular fact ("Morgue 1 was used as a homicidal gas chamber") and in the other case we deal with a general statement ("All swans are white"). Furthermore it was based on a false premise—namely that the slab was a fine example of "fair-faced concrete" which did not allow for "visually undetectable repairs." In fact, the slab that had covered Morgue 1 of Crematorium 3 was almost completely destroyed, and the slab that had covered Morgue 1 of Crematorium 2 was in such a bad state that it was very difficult to arrive at any positive or negative conclusion about whether or not repairs had been done on it. More important, I knew that there was much evidence that the holes had existed: both eyewitness testimony about them and one photo taken in early 1943 showing the roof of Morgue 1 before the Germans covered it with a layer of earth. It showed square objects on the roof which were clearly the small chimneys that provided access to the holes. And then there were the aerial photos taken in 1944 that showed four dots on the roof of Morgue 1 of both Crematorium 2 and 3. These dots were the holes.

But while there was sufficient evidence to argue that the holes had existed, the fact that they were not visible today remained a problem. Agreeing with Irving that Crematorium 2 was the obvious building to challenge was an asinine answer that gave him the opportunity to move from the anonymous architect's observations to Faurisson's motto "No holes, no Holocaust"—which in turn had been inspired by Langlois and Seignobos's maxim "No Documents, No History." If I had answered that the obvious building to challenge would be Crematorium 4 because it had been designed from the outset with homicidal gas chambers, I could have prevented much trouble. In the case of Crematorium 4, the "holes" measuring 30 by 40 centimeters were clearly marked in the blueprints, the request for the quick delivery of the gas-tight shutters to close those holes still survived, and three of these shutters could actually still be inspected. Yet I forgot to mention these facts, and so I stupidly agreed to Irving's suggestion to concentrate a large part of the cross-examination on Leichenkeller 1.

Pea-brained as I was, I had not lost all my wits. For Irving to fully exploit the issue of the holes, it was necessary for him to argue that the SS had not been able to make any modifications to the roof of Morgue 1 in the time between the cessation of the gassings and the evacuation of the camp. Irving tried to get me to admit that the SS would have had no time to make these modifications because the Russians were very close by and the Germans were "in a blue funk and in a terrible panic and just anxious to get away."[102] When I answered that between November 1944 and January 12, 1945, the front had been stationary, Irving asked me "How far away was the Russian front during that limbo period, in rough terms, 20 miles, 50 miles?" I guessed that the distance was between 70 to 90 miles—a guess that proved overly conservative, as I found out when I consulted a historical atlas later that week. Actually the front had been stationary at 100 miles east of Auschwitz.[103] With the Russians at such a distance, it was unlikely that the SS was in such a panic that they had no time to backfill the holes. Irving realized that the chronology did not support his version of events, so he responded with a "Very well," and withdrew from that particular issue.

In fact, at that time, Irving did not seem interested in pursuing Morgue 1 any further, which was fine with me. He turned to the surviving Sonderkommandos, suggesting that their testimonies could not be trusted because they were crushed by guilt and shame for having participated in the destruction process.[104] After trying to poison that well, Irving moved on to the German eyewitnesses, trying to discredit them also. From a discussion about the various tasks of the Sonderkommandos, Irving touched on the fact that the layout of Crematorium 2 did not resemble that of slaughterhouses and then expressed his surprise that the building of the crematoria had such a low priority that the completion of these buildings was delayed because of the shortage of electrical wires. Irving asked if the SS could not have speeded things up by telling the suppliers "Hey, we are carrying out the Führer's orders here. This is the annihilation of millions of Jews that the Führer has personally ordered. We demand top priority. This is the main plank of the national socialist programme."[105] In other words, from the memorandum of January 29, 1943, that discussed the meeting between an AEG representative and a member of the Central Construction Office in Auschwitz, Irving inferred that the SS was not carrying out the Führer's orders in Auschwitz, that Hitler had not ordered the annihilation of millions of Jews, and that the killing of Jews did not have top priority. However, Irving did not persuade Justice Gray that the problems the SS had in obtaining building supplies for Crematorium 3 meant that Hitler had not ordered the Final Solution.

We had reached one o'clock, and Justice Gray adjourned the proceedings for lunch. After lunch, Irving asked Justice Gray if he would allow for a somewhat shorter session, which would allow him to prepare in more detail for the next day. I took this as an indication that the afternoon would be relatively smooth and that the major battle would not yet begin. I was wrong. Initially the going seemed easy enough. Irving's cross-examination lacked focus and method, and it gave me ample opportunity to bring some important discussions contained in my report into open court. Irving mentioned Himmler's visit to Auschwitz in July 1942 and asked if I had any documentary proof that during this visit Himmler had ordered that the camp take a central role in the so-called Final Solution of the Jewish Problem. I replied that the minutes of a meeting held in the SS Central Construction Office in August 1942, which discussed the construction of two extra crematoria adjacent to the "Bathhouses for Special Actions," could be interpreted as a direct consequence of decisions taken during Himmler's visit. Irving argued that the expansion of incineration capacity was justified by the typhus epidemic which was raging in the camp that August. I answered that the increase of incineration capacity was so massive that it could not be justified by reference to fears for typhus and that I could demonstrate this by drawing a few graphs. Justice Gray invited me to make my argument, telling Irving that he would probably not like it, adding, however, that "it is something Professor van Pelt is entitled to do." Irving responded "My Lord, I am in your hands."[106]

Thus I got the opportunity to fully present the argument contained in Chapter 5 of this book. I concluded my presentation with a firm conclusion that it was absurd to provide Auschwitz with an incineration capacity of 120,000 corpses per month when the whole camp was only designed to hold 150,000 inmates. In other words, it did not make sense to be able to incinerate four-fifths of the camp population in one month. At the worst moment of typhus in August 1942, the disease had killed at most one-third of the camp population in a month, which would require at most an incineration capacity of 50,000—if the worst-case scenario of August 1942 were to be repeated.

> [van Pelt]: "The only point I want to make right now at this moment is that the incineration capacity in the camp on the monthly basis in Auschwitz in 1943 far and far exceeds the absolutely worst case scenario of typhus developing in this camp; and I have to stress here the worst case scenario because, in fact, the SS doctors have worked very hard to limit the possibility for typhus to occur."

> [Justice Gray]: "Right. Thank you very much then. That was all an answer, Mr Irving, to your question—actually I put it for you—whether the increase in capacity might have been nothing to do with Himmler's visit, but solely a response to the typhus epidemic. It was a long answer but that is what it was answering."

> [Irving]: "We share the guilt for inviting that answer, my Lord."

> [Justice Gray]: "Well, if 'guilt' is the right word."[107]

The discussion was not yet complete. Challenging my diagrams, Irving asked me about the projected incineration capacity for 120,000 people per month.

> [Irving]: "Approximately, so we get an idea what we are talking about here, that is four times Wembley stadium, that is 12,000 tonnes of people, 12,000 tonnes of cadavers, that you are going to have to cremate with these very limited installations? Am I getting it right?"

> [van Pelt]: "I do not want to speculate on how many tonnes and how many at Wembley stadium."

> Q.: "You do the calculation yourself. The human body is roughly

SPG of 1, is it not? Specific gravity of 1 because you float in water?"

A.: "Yes."

Q.: "Am I right?"

A.: "So where does this bring us?"

Q.: "Well, the human body weighs what, 100 kilograms? 10 people per tonne?"

A.: "I do not think after you have you been in Auschwitz very long you weigh 100 kilograms."

Q.: "OK. Say 12 people per tonne if you want to cavil, you are still going to end up with 10,000 tonnes of bodies to dispose of. This is bringing it home to you the size of the figures you are talking about there. That brings home to you the absurdity of the document you are relying on. Ten thousand tonnes of bodies. If you will take it from me that it takes 30 kilogrammes of coke to incinerate, as you say, one body, can you work out how many tonnes of coke we are going to put into those tiny coal bunkers that you can see on the aerial photographs to destroy, to incinerate, to cremate, 120,000 bodies? We are talking about train loads, if not ship loads of coke are going to have to go into Auschwitz, and there is no sign of the mountains of coke on the photographs, do you agree? There is no sign of the mountains—"[108]

Irving continued his speech, which was illustrated by an enlarged photograph of Crematoria 2 and 3. He pointed at a small structure which he claimed to be the Auschwitz coke bunker and argued that it was far too small to have been capable of accommodating the huge amount of coke which would have been needed for the incineration of thousands of bodies. I replied that each crematorium had its own coke storage bunker. Then I challenged Irving's assumption that tens of thousands of tonnes of coke were needed and presented to the court the argument which I had prepared in advance (which I have presented in Chapter 2). In court I stated that on the basis of wartime German documents, "we can calculate the amount of coke which is going to be used per corpse—which is not a happy calculation, I must say—but the bottom line is you come to three-and-a-half kilo of coke per corpse." Irving responded with scorn. "Do you really, sincerely believe that you can burn one corpse with enough coke that you could fit in one of these water bottles, is that what you are saying?"[109] I responded that German documents had led me to that conclusion.

This forced Irving to challenge Bischoff's letter of June 28, 1943, which officially established the incineration capacities of Crematoria 2 and 3 at 1,440 bodies per day each and of Crematoria 4 and 5 at 768 bodies per day each. I answered that I did not doubt its authenticity, and that there were two copies of it, one in Moscow and one in Dornburg in the former DDR. "This document has been known for many years, since shortly after the war," I concluded. "The document seems to be perfectly in line with other documents. . . . It seems to be sitting nice in its sequence of other documents. So I have no reason to doubt the integrity of the file or the integrity of the document itself."[110]

Then Irving began the attack which I had anticipated since that morning, but which I had assumed was postponed to the next day when Irving asked Justice Gray to shorten that afternoon's proceedings. Irving had

David Irving in his study at the time of the trial. Behind him is the aerial photo of the roof of the gas chamber of Crematorium 2. Photo by Paul Rogers. Courtesy The Times.

questioned me at length about the arrangement of the basement of Crematorium 2. My explanation of the position of the gas columns adjacent to the pillars in the gas chamber triggered an unexpected response:

> [Irving]: "Professor van Pelt, we are wasting our time really, are we not? There were never any holes in that roof. There are no holes in that roof today. There were never four holes through that roof. They cannot have poured cyanide capsules through that roof. The concrete evidence is still there. You yourself have stood on that roof and looked for those holes and not found them. Our experts have stood on that roof and not found them. The holes were never there. What do you have to say to that?"

> [van Pelt]: "I would just say why do we not put up the picture of the roof and look at the roof in the present condition? The roof is a mess. The roof is absolutely a mess. A large part of the roof is in fragments. The concrete has many different colours. You pretend that you are talking about a piece which is intact. It is not."[111]

As I was talking I looked at my watch. It was almost a quarter to four—time to adjourn. I realized to my relief how his impatience had brought Irving to trouble. Obviously he had planned to introduce the (negative) evidence of the holes the next day, but having introduced it now, he obviously wanted to exploit the momentum gained. But he had only minutes left. And I was not going to help him by hurrying along. Irving asked me to read what I had written about the present state of the roof of Morgue 1 of Crematorium 2, and I took my time to find the passage. As I was going through my report, Justice Gray told Irving that he was ready to adjourn the proceedings to the next day.

[Irving]: "My Lord, you may apprehend that the trap is now sprung and it would be a pity to put the mouse back in its cage."

[Justice Gray]: "The trap is what you have just asked?"

[Irving]: "Precisely it, my Lord. There are no holes in that roof. There were never any holes in that roof. All the eyewitnesses on whom he relies are therefore exposed as liars."

[Justice Gray]: "I am just identifying the trap."

[van Pelt]: "Now if I am sitting in the trap I will take a little longer to look for the information because—"

[Irving]: "Take as long as you like."

[van Pelt]: "—because I prefer to remain in the trap and eat the cheese while it lasts! OK, we are here at page 518, my Lord."

Q.: "518?"

A.: "Yes. The bottom two lines: 'Today, these four small holes that connected the wire-mesh columns and the chimneys cannot be observed in the ruined remains of the concrete slab. Yet does this mean they were never there? We know that after the cessation of the gassings in the fall of 1944 all the gassing equipment was removed, which implies both the wire-mesh columns and the chimneys. What would have remained would have been the four narrow holes and the slab. While there is no certainty in this particular matter, it would have been logical to attach at the location where the columns had been some formwork at the bottom of the gas chamber ceiling, and pour some concrete in the hole and thus restore the slab.'"

Q.: "Hold it there. So what you are saying is with the Red Army just over the River Vistula ever since November 1944 and about to invade and, as we found out earlier this morning, the personnel of Auschwitz concentration camp in a blue funk and destroying their records and doing what they can, some SS Rottenführer has been given the rotten job of getting up there with a bucket and spade and cementing in those four holes, in case after we have blown up the building they show?"

A.: "I would like to point out that the gas chamber was removed in November 1944."

Q.: "The gas chamber was removed?"

A.: "The gas chamber, the installations were removed. The installations in the gas chambers were removed. Also during the month of November and December 1944, because the Germans were still confident that they could hold back the Bolshevik horde from the East, they were creating gas type air-raid shelters in Auschwitz at that moment. They had started constructing these things just before. So there was still some local, small-term, small site construction activity going on. This was very primitive, but certainly the SS would have been able in November 1944, even December

1944, to repair the roof and to remove the evidence of the holes. The invasion, the offensive, only started on January 12th, as we have established before."[112]

With the trap set and sprung, Irving had played his ace—but he had no time to capitalize on it. Therefore, as the clock was ticking away the last seconds, he salvaged what he could by providing the journalists with some quotable quotes. Declaring the holes in the roof to be the "cardinal linch-pin of the Defence in this action," he inferred from the fact that the holes were invisible now that all "eyewitness evidence collapses" and that the people who had testified that these holes existed "are exposed for the liars they were."[113] With that, Justice Gray adjourned the proceedings until the next morning.

As I climbed down from the witness box, a smartly dressed man came down from the public gallery to meet me. I had noticed him before: every time I had offered a half-decent riposte to one of Irving's attacks he had smiled at me, sometimes even making a gesture of approval. He introduced himself: "I am Martin Gilbert." The eminent historian, who had not only written many books on the Holocaust but also the important *Auschwitz and the Allies,* which had been very important for my own research, sug-gested we go for tea at the nearby Waldorf Hotel. In the days that fol-lowed, his continuing presence in the public gallery and his appraisals of the exchanges at the end of each morning and afternoon proved a great support.

Over tea, I told Gilbert that Irving had shrewdly chosen the roof of the gas chamber of Crematorium 2 as his battleground. I knew that he could not win his argument, but neither could I destroy it because no blueprints exist that show either the holes or the hollow columns underneath which had been installed adjacent to four of the seven concrete structural columns carrying the roof. When Gilbert asked if there was any visual evidence for the holes, I told him of a photo taken of the outside of Crematorium 2 during construction which showed the box-like "chimneys" that gave access to the holes, air photos taken by allied reconnaissance planes in 1944 that showed the holes from the air, and several drawings created in 1945 by a surviving slave worker of Crematorium 3. The convergence of evidence showed that there had been holes in the roof. I also told Gilbert that my inability to positively identify remains of the holes in the ruined slab had in the past given me cause to question the evidence that there had been holes—the eyewitness testimony, the 1943 photo, the 1944 air pho-tos, and the 1945 drawings. However, I had been unable to come up with a plausible explanation of all of that evidence without the assumption of the holes, and therefore I had made the logical conclusion, which is that if all the evidence pointed to the wartime existence of the holes and the holes were not there anymore, they must have been closed at some time after the air photos taken in 1944. I admitted that I had failed to make this point clearly because Irving had the habit of constantly interrupting me. Gilbert asked me if I knew a way to move away from the holes, and I replied that the only option I saw was to shift the discussion to Crematoria 4 and 5. I explained that, unlike Crematoria 2 and 3, Crematoria 4 and 5 had been designed from the outset with a genocidal intent. They were simple and relatively cheap buildings, to be true, but all the functionally awkward aspects of Crematoria 2 and 3 as killing stations—the underground gas chamber that required mechanical ventilation, the elevator that connected the basement where the killing took place with the main floor where the incineration took place—had been dropped. Instead these buildings showed a very simple, functional layout on the same level, with aboveground gas chambers that could be ventilated by just opening a door.

It was essential to get an opportunity to discuss the one surviving blueprint of Crematorium 4 (and by implication of Crematorium 5): it clearly marked the 30 cm by 40 cm large "holes" through which the Zyklon B had been introduced. In this case, the blueprint, eyewitness testimony, work orders for "gas-tight shutters" measuring 30 cm by 40 cm, and the survival of several of these shutters in a storeroom of the Auschwitz museum converged at the one conclusion that, indeed, these "holes" had been used to introduce Zyklon B. Furthermore, the argument that these gas-tight shutters could be explained by calling the rooms that had them a gas-proof air-raid shelter was obviously absurd once one studied the blueprint of the building or glanced at the reconstruction: the walls of those spaces were thin, and the roof was of a very light construction. In the reconstructions of Crematorium 4 made by Braithwaite and Austin, I had taken care to choose these views so that it would be very clear that the roof was in no way blast-proof. But how to introduce this material, which was originally created for a lengthy examination-in-chief that Mr. Rampton had chosen not to conduct?

The next day, Irving began with the promise that no more traps would be sprung: "I am sure the Professor will appreciate advance notification. There are no more hidden booby-traps or mines."[114] I was not convinced. Irving then continued to question me about the roof of Morgue 1 of Crematorium 2, showing images taken from the underside taken by negationists. According to him, it did not show any tampering. The fact there were no holes "blows holes in the whole of the gas chamber story."

> If there are no holes in that roof, no holes in that roof, there are no holes now and there were no holes then, and that totally demolishes the evidence of your so-called eyewitnesses.[115]

Irving continued to incant variations of the "no holes, no holocaust" formula as if casting a spell. If anyone was entranced, it was only Irving himself. And so he went on, conjuring up a chimerical vision of the decade-long struggle between negationists and Holocaust scholars. Claiming that it was a common ground between the two sides that "the whole story rises and falls on the existence of holes," Irving expressed his astonishment that Holocaust scholars such as myself had not been "frantically looking for those holes to prove us wrong."

> They have not bothered to scrape off the rubble on the top to look for the evidence on top of the holes. They have not bothered to make any kind of survey clearing aside this brick mess underneath, digging deeper in, looking for evidence that those holes exist. Frankly, my Lord, I cannot accept the notion that the Nazis, in the last frantic days when we heard yesterday they were in a blue funk, blowing up buildings, taking out the equipment, dismantling everything nut and bolt, that they would have gone round with a bucket of cement filling in the holes of the buildings they were about to dynamite.[116]

Sitting in the public gallery, journalist James Dalrymple was stunned by the endless back and forth on the holes, and the fact that both Irving and I were still able to behave like "gentlemen and experts."

> At the lunchtime interval, wandering the court buildings and trying to come to terms with what I was seeing and hearing, I felt like a man in some kind of Kafkaesque dream. What was going on here? Was this some kind of grotesque Monty Python episode? Everybody seemed to be in such good spirits. As if they were taking part in some kind of historical parlour game. Spot the gas chamber for 20 points.[117]

On the stand, I shared Dalrymple's discomfort. I was not in good spirits and actually had great difficulty keeping my temper. But, in my breast pocket, I had the last letter written by my uncle before his deportation to Auschwitz and my grandmother's Yellow Star, more deadly than any verbal Yellow Star Irving may have suffered. It was not a parlor game for me.

Justice Gray did not seem very happy with the way Irving's cross-examination proceeded. It was amateurish and did not lead to any results. At a certain moment Irving raised the evidentiary value of the blueprints of Crematorium 2, and this promised a very long and detailed analysis of the various modifications of the plans of that basement which indicated a genocidal intent. Foreseeing an examination that could last hours, Justice Gray intervened, and told Irving that he wondered if this was a useful exercise if Irving's intention was to conclude at the end of all the testimony: "Oh well, that is very well, but it was just a delousing chamber or a disinfecting chamber."[118] Justice Gray stated that he did not want to spend a lot of time on what would be a purposeless discussion of the drawings. As an experienced cross-examiner, Rampton understood precisely Justice Gray's problem and immediately suggested that Irving be required to state his position on Morgue 1, "because otherwise, as your Lordship has just said, we could spend two hours going through the drawings and end up with the same conclusion as yesterday in cross-examination, 'Yes, it was a gas chamber, but not for live human beings.'" And he added: "If that is all that this examination is going to lead to, Mr Irving may as well come clean, say, 'Yes, I accept it was a gas chamber. Now, Mr van Pelt, how do you deal with the suggestion that [it] was for gassing corpses and clothes?'"[119] Justice Gray adopted Rampton's proposal and asked Irving what his position was going to be. Irving tried to evade the question, but Justice Gray insisted that he be given some idea of where Irving was going.

> [Justice Gray]: "Supposing that the evidence satisfies me that there is reason to believe that [what] was intended to be there was [a] gas chamber and not an air raid shelter, is that something you accept or dispute?"

> [Irving]: "It should be, with respect, my Lord, relatively easy for the witness to say there are two or three items, as he in fact said, which were to him, taken in conjunction with each other, adequate evidence that there was a sinister purpose."

> [Justice Gray]: "That is as may be, but I would like an answer to my question because I think you must come clean as to your position."

> [Irving]: "I do not think I am equivocating. My position on this particular room is that it was never used in the gas chamber sense, in the sense described by the eyewitnesses because of course the lack of holes proves that the eyewitnesses have lied."

> [Justice Gray]: "That is getting close to an answer but it is not

quite an answer. Are you accepting it was a gas chamber in the sense that it had the facility for gas to be inserted by whatever means, but contending that humans were never killed by gas in that chamber?"

[Irving]: "Certainly on one occasion it was referred to as a *Vergasungskeller* and also referred to as a *Sonderkeller,* a special cellar or special basement. That I also accept. What I do not accept is that it was going to be used for the mass killing of human beings by gas. This is a very clear statement. What I do postulate is that it was also simultaneously being held in prospect and even converted for use as an underground air raid shelter, being one of the very few subterranean buildings on the site in the event that mass attacks in this part of Poland also began, given the proximity of the IG Farben works."

[Justice Gray]: "I am sure I missed it, but was part of that answer that yes, you do accept that it was a gas chamber and that you accept that it was on occasion used for killing human beings?"

[Irving]: "I accepted it was referred to as there was gas chamber [*sic*], my Lord, which is not quite the same thing and there are documents—"

[Justice Gray]: "Are you accepting it was in fact there was [a] gas chamber?"

[Irving]: "That I have not seen evidence for."

[Justice Gray]: "So you are not accepting that?"

[Irving]: "I am not accepting that part of the statement because I have not seen any evidence that bears that part of the statement out. I have seen evidence that it was referred to by the German authorities as [a] *Vergasungskeller,* [a] room for gassing in."

[Justice Gray]: "But you still do not accept that it was in fact [a] gas chamber? Is that the position?"

[Irving]: "That is precisely my position, my Lord."[120]

After this surreal interchange it was time to consider the drawings. This proved my chance to reverse from defense to attack. That morning I had received from Canada the slides showing the reconstructions of the crematoria made by Braithwaite and Austin, and I suggested that it would be useful to show these slides in court, and slides of the blueprints. They would offer a convenient way to deal with this very difficult material. Justice Gray, who had made every indication before that he did not look forward to a slow, inept, and purposeless cross-examination on the plans, eagerly accepted my suggestion, and asked Irving if he could agree to it. Irving said yes, "provided it goes strictly to the issues that we have delineated." He rejected, however, a "Cook's tour of the building."[121] As I needed some time to prepare for the slide presentation, and as there was no projector in the courtroom, Justice Gray determined that the slide show would happen on the next court day, Friday, January 28.

The remainder of the afternoon proceeded without many surprises. Irving stayed close to the brief provided by the anonymous architect. The most important discussion concerned the elevator connecting the basement to the main floor of Crematorium 2. Several days earlier, when questioned about Bischoff's letter of February 11, 1943, which said that failure to deliver the blower for Morgue 1 would prevent the installation from being brought into operation, Irving had announced that the corpse elevator was to be the tool of "revenge." That tool had been forged for him by the anonymous architect. In his critique of my report, he had made a calculation of the total number of corpses that the elevator could hoist per day from the basement to the main floor. Assuming a carrying capacity of 200 kilos, assuming that the elevator would accommodate one attendant and one corpse, and assuming that one round trip would take 30 seconds, the anonymous architect went through the figures. He noted that the time increased by 1.5 sec for every additional passenger. Asking how long it would take for 2,000 people to travel up one floor, using a 2-person elevator, the architect came to (30 sec + 1.5 sec) × 1000 round trips = 31,500 seconds (or 8 hours 45 minutes). In a 3-person lift this would take 21,978 seconds (or 6 hours 6 minutes), in a 4-person lift 17,250 seconds (or 4 hours 48 minutes).

> Of course, live human passengers essentially loading themselves take significantly less time to load and unload than human cadavres, necessarily carefully placed on a delicate machine for fear of breaking it. Automatic controls will take significantly less time to operate than a manual cab control operated outside of the cab itself, by an operator on one floor who can only see the other floor by entering the lift shaft and peering up or down. Common sense alone tells us that each of the times given for the different loading capacities could be doubled or even tripled. It is also the undoubted fact that the smallest malfunction of the very heavily used and highly specialized lift machinery would bring the entire production line of killing and body disposal to a complete halt.[122]

I had read this reasoning the night before and had found that one of its flaws was the assumption that the elevator could only have carried 200 kilos. In fact, I had a copy of a document from February 1943 stipulating that the carrying capacity of the elevator should be doubled from 750 kilos to 1,500 kilos.

Taking the calculation of the anonymous architect as his point of departure, Irving presented the elevator as the crucial bottleneck in the whole operation.

> [Irving]: "You appreciate, do you not, that that lift shaft was the bottleneck through which all the victims of the Holocaust had to go, if we follow the standard version?"
>
> [van Pelt]: "I think most of the victims in the Holocaust died outside Auschwitz. So at least—"
>
> Q.: "These 500,000 you talk about?"
>
> A.: "—these people who went through that lift, that would have been a bottleneck between gassing and incineration."
>
> Q.: "I appreciate your earlier point. Of course far more people died than those 500,000 and I have never challenged that point, let there be no doubt about that. . . ."[123]

Whatever his view was, we were now at the bottleneck, and Irving asked if I could describe the speed of the "liquidation procedure—people being rammed into the gas chamber 2,000 at a time." I responded that the only "bottleneck" I could see was "the speed of incineration in the ovens."[124] But Irving remained with the elevator, and made the statement that it was the only connection between the basement and the ground floor. He asked me if I knew the carrying capacity of that elevator.

> [van Pelt]: "There is a document for that. The elevator, this document in March for that, I think it is March 1943, they carried the original one which was installed for 750 kilos."

> [Irving]: "750 kilos."

> A.: "They immediately asked to increase the carrying capacity of that elevator by providing extra cables to 1,500 kilos."[125]

Irving did not return to the carrying capacity. It was clear to me that an important assumption on which he planned to build his attack had been proven wrong. But Justice Gray did.

> [Justice Gray]: "Anyway, carrying a load of 1500 kilos, that would be how many corpses?"

> [van Pelt]: "An average [corpse would weigh] 60 kilos. It seems a little high, [but] that would be—the theoretical carrying capacity would be, let us say, 20 corpses, so that would be 20, 25 corpses."

> [Irving]: "The same question of course is how many people you can pack into a telephone box, but packing them in takes time. It would be difficult to envisage having a working lift system with people piled four or five or six or seven high, because quite simply the doors would not close."

> A.: "There were no doors."

> Q.: "There were no doors?"

> A.: "No. It was simply a platform which went up and down."

> Q.: "That would be even worse then. The bodies would presumably get jammed against the side of the lift shaft if they piled them too high. I am just looking at practicalities here, that although technically the final version of the lift, and I emphasise that, was going to have the 1500 kilogram capacity, in theory, when was that lift actually installed?"

> A.: "The 750 kilograms was installed by the time the building was finished and immediately they asked to double the capacity."

> Q.: "And the 1500 one was not of course installed at this time?"

> A.: "It was not immediately, but they asked immediately for the increase in the carrying capacity."[126]

Irving then asked how long it would take to make one round trip. I answered that there were too many variables and that I did not want to make a calculation right then and there. Irving did not agree, and forced me to make some "back-of-an-envelope" calculations. I was not able to provide much of an answer. My only comfort was that I realized that my answer did not really matter, as the whole purpose of cross-examination was to ask the right questions, and Irving's questions showed his lack of experience in cross-examining. Instead of leading me via a string of simple questions that could only be answered with a simple "yes" or "no" to the "inevitable" conclusion that the elevator could not have kept up with the ovens, he only sowed confusion, whereas it was incumbent on him to absolutely prove that the elevator was the bottleneck.

While I did not think much damage was done by my lackluster engagement with the elevator issue, I was thoroughly disgusted by the whole discussion. Others shared my anxiety. James Dalrymple described his own reaction in that Saturday's *Independent*.

> Irving gave him little leeway, and by late afternoon, with another verbal flourish, he suddenly produced what might be the main witness for his case. Not a human being—but something as mundane as the single lift-shaft connecting the "alleged" gas chamber with the crematorium ovens above. He called it the bottleneck. Or, as he put it, the bottleneck in the glass timing jar. The bottleneck that would blow holes in the Auschwitz story.
>
> Irving knows the value of a strong phrase, and the silence in Courtroom 73 seemed to deepen as he said it. We all knew what was coming. Even the judge murmured that he could see where this was leading. How could 500,000 bodies—the number estimated to have died in that one crematorium—be transported up a single lift-shaft, only about 9 ft square. Irving demanded that Van Pelt now do the arithmetic of nightmares. How much could the lift carry? 750 kilos, 1,500 kilos, 3,000 kilos? How many bodies would that be at, say 60 kilos a body? Were they in gurneys or were they just squeezed in, like people squashed into a telephone box? How long to take each batch up to the ovens? Ten minutes, or more, each batch? Twenty corpses at a time, or 25?
>
> Van Pelt entered into the exercise reluctantly, and his answers were unclear. It was not helpful to count the numbers of lift journeys, but rather the time it took to burn each batch. In the end, no conclusion was reached on this point. Nobody came up with a pat figure that would make such a logistics exercise possible or impossible during the years the crematorium was operational. But Irving repeated his phrase over and over again. The Bottleneck.
>
> And on the way home in the train that night, to my shame, I took out a pocket calculator and began to do some sums. Ten minutes for each batch of 25, I tapped in. That makes 150 an hour. Which gives 3,600 for each 24-hour period. Which gives 1,314,000 in a year. So that's fine. It could be done. Thank God, the numbers add up.
>
> When I realised what I was doing, I almost threw the little machine across the compartment in rage.

For Dalrymple, the exchange on the elevator revealed the character of that "strange and flourishing landscape that has come to be known as historical revisionism."

> It is an area of study with only one subject. The Holocaust. And it is a place where tiny flaws can be found—and magnified—in large structures, where great truths can be tainted and wounded by small discrepancies, where millions of dead people can be turned into a chimera. And where doubt can be planted like seed in the wind, to grow and fester as the screams of history grow fainter with the years.

A dark and dangerous place where even reasonable people start to do furtive sums on pocket calculators.[127]

Dalrymple was not the only one who took out his pocket calculator. Rampton felt that my answers on the elevator issue were less than clear and decided that in re-examination he would return to it. Indeed, after Irving finished his cross-examination on Friday afternoon, Rampton came back to it, but instead of approaching it from an engineer's point of view, as the anonymous architect had done, he looked at it from a different perspective. If the ovens could incinerate 1440 bodies in one day, was it feasible that the elevator would have been able to hoist that number of corpses from the basement to the incineration room? Also, unlike Irving, he offered me simple questions that could be answered with a simple "Yes" or "No."

[Rampton]: "Then the lift capacity. Tell me if I have the figures right. I think you said it could take 1500 kilograms?"

[van Pelt]: "They were expanding—the original one was 750 kilograms and they were ordering reinforcement of the cables so that it could take 1500 kilos."

Q.: "I am talking about their intentions."

A.: "Yes."

Q.: "This is all what I call intentional material. If the average corpse, balancing between young children and fat men, if you like, is, say, 60 kilograms, yes?"

A.: "Yes."

Q.: "Is that fair? I do not think in kilogrammes, you see, so I have to have your help."

A.: "Yes."

Q.: "60 kilograms, then the capacity for each hoist, each journey, would be about 25 corpses, would it not?"

A.: "Yes."

Q.: "The incineration capacity given in the letter of 28th June for all five crematoria, but for this one in particular, is 1440 corpses per 24 hours, is it not?"

A.: "Yes."

Q.: "That is, roughly speaking, if you take a 16 hour rather than a 24-hour period, about 90 corpses an hour, is it not?"

A.: "Yes."

Q.: "If it is 90 corpses an hour, then the lift can do more than that 90 in 15 minutes? If it can do 25 corpses a load?"

A.: "Yes."

Q.: "Then in an hour—"

[Justice Gray]: "More than four loads an hour?"

A.: "Certainly, sir, yes."

[Rampton]: "That is 50, roughly speaking, and you get to 90 before you got to the end of the hour?"

A.: "Yes."

Q.: "Does that seem to you feasible?"

A.: "Yes. It seems feasible to—certainly I think the elevator could keep up with the ovens."

Q.: "Yes. That is much more neatly put than I could have put it. Thank you."[128]

On January 28, 2000—the third day of my cross-examination—I arrived early in court to set up the projectors and load my slides. Irving also arrived early. He came up to me and asked how long my presentation would last. "One and half hours," I answered. "Very well," he replied, "it will allow me to take a decent nap."

I began my presentation with a number of axonometric representations of Crematorium 2, showing the building with its roofs removed. The point was to show the arrangement of the ventilation system that was designed to extract foul air from the incineration room, the autopsy rooms, and the basement, and to show arrangements of the ventilation system that was designed to introduce fresh air into Morgue 1, the basement space that was adapted into a gas chamber. Then I began what was effectively a walk-through of Crematorium 2. Justice Gray and Irving asked occasional questions. When I showed the entrance to the underground undressing room Irving asked "What kind of door would have been on that entrance?" I responded that neither the door nor the door frames had survived and that the drawings that depicted the entrance did not provide any information. Irving answered: "So it could have been an air raid shelter door?" "I don't know," I replied.[129] I was not surprised by Irving's question. Irving had suggested at various occasions that the basement spaces of Crematorium 2 had functioned as a gas-proof air-raid shelter. This explanation justified, according to him, why the door to Morgue 1 had been a "gas door," as was clearly stated in one of the letters sent by the Auschwitz construction office to a workshop. The problem with this explanation, as I had pointed out in my expert report, was that if the smaller Morgue 1, which eyewitnesses said had served as a gas chamber, had been an air-raid shelter, one would also have expected the larger Morgue 2, which served as an undressing room, to have served as an air-raid shelter, but there was no evidence that its two entrances had ever been equipped with gas doors. Rampton immediately realized that it would be good to establish this point, and at the end of the walk-through, before I turned to a discussion of the blueprints, he rose to ask a question.

[Rampton]: "Could I ask one question before we leave the picture? It is out of order. I know."

[Justice Gray]: "Mr Irving, I think this is sensible, do you not?"

[Irving]: "Perfectly, my Lord."

[Justice Gray]: "We are not exactly playing by the rules at the moment."

[Rampton]: "Professor van Pelt, can I do it now before you come to the plans and the documents? You showed us the new entrance to the undressing room in '43."

[van Pelt]: "Yes."

Q.: "Do you know of any document which refers to gas tight doors for *Leichenkeller 2?*"

A.: "No, I do not. The only document which refers to a gas tight door quite literally is in relationship to Morgue 1, not to Morgue 2."[130]

Having completed the walk-through of Crematorium 2, I turned to the blueprints of the basement, showing the modifications that clearly pointed at the adaptation of Morgue 1 into a gas chamber. One of the main changes in the arrangement of the basement of Crematorium 2 that pointed at the transformation of that space into a killing installation was the removal of the corpse-slide and the creation of an outside staircase leading down into the basement on the street side of the building.

[Irving]: "Just to be perfectly plain, the entrance which is moved to the street side of the building did not have a slide, did it?"

[van Pelt]: "No. . . . This other entrance does not have a slide."

Q.: "Would it not be a reasonable inference that the architects had decided that, being good architects, they ought to design a building where people had ways of getting in there where they might not have to mingle with corpses going in?"

A.: "Can you repeat that?"

Q.: "They decided that they need, for matters of taste and decency, to have a clean side of the building where people could go in without having to jostle with corpses that might be infected going down the steps and they decided, therefore, for pure hygienic reasons to move the staircase?"

A.: "That would perfectly—that would be perfectly fine. The problem is how do you then get the corpses into the building?"[131]

I hesitated initially because, of course, the whole suggestion that the Auschwitz architects had been concerned about matters of "taste and decency" in the design of the crematorium was not perfectly fine, but perfectly absurd. But I decided not to make that point, because that would have begun a rather useless discussion about the taste and decency of the men who ran Auschwitz. The more practical question of why the Germans would have replaced an efficient way of bringing corpses into the basement with a very awkward way of doing so seemed to offer greater opportunity to establish some clear, uncontroversial facts. I explained that the new access, with its tight turn at the end of the flight of stairs, did not allow for the easy movement of people carrying a stretcher. "It gets very, very tight," I explained. Immediately Justice Gray interjected: "So do you deduce that it is live people who are going down to that morgue?" "Yes," I answered. As I expected, Irving could not allow this point to pass by unchallenged: "But is there not an elevator or a hoist being installed which, we are told, is capable of carrying large numbers of bodies from the basement up to the furnaces? Could that elevator not also have been used to carry them down in the first place?"[132] It was an obvious point which could, however, be easily answered: the only access to the corpse elevator was through the autopsy rooms or the incineration room.

Friday afternoon Irving returned once again to the holes in the roof. He wondered if I had never felt the urge "to go and start scraping just where you know those holes would have been because you know approximately where, like a two or three foot patch of gravel to scrape away?"[133] I responded that I did not and that it violated my understanding of responsible preservation practices. Irving pressed on, and claimed that as "serious doubts have been raised as to the integrity of the gas chamber notion," it would be in everybody's interest if I would go to Auschwitz and scrape off the gravel from "the virgin concrete slab beneath to see if those holes were there."[134] Irving argued that it would be a very easy and cheap way to resolve a case that had already cost too much money, and that if I had done my homework on the roof, it would have saved everyone a lot of money and time. Rampton then interjected that the issue of the holes had come up only two days earlier. Justice Gray agreed. He noted that Irving's argument went nowhere "because if it was not raised as an issue until two days ago, how much money has been spent on it is really an irrelevant consideration." Irving replied that "if this matter had not occurred to the Defence, my Lord, then might I suggest with the utmost respect it ought to have occurred to the Defence."[135] But it was clear even to Irving that Justice Gray was not impressed, and so he suddenly announced that he would abandon the question of the holes in the roof, "which are central to my case." Rampton immediately rose to ask Irving what he meant when he said that the holes were central to his case. "I ask the question rhetorically, what case? This is a case about Mr Irving's state of mind at the time when he made certain utterances." The holes in the roof had never been an issue before, and therefore, Rampton argued, "they have really got very little to do with the case which your Lordship is trying."[136]

> [Irving]: "So suddenly once again the Defence is shifting its ground and suddenly what actually happened is of less moment."

> [Justice Gray]: "No, I think you are not doing justice to the point Mr Rampton is making. He is really making what is, I suppose, in a way an historical point. The case against you is that, historically, you have not approached the issue of the gas chambers in an honest, conscientious way as an historian. That is either right or wrong, looking at the history, but this holes in the roof point seems to have cropped up terribly recently and, although I might be entitled to draw inferences perhaps—"

> [Irving]: "My Lord, it has not cropped up recently."

> [Justice Gray]: "—about your approach from the way you are dealing with it, Mr Rampton is right, is he not?"[137]

Standing in the witness box, I perceived from Justice Gray's remark that he could draw inferences about Irving's approach from the way he had brought the holes into play. But Irving could not resist the temptation to grandstand once more on the issue of the holes:

> [Irving]: "And you do accept, do you not, that if you were to go to Auschwitz the day after tomorrow with a trowel and clean away the gravel and find a reinforced concrete hole where we anticipate it would be from your drawings, this would make an open and shut case and I would happily abandon my action immediately?"

> [van Pelt]: "I think I cannot comment on this. I am an expert on Auschwitz and not on the way you want to run your case."

Q.: "There is my offer. I would say that that would drive such a hole through my case that I would have no possible chance of defending it any further."

[Justice Gray]: "That is not really a question, is it?"

[Irving]: "Well, I am asking, the point I am making, my Lord, is that he has been to Auschwitz once a year for a number of years. The temptation must have occurred to him to go there with a trowel and scrape away the gravel and look for the hole, not just one but three of them, and he assures us that they were built-in holes, not just casual holes."

[Justice Gray]: "I think if he had been digging around with a trowel he would have got into trouble with the authorities, would he not?"

[Irving]: "It has been done by others, my Lord, I understand."

[Justice Gray]: "Well, with their permission. I do not think that is really a question in a way. You have made the point and I understand it, that nobody has actually done the excavation work or whatever you like to call it."

[Irving]: "This is, obviously, not the time to make submissions, so I will not, my Lord, and with that I will end my cross-examination of this witness with my many thanks. I wish you a pleasant flight home."[138]

This brought my cross-examination to a sudden and unexpected end. Rampton followed with a short re-examination, in which he set out, in his own words, to tie up some loose ends. As a skilled barrister, Rampton had no difficulty making his points. He presented me with Olère's plan of Morgue 1 of Crematorium 3 and the American aerial photo of 1944. Rampton asked me if I saw in Olère's drawing the alignment of the squares that represented the gas insertion columns. Then he asked me to consider the aerial photograph and asked: "How does the alignment of that photograph, those black dots, match what Olère has drawn?" I responded: "It seems identical."[139] Rampton asked me then if it was possible that Olère could have seen the photograph before he made that drawing. I answered that the photograph was only de-classified in 1979 and that Olère had made his drawing in 1945.

Rampton then turned to Irving's suggestion that Morgue 1 of Crematorium 2 had served as a gas chamber to delouse corpses and asked me if there were any contemporaneous documents referring to the gassing of corpses.

[van Pelt]: "I have never seen or heard of a document like that."

[Rampton]: "Are there any eyewitness accounts from either side or any side?"

A.: "No. There are no eyewitness accounts."

Q.: "Can you think of a reason why you would need to have, leaving aside the air raid question, we will come back to that, a double 8 millimetre thick glass spy hole to observe the gassing of corpses or clothes?"

A.: "I cannot think of any reason."

Q.: "Can you think of any reason why that door with the *Guck-loch* should have a metal grille on the inside of it?"

A.: "No. I cannot think of any reason."

Q.: "If it were an air raid shelter, can you think of any reason why the metal grilles should be on the inside?"

A.: "No, I cannot think of any reason."

Q.: "We will just have a look at the pictures in Pressac in a moment. You answered me this morning, I know, but I will repeat the question because it is connected. Are there any contemporaneous documents referring to the provision of gas stores or any similar equipment for *Leichenkeller 2*?"

A.: "No, there are no documents."

Q.: "What is the size of *Leichenkeller 2*, the *Auskleidekeller*, as I call it, as compared with *Leichenkeller 1*?"

A.: "[It is] one-third larger or maybe one-half larger than *Leich-enkeller 1*."

Q.: "Suppose Mr Irving's thesis is right, the corpses must have been undressed in the *Auskleidekeller* and then dragged through to *Leichenkeller 1* to be disinfested, yes?"

A.: "If he accepts it was an *Auskleidekeller*, yes."

Q.: "We can see it was from the documents. We do not have to argue about that. How would the clothes which had been removed from the corpses have been deloused in *Leichenkeller 2*?"

A.: "The only thing, I think, is to bring them also in *Leichenkeller 1*, to undress the corpses or maybe have the corpses dressed, deloused and then everything is deloused together, I do not know. The procedure seems to me so absurd to start with that—"

Q.: "I know. We just have to dot i's and cross t's sometimes. That is all. I said you would find these questions a bit silly, I am sure."[140]

As Rampton asked me clear questions that finally offered me the opportunity to give clear answers, I admired not only his great skill as a lawyer, but I also appreciated all the time we had spent together, in chambers, in Auschwitz, and, finally, at his house. He had gotten to know me well, and thus he was able to get the best out of me.

Finally I was released as a witness. I descended from the witness box and rejoined Rampton, Rogers, Jersak, and the others of the defense team. As I sat down I found a wonderful little doodle drawn by Rampton during my explanation of why the amount of coke delivered to Auschwitz would have sufficed to incinerate the alleged number of corpses. It showed a large battleship named SS Irving, with a tattered swastika flag, sinking after having been torpedoed by a submarine identified as the HMS van Pelt. When Justice Gray adjourned the proceedings to Monday, January 31, and I had the opportunity to ask Rampton why he had drawn that doodle during my refutation of Irving's thesis that there would not have been enough coke to incinerate the victims, he simply replied: "That moment, I believe, we won the case." I asked him how he knew. He replied: "I just watched Charles Gray's face."

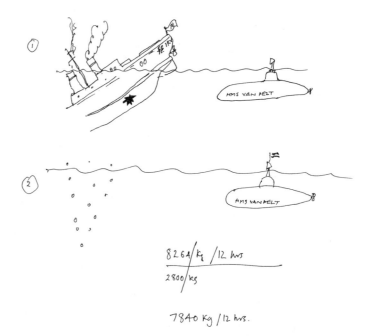

$$\frac{8264/k_2 \ /12 \ hrs}{2800/kg}$$

$$7840 \ Kg \ / 12 \ hrs.$$

Doodle, drawn by Richard
Rampton, January 26, 2000.

Richard Rampton.
26 . 1 . 00 .

We returned to Rampton's chambers. As we reviewed the days that had passed, it was clear that 95 percent of my report had not been challenged at all, and that it included the (for Irving) very damaging parts on negationist historiography in general and Leuchter in particular. Of the parts that had been attacked, most stood unscathed, and while I had not been able to produce the holes like a rabbit from a magician's hat, it seemed that in the end the argument about the holes had done Irving more damage than good. Rampton predicted that Justice Gray would not accept Irving's argument concerning the holes and that he would argue that as a historian, Irving, or for that matter I, had to weigh the evidence of the absence of signs of holes in the roof of the morgue against the opposing evidence that there were chimneys running through the roof. Rampton believed that I had done well to stress that it was difficult to verify by looking at the ruins whether or not holes had at one time existed and that my suggestion that the holes had been backfilled was plausible enough. He predicted that Justice Gray would take Tauber's evidence concerning the holes seriously, and that he would be particularly impressed by the convergence between Olère's drawings and the aerial photos. In short, Rampton thought that Justice Gray would determine that the apparent absence of evidence of holes in the roof of Morgue 1 of Crematorium 2 would fall short of providing sufficient reason to reject the convergence of evidence that the holes had existed.

That weekend my writing partner Debórah Dwork, who had crossed the ocean to give me spiritual support, and I enjoyed the many treats of London, the city where twenty years earlier we had met as graduate students. We were sure that the battle over Auschwitz had ended. We were wrong. When we returned to Courtroom 73 on Monday morning, Irving recalled me as a witness. He was to shoot his last torpedo. It concerned a central document in the case: Bischoff's letter of June 28, 1943, that listed the incineration capacity of the Auschwitz crematoria as 4,756 corpses in 24 hours. (See Chapter 5 for the full story about this challenge.)

During his own cross-examination a week earlier, Irving had first suggested that the letter was a forgery. When Rampton asked Irving why the camp needed such an excessive incineration capacity, Irving had responded that "this is one of the few documents whose integrity I am going to challenge."

[Rampton]: "Ah! On what basis, please tell us?"

[Irving]: "Well, I prefer to discuss this with one of the expert historians who you are calling as witnesses."

[Justice Gray]: "No."

[Rampton]: "No, absolutely not, Mr Irving. Do not keep your cards in your pocket, it is not allowed."

[Justice Gray]: "You have to explain why now."

A.: "Well, as I explained already to the court and we discussed this briefly with Professor Watt, all German documents of this character had to follow a standard layout, a German Civil Service layout, if you can put it like this. They were typed in a certain way. They had certain characteristics like the security classification and so on put in. Certain things were written in by hand. Certain things were typed in. There are I think five or six different versions of this document I have seen in the files over the last couple of years, and there are a number of discrepancies. I am only going to point to one discrepancy and this is right in the top left. The '31550' has been typed in."

[Justice Gray]: "Why is that a discrepancy?"

A.: "My Lord, if you go back to page 39 you will see that characteristically it would start off with 'Brief Tagebuch' BFTGB. This is a very good one for comparison. Then you follow with a handwritten number 24365 which was always handwritten on the documents, followed then by the '43' which is the year and that is missing in this page 49, the year is missing and the year is always there normally, followed by JA, and if it is supposed to be 'Janisch' it should be a JA with an umlaut, followed on page 49 by NE full stop, dash, and there is no other document in the entire Auschwitz archives which has a secretary initial 'NE.'"

[Justice Gray]: "Why do you say that is the secretary?"

A.: "The last initials to come there would always be the secretary who has typed the document. The one before it is the one who has dictated it. So that is the discrepancy, just in that one line. The line above the date we are missing the word 'Auschwitz.' So this is a document that I am very unhappy with, not to mention the fact that the figures do not tally with any of the established figures that are provided by the Topf company who actually manufactures these crematoria."

[Rampton]: "Yes, Mr Irving. That is what happens, is it not? You come across something absolutely insuperable, so immediately you cast doubt on its authenticity?"[141]

Irving promised in court many lines of enquiry which he in the end did not pursue. But the challenge to Bischoff's letter of June 28th did materialize. The first time he came back to it was on January 25th, after I had argued that the fear of typhus did not justify the absurdly high incineration capacity of the Auschwitz crematoria. As the letter of June 28, 1943, was a major piece of evidence in my argument, Irving decided to "poison the well" by throwing suspicion on it.

[Irving]: "Can I ask, Professor van Pelt, has it ever crossed your mind that this document of 28th June 1943 might not be authentic or a document of integrity? Did you ever investigate that possibility? Did you check any details about it? Did you just accept it at face value?"

[van Pelt]: "I think that the document is in perfect accordance with all the other documents."

Q.: "Do you know anything about the history of that document, where it came from?"

A.: "No, I do not know. Moscow, it has been in Moscow. It has been made available, for example, in the Vienna trial. It was available earlier. There was another copy of this document in a DDR archive in Do[rn]burg. This document has been known for many years, since shortly after the war. The document seems to be perfectly in line with other documents. It is a carbon copy. It is not on letterhead, like most of the copies in the *Zentralbauleitung*. It seems to be sitting nice in its sequence of other documents. So I have no reason to doubt the integrity of the file or the integrity of the document itself."

Q.: "Professor van Pelt, you were sitting in court yesterday when I challenged that document piece by piece, and indicated the discrepancies on the document which gave not just one discrepancy but several discrepancies which indicated there was every reason to doubt whether this was an original document or whether it is was, indeed, a true document?"

A.: "You can do that, but I have not changed my mind on this. I do not think that you have brought any kind of convincing evidence for me to change my mind on this document."[142]

That day Irving gave up trying to discredit the letter, but when he saw me back in court on Monday, as a spectator, he saw it as an opportunity to return to it. He called me back to the witness stand and presented me with the various observations that he made a week earlier, to which he added one other issue.

[Irving]: "Will you now look five or six lines lower down to the address: 'SS Wirtschafts-Verwaltungs-Hauptamt, Amtsgruppenchef C.' I draw your attention now to the following line. Is there anything missing from that line 'SS Brigadeführer u. Generalmajor'?"

[van Pelt]: "Generalmajor SS would have been normally—"

Q.: "Generalmajor der Waffen SS?"

A.: "Yes."

Q.: "Have you seen any other documents whatsoever in the entire construction files of the Auschwitz office, either in Moscow or in the Auschwitz archives now, in which the words 'Der Waffen SS' are omitted after the word 'Generalmajor'?"

A.: "I cannot comment on that."

Q.: "In other words, the address is improper in its present form; is that correct?"

[Justice Gray]: "Well, he cannot comment."[143]

Irving continued to make some comments about the contents of the document. The fact that Crematorium 1 was listed was suspicious, as it had just been taken out of commission. I responded that it was still intact and that it actually remained on standby throughout 1943. When Irving raised the point that at the end of June Crematorium 2 was also out of commission, I responded that the letter was an exercise in general accounting, reminding the court that the letter went back to a request which had been made early in January 1943, when Kommandant Höss requested an accounting of total cremation capacity in the camp.

That same day, Mr. Justice Gray also asked me some questions about the document.

[Justice Gray]: "You are quite right, it is. But I want to ask you a question which I hope does reflect the cross-examination, and that is this, Professor van Pelt. Taking on board, as it were, all the points that have been put to you by Mr Irving about the authenticity of this document, do you have a view about it? Are you doubtful about it?"

[van Pelt]: "If this document were to pop up right now, after having not been seen for 50 or 60 years, given the kind of challenges which have been made by Holocaust denier/revisionist historians, however one would want to call people who challenge the historical record, I would be more suspicious, because, you know, where does this document come from? The issue is, however, that this document has been in existence, and the records of these documents, before ever a challenge was being made to the incineration capacity of the crematoria. In fact, this document shows a much lower incineration capacity of the crematoria than we find in the testimonies of Höss and others.

So what I do not understand is what purpose would have been served, let us say, in the 1950s by, let us say, somebody who wants to make a case that Auschwitz was an extermination camp, by creating a document, by falsifying a document, which shows a lower incineration rate for the crematoria than that which has been attested to under oath by the German eyewitnesses. That is the discrepancy. So, given the fact that it is lower, and given the fact that it appeared at a time that no one was challenging the incineration capacity, because the German testimony on it was kind of self-evident, and given the fact also that this document, I think, shows a very good convergence with Tauber's testimony, and Tauber's testimony which after 1945 really was not published until Pressac did it—and Tauber describes in detail the way the corpses in the incinerators were incinerated, with many corpses at the time, and he gives times for this, and in fact Tauber's figures do converge with this one—I think there is absolutely no reason to doubt the authenticity of this document as far as the content is concerned."[144]

That same evening, I compared the letter of June 28, 1943, with a small collection of German documents which I had brought with me. The next day I returned to the witness box, armed with a sheaf of documents that addressed most of Irving's suspicions. During my examination-in-chief, I presented the court with the other version of the same letter, one that came from the Staatliche Archivverwaltung, Archivdepot Dornburg in the former GDR, which had been made available to the Auschwitz archive years earlier. I told the court that this copy had been introduced in the Dejaco/Ertl trial held in Vienna in the early 1970s. It was clear that the Dornburg copy was a typed copy of the original, as it was marked with the heading *Abschrift,* and on the bottom of the paper one could read "*Für die Richtigkeit der Abschrift*" which means "for the accuracy of this copy." I argued that given the fact that there were two different versions of the same letter in two different archives, it was very unlikely that they were forgeries. I also introduced many different letters which showed that, in contrast to Irving's assertion, there was no standard format in the way the registration line was made, the dates were written, and so on. I also showed that sometimes the registration number was written, and sometimes it was typed. I concluded that "the only conclusion one can draw out of this is that there was no standard procedure in the Zentralbauleitung."[145]

In cross-examination, Irving continued his attack on the document. He added a new reason to doubt the authenticity of the document.

[Irving]: "There is one final point, my Lord, which is a fourth question, which is possibly new and I would certainly be willing to let Mr Rampton come back on this one. The serial number of the document 31550, is that in sequence with the other documents of those days?"

A.: " In the file, you mean?"

Q.: "Yes."

A.: "I do not remember. I looked at the document in the file originally in relationship to the contents and not in relationship to the serial number. I am happy to go back, when I am back in North America, and have the whole file printed out, and then this thing could be reconsidered."

Q.: "Again, I have to ask the question this way. Would it surprise you to hear that the number is way out of sequence by several weeks?"[146]

This exchange marked the end of my testimony as an expert witness. I returned to Canada. Back home, I decided to have another look at

Bischoff's letter. I assumed that if the document was a Soviet forgery, it would have been made to serve a contemporary purpose. The only time that it could have served such a purpose was in 1945, when the Soviet State Extraordinary Commission for the Investigation of Fascist and Nazi Crimes ran a forensic investigation in Auschwitz. Remarkably enough, the Soviets did not use the document, and they did not publish it in their "Statement of the Extraordinary State Committee for the Ascertaining and Investigation of Crimes Committed by the German-fascist Invaders and Their Associates in the Oswiecim Death Camp" of May 6, 1945. It was not difficult to see why not: the Soviet investigators had assumed almost double the incineration rate mentioned in the letter.

Crematorium 1:	300 per day (Soviet) /	340 (German)
Crematorium 2:	3,000 per day (Soviet)/	1,440 (German)
Crematorium 3:	3,000 per day (Soviet)/	1,440 (German)
Crematorium 4:	1,500 per day (Soviet)/	768 (German)
Crematorium 5:	1,500 per day (Soviet)/	768 (German)
Total:	9,300 per day (Soviet)/	4,756 (German)

It is clear: the letter of June 28, 1943, did not serve the purposes of the Soviet State Extraordinary Commission for the Investigation of Fascist and Nazi Crimes, and it was not considered.

Nor did the letter support the conclusions of Professor Roman Dawidowski of the Polish committee of investigation, which did its investigations in the wake of the Soviet commission.

Crematorium 1:	300 per day (Polish)/	340 (German)
Crematorium 2:	2,500 per day (Polish)/	1,440 (German)
Crematorium 3:	2,500 per day (Polish)/	1,440 (German)
Crematorium 4:	1,500 per day (Polish)/	768 (German)
Crematorium 5:	1,500 per day (Polish)/	768 (German)
Total:	8,300 per day (Polish)/	4,756(German)

Hence, on February 8th, I faxed a short note with these figures to Rampton and added the rhetorical question:

> So the question is: why would they have created a document that would only support 50% or 55% of their own estimate—an estimate which had been basic in their determination that 4 million people had died in Auschwitz?

During my cross-examination, Irving had raised the issue of the serial number of the document: 31550. He had suggested that the number was "way out of sequence by several weeks." On my return home, I took a simple sample from my archive: file BW 30/7 BW 30/34, which includes various letters concerning the construction of the crematoria. This file contained a letter dated June 23 with the serial number 31370, and it contained a letter dated July 10 with the serial number 32372. In short, in seventeen days the Zentralbauleitung had produced 1,000 items with a serial number in the correspondence register, or an average of 59 items a day. This means that if the office had produced the same amount of letters every day, the item with the serial number 31550 would have been produced on either June 26 or 27 (31370 + 59 + 59 + 59 = 31547). In other words, if the letter was out of sequence at all—and it could well be that it was drafted on June 26 or 27 and that on that day the typist checked the serial numbers in the correspondence register—it was only out of sequence by one or two days. Irving's attempt to use the serial number to poison the well was not substantiated by the evidence. In fact, the serial number suggested that the letter had been drafted shortly before the date indicated on the letter, exactly as one would expect.

The final reason that made me decide that I had been right to trust the letter was the fact that in the Moscow file 314, in which it was preserved, it is followed by a translation made by a certain Wolynskaja. This translation is dated April 28, 1945. Remarkably enough, the translator Wolynskaja did pick up the mistake in Kammler's title. She (partly) corrected it in the translation, where she identifies Kammler as "SS-Brigadeführer and General Major SS." We saw that Irving had paid specific attention to the fact that there was a mistake in the title of Hans Kammler. Irving was right that such a mistake is unusual, but it was not completely impossible because the letter was drafted by Rudolf Jährling, a civilian heating engineer employed in the technical department of the Zentralbauleitung. What is interesting, however, is that the translator Wolynskaja picked up the mistake and partially corrected it. Because the mistake was recognized in April 1945, it is unlikely that if the document was a forgery it would have been allowed to sit with a mistake. This closed the case for me.

With Rampton's continuing cross-examination of Irving and Irving's cross-examination of Christopher Browning, Richard Evans, Peter Longerich and Hajo Funke, Auschwitz largely disappeared from the courtroom. Now Rampton pursued Irving's systematic distortion of Nazi history and focused on his racism and anti-Semitism, arguing that these beliefs had motivated his negationism. And Irving engaged Browning in a polite discussion on certain aspects of Operation Barbarossa, exchanged angry words with Evans on the latter's alleged dislike for him, unsuccessfully tried to trump Longerich on Hitler's role in the Final Solution of the Jewish Problem, and argued with Funke about the democratic credentials of German neo-Nazi organizations. But the fighting spirit had somehow left Irving when the battle of the holes had drawn to its inconclusive end.

The issue of Auschwitz returned to Courtroom 73 on March 15, the day of the closing statements. First Rampton presented the case for Auschwitz. He repeated from his opening speech information about how Leuchter had changed Irving's position. Then he quoted Irving's contention that "forensic chemistry is an exact science" and turned it against him, stating that the "small, but significant, traces of cyanide" that Leuchter had found in the walls of the homicidal gas chambers actually proved that these spaces had been used to kill human beings. "Despite this," Rampton asserted, "Mr Irving continued to cling, and still clings, to Leuchter's 'forensic chemistry' as the flagship of his Holocaust denial."[147] Stating that in the end Irving had made, in the face of overwhelming evidence, numerous concessions, Rampton presented Irving's last stand on Auschwitz, the suggestion that the gas chambers were used for gassing "objects and cadavers," as "ludicrous" and "entirely inconsistent with his continued adherence to Leuchter's chemical analysis as being conclusive evidence that *Leichenkeller 1* never was a gas chamber." Furthermore it was inconsistent with Irving's assertion that "*Leichenkeller 1* could never have been a gas chamber because the remains of the roof that can be seen at Birkenau do not show the holes through which the gas pellets were thrown." Mentioning the coincidence between two pieces of independent evidence which demonstrated conclusively the existence of these holes—the plan Olère drew in 1945 of Crematorium 3 and the aerial photograph taken by the Allies in 1944, which was not released to the world until 1979—Rampton concluded that "in the light of Mr Irving's concession that *Leichenkeller 1* was indeed a gas chamber and of the fact that it is clear that it was never intended for the gassing of corpses or other inanimate objects, or for use as an air-raid shelter, the stark conclusion can only be this: It must have been used for gassing people, live people."[148]

Rampton continued with a review of Irving's statements about the numbers of people murdered at Auschwitz-Birkenau. "This last barricade of Mr Irving's is based on three distinctly unstable legs," Rampton asserted: the death books, the British intercepts of SS radio traffic, and the incineration capacity. Rampton made clear that the death books did not record the deaths of unregistered deportees. Hence the "death books" did not record the deaths of perhaps 1 million people who were killed on arrival. Rampton noted that "for exactly the same reasons as the death books make no reference to those murdered on arrival, it is not reasonable to expect that the radio messages from Auschwitz would: people who were not registered on arrival at Auschwitz because they were not destined for work in the camp but, instead, for immediate death in the gas chambers, would obviously not be mentioned in messages about recorded deaths." Finally Rampton repeated my argument that the potential incineration capacity at Auschwitz-Birkenau in 1943 far exceeded any possible mortality rate among the registered inmates from "natural" causes, including typhus. Rampton dismissed Irving's challenge to the authenticity of the Bischoff letter that contained the official incineration capacity of the crematoria, noting that if it was a postwar communist forgery, it was a strange one, "as the incineration capacity shown in the document—that is 4,756 corpses per 24 hours—is very significantly lower than that estimated by the Soviets and the Poles (both communist regimes) shortly after the War." Finally, he addressed Irving's challenge of the incineration capacity on the grounds that the coke delivered to Auschwitz would not have been sufficient to meet the required rate of incineration. "As Professor van Pelt demonstrated, this challenge is demolished by two considerations which Mr Irving had evidently ignored: first, the procedure for incineration at Auschwitz involved the simultaneous incineration of up to four or five corpses . . . in every muffle of the ovens; and, second, in consequence, the corpses themselves served as fuel for the ovens, the more particularly so if, as they generally did, they included the comparatively well fed corpses of people recently arrived on the trains and gassed on arrival." In conclusion, Rampton defined Irving's negationism as a "fraud."

> It originated with a piece of so-called scientific research which, on analysis, turns out, if it has any value at all, to support the overwhelming historical evidence that Auschwitz was indeed a gigantic death factory. Mr Irving's later adornments to his gas chamber denial also turn out to be fragile conjectures based on no significant research at all: it should be noted that Mr Irving has never himself been to Auschwitz to examine the archeological remains or the documentary evidence contained in the archive. It follows that some other reason must be sought to explain his devotion, over many years, and even in this court, though his case has changed and changed back again throughout the trial, to the bizarre idea that no significant numbers of people were murdered in the homicidal gas chambers at Auschwitz-Birkenau. The reasons are not far to seek.

As the evidence in this court has shown, Mr Irving is a right-wing extremist, a racist and, in particular, a rabid anti-Semite.[149]

Thus ended the defense's case for Auschwitz.

In his own concluding speech, Irving stated that a judgment against him would cause a "paralysis in the writing of history" and would turn people away from studying the Holocaust. "From then on, discussion will revolve around 'safe' subjects, like sacred texts in the Middle Ages, or Marx in the old Soviet Union, or the Koran in some fundamentalist state today." He then turned to the trial itself and lamented the way Justice Gray had allowed the defendants to argue that what Irving ought to have known was relevant to the case. Describing the experts as people who "were more expert in reporting each other's opinions and those of people who agree with them than in what the archives actually contain and what they do not contain," Irving finally turned to Auschwitz, which he described as "a football of politicians and statesmen ever since World War II." He admitted that he had never been to Auschwitz, because the Auschwitz authorities had forbidden him access, "and they have every reason to know why they do not want to allow a David Irving to get his hands on their papers."[150]

Then Irving considered the evidence that was available to him. When Auschwitz was "overrun" by the Soviets, Hitler would have acknowledged that fact without any comment. Irving stated that "the court might find it significant that he did not prick up his ears and say something like, 'Herr Himmler, I hope you made sure the Russians will not find the slightest trace of what we have been up to.' (Or even, 'I hope you managed to get those holes in the roof slab of Crematorium No. 2 cemented over before you blew it up.')"[151] As expected, Irving devoted considerable attention to the holes. Because they could not be seen today, "the eyewitnesses have turned out to be liars." Irving recalled his "very grand offer and very generous offer to the Defendants in this case saying, 'Come back with photographs of those holes and I will stop the case within 24 hours because my position will be indefensible.' I made that offer, not once, but twice," and concluded that "the Defendants have not attempted this exercise" because "they know and they knew from the outset that I was right about that roof." And he concluded that "their entire case on Crematorium 2—the untruth that it was used as a factory of death, with SS guards tipping canisters of cyanide-soaked pellets into the building through those four (non-existent) man-holes—has caved in, as surely as that flat roof."[152]

Then Irving continued to attack all the documents in the archive. He recalled Neufert's suggestion that the temperature of the morgue be controlled by heating and cooling it "to avoid damage to the corpses" and stated that "document after document fell by the wayside in this manner." All of this built up to an attack on Bischoff's letter of June 28, 1943, concerning cremation capacities. "Logistic problems defeat the document," Irving concluded before repeating his argument about the elevator, "the bottleneck in the entire Crematorium 2 'factory of death' story."[153]

Irving then dismissed my attempt to look at the evolution of the basement design of Crematorium 2 as a way to reconstruct the way Morgue 1 was transformed into a gas chamber and explained that the changes pointed to the use of the space as an air-raid shelter. In response to Rampton's suggestion that the location of the air-raid shelter was impractical, Irving replied that there were early warning posts in Holland. "So they would provide more than adequate time for the SS to gallop that 1.5 miles to this building with the concrete roof." What Irving did not explain was whether or not the Auschwitz SS would then "gallop" to the morgue/

shelter every time bombers passed over Holland—bombers on their way to Cologne, Hamburg, Berlin, Leipzig, and other German cities.

Having begun his cross-examination of me by challenging my expertise, he ended by mocking my statement that the use of gas chambers at Auschwitz and Birkenau was a "moral certainty." "Three times in his report, three times in his report, he fell back upon that semi-religious phrase,"[154] Irving recalled. He did not mention that I also provided a precise epistemological definition of this term. "I call that Moral Certainty, which hath for its object such beings as are less simple, and do more depend upon mixed circumstances," the natural philosopher John Wilkins declared in the seventeenth century. "Which though they are not capable of the same kind of Evidence with the former, so as to necessitate every man's assent, though his judgement be never so much prejudiced against them; yet may be so plain, that every man whose judgement is free from prejudice will consent unto them. And though there be no natural necessity, that such things must be so, and that they cannot be possibly otherwise, without implying a Contradiction; yet may they be so certain as not to admit of any reasonable doubt concerning them."[155] This ended Irving's final submission on Auschwitz.

If the trial had been held in front of a jury, the conclusion would have been swift and simple. At the end of Irving's final speech, Justice Gray would have given the jurors their instructions and they would have withdrawn to decide either in favor of the plaintiff or the defendants—and that would have been it. However, without a jury, Justice Gray was at liberty to write a substantial judgment which not only gave his finding but also the arguments of the case. Recognizing the historic importance of the trial and the great public service of a substantial judgment, Justice Gray decided to make full use of the opportunity, and he withdrew to his study. He proved a remarkably productive writer: when he emerged from his seclusion four weeks later, he had written a judgment that encompassed in its published form 349 pages, of which 264 pages reproduced the arguments (largely compiled as the trial progressed) and 57 pages gave his findings (written in the weeks following the closing arguments). Gray took 42 pages to sum up the arguments about Auschwitz and 8 pages to present his findings on that camp.

While Justice Gray went through the transcripts, I boarded in Vienna's *Südbahnhof* the direct overnight train for Cracow, which has a scheduled stop in Oswiecim. It was my first visit to the camp after my cross-examination.

As I walked the killing fields once again, I was once again reminded of the power of the place and the absurdity of Irving's arguments. Everything did fit together: the stories of the eyewitnesses, the documents in the archive, and the place itself. But for all its power, the landscape of Birkenau appeared vulnerable also. As I surveyed the ruins, I felt a sudden pride for having been allowed to represent the history of that place in the British High Court. It was the pride a captain of an ocean-going tug must feel as his ship approaches the bright yellow line of the Dutch coast with a priceless salvage in tow.

From Oswiecim I returned to Vienna, and from there to London, to attend the thirty-third and last day of the trial. On Tuesday, April 11, I arrived at the Royal Courts of Justice to witness the final act. To accommodate the enormous crowd, a large and very dignified neo-Gothic courtroom had been assigned; even so, the crowd was so large that many people found standing room only. But the dense and disorderly crowd inside and outside the court certainly provided a sense of excitement, and if I had had any doubts during the many days of cross-examination about the importance of the case, they certainly disappeared when I saw Auschwitz survivor Michael Lee, and Sir Martin Gilbert, and all those other people who had chosen to attend the trial, day in and day out, because it was important to them. With no room to spare, I ended up on the plaintiff's side, right behind a place that was tagged with a big sign: "Mr Irving." Exactly at ten Irving came in, in shirtsleeves. He looked enraged. He had just been hit by an egg thrown by a demonstrator. I reached out to shake his hand—we had, after all, made our good-byes after my cross-examination had come to an end in a rather civil manner, with Irving actually offering me his Auschwitz file as it had ceased to be of use to him. This time he was in no mood to be civil. Angrily he told me that he had been presented the night before with an itemized bill of all of the defendants' costs and that my bill had been outrageous. He had posted it on his Web site so that the whole world could learn "for how much I could be bought." I just shrugged my shoulders.

"All rise," the usher called, and Justice Gray entered, slightly less impatiently than in the days when he sat through endless lectures on holes, elevators, and other details of the Auschwitz crematoria. The court was now absolutely silent—silent as only a great crowd can be. Justice Gray began by stating that he had written a judgment, and that normally it would be simply handed down without any reading. Yet, "because of the public interest in this case, it seems to me to be right that I should read at any rate part of it."[156] Justice Gray then summarized the essential issues.

> Irving complains that certain passages in the Defendants' book accuse him of being a Nazi apologist and an admirer of Hitler, who has resorted to the distortion of facts and to the manipulation of documents in support of his contention that the Holocaust did not take place. He contends that the Defendants' book is part of a concerted attempt to ruin his reputation as an historian and he seeks damages accordingly. The Defendants, whilst they do not accept the interpretation which Irving places on the passages complained of, assert that it is true that Irving is discredited as an historian by reason of his denial of the Holocaust and by reason of his persistent distortion of the historical record so as to depict Hitler in a favourable light. The Defendants maintain that the claim for damages for libel must in consequence fail.[157]

Given the fact that the issues to be determined aroused the strongest passions, Gray made it clear that he did not regard it as being his task as the trial judge "to make findings of fact as to what did and what did not occur during the Nazi regime in Germany." This was a task for historians. "It is important that those reading this judgment should bear well in mind the distinction between my judicial role in resolving the issues arising between these parties and the role of the historian seeking to provide an accurate narrative of past events."[158]

Justice Gray observed that the charges leveled at Irving's historiography were at the heart of what Lipstadt wrote about him in *Denying the Holocaust*. Hence, "the question which I shall have to decide is whether the Defendants have discharged the burden of establishing the substantial truth of their claim that Irving falsified the historical record." After a review of the evidence, Gray decided that the Defendants' criticisms were justified and that Irving had treated the historical evidence "in a manner which fell far short of the standard to be expected of a conscientious

Mr. Justice Gray reading his judgment. In the foreground are Deborah Lipstadt and David Irving. Behind them are Heather Rogers, Richard Rampton, and Anthony Julius. Drawing by Priscilla Coleman. Courtesy the Guardian.

historian. Irving in those respects misrepresented and distorted the evidence which was available to him."[159]

Justice Gray dealt separately with Irving's manipulation of evidence concerning Hitler's knowledge of and role in the Holocaust. His conclusion was that the evidence showed that there was substantial evidence that "Hitler was aware of the gassing in the Reinhard Camps" and that "he was consulted and approved the extermination."[160]

Then he turned to Auschwitz. After observing that Irving had made some valid comments, such as the point that contemporaneous documents yield little clear evidence of the existence of gas chambers designed to kill humans and the point that Bischoff's letter of June 28, 1943 had a number of curious features which raise the possibility that it is not authentic, and after acknowledging that there was a possibility that witnesses did not always tell the truth, Gray told all those assembled that, vulnerable though the individual categories of evidence may be to criticisms that were brought forward by Irving, "it appears to me that the cumulative effect of the documentary evidence for the genocidal operation of gas chambers at Auschwitz is considerable." He unequivocally stated that "few and far between though they may be, documents do exist for which it is difficult to find an innocent explanation." While he acknowledged that the reliability of the eyewitness evidence is variable, he stated clearly that "what is to me striking about that category of evidence is the similarity of the accounts and the extent to which they are consistent with the documentary evidence." In conclusion, Gray judged that "the various categories of evidence do 'converge' in the manner suggested by the Defendants," and that the totality of the evidence that Jews were killed in large numbers in the gas chambers at Auschwitz was so strong that "it would require exceedingly powerful reasons to reject it."[161] The Leuchter Report did not provide "sufficient reason for dismissing, or even doubting, the convergence of evidence on which the Defendants rely for the presence of homicidal gas chambers at Auschwitz."[162] As to the holes, Gray had this to say: "I consider that an objective historian, taking account of all the evidence, would conclude that the apparent absence of evidence of holes in the roof of the morgue at Crematorium 2 falls far short of being a good reason for rejecting the cumulative effect of the evidence on which the Defendants rely."[163]

Justice Gray also reviewed the suggestion that the gas chambers would have served as delousing rooms for objects and corpses. "I do not accept that an objective historian would be persuaded that the gas chambers served only the purposes of fumigation. The evidence points firmly in the direction of a homicidal use of the chambers as well."[164] And as to the air-raid shelter argument, he stated of the technical evidence that "there appear to me to be cogent pragmatic reasons for an historian to conclude that the evidence does not support the air-raid shelter argument." He dealt with the argument that it would have served the SS as follows: "I cannot accept that this argument comes anywhere near displacing the conclusion to be drawn from the convergent evidence relied on by the Defendants for their contention as to the object of the redesign work."[165]

All the subsidiary arguments, such as the death books, the decrypts of the radio messages published by Hinsley, and coke consumption did not impress Justice Gray, and he added "I do not consider that they would have impressed a dispassionate historian either." Deliberately slowing the pace with which he read his judgment, Gray came to his final conclusion:

> Having considered the various arguments advanced by Irving to assail the effect of the convergent evidence relied on by the Defendants, it is my conclusion that no objective, fair-minded historian would have serious cause to doubt that there were gas chambers at Auschwitz and that they were operated on a substantial scale to kill hundreds of thousands of Jews.[166]

He stopped and in the utter silence that followed it seemed that both he, and most of those present, paid their respects to those hundreds of thousands whose deaths had been denied.

The case for Auschwitz having been accepted by the judge, the rest of the judgment was equally scathing. Gray immediately turned to the general conclusion that Irving was a Holocaust denier "and that his denials are false."

Finally he came to his assessment of Irving as a historian. "Historians are human: they make mistakes, misread and misconstrue documents and overlook material evidence,"[167] Gray noted. Then he went on to state that Irving had misstated historical evidence, adopted positions which run counter to the weight of the evidence, given credence to unreliable evidence, and disregarded or dismissed credible evidence. In the case of Hitler, "I have seen no instance where Irving has misinterpreted the evidence or misstated the facts in a manner which is detrimental to Hitler. Irving appears to take every opportunity to exculpate Hitler."[168] He agreed with Evans that all Irving's historiographical "errors" converge, in the sense that they all tend to exonerate Hitler and to reflect Irving's partisanship for the Nazi leader. "If indeed they were genuine errors or mistakes, one would not expect to find this consistency."[169] Gray did not accept the argument that all of them were mistakes. Many were "so perverse and egregious that it is difficult to accept that it is inadvertence on his part." One example was Irving's rejection of the evidence for the existence of gas chambers at Auschwitz.

> Mistakes and misconceptions such as these appear to me by their nature unlikely to have been innocent. They are more consistent with a willingness on Irving's part knowingly to misrepresent or manipulate or put a "spin" on the evidence so as to make it conform with his own preconceptions. In my judgment the nature of these misstatements and misjudgments by Irving is a further pointer towards the conclusion that he has deliberately skewed the evidence to bring it into line with his political beliefs.[170]

Gray did not accept Irving's explanations. In fact, Irving's challenge of the Bischoff letter of June 28 turned out to be a boomerang.

> I accept that it is necessary for historians, not least historians of the Nazi era, to be on their guard against documents which are forged or otherwise unauthentic. But it appeared to me that in the course of these proceedings Irving challenged the authenticity of certain documents, not because there was any substantial reason for doubting their genuineness but because they did not fit in with his thesis.
>
> The prime example of this is Irving's dismissal of Bischoff's letter of 28 June 1943 dealing with the incineration capacity of the ovens at Auschwitz (to which I have referred above). As already stated, I agree with the assessment of van Pelt that there is little reason to doubt the authenticity of this document. Yet Irving argued strenuously that it should be dismissed as a forgery. In my judgment he did so because it does not conform to his ideological agenda.[171]

Irving's challenge to the letter stood in remarkable contrast to his unquestioning acceptance of a German document of uncertain provenance that suggested that in 1942 Hitler had postponed the "Final Solution" until after the war. In conclusion, Gray stated, "there is force in the Defendants' contention that Irving on occasion applies double standards to the documentary evidence, accepting documents which fit in with his thesis and rejecting those which do not." Irving also showed the same lack of evenhandedness in his treatment of eyewitnesses. Justice Gray noted that Irving took a highly skeptical approach toward the evidence of the survivors and camp officials at Auschwitz and elsewhere who confirm the genocidal operation of gas chambers at the camp, but he uncritically adopted the testimony of other witnesses (such as Hitler's adjutants, Christa Schroder and Voigt). "The double standards which Irving adopts to some of the documents and to some of the witnesses appear to me to be further evidence that Irving is seeking to manipulate the evidence rather than approaching it as a dispassionate, if sometimes mistaken, historian."[172]

Irving's concessions did not do him much good. Gray judged that it revealed Irving's motivation.

> It seems to me that the Defendants are justified in their contention that Irving's readiness to resile from positions he had adopted in what he has written and said about important aspects of the Holocaust demonstrates his willingness to make assertions about

the Nazi era which, as he must appreciate, are irreconcilable with the available evidence. I also consider that there is force in the Defendants' contention that Irving's retraction of some of his concessions, made when he was confronted with the evidence relied on by the Defendants, manifests a determination to adhere to his preferred version of history, even if the evidence does not support it.[173]

Gray accepted the proposition that Irving's manipulation of history was done because of his anti-Semitism. "The picture of Irving which emerges from the evidence of his extra-curricular activities reveals him to be a right-wing pro-Nazi polemicist. In my view the Defendants have established that Irving has a political agenda. It is one which, it is legitimate to infer, disposes him, where he deems it necessary, to manipulate the historical record in order to make it conform with his political beliefs."[174] He concluded that "for the most part the falsification of the historical record was deliberate and that Irving was motivated by a desire to present events in a manner consistent with his own ideological beliefs even if that involved distortion and manipulation of historical evidence." Gray judged the defense of justification to have succeeded. The verdict was only one short sentence: "It follows that there must be judgement for the Defendants."[175]

With this, the journalists began to leave the courtroom to telephone, fax, or e-mail their stories to the newsdesks of the world's media. After the journalists had left the courtroom, the usher restored order, and it was time to tie up the loose ends. Rampton rose with the request "to enter judgement for the Defendants and to make an order that the Claimant, Mr. Irving, pay the defendants' costs of these proceedings."[176] And with this, the post-trial battle began.

The rest of the day unfolded in a predictable fashion, with the media setting the agenda. Accompanied by German expert witness Hajo Funke and German researcher Tobias Jersak, Carolyn Rampton, Richard Rampton, Heather Rogers, and I had little inclination to celebrate in front of the world's cameras and separated ourselves from the crowd. Dinner that evening proved an unexpectedly melancholy occasion. Throughout the afternoon Rampton had been ashen-faced, but by the time the main course arrived, he burst into tears. "It doesn't make a difference," he lamented, "the judgment doesn't bring the dead back, it doesn't bring them back." Turning to me, he said:

> Auschwitz, that trip to Auschwitz, changed everything. I didn't realize. . . . For fifty years I thought I knew, but I did not really want to know. Six million: it was just a number. . . . Even when I took the case, I didn't think what it meant, I didn't think what the word "gas chamber" implied. And then you told me to go to Auschwitz, and see, and I did not think it necessary to go, because I had the documents, but you forced me to go, and we went, and then I understood. . . . I am deeply ashamed for all those years I thought I knew, and I did not—I am deeply ashamed.

We left our meal unfinished.

The next morning, I left for Canada. On my way to Heathrow, I stopped at a newsagent to gather the newspapers. Of all the reports, the editorial of the *Guardian* stood out, but a long reflection written by Dalrymple for the *Independent* touched me. Its subject was Auschwitz.

"The vast, sprawling complex of stone and steel that was once created so lovingly by the cream of Germany's architects and engineers is now an empty, silent mausoleum on the banks of a dark river in southern Poland," Dalrymple wrote, and thus he began a short account of the history of Auschwitz and Irving's denial of all the evidence. "Day after day I watched him at the Law Courts, doing what he likes doing most. Striding back and forth, letting his formidable imagination take over the control of his tongue, working an audience like a craftsman orator." Irving reminded Dalrymple of "a magician producing rabbits from a hat," only the rabbits were disturbing, puzzling, confusing, even bewildering questions meant to plant "tiny seeds of doubt."

> Why were there no holes in the roofs of the "Gas chambers" where the Zyklon B pellets were allegedly dropped? The buildings are still there, he roared at one point in his libel trial, and nobody can show me any holes.

Dalrymple noted that at the beginning of the trial many feared that it would open a Pandora's box and that it would give negationism respectability. Yet the worst fears had not been realized, and instead something of value had emerged from Courtroom 73 of the Royal Courts of Justice.

Deborah Lipstadt at the post-verdict press conference, April 11, 2000. Photo by Simon Walker. Courtesy The Times.

> The systematic slaughter of an entire generation of people who were neither combatants or even enemies, known as the Holocaust and perpetrated by one of the most civilised nations on earth, is unique in our history. There have been many acts of genocidal violence, both before and since, but they did not involve the transports of millions to industrial complexes built by ordinary German men and women with the single purpose of mass murder over a period of years. It is something that must not only be remembered. It must be studied endlessly, by each new generation, as they try to answer the unanswerable.
>
> And, again uniquely, the final flowering of this catastrophe is still in existence. The ghastly ruined abomination of Auschwitz-Birkenau still exists today, silent and forbidding in the open plains of Upper Silesia. It is only a couple of hours away from Heathrow Airport. It is a place to which we should, perhaps, take all our young men and women, when they are old enough to cope with the unique horror of it, so they may pass their memories to their own children.

Dalrymple concluded that the trial "in all its absurdity, has turned a great spotlight on this terrible place."

> And as he slinks away like a thief in the night into the oblivion he deserves, the lies of David Irving may have done history a kind of favour.

Epilogue

The trial was over, and normal life resumed. I returned to the history of the Holocaust I was writing with Debórah Dwork and decided to find a publisher interested in what was to become this record of the trial. I consigned my two-year involvement with negationism to the past. As a symbolic act of separation, I deleted the bookmark for Irving's Web site from my computer internet application.

Yet the past has a tendency to catch up with the present. On June 27, 2000, I received an electronic message from a Swedish acquaintance announcing "what appears to be a breakthrough in the study of the Krema II roof."

A team from The Holocaust History Project, see: http://www.holocaust-history.org inspected the roof (with permission from the museum) last week and think they have positively identified the original locations of holes number 1, 2, and 4 (south to north). Their placement seem to accord with Tauber's testimony. Number 3 is inaccessible without moving the rubble. The team is bringing back a lot of documentation so it will take some time before there is a full report. I could unfortunately not join because of ill health but have talked with them at length over the phone and feel convinced that they made important discoveries, one of them quite surprising. [. . . .] A preliminary short write-up with limited distribution should be ready within a few months. If you want to see it, please tell me where it should be sent.

Many months later I did receive a draft copy of a richly illustrated 24-page report, written by Daniel Keren, Jamie McCarthy, and Harry W. Mazal, entitled "A Report on Some Findings Concerning the Gas Chamber of Krematorium II in Auschwitz-Birkenau." From the introduction it became clear that their investigation had started in 1998 but that it had expanded in the aftermath of the trial. Using a computer model, the authors had analyzed the photo of Crematorium 2 showing the gas chamber with the chimneys before it was covered with dirt, and as a result had been able to identify precisely the location of the holes in the plan of the building. Taking into account the fact that the concrete slab that covered the gas chamber shifted when the Germans dynamited the pillars that supported it, they set out to look for evidence in the rubble. The problem, of course, was that there were many holes, all irregular. Their approach was sound: although the concrete revealed little about whether the hole had been intended or not, the reinforcement bars (rebars) that remained did. The team noticed that the rebars in the slab were spaced 15 centimeters apart. Believing that the holes had been larger than 15 centimeters square, they knew that the builders would have created the necessary opening by cutting one or two rebars on each side and hooking them back into the slab. While the straight edges of the holes had been blown away by the blast, there were places where the end of a rebar that had been hooked into the slab was still embedded in the concrete. This was the essential clue.

As I studied the report, it became clear that it could still serve a useful function in the judicial process. When Justice Gray handed down his verdict in favor of Penguin and Lipstadt, Irving immediately sought leave to appeal, which was refused at that time. In the late summer of 2000 Irving reapplied for leave to appeal, claiming, among other things, that not being a cremation engineer or a chemist, I should not have been allowed to testify as an expert witness on the Auschwitz crematoria. In response, barristers Rampton and Rogers defended my position that as a historian I had the duty to consider evidence concerning the existence of gas chambers at Auschwitz and the function of Auschwitz as a center of mass extermination from a variety of sources, including eyewitness accounts, contemporary documents, archaeological remains, photographic evidence, and chemical analysis.

> This is the necessary and normal function of an historian and the fact that the historian is not himself qualified as an expert in a particular discipline from which a particular piece of evidence is derived in no sense disqualifies him from considering it and its place in the evidence as a whole; on the contrary, it would be a breach of his duty as an historian not to do so. Thus, for example, the evidence yielded by chemical analysis of the remains of the gas chambers at Auschwitz-Birkenau (which van Pelt has studied in detail) is important evidence to which any objective and responsible historian must have regard if he is to give a full and fair account of the matter.[1]

In his rejection of Irving's application for a leave of appeal handed down in December, Lord Justice Sedley accepted this reasoning and reconfirmed my standing as an expert. On the substance of the Auschwitz issue itself, which Irving tried to appeal on the grounds that the holes in the roof of the gas chamber of Crematorium 2 through which the Zyklon B had been introduced in the chamber below were no longer visible, Lord Justice Sedley defined it as an essential piece of the case against Irving, as it clearly showed his attempt to marginalize the Holocaust.

> Here too the historical record is inevitably incomplete and in places unreliable; but here too the applicant has been betrayed by his own method, notably his reliance on the discredited Leuchter report. The judgment (J 8.17) sets out the solidity of the applicant's denial of mass homicide at Auschwitz, and sets in that context his recent focus on the "holes in the roof" issue (J 13.81–3). I accept readily that the latter argument may be none the worse for coming late in the day; but the evidence that there were no holes for the admission of cyanide pellets is at best inconclusive against the potent evidence that people were gassed there in tens of thousands. The controversy about methods and numbers may legitimately remain; but what the applicant has done is demonstrate once again his willingness to sacrifice objectivity in favour of anything which will support his chosen form of Holocaust denial.[2]

Lord Justice Sedley's decision proved not to be final: on January 17, 2001, the Appeal Court gave Irving an opportunity to make his case for an appeal in a hearing originally set for March 19, 2001, and later changed to a four-day period beginning June 20. If in that hearing Irving's application for permission to appeal were to be granted, the appeal itself would follow immediately. This meant, of course, that while it did not seem likely that the permission to appeal would be granted, both sides had to prepare as if it would. This issue touched me directly, as Irving announced that he would seek to adduce "new evidence" that Auschwitz could not have been an extermination camp—the only part of the case which he sought to appeal using new evidence. The court had given him four weeks to submit this new evidence with all supporting documents and skeleton arguments. On receipt of this material the defendants would also have four weeks to respond. I was told to expect a lot of new work.

In fact, when after six weeks the new evidence arrived at Lipstadt's law firm, Mishcon de Reya, and Penguin's solicitors, Davenport Lyons, it proved to be more than expected: 384 pages in total. The document was prepared by a German Holocaust denier named Germar Rudolf, the author of the so-called Rudolf Report (official English title: *An Expert Report on the Formation and Detection of Cyanide Compounds in the "Gas Chambers" of Auschwitz*), originally published in 1992. Immediately after the trial, Rudolf had gone on record in an article entitled "Critique of Claims Made by Robert Jan Van Pelt" that Irving had lost the case because he had "refused" to make use of his own expertise. The heading of the piece he posted on his Web site was "Those who choose to be their own lawyer choose a fool."

> David Irving refused to present Germar Rudolf as an expert witness. Here is the price he has to pay for it: He lost his lawsuit, and has to pay $3.2 (AP) or even $4.5 million (Reuters).
>
> Justice Gray made it pretty clear that refusing to present me as a witness forced him to reject Irving's lawsuit.[3]

Actually, Justice Gray did not mention Rudolf. In an autobiographical article entitled "The Hunt of Germar Rudolf," Rudolf makes it very clear that Irving asked him as early as 1996 to testify in his case against Penguin and Lipstadt. Rudolf agreed but Irving did not return to the issue until the fall of 1999. It was a difficult time for Rudolf: a few years earlier he had been convicted in Germany for Holocaust denial and had been on the run, since 1996, living in Great Britain under an assumed identity. Irving's request for help arrived at a time when Rudolf's whereabouts had become known, and he was preparing to move to the United States to seek political asylum. "That is the reason that I was only able to get Irving my comments shortly before the cross-examination of the most important witness, Professor van Pelt," Rudolf wrote. "Irving's trial likely suffered greatly because of that."[4]

In the aftermath of the verdict, it seems that Rudolf convinced Irving that, if given the opportunity, he could turn defeat into victory. But it was an uphill battle as any new evidence to be introduced at the appeal stage would have to fulfill three requirements that were established in an appeal granted in the 1954 case of *Ladd vs. Marshall,* which concerned the attempt by a certain Mr. Ladd to recover money he claimed to have paid as a down payment for a house bought from a certain Mr. Marshall. The judge had ruled for the defendant, but shortly after the verdict Mrs. Marshall, who had been called as a witness by the plaintiff and who had said that she did not know anything about the down payment, divorced Mr. Marshall and made a statement that, fearing a possible assault if she were to tell the truth, she had lied in court on his behalf and that she had seen Mr. Ladd paying the down payment to her husband. In deciding if Mrs. Marshall's reversal was sufficient to warrant an appeal, Lord Justice Tom Denning of the Court of Appeal laid down a test to be applied to the new evidence:

> To justify the reception of fresh evidence or a new trial, three conditions must be fufilled: first, it must be shown that the evidence could not have been obtained with reasonable diligence for use at the trial; secondly, the evidence must be such that, if given, it would probably have an important influence on the result, though it need not be decisive; thirdly, the evidence must be such as is presumably to be believed, or in other words, it must be apparently credible, though it need not be incontrovertible.[5]

In the end the Court of Appeal decided that the new evidence did not pass this test because Mrs. Marshall had confessed that she lied and could not be trusted not to lie now. The rule concerning the admissibility of new evidence laid down in that case by Lord Justice Denning became a standard test. Irving would therefore have to prove that the new evidence he sought to introduce was and could not have been available at the trial, that in all likelihood it would have influenced the outcome of the trial, and that it was unambiguous.

Remarkably enough, in Irving's "skeleton argument re an application to adduce new evidence," the Rudolf affidavit is said to be "founded upon the same author's earlier analysis of the improbability or outright impossibility of the established historiography of Auschwitz."[6] Indeed, upon inspection, the bulk of the text proved to be a rehash of old arguments which Irving could have brought up at the trial. It meant that, in theory, it ought to be refused on the basis of the first requirement of the *Ladd vs. Marshall* test. In order to provide the lawyers with the material to kill the Rudolf report on procedural grounds, I had to date all the arguments and show that all the material could have been available during the trial. It was a tedious job, but with the help of others it was accomplished.

As to the second requirement of the *Ladd vs. Marshall* test, Rampton and Rogers reminded the Court of Appeal that Irving challenged only the evidence concerning Auschwitz, and because the case had involved many issues not related to Auschwitz, Irving would still have lost even if he had been able during the trial to challenge successfully the historical record concerning that camp or if he were to be able to do so in an appeal.

Most of my own work concerned the issue of whether the affidavit could pass the third requirement of the *Ladd vs. Marshall* test—namely whether the so-called evidence was "apparently credible." In practice this meant that I had to engage in a full-scale rebuttal of the affidavit. Most of the arguments that Rudolf presented I was able to deal with, as they concerned the validity of evidence given by eyewitnesses or the interpretation of documents. But some seventy-three pages concerned the interpretation of samples of residual cyanide in the form of so-called Prussian blue or ferro-ferri cyanide taken at various times by various people from the ruined walls of the homicidal gas chambers in the crematoria and from largely intact delousing chambers elsewhere in Birkenau. I asked and received help from Richard Green, who holds a Ph.D. in chemistry from Stanford University and who in the late 1990s published several articles about Rudolf's chemistry on the Web site www.Holocaust.org., set up and maintained by Harry Mazal.[7] Green produced an excellent 65-page report in which he demolished point-for-point Rudolf's attempt to use chemistry to trump knowledge based on a convergence of both eyewitness and documentary evidence.[8] One of Green's most important arguments was that Rudolf was wrong to assume that a similar exposure to cyanide should produce an equivalent amount of Prussian blue in the homicidal gas chambers as in the delousing chambers, and that therefore a relatively low concentration of Prussian blue in the samples taken from the gas chambers, compared to the higher concentration in the samples taken from the delousing chambers, did not prove that the former spaces had not been systematically used as execution chambers. "The effort to disprove history on chemical grounds failed," Green concluded; remarkably, Rudolf had admitted just that in one of his responses to Green's criticism posted on his own Web site, www.vho.org: "Chemistry is not the science which can prove or refute any allegations about the Holocaust 'rigorously,'"[9] Rudolf had written before the Irving trial had started. Green ended his report by concluding that "the only explanation that is consistent with all of the evidence, physical and historical, is that mass murder by poison gas at Auschwitz and Birkenau did in fact take place."[10]

Besides engaging Green to submit an expert report on the chemistry, I also ensured that the recent research by Keren, McCarthy and Mazal on the "holes" was made available to the Court of Appeal. Because Rudolf had raised this issue in his affidavit, this gave me an opportunity to submit the Keren, McCarthy, and Mazal report as an appendix to my rebuttal of Rudolf.[11] I added a second report written by Paul Zucchi of Yolles Engineering in Toronto. I had asked Zucchi to review the report on the holes, and he had suggested engaging in a series of engineering calculations on what would have been the most likely place for holes to be inserted in the reinforced concrete slab that covered the gas chamber. Zucchi concluded that "the authors present a strong and sustainable case that openings described as Zyklon vents 1, 2, and 4 were installed in the roof of the building during the course of construction."[12] With such support, I felt justified in keeping my comment on Rudolf's assertions to a minimum.

While the "discovery" of three of the four holes had effectively answered Irving's challenge made on the eleventh day of the trial, I judged it wise to provide the Appeal Court with the historical context of the issue. The holes were, so to speak, the fig leaf to hide the nakedness of the negationists. In order to develop my argument, I returned to the basics of gas chamber design: to have a homicidal gas chamber, one needs a room in which one first locks the victims to be killed and then introduces gas. In the case of a delousing gas chamber, it is possible to bring in the items to be fumigated, enter the room with a closed tin of Zyklon B pellets, don a gas mask, open the tin, spread the contents on the floor, quickly leave the room, and close and lock the door. This procedure is, of course, impossible if the room is filled with human beings. So the question is: "How to introduce the gas?"

I explained that in the case of the carbon monoxide gas chambers used by the Nazis in the T4 program to kill the mentally ill and in the Operation Reinhard camps of Belzec, Sobibor and Treblinka, the gas which was supplied by means of bottles (T4) or engines (Operation Reinhard camps) was piped into the gas chambers. In Auschwitz the chemical used was Zyklon B, a generally available delousing agent in which cyanide was absorbed in some carrier such as a porous granular substance or paper disks. Zyklon B was shipped in tins of various sizes. When the tin was opened, the cyanide would begin to evaporate from the carrier. To introduce the cyanide into a room, one therefore needed apertures through which the contents of a can of Zyklon B could be thrown into the chamber, but which were designed in such a way that the people locked inside the room could not interfere with the process or use the apertures as a means of escape. In the case of the above-ground gas chambers of Crematoria 4 and 5, these apertures were located close to the ceiling of the gas chamber; in the case of the underground gas chambers of Crematoria 2 and 3, these apertures were located in the ceiling. Connected to the apertures were some wire-mesh columns that ran from the floor of the gas chamber to the holes in the ceiling. A movable element in the center of the column collected the Zyklon B pellets and allowed the removal of the carrier (from which the cyanide degassed for twenty-four hours after the tin had been opened) after the twenty minutes or so it took to kill the people inside the gas chamber. With the Zyklon B removed and the ventilators turned on, it was possible to enter the gas chamber about half an hour later to begin the process of removing and incinerating the corpses. I also reminded the Court of Appeal that the gassing installations of Crematoria 2 and 3, consisting of the holes and the wire-mesh columns, were designed only after these buildings were already under construction; as a result they were not included in the original set of blueprints.

Then I turned to the question of why Irving had made such an issue of his claim that his whole case depended on the existence of holes in the ruined roof of Morgue 1 of Crematorium 2. I showed that Irving's attempt to use negative evidence as a means to push his case reflected the general negationist tendency to rely on negative evidence. From the mid-1970s they claimed that there were no blueprints that designated a specific room in the crematoria as a "gas chamber"; when the detailed studies by Jean-Claude Pressac showed that there were many references in the Auschwitz building archive to gas chambers, Holocaust deniers turned to the absence of large quantities of residual cyanide in the ruined walls of the gas chamber as a proof that these spaces had not been used for genocidal purposes. This approach conveniently ignored the fundamental premise of historical research that negative evidence means precisely that: a lack of evidence, and nothing more. I recalled that in 1988 Irving interpreted negative evidence as positive evidence for the nonexistence of the gas chambers when he accepted Leuchter's conclusion that the absence of residual cyanide in the walls of the gas chambers proved that these gas chambers were a myth

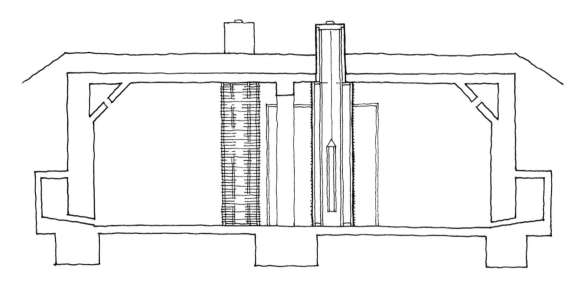

Section of the gas chamber of Crematorium 2. Drawing by Marc Downing.

The remains of hole #4, Crematorium 2. The hole is located where the slab quite literally folded as a result of the explosion when the SS dynamited the gas chamber. At the hole the rebars were cut during the construction, and bent back. Courtesy Mazal Library.

created by British propaganda, and that in the early 1990s Germar Rudolf published a report that replicated Leuchter's approach. I added that, by the end of that decade, Rudolf was forced to backtrack, partly in response to Green's incisive criticism. In August 1998 Rudolf concluded a paper given at the first Australian Revisionist Conference with the remark that "chemistry is not the science which can prove or refute any allegations about the Holocaust rigorously. . . . [O]n the chemical argument no absolute certainty can be built." Yet this did not mean that Rudolf rejected negative evidence: abandoning the chemical argument, he invoked another piece of crucial evidence that appeared to be missing: the holes. "Without holes, no gassings according to the scenario as described by the eye witnesses, without such gassings no reliable eye witnesses, and without reliable eye witnesses no evidence for the Holocaust. Or, as Robert [Faurisson] put it: 'NO HOLES, NO HOLOCAUST.'"[13] I concluded that, in the same way that in the late 1980s the argument concerning the alleged lack of residual cyanide in the walls of the gas chambers was to compensate for the fact that the negationist attempts to discredit the documentary evidence had failed, so in the late 1990s the argument concerning the alleged lack of holes was to compensate for the retreat on the alleged chemical proof.

Having settled the issue of the holes did not liberate me from the obligation of responding in detail to over 200 pages of Rudolf's affidavit. Upon close inspection, it became apparent that, for all its bulk, it was mainly irrelevant as a means to overturn Justice Gray's conclusions concerning Auschwitz, which had been largely based on my own expert report and testimony in court. Rudolf did not address the systematic way in which I tried to establish the evidentiary foundations of the "established historiography" of Auschwitz, nor did he challenge the historiographical principle that was central to my approach—one that reflects proper historiographical practice: namely that one piece of evidence does not suffice to prove or disprove a fact, but that various pieces of evidence of many different kinds and classes converge toward a conclusion, and that if there are apparent contradictions among different pieces of evidence, then the interrogator of the evidence must ask tough questions. Perhaps an eyewitness was mistaken, or perhaps the calculation was wrong, or perhaps both the testimony and the experiment were wrong. Rudolf, however, simply dismissed one category of evidence—the eyewitnesses—when it seemed to contradict a laboratory experiment or a calculation concerning some technical point.

I established that Rudolf produced a number of unrelated attacks on some selected parts of the evidence that Auschwitz was an extermination camp equipped with homicidal gas chambers, and that he had proposed some mutually exclusive alternative explanations for selected pieces of evidence. At no point did Rudolf actually begin to revise the history of Auschwitz, or any part of it, nor had he created even the beginning of a plausible narrative with which one could engage. I also noted that Rudolf's attacks not only were unrelated and failed to add up to a plausible narrative but they were actually contradictory. Thus, Rudolf maintained at one point that the alleged gas chambers of Crematoria 2 and 3 were delousing cellars for objects; at other times he asserted that they were morgues for corpses of victims who had succumbed to infectious diseases or showering rooms for either living or dead inmates, or air-raid shelters. In two consecutive paragraphs he claimed that the undressing rooms in the basements of Crematoria 2 and 3 were places to undress the corpses of people who had died elsewhere in the camp and that they served as undressing rooms for inmates who were to shower in the basements of these very crematoria. In his attacks on the evidence, Rudolf was forced to bring forward various alternative suggestions as to what the gas chambers in the basements of Crematoria 2 and 3 actually were, since not one of his suggested alternatives actually provided an explanation of all the curious features that indicate that these spaces were actually cellars that had originally been designed as morgues but that had been transformed in a process of adaptive re-use into homicidal gas chambers.

Quite apart from the many historical errors, it was easy to show that the various alternative explanations of the evidence offered by Rudolf could not be unified in any coherent proposition that offers a plausible alternative to such histories of Auschwitz as were written some fifty years ago by Judge Jan Sehn, or as recently as six years ago by Debórah Dwork and me. As to the various suggestions he made to neutralize inconvenient evidence, Rudolf proved unable to support these various possibilities with a single piece of eyewitness or even significant non-intentional evidence. Whereas eyewitnesses such as Höss, Broad, Stark, Tauber, and others attested that Morgue 1 of Crematorium 2 served as a homocidal gas chamber, Rudolf offered no statements by SS officials, or camp inmates, or civilians to support his allegations that it was a delousing cellar, an air-raid shelter, or an actual morgue for people who died of "natural" causes. Nor did he provide any documents that clearly supported his suggestion. And he ignored the convergence of evidence that supports the interpretation that Morgue 1 was, as the eyewitnesses testified, a homicidal gas chamber.

I also demonstrated that Rudolf tried to pass over inconvenient evidence. The case of Crematoria 4 and 5 was an obvious example. Unlike Crematoria 2 and 3, Crematoria 4 and 5 were from the very beginning designed as killing installations. If in Crematoria 2 and 3 the underground cellars were transformed in a late stage of the construction from morgues into a sequence of rooms that included an undressing room and a gas chamber—an example of adaptive re-use that necessitated some awkward compromises—Crematoria 4 and 5 were efficient and economic killing machines. Both crematoria had three gas chambers. Rudolf did admit that these rooms were intended to be used as gas chambers, but he then argued that these gas chambers would have been Zyklon B delousing chambers, invoking an alleged item in the plan of the building which I have been unable to find. He did not address the fact that there is absolutely no eyewitness testimony that supports this suggestion, and that there is not a single document that supports the suggestion that these gas chambers were in fact delousing chambers. Moreover, he ignored a curious feature of these gas chambers which one does not find in any of the delousing chambers in Auschwitz: the presence of the small gas-tight shutters, measuring 30 by 40 cm. These were located close to the ceiling. When opened, these gas-tight shutters allowed the SS to introduce Zyklon B into the gas chamber without having to enter that space. Such shutters were not necessary in delousing rooms, as a person equipped with a gas mask could enter such spaces, open a can with Zyklon B, pour the contents on the floor, and quickly leave, shutting the gas-tight door behind him. But if the room was filled with people, this procedure was impossible, and therefore the presence of the small, gas-tight shutters, located above the heads of the victims, was required.

Rudolf also did not address the remarkable convergence of evidence that occurs in the case of, for example, the existence of the gas columns and their attendant "holes" in the gas chambers of Crematoria 2 and 3. In my expert report and during my testimony at the trial, I pointed out that the existence of these columns, which were an essential part of the machinery of destruction of Crematoria 2 and 3, could be established on the basis of the convergence of independent eyewitness evidence given by Henryk Tauber and Michael Kula in Poland in the spring of 1945, drawings made by David Olère in France in the spring of 1945 and early 1946, drawings made by Yehuda Bacon in Austria and Czechoslovakia in the spring of 1945, and non-intentional evidence such as a photo of Crematorium 2 taken in early 1943 and American air photos of Auschwitz taken in the spring and summer of 1944. These various pieces of evidence have some remarkable details in common, such as, for example, the fact that according to Tauber, Olère, the German photo from 1943, and the American air photos from 1944, the gas columns were arranged in a zig-zag pattern. Rudolf did not deal with the convergence of this evidence at all and did not address these remarkable resemblances. Furthermore, he ignored important evidence that does support the existence of these gas columns, such as an inventory of Crematorium 2 that mentions in Morgue 1 four instruments identified as *Drahtnetzeinschiebvorrichtung[en],* which translates as wire mesh introduction device[s].

Arguing that Holocaust deniers regularly and systematically dismiss whole categories of perfectly acceptable evidence by maintaining in each particular case that another explanation of selected pieces of evidence may be possible and by ignoring the obvious explanation that is supported by other evidence, I showed that Rudolf did exactly the same. I concluded, at the end of a 250-page rebuttal, that if the Rudolf affidavit had been introduced at the trial, it might have slowed the proceedings but it would not have made a difference.

Work on the appeal, as on the main case, was tedious, as the following example of Rudolf's methodology demonstrates. In one paragraph Rudolf asserts that all the eyewitnesses of mass killing in Auschwitz were mistaken because their testimonies contain absurd and technically impossible claims. Thus, eyewitnesses of the incinerations claimed that the Germans were able to reach a high rate of incineration by means of multi-corpse incineration. Rudolf asserted that "multi-corps [*sic*] incineration result in a drastic reduction of efficiency (i.e., in a massive increase of coke consumption) and only little advantage in speed increase compared to several consecutive single corpse incinerations, so nobody does this."[14] Or he stated that eyewitnesses who reported that the Auschwitz crematoria smoked are exposed as liars because "only during the ignition phase of a fire do crematoria develop smoke, but not during normal operation, nor do they develop any stench."[15] He did not substantiate any of his claims with any references to sources.

In response, I was forced to research such issues in some depth. In the case of multi-corpse incineration—that is, the illegal practice of reducing two or more corpses to ashes in the same oven—I found in Kenneth V. Iserson's standard work on corpse disposal, *Death To Dust* (1994), that one California crematorium had to settle a suit by 25,000 people "who claimed that their relatives' bodies have been cremated en masse, rather than separately. Another southern California firm [. . .] routinely packed nine to fifteen bodies into each oven, which was about the size of the interior of a typical American sedan."[16] These cases suggested that Rudolf was wrong. To answer his challenge that cremations do not produce smoke, I studied the history of cremation technology. The report of the first cremation undertaken in the United States on October 16, 1879, recorded that "a dense volume of black smoke rose from the chimney, and the odor of burning flesh greeted the olfactories of the few persons who remained outside."[17] As I researched the literature, it became clear that black smoke emanating from crematoria chimneys remained a real problem, if only because it did not support the propaganda by the advocates of cremation that it was a clean way to dispose of corpses. In 1912 Lawrence Moore, who had been appointed manager of the California Crematorium in Oakland, California, toured with his wife all over the United States to visit crematoria with a view to improving operation. In 1940 he recalled in a lecture given for the annual meeting of the Association of American Cemetery Superintendents the situation he encountered. "The impressions gained at that time are still vividly clear to both of us. Nearly all crematories were characterized by spectacular high smokestacks, black smoke, furnaces red hot to receive caskets and bodies. . . . No loveliness, no charm were anywhere, we thought."[18] The *Proceedings* of the Association of American Cemetery Superintendents provided ample evidence of the continuous search by crematory engineers to control the smoke, and that only by 1940 was the problem solved by a combination of practices that included using oil and gas instead of coke as fuel, inserting the corpse into a cold instead of a preheated oven, slowing down the incineration, installing afterburners and air-pollution control scrubbers, and establishing procedures for regular maintenance. None of these practices applied to the Auschwitz crematoria. While designed for oil, they had been modified for coke use as oil was in short supply in the German war economy. The ovens of the Auschwitz crematoria were preheated before the corpses were introduced. Furthermore, those who operated the crematoria did their best to shorten the incineration time as much as possible. These crematoria were not supplied with either afterburners or air-pollution control scrubbers. Finally, the furnaces were intensively operated with what seems to have been little regard for maintenance. Thus, one of Rudolf's sentences—"only during the ignition phase of a fire do crematoria develop smoke, but not during normal operation"—forced me to research a large topic and write many pages. Since Rudolf produced many such attempts to discredit eyewitness evidence, I devoted much time to proving the obvious.

Working on the Rudolf affidavit had its lighter moments. Having been subjected to many attempts at character assassination by Irving both within and outside the court, I was surprised that Irving had volunteered an individual who was vulnerable, to say the least. A quick search on the internet revealed that Rudolf bragged that, in the past, he had intentionally tried to deceive a court of law by inventing various personae who could serve as expert witnesses.[19] This resulted in a confused bibliography in which Rudolf had published under his original name, Germar Rudolf, under the assumed names of a number of men claiming to hold doctorates —Dr. Ernst Gauss (engineer?), Dr. Werner Kretschmer (lawyer), Dr. Christian Konrad (historian)—one man claiming no less than two doctorates: Dr. Rainer Scholz (chemist and pharmacologist), under the names of a few individuals without doctorates—Jakob Sprenger, Wilhelm Schlesiger, Manfred Koehler, Lennard Rose—and under his adopted name of Germar Scheerer. For the record: Rudolf does not hold a Ph.D. By appropriating a doctoral dignity for Drs. Gauss, Kretschmer, and Konrad, and by pretending to multiple doctoral dignities for Scholz, one must conclude that Rudolf violated the basic principles of academic decorum and decency. To make matters worse, he undermined the principles of scholarship by deploying these different identities in support of each other: Dr. Gauss quotes Mr. Rudolf, Mr. Rudolf co-authors an article with Dr. Gauss, and so on. Trying to work my way through the maze of Rudolf's identities, I began to imagine the way Rampton would commence a caustic and trenchant cross-examination of Rudolf. And I almost hoped that I would be able to enjoy that spectacle.

It has not come so far. On June 21, 2001, Irving's barrister, Adrian Davies, told a three-judge panel of the Court of Appeal, sitting in the same Court 73 of the Royal Courts of Justice where Mr. Justice Gray had heard the case, that he would not submit the Rudolf affidavit in his attempt to obtain an appeal. He did not offer an explanation. Perhaps it was the force of my rebuttal, or perhaps it was the discovery of the holes that led Irving to scuttle the battleship Rudolf. Whatever the reason, despite the decision not to submit the Rudolf material to the Court of Appeal, Auschwitz was still to be the hinge in Irving's case, as it had been seventeen months earlier when Irving had offered to drop his suit if I were to be able to show him the holes. Davies now argued that if the Court of Appeal determined that at no time since 1988 did Irving's "doubts" concerning Auschwitz have any justification, it would have no choice but to reject Irving's request to obtain an appeal.

Seated in my old place in the courtroom behind Rampton and Rogers, I was reminded of Marx's observation that all (world)-historical events occur the first time as tragedy, the second as farce. For all the madness of Irving's arguments, the original trial had provided one with the sense that something important was at stake. In the months before the hearing on the appeal, Irving had tried to convince his supporters, and possibly even himself, that the appeal would have an even greater impact. In his Action Report 18, issued three months before the hearing, he announced that the appeal would be "the Big One," and that "the opposing lines drawn up are in some ways more formidable than at Agincourt, or Waterloo, or Kursk." Irving predicted that the appeal would once again draw the media to London. "TV cameras, satellite transmitters, news teams and photographers, will line up all the way down the street outside the Law Courts."[20] But Davies proved no match for Rampton, the Court of Appeal did not resemble either Agincourt, Waterloo or Kursk, and the media did not pay attention.

But even if the world had turned its back on Irving's quest for an appeal, Irving and his barrister persisted in casting themselves as heroes in their own Wagnerian *Götterdämmerung*. More than twelve years before, Irving had opened the chapter of his life that was to become the occasion of this book by identifying Auschwitz as the "great battleship" that prevented a negationist breakthrough and thus issued the call to "Sink the Auschwitz." The strategy of Rampton, Rogers and Julius had been to transform the plaintiff into the defendant, the accuser into the accused. It had worked well. At the end of the third day at the Court of Appeal Irving noted in his diary that earlier that day, when the hearing was adjourned until the next Tuesday, Davies told him that he had lost.

> Adrian gathers up his things and turns round to say to me, "So on Tuesday we can at least go down with guns firing like the Bismarck." "Go down?" He says firmly and knowledgeably, "We're going down."[21]

And so, indeed, they did. On July 20, 2001, the Court of Appeal handed down its 32-page verdict in a session that lasted less than one hour, and which Irving chose not to attend. Given all the attacks on my credibility that Irving and his supporters had made since the beginning of the trial, I was pleased to note that Lord Justices Sir Malcolm Pill, Sir Charles Mantell, and Sir Richard Buxton explicitly vindicated my standing as an expert.

Professor van Pelt plainly had considerable knowledge and expertise in the design of buildings and the uses to which they can be put. The absence of a professional qualification in architecture did not preclude him from giving evidence on architectural matters when the issues were those in this case. One does not have to be a qualified lawyer to express views on legal history. There must of course be a limit to the extent to which someone whose profession is that of historian can express views of his own on highly technical matters. The witness is however entitled to consult, refer to and rely on source material in support of an opinion. Military historians frequently express opinions about the effectiveness of weapons and the effect of their use in battle and can do so without their being experts, for example, in ballistics or metallurgy.[22]

The last sentence directly referred to an argument made by Davies on the second day of the appeal in which he had attacked my standing as an expert by means of a lengthy consideration on the question of whether a naval historian who was not trained as a gunnery officer could determine if a 15-inch shell fired by the battleship *Bismarck* or an 8-inch shell fired by the cruiser *Prinz Eugen* had sunk the battle cruiser HMS *Hood*. Davies had proposed that a naval historian could not make such a determination, and that therefore I should not have been allowed to comment on the incineration capacity of the crematoria. The Court of Appeal obviously disagreed.

Lord Justices Pill, Mantell, and Buxton also expressed their "dismay" about the last-minute withdrawal of the Rudolf affidavit, since Irving's stated intention to submit it had caused Green and me to prepare "voluminous evidence in reply," exposed Penguin and Lipstadt "to great expense," and forced them "to considerable pre-hearing reading."[23]

Reviewing the case as a whole, the Court of Appeal considered it remarkable that whereas Irving had insisted that in all other aspects of the case the contents of his books ought to be assessed on the basis of evidence available at the time of publication, with reference to Auschwitz he demanded a consideration of his current views; thus, Irving had maintained that the issue of the holes was relevant, and consequently that his refusal to accept the systematic use of gas chambers to kill large numbers of Jews could not be described as perverse. The Court of Appeal ruled that Justice Gray had taken Irving's objections seriously, handicapped as he was by the fact that Irving's position on Auschwitz during the trial was different from what it had been at the time covered in Lipstadt's book, and that he had handled this part of the case in an appropriate fashion. After a review of the other issues raised in the hearing, the Court of Appeal came to the conclusion that Justice Gray had reached a sound conclusion on all issues that Davies had raised, and that the defense of justification had succeeded. The Court of Appeal decided that "it is not arguable that an appeal against the judge's verdict would succeed. The application for permission to appeal is refused."[24]

With this, my effort to present the case for Auschwitz has come to a close, and *The Case for Auschwitz* can go into production.

Toronto, July 20, 2001

Abbreviations

AABSMO	Archive of the Auschwitz-Birkenau State Museum in Oswiecim
AEMS	Archive Erfurter Malzerei und Speicherbau (Topf & Sons company archive)
BW	Bauwerke (section of archive of AABSMO)
CDC	Cracow District Commission for the Investigation of German War Crimes
COA	Court of Appeal
DCO: HMQvEZ'85	District Court of Ontario, Her Majesty the Queen versus Ernst Zündel, 1985 (first Zündel Trial)
DCO: HMQvEZ'88	District Court of Ontario, Her Majesty the Queen versus Ernst Zündel, 1988 (second Zündel Trial)
HCJ/QB: IvP&L	In the High Court of Justice, Queen's Bench Division, 1996–I-No. 1113, Irving versus Penguin and Lipstadt
IHR	Institute for Historical Review
IMT	International Military Tribunal
JHR	Journal of Historical Review
LSW	Landesgericht für Strafsachen, Vienna, Austria
OAM	Osobyi Archive Moscow
PRO/FO	Public Record Office/Foreign Office, London
PRO/WO	Public Record Office/ War Office, London
USA	United States of America
USHRI	United States Holocaust Research Institute, Washington, D.C.
USSR	Union of Soviet Socialist Republics
ZBL	Zentralbauleitung (Central Construction Office)

Preface

1. HCJ/QB: IvP&L, transcripts, day 33 (Tuesday, 11 April 2000), 43.
2. "The Bad History Man."
3. Davis, "British Court Slams Irving as Holocaust Denier."
4. Lyall, "Critic of a Holocaust Denier Is Cleared in British Libel Suit."
5. Moss, "History's Verdict on Holocaust Upheld."
6. "David Irving Lost His Case—and We Can Celebrate a Victory for Free Speech."
7. "Holocaust Denial."
8. "Truth's Sheer Weight."
9. Hoffman, "David Irving and the Verdict of History."
10. Lipstadt, *Denying the Holocaust,* 26.

1. The Negationists' Challenge to Auschwitz

1. HCJ/QB: IvP&L daily transcripts, day 1 (11 January 2000), 100–101.
2. Ibid., 25–26.
3. Van Pelt, "Expert Opinion," 518–519.
4. HCJ/QB: IvP&L, day 11 (28 January 2000), 151.
5. "Testimony of Rudolf Hoess Taken at Nurnberg, on 1 April 1946, 1430 to 1730," in *The Holocaust,* ed. Mendelsohn and Detwiler, 12: 72.
6. Probably Höss referred with "Wolzek" to Sobibor, the third Operation Reinhard extermination camp.
7. Document 3868–PS, "Affidavit of Rudolf Franz Ferdinand Hoess," in IMT, *Trial of the Major War Criminals,* 33: 275ff.
8. Proceedings of Monday, 15 April 1946 in IMT, *Trial of the Major War Criminals,* 11: 414.
9. Butz, *The Hoax of the Twentieth Century* (2nd edition), 363–364.
10. Irving, "Battleship Auschwitz," 499.
11. Adorno, "Kulturkritik und Gesellschaft," 33.
12. Jonas, "The Concept of God after Auschwitz," 292.
13. See, for example, Maybaum, *The Face of God after Auschwitz;* Rubenstein, *After Auschwitz;* Neher, *L'exil de la Parole;* Jansen, *Christelijke theologie na Auschwitz;* Mosler, ed., *Schreiben nach Auschwitz;* Hirsch, *The Deconstruction of Literature.*
14. Habermas, "Historical Consciousness and Post-Traditional Identity," 251.

15. Wiesel, *Legends of Our Time,* 183.

16. Hilberg, *The Destruction of the European Jews,* 3: 1219.

17. Hungary (438,000); Poland (300,000); France (69,000); The Netherlands (60,000); Greece (55,000); Bohemia and Moravia, Theresienstadt (46,000); Slovakia (27,000); Belgium (25,000); Germany and Austria (23,000); Yugoslavia (10,000); Italy (7,500); Norway (69,000). See Piper, *Die Zahl der Opfer von Auschwitz,* Table D (between pp. 144–145).

18. Rosenzweig, *The Star of Redemption,* 298.

19. Wiesel, *Messengers of God,* 32.

20. Levi, *The Drowned and the Saved,* 78.

21. Ibid., 86.

22. Feingold, "How Unique Is the Holocaust?," 398.

23. Littell, "The Credibility Crisis of the Modern University," 274.

24. Hochhuth, *The Deputy,* 248.

25. Vidal-Naquet, *The Jews,* 148–149.

26. Ibid.

27. Rubenstein, *The Cunning of History,* 46–47.

28. Ibid., 6, 79.

29. Irving, "On Contemporary History and Historiography," 274.

30. Cayrol, "Night and Fog," 240–241.

31. HCJ/QB: IvP&L, day 1 (11 January 2000), 95ff.

32. Irving, *The Destruction of Dresden,* 234.

33. Irving, *Hitler's War,* 3.

34. Ibid., xiv.

35. Ibid., 332.

36. Ibid., xiv.

37. Ibid., 505.

38. Ibid.

39. Ibid., 332.

40. Ibid., 391.

41. Ibid., 392.

42. Ibid., 632.

43. Ibid., 660.

44. Trevor-Roper, "Hitler: Does History Offer a Defence?"

45. Sydnor, "The Selling of Adolf Hitler," 195, 176, 198.

46. Lewis Brandon to David Irving, 27 February 1980, in Van Pelt, "Expert Opinion," 561.

47. David Irving to Lewis Brandon, 4 March 1980, in Van Pelt, "Expert Opinion," 562.

48. Harris, *Selling Hitler,* 322–323.

49. Lecture given by David Irving in Toronto, August 1988, in Van Pelt, "Expert Opinion," 589.

50. Harris, *Selling Hitler,* 359.

51. Irving, "On Contemporary History and Historiography," 253.

52. Ibid., 274.

53. Ibid., 279.

54. Ibid., 282.

55. Berg, "The Diesel Gas Chambers," 41, 43.

56. Irving, "On Contemporary History and Historiography," 283.

57. Wimsatt, *Day of Leopards,* 12.

58. Robert Faurisson in interview with *Nouvelles littéraires* (10–17 February 1977), as quoted in Thion, *Vérité historique ou vérité politique?,* 54.

59. Langlois and Seignobos, *Introduction to the Study of History,* 17.

60. Ibid., 69.

61. Ibid., 115.

62. Ibid., 143.

63. DCO: HMQvEZ'85, transcripts, 2411–2412.

64. Langlois and Seignobos, *Introduction to the Study of History*, 131.

65. Wimsatt and Beardsley, "The Intentional Fallacy," in Wimsatt, *The Verbal Icon*, 4–5.

66. Rassinier developed these ideas in a number of books: *Le Passage de la ligne* (1949), *Le Mensonge d'Ulysse* (1950), *Ulysse trahi par les siens* (1961), and *Le Drama des Juifs européens* (1964). An English-language compilation of selected portions of these books appeared in 1978 under the title *The Holocaust Story and the Lies of Ulysses*. Officially designated "the only authorized edition available in the English language," this book quickly became, and has remained to this day, a negationist best-seller.

67. Rassinier, *The Holocaust and the Lies of Ulysses*, 109.

68. Ibid., 34.

69. Ibid., 53.

70. Ibid., 35.

71. Ibid., 112.

72. See Malaurie with Terrée, *L'affaire Kravchenko*; Berberova, *L'affaire Kravtchenko*.

73. Brayard, *Comment l'idée vint à M. Rassinier*, 438–439.

74. Printed in Thion, *Vérité historique ou vérité politique?*, 83–89.

75. Ibid., 89.

76. Wellers, "Reply to the Neo-Nazi Falsification of Historical Facts Concerning the Holocaust," 108.

77. Seidel, *The Holocaust Denial*, 99.

78. As quoted in Seidel, *The Holocaust Denial*, 101.

79. Faurisson to *Le Monde*, 29 December 1978, as quoted in Faurisson, *Mémoire en Défense*, 73.

80. Ibid., 75.

81. Faurisson to *Le Monde*, 16 January 1979, as quoted in Faurisson, *Mémoire en Défense*, 84.

82. "La politique hitlérienne d'extermination. Une décleration d'historiens," *Le Monde*, 21 February 1979.

83. Faurisson to *Le Monde*, 26 February 1979, as printed in Faurisson, *Mémoire en Défense*, 100.

84. Thion, *Vérité historique ou vérité politique?*, 189–190.

85. Ibid.

86. Ibid., 163.

87. Chomsky and Herman, *After the Cataclysm*, 24.

88. Faurisson, "The Mechanics of Gassing," 24.

89. Ibid., 30.

90. Ibid., 27.

91. Ibid., 29.

92. Faurisson testimony, DCO: HMQvEZ'88, transcripts, 8490ff.

93. Ibid., 8498.

94. As quoted in Jeffery Mehlman, "Foreword," in Vidal-Naquet, *Assassins of Memory*, xv.

95. Chomsky and Herman, *After the Cataclysm*, 295.

96. Finkelkraut, *The Future of a Negation*, 24–25.

97. Nietzsche, "On Truth and Lie in an Extra-Moral Sense," 219.

98. Kristeva, *Strangers to Ourselves*, 1.

99. Lyotard, *The Differend*, 3–4.

100. Thion, *Vérité historique ou vérité politique?*, 14.

101. Ibid., 33–34.

102. Noam Chomsky, "Quelques commentaires elementaires sur le droit a la liberté d'expression," in Faurisson, *Memoire en Defense*, xii.

103. Ibid., xiv.

104. Kuesters, "Encountering the Revisionists," 319.

105. Faurisson, "A Challenge to David Irving," 291.

106. Ibid., 292.

107. Ibid., 294.

108. Ibid., 302–303.

109. Harwood, *Did Six Million Really Die?*, 5.

110. David Irving to Ernst Zündel, 16 August 1984, in Van Pelt, "Expert Opinion," 566.

111. Felderer testimony, DCO: HMQvEZ'85, transcripts, 3255ff.

112. Leland Harrison to Secretary of State, 6 July 1944, telegram containing a copy of Roswell McClelland's summary of the Vrba-Wetzlar report to War Refugee Board of the same date, in *America and the Holocaust*, ed. Wyman, 12: 72–73.

113. Faurisson testimony, DCO: HMQvEZ'85, transcripts, 2390.

114. Ibid., 2530–2531.

115. Vrba testimony, DCO: HMQvEZ'85, transcripts, 1478–1479.

116. Lindsey, "Zyklon B, Auschwitz, and the Trial of Dr. Bruno Tesch," 287–288.

117. Lindsey testimony, DCO: HMQvEZ'85, transcripts, 3085.

118. Hoffman, *The Great Holocaust Trial*, 7ff.

119. David Irving, "Censorship of History," lecture given in Runnymead, Australia, 18 March 1986, in Van Pelt, "Expert Opinion," 567.

120. David Irving interviewed by Terry Lane, of ABC 3LO Radio, 18 March 1986, in Van Pelt, "Expert Opinion," 568.

121. Ibid.

122. Nolte, *Der europäische Bürgerkrieg 1917–1945*, 515.

123. Ibid., 513.

124. Ibid., 592.

125. Zündel, "The David Irving/Eichmann Memoirs Controversy!," 1.

126. Ernst Zündel to David Irving, 21 May 1986, in Van Pelt, "Expert Opinion," 569.

127. Ernst Zündel to David Irving, 9 November 1987, in Van Pelt, "Expert Opinion," 571.

128. Ernst Zündel to David Irving, 4 January 1988, in Van Pelt, "Expert Opinion," 572.

129. David Irving to Ernst Zündel, 17 January 1988, in Van Pelt, "Expert Opinion," 855.

130. Bill Armontraut to Barbara Kulaszka, 13 January 1988, in Van Pelt, "Expert Opinion," 498.

131. Leuchter, "The Leuchter Report: The How and the Why," 133.

132. Ibid., 135.

133. Ernst Zündel to David Irving, 12 March 1988, in Van Pelt, "Expert Opinion," 573.

134. Leuchter, *The Leuchter Report*, 7.

135. Ernst Zündel in interview with Errol Morris, 9 September 1998, transcript, Black Bulldog Productions.

136. Irving testimony, DCO: HMQvEZ'88, transcripts, 9388.

137. Ibid., 9403–9404.

138. Ibid., 9390–9391.

139. Ibid., 9391.

140. Ibid., 9471ff.

141. Leuchter, *The Leuchter Report,* 7.

142. Irving testimony, DCO: HMQvEZ'88, transcripts, 9414, 9423.

143. Irving, "Battleship Auschwitz," 498–499.

144. "The Second Trial of the Indefatigable Ernst Zündel," *Instauration,* July 1988, 6.

145. Willis A. Carto to David Irving, 2 April 1989, in Van Pelt, "Expert Opinion," 587.

146. Lecture given by David Irving in Toronto, August 1988, in Van Pelt, "Expert Opinion," 588.

147. Ibid.

148. Mayer, *Why Did the Heavens Not Darken?,* 35.

149. Ibid., 365.

150. Ibid.

151. Goldhagen, "False Witness," 39.

152. Ibid., 44.

153. "The Holocaust: A Sinking Ship," *IHR Newsletter* 66 (May 1989): 2.

154. Ibid.

155. Mayer, *Why Did the Heavens Not Darken?,* 362.

156. Faurisson, Review of *Why Did the Heavens Not Darken?,* 379.

157. David Irving to Robert Countess, 2 July 1989, in Van Pelt, "Expert Opinion," 596.

158. Focal Point Publications, "Press Statement: The Leuchter Report, The First Forensic Examination of Auschwitz," June 1989, in Van Pelt, "Expert Opinion," 596–597.

159. Irving, "Foreword," in Leuchter, *Auschwitz: The End of the Line,* 6.

160. Ibid.

161. House of Commons—Early Day Motion, Tuesday 20th June 1989; Member—Hugh Dykes; Title—David Irving and Holocaust Denial, in Van Pelt, "Expert Opinion," 599.

162. David Irving to Hugh Dykes, 30 June 1989, in Van Pelt, "Expert Opinion," 600.

163. David Irving to the Earl of Kitchener, 14 June 1990, in Van Pelt, "Expert Opinion," 622.

164. Gray, *The Irving Judgement,* 234–235.

165. David A. Crabtree to David Irving, 14 July 1989, in Van Pelt, "Expert Opinion," 916.

166. David A. Crabtree, "The Leuchter Report—proposals for amendments to be incorporated in the second edition, Together with reasoned substantiation thereof," 2, in Van Pelt, "Expert Report," 604.

167. Ernst Zündel to David Irving, 1 August 1989, in Van Pelt, "Expert Opinion," 606.

168. Ibid.

169. Wegner, "Keine Massenvergasungen in Auschwitz?," 450ff. Because the printed version of Wegner's article is not identical with the manuscript Weber sent to Irving, I will refer to the manuscript version of Wegner's article.

170. Mark Weber to David Irving, 31 July 1989, in Van Pelt, "Expert Opinion," 608.

171. "Kritische Stellungnahme zum sogen. Leuchter-Dokument," 12–13, in Van Pelt, "Expert Opinion," 608.

172. David Irving to Mark Weber, 4 September 1989, in Van Pelt, "Expert Opinion," 609–610.

173. It is unclear whether Colin Beer was the author of the critique or

only the conduit of the report from the unknown author to Irving. Irving's 12 January 1990 letter to Colin Beer suggests the latter possibility; Irving wrote "Dear Mr. Beer: Thank you so much for sending me that anonymous treatise on the *Leuchter Report.*" However, in a letter Irving wrote that same day to Zündel, there is a suggestion that he thought that Beer was actually the author: "Dear Ernst: The Leuchter Report continues to attract much attention, and several learned responses. I thought you might like to see the latest, from Colin Beer, in England, and my humble response." David Irving to Colin M. Beer, 12 January 1990; and David Irving to Ernst Zündel, 12 January 1990, in Van Pelt, "Expert Opinion," 612.

174. Anonymous, "Critique of Forensic Examinations of Auschwitz by Leuchter," unpublished manuscript, 5–6, in Van Pelt, "Expert Opinion," 615–616.

175. David Irving to Colin M. Beer, 12 January 1990, in Van Pelt, "Expert Opinion," 616–617.

176. Witte, et al., eds., *Der Dienstkalender Heinrich Himmler's 1941/42,* 492.

177. Höss, *Death Dealer,* 32–33.

178. Irving, *Hitler's War* (1991 edition), 466.

179. Irving, *Hitler's War* (1977 edition), 632.

180. Irving, *Hitler's War* (1991 edition), 620.

181. Irving, *Hitler's War* (1977 edition), 660.

182. Irving, *Hitler's War* (1991 edition), 654.

183. Kossoff, "Keep Holocaust 'Apologists' out of Britain, Home Secretary Is Told," 1.

184. Immigration and Nationality Department to Fred Leuchter, 1 October 1991, in Van Pelt, "Expert Opinion," 643.

185. "Leuchter is Coming," Flyer published by Focal Point Publications, 1991, in Van Pelt, "Expert Opinion," 646.

186. The Chelsea Old Town Hall Meeting, "This Week" program, 28 November 1991, in Van Pelt, "Expert Opinion," 646.

187. David Irving, "Robert Faurisson," introductory remarks to a lecture by Faurisson given in London, Friday 15 November 1991, in Van Pelt, "Expert Opinion," 646–647.

188. Farrell, "Death's Salesman Cut Off before His Time."

189. Ibid.

190. Press statement made by Fred Leuchter, 17 November 1991, in Van Pelt, "Expert Opinion," 648.

191. Sereny, "David Irving Resells Hitler's War."

192. Lecture, David Irving in Toronto, 8 November 1990, in Van Pelt, "Expert Opinion," 640–641.

193. Lecture, David Irving in Moers, Germany, 5 March 1990, in Van Pelt, "Expert Opinion," 621.

194. HCJ/QB: IvP&L, "Defence of the Second Defendant," 7.

195. Ibid., 8.

196. Kossoff, "Hitler Innocent, Says Irving, Despite 'Discovery' of Eichmann Documents," 1.

197. David Irving to Ernst Zündel, 27 January 1993, in Van Pelt, "Expert Opinion," 668.

198. David Irving, "The Search for Truth in History Banned," 1993, in Van Pelt, "Expert Opinion," 670.

199. Ball, *Air Photo Evidence,* 1.

200. Ibid., 113.

201. "The Ball Report," insert in Ball, *Air Photo Evidence,* 1.

202. David Irving to Ernst Zündel, 15 December 1993, in Van Pelt, "Expert Opinion," 673.

203. David Irving's lecture in Milton, Ontario, 5 October 1991, in Van Pelt, "Expert Opinion," 644.

204. Irving, "Opinion."

205. Rosenbaum, *Explaining Hitler,* 233.

206. Conan, "Auschwitz: La mémoire du mal," 54ff.

207. Ibid., 57.

208. Ibid., 60.

209. Ibid., 68.

210. Irving, "French Make a Clean Breast," 1.

211. Ibid., 4.

212. *David Irving's Action Report,* no. 9 (May 1995), 4.

213. David Irving in interview with Ron Casey, 27 July 1995, Station 2GB, *Media Monitors* (Sydney, Melbourne etc.): Broadcast Transcript S36962003, in Van Pelt, "Expert Opinion," 684–685.

214. Hilberg, *The Destruction of the European Jews,* 3: 1219.

215. Faurisson to Irving, 29 September 1995, faxed letter, in Van Pelt, "Expert Opinion," 685–686.

216. Irving to Faurisson, 28 November 1995, in Van Pelt, "Expert Opinion," 686.

217. Faurisson to Irving, 1 December 1995, faxed letter, in Van Pelt, "Expert Opinion," 686–687.

218. Faurisson, "On David Irving," 1.

219. Lipstadt, "A Proposal for Research: The Historical and Historiographic Methodology of the Holocaust Deniers" (1984), unpublished manuscript in possession of Deborah Lipstadt.

220. Yehuda Bauer to Deborah Lipstadt, 27 November 1992, in possession of Deborah Lipstadt.

221. Lipstadt, *Denying the Holocaust,* 181.

222. David Irving, fax to his supporters, 12 November 1994. Posted on his Web site fpp.co.ok under the title "The Day Deborah Lipstadt Found Herself Face to Face with David Irving" on 9 October 1998.

223. Irving, "The Life and Death of 'Dr Goebbels,'" 7.

224. Lipstadt, *Denying the Holocaust,* 161.

225. Ibid., 179.

226. HCJ/QB: IvP&L, "Statement of Claim," lines 261–275.

227. Ibid., lines 285–295.

228. Ibid., lines 318–324.

229. Ibid., lines 379–390.

2. Marshaling the Evidence for Auschwitz

1. Jaspers, *On the Origin and Goal of History,* 147.

2. Ibid., 148.

3. Van Pelt and Westfall, *Architectural Principles,* 405.

4. Apfelbaum, "Forgetting the Past," 612.

5. Van Pelt, "A Site in Search of a Mission," 93.

6. As quoted in Dawidowicz, ed., *A Holocaust Reader,* 131ff.

7. Levi, *The Drowned and the Saved,* 11–12.

8. Donat, *The Holocaust Kingdom,* 183, 211.

9. Wyschogrod, *An Ethics of Remembering,* 3.

10. Faurisson to *Le Monde,* 26 February 1979, as printed in Faurisson, *Mémoire en Défense,* 100.

11. Pressac, *Auschwitz: Technique and Operation of the Gas Chambers,* 429ff.

12. Shermer and Grobman, *Denying History,* 34.

13. Shermer, "Proving the Holocaust," 42–43.

14. Brugioni and Poirier, *The Holocaust Revisited,* 10–11.

15. Lipstadt, "The Mundane Face of Evil," C1.

16. Leuchter, *The Leuchter Report,* 11.

17. HCJ/QB: IvP&L, "Defence of Second Defendant," 2.

18. Harriet Benson of Mishcon de Reya to Robert Jan van Pelt, 9 June 1998.

19. HCJ/QB: IvP&L, "Defence of Second Defendant," 5.

20. HCJ/QB: IvP&L, "Reply to Defence of Second Defendant," 5.

21. Information Service, Republic of Poland, "Documents from Poland," 2.

22. Bloch, *The Historian's Craft,* 67.

23. Wilkins, *Of the Principles and Duties of Natural Religion,* 22ff.

24. Iwaszko, "Les Détenus 'E' d'Auschwitz."

25. For a collection of excellent oral histories of surviving Sonderkommandos see Greif, *Wir weinten tränenlos.*

26. HCJ/QB: IvP&L, "Defence of Second Defendant," 6.

27. HCJ/QB: IvP&L, "Reply to Defence of Second Defendant," 5.

28. HCJ/QB: IvP&L, "Defence of Second Defendant," 8.

29. Ibid., 11; Mark Weber, introductory remarks, in Irving, "Battleship Auschwitz," 492ff.

30. HCJ/QB: IvP&L, "Defence of Second Defendant," 11–12; Irving, "Battleship Auschwitz," 498–499.

31. Irving, "Battleship Auschwitz," 500.

32. HCJ/QB: IvP&L, "Reply to Defence of Second Defendant," 9.

33. HCJ/QB: IvP&L, "Defence of Second Defendant," 16.

34. HCJ/QB: IvP&L, "Reply to Defence of Second Defendant," 9.

35. HCJ/QB: IvP&L, "Defence of Second Defendant," 17; also Irving, "Foreword," in Leuchter, *Auschwitz: The End of the Line,* 6.

36. Ibid.

37. HCJ/QB: IvP&L, "Reply to Defence of Second Defendant," 10.

38. Ibid., 20.

39. Aschenauer, ed., *Ich, Adolf Eichmann,* 496.

40. As quoted in State of Israel, *The Trial of Adolf Eichmann,* 3: 1310.

41. "Testimony of Rudolf Hoess Taken at Nurnberg, on 1 April 1946," in Mendelson and Detwiler, *The Holocaust,* 12: 72.

42. Document 3868–PS, "Affidavit of Rudolf Franz Ferdinand Hoess," in IMT, *Trial of the Major War Criminals,* 33: 275–276.

43. Gilbert, *Nuremberg Diary,* 249.

44. State of Israel, *The Trial of Adolf Eichmann,* 3: 1005–1006.

45. Ibid., 38–39.

46. Kevin Bays of Davenport Lyons to Robert Jan van Pelt, 21 August 1998.

47. "Aharon Appelfeld," in Lewis, *Art out of Agony,* 16.

48. Wiesel, "Why I Write," 201.

49. Levi, *The Drowned and the Saved,* 83–84.

50. Boder, *I Did Not Interview the Dead.*

51. Lyotard, *The Differend,* 56–57.

52. Ibid., 58.

53. Bloch, *The Historian's Craft,* 61.

54. Ibid., 101.

55. Hume, *A Treatise of Human Nature,* 130–131.

56. De Tocqueville, *Democracy in America,* 2: 9.

57. See Pompa, *Human Nature and Historical Knowledge,* 27–28.

58. Ibid., 197.

59. Ibid., 200–201.

60. Lecture by David Irving in Moers, Germany, 5 March 1990, in Van Pelt, "Expert Opinion," 621.

61. Irving, "Battleship Auschwitz," 500.

62. State Museum of Auschwitz-Birkenau, *Death Books from Auschwitz,* 1: 212ff.

63. Irving, *Hitler's War* (1977), 391.

64. Ibid., 500.

65. David Irving, "The Search for Truth in History Banned," 1993, in Van Pelt, "Expert Opinion," 670.

66. Broad, "Reminiscences," 142.

67. State of Israel, *The Trial of Adolf Eichmann,* 3: 1005–1006.

68. USA, *Trials of War Criminals Before the Nuernberg Military Tribunals,* 5: 433.

69. See USSR, "Statement . . . on Crimes Committed by the German-fascist Invaders in the Oswiecim Death Camp," 8.

70. Ibid.

71. Expert Opinion of Nachman Blumental, Höss Trial, 29: 153ff.; 31: 47ff., AABSMO.

72. Reitlinger, *The Final Solution,* 460–461.

73. Ibid., 489.

74. Ibid., 488.

75. For the higher figure, see Document 3868–PS, "Affidavit of Rudolf Franz Ferdinand Hoess," in IMT, *Trial of the Major War Criminals,* 33: 275–276; see also Gilbert, *Nuremberg Diary,* 249. For the lower figure, see "Testimony of Rudolf Hoess Taken at Nurnberg, on 1 April 1946, 1430 to 1730," in Mendelson and Detwiler, *The Holocaust,* 12: 72; State of Israel, *The Trial of Adolf Eichmann,* 3: 1005–1006; Höss, "The Final Solution to the Jewish Question," in *Death Dealer,* 38–39.

76. Hilberg, *The Destruction of the European Jews,* 3: 1219.

77. Yad Vashem published his findings in 1991: see Piper, "Estimating the Number of Deportees to and Victims of the Auschwitz-Birkenau Camp." The United States Holocaust Research Institute published Piper's findings in 1994: see Piper, "The Number of Victims."

78. See Piper, *Die Zahl der Opfer von Auschwitz,* 65ff.

79. Broad, "Reminiscences," 142.

80. See Kern, "The Family Camp," 428ff.

81. Bischoff to Kammler, 28 June 1943, Osobyi Moscow, ms. 502/1–314; USHRI Washington, microfilm RG 11.001M.03–41.

82. See Piper, *Die Zahl der Opfer von Auschwitz,* 100.

83. Czech, *Auschwitz Chronicle: 1939–1945.*

84. Ibid., 268–269.

85. Lestschinsky, "Bilan d'extermination," 19–20.

86. Pressac, *Les crématoires d'Auschwitz,* 147.

87. Ibid.

88. Ibid., 148.

89. Pressac, *Die Krematorien von Auschwitz,* 197ff.

90. Bischoff to Kammler, 28 June 1943, Osobyi Moscow, ms. 502/1–314; USHRI Washington, microfilm RG 11.001M.03–41.

91. Pressac, *Die Krematorien von Auschwitz,* 196–197.

92. Richard Evans to Robert Jan van Pelt, e-mail message, 17 June 1998.

93. Robert Jan van Pelt to Richard Evans, e-mail message, 17 June 1998, 8:48 AM.

94. Richard Evans to Robert Jan van Pelt, e-mail message, 17 June 1998, 9:55 AM.

95. David Irving to Robert Jan van Pelt, Chicago, 29 May 1997, www.fpp.co.uk/Auschwitz/Pelt/query290597.html.

96. Focal Point Publications, "Press Statement: The Leuchter Report, The First Forensic Examination of Auschwitz," June 1989, in Van Pelt, "Expert Opinion," 596–597.

97. Irving, "Foreword," in Leuchter, *Auschwitz: The End of the Line*, 6.

98. "Leuchter Report Press Conference," London, 23 June 1989, in Van Pelt, "Expert Opinion," 601.

99. Lecture, David Irving in Moers, Germany, 5 March 1990, in Van Pelt, "Expert Opinion," 621.

100. Telegram 1189, "From Foreign Office to Moscow," 26 August 1943, PRO/FO 371/34551.

101. Telegram 1190, "From Foreign Office to Moscow," 26 August 1943, PRO/FO 371/34551.

102. Victor Cavendish-Bentinck Minute, 27 August 1943, PRO/FO 371/34551.

103. Trevor-Roper, *History and Imagination*, 15–16.

104. Ponsonby, *Falsehood in War-Time*, 161.

105. Read, *Atrocity Propaganda 1914–1919*, 25.

106. Ponsonby, *Falsehood in War-Time*, 25ff.

107. Viereck, *Spreading Germs of Hate*, 153–154.

108. "The Corpse Factory," *The Times*, 17 April 1917.

109. "Cannon-Fodder—and After," *Punch*, 152 (25 April 1917).

110. Kushner, *The Holocaust and the Liberal Imagination*, 56.

111. *Time* (18 September 1939), 59, as quoted in Lipstadt, *Beyond Belief*, 137.

112. *Peoria Journal Transcript*, 9 March 1940, as quoted in Lipstadt, *Beyond Belief*, 137.

113. Wasserstein, *Britain and the Jews of Europe*, 166–167.

114. As quoted in Hamilton, *Koestler*, 77.

115. Koestler, *The Yogi and the Commissar*, 94–95.

116. Lawrence, "50,000 Kiev Jews Reported Killed," 3.

117. Lawrence, *Six Presidents, Too Many Wars*, 90–91.

118. Diary 5358, 20 April 1945, as quoted in Reilly, *Belsen*, 66.

119. Chandler and Ambrose, eds., *Papers of Dwight David Eisenhower*, 4: 2615–2616.

120. Ibid., 2623.

121. As quoted in Frei, "'Wir waren blind, ungläubig und langsam," 390.

122. Ibid., 390–391.

123. As quoted in Lipstadt, *Beyond Belief*, 249.

124. As quoted in Lipstadt, *Beyond Belief*, 274.

125. Churchill, "The War Situation IV," in *Blood, Sweat, and Tears*, 391.

126. Churchill, "Their Finest Hour," in *Blood, Sweat, and Tears*, 314.

127. Adorno, *Minima Moralia*, 108.

128. Ibid., 109.

129. Judge Michael A. Musmanno, "Concurring Opinion," in USA, *Trials of War Criminals Before the Nuernberg Military Tribunal*, 5: 1128–1129.

3. Intentional Evidence

1. HCJ/QB: IvP&L, transcripts, day 6 (19 January 2000), 45–46.

2. Ibid., 193–194.

3. Trevor-Roper, "Hitler: Does History Offer a Defence?"

4. Crowell, "The Gas Chamber of Sherlock Holmes," Section 1, at http:/www.fpp.co.uk/Auschwitz/Auschw.html.

5. Showalter, *Hystories*, 6.

6. Crowell, "The Gas Chamber of Sherlock Holmes," Section 1.

7. Ibid.

8. Crowell, "The Gas Chamber of Sherlock Holmes," Section 16.

9. Wilhelm Stäglich, "My Impressions of the Auschwitz Concentration Camp in 1944," as published in Stäglich, *The Auschwitz Myth*, 293.

10. Stäglich, *The Auschwitz Myth*, 2–3.

11. Ibid., 109–110.

12. Ibid., 114.

13. Ibid.

14. Ibid., 115–116.

15. Le Bon, *Psychologie des foules*, 124.

16. Stäglich, *The Auschwitz Myth*,116.

17. Kautsky, *Teufel und Verdammte*, 273.

18. Stäglich, *The Auschwitz Myth*,117.

19. Irving testimony, DCO: HMQvEZ'88, transcripts, 9403–9404.

20. Stäglich, *The Auschwitz Myth*, 118.

21. HCJ/QB: IvP&L, transcripts, day 7 (20 January 2000), 152.

22. Crowell, "The Gas Chamber of Sherlock Holmes," Section 2.

23. Republic of Poland, "Documents from Poland: German Attempts to Murder a Nation," 2.

24. Ibid.

25. See Barcz, "Die erste Vergasung," 17–18.

26. Republic of Poland, "German Crimes Arraigned," 3, and "A Press Conference at the Ministry of Information," 5.

27. Republic of Poland, "Extermination of the Polish Jewry: What Happened in the Warsaw Ghetto," 3.

28. Republic of Poland, "Extraordinary Report from the Jew-extermination Camp at Belzec," 4.

29. Republic of Poland, *The Mass Extermination of Jews in German Occupied Poland*.

30. As quoted in Swiebocki, *London Has Been Informed*, 77.

31. Gilbert, *Auschwitz and the Allies*, 129.

32. Gilbert, "What Was Known and Why," 540.

33. As quoted in Gilbert, *Auschwitz and the Allies*, 234.

34. Gilbert, *Auschwitz and the Allies*, 130.

35. "Underground Poland," in Polish Labor Group, *Oswiecim Camp of Death*, 33–34.

36. Nansen, *From Day to Day*, 341.

37. Ibid., 349.

38. Ibid.

39. War Refugee Board, "The Extermination Camps of Auschwitz (Oswiecim) and Birkenau in Upper Silesia," in *America and the Holocaust*, ed. Wyman, 12: 13.

40. Ibid., 18.

41. Ibid., 19–20.

42. Vrba and Bestic, *I Cannot Forgive*, 175, 271.

43. Müller, with Freitag, *Eyewitness Auschwitz,* 121–122.

44. Vrba testimony, DCO: HMQvEZ'85, transcripts, 1478–1479.

45. War Refugee Board, "The Extermination Camps of Auschwitz (Oswiecim) and Birkenau in Upper Silesia," in *America and the Holocaust,* ed. Wyman, 12: 20.

46. Ibid.

47. As quoted in Gilbert, *Auschwitz and the Allies,* 234.

48. Ibid., 236.

49. Swiebocki, "Die lagernahe Widerstandsbewegung," 118–119, 142, 174ff.

50. War Refugee Board, "The Extermination Camps of Auschwitz (Oswiecim) and Birkenau in Upper Silesia," in *America and the Holocaust,* ed. Wyman, 12: 58.

51. Ibid., 58.

52. As quoted in Gilbert, *Auschwitz and the Allies,* 251. Gilbert notes that the figure of 60,000 was a "telegraphic error" and that the correct figure, given in the original message Lichtheim drafted, was 12,000.

53. For the text of the summary, see Gilbert, *Auschwitz and the Allies,* 262ff.

54. As quoted in Gilbert, *Auschwitz and the Allies,* 246.

55. Leland Harrison to Secretary of State, 6 July 1944, telegram containing a copy of Roswell McClelland's telegram to War Refugee Board of the same date, in *America and the Holocaust,* ed. Wyman, 12: 67.

56. Roswell D. McClelland to John Pehle, Director, War Refugee Board, 12 October 1944, in *America and the Holocaust,* ed. Wyman, 12: 75–76.

57. Leland Harrison to Secretary of State, 6 July 1944, telegram containing a copy of Roswell McClelland's summary of the Vrba-Wetzlar report to War Refugee Board of the same date, in *America and the Holocaust,* ed. Wyman, 12: 71.

58. Ibid.

59. Ibid., 72–73.

60. Ibid., 74.

61. "Czechs Report Massacre," *New York Times,* 20 June 1944, 5.

62. Brigham, "Two Death Camps: Places of Horror," 6.

63. Simonov, "Lublin Annihilation Camp," 5.

64. Ibid., 7–8.

65. Simonov, "Lublin Annihilation Camp, Part II," 5.

66. Ibid., 5–6.

67. The term "River Rouge" referred to the highly mechanized Ford plant on the Rouge River near Detroit, which in the 1930s and 1940s had become to Americans a symbol of the most advanced system of mechanized production.

68. Lawrence, "Nazi Mass Killing Laid Bare in Camp," 1, 9.

69. "Biggest Atrocity Story Breaks in Poland," 1045.

70. "Vernichtungslager," 36.

71. Lauterbach, "Murder, Inc.," 36.

72. Ibid.

73. Lauterbach, "Sunday in Poland," 17.

74. See *Soviet Government Statements on Nazi Atrocities.*

75. Union of Soviet Socialist Republics, "Statement of the Polish-Soviet Extraordinary Commission for the Investigation of Crimes Committed by the Germans in the Extermination Camp of Maidanek in the Town of Lublin," 1–8.

76. "Statement of the Polish-Soviet Extraordinary Commission," 1.

77. Ibid., 5.

78. Ibid., 6.

79. Marszalek, *Majdanek,* 8.

80. Affidavit given by SS-Standartenführer Kurt Becher in Nuremberg, 8 March 1946, PS-3762, IMT, *Trial of the Major War Criminals,* 23: 68.

81. Crowell, "The Gas Chamber of Sherlock Holmes," Section 4.

82. Ibid.

83. War Refugee Board, "German Extermination Camps of Auschwitz (Oswiecim) and Birkenau," in *America and the Holocaust,* ed. Wyman, 12: 1.

84. Levi, *The Reawakening,* 11–12.

85. Boris Polevoi, "The Factory of Death at Auschwitz," *Pravda,* 2 February 1945, as translated by "Samuel Crowell" and published on David Irving's Web site, http://w.w.w.fpp.co.uk/Auschwitz/Auschw.html.

86. Polevoi, "The Factory of Death at Auschwitz."

87. J. A. Topf & Söhne, Erfurt, Patent Application, "Kontinuierliche arbeitender Leichen-Verbrennungsofen für Massenbetrieb," AABSMO, ZBL/BW 30/44.

88. "Samuel Crowell," Introduction to Polevoi, "The Factory of Death at Auschwitz."

89. "Poland's Jewish Survivors," 1.

90. "Oswiecim Revelations," 1.

91. See Nathan Cohen, "Diaries of the *Sonderkommando,*" in Gutman and Berenbaum, *Anatomy of the Auschwitz Death Camp,* 523ff.

92. Salmen Gradowski, Letter, in *Amidst a Nightmare of Crime,* ed. Bezwinska and Czech, 75ff.

93. Cohen, "Diaries of the *Sonderkommando,*" in Gutman and Berenbaum, *Anatomy of the Auschwitz Death Camp,* 523.

94. Treblinka was located on a side line some six miles from the main railway line connecting Bialystok and Warsaw.

95. Gradowski, "Diary," in *Amidst a Nightmare of Crime,* ed. Bezwinska and Czech, 81.

96. Ibid., 82ff.

97. Ibid., 94.

98. Ibid., 95.

99. Gradowski, "Diary," in *Amidst a Nightmare of Crime,* ed. Bezwinska and Czech, 99ff.

100. As quoted in Hawkins, ed., *War Report: D-Day to VE-Day,* 318.

101. As quoted in Lipstadt, *Beyond Belief,* 259.

102. Republic of Poland, "Polish Women in German Concentration Camps," 1.

103. Padover, *Experiment in Germany,* 358.

104. Heym, *Reden an den Feind,* 334–335.

105. "The Horrors of Buchenwald," 2.

106. Document 159, "Experiences of a Fifteen-Year-Old in Birkenau," in *The Buchenwald Report,* ed. Hackett, 349.

107. Stäglich, *The Auschwitz Myth,* 115–116.

108. Document 157, "Selections in Birkenau," in *The Buchenwald Report,* ed. Hackett, 346–347.

109. Ibid., 2.

110. Ibid., 5–6.

111. Ibid., 8.

112. State of Israel, *The Trial of Adolf Eichmann,* 3: 1247.

113. Information given to the author by Yehuda Bacon, 16 November 2000.

114. State of Israel, *The Trial of Adolf Eichmann,* 3: 1251.

115. Ibid.

116. As quoted in Klarsfeld, *David Olère 1902–1985,* 8.

117. Both drawings are in the collection of the museum of the Ghetto Fighters' House Holocaust and Jewish Resistance Heritage Museum, Kibbutz Lohamei-Haghettaot, Israel.

118. USSR, "Statement of the Extraordinary State Committee for the Ascertaining and Investigation of Crimes Committed by the German-fascist Invaders and Their Associates in the Oswiecim Death Camp," 1.

119. Ibid., 8.

120. Crowell, "The Gas Chamber of Sherlock Holmes," Section 6.

121. "Samuel Crowell," Introduction to Polevoi, "The Factory of Death at Auschwitz."

122. Crowell, "The Gas Chamber of Sherlock Holmes," Section 6.

123. Ibid.

124. Ibid.

125. Central Commission for Investigation of German Crimes in Poland, *German Crimes in Poland,* 1: 7.

126. Stanislaw Jankowski, "Deposition," in *Amidst a Nightmare of Crime,* ed. Bezwinska and Czech, 45ff.

127. Ibid., 53ff.

128. Ibid., 63.

129. Ibid., 56.

130. Protocol testimony of Shlomo Dragon, 10 and 11 May 1945, added as Appendix 17 to CDC, "Protocol on the Machinery of Mass Extermination of Humans in Birkenau," 26 November 1946, trans. Roman Sas-Zalaziocky, in LSW, Case 20 Vr 3806/64 (Ertl/Dejaco), ON 264, 393y to 393z.

131. Protocol testimony of Shlomo Dragon, 10 and 11 May 1945, in LSW, Case 20 Vr 3806/64 (Ertl/Dejaco), ON 264, 393cc.

132. Ibid.

133. Deposition of Henry Tauber, as quoted in Pressac, *Auschwitz: Technique and Operation of the Gas Chambers,* 483.

134. Ibid., 483.

135. Pery Broad, "Reminiscences," in Auschwitz-Birkenau State Museum in Oswiecim, *KL Auschwitz Seen by the SS,* 128ff.

136. Ibid., 483–484.

137. Fromer, *The Holocaust Odyssey of Daniel Bennahmias, Sonderkommando,* 52–53.

138. Ibid., 483–484.

139. Ibid., 488.

140. Chamotte is fired clay or firebrick.

141. Deposition of Henry Tauber, as quoted in Pressac, *Auschwitz: Technique and Operation of the Gas Chambers,* 489.

142. Ibid.

143. Ibid.

144. Ibid.

145. Ibid., 489.

146. Ibid., 494.

147. Ibid.

148. Ibid., 495.

149. Ibid.

150. Ibid., 498, 500–501.

151. Ibid., 502.

152. Eknes, "Crematoriums II and III," 315.

153. Ibid., 315–316.

154. Protocol testimony of Michael Kula, 11 June 1945, added as Appendix 16 to CDC, "Protocol on the Machinery of Mass Extermination of Humans in Birkenau," 26 November 1946, trans. Roman Sas-Zalaziocky, in LSW, Case 20 Vr 3806/64 (Ertl/Dejaco), ON 264, 393u (r).

155. Ibid., 393u (v).

156. Ibid., 393v (r & v).

157. Report 15 December 1945 of the Forensic Laboratory at Cracow, signed by its director, Dr. Jan Z. Robel, added as Appendix 12 to CDC, "Protocol on the Machinery of Mass Extermination of Humans in Birkenau," 26 November 1946, trans. Roman Sas-Zalaziocky, in LSW, Case 20 Vr 3806/64 (Ertl/Dejaco), ON 264, 393g (r) to 393h (r).

158. The crematorium in the main camp was assigned the number BW 11; those in Birkenau were all put under the general heading of BW 30— Crematorium 2 as BW 30, Crematorium 3 as BW 30/a, Crematorium 4 as BW 30/b, and Crematorium 5 as BW 30/c.

159. CDC, "Protocol on the Machinery of Mass Extermination of Humans in Birkenau," 26 November 1946, trans. Roman Sas-Zalaziocky, in LSW, Case 20 Vr 3806/64 (Ertl/Dejaco), ON 220, 309–353 and 393a–393f.

160. CDC, "Protocol on the Machinery of Mass Extermination of Humans in Birkenau," 311.

161. See Kogon, Langbein, and Rückerl, eds., Nazi Mass Murder, 5ff.

162. CDC, "Protocol on the Machinery of Mass Extermination of Humans in Birkenau," 314ff.

163. Ibid., 315–316.

164. Ibid., 323 verso.

165. Ibid., 330 recto–331.

166. Ibid., 334.

167. Ibid., 335 recto–336.

168. Ibid., 340 verso–341.

169. Ibid., 351ff.

170. Ibid., 393e.

171. Jan Sehn, "Concentration and Extermination Camp at Oswiecim (Auschwitz-Birkenau)," in Central Commission for Investigation of German Crimes in Poland, German Crimes in Poland, 1: 27–28.

172. Ibid., 28.

173. Ibid., 32–33.

174. Ibid., 83–84.

175. Ibid., 85–86.

176. Ibid., 88.

177. Ibid., 90.

178. Ibid., 91.

179. Ibid., 92.

180. Kraus and Schön, Továrna na Smrt.

181. Ibid., 116.

182. Ibid., 119.

183. Ibid.

184. Ibid., 120; the blueprints are printed on a fold-out page between pages 144 and 145.

185. Ibid., 120–121.

186. Ibid., 121–122.

187. Ibid., between pages 144 and 145.

188. Ibid., figures 22 and 23, between pages 160 and 161.

189. Ibid., 125–126.

4. Confessions and Trials

1. Langbein, *Der Auschwitz Prozeß*, 1: 538.

2. Ibid., 537.

3. Ibid., 538–539.

4. Pery Broad, "Reminiscences," in Auschwitz-Birkenau State Museum in Oswiecim, *KL Auschwitz Seen by the SS*, 128ff.

5. Ibid., 134.

6. Ibid., 135.

7. Ibid., 136.

8. Ibid., 142.

9. As quoted in Silets, "Facts Written in Blood," 98.

10. Ibid., 100ff.

11. Ibid.

12. David Irving to Tom Marcellus, 4 June 1992, in Van Pelt, "Expert Opinion," 657.

13. Irving, *Nuremberg*, 353–354.

14. Höss, *Death Dealer*, 231.

15. Statement of Hans Aumeier 29 June 1945, PRO/WO 208/4661, 3ff.

16. Handwritten account by Hans Aumeier, 25 July 1945, 3ff., PRO/WO 208/4661.

17. http://www.fpp.co.uk/Auschwitz/Aumeier/Crowell280199.html.

18. Aumeier refers here to Crematorium 4, which came into operation shortly after Crematorium 2 but before Crematorium 3. He is confused about the number of ovens. Crematorium 4 had one double-four-muffle oven, while Crematorium 2 had five triple-muffle ovens—in other words, he seems to have switched the oven arrangement in his memory. But he is right in his description of the aboveground gas chambers of Crematorium 4, which had openings in the gas-tight shutters through which the Zyklon was inserted into the gas chambers.

19. Handwritten account by Hans Aumeier, 25 July 1945, 3ff., PRO/WO 208/4661.

20. "Aussiedlung der Juden," typed account by Hans Aumeier dated Oslo, 8 October 1945, PRO/WO 208/4661, 10.

21. Undated account by Hans Aumeier, PRO/WO 208/6441, 43.

22. As quoted in Phillips, ed., *Trial of Josef Kramer*, 17.

23. Ibid., 66.

24. Ibid., 68.

25. Ibid., 742.

26. Ibid., 131–132.

27. Ibid., 134.

28. Ibid., 731.

29. Ibid., 738.

30. Ibid., 157.

31. Ibid., 173–174.

32. Ibid., 157–158.

33. Ibid., 183.

34. Ibid., 717.

35. Ibid., 184.

36. Ibid.

37. Ibid., 714–715.

38. Ibid., 196.

39. Ibid., 156.

40. Ibid., 148.

41. Ibid., 149. In the official published version of Winwood's opening speech, he limited himself to stating that "the type of internee who came to these concentration camps was low, and had very little idea of doing what they were told." It seems, however, that Winwood used slightly different words during his actual submission. "The concentration camps of Germany came to contain the dregs of the ghettoes of central Europe—people who had very little idea how to behave in ordinary life or of doing what they were told." This statement led to a formal protest by the Executive of the Board of Deputies, which noted that Winwood's statement "besmirches the memory of millions of men, women and children who died amid unspeakable horrors or were murdered for no fault but that they were Jews." See "The Belsen Trial," 9.

42. Phillips, ed., *Trial of Josef Kramer,* 538–539.

43. Ibid., 244.

44. Ibid., 494.

45. Ibid., 505.

46. "A Spectator's Notebook," 304.

47. Bentwich, "Nuremberg Issues," 450.

48. As quoted in Phillips, ed., *Trial of Josef Kramer,* 595–596.

49. Ibid., 599.

50. Ibid., 632–633.

51. Ibid., 640–641.

52. Ibid., xlv.

53. "Belsen and Nuremberg," 478.

54. Phillips, ed., *Trial of Josef Kramer,* 599.

55. Lindsey, "Zyklon B, Auschwitz, and the Trial of Dr. Bruno Tesch," 264.

56. IMT, *Trial of the Major War Criminals,* 4: 364–365.

57. Ibid., 365.

58. Ibid., 369.

59. IMT, *Trial of the Major War Criminals,* 5: 373ff.

60. IMT, *Trial of the Major War Criminals,* 6: 214ff.

61. As quoted in Taylor, *The Anatomy of the Nuremberg Trials,* 306.

62. IMT, *Trial of the Major War Criminals,* 8: 319–320.

63. Gilbert, *Nuremberg Diary,* 174–175.

64. As quoted in State of Israel, *The Trial of Adolf Eichmann,* 3: 1310.

65. "Testimony of Rudolf Hoess Taken at Nurnberg, on 1 April 1946, 1430 to 1730," in Mendelson and Detwiler, *The Holocaust,* 12: 72.

66. Document 3868–PS, "Affidavit of Rudolf Franz Ferdinand Hoess," in IMT, *Trial of the Major War Criminals,* 33: 275ff.

67. Proceedings of Monday, 15 April 1946 in IMT, *Trial of the Major War Criminals,* 11: 402.

68. Ibid., 414.

69. Gilbert, *Nuremberg Diary,* 266.

70. Ibid., 249–250.

71. State of Israel, *The Trial of Adolf Eichmann,* 3: 1005–1006.

72. Gilbert, *Nuremberg Diary,* 260.

73. Höss, "The Final Solution," in *Death Dealer,* 30.

74. Ibid., 31.

75. Ibid., 32–33.

76. Ibid., 32.

77. Ibid., 36.

78. Ibid., 43ff.

79. Ibid., 37.

80. Ibid., 38–39.

81. Höss, "Gravits," in *Death Dealer,* 264.

82. Langbein, *Der Auschwitz-Prozeß,* 1: 211.

83. Höss, "Gravits," in *Death Dealer,* 264–265.

84. Höss, "Rules and Regulations for Concentration Camps," in *Death Dealer,* 223–224.

85. Höss, "Himmler," in *Death Dealer,* 287.

86. Ibid., 290.

87. Höss testimony, given in Cracow on 11 January 1947, AABSMO, Höss Trial, 21g: 151.

88. Ibid., 152–153.

89. Ibid., 153.

90. Ibid., 154ff.

91. Ibid., 156–157.

92. Ibid., 157.

93. Ibid., 158.

94. Ibid., 159.

95. AABSMO, Höss Trial, 26b: 168ff.

96. AABSMO, Höss Trial, 32: 6.

97. Ibid., 115–116.

98. Ibid., 237–238.

99. Rassinier, *The Holocaust and the Lies of Ulysses,* 238–239.

100. Höss, "The Final Solution," in *Death Dealer,* 31.

101. Ibid., 37.

102. Rassinier, *The Holocaust and the Lies of Ulysses,* 239.

103. Proceedings of Monday, 15 April 1946 in IMT, *Trial of the Major War Criminals,* 11: 399–400.

104. Rassinier, *The Holocaust and the Lies of Ulysses,* 239.

105. Höss, "[My Life]," in *Death Dealer,* 159.

106. Höss, *Kommandant in Auschwitz,* 129.

107. Höss, "The Final Solution," 32, and "[My Life]," 136, 145, 147, both in *Death Dealer.*

108. Ibid., 32–33.

109. Ibid., 287.

110. Rassinier, *The Holocaust and the Lies of Ulysses,* 240.

111. Because of the confusing substitution of terms in Pollinger's translation, I have retranslated this section from the German original. Höss, *Kommandant in Auschwitz,* 165.

112. Rassinier, *The Holocaust and the Lies of Ulysses,* 240–241.

113. Höss, "The Final Solution," in *Death Dealer,* 32.

114. Rassinier, *The Holocaust and the Lies of Ulysses,* 241.

115. Ibid., 115–116.

116. Butz, *The Hoax of the Twentieth Century.*

117. Document 3868–PS, "Affidavit of Rudolf Franz Ferdinand Hoess," in IMT, *Trial of the Major War Criminals,* 33: 276.

118. Butz, *The Hoax of the Twentieth Century,* 103.

119. Ibid.

120. Document 3868–PS, "Affidavit of Rudolf Franz Ferdinand Hoess," in IMT, *Trial of the Major War Criminals,* 33: 276.

121. Butz, *The Hoax of the Twentieth Century,* 103–104.

122. Ibid., 105.

123. Ibid., 109.

124. Ibid.

125. Ibid., 111.

126. Ibid., 115.

127. Höss, "The Final Solution of the Jewish Question in Concentration Camp Auschwitz," in *Death Dealer*, 44.

128. Höss, "[My Life]," in *Death Dealer*, 160.

129. Faurisson, *Mémoire en Défense*, 161.

130. Ibid., 160, 164.

131. Irving, *Nuremberg*, 241.

132. Document 3868–PS, "Affidavit of Rudolf Franz Ferdinand Hoess," in IMT, *Trial of the Major War Criminals*, 33: 275ff.

133. IMT *Trial of the Major War Criminals*, 11: 414.

134. Ibid., 418.

135. Irving, *Nuremberg*, 244.

136. Höss, *Death Dealer*, 74.

137. State of Israel, *The Trial of Adolf Eichmann*, 3: 1001.

138. Ibid., 1026.

139. Gilbert, *Nuremberg Diary*, 249–250.

140. Ibid., 258–259.

141. Ibid., 260.

142. State of Israel, *The Trial of Adolf Eichmann*, 3: 1008.

143. Ibid., 1008–1009.

144. Johann Paul Kremer, "Diary," in Auschwitz-Birkenau State Museum in Oswiecim, *KL Auschwitz Seen by the SS*, 161–162.

145. Kremer testimony, 18 August 1947, in Auschwitz-Birkenau State Museum in Oswiecim, *KL Auschwitz Seen by the SS*, 162.

146. Kremer, "Diary," in Auschwitz-Birkenau State Museum in Oswiecim, *KL Auschwitz Seen by the SS*, 162–163.

147. Kremer testimony, 17 July 1947, in Auschwitz-Birkenau State Museum in Oswiecim, *KL Auschwitz Seen by the SS*, 163.

148. Kremer, "Diary," in Auschwitz-Birkenau State Museum in Oswiecim, *KL Auschwitz Seen by the SS*, 163.

149. Ibid., 167.

150. Kremer testimony, 30 July 1947, in Auschwitz-Birkenau State Museum in Oswiecim, *KL Auschwitz Seen by the SS*, 167.

151. Kremer, "Diary," in Auschwitz-Birkenau State Museum in Oswiecim, *KL Auschwitz Seen by the SS*, 168.

152. Kremer testimony, 18 July 1947, in Auschwitz-Birkenau State Museum in Oswiecim, *KL Auschwitz Seen by the SS*, 168.

153. Kremer, "Diary," in Auschwitz-Birkenau State Museum in Oswiecim, *KL Auschwitz Seen by the SS*, 169.

154. Kremer testimony, 18 July 1947, in Auschwitz-Birkenau State Museum in Oswiecim, *KL Auschwitz Seen by the SS*, 169.

155. Faurisson, *Mémoire en Défense*, 13–64.

156. Ibid., 14.

157. Kremer, "Diary," in Auschwitz-Birkenau State Museum in Oswiecim, *KL Auschwitz Seen by the SS*, 177.

158. Ibid.

159. Kremer, "Diary," in Auschwitz-Birkenau State Museum in Oswiecim, *KL Auschwitz Seen by the SS*, 162.

160. Faurisson, *Mémoire en Défense*, 22.

161. Ibid., 23–24.

162. Kremer, "Diary," in Auschwitz-Birkenau State Museum in Oswiecim, *KL Auschwitz Seen by the SS*, 161–162.

163. Faurisson, *Mémoire en Défense*, 31–32.

164. Ibid., 55–56.

165. Ibid., 56.

166. Kremer, "Diary," in Auschwitz-Birkenau State Museum in Oswiecim, *KL Auschwitz Seen by the SS*, 168. In the Lüneburg Trial, Hössler admitted that he was present at selections for the gas chambers. See Phillips, ed., *Trial of Josef Kramer*, 196, 714–715.

167. As quoted in Vidal-Naquet, *Assassins of Memory*, 113.

168. Faurisson, *Mémoire en Défense*, 37.

169. As quoted in Kravchenko, *I Chose Justice*, 136.

170. Faurisson, *Mémoire en Défense*, 37.

171. Protocol testimony of Shlomo Dragon, 10 and 11 May 1945, added as Appendix 17 to CDC, "Protocol on the Machinery of Mass Extermination of Humans in Birkenau," 26 November 1946, trans. Roman Sas-Zalaziocky, in LSW, Case 20 Vr 3806/64 (Ertl/Dejaco), ON 264, 393y to 393z.

172. Ibid., 393aa.

173. Pery Broad, "Reminiscences," in Auschwitz-Birkenau State Museum in Oswiecim, *KL Auschwitz Seen by the SS*, 132. The translation quoted is similar to the one read in the Frankfurt court in 1964. See Naumann, *Auschwitz*, 162–182.

174. Faurisson to *Le Monde*, 16 January 1979, as printed in Faurisson, *Mémoire en Défense*, 85–86; the English translation given here can be found in Vidal-Naquet, *Assassins of Memory*, 148.

175. Vidal-Naquet, *Assassins of Memory*, 49–50.

176. Josef Klehr in interview, in *Auschwitz—"Direkt von der Rampe weg,"* ed. Demant, 114.

177. Frankfurter, ed., *Die Begegnung: Auschwitz*, 102.

178. [Gray], *The Irving Judgement*, 217.

179. Ibid., 218.

5. "Witnesses Despite Themselves"

1. Bloch, *The Historian's Craft*, 61.

2. Lipstadt, *Denying the Holocaust*, 181.

3. Stäglich, *The Auschwitz Myth*, 293.

4. Christophersen, *Auschwitz: A Personal Account*, 3.

5. Ibid., 13.

6. Ibid., 15–16.

7. Ibid., 19.

8. Harwood, *Did Six Million Really Die?*, 16.

9. LSW, Case 20 Vr 3806/64 (Ertl/Dejaco), ON 484, proceedings of 21 January 1972, 113.

10. Ibid., 124.

11. Ibid., 125.

12. Karl Bischoff to Hans Kammler, 29 January 1943, AABSMO/ZBL, BW 30/34.

13. LSW, Case 20 Vr 3806/64 (Ertl/Dejaco), ON 484, proceedings 21 January 1972, 125–126.

14. "Aktenvermerk Betr.: Anwesenheit von Obering. Prüfer der Fa. Topf u. Söhne Erfurt, bezüglich Ausbau der Einäscherungsanlagen im K.G.L. Auschwitz," AABSMO/ZBL, BW 30/27, 38–39.

15. Fritz Ertl testimony, 21 January 1972, LSW, Case 20 Vr 3806/64 (Ertl/Dejaco), ON 484, 120.

16. David Irving, "The Controversy on Auschwitz and the Dangers

of Censorship," Speech given to the Free Speech League at Victoria B.C., 27 October 1990, in Van Pelt, "Expert Opinion," 632.

17. Irving testimony, DCO: HMQvEZ'88, transcripts, 9738–9739.

18. Ibid., 9739ff.

19. Ibid., 9743ff.

20. IMT, *Trial of the Major War Criminals*, 23: 68–69.

21. Aschenauer, ed., *Ich, Adolf Eichmann*, 150.

22. Walther Dejaco testimony, 19 January 1972, LSW, Case 20 Vr 3806/64 (Ertl/Dejaco), ON 484, 27.

23. Ibid., 120.

24. Butz, *The Hoax of the Twentieth Century*, 120–121.

25. Fischer, *Historians' Fallacies*, 53.

26. Butz, *The Hoax of the Twentieth Century* (1992 ed.), 380.

27. Ibid., 381.

28. Ibid.

29. Ibid., 118.

30. Ibid., 381–382.

31. Ibid., 382.

32. Ibid., 383.

33. Graf, *Der Holocaust auf dem Prüfstand*, 112.

34. Butz, *The Hoax of the Twentieth Century* (1992 ed.), 383.

35. Ibid., 385.

36. The many plans and construction documents for the sewage treatment plants are preserved in the AABSMO/ZBL, BW 29.

37. Butz, "The Nagging 'Gassing Cellar' Problem," 20.

38. Ibid., 21.

39. Stäglich, *The Auschwitz Myth*, 46–47.

40. Ibid., 47.

41. See Dwork and van Pelt, *Auschwitz: 1270 to the Present*, 220ff.

42. Stäglich, *The Auschwitz Myth*, 47.

43. Timesheet Riedel, 28 February 1943, AABSMO/ZBL, BW 30/28.

44. Timesheet Riedel, 2 March 1943, AABSMO/ZBL, BW 30/28.

45. Timesheet Topf, 13–22 April 1943, AABSMO/ZBL, BW 30/241.

46. SS-Untersturmführer Pollok to Topf & Sons, telegram, 26 February 1943, AABSMO/ZBL, BW 30/34.

47. Faurisson, "Auschwitz: Technique & Operation of the Gas Chambers," 59.

48. Topf & Sons to Central Construction Office, Auschwitz, 2 March 1943, OAM, ms. 502/1–313; USHRI Washington, microfilm RG 11.001M.03—41. As printed in Pressac and van Pelt, "The Machinery of Mass Murder at Auschwitz," 230–231.

49. Faurisson, "Jean-Claude Pressac's New Auschwitz Book, " 23.

50. Butz, "Gas Detectors in Auschwitz Crematory II," 24.

51. The barracks in Birkenau were not equipped with either bed linen or mattresses, and camp uniforms were in such short supply that they were worn until they were rags.

52. Butz, "Gas Detectors in Auschwitz Crematory II," 26.

53. Ibid., 27.

54. Ibid., 29.

55. There are two (carbon) copies of the letter. In both, the word for doors is misspelled: instead of *Türe*, the writer typed *Türme*. The word *Türme* literally means "towers." In one of the two copies, the mistake was noticed and hand-corrected: "*Türme*." Negationists have tried to use this typo to deny the obvious meaning of the letter, which is reinforced by the

subsequent order in the second paragraph for another "gasdoor"—"*Gas-tür*" for Morgue 1 of Crematorium 3.

56. Building BW—"*Bauwerk*"—30b refers to Crematorium 4, BW 30c to Crematorium 5.

57. Karl Bischoff to German Armament Works, 31 March 1943, AABSMO/ZBL, BW 30/34.

58. Stäglich, *The Auschwitz Myth,* 53.

59. Ibid.

60. Crowell, "The Gas Chamber of Sherlock Holmes," Section 12.

61. Crowell, "The Gas Chamber of Sherlock Holmes," Section 14.

62. Crowell's article seems to be regularly updated. I picked up this particular footnote as footnote 408 in the version of "The Gas Chamber of Sherlock Holmes" published on http://www.codoh.com/incon/incon-shrnotes.html—a site that is linked by means of a hyperlink to Irving's Web site.

63. Crowell, "The Gas Chamber of Sherlock Holmes," Section 14.

64. I picked up this particular footnote as footnote 409 in the version of "The Gas Chamber of Sherlock Holmes" published at http:/www.codoh.com/incon/inconshrnotes.html.

65. "Documents on Auschwitz," http://www.fpp.co.uk/Auschwitz/documents/LSKeller/MoscowDocs.html.

66. "Luftschutzdeckungsgrabe für des SS-Truppenlazaret—Infektions-abteilung," and "Luftschutzbunker für cca 20 Pers, mit Operationsalnage, Truppenlazarett im K.L. II," AABSMO/ZBL, BW 14/1–2.

67. For the regulations concerning air-raid shelter design, see Neufert, *Bau-Entwurfslehre,* 255ff.

68. "Edited comments of Author 'Samuel Crowell'" (19 February 1998), attached to "Documents on Auschwitz," http://www.fpp.co.uk/Auschwitz/documents/LSKeller/MoscowDocs.html.

69. Ibid.

70. Memorandum Meeting held on November 9, 1943 at the Central Construction Office, OAM, ms. 502/1–401. USHRI Washington, micro-film RG 11.001 M.03–47.

71. Memorandum Meeting held on June 26, 1944 at the Central Construction Office, OAM, ms. 502/1–401. USHRI Washington, micro-film RG 11.001 M.03–47.

72. Levi, *Survival in Auschwitz,*118–119.

73. HCJ/QB: IvP&L, transcripts, day 8 (24 January 2000), 85ff.

74. HCJ/QB: IvP&L daily transcripts, day 8 (11 January 2000), 99–100.

75. HCJ/QB: IvP&L daily transcripts, day 32 (15 March 2000), 177–178.

76. "Preliminary Finding Aid," RG-11.001M.03, Records of the Zentralbauleitung der Waffen-SS und Polizei in Auschwitz (Osobyi fond # 502), USHRI Washington.

77. OAM, 502/1–400; USHRI RG 11.001 M.03—47.

78. Ibid.

79. OAM, 502/1–401; USHRI RG 11.001 M.03—47.

80. Trevor-Roper, "Hitler: Does History Offer a Defence?"

81. OAM, 502/1—26; USHRI Washington, RG 11.001M.03—20.

82. Karl Bischoff to German Armament Works, 29 January 1943, AABSMO/ZBL, BW 30/34.

83. "How a Major Holocaust Historian Manipulates Facts: Gerald Fleming's Distortions," 11.

84. Statement of Hans Aumeier, 25 July 1945, 3ff. PRO/WO 208/4661.

85. Fischer, *Historians' Fallacies,* 63.

86. Faurisson to *Le Monde,* 26 February 1979, as printed in Faurisson, *Mémoire en Défense,* 100.

87. Order Central Construction Office to German Armament Works, February 13, 1943, and calculation of materials to be used by German Armament Works on the back of the original order, February 24, 1943. AABSMO/ZBL, BW 30/31, 385 and 385a.

88. Deposition of Henry Tauber, as quoted in Pressac, *Auschwitz: Technique and Operation of the Gas Chambers,* 498, 500–501.

89. Karl Bischoff to Hans Kammler, 28 June 1943, OAM, 502/1—314; USHRI Washington, microfilm RG 11.001M.03—41.

90. Elton, *The Practice of History,* 75.

91. Stäglich, *The Auschwitz Myth,* 49.

92. Deposition of Henry Tauber, as quoted in Pressac, *Auschwitz: Technique and Operation of the Gas Chambers,* 483.

93. Ibid., 489.

94. Ibid.

95. Ibid.

96. Höss, "The Final Solution," in *Death Dealer,* 36.

97. Ibid., 45.

98. J. A. Topf & Söhne, Erfurt, Patent Application, "Kontinuierliche arbeitender Leichen-Verbrennungsofen für Massenbetrieb," AABSMO/ZBL, BW 30/44, 1–2.

99. Report of Klaus and Christel Kunz, 25 April 1985, on patent application T 58240 Kl. 24 for a "Kontinuierliche arbeitender Leichen-Verbrennungsofen für Massenbetrieb," AABSMO/ZBL, BW 30/44.

100. AEMS, file 241.

101. Brugioni and Poirier, *The Holocaust Revisited,* 10–11.

102. Information given to me by Michael Shermer.

103. Czech, *Auschwitz Chronicle,* 637.

104. Markiewicz, Gubala, and Labedz, "A Study of the Cyanide Compounds," tables 1–4.

105. Ibid.

106. Ibid.

107. Ibid., 193–194.

108. Lipstadt, *Denying the Holocaust,* 181.

109. Focal Point Publications, "Press Statement: The Leuchter Report, The First Forensic Examination of Auschwitz," June 1989, in Van Pelt, "Expert Opinion," 596–597.

110. Ibid.

111. Leuchter testimony, DCO: HMQvEZ'88, transcripts, 9015ff.

112. Leuchter, *The Leuchter Report,* 7.

113. Ibid., 7.

114. Leuchter testimony, DCO: HMQvEZ'88, transcripts, 8955ff.

115. Leuchter, *The Leuchter Report,* 11.

116. Leuchter testimony, DCO: HMQvEZ'88, transcripts, 9230; Leuchter, "The Leuchter Report: The How and the Why," 136.

117. Leuchter testimony, DCO: HMQvEZ'88, transcripts, 9020.

118. Ibid., 9021.

119. Ibid., 9249–9250.

120. David A. Crabtree, "The Leuchter Report—proposals for amendments to be incorporated in the second edition, Together with reasoned substantiation thereof," 4, in Van Pelt, "Expert Opinion," 605.

121. Leuchter testimony, DCO: HMQvEZ'88, transcripts, 8988–8989.

122. German army survey of Zasole, December 1939, AABSMO/ZBL, BW 2/, file 2/1. See also Plate 1 in Dwork and van Pelt, *Auschwitz: 1270 to the Present,* between 320 and 321.

123. Leuchter testimony, DCO: HMQvEZ'88, transcripts, 9083.

124. Ibid., 9085.

125. Ibid., 9241–9242.

126. Faurisson, "The Mechanics of Gassing," 26.

127. Green and McCarthy, "Chemistry Is Not the Science: Rudolf, Rhetoric and Reduction."

128. Piper, "Gas Chambers and Crematoria," 166.

129. Pressac with van Pelt, "The Machinery of Mass Murder at Auschwitz," 210.

130. American Conference of Governmental Industrial Hygienists Web site, at http://www.acgih.org previously had a free version of this calculator.

131. DuPont, *Hydrogen Cyanide.*

132. Deposition of Henry Tauber, as quoted in Pressac, *Auschwitz: Technique and Operation of the Gas Chambers,* 483–484.

133. Leuchter testimony, DCO: HMQvEZ'88, transcripts 8981.

134. As quoted in Klee, Dressen, and Riess, *"The Good Old Days,"* 252–253.

135. Ibid., 255.

136. Ibid.

137. Deposition of Henry Tauber, as quoted in Pressac, *Auschwitz: Technique and Operation of the Gas Chambers,* 483–484.

138. Inventory Huta drawings, AABSMO/ZBL, BW 30/25, 27.

139. Pressac, *Auschwitz: Technique and Operation of the Gas Chambers,* 318.

140. Deposition of Henry Tauber, as quoted in Pressac, *Auschwitz: Technique and Operation of the Gas Chambers,* 483–484.

141. Ibid., 494.

142. Leuchter testimony, DCO: HMQvEZ'88, 9205–9206.

143. Ibid., 8998.

144. Ibid., 8999.

145. State of Israel, *The Trial of Adolf Eichmann,* 3: 1247.

146. Karl Bischoff to Topf & Sons, 6 March 1943, AABSMO/ZBL, BW 30/25, 7.

147. Leuchter testimony, DCO: HMQvEZ'88, 9255.

148. "Kritische Stellungnahme zum sogen. Leuchter-Dokument," 12–13, in Van Pelt, "Expert Report," 608.

149. David A. Crabtree, "The Leuchter Report," 3, in Van Pelt, "Expert Opinion," 604.

150. Leuchter testimony, DCO: HMQvEZ'88, transcripts, 9077.

151. Ibid., 9253–9254.

152. Deposition of Henry Tauber, as quoted in Pressac, *Auschwitz: Technique and Operation of the Gas Chambers,* 483–484.

153. Leuchter testimony, DCO: HMQvEZ'88, transcripts, 8973–8974.

154. Lesy, *The Forbidden Zone,* 140.

155. Leuchter, *The Leuchter Report: The End of a Myth,* 15.

156. Ibid., 15ff.; Tables V, VI and VIII.

157. Leuchter, *The Leuchter Report,* 12–13.

158. Leuchter testimony, DCO: HMQvEZ'88, transcripts, 8975ff.

159. Leuchter, *The Leuchter Report,* 12–13.

160. Ibid., Table VIII.

161. Hilberg, *The Destruction of the European Jews,* 3: 978.

162. Karl Bischoff to Hans Kammler, 28 June 1943, OAM 502/1—314; USHRI Washington, microfilm RG 11.001M.03—41.

163. Leuchter testimony, DCO: HMQvEZ'88, 9010.

164. Ibid., 9005–9006.

165. Ibid., 8998.

166. Ibid., 9203–9204.

167. Leuchter, *The Leuchter Report,* 14; see also Leuchter, "The Leuchter Report: The How and the Why," 139.

168. Anonymous, "Critique of Forensic Examinations of Auschwitz by Leuchter," unpublished manuscript, 2, in van Pelt, "Expert Report," 612.

169. Ibid.

170. "Critique," 3, in van Pelt, "Expert Opinion," 613–614.

171. "Critique," 4, in van Pelt, "Expert Opinion," 614.

172. Ibid.

173. "Critique," 5–6, in van Pelt, "Expert Opinion," 615–616.

174. Statement by Dr. Jim Roth, the chemist who analyzed Leuchter's samples in 1988, in Errol Morris's film *Mr. Death: The Rise and Fall of Fred A. Leuchter, Jr.*

175. Ibid.

176. Ibid.

177. Jan Markiewicz to Mark Weber, 7 June 1991, as printed in "An Official Polish Report on the Auschwitz 'Gas Chambers,'" 215.

178. Ibid., 216.

179. Markiewicz, Gubala, and Labedz, "A Study of the Cyanide Compounds," 19ff.

180. Ibid., 25–26.

181. Ibid., 25.

182. Ibid.

183. Ibid., 18.

184. Ibid., 27.

6. Auschwitz at the Irving Trial

1. Doyle, "The Adventure of the Beryl Coronet," 164.

2. HCJ/QB: IvP&L, Kevin Macdonald, "Statement."

3. HCJ/QB: IvP&L, "Interrogatories," part one, 4–5.

4. Ibid., 42ff.

5. Ibid., 50ff.

6. Ibid., 56.

7. HCJ/QB: IvP&L, Statement of Case, Section 1, 1.1.

8. Ibid., Section 1, 4.1.

9. Ibid., Section 1, 5.1.

10. Ibid., Section 1, 6.1.

11. Ibid., Section 1, 7.1.

12. Ibid., Section 2.1.

13. Ibid., Section 2.1, 1–20.

14. Ibid., Section 2.1, 16, i–xx.

15. Ibid., Section 2.1., iii, a–h.

16. Ibid., Section 2.1., iv, a–j.

17. Ibid., Section 3, 21.

18. David Irving to James Libson of Mishcon de Reya, Solicitors, and to Mark Bateman of Davenport Lyons, Solicitors, 19 December 1999.

19. HCJ/QB: IvP&L, van Pelt, "Deliveries of Zyklon B to Auschwitz and Consumption Rates of Zyklon B in Auschwitz and Other Camps," 20.

20. See Trial by a Military Court of Bruno Tesch, Joachim Droshin and Karl Weinbacher, PRO/WO (Judge Advocate General's Office—War of 1939–45; War Crimes Papers) WO 235/Case no. 83, 146972 (1–8 March 1946).

21. See NI 9912, Health Institution of the Protectorate of Bohemia and Moravia in Prague, "Directives for the Use of Prussic Acid (Zyklon) for the Destruction of Vermin (Disinfestation)," in *The Holocaust*, ed. Friedlander. Vol. 12, *The "Final Solution,"* 136.

22. Gerstein, "The Gerstein Report," in Léon Poliakov, "Le Dossier Kurt Gerstein," *Le Monde Juif* 19 (Jan.–March 1964), 11.

23. [Gray], *Irving Judgement,* 316–317.

24. HCJ/QB: IvP&L, transcripts, day 1 (11 January 2000), 3.

25. Ibid., 5.

26. Ibid., 29–30.

27. Ibid., 15–16.

28. Ibid., 34.

29. Ibid., 87ff.

30. HCJ/QB: IvP&L, transcripts, day 2 (12 January 2000), 105–106.

31. Ibid., 107–108.

32. Ibid., 121.

33. Ibid.

34. Ibid., 157.

35. Ibid.

36. Ibid., 225.

37. Ibid., 229–230.

38. Ibid., 233.

39. Ibid., 34.

40. Ibid., 235.

41. Ibid., 241–242.

42. Ibid., 250.

43. HCJ/QB: IvP&L, transcripts, day 5 (18 January 2000), 90.

44. Ibid., 93–94.

45. Ibid., 126–127.

46. Ibid., 130.

47. Ibid., 141ff.

48. Ibid., 185.

49. HCJ/QB: IvP&L, transcripts, day 6 (19 January 2000), 42–43.

50. Ibid., 83–84.

51. HCJ/QB: IvP&L, transcripts, day 6 (19 January 2000), 193–194.

52. HCJ/QB: IvP&L, transcripts, day 7 (20 January 2000), 48.

53. Ibid., 83.

54. Ibid., 83ff.

55. Ibid., 101.

56. HCJ/QB: IvP&L, transcript ruling, day 7 (20 January 2000), 3–4.

57. HCJ/QB: IvP&L, transcripts, day 7 (20 January 2000), 109.

58. Ibid., 113.

59. Ibid., 117.

60. Ibid., 118.

61. Ibid., 124.

62. Ibid., 140.

63. Ibid., 146.

64. Ibid., 153ff.

65. Ibid., 156–157.

66. Ibid., 159–160.

67. Roddy, "New Twists on History," http://www.post-gazette.com:
80/columnists/20000122roddy.asp.

68. Anonymous, "Critique of the Pelt Report by Robert Jan van Pelt,
1999," (1).

69. Ibid.

70. Ibid., 2.

71. HCJ/QB: IvP&L, transcripts, day 8 (24 January 2000), 44–45.

72. Ibid., 50–51.

73. Ibid., 51–52.

74. Ibid., 74–75.

75. Anonymous, "Critique of the Pelt Report by Robert Jan van Pelt,
1999," 8.

76. Ibid., 6.

77. Ibid., 8–9.

78. Ibid., 9.

79. Ibid.

80. Nyiszli, *Auschwitz: A Doctor's Eyewitness Account,* 94ff.

81. HCJ/QB: IvP&L, transcripts, day 8 (24 January 2000), 101ff.

82. Ibid., 109.

83. Neufert, *Bau-Entwurfslehre,* 271.

84. HCJ/QB: IvP&L, transcripts, day 8 (24 January 2000), 113–114.

85. Ibid., 126ff.

86. Ibid., 134ff.

87. AABSMO/ZBL, BW 30/7, 30/34.

88. HCJ/QB: IvP&L, transcripts, day 8 (24 January 2000), 145–146.

89. Ibid., 188–189.

90. Anonymous, "Critique of the Pelt Report by Robert Jan van Pelt,
1999," 14.

91. Ibid., 15.

92. Ibid., 15–16.

93. HCJ/QB: IvP&L, transcripts, day 9 (25 January 2000), 6ff.

94. Ibid., 38–39.

95. Ibid., 40.

96. Ibid., 42.

97. "Round Two to Go to the UK Court of Appeal," *David Irving's
Action Report,* no. 17 (20 July 2000), 1.

98. HCJ/QB: IvP&L, transcripts, day 9 (25 January 2000), 47.

99. Ibid., 53.

100. Anonymous, "Critique of the Pelt Report by Robert Jan van Pelt,
1999," 26.

101. Ibid., 27.

102. HCJ/QB: IvP&L, transcripts, day 9 (25 January 2000), 81.

103. Keegan, ed., *Times Atlas of the Second World War,* 175–176.

104. HCJ/QB: IvP&L, transcripts, day 9 (25 January 2000), 91.

105. Ibid., 98.

106. Ibid., 131.

107. Ibid., 136–137.

108. Ibid., 141–142.

109. Ibid., 147–148.

110. Ibid., 148–149.

111. Ibid., 185.

112. Ibid., 187ff.

113. Ibid., 193.
114. HCJ/QB: IvP&L, transcripts, day 10 (26 January 2000), 4.
115. Ibid., 12.
116. Ibid., 22.
117. Dalrymple, "The Curse of Revisionism."
118. HCJ/QB: IvP&L, transcripts, day 10 (26 January 2000), 151.
119. Ibid., 152–153.
120. Ibid., 154ff.
121. Ibid., 158.
122. Anonymous, "Critique of the Pelt Report by Robert Jan van Pelt, 1999," 21.
123. HCJ/QB: IvP&L, transcripts, day 10 (26 January 2000), 180–181.
124. Ibid., 182–183.
125. Ibid., 183–184.
126. Ibid., 184–185.
127. Dalrymple, "The Curse of Revisionism."
128. HCJ/QB: IvP&L, transcripts, day 11 (28 January 2000), 187ff.
129. Ibid., 21.
130. Ibid., 26–27.
131. Ibid., 47.
132. Ibid., 48.
133. Ibid., 133.
134. Ibid., 134.
135. Ibid., 136.
136. Ibid., 138.
137. Ibid., 139.
138. Ibid., 151–152.
139. Ibid., 182.
140. Ibid., 185ff.
141. HCJ/QB: IvP&L daily transcripts, day 8 (January 24, 2000), 149ff.
142. HCJ/QB: IvP&L daily transcripts, day 9 (January 25, 2000), 147–148.
143. HCJ/QB: IvP&L daily transcripts, day 13 (February 1, 2000), 8–9.
144. Ibid., 15.
145. HCJ/QB: IvP&L daily transcripts, day 14 (February 2, 2000), 9.
146. Ibid., 12.
147. HCJ/QB: IvP&L, transcripts, day 32 (15 March 2000), 20ff.
148. Ibid., 22ff.
149. Ibid., 27ff.
150. Ibid., 144–145.
151. Ibid., 145.
152. Ibid., 169–170.
153. Ibid., 173–174.
154. Ibid., 181.
155. Wilkins, *Of the Principles and Duties of Natural Religion*, 7–8.
156. HCJ/QB: IvP&L, transcripts, day 33 (Tuesday, 11 April 2000), 2.
157. Ibid.
158. Ibid., 3.
159. Ibid., 25.
160. Ibid., 32.
161. Ibid., 37.

162. Ibid., 38.
163. Ibid., 40.
164. Ibid., 41.
165. Ibid.
166. Ibid., 43.
167. Ibid., 49.
168. Ibid., 50.
169. Ibid.
170. Ibid., 51.
171. Ibid., 53–54.
172. Ibid., 55.
173. Ibid., 55–56.
174. Ibid., 57.
175. Ibid., 59.
176. Ibid.

Epilogue

1. COA: HCJ/QB: IvP&L, "Defendants' submissions in accordance with the directions of Sedley LJ dated 6 September 2000," 6.

2. COA: HCJ/QB: IvP&L, Lord Justice Sedley, "Irving v Penguin Books: Reasons."

3. Germar Rudolf, "Critique of Claims Made by Robert Jan Van Pelt."

4. Germar Rudolf, "The Hunt of Germar Rudolf."

5. "Ladd v. Marshall," 1491.

6. COA: HCJ/QB: IvP&L, "Skeleton Argument Re An Application to Adduce New Evidence."

7. Richard J. Green, "Leuchter, Rudolf and the Iron Blues" (1998); Richard J. Green and Jamie McCarthy, "Chemistry is not the Science: Rudolf, Rhetoric and Reduction" (1999); Richard J. Green, "Postscript to Chemistry is not the Science" (2000).

8. COA: HCJ/QB: IvP&L, Richard Green, "Expert Report."

9. Germar Rudolf, "Some considerations about the Gas Chambers of Auschwitz and Birkenau."

10. COA: HCJ/QB: IvP&L, Richard Green, "Expert Report."

11. COA: HCJ/QB: IvP&L, Daniel Keren, Jamie McCarthy, and Harry W. Mazal, "A Report on Some Findings Concerning the Gas Chamber of Krematorium II in Auschwitz-Birkenau," attached as an appendix to Robert Jan van Pelt, "Expert Report."

12. COA: HCJ/QB: IvP&L, Paul Zucchi, Letter to Robert Jan van Pelt: Auschwitz-Birkenau Krematorium II Roof Openings—[Yolles] Reference No. T010539, March 11, 2001, attached as an appendix to Robert Jan van Pelt, "Expert Report."

13. Germar Rudolf, "Some considerations about the Gas Chambers of Auschwitz and Birkenau."

14. COA: HCJ/QB: IvP&L, Germar Scheerer [Rudolf], "Affidavit," 169.

15. Ibid.

16. Kenneth V. Iserson, *Death to Dust: What Happens to Dead Bodies?* (Tucson: Galen Press, 1994), 264f.

17. "LeMoyne Cremated," *Chicago Tribune,* Oct. 17, 1879.

18. Lawrence F. Moore, "Technology of Cremation," Association of American Cemetery Superintendents, *Proceedings,* vol. 54 (1940), 67.

19. Germar Rudolf, "Character Assasins."

20. Irving, "A Final Big Appeal by David Irving to all his supporters," 1, 3.

21. Irving, "Radical's Diary," June 22, 2001.

22. COA: HCJ/QB: IvP&L, Judgment, July 20, 2001, 7.

23. Ibid., 8.

24. Ibid., 32.

Adler, H. G. *Theresienstadt 1941–1945.* Tübingen: J.C.B. Mohr, 1955.

Adorno, Theodor. "Kulturkritik und Gesellschaft." In *Kulturkritik und Gesellschaft I: Prismen Ohne Leitbild.* Frankfurt am Main: Suhrkamp, 1977.

———. *Minima Moralia.* Trans. E. F. N. Jephcott. London: Verso, 1978.

Aly, Götz. "Auschwitz und die Zahlen: Was Historiker längst wußten, ist jetzt öffentlich." *Die Tageszeitung,* 18 July 1990.

———. "Auschwitz und die Leichenarithmetik." *Die Tageszeitung,* 13 August 1990.

Anissomov, Myriam. *Primo Levi: Tragedy of an Optimist.* Trans. Steve Cox. Woodstock: The Overlook Press, 1999.

Apfelbaum, Erika. "Forgetting the Past." *Partisan Review* 48 (1981): 608–617.

Arendt, Hannah. *Essays in Understanding, 1930–1954.* Ed. Jerome Kohn. New York, San Diego, and London: Harcourt Brace & Company, 1994.

Aschenauer, Rudolf, ed. *Ich, Adolf Eichmann: Ein historischer Zeugenbericht.* Leoni am Starberger See: Druffel, 1980.

Ascherson, Neil. "Last Battle of Hitler's Historians." *Observer,* 16 January 2000.

"The Bad History Man," *The Daily Telegraph,* 12 April 2000.

Ball, John C. *Air Photo Evidence.* Delta, B.C.: Ball Resource Services, 1992.

Barcz, Wojciech Barcz. "Die erste Vergasung." In *Auschwitz: Zeugnisse und Berichte,* ed. Hans Günther Adler, Hans Langbein, and Ella Lingens-Reiner, 30–31. Frankfurt: Atheneum, 1988.

Beardsley, Monroe C. *Aesthetics: Problems in the Philosophy of Criticism.* New York, Chicago, and Burlington: Brace & World, 1958.

"Belsen and Nuremberg." *The Spectator* 175 (23 November 1945): 478.

"The Belsen Trial: Defence Counsel's Astounding Statement." *The Jewish Chronicle* 104 (12 October 1945): 9.

Bentwich, Norman. "Nuremberg Issues." *The Spectator* 175 (16 November 1945): 450.

Berberova, Nina. *L'affaire Kravtchenko.* Trans. Irène and André Markowicz. Arles: Actes Sud, 1990.

Berg, Friedrich Paul. "The Diesel Gas Chambers: Myth within a Myth." *Journal of Historical Review* 5 (Spring 1984): 15–46.

Berlin, Isaiah. "Winston Churchill in 1940." In *The Proper Study of*

Mankind: An Anthology of Essays, ed. Henry Hardy and Roger Hausheer, 605–627. New York: Farrar, Straus and Giroux, 1998.

Bezwinska, Jadwiga, and Danuta Czech, eds. *Amidst a Nightmare of Crime: Manuscripts of Members of Sonderkommando.* Trans. Krystyna Michalik. Oswiecim: State Museum at Oswiecim, 1973.

"Biggest Atrocity Story Breaks in Poland." *The Christian Century* 61 (13 September 1944): 1045.

Bloch, Marc. *The Historian's Craft.* New York: Vintage, 1953.

Boder, David P. *I Did Not Interview the Dead.* Urbana: University of Illinois Press, 1949.

Borowski, Tadeusz. "Auschwitz, Our Home (A Letter)." In *This Way for the Gas, Ladies and Gentlemen,* trans. Barbara Vedder, 98–142. Harmondsworth: Penguin, 1976.

Brayard, Florent. *Comment l'idée vint à M. Rassinier: Naissance du révisionnisme.* Paris: Fayard, 1996.

Brigham, Daniel T. "Two Death Camps: Places of Horror." *The New York Times,* 6 July 1944, 6.

Broad, Pery. "Reminiscences." In *KL Auschwitz Seen by the SS: Rudolf Höss, Pery Broad, Johann Paul Kremer,* by Auschwitz-Birkenau State Museum in Oswiecim, 103–147. Trans. Constantine FitzGibbon and Krystyna Michalik. Warsaw: Interpress, 1991.

Brugioni, Dino A., and Robert G. Poirier. *The Holocaust Revisited: A Retrospective Analysis of the Auschwitz-Birkenau Extermination Complex.* Washington, D.C.: Central Intelligence Agency, 1979.

Butz, Arthur R. "Gas Detectors in Auschwitz Crematory II." *The Journal of Historical Review* 16 (September/October 1997): 24–30.

———. *The Hoax of the Twentieth Century: The Case against the Presumed Extermination of European Jewry.* Torrance, Calif.: Institute for Historical Review, 1976.

———. *The Hoax of the Twentieth Century: The Case against the Presumed Extermination of European Jewry.* 2nd ed. Torrance, Calif.: Institute for Historical Review, 1992.

———. "The Nagging 'Gassing Cellar' Problem." *The Journal of Historical Review* 16 (July/August 1997): 20–22.

Cayrol, Jean. "Night and Fog." In *Film. Book 2: Films of Peace and War,* ed. Robert Hughes, 234–257. New York: Grove Press, 1962.

Central Commission for Investigation of German Crimes in Poland. *German Crimes in Poland.* 2 vols. Warsaw: Central Commission for Investigation of German Crimes in Poland, 1946–1947.

Chandler, Alfred D., Jr., and Stephen Ambrose, eds. *Papers of Dwight David Eisenhower: The War Years.* 5 vols. Baltimore: Johns Hopkins University Press, 1976.

Chomsky, Noam, and Edward S. Herman. *After the Cataclysm: Postwar Indochina and the Reconstruction of Imperial Ideology.* Montréal: Black Rose Books, 1979.

Christophersen, Thies. *Auschwitz: A Personal Account.* Rev. ed. Introduction by Manfred Roeder. Reedy, W.Va.: Liberty Bell Publications, 1979.

Churchill, Winston. *Blood, Sweat, and Tears.* New York: G. P. Putnam's Sons, 1941.

Cohen, Arthur A. *The Tremendum: A Theological Interpretation of the Holocaust.* New York: Crossroads, 1981.

Cohen, Nathan. "Diaries of the *Sonderkommando.*" In *Anatomy of the Auschwitz Death Camp,* ed. Yisrael Gutman and Michael Berenbaum,

522–534. Washington, D.C., Bloomington, and Indianapolis: United States Holocaust Memorial Museum and Indiana University Press, 1994.

Conan, Eric. "Auschwitz: La mémoire du mal." *L'Express,* 19 January 1995, 54–73.

Crowell, Samuel. "The Gas Chamber of Sherlock Holmes." http://www.fpp.co.uk/Auschwitz/Auschw.html.

Czech, Danuta. *Auschwitz Chronicle: 1939–1945.* Trans. Barbara Harshav, Martha Humphreys, and Stephen Shearier. New York: Henry Holt and Company, 1990.

"Czechs Report Massacre." *The New York Times,* 20 June 1944, 5.

Dalrymple, James. "The Curse of Revisionism." *The Independent,* 29 January 2000.

———. "He Says Auschwitz Is a Myth, But He Has Never Set Foot in the Place, Never Seen the Evidence." *The Independent,* 12 April 2000.

"David Irving Lost His Case—and We Can Celebrate a Victory for Free Speech." *The Independent,* April 12, 2000.

Davis, Douglas. "British Court Slams Irving as Holocaust Denier." *The Jerusalem Post,* 12 April 2000.

Dawidowicz, Lucy S., ed. *A Holocaust Reader.* New York: Behrman House, 1976.

Demant, Ebbo, ed. *Auschwitz—"Direkt von der Rampe weg . . ." Kaduk, Erber, Klehr: Drei Täter geben zu Protokoll.* Hamburg: Rowohlt, 1979.

de Tocqueville, Alexis. *Democracy in America.* Ed. Phillips Bradley, trans. Henry Reeve. 2 vols. New York: Vintage Classics, 1990.

"Die Toten von Auschwitz." *Auschwitz Information: Bulletin der Österreichischen Lagergemeinschaft Auschwitz,* June 1990.

Donat, Alexander. *The Holocaust Kingdom.* New York: Holocaust Library, 1978.

Doyle, Arthur Conan. "The Adventure of the Beryl Coronet." In *The Original Illustrated Sherlock Holmes.* Secaucus, N.J.: Castle, n.d.

DuPont. *Hydrogen Cyanide: Properties, Uses, Storage, and Handling.* Wilmington, Del.: DuPont, 1991.

Dwork, Debórah, and Robert Jan van Pelt. *Auschwitz: 1270 to the Present.* New York and London: W. W. Norton, 1996.

Eknes, Enrique Aynat. "Crematoriums II and III: A Critical Study." *The Journal of Historical Review* 8 (Fall 1988): 303–352.

Elton, Geoffrey Rudolph. *The Practice of History.* London: Methuen, 1967.

Farrell, Nicholas. "Death's Salesman Cut Off before His Time." *Sunday Telegraph,* 17 November 1991.

Faurisson, Robert. *A-t-on lu Lautréamont?* Paris: Gallimard, 1972.

———. *Mémoire en Défense contre ceux qui m'accusent de falsifier l'histoire/La question des chambres à gaz.* Preface by Noam Chomsky. Paris: La Veille Taupe, 1980.

———. "The Mechanics of Gassing." *The Journal of Historical Review* 1 (1980): 23–30.

———. "A Challenge to David Irving." *The Journal of Historical Review* 5 (Winter 1984): 289–305.

———. Review of *Why Did the Heavens Not Darken? The Journal of Historical Review* 9 (Fall 1989): 361–379.

———. "Auschwitz: Technique & Operation of the Gas Chambers; or, Improvised Gas Chambers & Casual Gassings at Auschwitz & Birkenau According to J.C. Pressac (1989), Part 1." *The Journal of Historical Review* 11 (Spring 1991): 25–66.

———. "Jean-Claude Pressac's New Auschwitz Book." *The Journal of Historical Review* 14 (January/February 1994): 23–24.

———. "On David Irving." *Adelaide Institute* 43 (August 1996): 1

Feingold, Henry L. "How Unique Is the Holocaust?" In *Genocide: Critical Issues of the Holocaust,* ed. Alex Goodman and Daniel Landes. Los Angeles: The Simon Wiesenthal Center, 1983.

Finkelkraut, Alain. *The Future of a Negation: Reflections on the Question of Genocide.* Trans. Mary Byrd Kelly. Lincoln and London: University of Nebraska Press, 1998.

Fischer, David Hackett. *Historians' Fallacies: Toward a Logic of Historical Thought.* New York and Evanston: Harper Torchbooks, 1970.

Forester, C. S. *The Ship.* Toronto: S. J. Reginald Saunders, 1943.

Frankfurter, Bernhard, ed. *Die Begegnung: Auschwitz—Ein Opfer und ein Täter im Gespräch.* Vienna: Verlag für Gesellschaftskritik, 1995.

Frei, Norbert. "'Wir waren blind, ungläubig und langsam': Buchenwald, Dachau und die amerikanischen Medien im Frühjahr 1945." *Vierteljahrshefte für Zeitgeschichte* 35 (1987): 385–401.

Friedlander, Henry, ed. *The Holocaust.* Vol. 12, *The "Final Solution" in the Extermination Camps and the Aftermath.* New York and London: Garland, 1982.

Friedman, Filip, and Tadeusz Holuj. *Oswiecim.* Warsaw: Spoldzielnia Wydawicza Ksiazka, 1946.

Fromer, Rebecca Camhi. *The Holocaust Odyssey of Daniel Bennahmias, Sonderkommando.* Tuscaloosa and London: University of Alabama Press, 1993.

Gerstein, Kurt. "The Gerstein Report." In Léon Poliakov, "Le Dossier Kurt Gerstein." *Le Monde Juif* 19 (Jan.–March 1964): 4–20.

Gilbert, Gustave M. *Nuremberg Diary.* New York: Farrar, Straus and Company, 1947.

Gilbert, Martin. *Auschwitz and the Allies.* London: Michael Joseph/Rainbird, 1981.

———. "What Was Known and Why." In *Anatomy of the Auschwitz Death Camp,* ed. Yisrael Gutman and Michael Berenbaum, 539–552. Washington, D.C., Bloomington, and Indianapolis: United States Holocaust Memorial Museum and Indiana University Press, 1994.

Goldhagen, Daniel Jonah. "False Witness." *The New Republic* (April 17, 1989), 39–44.

Graf, Jürgen. *Der Holocaust auf dem Prüfstand: Augenzeugenberichte versus Naturgesetze.* Basel: Guideon Burg Verlag, 1992.

Gray, Charles. *The Irving Judgement: David Irving v. Penguin Books and Professor Deborah Lipstadt.* Harmondsworth: Penguin Books, 2000.

Green, Richard J. "Leuchter, Rudolf and the Iron Blues" (1988), www.holocaust-history.org/auschwitz/chemistry/blue

———. "Postscript to Chemistry Is Not the Science" (2000), www.holocaust-history.org/auschwitz/chemistry/not-the-science/postscript

———. "Expert Report," written to assist the Court of Appeal (Civil Division) in the Supreme Court of Judicature in London in the Case between John Cawdell Irving, Applicant, and Penguin Books Limited and Deborah E. Lipstadt, Respondents.

Green, Richard J., and Jamie McCarthy. "Chemistry Is Not the Science: Rudolf, Rhetoric and Reduction" (1999). At http://www.holocaust-history.org/auschwitz/chemistry/not-the-science

Greif, Gideon. *Wir weinten tränenlos: Augenzeugenberichte der jüdischen "Sonderkommandos" in Auschwitz.* Cologne, Weimar, and Vienna: Böhlau, 1995.

Gutenplan, Don. "The Holocaust on Trial." *Atlantic Monthly* (February 2000), 45–66.

Gutman, Yisrael, and Michael Berenbaum, eds. *Anatomy of the Auschwitz Death Camp.* Washington, D.C., Bloomington, and Indianapolis: United States Holocaust Memorial Museum and Indiana University Press, 1994.

Habermas, Jürgen. "Historical Consciousness and Post-Traditional Identity." In *The New Conservatism: Cultural Criticism and the Historians' Debate,* trans. Shierry Weber Nicholson, 249–267. Cambridge: MIT Press, 1989.

Hackett, David A., ed. *The Buchenwald Report.* Boulder, San Francisco, and Oxford: Westview Press, 1995.

Hamilton, Iain. *Koestler: A Biography.* London: Secker & Warburg, 1982.

Harris, Jay. "Visiting Auschwitz before the Ovens." *Forward* (1 November 1996).

Harris, Robert. *Selling Hitler.* New York: Pantheon Books, 1986.

Harwood, Richard E. *Did Six Million Really Die?* Toronto: Samisdat, n.d.

Hawkins, Desmond, ed. *War Report: D-Day to VE-Day.* London: BBC Books, 1994.

Heym, Stefan. *Reden an den Feind.* Ed. Peter Mallwitz. Munich: C. Bertelsmann, 1986.

Hilberg, Raul. *The Destruction of the European Jews.* Revised and definitive edition. 3 vols. New York and London: Holmes and Meier, 1985.

Hirsch, David H. *The Deconstruction of Literature: Criticism after Auschwitz.* Hanover and London: Brown University Press, 1991.

Hochhuth, Rolf. *The Deputy.* Trans. Richard and Clara Winston. New York: Grove Press, 1964.

Hoffman, Michael. *The Great Holocaust Trial.* Torrance, Calif.: Institute for Historical Review, 1985.

———. "David Irving and the Verdict of History," www.hoffman-info.com (April 13, 2000).

"The Holocaust: A Sinking Ship." *IHR Newsletter* 66 (May 1989): 2.

"Holocaust Denial." *The Irish Times,* 12 April 2000.

"The Horrors of Buchenwald." *The Times,* 28 April 1945, 2.

Horsnell, Michael. "Auschwitz Death Chambers 'A Moral Certainty.'" *The Times,* 26 January 2000.

Höss, Rudolf. *Death Dealer: The Memoirs of the SS Kommandant at Auschwitz.* Ed. Steven Paskuly, trans. Andrew Pollinger. Buffalo, N.Y.: Prometheus Books, 1992.

———. *Kommandant in Auschwitz.* Ed. Martin Broszat. Munich: DTV, 1987.

"How a Major Holocaust Historian Manipulates Facts: Gerald Fleming's Distortions." *The Journal of Historical Review* 16 (November/December 1997): 11–12.

Hume, David. *A Treatise of Human Nature.* Ed. Ernest C. Mossner. Harmondsworth: Penguin, 1985.

Hyman, Stanley E. *The Armed Vision.* New York: Knopf, 1948.

International Military Tribunal. *Trial of the Major War Criminals.* 41 vols. Nuremberg: Secretariat of the Tribunal, 1947–1949.

Irving, David. *The Destruction of Dresden.* London: William Kimber, 1963.

————. *Hitler's War.* New York: Viking, 1977.

————. "On Contemporary History and Historiography." *Journal of Historical Review* 5 (Winter 1984): 251–288.

————. "Battleship Auschwitz." *The Journal of Historical Review* 10 (1990): 491–508.

————. *Hitler's War.* 2nd ed. London: Focal Point Publications, 1991.

————. "Opinion." *David Irving's Action Report,* September 1994.

————. "French Make a Clean Breast: Admit Fifty-Seven Year Auschwitz 'Gas-Chamber' Fraud." *David Irving's Action Report* 9 (May 1995): 1.

————. "The Life and Death of 'Dr Goebbels': How a Powerful U.S. Lobby Killed That Book." *David Irving's Action Report* 10 (July 1996): 7.

————. *Nuremberg: The Last Battle.* London: Focal Point, 1996.

————. "A Final Big Appeal by David Irving to all his supporters," *David Irving's Action Report* 18 (March 24, 2001), 1, 3.

————. Radical's Diary, June 22, 2001, as posted on Tuesday, June 24, 2001 on www.fpp.co.uk/Legal/Penguin/Appeal/RadDi22601.htm

Iserson, Kenneth V. *Death to Dust: What Happens to Dead Bodies?* Tucson: Galen Press, 1994.

Iwaszko, Tadeusz. "Les Détenus 'E' d'Auschwitz." *Bulletin d'Information. Comité internationale d'Auschwitz* 9/10, no. 4 (1977); 1, no. 4 (1978); and 2, no. 4 (1978).

Jansen, Hans. *Christelijke theologie na Auschwitz: Theologische en kerkelijke wortels van het antisemitisme.* The Hague: Boekencentrum, 1982.

Jaspers, Karl. *On the Origin and Goal of History.* Trans. Michael Bullock. London: Routledge & Kegan Paul, 1953.

Jonas, Hans. "The Concept of God after Auschwitz." In *Echoes from the Holocaust: Philosophical Reflections on a Dark Time,* ed. Alan Rosenberg and Gerald E. Myers, 292–305. Philadelphia: Temple University Press, 1988.

Kautsky, Benedikt. *Teufel und Verdammte.* Zürich: Büchergilde Gutenberg, 1946.

Keegan, John, ed. *Times Atlas of the Second World War.* London: Times Books, 1989.

Keren, Daniel, Jamie McCarthy, and Harry W. Mazal. "A Report on Some Findings Concerning the Gas Chamber of Krematorium II in Auschwitz-Birkenau," attached as an appendix to Robert Jan van Pelt, "Expert Report," written to assist the Court of Appeal (Civil Division) in the Supreme Court of Judicature in London in the Case between John Cawdell Irving, Applicant, and Penguin Books Limited and Deborah E. Lipstadt, Respondents.

Kern, Nili. "The Family Camp." In *Anatomy of the Auschwitz Death Camp,* ed. Yisrael Gutman and Michael Berenbaum, 428–440. Washington, D.C., Bloomington, and Indianapolis: United States Holocaust Memorial Museum and Indiana University Press, 1994.

Klarsfeld, Serge. *David Olère 1902–1985: Un peintre au sonderkommando à Auschwitz.* New York: The Beate Klarsfeld Foundation, 1989.

Klee, Ernst, Willi Dressen, and Volker Riess, eds. *"The Good Old Days": The Holocaust as Seen by the Perpetrators and Bystanders.* Trans. Deborah Burnstone. London: Hamish Hamilton, 1993.

Koestler, Arthur. *The Yogi and the Commissar, and Other Essays.* London: Jonathan Cape, 1945.

Kogon, Eugen, Hermann Langbein, and Adalbert Rückerl, eds. *Nazi Mass Murder: A Documentary History of the Use of Poison Gas.* English edition ed. Pierre Serge Choumoff. Trans. Mary Scott and Caroline Lloyd-Morris. New Haven and London: Yale University Press, 1994.

Kossoff, Julian. "Keep Holocaust 'Apologists' Out of Britain, Home Secretary Is Told." *Jewish Chronicle,* 12 July 1991.

———. "Hitler Innocent, Says Irving, Despite 'Discovery' of Eichmann Documents." *Jewish Chronicle,* 17 January 1992.

Kraus, Ota, and Erich Schön. *Továrna na Smrt.* Prague: Cin, 1946.

Kravchenko, Victor A. *I Chose Justice.* New Brunswick and Oxford: Transaction Publishers, 1989.

Kremer, Johann Paul. "Diary." In *KL Auschwitz Seen by the SS: Rudolf Höss, Pery Broad, Johann Paul Kremer,* by Auschwitz-Birkenau State Museum in Oswiecim, trans. Constantine FitzGibbon and Krystyna Michalik, 149–215. Warsaw: Interpress, 1991.

Kristeva, Julia. *Strangers to Ourselves.* Trans. Leon S. Roudiez. New York: Columbia University Press, 1991.

Kuesters, Elisabeth. "Encountering the Revisionists: An Outside-Inside Report on the 1983 International Revisionist Conference." *The Journal of Historical Review* 5 (Winter 1984): 307–323.

Kühnrich, Heinz. *Der KZ-Staat: 1933–1945.* Berlin: Dietz, 1988.

Kushner, Tony. *The Holocaust and the Liberal Imagination.* Oxford: Blackwell, 1994.

"La politique hitlérienne d'extermination. Une décleration d'historiens." *Le Monde,* 21 February 1979.

"Ladd v. Marshall," *The Weekly Law Reports* (1954), vol. 1, 1491.

Langbein, Hermann. *Der Auschwitz Prozeß: Eine Dokumentation.* 2 vols. Frankfurt am Main: Verlag Neue Kritik, 1995.

Langlois, Ch. V., and Ch. Seignobos. *Introduction to the Study of History.* Trans. G. G. Berry. London: Duckworth, 1898.

Lauterbach, Richard. "Murder, Inc." *Time* 44 (11 September 1944): 36.

———. "Sunday in Poland." *Life* 17 (18 September 1944): 17.

Lawrence, William H. "50,000 Kiev Jews Reported Killed." *The New York Times,* 29 November 1943.

———. "Nazi Mass Killing Laid Bare in Camp." *The New York Times,* 30 August 1944.

———. *Six Presidents, Too Many Wars.* New York: Saturday Review Press, 1972.

Le Bon, Gustave. *Psychologie des foules.* Paris: Presses Universitaires de France, 1963.

"LeMoyne Cremated," *Chicago Tribune,* Oct. 17, 1879.

Lessing, Gotthold Ephraim. *Nathan the Wise.* Trans. Bayard Quincy Morgan. New York: Ungar, 1955.

Lestschinsky, Jacob. "Bilan d'extermination." *Le Monde Juif,* March 1947.

Lesy, Michael. *The Forbidden Zone.* New York: Anchor, 1989.

Leuchter, Fred A. *The Leuchter Report: The End of a Myth—An Engineering Report on the Alleged Execution Gas Chambers at Auschwitz, Birkenau and Majdanek, Poland.* Foreword by Dr. Robert Faurisson. Decatur, Ala.: David Clark, n.d.

———. *Auschwitz: The End of the Line—The Leuchter Report: The First Forensic Examination of Auschwitz.* Foreword by David Irving. London: Focal Point, 1989.

———. "The Leuchter Report: The How and the Why." *The Journal of Historical Review* 9 (Summer 1989): 133–140.

Levi, Primo. *The Reawakening.* Trans. Stuart Woolf. Boston: Little, Brown and Co., 1965.

———. *The Drowned and the Saved*. Trans. Raymond Rosenthal. New York: Summit Books, 1988.

———. *Survival in Auschwitz*. Trans. Stuart Woolf. New York: Collier/ Macmillan, 1993.

Lewis, Stephen. *Art Out of Agony: The Holocaust Theme in Literature, Sculpture and Film*. Montreal: CBC Enterprises, 1984.

Lindsey, William C. "Zyklon B, Auschwitz, and the Trial of Dr. Bruno Tesch." *The Journal of Historical Review* 4 (1984): 261–303.

Lipstadt, Deborah. *Beyond Belief: The American Press and the Coming of the Holocaust, 1933–1945*. New York: The Free Press, 1986.

———. *Denying the Holocaust: The Growing Assault on Truth and Memory*. New York: The Free Press, 1993.

———. "The Mundane Face of Evil." *New York Newsday*, 4 August 1996.

Littell, Franklin H. "The Credibility Crisis of the Modern University." In *The Holocaust: Ideology, Bureaucracy, and Genocide,* ed. Henry Friedlander and Sybil Milton, 271–284. Millwood: Kraus, 1980.

Lyall, Sarah. "Critic of a Holocaust Denier Is Cleared in British Libel Suit." *The New York Times,* 12 April 2000.

Lyotard, Jean-François. *The Differend: Phrases in Dispute*. Trans. Georges Van Den Abbeele. Minneapolis: University of Minnesota Press, 1988.

Malaurie, Guillaume, with Emmanuel Terrée. *L'affaire Kravchenko: Paris 1949—Le Goulag en correctionnelle*. Paris: Robert Lafont, 1982.

Markiewicz, Jan, Wojciech Gubala, and Jerzy Labedz. "A Study of the Cyanide Compounds Content in the Walls of the Gas Chambers in the Former Auschwitz and Birkenau Concentration Camps." *Z Zagadnien Nauk Sadowych/Problems of Forensic Science* 30 (1994): 19–27.

Marszalek, Jozef. *Majdanek: The Concentration Camp in Lublin*. Warsaw: Interpress, 1986.

Maybaum, Ignaz. *The Face of God after Auschwitz*. Amsterdam: Polak and Van Gennep, 1965.

Mayer, Arno J. *Why Did the Heavens Not Darken? The "Final Solution" in History*. New York: Pantheon, 1988.

McElvoy, Anne. "Unfortunately, Holocaust Denial Will Not End Here." *The Independent,* 12 April 2000.

Menasse, Eva. "Es knistert aus dem Irving-Prozess: Taktische Konzessionen des Klägers." *Frankfurter Allgemeine Zeitung,* 16 February 2000.

Mendelsohn, John, and Donald S. Detwiler, eds. *The Holocaust: Selected Documents in Eighteen Volumes*. New York and London: Garland, 1982.

Monsarrat, Nicholas. *The Cruel Sea*. New York: Knopf, 1951.

Moore, Lawrence F. "Technology of Cremation," Association of American Cemetery Superintendents, *Proceedings* 54 (1940), 67.

Mosler, Peter, ed. *Schreiben nach Auschwitz*. Cologne: Bund Verlag, 1989.

Moss, Stephen. "History's Verdict on Holocaust Upheld." *The Guardian,* 12 April 2000.

Müller, Filip, with Helmut Freitag. *Eyewitness Auschwitz: Three Years in the Gas Chambers*. Trans. Susanne Flatauer. Chicago: Ivan R. Dee, 1999.

Nansen, Odd. *From Day to Day*. Trans. Katherine John. New York: G. P. Putnam's Sons, 1949.

Naumann, Bernd. *Auschwitz: A Report on the Proceedings against Robert Ludwig Mulka and Others before the Court at Frankfurt*. Trans. Jean Steinberg. Introduction by Hannah Arendt. New York, Washington, D.C., and London: Frederick A. Praeger, 1966.

Neher, André. *L'exil de la Parole: du silence biblique au silence d'Ausch-witz*. Paris: Éditions du Seuil, 1970.

Neufert, Ernst. *Bau-Entwurfslehre: Handbuch für den Baufachmann, Bau-herrn, Lehrenden und Lernended*. Berlin: Bauwelt-Verlag, 1944.

Nietzsche, Friedrich. "On Truth and Lie in an Extra-Moral Sense." In *Deconstruction in Context: Literature and Philosophy*, ed. Mark C. Taylor, 216–219. Chicago and London: University of Chicago Press, 1986.

Nolte, Ernst. *Der europäische Bürgerkrieg 1917–1945*. Frankfurt: Pro-pyläen, 1987.

Nyiszli, Miklos. *Auschwitz: A Doctor's Eyewitness Account*. New York: Arcade, 1993.

"An Official Polish Report on the Auschwitz 'Gas Chambers': Krakow Forensic Institute Bolsters Leuchter's Findings." *The Journal of Historical Review* 11 (Summer 1991): 207–216.

"Oswiecim Revelations." *The Jewish Chronicle* 104, no. 3,957 (9 February 1945): 1.

Padover, Saul K. *Experiment in Germany: The Story of an American Intelligence Officer*. New York: Duell, Sloan and Pearce, 1946.

Phillips, Raymond, ed. *Trial of Josef Kramer and Forty-Four Others (The Belsen Trial)*. London, Edinburgh and Glasgow: William Hodge and Company, 1949.

Piper, Franciszek. "Estimating the Number of Deportees to and Victims of the Auschwitz-Birkenau Camp." *Yad Vashem Studies* 21 (1991): 49–103.

———. *Die Zahl der Opfer von Auschwitz Aufgrund der Quellen und der Erträge der Forschung 1945 bis 1990*. Oswiecim: The Auschwitz-Birkenau State Museum in Oswiecim, 1993.

———. "Gas Chambers and Crematoria." In *Anatomy of the Auschwitz Death Camp*, ed. Yisrael Gutman and Michael Berenbaum, 157–182. Washington, D.C., Bloomington, and Indianapolis: United States Holocaust Memorial Museum and Indiana University Press, 1994.

———. "The Number of Victims." In *Anatomy of the Auschwitz Death Camp*, ed. Yisrael Gutman and Michael Berenbaum, 61–76. Washington D.C., Bloomington, and Indianapolis: United States Holocaust Memorial Museum and Indiana University Press, 1994.

Pohl, Dieter. "Die großen Zwangarbeitslager der SS-und Polizeiführer für Juden im Generalgouvernement 1942–1945." In *Die nationalsozial-istischen Konzentrationslager: Entwicklung und Struktur*, ed. Ulrich Herbert, Karin Orth, and Christoph Dieckmann. 2 vols. Göttingen: Wallstein, 1998.

"Poland's Jewish Survivors." *The Jewish Chronicle* 104, no. 3,956 (2 February 1945): 1.

Polevoi, Boris. "The Factory of Death at Auschwitz," http://www.fpp.co.uk/Auschwitz/Auschw.html

Polish Labour Group. *Oswiecim Camp of Death (Underground Report)*. New York: Polish Labour Group, 1944.

Pompa, Leon. *Human Nature and Historical Knowledge: Hume, Hegel and Vico*. Cambridge: Cambridge University Press, 1990.

Ponsonby, Arthur. *Falsehood in War-Time: Containing an Assortment of Lies Circulated Throughout the Nations during the Great War*. London: George Allan & Unwin, 1928.

Pressac, Jean-Claude. *Auschwitz: Technique and Operation of the Gas Chambers*. New York: The Beate Klarsfeld Foundation, 1989.

———. *Les crématoires d'Auschwitz: la machinerie du meurtre de masse.* Paris: CNRS Éditions, 1993.

———. *Die Krematorien von Auschwitz: Die Technik des Massenmordes.* Trans. Eliana Hagedorn and Barbare Reitz. München and Zürich: Piper, 1994.

Pressac, Jean-Claude, and Robert Jan van Pelt. "The Machinery of Mass Murder at Auschwitz." In *Anatomy of the Auschwitz Death Camp,* ed. Yisrael Gutman and Michael Berenbaum, 183–245. Washington, D.C., Bloomington, and Indianapolis: United States Holocaust Memorial Museum and Indiana University Press, 1994.

Protectorate of Bohemia and Moravia, Health Institution. "Directives for the Use of Prussic Acid (Zyklon) for the Destruction of Vermin (Disinfestation)." In *The Holocaust,* ed. Henry Friedlander. Vol. 12, *The "Final Solution" in the Extermination Camps and the Aftermath.* New York and London: Garland, 1982.

Rassinier, Paul. *The Holocaust and the Lies of Ulysses.* Trans. Adam Robbins. Costa Mesa: The Institute for Historical Review, 1978.

Read, James Morgan. *Atrocity Propaganda 1914–1919.* New Haven: Yale University Press, 1941.

Reed, Douglas. *Lest We Regret.* London: Jonathan Cape, 1943.

Reilly, Joanne. *Belsen: The Liberation of a Concentration Camp.* London and New York: Routledge, 1998.

Reitlinger, Gerald. *The Final Solution: The Attempt to Exterminate the Jews of Europe 1939–1945.* London: Valentine, Mitchell & Co., 1953.

Republic of Poland, Information Service. "Documents from Poland: German Attempts to Murder a Nation." *Polish Fortnightly Review* 47 (1 July 1942): 2.

———. "German Crimes Arraigned" and "A Press Conference at the Ministry of Information." *Polish Fortnightly Review* 48 (15 July 1942).

———. "Extermination of the Polish Jewry: What Happened in the Warsaw Ghetto." *Polish Fortnightly Review* 57 (1 December 1942).

———. "Extraordinary Report from the Jew-Extermination Camp at Belzec." *Polish Fortnightly Review* 57 (1 December 1942): 4.

———. "Polish Women in German Concentration Camps." *Polish Fortnightly Review* 115 (1 May 1945): 1.

Republic of Poland, Ministry of Foreign Affairs. *The Mass Extermination of Jews in German Occupied Poland.* London: Hutchinson & Co., 1942.

Roberts, Andrew. "David Irving, Truth, and the Holocaust." *Sunday Telegraph,* 16 January 2000.

Roddy, Dennis. "New Twists on History." *Pittsburgh Post Gazette,* 22 January 2000.

Rosenbaum, Ron. *Explaining Hitler: The Search for the Origins of His Evil.* New York: Random House, 1998.

Rosenzweig, Franz. *The Star of Redemption.* Trans. William H. Hallo. London: Routledge and Kegan Paul, 1971.

"Round Two to Go to the UK Court of Appeal." *David Irving's Action Report* 17 (20 July 2000).

Rousset, David. *The Other Kingdom.* Trans. Ramon Guthrie. New York: Reynal & Hitchcock, 1947.

Rubenstein, Richard L. *After Auschwitz: Radical Theology and Contemporary Judaism.* Indianapolis: Bobbs-Merrill, 1966.

————. *The Cunning of History: The Holocaust and the American Future.* New York: Harper Colophon Books, 1978.

Rudolf, Germar. "Critique of Claims Made by Robert Jan Van Pelt," www.vho.org/GB/c/GR/RudolfOnVanPelt.html

————. "The Hunt of Germar Rudolf," www.vho.org/VffG/2000/3/Rudolf393-409.html

————. "Some considerations about the Gas Chambers of Auschwitz and Birkenau," www.vho.org/GB/c/GR/Green

————. "Character Assassins," www.vho.org/GB/c/GR/CharacterAssassins

————. "Affidavit," written to assist the Court of Appeal (Civil Divison) in the Supreme Court of Judicature in London in the Case between John Cawdell Irving, Applicant, and Penguin Books Limited and Deborah E. Lipstadt, Respondents (withdrawn on June 21, 2001).

Sack, John. "Inside the Bunker." *Esquire* (February 2001), 99–103, 138–140.

"The Second Trial of the Indefatigable Ernst Zündel." *Instauration,* July 1988, 6.

Sehn, Jan. "Concentration and Extermination Camp at Oswiecim (Auschwitz-Birkenau)." In *German Crimes in Poland,* by Central Commission for Investigation of German Crimes in Poland, vol. 1, 27–92. Warsaw: Central Commission for Investigation of German Crimes in Poland, 1946–1947.

Seidel, Gill. *The Holocaust Denial: Antisemitism, Racism and the New Right.* Leeds: Beyond the Pale Collective, 1986.

Sereny, Gitta. "David Irving Resells Hitler's War." *The Independent,* 27 November 1991.

Shermer, Michael. "Proving the Holocaust: The Refutation of Revisionism and the Restoration of History." *Skeptic* 2, no. 4 (1994): 32–57.

Shermer, Michael, and Alex Grobman. *Denying History: Who Says The Holocaust Never Happened and Why Do They Say It?* Berkeley, Los Angeles, and London: University of California Press, 2000.

Showalter, Elaine. *Hystories.* New York: Columbia University Press, 1997.

Silets, H. L. "Facts Written in Blood: The Zyklon B Trial of Bruno Tesch." In *Truth Prevails: Demolishing Holocaust Denial—The End of "The Leuchter Report,"* ed. Shelly Shapiro, 95–104. New York: The Beate Klarsfeld Foundation, 1990.

Simonov, Konstantin. "Lublin Annihilation Camp." *Information Bulletin, Embassy of the Soviet Socialist Republics (Washington D.C.)* 4, no. 97 (29 August 1944): 5.

————. "Lublin Annihilation Camp, Part II." *Information Bulletin, Embassy of the Soviet Socialist Republics (Washington D.C.)* 4, no. 98 (1 September 1944): 5.

Sofsky, Wolfgang. *Die Ordnung des Terrors: Das Konzentrationslager.* Frankfurt am Main: Fischer, 1993.

Solzhenitsyn, Aleksandr I. *The Gulag Archipelago, 1918–1956: An Experiment in Literary Investigation.* Trans. Thomas P. Whitney. 3 vols. New York: Harper & Row, 1975.

"A Spectator's Notebook." *The Spectator* 175 (5 October 1945): 304.

Stäglich, Wilhelm. *The Auschwitz Myth: A Judge Looks at the Evidence.* [Costa Mesa, Calif.]: Institute for Historical Review, 1986.

State of Israel, Ministry of Justice. *The Trial of Adolf Eichmann: Record of Proceedings in the District Court of Jerusalem.* 5 vols. Jerusalem: The Trust for the Publication of the Eichmann Trial, 1992.

State Museum of Auschwitz-Birkenau. *Death Books from Auschwitz:*

Remnants. 3 vols. Munich, New Providence, London, and Paris: K. G. Saur, 1995.

Swiebocki, Henryk. "Die lagernahe Widerstandsbewegung und ihre Hilfs-aktionen für die Häftlinge des KL Auschwitz." *Hefte von Auschwitz* 19 (1995): 5–187.

———. *London Has Been Informed: Reports by Auschwitz Escapees.* Trans. Michael Jacobs and Laurence Weinbaum. Oswiecim: The Auschwitz-Birkenau State Museum, 1997.

Sydnor, Charles W., Jr. "The Selling of Adolf Hitler: David Irving's *Hitler's War." Central European History* 12, no. 2 (June 1979): 169–199.

Taylor, Telford. *The Anatomy of the Nuremberg Trials: A Personal Memoir.* New York: Knopf, 1992.

Thion, Serge. *Vérité historique ou vérité politique? La dossier de l'affaire Faurisson. La question des chambres à gaz.* Paris: La Veille Taupe, 1980.

Trevor-Roper, Hugh. "Hitler: Does History Offer a Defence?" *The Sunday Times,* 12 June 1977.

———. *History and Imagination: A Valedictory Lecture.* Oxford: Clarendon Press, 1980.

"Truth's Sheer Weight: Irving Was the Deniers' Best Shot." *The Guardian,* 12 April 2000.

Union of Soviet Socialist Republics. "Statement of the Polish-Soviet Extraordinary Commission for the Investigation of Crimes Committed by the Germans in the Extermination Camp of Maidanek in the Town of Lublin." *Information Bulletin, Embassy of the Soviet Socialist Republics (Washington D.C.)* 4, no. 111 (17 October 1944): 1–8.

———. "Statement of the Extraordinary State Committee for the Ascertaining and Investigation of Crimes Committed by the German-fascist Invaders and Their Associates in the Oswiecim Death Camp." *Information Bulletin, Embassy of the Soviet Socialist Republics (Washington D.C.)* 5, no. 54 (29 May 1945): 1–8.

———. *Soviet Government Statements on Nazi Atrocities.* London: Hutchinson & Co., n.d.

United States of America. *Trials of War Criminals before the Nuernberg Military Tribunals Under Control Council Law No. 10.* 10 vols. Washington, D.C.: United States Government Printing Office, 1950.

van Pelt, Robert Jan. "(Deliveries of Zyklon B to Auschwitz and Consumption Rates of Zyklon B in Auschwitz and Other Camps) Supplement to the Expert Opinion written by Robert Jan van Pelt, D.Lit., Professor of Architecture at the University of Waterloo, Canada, on Instructions of Davenport Lyons and Mishcon de Reya, Solicitors, for the Purposes of Assisting the Queen's Bench Division in the High Court in London in the Case between David John Cawdell Irving, Plaintiff, and Penguin Books Limited and Deborah E. Lipstadt, Defendants."

———. "Expert Opinion written by Robert Jan van Pelt, D.Lit., Professor of Architecture at the University of Waterloo, Canada, on Instructions of Davenport Lyons and Mishcon de Reya, Solicitors, for the Purposes of Assisting the Queen's Bench Division in the High Court in London in the Case between David John Cawdell Irving, Plaintiff, and Penguin Books Limited and Deborah E. Lipstadt, Defendants."

———. "A Site in Search of a Mission." In *Anatomy of the Auschwitz Death Camp,* ed. Yisrael Gutman and Michael Berenbaum, 93–156. Washington, D.C., Bloomington, and Indianapolis: United States Holocaust Memorial Museum and Indiana University Press, 1994.

van Pelt, Robert Jan, and Carroll William Westfall. *Architectural Principles in the Age of Historicism.* New Haven and London: Yale University Press, 1991.

"Vernichtungslager." *Time* 44 (21 August 1944), 36.

Vidal-Naquet, Pierre. *Assassins of Memory: Essays on the Denial of the Holocaust.* Trans. Jeffery Mehlman. New York: Columbia University Press, 1992.

————. *The Jews: History, Memory, and the Present.* Trans. David Ames Curtis. New York: Columbia University Press, 1996.

Vierick, George Sylvester. *Spreading Germs of Hate.* New York: H. Liveright, 1930.

Voltaire (François-Marie Arouet). *Candide.* Trans. John Butt. Harmondsworth: Penguin Books, 1947.

Vrba, Rudolf, and Alan Bestic. *I Cannot Forgive.* London: Sidgwick and Jackson, 1963.

Walendy, Udo. *Auschwitz im IG-Farben Prozeß—Holocaust-Dokumente?* Vlotho: Verlag für Volkstum und Zeitgeschichtsforschung, 1981.

War Refugee Board. "The Extermination Camps of Auschwitz (Oswiecim) and Birkenau in Upper Silesia." In *America and the Holocaust,* ed. David S. Wyman, vol. 12, 3–43. New York and London: Garland, 1990.

————. "German Extermination Camps—Auschwitz and Birkenau." In *America and the Holocaust,* ed. David S. Wyman, vol. 12, 44–65. New York and London: Garland, 1990.

Wasserstein, Bernard. *Britain and the Jews of Europe, 1939–1945.* Oxford: Clarendon Press, 1979.

Wegner, Werner. "Keine Massenvergasungen in Auschwitz? Zur Kritik des Leuchter-Gutachtens." In *Die Schatten der Vergangenheit: Impulse zur Historisierung des nationalsozialismus,* ed. Uwe Backes, Eckhard Jesse, and Rainer Zitelmann, 450–476. Frankfurt am Main: Propyläen, 1990.

Wellers, Georges. "Reply to the Neo-Nazi Falsification of Historical Facts concerning the Holocaust." In *The Holocaust and the Neo-Nazi Mythomania,* ed. Serge Klarsfeld, trans. Barbara Rucci, 107–162. New York: The Beate Klarsfeld Foundation, 1978.

————. *Les chambrez à gaz ont existé: Des documents, des témoignages, des chiffres.* Paris: Gallimard, 1981.

Wiesel, Elie. *Messengers of God: Biblical Portraits and Legends.* Trans. Marion Wiesel. New York: Summit Books, 1976.

————. "Why I Write." In *Confronting the Holocaust: The Impact of Elie Wiesel,* ed. Alvin Rosenfeld and Irving Greenberg, 200–206. Bloomington: Indiana University Press, 1978.

————. *Legends of Our Time.* New York: Schocken Books, 1982.

Wilkins, John. *Of the Principles and Duties of Natural Religion.* London: A. Maxwell, 1675.

Wimsatt, William K. *The Verbal Icon.* Lexington: University Press of Kentucky, 1954.

————. *Day of Leopards: Essays in Defense of Poems.* New Haven and London: Yale University Press, 1976.

Witte, Peter, Michael Wildt, Martina Voigt, Dieter Pohl, Peter Klein, Christian Gerlach, Christoph Dieckmann, and Andrej Angrich, eds. *Der Dienstkalender Heinrich Himmler's 1941/42.* Hamburg: Christians, 1999.

Wyman, David S., ed. *America and the Holocaust.* 13 vols. New York and London: Garland, 1990.

Wyschogrod, Edith. *An Ethics of Remembering.* Chicago and London: University of Chicago Press, 1998.

Zündel, Ernst. "The David Irving/Eichmann Memoirs Controversy!" *Power,* 30 January 1992, 1.

Index

historical revisionism, 2, 471–472

Historical Truth or Political Truth? (Thion), 32

historiography, 67

Hitler, Adolf: in chain of command, 249; concentration camp policy of, 241–242; delegation of powers to Himmler, 242; exploitation by French ultra-left, 32; Faurisson on, 29–30; and Final Solution, 447; Gray on, 489, 490–491; Irving on, 18–21, 23, 44, 45, 52; in Irving trial testimony, 460; Irving's early interest in, 18; knowledge of Himmler's role, 40; as law, 242; loyalty of officers to, 237; Mayer on, 47; *Mein Kampf,* 18; peace offer to Churchill, 59; transcribed conversations of, 44

Hitler diaries, 21–23, 42, 45–46, 48, 439

Hitler's War (Irving), 14, 18–21, 23, 44–45, 52–54, 57, 105, 431–433, 437

The Hoax of the Twentieth Century (Butz), 303, 357

Hochhuth, Rolf, 8

Hoffmann, Albert, 53

holes. *See* Zyklon B, insertion points for

Holocaust: accepted sense of term, 412; Auschwitz as symbolic center of, 6–8, 14; confessions by German officers, 3–5; consensus on, 12; in "Defendants' Statement of Case," 420–421; denial as punishable offence in Germany, 55; disagreement on, 12; Faurisson on, 35; Harwood on, 35, 44; Irving on, 2, 40, 45, 55, 57, 59, 430, 432, 438, 439; Jewish lives claimed by, 6; Lindsey on, 38; Mayer on, 46–48; Nolte on, 41; peak of killing, 80; and ultra-left ideologists, 32; Web site, 498

"The Holocaust: A Sinking Ship?" (Institute for Historical Review), 47–48

The Holocaust and the Liberal Imagination (Kushner), 132

The Holocaust and the Neo-Nazi Mythomania, 27–28

Holocaust History Project, 494–495

Holocaust Hoax, 3, 39, 57

The Holocaust Kingdom (Donat), 82

Holocaust Memorial Museum, Washington, D.C., 109

The Holocaust Revisited (Brugioni and Poirier), 84, 352–353

Hoessler, Franz, 225–226, 231, *239,* 239–240, 244, *255*

Höss, Rudolf, *4, 98, 251;* and Aumeier, 230; Aumeier on, 332; autobiography of, 263, *264;* Butz on, 272–274, 303; confession of, 3–5, 111, 217; on corpse disposal, 254–255; correspondence of, *447;* corroboration of others, 348; doubts of, 261; Eichmann's challenge of, 97; essays of, 254–257; extradition to Poland, 254; eyewitness testimony of, 502; Faurisson on, 274–275; on Final Solution, 4–5, 254, 257, 259–261, 262–263; on gas chambers, 30; on Himmler, 259; and Hoessler, 239–240; importance of testimony, 253–254; inconsistencies in memoirs, 97; on institutional structure of Auschwitz, 258–259; in interrogatories, 414; Irving on, 97, 99–100, 275–279, 431; in Irving trial testimony, 481; on killing procedures, 255–256; and Josef Kramer, 236, 237–238; Johann Paul Kremer on, 283; lack of empathy, 253; mentioned in "Defence of Second Defendant," 96–97; not allowed to keep records, 106; Nuremberg testimony, 250–253; Polish resistance reports corroboration, 146; prisoner statistics reports of, 92; psychological profile of, 254; Rassinier on, 263, 265–271; role in exterminations, 260; sense of duty, 261; statement to Gilbert, 251–253; on ventilation, 365; victim count estimates, 3, 27, 97–99, 108–109, 250, 251, 257, 261; on Zyklon B, 4, 250, 252, 258

human bell clapper propaganda spoof, 129–130, 131

human experiments, 181–182, 234, 247, 283, 445

Hume, David, 103, 104

Hungarian Action: Auschwitz as selection station, 118; crematoria capacity exceeded during, 256; crowding of crematoria during, 205; frenzy of killing, 256; Irving on, 20; peak of killing, 186–187

hydrogen cyanide: circulation in gas chamber, 377, 379; detectors for, 311–313; diffusion of, 365–366; forensic investigation on residue, 43, 354–355, 359, 390–393, *394,* 395–398, 496, 498–499; in interrogatories, 413–414, 415,

diverted from Auschwitz to, 329; transformed from extermination camp, 128; victim counts, 80

Trevor-Roper, Hugh, 20, 21, 22, 128, 138, 328

trials. *See* Auschwitz trial, Cracow; Belsen trial; Dejaco-Ertl trial; Eichmann trial; Frankfurt Auschwitz trial; Irving trial; Nuremberg Military Tribunal; Supreme National Tribunal, Cracow; Zündel trials

Truman, Harry S., 133

truth, perceptions of, 135

twin experiments of Mengele, 234, 247, 445

typhus: author on, 122, 125, 444–445; Faurisson on, 284, 286, 288–289; Irving on, 40, 59, 434, 453, 462; Kremer on, 281, 283; Mayer on, 47

UFOs: Nazi Secret Weapons (Zündel), 94

Uhlenbrock, Kurt, 280

ultra-left ideologists, 32

undressing rooms: anonymous architect on, 444; author on, 473; Irving on, 446; Olère's depictions of, 173, *173*, 174, *176–177*, *178*, 180; Rudolf on, 501; Tauber on, 189–191, 193–194, 202

"unfit for work" deportee classification, 110

United States, knowledge of atrocities, 153

University of Virginia, 66–68

Vaillant-Couturier, Marie Claude, 246–248, 275, 292

van het Kaar, Cornelis, 224

van Pelt, Robert Jan, *401, 409, 411*; about, 66; ad hominem attack on, 441; *Architectural Principles in the Age of Historicism*, 69–71; *Auschwitz: 1270 to the Present*, 80, 82–83, 85, 89, 100, 119–120, 409; in BBC documentary, 331; Crematorium 2 thesis, 66–69; cross-examination by Irving, 456–465, 466–473, 473–476, 480–482; as expert witness, 3, 86–87, 100, 457–458, 495, 505–506; and Irving, 436, 488; and Irving appeal, 498–499, 501–506; Irving on, 429; personal involvement with Auschwitz, 467; pre-trial preparation of, 399–401, 406, 408–412; re-examination by Rampton, 472–

473, 473–474, 476–477; Rudolf critique of, 496–497; swearing in, 455

Vaupel (SS Hauptscharführer), 225

Verall, Richard, 35. *See also* Harwood, Richard (pseudonym of Verall)

Vergasungskeller: appearance of term, 209, 211; Bischoff's mention of, 296–297, 299, 401; Butz on, 303–304; Crowell on, 317–318; interpretation of term, 305–311; Irving on terminology, 299–300, 302–304, 324, 468; in Irving trial testimony, 443, 454; sewage treatment theory, 309–310; Stäglich on, 310–311

victim counts: Aumeier on, 232; Auschwitz, 80, 106–119; Austrian Jews, 114, 115; Belzec, 80; Broad on, 229; Butz on, 272–273; by country of origin, 99, 107; deportations by country, 113; dispute over, 27, 114–115; Eichmann on, 97–98, 99, 108–109, 135, 253, 261; German Jews, 114–115; Höss on, 3, 27, 97–99, 108–109, 250, 251, 257, 261; Hungarian Jews, 116; Irving on, 40, 55, 56, 59, 105–106; in Irving trial, 485; by location, 80; Maidanek as measuring stick for, 183; in Nuremberg indictment, 108; Polish Jews, 114, 116; Polish resistance report, 145; Rassinier on, 263–267, 270–271; Reitlinger on, 27; scholarship of, 106–119; Sonderkommando estimates, 184–185; Soviet estimates, 183, 257; Soviet-Polish commission report, 157; Tauber on, 188; Yugoslavian Jews, 115

victim possessions: artificial limbs, *160*; clothing, 159, 182, 232; confiscation of valuables, 232, 252; jewelry, 197; shoes, *155*, 156, 157, 159

Vidal-Naquet, Pierre, 8–9, 29, 289–290

Vrba, Rudi, 37–38, 53, 145–146, 147, 149–152

Vrba/Wetzlar reports, 145–146, 147, 149–152, 153, 158

Wannsee Conference, 41, 72

War Refugee Board, 12, 153

War Refugee Board report, 37, 158, 184

Warsaw ghetto, 30, 146

watchtowers, 202

Watt, Donald Cameron, 437, 479

ROBERT JAN VAN PELT is professor of architecture at the University of Waterloo, Canada. He is co-author (with Debórah Dwork) of *Auschwitz: 1270 to the Present*.